REFERENCE

Short Stories
for Students

National Advisory Board

Short Stories for Students

Presenting Analysis, Context, and Criticism on Commonly Studied Short Stories

Volume 12

Jennifer Smith, Editor

GALE GROUP

Detroit
New York
San Francisco
London
Boston
Woodbridge, CT

Short Stories for Students

Staff

Editor: Jennifer Smith.

Contributing Editors: Anne Marie Hacht, Michael L. LaBlanc, Ira Mark Milne, Elizabeth Thomason.

Managing Editor, Literature Content: Dwayne D. Hayes.

Managing Editor, Literature Product: David Galens.

Publisher, Literature Product: Mark Scott.

Content Capture: Joyce Nakamura, *Managing Editor.* Michelle Poole, *Associate Editor.*

Research: Victoria B. Cariappa, *Research Manager.* Cheryl Warnock, *Research Specialist.* Tamara Nott, Tracie A. Richardson, *Research Associates.* Nicodemus Ford, Sarah Genik, Timothy Lehnerer, Ron Morelli, *Research Assistants.*

Permissions: Maria Franklin, *Permissions Manager.* Jacqueline Jones, Julie Juengling, *Permissions Assistants.*

Manufacturing: Mary Beth Trimper, *Manager, Composition and Electronic Prepress.* Evi Seoud, *Assistant Manager, Composition Purchasing and Electronic Prepress.* Stacy Melson, *Buyer.*

Imaging and Multimedia Content Team: Barbara Yarrow, *Manager.* Randy Bassett, *Imaging Supervisor.* Robert Duncan, Dan Newell, *Imaging Specialists.* Pamela A. Reed, *Imaging Coordinator .* Leitha Etheridge-Sims, Mary Grimes, David G. Oblender, *Image Catalogers.* Robyn V. Young, *Project Manager.* Dean Dauphinais, *Senior Image Editor.* Kelly A. Quin, *Image Editor.*

Product Design Team: Kenn Zorn, *Product Design Manager.* Pamela A. E. Galbreath, *Senior Art Director.* Michael Logusz, *Graphic Artist.*

Copyright Notice

Table of Contents

Why Study Literature At All?

Short Stories for Students is designed to provide readers with information and discussion about a wide range of important contemporary and historical works of short fiction, and it does that job very well. However, I want to use this guest foreword to address a question that it does *not* take up. It is a fundamental question that is often ignored in high school and college English classes as well as research texts, and one that causes frustration among students at all levels, namely—why study literature at all? Isn't it enough to read a story, enjoy it, and go about one's business? My answer (to be expected from a literary professional, I suppose) is no. It is not enough. It is a start; but it is not enough. Here's why.

First, literature is the only part of the educational curriculum that deals directly with the actual world of lived experience. The philosopher Edmund Husserl used the apt German term *die Lebenswelt*, "the living world," to denote this realm. All the other content areas of the modern American educational system avoid the subjective, present reality of everyday life. Science (both the natural and the social varieties) objectifies, the fine arts create and/or perform, history reconstructs. Only literary study persists in posing those questions we all asked before our schooling taught us to give up on them. Only literature gives credibility to personal perceptions, feelings, dreams, and the "stream of consciousness" that is our inner voice. Literature wonders about infinity, wonders why God permits evil, wonders what will happen to us after we die. Literature admits that we get our hearts broken, that people sometimes cheat and get away with it, that the world is a strange and probably incomprehensible place. Literature, in other words, takes on all the big and small issues of what it means to be human. So my first answer is that of the humanist—we should read literature and study it and take it seriously because it enriches us as human beings. We develop our moral imagination, our capacity to sympathize with other people, and our ability to understand our existence through the experience of fiction.

My second answer is more practical. By studying literature we can learn how to explore and analyze texts. Fiction may be about *die Lebenswelt*, but it is a construct of words put together in a certain order by an artist using the medium of language. By examining and studying those constructions, we can learn about language as a medium. We can become more sophisticated about word associations and connotations, about the manipulation of symbols, and about style and atmosphere. We can grasp how ambiguous language is and how important context and texture is to meaning. In our first encounter with a work of literature, of course, we are not supposed to catch all of these things. We are spellbound, just as the writer wanted us to be. It is as serious students of the writer's art that we begin to see how the tricks are done.

Seeing the tricks, which is another way of saying "developing analytical and close reading skills," is important above and beyond its intrinsic literary educational value. These skills transfer to other fields and enhance critical thinking of any kind. Understanding how language is used to construct texts is powerful knowledge. It makes engineers better problem solvers, lawyers better advocates and courtroom practitioners, politicians better rhetoricians, marketing and advertising agents better sellers, and citizens more aware consumers as well as better participants in democracy. This last point is especially important, because rhetorical skill works both ways—when we learn how language is manipulated in the making of texts the result is that we become less susceptible when language is used to manipulate us.

My third reason is related to the second. When we begin to see literature as created artifacts of language, we become more sensitive to good writing in general. We get a stronger sense of the importance of individual words, even the sounds of words and word combinations. We begin to understand Mark Twain's delicious proverb—"The difference between the right word and the almost right word is the difference between lightning and a lightning bug." Getting beyond the "enjoyment only" stage of literature gets us closer to becoming makers of word art ourselves. I am not saying that studying fiction will turn every student into a Faulkner or a Shakespeare. But it will make us more adaptable and effective writers, even if our art form ends up being the office memo or the corporate annual report.

Studying short stories, then, can help students become better readers, better writers, and even better human beings. But I want to close with a warning. If your study and exploration of the craft, history, context, symbolism, or anything else about a story starts to rob it of the magic you felt when you first read it, it is time to stop. Take a break, study another subject, shoot some hoops, or go for a run. Love of reading is too important to be ruined by school. The early twentieth century writer Willa Cather, in her novel *My Antonia*, has her narrator Jack Burden tell a story that he and Antonia heard from two old Russian immigrants when they were teenagers. These immigrants, Pavel and Peter, told about an incident from their youth back in Russia that the narrator could recall in vivid detail thirty years later. It was a harrowing story of a wedding party starting home in sleds and being chased by starving wolves. Hundreds of wolves attacked the group's sleds one by one as they sped across the snow trying to reach their village. In a horrible revelation, the old Russians revealed that the groom eventually threw his own bride to the wolves to save himself. There was even a hint that one of the old immigrants might have been the groom mentioned in the story. Cather has her narrator conclude with his feelings about the story. "We did not tell Pavel's secret to anyone, but guarded it jealously—as if the wolves of the Ukraine had gathered that night long ago, and the wedding party had been sacrificed, just to give us a painful and peculiar pleasure." That feeling, that painful and peculiar pleasure, is the most important thing about literature. Study and research should enhance that feeling and never be allowed to overwhelm it.

Thomas E. Barden
Professor of English and
Director of Graduate English Studies
The University of Toledo

Introduction

Purpose of the Book

The purpose of *Short Stories for Students* (*SSfS*) is to provide readers with a guide to understanding, enjoying, and studying short stories by giving them easy access to information about the work. Part of Gale's "For Students" Literature line, *SSfS* is specifically designed to meet the curricular needs of high school and undergraduate college students and their teachers, as well as the interests of general readers and researchers considering specific short fiction. While each volume contains entries on "classic" stories frequently studied in classrooms, there are also entries containing hard-to-find information on contemporary stories, including works by multicultural, international, and women writers.

The information covered in each entry includes an introduction to the story and the story's author; a plot summary, to help readers unravel and understand the events in the work; descriptions of important characters, including explanation of a given character's role in the narrative as well as discussion about that character's relationship to other characters in the story; analysis of important themes in the story; and an explanation of important literary techniques and movements as they are demonstrated in the work.

In addition to this material, which helps the readers analyze the story itself, students are also provided with important information on the literary and historical background informing each work. This includes a historical context essay, a box comparing the time or place the story was written to modern Western culture, a critical overview essay, and excerpts from critical essays on the story or author (if available). A unique feature of *SSfS* is a specially commissioned overview essay on each story, targeted toward the student reader.

To further aid the student in studying and enjoying each story, information on media adaptations is provided, as well as reading suggestions for works of fiction and nonfiction on similar themes and topics. Classroom aids include ideas for research papers and lists of critical sources that provide additional material on the work.

Selection Criteria

The titles for each volume of *SSfS* were selected by surveying numerous sources on teaching literature and analyzing course curricula for various school districts. Some of the sources surveyed include: literature anthologies, *Reading Lists for College-Bound Students: The Books Most Recommended by America's Top Colleges*; *Teaching the Short Story: A Guide to Using Stories from Around the World*, by the National Council of Teachers of English (NCTE); and "A Study of High School Literature Anthologies," conducted by Arthur Applebee at the Center for the Learning and Teaching of Literature and sponsored by the National Endowment for the Arts and the Office of Educational Research and Improvement.

Input was also solicited from our advisory board, as well as educators from various areas. From these discussions, it was determined that each volume should have a mix of "classic" stories (those works commonly taught in literature classes) and contemporary stories for which information is often hard to find. Because of the interest in expanding the canon of literature, an emphasis was also placed on including works by international, multicultural, and women authors. Our advisory board members—educational professionals—helped pare down the list for each volume. Works not selected for the present volume were noted as possibilities for future volumes. As always, the editor welcomes suggestions for titles to be included in future volumes.

How Each Entry Is Organized

Each entry, or chapter, in *SSfS* focuses on one story. Each entry heading lists the title of the story, the author's name, and the date of the story's publication. The following elements are contained in each entry:

- **Introduction:** a brief overview of the story which provides information about its first appearance, its literary standing, any controversies surrounding the work, and major conflicts or themes within the work.

- **Author Biography:** this section includes basic facts about the author's life, and focuses on events and times in the author's life that may have inspired the story in question.

- **Plot Summary:** a description of the events in the story.

- **Characters:** an alphabetical listing of the characters who appear in the story. Each character name is followed by a brief to an extensive description of the character's role in the story, as well as discussion of the character's actions, relationships, and possible motivation.

  Characters are listed alphabetically by last name. If a character is unnamed—for instance, the narrator in "The Eatonville Anthology"—the character is listed as "The Narrator" and alphabetized as "Narrator." If a character's first name is the only one given, the name will appear alphabetically by that name.

- **Themes:** a thorough overview of how the topics, themes, and issues are addressed within the story. Each theme discussed appears in a sepa-

rate subhead, and is easily accessed through the boldface entries in the Subject/Theme Index.

- **Style:** this section addresses important style elements of the story, such as setting, point of view, and narration; important literary devices used, such as imagery, foreshadowing, symbolism; and, if applicable, genres to which the work might have belonged, such as Gothicism or Romanticism. Literary terms are explained within the entry, but can also be found in the Glossary.

- **Historical Context:** this section outlines the social, political, and cultural climate *in which the author lived and the work was created.* This section may include descriptions of related historical events, pertinent aspects of daily life in the culture, and the artistic and literary sensibilities of the time in which the work was written. If the story is historical in nature, information regarding the time in which the story is set is also included. Long sections are broken down with helpful subheads.

- **Critical Overview:** this section provides background on the critical reputation of the author and the story, including bannings or any other public controversies surrounding the work. For older works, this section may include a history of how the story was first received and how perceptions of it may have changed over the years; for more recent works, direct quotes from early reviews may also be included.

- **Criticism:** an essay commissioned by *SSfS* which specifically deals with the story and is written specifically for the student audience, as well as excerpts from previously published criticism on the work (if available).

- **Sources:** an alphabetical list of critical material quoted in the entry, with bibliographical information.

- **Further Reading:** an alphabetical list of other critical sources which may prove useful for the student. Includes full bibliographical information and a brief annotation.

  In addition, each entry contains the following highlighted sections, set separate from the main text:

- **Media Adaptations:** where applicable, a list of film and television adaptations of the story, including source information. The list also includes stage adaptations, audio recordings, musical adaptations, etc.

- **Topics for Further Study:** a list of potential study questions or research topics dealing with the story. This section includes questions related to other disciplines the student may be studying, such as American history, world history, science, math, government, business, geography, economics, psychology, etc.

- **Compare and Contrast Box:** an ''at-a-glance'' comparison of the cultural and historical differences between the author's time and culture and late twentieth-century Western culture. This box includes pertinent parallels between the major scientific, political, and cultural movements of the time or place the story was written, the time or place the story was set (if a historical work), and modern Western culture. Works written after the mid-1970s may not have this box.

- **What Do I Read Next?:** a list of works that might complement the featured story or serve as a contrast to it. This includes works by the same author and others, works of fiction and nonfiction, and works from various genres, cultures, and eras.

Other Features

SSfS includes ''Why Study Literature At All?,'' a guest foreword by Thomas E. Barden, Professor of English and Director of Graduate English Studies at the University of Toledo. This essay provides a number of very fundamental reasons for studying literature and, therefore, reasons why a book such as *SSfS*, designed to facilitate the study of litererture, is useful.

A Cumulative Author/Title Index lists the authors and titles covered in each volume of the *SSfS* series.

A Cumulative Nationality/Ethnicity Index breaks down the authors and titles covered in each volume of the *SSfS* series by nationality and ethnicity.

A Subject/Theme Index, specific to each volume, provides easy reference for users who may be studying a particular subject or theme rather than a single work. Significant subjects from events to broad themes are included, and the entries pointing to the specific theme discussions in each entry are indicated in **boldface.**

Entries may include illustrations, including an author portrait, stills from film adaptations (if available), maps, and/or photos of key historical events.

Citing Short Stories for Students

When writing papers, students who quote directly from any volume of *SSfS* may use the following general forms to document their source. These examples are based on MLA style; teachers may request that students adhere to a different style, thus, the following examples may be adapted as needed.

When citing text from *SSfS* that is not attributed to a particular author (for example, the Themes, Style, Historical Context sections, etc.), the following format may be used:

> ''The Celebrated Jumping Frog of Calavaras County.'' *Short Stories for Students*. Ed. Kathleen Wilson. Vol. 1. Detroit: Gale, 1997, pp. 19-20.

When quoting the specially commissioned essay from *SSfS* (usually the first essay under the Criticism subhead), the following format may be used:

> Korb, Rena. Essay on ''Children of the Sea.'' *Short Stories for Students*. Ed. Kathleen Wilson. Vol. 1. Detroit: Gale, 1997, p. 42.

When quoting a journal essay that is reprinted in a volume of *Short Stories for Students,* the following form may be used:

> Schmidt, Paul. ''The Deadpan on Simon Wheeler.'' *The Southwest Review* Vol. XLI, No. 3 (Summer, 1956), pp. 270-77; excerpted and reprinted in *Short Stories for Students,* Vol. 1, ed. Kathleen Wilson. (Detroit: Gale, 1997), pp. 29-31.

When quoting material from a book that is reprinted in a volume of *SSfS,* the following form may be used:

> Bell-Villada, Gene H. ''The Master of Short Forms,'' in *Garcia Marquez: The Man and His Work* (University of North Carolina Press, 1990); excerpted and reprinted in *Short Stories for Students,* Vol. 1, ed. Kathleen Wilson. (Detroit: Gale, 1997), pp. 90- 91.

We Welcome Your Suggestions

The editor of *Short Stories for Students* welcomes your comments and ideas. Readers who wish to suggest short stories to appear in future volumes, or who have other suggestions, are cordially invited to contact the editor. You may contact the editor via e-mail at **ForStudentsEditors@galegroup.com.** Or write to the editor at:

Editor, *Short Stories for Students*
Gale Group
27500 Drake Road
Farmington Hills, MI 48331-3535

Literary Chronology

1857: Joseph Conrad is born Jozef Teodor Konrad Korzeniowski on December 3, in Berdiczew, Podolia (then part of Russia).

1882: Virginia Woolf is born on January 25 in London, England.

1883: Franz Kafka is born on July 3 in Prague, Czechoslovakia.

1893: Dorothy L. Sayers is born in Oxford, England.

1897: William Faulkner is born William Cuthbert Falkner on September 25 in New Albany, Mississippi.

1899: Joseph Conrad's ''Heart of Darkness'' is published for the first time.

1904: Isaac Bashevis Singer is born in Radzymin, Poland (then part of Russia).

1915: Saul Bellow is born Solomon Bellows in Quebec, Canada.

1915: Franz Kafka's ''Metamorphosis'' is published.

1919: Virginia Woolf's ''Kew Gardens'' is published.

1919: Doris Lessing is born Doris May Tayler on October 22 in Persia.

1923: Italo Calvino is born on October 15 in Cuba.

1924: Joseph Conrad dies of a heart attack on August 3.

1924: Franz Kafka dies of tuberculosis on June 3, a month before his forty-first birthday.

1925: Yukio Mishima is born Hiroka Kimitake in Tokyo, Japan.

1928: Cynthia Ozick is born April 17 in New York City, New York.

1931: William Faulkner's ''That Evening Sun'' is published for the first time.

1933: Philip Roth is born on March 19 in Newark, New Jersey.

1938: Raymond Carver is born on May 25 in Clatskanie, Oregon.

1939: Toni Cade Bambara is born on March 25 in Harlem in New York City, New York.

1939: Dorothy L. Sayers's ''Suspicion'' is published.

1940: Angela Carter is born in Eastborne, England.

1941: Virginia Woolf commits suicide on March 28.

1941: John Edgar Wideman is born in Washington, D.C.

1947: Saul Bellow wins a Guggenheim Fellowship.

1949: William Faulkner wins the Nobel Prize for literature.

1956: Italo Calvino's ''The Feathered Ogre'' is published.

1957: Saul Bellow's ''Leaving the Yellow House'' is published.

1957: Dorothy L. Sayers dies of a stroke.

1959: Philip Roth's ''Goodbye, Columbus'' is published.

1959: Philip Roth wins a National Book Award for *Goodbye, Columbus and Five Short Stories.*

1961: Isaac Bashevis Singer's ''Spinoza of Market Street'' is published.

1962: William Faulkner dies of a heart attack.

1963: John Edgar Wideman wins a Rhodes scholarship.

1963: Yukio Mishima's ''Fountains in the Rain'' is published.

1970: Yukio Mishima commits ritual suicide (*seppuku*) November 25.

1971: Cynthia Ozick's ''The Pagan Rabbi'' is published.

1972: Toni Cade Bambara's ''The Lesson'' is published.

1973: Raymond Carver wins the O. Henry Award (also in 1974, 1975, and 1983).

1974: Isaac Bashevis Singer wins the National Book Award.

1976: Saul Bellow wins the Nobel Prize for literature.

1978: Isaac Bashevis Singer wins the Nobel Prize for literature.

1979: Angela Carter's ''The Erlking'' is published.

1981: John Edgar Wideman's ''The Beginning of Homewood'' is published.

1981: Raymond Carver's ''What We Talk About When We Talk About Love'' is published.

1985: Italo Calvino dies of a stroke on September 19 in Rome.

1987: Doris Lessing's ''Debbie and Julie'' is published.

1988: Raymond Carver dies of lung cancer at the age of fifty.

1991: Isaac Bashevis Singer dies in Florida on July 24 after a series of strokes.

1992: Angela Carter dies of lung cancer.

1995: Toni Cade Bambara dies of colon cancer in December.

Acknowledgments

The editors wish to thank the copyright holders of the excerpted criticism included in this volume and the permissions managers of many book and magazine publishing companies for assisting us in securing reproduction rights. We are also grateful to the staffs of the Detroit Public Library, the Library of Congress, the University of Detroit Mercy Library, Wayne State University Purdy/Kresge Library Complex, and the University of Michigan Libraries for making their resources available to us. Following is a list of the copyright holders who have granted us permission to reproduce material in this volume of *Short Stories for Students (SSfS)*. Every effort has been made to trace copyright, but if omissions have been made, please let us know.

COPYRIGHTED MATERIAL IN *SSfS*, VOLUME 12, WERE REPRODUCED FROM THE FOLLOWING PERIODICALS:

African American Review, v. 26, Fall, 1992 for "Home: An Interview with John Edgar Wideman" by Jessica Lustig. © 1992 Jessica Lustig. Reproduced by permission of the authors.—*English Studies,* v. 68, February, 1987; v. 68, June, 1987. Swets & Zeitlinger, 1987. Copyright © 1987 by Swets & Zeitlinger. Reproduced by permission.—*The International Fiction Review,* v. 12, Summer, 1985. © Copyright 1985 International Fiction Association. Reproduced by permission.—*Studies in Short Fiction,* v. XIII, Summer, 1975; v. 19, Summer, 1982; v. 22, Summer, 1985. Copyright 1975, 1977, 1982, 1985 by Newberry College. All reproduced by permission.

COPYRIGHTED MATERIALS IN *SSfS*, VOLUME 12, WERE PRODUCED FROM THE FOLLOWING BOOKS:

Alexander, Edward. From *Isaac Bashevis Singer: A Study of the Short Fiction.* Twayne Publishers, 1990. Copyright 1990 by G. K. Hall & Co. All rights reserved. The Gale Group.—Billy, Ted. From *A Wilderness of Words: Closure and Disclosure in Conrad's Short Fiction.* Texas Tech University Press, 1997. © Copyright 1997 Texas Tech University Press. All rights reserved. Reproduced by permission of the publisher.—Campbell, Ewing. From *Raymond Carver: A Study of the Short Fiction.* Twayne Publishers, 1992. Copyright © 1992 by Twayne Publishers. All rights reserved. The Gale Group.—Fleishman, Avrom. From *Virginia Woolf: Revaluation and Continuity.* University of California Press, 1980. Copyright © 1980 by The Regents of the University of California. Reproduced by permission of the University of California Press and the author.—Friedman, Lawrence S. From *Understanding Cynthia Ozick.* University of South Carolina Press, 1991. Copyright © University of South Carolina 1991. Reproduced by permission.—Gillon, Adam. From *Joseph Conrad.* Twayne Publishers, 1982. Copyright © 1982 by Twayne Publishers. The Gale Group.—Halio, Jay L. From *Philip Roth Revisited.* Twayne Publishers, 1992. Copyright © 1992 by Twayne Publishers. All rights reserved. The Gale Group.—Hargrove, Nancy D. From ''Youth in Toni Cade Bambara's 'Gorilla, My Love,''' in *Women Writers of the Contemporary South*. Edited by Peggy Whitman Prenshaw. University Press of Mississippi, 1984. Copyright © 1984 by the University Press of Mississippi. Reproduced by permission.—Jones, Diane Brown. From *A Reader's Guide to the Short Stories of William Faulkner*. G. K. Hall & Company, 1994. Copyright © 1994 by Diane Brown Jones. All rights reserved. The Gale Group.—Kauvar, Elaine M. From *Cynthia Ozick's Fiction: Tradition and Invention.* Indiana University Press, 1993. © 1993 by Elaine M. Kauvar. All rights reserved. Reproduced by permission.—Kloepfer, Deborah Kelly. From ''Kew Gardens: Overview,'' in *Reference Guide to Short Fiction.* St. James Press, 1994. Edited by Noelle Watson. The Gale Group.—Lowin, Joseph. From *Cynthia Ozick.* Twayne Publishers, 1988. Copyright 1988 by G. K. Hall & Co. All rights reserved. The Gale Group.—Malin, Irving. From *Isaac Bashevis Singer.* Frederick Ungar Publishing Company, 1972. Copyright © 1972 by Frederick Ungar Publishing Co., Inc. Reproduced by permission.—Meyer, Adam. From *Raymond Carver.* Twayne Publishers, 1995. Copyright © 1995 by Twayne Publishers. All rights reserved. The Gale Group.—Spann, Meno. From *Franz Kafka.* Twayne Publishers, 1958. Copyright © 1958 by G. K. Hall & Co. All rights reserved. The Gale Group.—Vertreace, Martha M. From ''The Dance of Character and Community,'' in *American Women Writing Fiction: Memory, Identity, Family, Space.* Edited by Mickey Pearlman. University of Kentucky, 1989. Copyright © 1989 by The University Press of Kentucky. Reproduced by permission.

PHOTOGRAPHS AND ILLUSTRATIONS APPEARING IN *SSfS*, VOLUME 12, WERE RECEIVED FROM THE FOLLOWING SOURCES:

Bambara, Toni Cade, 1977, photograph by Sandra L. Swans. Reproduced by permission.—Bellow, Saul, photograph. The Library of Congress.—Calvino, Italo, photograph by Jerry Bauer. © Jerry Bauer. Reproduced by permission.—Carter, Angela, photograph by Jerry Bauer. © Jerry Bauer. Reproduced by permission.—Carver, Raymond, photograph. Archive Photos, Inc. Reproduced by permission.—Conrad, Joseph, photograph. The Library of Congress.—Ellmann, Richard, Robert Lowell, Philip Roth, New York City, 1960, photograph. AP/Wide World Photos. Reproduced by permission.—''Family Picture,'' 1920, oil on canvas, 25 5/8'' x 39 3/4'', painting by Max Beckmann. From a cover of *The Metamorphosis*, by Franz Kafka. Collection, The Museum of Modern Art, New York. Gift of Abby Aldrich Rockefeller. © The Museum of Modern Art, New York, 1986. Reproduced by permission of Bantam Books, a division of Random House, Inc.—Faulkner, William, photograph. Archive Photos, Inc. Reproduced by permission.—''The Giant of Yewdale,'' illustration from cigarette card, giant kidnapping Barbara, maid to Lady Eva le Fleming. Mary Evans Picture Library. Reproduced by permission.—Kafka, Franz, photograph. AP/Wide World Photos. Reproduced by permission.—Lessing, Doris, photograph by Jerry Bauer. © Jerry Bauer. Reproduced by permission.—Mencken, H. L., photograph. Corbis-Bettmann. Reproduced by permission.—Mishima, Yukio, Tokyo, Japan, 1966, photograph by Nobuyuki Masaki. AP/Wide World Photos. Reproduced by permission.—Ozick, Cynthia, photograph. Corbis-Bettmann. Reproduced by permission.—Roth, Phillip, photograph. AP/Wide World Photos, Inc. Reproduced by permission.—Roth, Tim, as Marlow, television still from movie ''Heart of Darkness.'' Archive Photos, Inc. Reproduced by permission.—Sayers, Dorothy L., photograph. Archive Photos, Inc. Reproduced by permission.—Singer, Isaac Bashevis, photograph. Corbis-Bettmann. Reproduced by permission.—Spinoza, Baruch, engraving.—Wideman, John Edgar, photograph by Jerry Bauer. © Jerry Bauer. Reproduced by permission.—Woolf, Virginia, photograph. AP/Wide World Photos. Reproduced by permission.

Contributors

Greg Barnhisel: Barnhisel holds a Ph.D. in English and American literature and currently teaches writing at Southwestern University in Georgetown, Texas. Entry on "That Evening Sun." Original essay on "That Evening Sun."

Liz Brent: Brent has a Ph.D. in American Culture, specializing in film studies, from the University of Michigan. She is a freelance writer and teaches courses in the history of American cinema. Entries on "The Feathered Ogre," "Goodbye, Columbus," "Heart of Darkness," "The Pagan Rabbi," "Spinoza of Market Street," and "What We Talk About When We Talk About Love." Original essays on "The Feathered Ogre," "Goodbye, Columbus," "Heart of Darkness," "The Pagan Rabbi," "Spinoza of Market Street," and "What We Talk About When We Talk About Love."

James Frazier: Frazier is an instructor of high school and college English literature and composition. Original essay on "The Beginning of Homewood."

Sheldon Goldfarb: Goldfarb has a Ph.D. in English and has published two books on the Victorian author William Makepeace Thackeray. Entry on "Metamorphosis." Original essay on "Metamorphosis."

Carole Hamilton: Hamilton is an English teacher at Cary Academy, an innovative private school in Cary, North Carolina. Original essay on "The Feathered Ogre."

Joyce Hart: Hart has degrees in English literature and creative writing and is a copyeditor and published writer. Original essays on "The Erlking" and "Fountains in the Rain."

Kendall Johnson: Johnson teaches American literature at the University of Pennsylvania where he recently received his Ph.D. Entry on "Kew Gardens." Original essay on "Kew Gardens."

Lois Kerschen: Kerschen is a writer and public school district administrator. Original essay on "Spinoza of Market Street."

Rena Korb: Korb has a master's degree in English literature and creative writing and has written for a wide variety of educational publishers. Entries on "Fountains in the Rain," "Leaving the Yellow House," "The Lesson," and "Suspicion." Original essays on "Debbie and Julie," "The Erlking," "The Feathered Ogre," "Fountains in the Rain," "Leaving the Yellow House," "The Lesson," and "Suspicion."

Sarah Madsen Hardy: Madsen Hardy has a doctorate in English literature and is a freelance writer and editor. Entries on "Debbie and Julie" and "The Erlking." Original essays on "Debbie and Julie" and "The Erlking."

Daniel Moran: Moran is a secondary-school teacher of English and American literature. He has contributed several entries and essays to the Gale series *Drama for Students*. Original essay on ''Suspicion.''

Wendy Perkins: Perkins is Assistant Professor of English, Prince George's Community College, Maryland; Ph.D. in English, University of Delaware. Original essays on ''Debbie and Julie,'' ''Leaving the Yellow House,'' and ''Suspicion.''

Doreen Piano: Piano is a Ph.D. candidate in English at Bowling Green State University. Original essay on ''Fountains in the Rain.''

Elisabeth Piedmont-Marton: Piedmont-Marton teaches American literature and directs the writing center at Southwestern University in Texas. She writes frequently about the modern short story. Entry on ''The Beginning of Homewood.'' Original essay on ''The Beginning of Homewood.''

The Beginning of Homewood

John Edgar Wideman is the author of dozens of books and stories and has in the last two decades claimed his rightful place among the most important contemporary American authors. Central to his legacy, the Homewood books, originally published as separate volumes, *Damballah*, *Hiding Place*, and *Sent For You Yesterday*, were collected under the title *The Homewood Trilogy* and published in 1985. ''The Beginning of Homewood'' has emerged as the most anthologized of all the stories in the volume.

''The Beginning of Homewood'' employs Wideman's call and response narrative technique to blend the stories of his ancestor Sybela Owens, his elderly aunt May, and his own incarcerated brother, Robby. In the story, which he confesses has ''something wrong with it,'' he poses the question whether Sybela's crime (of escaping slavery) can be weighed against Robby's. Though Wideman never offers a resolution for this thorny problem, by juxtaposing these two images of freedom and bondage, he encourages readers to explore the complex and deeply ambiguous moral landscape that all of the characters inhabit.

John Edgar Wideman

1981

Author Biography

Born in Washington, D.C., in 1941, John Edgar Wideman has led a life filled with remarkable achievement and terrible tragedy. He is the author

of seven novels, three collections of short stories, and two books of nonfiction. He has taught at the University of Pennsylvania, the University of Wyoming, and the University of Massachusetts, where he is currently a member of the faculty.

When Wideman was still a baby, his family moved from Washington to Pittsburgh and settled in Homewood, a black neighborhood with a rich history that would later inspire several books. Within a decade, however, Wideman's family moved from Homewood to the predominantly white, upper-class neighborhood of Shadyside. John flourished in school, becoming captain of the basketball team and the class valedictorian. In 1959, he entered the University of Pennsylvania on a scholarship, intending to be a psychology major. After switching to English as a major, he continued to excel as both a student and an athlete, winning election to Phi Beta Kappa and all Ivy-league in basketball. By his senior year Wideman had decided to become a writer.

After graduation in 1963, Wideman became the first African American to win a Rhodes Scholarship since Alain Locke in 1905. At Oxford he continued to study literature and began his teaching career in the summer term at Howard University in Washington, D.C. In 1965, he married Judith Ann Goldman and the next year received his degree from Oxford. After attending the famous University of Iowa's Writer's Workshop and publishing his first novel, *A Glance Away*, Wideman returned to the University of Pennsylvania to teach. After students asked him to teach a course in African-American literature, Wideman began his own personal exploration of black literature and reconsidered his own voice as an African-American writer. After publishing two more novels, Widmean entered an eight-year fallow period.

In the mid-1970s two things happened that changed the course of Wideman's life. He accepted an offer from the University of Wyoming and moved away from his roots and history to the virtually all-white world of Laramie. Within a year, his brother Robby, who had remained in the Pittsburgh area, was sentenced to life imprisonment for armed robbery and murder. After an exceptionally productive ten-year period, Wideman and his family moved back east and he began teaching at the University of Massachusetts in Amorist, a position he continues to hold. The same year in which they moved east, 1986, the Wideman family experienced yet another tragedy when his middle child, Jacob, confessed to killing a roommate at summer camp and, at eighteen years old, was sentenced to life in prison.

Plot Summary

The story opens as the narrator tries to explain how the story came into being. It began, he says, as a letter to his brother, which he "began writing on a Greek island two years ago, but never finished, never sent." Addressing his absent brother, he then proceeds to tell "the story that came before the letter," the story about his great-great-great-grandmother Sybela Owens and how she escaped slavery and settled in Pittsburgh in what is now known as Homewood.

At his grandfather's funeral, the narrator had heard the elderly aunts talk of Sybela and the beginnings of Homewood. Through the intervening voices of his aunt May and Bess, the narrator relates the story of Sybela's "escape, her five-hundred-mile flight through hostile, dangerous territory."

Having been a slave on a plantation near Cumberland, Maryland, Sybela escaped one night with her two small children and Charlie Bell, the white man and son of the owner, who "stole" her when he learned that his father planned to sell her. The year was 1859; Sybela was around eighteen years old, and Charlie was the father of the children. Charlie and Sybela went on to have eighteen more children. Eventually, as Aunt May relates, "the other white men let Charlie know they didn't want one of their kind living with no black woman so Charlie up and moved." And the neighborhood where he moved, "way up on Bruston Hill where nobody 'round trying to mind his business," marked the beginning of Homewood.

Sybela was remarkable, not only because of her courageous escape from slavery but also because of her legendary ability to refuse to internalize her status as slave. She was known throughout the plantation as a woman of exceptional pride and reminded old-timers of another woman who maintained the autonomy of her body against the all common sexual advantages of white owners by wearing a cage around her torso.

After Aunt May and Mother Bess finish telling their story about Sybela and the old days, the narrator's voice returns in the final paragraphs. Again, he addresses his brother, whom he last saw "in chains . . . old-time leg irons and wrist shackles and twenty pounds of iron dragged through the marble corridors in Fort Collins.'' He wonders if there is a larger scale of justice at work, if the ''Court could set your crime against Sybela's, the price of our freedom against yours.''

Characters

Charlie Bell

Charlie Bell is the white man whose family owns Sybela Owens. As was the cruel custom among slave-holding men, he has forced Sybela to be his concubine. One night he comes to her cabin and ''steals'' her and her two children, of whom he is the father, and together they run north toward Pittsburgh where the neighborhood in which they settle becomes known as Homewood.

Bess

Called Mother Bess, she's May's sister and fellow caretaker of Sybela's spirit and the family's history.

Maggie

Maggie is the oldest of Sybela's two children who accompany her in her flight from slavery (with Charlie Bell). The story does not specify, but it is reasonable to suppose that they are Bell's children as well.

May

Called Aunt May most of the time by the narrator, she, like Mother Bess, belongs to an intermediate generation of women. She is old enough to remember Sybela as an old woman and takes it as her responsibility to tell the old stories to the younger generations. The narrator hears her tell these stories at his grandfather's funeral, and it plants the idea of this story in his head. May also has a certain way of talking that the narrator finds fascinating, and he attempts to imitate it in his prose.

Narrator

The narrator is the great-great-great-grandson of Sybela Owens. This story is a letter he's writing

John Edgar Wideman

from a Greek island to his brother who is in prison and is his self-conscious attempt to connect her story to his.

Sybela Owens

Sybela is the narrator's (and the un-named ''you'' to whom the story is told, the narrator's brother's) great-great-great-grandmother. A ''black woman who in 1859 was approximately eighteen years old,'' she's the ancestor that helped establish the African-American community of Homewood when she settled there with Charlie Bell. Sybela went on to have eighteen more children in addition to the two she brought with her when she escaped from slavery. She's a kind of spiritual leader of the family, and the older women, Aunt May and Mother Bess, tell stories about her courage and strength in order to keep her memory alive and the family history known to the younger generations. Wideman uses the story of her captivity and flight as a contrast to his brother's flight and captivity in the criminal justice system.

Thomas

Thomas is Maggie's younger brother.

Topics for Further Study

- How common was it for runaway slaves to make it to freedom and establish permanent homes in the North? Do some research to see if Sybela's story is typical. Identify through research other areas in Northern cities like Homewood.

- What's the significance of Greece and the Greek island in the story? How does it relate to the Sybil, which the narrator identifies with Sybela?

- Compare Wideman's narrative technique of weaving together multiple voices with the narrative technique of another story you have read.

- Explain your opinions on Wideman's comparison of his brother to a runaway slave? What questions about fairness and the criminal justice system are raised by this story? Try to answer this question by looking at the issues from several perspectives.

Themes

Afrocentricity

"The Beginning of Homewood" and the volume of short stories of which it is a part, *Damballah*, belongs to the stage of Wideman's career when he began to write from an Afrocentric perspective. After the eight year hiatus following the publication of the novel *The Lynchers*, Wideman moved his family back East and shifted his literary interest to stories more connected to his own life and to African-American culture and history.

Critic Doreatha Drummond Mbalia explains that this process is necessarily incremental. Wideman's literary education, Mbalia explains, was Eurocentric. That is, he was taught to view the world from a European, or white, point of view and came to internalized European standards and values for art and literature. Thus, when he began his career as a writer, he emulated white writers like William Faulkner and James Joyce. According to Mbalia, Wideman, like so many African-American authors,

needed to "reclaim his African personality." This process "occurred in developmental stages, she continues, "caused by a quantitative buildup of a number of factors, largely negative, involving family members, race concerns, and the writing process itself." For Wideman, the most influential of these factors was his brother Robby's arrest for murder, which brought him back into the fold of his family for the first time in years. He writes about this experience in the memoir *Brothers and Keepers*: "The distance I'd put between my brother's world and mine suddenly collapsed. The two thousand miles between Laramie, Wyoming, and Pittsburgh, Pennsylvania, my years of willed ignorance, of flight and hiding, has not changed a simple truth: I could not run fast enough or far enough. Robby was inside me. Wherever he was, running for his life, he carried part of me with him." "The Beginning of Homewood," then, is a story about his own ancestor, Sybela Owens, who came to Homewood in 1859 but is addressed to a fictionalized version of his incarcerated brother. The story is about both Sybela's and Tommy's (Robby's) flights from bondage—hers from slavery, his as a fugitive—but it is also about Wideman's narrator's struggle to reconcile these two stories and to locate his own voice in them.

Freedom and Bondage

Images of freedom and bondage animate the narrative of "The Beginning of Homewood." Wideman juxtaposes the story of his great-great-great grandmother Sybela Owens with the story of his brother, to whom the story is addressed as a letter, in order to challenge readers' assumptions about what freedom and bondage signify in the African-American experience. Moreover, the narrator explores the ways in which he is *bound* to his family's history and, conversely, how *free* he is to tell the story. In this sense, Wideman's relationship with the material for his story is problematic. Critic Barbara Seidman explains that "by embedding Sybela's story of physical and spiritual redemption within a meditation on his brother's grim circumstances, the narrator conveys the continued urgency of such issues for African Americans; he also engages the metafictional self-reflexiveness that characterizes his generation of American writers as he muses over the act of writing and its problematic relationship to living events."

Sybela's narrative moves nominally from bondage to freedom as she escapes from slavery in the South to the free black communities of Pittsburgh in the North. But crossing over from slavery to freedom, Wideman suggests, is never as simple and absolute as it appears. Sybela's freedom is compromised by her dependence on Charlie Bell, the white man who ''stole'' her and her children. She may have escaped slavery, but her status as his property is fundamentally unchanged. Sybela's story is one of gradual self-emancipation from the psychological bonds of slavery, and her presence in May's and Bess's narratives testifies that she has finally found freedom: she belongs to them.

Tommy's (Robby's) trajectory, on the other hand, is the opposite of Sybela's. He moves from freedom to captivity in the criminal justice system. In a gesture analogous to the portrayal of the ambiguity of Sybela's freedom, Wideman's story suggests that Tommy's prior freedom was already constrained, as it is for most African-American males, and that his captivity is merely superficial because his defiance keeps him free to some extent.

The narrator, as well, is caught up in the shifting valences of freedom and bondage. While he presumes to write to his brother from the safe and remote location of Greece, he is ineluctably drawn into the stories of both his ancestors and his brother. It's as if he isn't free to tell other stories; he must tell these. Furthermore, as he explains in the opening paragraph of ''The Beginning of Homewood,'' one story is held captive by another: ''The letter [to his brother] remains inside the story, buried, bleeding through when I read.''

Style

Narration: Oral Tradition

Wideman's narrative technique in ''The Beginning of Homewood'' is related to the development of his Afrocentric point of view. By the time in his career when he was writing the stories that make up *Damballah*, Wideman had shaken off the single narrator perspective of his earlier fiction and had merged his interest in the modernist prose of Faulkner and James Joyce with his concern to write about the African-American experience. The resulting narrative technique attempts to render in prose aspects of the African-American oral traditions of storytelling and call and response. In an interview with James Coleman, Wideman explains how he came to adopt these new techniques: ''In the later books also I began to understand how in using Afro-American

folklore and language I didn't have to give up any of the goals that I was after when I was using more Europeanized and more traditional—literary traditional—devices and techniques.''

''The Beginning of Homewood,'' as the final story in *Damballah*, makes particularly good use of these Afrocentric literary techniques. In the words of critic Seidmann, Wideman's narrator ''creates a wall of sound from the voices he has unloosed in the preceding stories; writing to his brother in prison, he acknowledges that his real task as a writer has been to hear and synthesize those women's testimonials to the community's history of defeat and transcendence.'' In other words, he allows Sybela and May and Bess to speak through him, to use him as an instrument to tell their stories across barriers of time, culture, and geography. To choose this technique is also to comment on the role of the storyteller, or writer, in the African-American culture. To some extent, this kind of self-consciousness about the role of the writer is a feature of all modern literature, as Seidmann explains. Like many of his contemporaries, Wideman ''engages in the metafictional self-reflexiveness that characterizes his generation of American writers as he muses over the act of writing and its problematic relationship to lived events.'' But as Wideman himself explains in the interview with James Coleman, there is something more at stake for African-American writers. ''Storytellers are always inside and outside the story by definition. Sometimes in Afro-American culture there are these little doors, there are these wonderful windows by which the storyteller gets pulled back, so he doesn't feel too lonely, doesn't feel left out . . .''

Setting: Mythical Spaces

Just as Wideman's use of many narrative voices, or poly-vocality, allows him to tell the story from several perspectives, his use of diffuse and multiple settings for the story adds to its power and range. It's difficult to say where the story takes place. Is it the place from which the narrator is writing the letter to his brother? Is it the plantation in Maryland? Is it Homewood of the mid-nineteenth century, or Homewood of the 1970s and 1980s? Is it the Fort Collins courtroom where the narrator last sees his brother? Or even the Greek island where the narrator first begins thinking about these stories? Wideman's point is that the story is set in all these places and times, but its true force does not emerge until they come together, layered upon and woven around each other.

As a result of this layered or woven construction, Wideman's narrative settings take on more mythic dimensions than they otherwise would. The character of Sybela, for example, resonates with the legend of a slave woman, named Belle, from an earlier era, as well as with the Greek legend of the Sybil, who, when asked what she wanted, replied "I want to die." The intermingling of these identities and stories helps to imbue Homewood with a history and significance that would have been lost without the intervention of the storytellers.

Historical Context

Life under Slavery

The institution of slavery placed enormous physical and psychological burdens on the body of the slave population in the American South. In addition to the hideous cruelties of forced labor, slaves faced a constant threat of being sold. This meant that slaves lived with a gnawing instability, as families could be broken up against their will.

Female slaves endured yet another hardship as they frequently became the objects of unwanted and often violent sexual advances from white owners and overseers. In fact, many white owners who viewed their slaves as property, considered sexual appropriation of black women to be their right. As a result, there were many white men who had two families: one in the big house and another down in the slave quarters. To make matters even worse, the children of these unions, mulattos, were treated even worse. Linda Brent, a slave whose autobiography, *Incidents in the Life of a Slave Girl*, was originally published in 1861, wrote that "slavery was terrible for me, but it is far more terrible for women." Walter Teller explains in his introduction to a new edition to Brent's book in 1973 that "while all female slaves were subject to sexual abuse, mulattos in particular were exploited sexually." The subject was rarely discussed, even among anti-slavery activists. In fact, when a white woman, L. Marie Child, helped to bring Brent's narrative into print, she felt compelled to warn her readers in a preface about the "indelicate" subject matter contained in the book: "This peculiar phase of slavery has generally been kept veiled; but the public ought to be made acquainted with its monstrous features, and I willingly take responsibility of presenting them with the veil withdrawn. I do this for the sake of my sisters in bondage, who are suffering wrongs so foul, that our ears are too delicate to listen to them."

Homewood and African-American Enclaves

An enclave is a section or an area of a city or town in which members of an ethnic group settle. As opposed to a ghetto, where members of ethnic or religious groups are forced to live, enclaves are created by members of these groups and tend to cultivate community support networks and other economic structures. Of course, runaway slaves and free Blacks would not necessarily have their pick of prime real estate in cities like Pittsburgh in the mid-nineteenth century. Nor would the residents of Homewood, or enclaves like it in other cities, have much economic power to wield. The value of enclaves like Homewood, Wideman explains, is in their power to preserve and reproduce culture and tradition. In an interview with Jessica Lusting in 1992, he explains that the appeal of Homewood is "not so much with bricks and boards," but in the people's "sense of values and the way they treated one another and the way they treated the place." Wideman elaborates on how African-American enclaves like Homewood are so important: "Africans couldn't bring African buildings, ecology, languages wholesale, in the material sense, to the New World. But they brought the invisible dimensions of their society, of our culture, to this land."

Critical Overview

As many of his critics have pointed out, the novel *Damballah*, of which "The Beginning of Homewood" is a part, marks the end of a fallow period for Wideman and signals the beginning of a new phase for him as a writer. Not surprisingly, then, some critics, expecting more of the same from the accomplished college professor and Rhodes scholar, were somewhat put off by his new thematic interests and stylistic innovations. On the other hand, some reviewers and critics saw the book as the culmination of Wideman's career up to that point.

Writing in the *New York Times*, reviewer Mel Watkins says that Wideman's latest work contains "the high regard for language and craft demonstrated in [his] previous books." He goes on to praise *Damballah* for its formal daring and departure from the rules of the novel. The book, he says, "is something of a departure for him, and in freeing his voice from the confines of the novel form, he has written what is possibly his most impressive work." Watkins concludes that "Wideman is one of America's premier writers of fiction." Finally, he sounds a note that other reviewers and critics have also echoed: "That they [*Damballah* and *Hiding Place*] were published originally in paperback perhaps suggests that he is also one of our most underrated writers."

Also writing in the *New York Times*, reviewer John Leonard praises both *Damballah* and *Hiding Place*, but decries their paperback status. Suggesting that the publishing world does not acknowledge the literary permanence of many black writers, Leonard wonders if publishers aren't guilty of "a new 'aesthetic' of bad faith." He concludes: "That his two new books will fall apart after a second reading is a scandal." But in an interview in the *New York Times* with Edwin McDowell, Wideman explains that it was his decision to bring the books out in paperback. Citing the modest hardcover sales of his earlier work, Wideman explained: "I spend an enormous amount of time and energy writing and I want to write good books, but I also want people to read them."

Among the stories in *Damballah*, "The Beginning of Homewood" is often singled out by critics and reviewers as a particularly successful example of the kinds of stories Wideman was writing during this period. "The Beginning of Homewood," because it links the stories set in Africa with those set in Pittsburgh that will follow in the next volume, seems to best embody the features that reviewer Randall Kenan identified as Wideman's strength during the Homewood period: "It is as if he wrote his stories and then compressed them to a third of their original size. Eschewing quotation marks, Wideman has his speakers shift and shift and at times meld—as if into one mind, one voice."

Literary critics recognized in these collage-like techniques, despite the African-American setting and allusions to an oral literature, the hallmarks of literary modernism as practiced by the likes of James Joyce and William Faulkner. Despite the praise he received for the Homewood stories, Wideman continued to develop his experimental techniques and Afrocentric perspectives. This trend, as Mbalia points out, has caused some members of the literary establishment to dismiss his more recent work as not quite up to the standards of the Homewood stories. In her estimation, reviewers "emphasized the beauty of the Homewood sto-

ries," and implied that they "were more lyrical and thus more powerful works of art than the more recent ones."

Criticism

Elisabeth Piedmont-Marton

Piedmont-Marton teaches literature and writing classes at Southwestern University in Texas. She writes frequently about the modern short story. In this essay she explores the moral ambiguity at work in "The Beginning of Homewood."

Like William Faulkner does in his novels and stories set in the fictional world of Yoknapatawpha, Wideman creates a complex landscape in "The Beginning of Homewood" that allows him to enmesh his characters in webs of moral ambiguities. The community of Homewood founded by runaway slave Sybela Owens, the narrator's great-great-great-grandmother, is certainly not an unqualified safe-haven. Though life in Homewood is preferable to life as a slave in Maryland, Sybela's escape from freedom, Wideman's story suggests, is compromised by her alliance with Charlie Bell, the white man and father of her children who stole her from his own father and brought her to Pittsburgh. The story's theme of moral ambiguity is dramatized by the narrator's comparison between Sybela's escape from slavery and his own brother's captivity. By asking himself and readers to weigh her crime against his, he suggests that her emancipation is incomplete and the crimes committed against her are not yet fully redressed. Thus the story leads readers into extremely ambiguous moral territory—intimating that the narrator's brother's crime is caused or balanced by the legacy of slavery. But the narrator's own reticence and ambivalence about asking these questions, about even telling the story, encourages readers to contemplate the troubling issues that the story raises rather than just turn away from them.

The opening paragraph of the story sets the tone of moral ambiguity and introduces the narrator as a troubled mediator, as someone stuck in the middle. He describes the story to follow as unfinished, as having something wrong with it. He identifies himself as reader as well as author of the text: "I have just finished reading a story which began as a letter to you." The letter, which was never finished and never sent, was written from a Greek island two

What Do I Read Next?

- *Incidents in the Life of a Slave Girl* (1973) by Linda Brent was originally published with the assistance of a white woman named L. Maria Child in 1861. This book has become a crucial piece in nineteenth-century American literature. Though the slave narrative constitutes its own genre, Brent's book is one of the few written by a woman.

- ''Everyday Use'' by Alice Walker is a short story that explores many of the same themes about African-American culture that Wideman's stories do. Walker also experiments with the same techniques of integrating oral culture into the story format.

- *Cane* (1923) by Jean Toomer uses experimental techniques drawn both from literary modernism and from traditional African-American culture. Toomer renders a richly textured and powerful portrait of the lives of African Americans in the South. This is one of the books that Wideman cites as an influence on his work.

---

years earlier. The narrator's distance—and alienation—from home is significant and will figure into the complex moral equations he explores regarding ethics of escape. But readers don't know now to whom the narrator is writing, nor why ''there is something wrong about the story nothing can fix.''

Soon, however, the narrator begins to explain how one story overtook another, how the letter he never finished became the story he's telling now. He also maps out some of the moral territory across which his narrative and intellectual journey will take place. First, he says, he wanted to tell Aunt May's story, let her voice come through him to tell the tale of great-great-great-grandmother Sybela Owens' flight to freedom. But as clearly as he hears May's voice working through him, he is also nagged by the question why he ''was on a Greek island and why you were six thousand miles away in prison and what all that meant and what I could say to you about it.'' At first, telling May's and Sybela's story seemed as simple as it was important: ''the theme was to be the urge for freedom, the resolve of the runaway to live free or die.'' But the narrator soon discovers the disquieting fact that when he tries to connect Sybela's story to his brother's, he's unable to maintain the safety of his objective storytelling stance: ''I couldn't tell either story without implicating myself.'' What he runs up against is ''the matter of guilt, of responsibility,'' and he finds he must include himself in the reckoning. Then movement of his narrative from the café in the Greek islands back to Homewood, back, in fact, to Sybela Owens and the beginning of Homewood, is a return to the place from which he believed he had escaped. But in returning he finds that he must face matters of guilt and responsibility; he must, as the storyteller, set his brother's crime against ''the crime of this female runaway.''

The narrator's reckoning process requires that he reconsider Sybela's story in light of both his own and his brother's life. When he revisits her ''dash for freedom,'' he finds that he wants to dwell on her first day of freedom, but cannot. The reason his imagination won't stay fixed on how Sybela felt and what she thought that first day when she isn't awakened by the sound of the conch shell is that her freedom is compromised and mediated, not simple, as he had always thought it was. Sybela's freedom is incomplete, and her autonomy limited. She trades absolute freedom—and the risk of death and capture—for the protection she gets from remaining with Charlie Bell. On her first day of freedom, Sybela ''misses the moaning horn and hates the white man, her lover, her liberator, her children's father sleeping beside her.'' In other words, the line between slavery and freedom is not absolute, nor is the boundary between evil and good, and hate and love. Sybela's freedom, upon which the narrator's entire family's existence depends, is not the result of a singular, heroic act. Rather, she's free because of an infinite number of calculations and compromises, all of which have consequences. She may have escaped the plantation and some of the strictures of slavery, but she remains bound to Charlie, at first because he knows where they're going and later because he can offer her and her children protection. He knows his way in the world and she does not: "All white men seemed to know that magic that connected the plantation to the rest of the world, a world which for her was no more than a handful of words she had heard others use."

When the narrator imagines what would happen to Sybela if she had been caught, "a funky, dirty, black woman, caught and humbled, marched through like the prize of war she is," he is compelled to ask himself "why not me." And then he addresses his questions to his brother's situation, also "paraded . . . costumed, fettered through the halls," and wonders if he "could have run away without committing a crime." Will running away always be a crime for descendants of Sybela Owens, the woman who never managed to quite run far enough? The narrator wonders if his own distance from, or escape from, Homewood constitutes a crime, or if it is compensated by his brother's crime.

The narrator suggests that his brother's incarceration is a consequence of Homewood's history. According to May's account, the land on which Sybela and Charlie originally settled is "fixed," or cursed. She explains: "That spiteful piece of property been the downfall of so many I done forgot half the troubles come to people try to live there." She describes how the beautiful babies she remembers later become men about whom there always seems to be some terrible story to tell: "I remembers the babies. How beautiful they were. Then somebody tells me this one's dead, or that one's dying or Rashad going to court today or they gave Tommy life."

Though it stops short of drawing conclusions, Wideman's story suggests that even today in Homewood, a community founded by a runaway slave and her white lover, determining guilt and innocence is no simple matter. By setting up the comparison between Sybela's incarceration under the institution of slavery and her moral but illegal escape on the one hand, and Robby's flight from the law and subsequent imprisonment on the other hand, Wideman asks some troubling questions about

> By setting up the comparison between Sybela's incarceration under the institution of slavery and her moral but illegal escape on the one hand, and Robby's flight from the law and subsequent imprisonment on the other hand, Wideman asks some troubling questions about justice and accountability."

justice and accountability. Is Robby's criminalization inevitable? Is his flight from justice preordained and his imprisonment an instance of the historical desire of white America to subdue rebellious black Americans like Sybela? By examining his own role in the family and his safe, privileged distance from the kind of life his brother has led, the narrator wonders if his freedom had been purchased by his brother's. The story implies that the curse of the piece of land on which Sybela and Charlie settled insists that the family has not yet paid for Sybela's crime of resistance, and that it demands that every generation must offer up one of its own to white authority to compensate for Sybela's refusal to give herself and her children up.

Just as the narrative landscape of Wideman's story proves to be more complex than meets the eye, so does it's moral terrain. Wideman challenges readers to sort out one voice from the next and leaves readers to wrestle with gaps and unanswered questions. On a moral level, however, his story has an even more profoundly destabilizing effect by linking Sybela's "crime" of escaping slavery, to Robby's crime and capture, to the narrator's "escape" from the life his brother and so many others have been consigned to live.

Source: Elisabeth Piedmont-Marton, Critical Essay on "The Beginning of Homewood," in *Short Stories for Students*, The Gale Group, 2001.

James Frazier

Frazier is an instructor of high school and college English literature and composition. In this essay, he analyzes the relation of Wideman's structure to his themes.

John Edgar Wideman's short story, "The Beginning of Homewood," is a complex assembly of smaller stories that the narrator attempts to meaningfully string together. The many stories he tells appear in the letter written from the narrator to his brother, imprisoned for life for a murder to which he was an accomplice. That letter is the short story "The Beginning of Homewood." His brother's fate prompts the narrator into "trying to figure out why I was on a Greek island and why you were six thousand miles away in prison and what all that meant and what I could say to you about it." Feeling he must say something to his brother ("the only person I needed to write was you"), he begins a letter, but "five or six sentences addressed to you and then the story took over." The narrator never finishes this original letter or its story. He does, however, later re-read it and is provoked to write the second letter—the present story. The first story the narrator tells, about a letter becoming a story but never getting sent, establishes one of the major themes of "The Beginning of Homewood," namely, the attempt to make sense of events through telling stories. Additionally, the structure here serves to blur the generic distinctions between letters and stories, suggesting that stories take on much of their meaning through whomever the writer is addressing, and that, conversely, letters to others may be not very different from stories we want to tell them, specifically and individually.

The second story the narrator wants to tell his brother, that of their great-great-great-grandmother Sybela Owens, he calls both a story and a meditation. Moreover, it is a meditation that he "had wanted to decorate with the trappings of a story." As the short story "The Beginning of Homewood" is both story and letter, here the story of Sybela is both story and meditation meant to look like a story. The effect is a further blurring of genre distinctions, which here suggests that stories might be characterized as meditations, instruments for thought processes that change the reader or listener. With that invitation to meditate on Sybela's story, the narrator proceeds. Sybela had been a runaway slave, and the theme of the story as the narrator wants to tell it is "the urge for freedom," presumably because his brother feels the same urge. But this application gets too complicated. His attempt "to tell Sybela's story as it connected with yours," proves difficult since she ran away from slavery, and his brother ran away from the scene of a murder he committed. It would seem obvious that a slave who runs away is certainly less a criminal than a man who commits murder and runs from the law. Therefore, there is an initial impulse to say something to his brother with this story, but the message is deferred because the narrator is uncertain how to make sense of it; the parallels between the stories of Sybela and his brother seem difficult to maintain. Still, in the face of this frustration, he persists, faithful that telling the story will yield some meaning, some understanding for his brother and him. Straining to relate his brother's story to Sybela's, he wonders whether the difference might be one of language, whether there are "names other than 'outlaw' to call you," whether "words other than 'crime'" might "define" his brother's actions. Though during slavery a slave who ran away was, legally speaking, committing a crime, few people would today call a runaway slave a criminal. Perhaps such a change in perception could redeem his brother. But imagining such a change is a difficult and complex task. The narrator wants to tell a story that can console his brother, offer him some kind of redemption, some kind of connection, but there are parts that don't fit, that he can't make sense of. This is presumably why the original letter was deferred for so long.

Yet Aunt May's voice, which echoes throughout "The Beginning of Homewood," gets him "started on the story" of Sybela. Like Aunt May, the narrator allows himself to make "digressions within digressions." Imitating Aunt May's stories that "exist because of their parts and each part is a story worth telling, worth examining to find the stories it contains," the narrator takes two important "digressions" off the Sybela story, seeking "to recover everything." These are the stories of Sybil and Belle. Sybela's very identity—her name—preserves both of these women's stories. Sybela and Sybil the Greek priestess are both imprisoned, but Sybela overcomes the death of spirit that comes from being caged, while Sybil begs for death. Thus, Sybela's triumph of spirit is highlighted through contrast. It becomes an example the narrator wants to hold up for his brother. Sybil's story contributes meaning to Sybela's and, by extension, to the story of the narrator's brother. Sybela, Sybil, and Belle—who encloses her head in a bird cage to ward off the sexual advances of white men—all struggle with captivity and the waiting it entails. They raise the possibility of, and complicate the issue of, dignity within captivity. In the worst case scenario, captivity might finally allow no hope except the "hauntingly human expressiveness" with which one can sing Sybil's song, "I want to die." As these stories provided ways for her fellow slaves to interpret Sybela, so they all three might provide interpretations for the situation in which the narrator and his brother find themselves. The quick complications the narrator brings together with this grouping of stories—those of Sybela, Sybil, Belle, and his brother—demonstrate his readiness to concede that there are no easy answers and to deal with the difficulties directly. Striving to be the kind of storyteller Aunt May is, one whose stories take shape in the process of telling, he has faith that the stories, however disparate, can be pieced together into a unified and meaningful whole. And so he continues to tell them.

Around the middle of "The Beginning of Homewood," the narrator writes his own version of a piece of his brother's story, the scene at the courthouse in Fort Collins, Colorado. The imagery in this account provides links to the other stories, inviting comparisons. For example, details such as the hallway that "some other black prisoner mopped" and the "drag of the iron" that binds their legs suggest the slavery and bondage of the narrator's brother's ancestors. The narrator's brother and accomplice pretend no awareness of the chains that cage them at the courthouse, creating around themselves a "glass cage," in which they perform for the onlookers, and asserting their spiritual independence from the physical chains that bind them. This "glass cage" is part of a pattern of cage imagery that links many of the stories, and how these characters respond to the cages is a good point of contrast. The image of the cage recalls the self-imposed cage worn on Belle's head, which became a symbol of self-rule and dignity to protect her from the sexual advances of the white men. Sybil is caged by the magician and wants to die. Sybela flees her cage, and escapes. Yet the most important cage is the prison that holds the narrator's brother, and the question that drives this story is: What should my reaction to this cage be? It's a question as urgent to his brother as to the narrator.

In the project of telling stories to find meaning and order, the narrator might also hypothesize variations on those stories. For example, he realizes that Sybela is a much closer parallel to himself than to his brother since he and Sybela both escaped—she the slavery, he the conditions that have landed his brother in jail. So by imagining her getting caught,

> " The first story the narrator tells, about a letter becoming a story but never getting sent, establishes one of the major themes of 'The Beginning of Homewood,' namely, the attempt to make sense of events through telling stories."

he distances himself and turns Sybela's story, once more, into his brother's: "I ask myself again *why not me*, why is it the two of you skewered and displayed like she would have been if she hadn't kept running." In this comparison, his brother becomes a victim of the social forces around him, as sympathetic as a runaway slave. Tinkering with the story allows the narrator to wonder, to question the society that has jailed his brother. Yet, the tone is not argumentative. It is openly exploratory, not angrily condemnatory. He wonders "if you really had any chance, if anything had changed between her crime and yours." The tension is not relieved, but the hypothesized story creates new possibilities for the narrator to consider in trying to make sense of his brother's situation, and thus the layering of these stories continues to fulfill an important purpose.

Yet another story, that of Sybela's life at Homewood, finally shows the significance of the title, "The Beginning of Homewood." Like most of the stories the narrator tells, this one has no real conclusion; it ends in a kind of limbo. Racists in the community run Sybela and Charlie Bell off the property at Hamilton Avenue, and legend says that "Grandmother Owens cursed it." As evidence of this curse, Aunt May offers two more stories, one of a "crazy woman" that tried to live there and "strangled her babies and slit her own throat," and another of a Jehovah's Witness church there that "burned to the ground." The property is "still empty 'cept for ashes and black stones." All of these details suggest that things have not yet been set right. The land from which this family springs is still cursed and at odds with its surroundings, and no one knows how to release it. There is sterility, lack of peace, and discord. The story is called "The Beginning of Homewood," because this beginning is what still determines the lives of these family members, and the story has no end yet. Still in the beginning stages of making sense of Homewood and its people, they wait for an authentic resolution.

This theme of waiting pervades "The Beginning of Homewood." In the first paragraph, the narrator's report that he has delayed the writing of the letter—the telling of the story—establishes the mood of "The Beginning of Homewood," one of uncertain waiting and incompletion. Furthermore, the narrator's brother waits in prison. Sybil waits in a cage. The isle of Delos waits in a barren limbo with no death and no birth. The narrator has just visited Dachau, where prisoners waited and died, hopelessly. Aunt May's plea in her song for the lord to come down and touch her expresses a reverent waiting. May and Sybela Owens wait for each other in their exchange of gazes, wait to share the truth, wait to hear it, wait upon each other. The narrator wonders whether he would have tried to escape slavery, or waited in its hold. The narrator ends this letter to his brother with the words, "Hold on."

In the last story the narrator tells, people wait to hear the Supreme Court. The Court will be hearing a story to which it must offer some kind of resolution, a case involving prison conditions and inmate rights. Though it does not seem that this case would directly affect the narrator's brother, it offers hope because the Court may be able to re-conceptualize human rights; it has "a chance to author its version of the Emancipation Proclamation." The simple hearing of an unusual story might cause the Court to see things differently, the narrator hopes, to probe deeper than present ideas of "crime," to "ask why you are where you are, and why the rest of us are here." For the narrator, there is no simple conviction that everything will turn out well, but his faith in storytelling allows him to have faith in the institutions of justice that have imprisoned his brother. Given the circumstances, that is a tremendous accomplishment.

At the conclusion of "The Beginning of Homewood," none of the stories end. There is still waiting to be done, everyone must "hold on." They will all wait for some resolution, for some new version of the Emancipation Proclamation, for the Judgment Day that Sybela's neighbors saw portended in the falling of stars, stars who come to symbolize her descendants and their falls. While that waiting is uncertain in nature, the stories told can begin "to cohere" and offer hope that their lives may finally do the same.

Source: James Frazier, Critical Essay on "The Beginning of Homewood," in *Short Stories for Students*, The Gale Group, 2001.

Jessica Lustig

In the following interview, Wideman discusses how the fictional Homewood portrayed in his stories relates to the real Homewood, his hometown.

I went to Amherst, Massachusetts, on April 23, 1992, to talk with John Edgar Wideman on the U Mass campus, where he teaches a graduate course in creative writing. Wideman's literary mapping and charting of Homewood's neighborhood streets and people indicate the complexities and paradoxes of contemporary American urban literature. In discussing his portraits of Homewood in *Damballah*, *Hiding Place*, *Sent for You Yesterday*, and *Reuben*, we explored the ways in which fictional, constructed landscapes can be read.

[Lustig:] You moved from Homewood when you were twelve, yet it's the place that you keep circling back to. I find it interesting that, despite all those years away, it's the primary place in your work, that you keep going back to it as defining home. Maybe you could talk a little about that.

[Wideman:] Okay, but let me start with a distinction. There is a neighborhood in Pittsburgh called Homewood. It was there before I was born, and probably when I'm dead it will still be called that. It's considered a number of streets, houses, population changes—people get old and die. It's a real place in that sense. Now, for many of the years between birth and about twelve, I lived in Homewood. Other times I've lived in Shadyside, which is a completely different neighborhood. That's the level of fact. The distinction I want to make is that, once I started to write, I was creating a place based partly on memories of the actual place I lived in, and partly on the exigencies or needs of the fiction I was creating. Once I began to write, to create, I felt no compunction to stay within the bounds of Homewood. Now how that fictional place relates to the actual Homewood is very problematic. And, depending on the questions you ask, that relationship will be important or irrelevant, superfluous.

If I were to tell the story of your life in my fiction, I might talk about your height, and keep you tall, but I also might make your hair dark, because I want a heroine who has dark hair. And I might know your parents well, or know just a tiny bit about them, but I could make one a sailor, and the other a college teacher, just because that's what I need in my fiction. People could then go back and say, well now, what did Wideman know about this young woman named Jessica, and how long did he know her, and how tall is she really, and what do her parents do? But all that might or might not have anything to do with the particular book in which you appear. So although I have lived in other places, the Homewood which I make in my books has continued to grow and be confident. It has its own laws of accretion and growth and reality.

What I think is really interesting about the way this Homewood, in your books, is figured is that the post-1970 landscape has been in a lot of ways devastated. Your characters—and you, for that matter—talk about Homewood Avenue as it is now, as opposed to what it was in the '50s, or the '40s. And yet the way in which the people relate to each other makes it feel almost like a rural place, like a small town. I think that a neighborhood is an urban construct, so I'm very interested in the way that these people seem to interrelate as a small-town community.

I go in the other direction. I think it's the people who make the neighborhood. That's the difference between learning about Homewood through my writing and learning about Homewood from sociologists. There have been interesting books written about Homewood, but the people make the place. They literally *make* it. Yes, Homewood Avenue is devastated, but when the character in ''Solitary'' walks down that street, she sees the street at various times in its history. So it's populated by the fish store, by five-and-tens. She remembers places that were there when she was a little girl. Characters do that all the time. They walk through the landscape which, from the point of view of some person who's either following them with a camera or looking at them from a distance, is just vacant lots, but the person in the story sees something else. What counts most is what the person inside the story sees. That's where the life proceeds; that's where Homewood has a definition.

In other places in my writing I talk about how the old people *made*, created the town. But they created it not so much with bricks and boards; a lot of them simply moved into houses where other people had lived. They created it through their sense of values and the way they treated one another, and

> **If I were to tell the story of your life in my fiction, I might talk about your height, and keep you tall, but I also might make your hair dark, because I want a heroine who has dark hair."**

the way they treated the place. That's *crucial* to the strength of Homewood, and it's something very basic about African-American culture. Africans couldn't bring African buildings, ecology, languages wholesale, in the material sense, to the New World. But they brought the invisible dimensions of their society, of our culture, to this land. That's what you have to recognize: This world that's carried around in people's heads overlays and transcends and transforms whatever the people happen to be. So it's not anything that people in Homewood invented. To make something from nothing is almost a tradition.

Home, what could be called territory or turf, in your books, is often shaped by streets. You know, some of your characters will sort of read a litany of streets. I know that's so in Hiding Place. That seems to me like the equivalent of boundaries or property lines in rural or suburban areas, like a sense of possession, or of defining your place, your landscape.

Absolutely, and I'd take your point a step further. That litany, or *incantation*, is a way of *possessing* the turf. You name it, you claim it. There isn't that much physical description, I don't think, of Homewood. It's mostly the inner geography, and then street names as the most concrete manifestation of that geography. The street names are there, I think, because they have a magic. They have an evocative quality, and that's something that can be shared when you speak. There are streets, and when I say them to you and you walk down them, that's the opening. It's no coincidence that some of the great catalogues that occur in classical literature have to do with the names of the ships, the names of places. For sailors or voyagers or travelers, naming is a way, literally, of grounding themselves.

Talking about streets, or a neighborhood, in connection with this whole idea of memory and memory links, and evocation, and incantation . . . what I find so striking is what you do with time, and how much of your work starts or is set in the present and then goes back, and back, and back. And a lot of the time the look of the present is very different from that of the past, especially since urban renewal. You often refer to the effects of urban renewal as having devastated whole blocks or houses that you used to live in or live next to. I think that could be an interesting argument against urban renewal, because of the idea of memory, those memory links, the tangible memory links or the physical memory links, to the past.

I don't know that it's so much an argument against urban renewal, because urban renewal is a big political decision, and lots of factors go into it— and some of the reasons for doing it are very good indeed. I mean, if you take that preservationist argument to its logical conclusion, then there's a good reason for keeping the slave barracks in the South behind the big house. You don't want to lock yourself into some ghettoized existence.

There's nothing essential about things; it's how people see them, how people treat them. You could have the same attachment to a shiny new house, if you really felt it was yours, if you felt you had experience in it. For instance, the house that the Tates live in in *Sent For Your Yesterday*, that's a big house, a roomy house. And there are obviously well-put-together staircases and stuff like that. It might even be a house that *had* been urban-renewed, at least remodeled, et cetera. And it's a perfectly good situation, although it's kind of haunted and scary, too.

Well, I'm thinking more of urban renewal as it was conceived of in the late '50s and during the '60s, as it involved the razing of blocks and sometimes of entire neighborhoods.

The impetus behind that kind of urban renewal was a simple-minded remaking of people by changing their external circumstances.

Or slum clearance, as it was sometimes called.

What that really was about was turning black people into white people, without a critique of what was wrong with white people, what was wrong with the world that blacks were being asked to become part of. That's the whole integration-into-a-burning-building kind of thing. That's why it didn't

make any sense, and why it was devastating. Nobody asked what was important, what was valuable about the black community that shouldn't go, that should resist the bulldozers. There was just a wholesale exchange. We'll give you these external circumstances because we think they're good, because our lives are prospering. We'll plunk this down on you, and it'll become your world. When you examine it that way, then the real problems behind urban renewal become clearer.

You say, I think it's in Brothers and Keepers, that your grandmother's house on Finance was your link to Homewood at the stage when that book was being written, the early '80s, and you were remembering the railroad tracks going overhead. I know this isn't a fictional work, but that image sticks out for me because it's very evocative, because I understand the sense of this place that is yours, that you're linked into through your grandmother, because I have that with two neighborhoods in Brooklyn that were home to me. I'd like to hear more about why it's a Homewood, and not parts of Philadelphia, not parts of Laramie, that you write about. You've been in many places that you could write about as, figure as, home—many places in which you could absorb the stories. A lot of times it seems that your places are alive because of the stories that people tell about the places, continually, to keep them alive.

Well, there's something simple going on here. Those elements of Philadelphia that I came to appreciate and enjoy, and the same with Laramie, I plug into Homewood. They're in there, although they're kind of disguised. If I met somebody yesterday who had some quality that I felt was fascinating, and it either reminded me of my grandfather or suddenly opened up some mystery that I had in my mind, well, I might stick that in. It's not like there's this well of Homewood experiences that I keep drawing from; it's stuff in the future that I'm also locating there. It has to happen that way, or else the work would become static, a moldy thing, nostalgic. The neighborhood, the place, is an artistic contrivance for capturing *all* kinds of experience, and it works to the degree that it is permeable, that things that happen outside Homewood continue to grow up.

That makes sense. The idea of plugging in the different parts is an elegant way of putting the writing process, or the writerly process. But if we're talking about the neighborhood as sort of this artistic crucible for you, I'm interested in the environment that you create in your books; that is,

Homewood. Am I correct in understanding that the environment forces some of your characters into situations? I read Tommy, in Hiding Place, as having been forced into his situation through an accumulation of circumstances.

I think it's safer, and it's always more productive and useful, to look at the individual case. That's, again, the break in the fictional from the sociological. The play of environment versus character, versus the individual, to me is pretty meaningless when translated into the statistical terms that you use for gas molecules. You know, where and how they separate, how many will end up in this corner. That's sort of silly when you only have one life and your life pushes you in the way that it does. It's also kind of dangerous to generalize from one life. I want to examine the interplay of environment and character at the level at which it's meaningful, and that is the individual life. What part does biology play, what part does nature, as opposed to nurture, play? You can only answer that, and even then in a very tentative way, by looking at the individual life. I'm not making any case, except the case of the person.

And so this play of the place, and the individual, is going to create different stories for each of the persons in that place?

Exactly. I mean, it's not because Robby gave in, because something in the shape of Robby's life was the shape it was. I had other brothers; there were lots of other kids like Robby who turned out a different way.

I understand. Let me ask you another question about Hiding Place. The last line of that book is, "They better make sure it doesn't happen so easy ever again." It's Mother Bess, you know, talking about Tommy's situation. I think that can be really interesting in conjunction with what you said about incantation, and litany. That line, for me, embodies what I see you doing with different memory links as stories passed between people, and between generations, because I think one of the most important things about this place that you create in this book is that it's generational. It's an established neighborhood that's generational, that continues to exist with links between generations. As a reader you wonder, what's going to happen in this place? What is happening with the new generation? I'm not asking you to say, here's what's happening, here's the news, you know, but that kind of line, coming from a representative of the older generation, not

the younger one . . . as readers, can we infer that you are saying that, for these people, a memory link has got to be established, and strong, or else the nature of Homewood will be lost, as a place, as a home?

I think that's fair enough, if I understand what you're saying. The learning goes in both directions: Older people teach younger people, and younger people also teach their elders. I wanted Bess's last words to reverberate. I wanted almost to make hers a kind of avenging, or a threatening, voice. The community has learned something, she has learned something, and now it's in the air, it's out there, that idea *should* be out there. And if that idea *is* out there, an idea that has a certain amount of anger, because of what's happened to this relative of hers and, knowing something about his life circumstances, the rotten dead he got, the love she has for him . . . these are things that are very powerful. They can only be allowed to fester, or be ignored, at one's peril. She's arming the community with a knowledge of itself which will hopefully open the door to a healthier future. The singer, or the storyteller, if he or she is functioning the way he or she should, traditionally, should arm, should enlighten, should tell you what's *happening*, tell you what you need to do, what your choices are. That's the stage I wanted to take Bess to, in that book—and, with her, the reader and the community. Bess inhabits the same world the little fairy who helps to burn things down in *Hiding Place* inhabits. Hers is a *blood* knowledge, it's very palpable, but it's also a world of the spirit.

It's what you can call upon.

Yeah.

Source: Jessica Lustig, "Home: An Interview with John Edgar Wideman," in *African American Review*, Vol. 26, No. 3. Fall 1992.

Sources

Brent, Linda, *Incidents in the Life of a Slave Girl*, Harcourt Brace, 1973.

Kenan, Randall, "A Most Righteous Prayer," in *The Nation*, Vol. 250, No. 1, January 1, 1990, pp. 25–27.

Leonard, John, Review in *New York Times*, November 27, 1981, p. 23, col. 1.

Lustig, Jessica, "Home: An Interview with John Edgar Wideman," in *Conversations with John Edgar Wideman*, edited by Bonnie TuSmith, University Press of Mississippi, 1998.

Mbalia, Doreatha Drummond, *John Edgar Wideman: Reclaiming the African Personality*, Susquehanna University Press, 1995.

McDowell, Edwin, Review in *New York Times Book Review*, November 13, 1994, p. 11.

O'Brien, John, "John Wideman," in *Conversations with John Edgar Wideman*, edited by Bonnie TuSmith, University Press of Mississippi, 1998.

Watkins, Mel, Review in *New York Times Book Review*, April 11, 1982, p. 6.

Further Reading

Coleman, James, *Blackness and Modernism: The Literary Career of John Edgar Wideman*, University Press of Mississippi, 1989.
    This study takes on the complicated issues that arise when the Eurocentric models of modernism are applied to African-American writing.

Du Bois, W. E. B., *The Souls of Black Folk*, 1903.
    This essay is one of the classics in the study of African-American literature. In it Du Bois explains his theories of second sight.

Hurston, Zora Neale, *Mules and Men*, Perennial Library, 1990.
    This pioneering work by the anthropologist and writer remains the landmark study of African-American culture in the post-reconstruction South.

Debbie and Julie

Doris Lessing
1987

''Debbie and Julie,'' a matter-of-fact fictional account of teenage pregnancy, opens Doris Lessing's 1989 collection of stories and sketches about London titled *The Real Thing*. This volume, written toward the end of Lessing's long, varied, and prolific career, represents a return to the realistic style with which she first gained her literary reputation in the 1950s and '60s. Though *The Real Thing* is not considered to be among Lessing's most significant works, critics have singled out ''Debbie and Julie'' for praise as a well-crafted and emotionally wrenching example of Lessing's talent. The story touches on highly relevant issues, such as teen pregnancy, runaways, and parent-child relationships, and serves as an excellent introduction to Lessing's lengthy body of work.

The story opens with Julie, the protagonist, in labor and leaving the London apartment of Debbie, a prostitute who took her in when she ran away from home five months earlier. Throughout the dramatic events that follow—Julie's solitary delivery and abandonment of a baby girl and her return to the cold and conservative home of her parents—Julie thinks about all she has learned from her trusting and frank relationship with Debbie. Throughout her many experiments with fiction, Lessing has shown an abiding interest in how individuals—especially women and girls—cope psychologically and practically with society's labels, assumptions, and unwritten rules. Lessing portrays Julie's thought process in an understated, realistic style, using the

teenager's harrowing experience to explore issues of intimacy, morality, and identity in a way that is both accessible and complex.

Author Biography

On October 22, 1919, Lessing was born Doris May Tayler in Persia (now Iran), where her parents, both British citizens, were living at the time. Her father, a disabled veteran of World War I, worked at a British bank there until moving the family, when Lessing was five, to colonial Southern Rhodesia (now Zimbabwe) with the hopes of getting rich on farming and panning for gold. However, the family continued to struggle financially. Of Lessing's African childhood, critic Mona Knapp writes in her critical study *Doris Lessing*, "Her solitary hours roughing it in the bush were an antidote to the maternal pressure to be dainty and ladylike. During these years, distaste for traditional feminine roles was instilled in young Doris Tayler—an aversion the later Doris Lessing will never lose."

In Southern Rhodesia, Lessing was educated first at a convent school, then at an all-girl's school run by the government. She was an avid reader and an excellent student but dropped out of school at age thirteen, never to continue her formal education. Committed to writing, she began to publish short stories at age eighteen. When she was twenty, Lessing married Frank Wisdom, a much older man. They quickly had two children, then divorced four years later, in 1943. Her first novel, *The Grass Is Singing* (1950), is based closely upon the failed marriage. In the early 1940s, Lessing became involved in the Communist Party, with which she dissolved all ties a decade later. In connection to her political activities, she met Gottfried Lessing. They were married from 1945 to 1949 and had one son.

In 1949 Lessing left Africa and her family—including the two children from her first marriage—behind. She settled in London, which was to become her beloved adopted home. However, she drew on the scenes and settings of her colonial African childhood throughout her career as a writer. Her outspoken views on colonialism, racism, and feminism grew out of these formative early experiences. In cosmopolitan London, Lessing began life anew as a writer. Her debut novel, *The Grass Is Singing*, was met with strong critical praise. Lessing moved on to publish the five novels of her autobiographical "Children of Violence" series in less than a decade. She followed with *The Golden Notebook*, published in 1962, an experimental narrative in diary form that became her best known work. While she earned her literary reputation on psychologically honest realism, Lessing's numerous novels of the 1970s and 1980s became more mystical. She also wrote a number of what she calls "inner space" science fiction novels, including her "Canopus in Argos" series.

Lessing has continued to publish prolifically into her old age, moving freely from science fiction, nonfiction, and drama back to the autobiography and psychological realism of her roots. She is the recipient of numerous awards and honors. Throughout her many works, Lessing has maintained an interest in ideology and the assumptions underlying people's most basic life choices.

Plot Summary

The story opens with Julie, the pregnant teenager who is its protagonist, looking at herself in the mirror. She is in the London apartment of Debbie, a prostitute who took her in five months earlier, when she ran away from home to hide her condition from her parents. Julie is now in labor, and Debbie, who had promised to help her, is out of the country with a man. Julie is surprised that the other people in the apartment—from whom she has managed to keep her pregnancy a secret—do not seem to notice that her water has broken and that she is soaked with sweat. She leaves a note for Debbie with her home address and gets a bag she had prepared ahead of time. As she is about to leave, she goes back and takes extra towels from Debbie's bathroom, reflecting on the older woman's generosity toward her.

According to her plan, Julie takes a bus to another part of town where she knows there is an unlocked shed in an abandoned lot. It is sleeting, and she is in pain. When she gets to the shed, there is a large dog in front of the door. She throws a brick at it, and the dog runs into the shed where she is planning to give birth. She soon realizes that it is a starving stray and allows it to stay with her. She doesn't know what to do next. She takes off her underwear and calls out quietly for Debbie. She is in agony and feels very lonely. She squats against the wall and soon delivers the baby.

She has supplies for wrapping the baby and cutting its umbilical cord. When she picks up the baby, she is surprised that she feels happy and proud. She examines it, seeing that it is healthy and noticing that it is a girl. She delivers the afterbirth, which she allows the hungry dog to devour. She dresses, puts the bundled baby inside of her coat, and goes out into the street. She goes into a phone booth, puts the baby on the floor, and leaves.

Julie then goes to a nearby pub and uses its bathroom to clean herself up. She watches through the pub's window as a couple goes into the phone booth, finds the baby, and calls for an ambulance. It had been her plan for the baby to be found and taken somewhere safe, but Julie nevertheless feels sad and empty as she heads back out into the rain. She gets on the subway and heads home to her parents' house in a nearby suburb.

When Julie arrives home, her father, Len, answers the door. She is surprised by how small and ordinary he looks; her fear of him is what drove her to run away from home in the first place. Len calls for her mother, and they invite her in. Her parents are crying. They treat her politely, promising not to ask her ''awkward questions.'' Julie asks for something to eat and a bath. She bathes quickly and goes back downstairs to her parents. As she eats the meager sandwich her mother has prepared, she thinks of the exotic and plentiful food that Debbie provided her while she was pregnant. Julie tells her parents she'd been staying with a girl, and they are relieved that she was not with a boyfriend. At this point, Julie reflects back on the single sexual encounter that led to her pregnancy.

Julie feels that she can see her parents more clearly now. Compared to Debbie, they seem repressed and cold. She thinks about Debbie's situation as a prostitute and her reasons for taking Julie in and caring for her. She remembers spending the night in Debbie's bed and thinks about the lack of physical affection in her own family. A news item comes on the television. It is about an abandoned baby found in a phone booth, Julie's baby. Julie is worried that her parents will put the pieces together, but they do not. Instead, her father mentions Julie's aunt, Jessie, who, he reveals, got pregnant out of wedlock as a teenager and kept the baby. Len cries as he tells the story. He had feared that this was what had happened to Julie and is now relieved because he thinks that it did not. Julie is shocked by this revelation. To keep herself from crying, she excuses herself to go to bed. She first apologizes to her parents, and they accept. She is confused because she realizes that if she had told her parents about her

Doris Lessing

pregnancy, they would not have kicked her out. She wonders about her own future and tries to imagine a life with her baby, living either with Debbie or with her parents. She dismisses both options and starts thinking about moving to London as soon as she has finished high school. As she drifts off to sleep, she tries to reassure herself that she has proven that she can do anything she wants to do.

Characters

American Man

When Julie goes into labor, Debbie is not there to help her as she had promised. Instead, she has extended a trip with a client, an American television producer, who seems like a promising prospect. Debbie has always wished for ''just one regular customer'' or ''just one man.''

Anne

Anne is Julie's mother. She and her husband, Len, accept Julie back into their home when she returns after a five-month absence. She encourages Len not to ask Julie any questions about where she has been. Anne is a figure of repressed emotion. Anne and Len sleep in separate beds. They are quiet and seldom express emotion. Anne is frugal with food and physically undemonstrative. She was older when she had Julie, a fact that Julie thinks might explain the lack of vitality and affection in her upbringing. Comparing her with Debbie, the mother figure who took her in, Anne seems "empty and sad" to Julie.

The Baby

The baby, also known as Rosie, is the name the nurses give to Julie's baby after she is discovered abandoned in a telephone booth and brought to the hospital. Julie has mixed feelings toward the baby. She tries not to look at her so she will not love her, but when she first holds her, she can't help feeling proud and happy. She later thinks of the baby by name and tries to imagine a future with her, but cannot.

Uncle Bob

Uncle Bob is Auntie Jessie's husband. It is revealed that he married her despite the fact that she had already given birth to another man's child out of wedlock. Julie sees Uncle Bob as unimpressive, "Auntie Jessie's shadow, not up to much." She now understands why her aunt agreed to marry him.

Debbie

Debbie is a call girl, a high-status prostitute. She does not have a pimp but runs her own business out of the apartment that she shares with Julie. She appears to Julie to be independent and in control, despite the fact that she does not have what she wants out of life. Debbie is considerably older than Julie, with a painful past that she will not discuss. She is worldly and uninhibited—a figure of knowledge, teaching Julie "what things cost, the value of everything, and of people, of what you did for them and what they did for you." Despite a sharp and savvy exterior, she is warm, protective, and generous toward Julie, giving to her freely and never asking for anything in return.

Debbie extends a trip with one of her clients and is therefore not available to help Julie when she goes into labor as she had promised to do. Julie is disappointed in her and feels lonely, but she also understands Debbie's needs and priorities. Julie misses Debbie greatly during her labor and after she returns to her repressive family home. An unconventional mother figure, Debbie stands in vital contrast to Julie's own bloodless, undemonstrative

mother. Julie is grateful to Debbie for the wisdom she has imparted.

Derek

Derek is Debbie's "real" boyfriend—not one of her clients. Derek likes Julie, but she does not like him, thinking him not good enough for Debbie.

Freda

Freda is Julie's cousin. Julie learns that she is a "love child," born out of wedlock to her aunt Jessie when she was a teenager.

Billy Jayson

Billy Jayson is the boy who impregnated Julie during one brief sexual encounter in their school cloak room. Julie never told him about her pregnancy and assumes that he never suspected it.

Auntie Jessie

Jessie is Julie's aunt. At the end of the story, Julie's father reveals to her that Jessie had given birth to her first child, cousin Freda, out of wedlock at age seventeen. This limited her prospects, and she married soon after. Auntie Jessie represents an option that Julie has not taken. Jessie's noisy, exciting house reminds her in some way of Debbie's.

Julie

Julie is the protagonist of the story. She is a teenager from a London suburb who runs away from home when she is four months pregnant, fearing her father's wrath and her family's rejection. She is taken in by Debbie, a call girl, who identifies with her plight and protects and nurtures her during her pregnancy. The story relates the events of Julie's labor and childbirth and her subsequent return to her family home.

Julie, a "sensible girl" from a conservative family, flees to London, lives with a prostitute, and then gives birth alone in an abandoned shed. She leaves home an innocent and returns with a new ability to understand her family and herself. Though Debbie never appears in the story, the narrative centers on her influence on Julie as she makes this passage. Julie learns from Debbie an attitude of autonomy and toughness but, more importantly, the value of intimacy and emotional expressiveness. Julie has been raised in a cold, repressive family. Her first sexual encounter is devoid of love or meaning. Debbie forges an important emotional connection with Julie, which gives the girl the strength to act in her own best interest and allows her to see her parents' weaknesses and limitations.

Lebanese Man

One of the shady figures who hang around at Debbie's apartment is a Lebanese man who is a drug dealer. Oblivious to her pregnancy, he is there when Julie, in the midst of labor pains, leaves the apartment to give birth and then go home. He had once tried to procure Julie from Debbie for sex, but Debbie refused him. Julie is afraid of him.

Len

Len is Julie's father. She attributes her original motivation to run away to him, assuming that if he learned of her pregnancy, he would kick her out anyway. She is intimidated by him, seeing him as powerful, but this changes when she returns home after she has given birth. He looks old and gray to her, and she sees him, for the first time, as vulnerable. He cries, and she can tell that she has hurt him. She understands that he feared her moral corruption, and she lets him believe that this fear was groundless by assuring him that she had been staying with a girl, not a boyfriend, for the past months. He accedes to his wife's admonishments not to ask Julie any uncomfortable questions, but at the story's end, he reveals a shocking skeleton in the family closet—that Julie's aunt Jessie had gotten pregnant out of wedlock as a teenager.

Rosie

See The Baby

Themes

Knowledge and Ignorance

''Debbie and Julie'' tells of the knowledge that is earned through the trials of life experience. Julie, its teenage protagonist, runs away from her conservative parents in order to hide her pregnancy from them. She is taken in by a kind prostitute and survives the terrifying ordeal of giving birth alone in an abandoned shed. After a five-month absence, she returns home, a more mature and insightful person. Most significantly, she is now able to see her parents with more critical distance and more sympa-

Topics for Further Study

- Do you think that Julie made the right choice to abandon her infant daughter? Why or why not?

- Julie sees Debbie as a positive force in her life and compares her favorably to her own parents. Do you think that Debbie is a positive model for Julie? Explain why. If you do not think Debbie is a positive role model for Julie, explain why you think this.

- Compare the characters of Julie, Debbie, Anne, and Jessie to female characters in other stories in *The Real Thing*. What are some of Lessing's most important points about women's place in society and their relationships to one another?

- Do some research about the most prevalent social perceptions of teen mothers in the 1980s, when the story takes place, and compare them to those a generation earlier, when Julie's Auntie Jessie gave birth.

- Find some American and British magazine articles from the 1980s about the issue of teen pregnancy. How were public debates about sexual morality different in the two countries?

thetic understanding. At the end of the story, she is in a position to consider her future options with greater freedom and realism than she was before her accidental pregnancy.

Julie attributes much of her newfound knowledge to Debbie, the woman who took her in. Debbie is worldly. She has had a hard life as a prostitute but has won a measure of independence with her own business. When Julie arrived in London, she was ''innocent and silly.'' She has learned from Debbie ''the value of everything'' and ''what had to be paid.'' In addition to this lesson in pragmatic self-preservation, however, she has also learned the value of emotional openness and expressiveness. Debbie is uninhibited and nonjudgmental—a stark contrast to Julie's parents, who live a narrow and repressed existence. Julie realizes that her parents are ignorant of many of life's pleasures and opportunities and that they choose to remain blinded to some of life's agonies, as well: "It was as if they had switched themselves off."

Love and Intimacy

The title names the relationship between Debbie and Julie as the most significant one in the story, despite the fact that Debbie is absent throughout the events of the narrative. The love between Debbie and Julie is stronger than the love between Julie and her mother or her newborn baby, let alone the boy who impregnated her. Debbie helps Julie when she is in need, accepts her without judgment, and is demonstrative and generous in her love. In return, Julie understands Debbie's vulnerabilities: she "knew she was the only person who really understood Debbie." She also holds up Debbie as a model, having learned from her the value of trust and intimacy. There is some irony in this fact, since Debbie—looking out for her own interests—abandons Julie when she is most in need. This can be seen as a thematic echo of Julie's pragmatic decision to abandon her newborn daughter.

In the months preceding the events of the story, Debbie has taken on a mothering role, protecting Julie and nurturing her physically and emotionally through her pregnancy. Julie longingly recalls Debbie's warmth and love after she has returned home to her own parents. At several points, she makes explicit comparisons between her mother's capacity for love and Debbie's. She recalls curling up with Debbie when she was afraid to sleep alone and the intimate gesture of Debbie's hand touching her pregnant belly. Upon her return home, Julie reflects that her mother would be embarrassed if Julie asked to share her bed with her. "In this family, they simply did not touch each other." Julie was not able even to tell her mother about her pregnancy, let alone share mutual emotional vulnerabilities and comfort.

Choices and Consequences

Julie is a character who has faced the difficult consequences of her choices. She becomes pregnant accidentally and decides that she must leave home to avoid having her condition discovered by her parents, an option she considers unthinkable. When Debbie sees Julie arrive on a London train platform, she seems to understand implicitly how narrow and dangerous Julie's choices are and offers to take her in. Debbie, who has had a difficult past, represents one set of consequences for being a sexually active woman: she has become a prostitute and relies on men for her livelihood, if not for her emotional sustenance. Julie's Auntie Jessie represents a different set of consequences: as a teenager, she admitted to her parents that she was pregnant, kept the baby, and later married a man who was not good enough for her. She too is dependent on a man, though she lives a "respectable" life, and her options and limitations are very different from Debbie's. At the story's close, Julie tries to imagine a range of different options for her future, reassuring herself that she is strong and, perhaps, capable of independence that will be greater than either Debbie's or Jessie's. She also recognizes what her choices have cost her; she cannot imagine a way to include her newborn daughter in her future.

Style

Point of View

"Debbie and Julie" opens with the image of Julie looking in the mirror and closes with her private thoughts as she drifts off to sleep, suggesting that the story is centrally concerned with Julie's consciousness and self-perception. It is narrated from a third-person point of view. The narrator is not a participant in the events described but has a point of view closely aligned with that of Julie, with full access to her inner thoughts and feelings. This is described in literary terms as limited omniscience. The narrator's omniscience or "all-knowingness" is limited because it does not extend beyond Julie's consciousness. For example, readers aren't given access to Julie's father's experience of her homecoming, only Julie's perceptions of his experience.

Structure

"Debbie and Julie" concerns extreme changes taking place in the protagonist's life and in her outlook, and its plot reflects these changes. Julie is a "plump, fresh-faced girl" who has always done well in her suburban school. Her parents consider her "sensible," a "good girl." When she gets pregnant, runs away to London, and becomes part of Debbie's unconventional lifestyle, she discovers a new part of herself and new ways of understanding other people. The story has two distinct parts, highlighting the strong contrast between Julie's experiences and identity in London and her experiences and identity at home.

In the first part, Julie has the extreme experience of giving birth alone in an abandoned shed. This terrifying episode concludes her eye-opening, five-month stay in London with Debbie, which is described throughout the story in brief flashbacks and recollections. In the second part, Julie takes a subway ride and returns to the "normal" life she had always known with her parents, who, themselves largely unchanged, remain ignorant of all that she has been through. "It was hard enough for her to believe that she could sit here in her pretty little dressing gown, smelling of bath powder, when she had given birth by herself in a dirty shed with only a dog for company." Much of the story's drama is based on the contrast between its two parts, particularly the difference between how Julie now sees herself and how her parents will continue seeing her.

Symbolism

Though the story is narrated in a realistic mode, with attention to concrete detail and closely observed behavior, Lessing also employs understated symbolism to amplify her ideas about the characters and their situations. Like its structure, the symbolism in "Debbie and Julie" is based on contrast. For example, at the beginning of the story, Julie is wearing a once-fashionable sky-blue coat borrowed from Debbie. It reflects her worldly, sometimes shocking, experiences in London, as well as her close friendship with Debbie. Debbie lends her part of her identity, and this helps Julie through her solitary trial of labor and delivery. Julie sheds the coat just before entering her parents' house, soon taking a bath and changing into a pretty and childish-looking pink dressing gown. This suggests a return to her former identity, which is meant to reassure as well as to deceive her parents. Whereas Debbie and Julie shared everything, from clothes to feelings, Julie and her parents maintain a cautious distance from each other.

Throughout the story, Lessing endows dirt and cleanliness with symbolic meaning. Julie worries about her post-labor bleeding dirtying the "fluffy pink towels, which her mother changed three times a week." These towels are implicitly contrasted with those she takes freely from Debbie's apartment just before she leaves, knowing that she will bleed all over them. Dirtiness is an intrinsic part of life in London with Debbie, reflecting Debbie's "dirty" profession and Julie's own compromised situation. It is, however, in many ways a relief compared to the clean, orderly, respectable life Julie had always known with her parents, who are cold and rigid. The order and tidiness of Len and Anne's house is contrasted not only with Debbie's apartment but also with the more extreme and literal dirtiness of the shed where Julie gives birth. Julie's parents shy away from the symbolic messiness of intimacy, creating a home that is emotionally sterile.

Historical Context

Teen Runaways in Great Britain

In 1989, the same year that Lessing published "Debbie and Julie," the British government recognized the problem of teen runaways by passing the Children Act, which made provisions for outreach to runaways and offered some sources of refuge for them. However, the great majority of British runaways do not receive aid from any agency or organization. Because of their wariness of authority figures, runaways are notoriously hard to trace or study. Based on police reports, approximately 43,000 children and teenagers under the age of sixteen run away from home each year in Great Britain. However, there is evidence that this statistic may minimize the problem, since many runaways are not reported missing by their families.

The majority of runaways in Great Britain are between fourteen and sixteen years old, with the gender ratio of these roughly equal. (Younger runaways are more likely to be boys.) Problems at home are the most frequently cited reasons for running away. Many runaways report arguments, sexual and emotional abuse, and domestic violence in the homes from which they flee. At least sixty percent of runaways come from homes where a divorce or other split has occurred. A high proportion of children and teens in foster care also run away.

Though runaways describe some positive results of the decision to leave home, they are a highly vulnerable population, subject to many risks. A majority of young people reported being frightened, a quarter physically injured, and one in nine sexually assaulted while on the run. Many were hungry or otherwise physically deprived, leading more than half to admit to stealing. Furthermore, a high incidence of self-destructive behavior, including suicide attempts and drug use, reflects the emotional toll on the life of a runaway.

Julie's experience as a runaway is quite atypical. First, she runs away from a stable family.

Second, she quickly finds a relatively safe and secure place to stay. However, her decision-making process reflects a feeling characteristic among runaways that staying at home is an intolerable option. Despite her luck in finding a place to live, Julie is particularly vulnerable because her pregnancy places her at a greater physical and emotional risk than the average runaway.

Teen Pregnancy on the Rise

Julie's pregnancy reflects a dramatic demographic trend. In the 1980s the teen pregnancy rate in Great Britain rose to become one of the highest in Europe. Only a decade earlier, the country's teen pregnancy rate was reported as average for the continent. Some experts attributed the troubling rise to Britain's economic problems, supported by the fact that poorer areas had far higher teen pregnancy rates than the rest of the country. Youngsters with few hopes for the future saw little reason not to get pregnant. Several cases involving pregnant pre-teens were highlighted in the press, bringing widespread attention to the problem. Though this was a period of social conservatism, such publicity led to activism for earlier and more extensive sex education and easier access to contraception for teens.

Though she apparently did not consider it, abortion would have been a legal option for Julie. Abortion has been legal in Great Britain since 1968 and may be performed up to twenty-eight weeks into the pregnancy, or through the second trimester. It is covered as a medical procedure under the public health care system, in which anyone over the age of sixteen can consent to his or her own medical treatment. Girls under sixteen may also decide independently on abortion if their doctors find them capable of making such a decision, but most doctors require parental consent.

Critical Overview

Lessing earned critical success with her very first novel, 1950's *The Grass is Singing*, and has, in the half century since, grown in stature to be considered one of the most important writers of her time. She has never rested on her laurels, instead continuing to write at a furious pace and to experiment with both style and subject matter.

Her fame reached a high point in 1962 with the publication of her seventeenth book. *The Golden Notebook* takes the form of a diary, revealing the tensions in one modern woman's relationships and commitments and expressing her disillusionment with feminism, Communism, and other collective movements. Though critical of organized feminism, the novel was embraced by feminists around the world. This was the first of Lessing's works to be published in many languages, and it brought her significant international prominence. It remains Lessing's best known and most highly esteemed effort.

While her early works, including *The Golden Notebook*, were grounded in social and psychological realism and centrally concerned with her characters' relationships to social and ideological movements, in the late 1960s, Lessing's work underwent an important change. Beginning with 1969's *Four-Gated City* (the last volume in her autobiographical "Children of Violence" series), her writing became more mystical and preoccupied with the expansion of consciousness. Critics attribute this shift to Lessing's growing interest in Sufism, an ancient cult of mysticism. Some also see connections between her ideas in this period and those of contemporary theories of psychiatry. In the 1970s she continued to pursue this path, publishing a number of "inner space" books that explore concepts of consciousness, madness, and sanity. While these novels have a pessimistic tone, her next series, begun in 1979, begins to envision positive alternatives. The science fiction "Canopus in Argos: Archives" series represents a bold step further away from the realism of Lessing's literary roots. "With this series," writes Mona Knapp in *Doris Lessing*, "it is necessary to draw an unavoidably simplistic line between the 'old,' realist Lessing and the 'new' Lessing." She goes on to say that "most of her readers identify with one or the other," while few embrace both styles.

After undergoing this dramatic mid-career change in literary identity, Lessing continued to foil those who would wish to label her or her writing. For example, in 1984 she wrote *The Diaries of Jane Sommers* under a pen name in order to dramatize the difficulties that young, unknown authors have getting published. This work echoes the diary form as well as some of the concerns of *The Golden Notebook*. She also returned to autobiography, publishing a two-volume account of her life. Her 1989 publication, *The Real Thing: Stories and Sketches*, can be understood as part of this shift back toward realism.

This volume, in which "Debbie and Julie" appears, combines fiction and nonfiction portraits of life in London. It makes her "beloved adopted home seem like a character in its own right," writes *Maclean's* John Belrose. Many critics responded more favorably to the stories than the sketches. The reviewer for *Publishers Weekly* opines that overall the volume is "less than substantial, satisfying in short takes, but not a major contribution to her works," while naming "Debbie and Julie" as a "splendid example of Lessing's iridescent prose . . . consist[ing] of tantalizingly unresolved scraps of character and situation." In a warmer review, Eils Lotozo of *The New York Times Book Review* singles out "Debbie and Julie" as "harrowing" and praises Lessing for how, "as always, [she] expertly deciphers the complex relationships that characterize modern life." The *Kirkus Review* also makes note of "Debbie and Julie" as an "especially fine" contribution to the collection, characterizing the story as "almost clinical in the telling but devastating in effect."

Due in part to Lessing's stellar reputation, *The Real Thing* was reviewed widely, but it is generally considered a side note to Lessing's long and varied career, and little critical attention has been paid to the book since its publication. However, in recent years Lessing's reputation overall has continued to shine among scholars. She is the subject of numerous critical studies and dissertations, the recipient of many awards, and she has diverse and loyal fans. Knapp writes that Lessing "thwarts the 'isms' that would otherwise divide her readership. This is the natural result of her books' focus, unchanged over thirty years: they attack compartmentalized thinking and strive toward a vision of the whole rather than the particular."

Criticism

Sarah Madsen Hardy

Madsen Hardy has a doctorate in English literature and is a freelance writer and editor. In the following essay, she discusses the theme of motherhood and the contrast between Debbie and Anne as maternal figures.

"Debbie and Julie" concerns a teenager's decision not to take on the responsibilities of motherhood.

Julie, the adolescent protagonist of the story, gives birth to a baby daughter and, resisting the positive feelings she has toward the infant, abandons her in telephone booth, a place in which she hopes the baby will be quickly found. Relinquishing her own role as a mother is only one of the ways in which Julie learns hard lessons about motherhood over the course of the events that the story describes. The narrative characterizes Debbie, the prostitute who took Julie in when she ran away from home, as a mother figure and compares her to Anne, the respectable but repressed mother in whom Julie dared not confide.

That Debbie is a mother figure is supported by the fact that she recognizes Julie's vulnerability, takes her into her home, and nurtures her physically and emotionally. Furthermore, Julie speculates that Debbie probably ended a pregnancy or gave up a newborn when she, like Julie, was a vulnerable and impractical teenager. As Debbie is significantly older than Julie, with "wear under her eyes," Julie might now be just about the age Debbie's child would have been. This suggests that their relationship fulfills a mother-daughter intimacy that both have felt missing in their lives. Debbie's maternal qualities are further highlighted through explicit and implicit comparisons between Debbie and Julie's mother, Anne. Debbie and Anne are both flawed mothers. However, the story centers on the positive lessons Debbie has taught Julie about vulnerability and nurturing. In this essay, Debbie and Anne's capacities for mothering will be compared, and the language Lessing uses to characterize love and intimacy will be explored.

The contrast between the characters of Debbie and Anne could hardly be stronger: Debbie is an urban prostitute; Anne is a proper suburban wife. Anne is middle-aged and gray-haired but appears "almost girlish" with "blue eyes full of wounded and uncomprehending innocence"; Debbie has "scarlet lips," "black eyes," and an assertive, knowing attitude. "She made up her lips to be thin and scarlet, just right for the lashing, slashing tongue behind them." Anne wears a "pretty pale blue dress with its nice little collar and the little pearl buttons down the front;" Debbie "might answer the door in her satin camiknickers, those great breasts of hers lolling about." According to these descriptions, Anne probably fits most people's mental image of a "good mother" much more closely than Debbie does. As Anne's appearance suggests, she is predictable, emotionally contained, and traditional.

What Do I Read Next?

- *The Doris Lessing Reader* (1988) makes an excellent introduction to Lessing's varied body of work. It includes short stories, novel excerpts, and nonfiction essays that highlight Lessing's long career.

- *The Golden Notebook* (1962), Lessing's best known work, is widely considered a masterpiece. An inventive narrative based on the diary form, the novel frankly reveals a modern woman's political and interpersonal struggles.

- *Victoria Line, Central Station* (1978), by Maeve Binchy, is a collection of twenty-five short stories exploring the variety and vitality of life in London. Each story is related to one of London's "Tube" subway stops.

- *The Magic Toyshop* (1967), a gothic novel by Angela Carter, narrates an adolescent girl's experiences when she is sent to London to live with relatives after her parents' death. It gives the themes of sexuality and family dynamics a dark and fantastical twist.

- *Due East* (1987), by Valerie Sayers, is set in small-town South Carolina and tells of the struggles of a fifteen-year-old girl who gets pregnant and decides to keep her baby.

- *Local Girls* (1999) is Alice Hoffman's cycle of interconnected short stories centering on the relationships among two teenage girls and two adult women. Set in Long Island, the stories take up issues of friendship, divorce, and illness.

Debbie, on the other hand, is tough, passionate, and unconventional. Furthermore, she exudes an overt sexuality that is conventionally seen as antithetical to motherhood. Through Julie's perceptions, however, Lessing suggests that Debbie's qualities make her a more fit mother than Anne is.

One of the ways that Lessing expresses the difference between Anne's ability to take care of Julie and Debbie's is through their attitudes toward food and feeding, which are closely associated with mothering. When Julie arrives at her parents' doorstep and, famished after her ordeal, asks for a sandwich, she immediately recognizes that her needs are interfering with her mother's sense of order and propriety. "She knew what had been on those plates was exactly calculated, not a pea or a bit of potato left over," Julie says of the dinner that Len and Anne had eaten earlier. She also knew that "the next proper meal (lunch, tomorrow) would already be on a plate ready to cook, with a plastic film on it, in the fridge." There is nothing in the story to suggest that Julie's family is so poor that they have to count every pea; rather Anne plans the family meals so carefully in order to give her life the structure and predictability that she considers proper.

This sense of "right" behavior overrides Anne's ability to recognize and respond to her daughter's particular and changing needs. The coldness and sterility of the imagery in this passage echoes the coldness of the family's interpersonal behavior. It is as if they interact with a "plastic film" between them. They never touch each other, and they never argue. Thus it is not so much that Anne is callous to Julie's needs—whether to her hunger (physical *or* emotional) or to the terrible dilemma presented by her pregnancy—but that she is simply too far removed from her daughter to ever find out about her needs.

As Julie eats the simple snack of bread, jam, and tea that her mother has brought from the kitchen for her, she remembers the "feasts" that Debbie had provided: "the pizzas that arrived all hours of the day and the night from almost next door, the Kentucky chicken, the special steak feeds when Debbie got hungry, which was often." The word *feasts* suggests extravagance and celebration, and part of the food's appeal lay in its variety and spontaneity. Debbie is a woman of appetites— physical, sexual, and emotional. She recognizes Julie's literal and symbolic "hungers" because she is in touch with her own: ''In the little kitchen was a bowl from Morocco kept piled with fruit. . . . 'You must get enough vitamins,' Debbie kept saying, and brought in more grapes, more apples and pears, let alone fruit Julie had never heard of, like pomegranates and pawpaws.'' In Anne's kitchen predictability and familiarity are valued; in contrast, Debbie's offerings are a testament to her willingness to experience life in all of its variety. Her wisdom comes from having taken risks and survived trying times; because of this, she is, unlike Julie's real mother, able to understand Julie's plight implicitly and the needs that arise from it.

Anne is responsible in practical ways but inept at intimacy. Though she is as dependable as clockwork in her domestic routine, she is revealed as having been emotionally absent as a mother. Upon returning home, Julie realizes that she has never been able to turn to her mother for the many simple comforts that Debbie spontaneously offered. ''I wish I could just snuggle up to Mum and she could hold me and I could go to sleep,'' Julie thinks at the end of her harrowing day of labor and her uncomfortable homecoming. ''Surely this must have happened when [I] was small,'' she goes on to speculate, ''but she could not remember it. In this family, they simply did not touch each other.'' The only response she can imagine from her mother is embarrassment. The distance and repression in the mother-daughter relationship is echoed in the marriage between Anne and Len. ''Each day was a pattern of cups of tea, meals, cups of coffee and biscuits, always at exactly the same times, with bedtime as a goal,'' when the husband and wife go to sleep in separate beds. Though they provide what is often valued as an wholesome home environment, Anne and Len seem to have ''switched themselves off,'' leaving little opportunity for emotional connection between parent and child.

While Debbie presents the world with the face of a wily prostitute, someone who has learned, the hard way, the rules of ''what things cost, the value of everything, and of people, of what you did for them, and what they did for you,'' she is also, to Julie, a source of the kind of primal maternal comfort her own mother denied her. Julie sometimes spends the night in Debbie's bed, not at Julie's request but at Debbie's, asked there to assuage Debbie's fear of being alone—a real enough fear for a call girl who is no longer young. Debbie reveals her vulnerabilities to Julie and, in return, is sensitive to Julie's. This mutuality and openness is the key to

> '' In Anne's kitchen predictability and familiarity are valued; in contrast, Debbie's offerings are a testament to her willingness to experience life in all of its variety.''

the intimacy that they share: ''Julie lay entangled with Debbie, and they were like two cats that have just finished washing each other and gone to sleep, and Julie knew how terribly she had been deprived at home, and how empty and sad her parents were.'' Likewise, Debbie receives from Julie a kind of closeness of which she is deprived in her relationships with men, whom she relates to in terms of contractual exchange. Thus Debbie represents two diametrically opposed concepts of intimacy—one, in relation to men, that is a set of carefully negotiated conditions, and the other, in relation to Julie, that is spontaneous and mutual. Debbie gives Julie a sky blue coat, some towels, and a safe place to stay. She assigns a price tag to the most intimate physical acts, but she refuses to take a penny in rent from the teenager, seeming to find reward enough in the friendship that they share and in the promise of Julie's brighter future.

Though Debbie, the amoral prostitute, is revealed as a nurturing woman who teaches Julie some very wholesome lessons about love, she remains a flawed mother figure. Before Julie abandons her infant child in a phone booth, she had been abandoned by her own two mother figures. She has long been abandoned by Anne, by the emotional distance that Anne has established, and she is once again abandoned by Debbie, now in geographical distance. Debbie is out of the country with a client when Julie goes into labor. Though she had promised to help Julie in this time of great need, Debbie is not available for her. She is, instead, catering to her own need to gain security though her sexual relationships with men. Thus, on a cold and rainy night, Julie makes the painful passage into motherhood, alone, in a dirty shed, with only a stray dog for company. Her own shortcomings in fulfilling this momentous role can be attributed to the mother figures that let her down. But it is Debbie's name Julie cries out in the dark.

Source: Sarah Madsen Hardy, Critical Essay on ''Debbie and Julie,'' in *Short Stories for Students*, The Gale Group, 2001.

Rena Korb

Korb has a master's degree in English literature and creative writing and has written for a wide variety of educational publishers. In the following essay, she analyzes the unraveling of the character ''Julie.''

''Debbie and Julie'' is one of the so-called ''London stories'' collected in Lessing's *The Real Thing*. A reviewer for *Publishers Weekly* called the eighteen pieces in the volume ''splendid examples of Lessing's iridescent prose.'' The reviewer noted, however, that ''most consist of tantalizingly unresolved scraps of character and situation.'' As one of these sketches, the reviewer singled out ''Debbie and Julie,'' which is described as ''a grim story about a girl who gives birth alone in a shed.'' This story, though long at about twenty-five pages, indeed reveals only bare scraps about its main characters and their motivations.

Although Debbie and Julie share title billing, Debbie never actually appears on the pages; away in America as the drama plays out, Debbie exists only in Julie's memory. The action of the story focuses on Julie; the eye of the writer follows her from Debbie's lively apartment, to the decrepit shed where she gives birth, and then back to her parents' silent home outside of London. This eye is distant, however, so Julie's feelings about the cataclysmic events taking place are difficult to gauge. Not until the end of the story is any true glimpse into Julie's personality seen. Another challenge the text poses is its extremely gradual revelation of key characteristics. The story falls into place as the pieces of a puzzle slowly interlock; only upon completion is a cohesive picture created.

The story's opening is a prime example of Lessing's deliberate narrative blurring: ''The fat girl in the sky-blue coat again took herself to the mirror.'' Here Lessing indulges in misrepresentation; as the author, Lessing knows that Julie is not fat but is pregnant. Theoretically, however, the reader may not become aware of this fact until several pages into the story, when Julie is on the cusp of giving birth. The third paragraph begins with another misleading, potentially confusing description. Julie, ''so wet she was afraid she would start squelching,'' worries about ''the wet'' bleeding through to her coat. Where is the wet coming from? A reader might logically assume that Julie has been outside, but this makes no sense. First, her coat is not wet but her dress is. Second, why would she be concerned that her outer garment gets wet? Third, the reader is told that Julie has been inside all along—she ''knew it was cold outside, for she had opened a window to check.'' The lack of clarity of the opening details challenges the reader early on to take an active role in understanding the story.

And there is a lot to sort out. One issue the reader must grapple with is Julie's place in Debbie's world. It is immediately apparent that Debbie is a prostitute. As Julie recalls in the second paragraph, ''[P]eople (men) from everywhere'' came to Debbie's flat. As the story opens, Debbie is not present, but a host of other characters are. For example, the ''man she [Julie] was afraid of, and who had tried to 'get' her''; a girl who worked for a drug dealer; and ''two girls Julie had never seen before, and she supposed they were innocents, as she had been.'' Julie's subsequent musings on her relationship with Debbie seem somewhat contradictory. In her five months in London, Julie learned from Debbie ''what things cost, the value of everything, and of people, of what you did for them, and what they did for you.'' Still, ''Debbie had never allowed her to pay for anything.''

Despite Julie's assertions, a hint of sexual payoff floats in and out of the story. First, and most obviously, Debbie is a prostitute, and the other girls in the story seem well on their way to becoming prostitutes also—the two new girls whom Julie characterizes as ''all giggly and anxious to please.'' Also, Debbie and Julie sometimes shared Debbie's bed, and ''if Debbie woke in the night, she might turn to Julie and draw her into an embrace.'' Even though Debbie ''never actually 'did' anything,'' Julie waited, ''for 'something' to happen.'' An implication that Julie would not be adverse to a sexual relationship with Debbie also arises in different places throughout the story. For one thing, although Julie is pregnant, she is not sexually promiscuous. The ''incident in the school cloakroom'' that led to her pregnancy she equates more with a ''virgin birth.'' As Julie told Debbie, ''He hardly got it in. . . . I didn't think anything had really happened.'' Julie also is possessive of Debbie, believing that her boyfriend is ''not good enough'' for her.

Despite these allusions, what Julie offers Debbie has nothing to do with sex; rather, it is all about helping out a girl who is young, alone, and pregnant, as Debbie once had been. Although Debbie never talked about it, Julie surmises that she had once ''stood very late in a railway station, pregnant, her head full of rubbish about how she would get a job, have the baby, bring it up, find a man who would love her and the baby.'' Although she rebels against the truth, Julie knows, ''It was not she, Julie, who had earned five months of Debbie's love and protection, it was pregnant Julie, helpless and alone.'' Because of this, Julie has no choice but to return home after giving birth; she cannot stay with Debbie.

Another issue that arises after Julie leaves London is how she feels about the baby whom she deserted in the phone booth. She knows that physically the baby will be cared for, or as she puts it, ''safe.'' However, she thinks little about the child. Instead, upon arriving home, she is concerned with bathing, eating, keeping her pregnancy secret, and, most importantly, seeing her parents through new eyes—Debbie's eyes. When her father opens the door, she thinks,

> That can't be him, that can't be my *father*—for he had shrunk and become grey and ordinary, and . . . *what on earth had she been afraid of?* She could just hear what Debbie would say about him! Why, he was nothing at all.

Not until later that evening, when she and her parents are watching television, do her thoughts return to the newborn infant. A newscast announces that a child has been found in a phone booth. ''The nurses have called her Rosie,'' the anchor reports, causing in Julie ''[h]ot waves of jealously . . . when she saw how the nurse smiled down at the little face.'' Julie is even more taken aback by the conversation the report provokes among her and her parents. She learns that her aunt Jessie had been an unwed, teenaged mother herself and had stayed at home with the child until she married and moved into a house with her new husband.

The implications of the long-held family secret put Julie into a brief turmoil as she realizes that ''she could be sitting here now, with her baby Rosie,'' and that ''they [her parents] wouldn't have thrown her out.'' However, Julie soon acknowledges the truth, that ''Rosie her daughter could not come here, because she, Julie, could not stand it.'' With these blunt revelations, Julie's selfishness emerges. She has hurt others: the baby deserted on a rainy night and crying out its ''short angry spasms,'' the disheartened parents, who even upon her return ''weep,

> ❝ She has hurt others: the baby deserted on a rainy night and crying out its 'short angry spasms,' the disheartened parents, who even upon her return 'weep, their bitter faces full of loss,' left behind without a word.''

their bitter faces full of loss,'' left behind without a word. Julie could never bring Rosie to her parents' home because if she did so, she would have to stay there, just like Aunt Jessie, until she found some weak-willed ''shadow'' of a man who was willing to marry her.

With these realizations, the pieces of Julie's puzzle—her own true character—fall into place. Julie's intense isolation becomes stark. At her parents' home, in her family, ''they simply did not touch each other.'' Debbie hugged Julie and lavished affection upon her, but now Debbie has no use for Julie. Although she does not admit it, Julie knows that her perception of Debbie was only a fantasy. Debbie did not even bother to return to England in time to help Julie give birth, although ''she had promised'' to do so. She had assured Julie for months that she would be there to ''see everything's all right.'' Instead, she left Julie completely alone to give birth to her child in a shed, her only companion a stray dog eager to eat the afterbirth. The tears that Julie cries at home are for herself—for her own loss of the artificial closeness she had once shared with Debbie—not for anyone else. Debbie would not take her in now.

In her childhood bed that night, clutching a panda bear, Julie goes over future plans, but these plans, steeped in a bitter acceptance of reality, will only further serve to isolate her. She falsely builds herself up and attempts to deceive herself in her ability to start a new life independently. The ''accomplishments'' that she uses to praise herself are hardly accomplishments at all. She ''lived in Debbie's flat, and didn't get hurt by them.'' More significantly, she tells herself,'' [I] had Rosie by myself in that shed with only a dog to help me, and then I put Rosie in a safe place and now she's all right.'' Julie completely overlooks any moral implications of her actions in deserting and endangering a helpless child. She can only think of her own wants. Her final thought before she falls asleep reveals the self-absorbed, delusional, and yet extremely lonely child who remains inside Julie: ''I can do anything I want to do, I've proved that.''

Source: Rena Korb, Critical Essay on ''Debbie and Julie,'' in *Short Stories for Students*, The Gale Group, 2001.

Wendy Perkins

Perkins is an associate professor of English at Prince George's Community College in Maryland. In the following essay she focuses on how the structure of Doris Lessing's ''Debbie and Julie'' illuminates the story's themes.

In the short sketch ''Storms,'' one of the collected pieces published in Doris Lessing's *The Real Thing*, a passenger in a London cab expresses her feelings for the city: ''It was like a great theater, I said; you could watch what went on all day, and sometimes I did. You could sit for hours in a cafe or on a bench and just watch. Always something remarkable, or amusing.'' The collection of stories in *The Real Thing* have been heralded for their realistic snap-shots of London and Londoners. In one of the darker stories in the collection ''Debbie and Julie,'' Lessing presents a harrowing portrait of a young Londoner, who finds herself quite alone as she faces the impending birth of her child. Lessing's clear, direct prose and tight narrative structure illuminate the story's exploration of the methods and consequences of survival.

A *Publishers Weekly* reviewer noted that ''the fiction pieces [in *The Real Thing*] are splendid examples of Lessing's iridescent prose, though most consist of tantalizingly unresolved scraps of character and situation.'' The reviewer argues that the pieces in the collection ''tease with implications that they do not fully explore.'' Lessing employs this ''teasing'' to full advantage in ''Debbie and Julie,'' as she focuses on the main character's powerful urge for self-preservation. She does not flesh out Julie's story because Julie herself feels compelled to ignore or suppress some of the painful realities of her life.

The story opens with Julie observing herself in the mirror—an appropriate beginning to a story about a woman who must focus on her own needs in order to survive. Lessing begins in the middle of things, with Julie alone, cut off from her family, from her friend Debbie, from everyone, facing the unconscionable prospect of delivering her baby on her own. In order to survive this event, Julie must not think about what she is doing, other than to concentrate upon the purely mechanical acts she must complete so that she and the baby will stay alive. Lessing's spare style and matter-of-fact reportorial prose reflect Julie's desperate attempt to control her emotions and to make it through the experience. At this point, she gives us no details about how Julie got into this situation. Her focus is only on the measures Julie must take for her own self-preservation.

Julie's sense of isolation is compounded by the fact that no one in Debbie's apartment notices her. ''She thought they did not see her,'' but recognizes that since Debbie let it be known that she would be protecting Julie, the ''dangerous'' people who come and go there ''got nothing out of noticing her.'' When she comes out of her room, the people in the apartment do not even look at her.

Her loneliness grows when she thinks of Debbie's absence. Lessing never allows us to meet Debbie; we only know her through Julie's subjective point of view, which reinforces what the woman meant to her. Debbie has provided her with much needed comfort and has taught her how to survive on her own. She remembers how Debbie and she would joke about ''how little people noticed about other people.'' As her labor begins, however, some of her buried emotions surface. She longs for her friend and feels ''she could not bear to go without seeing her.''

As the labor intensifies, Julie prepares to leave for the shack, mentally ticking off a detailed list of the contents of her bag, rather than focusing on what she has decided to do with the baby after it is born. Something, however, nags at her as she admits, ''She felt ill-prepared, she did not have enough of something, but what could it be?'' At this point she remembers Debbie's philosophy: ''take what you want and don't pay for it.'' But Julie had learned from Debbie ''what things cost, the value of everything, and of people, of what you did for them, and what they did for you.'' Before she ''hadn't known what had to be paid.'' She now knows that she must pay for the price of survival, by giving up her child.

Julie focuses on what is happening to her body and it frightens her. Lessing's descriptions of the labor and birth reflect Julie's internal torment. Alone, she stumbles down a dark alley in the frozen rain to a broken-down, filthy shack inhabited by a starving, mangy dog. The dog, focused, like Julie, solely on self-preservation, will eat the bloody afterbirth. Julie notes, "Its eyes were saying, Please, please. . . . It was gulping and licking its lips, because of all the blood, when it was so hungry."

As the pain gets worse, she thinks about Debbie, chanting her name like a mantra, but notes that even though her friend insisted that she would stay with her to "see everything's all right," she had left with a man. While Julie makes herself think, "I don't blame her," she groans, "Oh, Debbie, Debbie, why did you leave me?" She acknowledges that "Debbie had left her to cope on her own, after providing everything from shelter and food and visits to a doctor, to the clothes." Just before the birth, Julie admits "the pain was awful, but that wasn't the worst of it. She felt so alone, so lonely."

Julie's feelings about her baby emerge in Lessing's narration after the birth. Although the baby appears gray and bloody, Julie recognizes the connection between them as she picks up the umbilical cord, "a thick twisted rope of flesh, full of life, hot and pulsing in her hand." While looking at her daughter, she admits "its wriggling strength, its warmth, the life she could feel beating there, astonished and pleased her. Unexpectedly she was full of pleasure and pride." Her suppression of the decision she has made about giving up her baby results in momentary confusion. After she cuts the cord, she worries because she is "getting something wrong, but [can't] remember what it was."

Her confusion causes her to consider leaving the baby in the shack, but she decides that would be unwise because of the presence of the dog. Yet as she considers her options, she looks at her child and struggles to contain her feelings for her. Julie observes the baby stop crying and lie "quietly looking at her," and resolves "she wasn't going to look back, she wasn't going to love it." Her determination plays out as she places her daughter in a telephone box and walks toward the "brilliant lights of the pub at the corner" without looking back. Yet, once inside the pub, she finds a window that she can sit beside and view "the bundle, a small pathetic thing." Even after she watches a young woman and her companion find her baby and make a phone call, presumably for an ambulance, she decides "she ought to leave . . . she ought not to stand here . . . but she stayed, watching, while the noise of the pub beat

around her," at a safe distance from her painful reality.

In an effort to gain control of her emotions, Julie observes in an objective, reportorial tone the details of her daughter's departure in an ambulance with the couple who found her. She reports, "So the baby was safe. It was done. She had done it." Yet her sorrow emerges "as she went out into the sleety rain." As "she saw the ambulance lights vanish . . . her heart plunged into loss and became empty and bitter, in the way she had been determined would not happen." In an effort to cope with her loss, with "the tears running, she calls . . . 'Where are you Debbie?'"

Lessing fills in some of the narrative details when Debbie returns to her parents. Julie had been sure that her father would have thrown her out after discovering she was pregnant. Yet when she sees him looking "small and weak," she wonders "what on earth had she been afraid of?" Her parents are unable to offer her any consolation as they sit weeping "each in a chair well apart from the other, not comforting each other, or holding her, or wanting to hold each other, or to hold her." Later she admits, "I wish I could just snuggle up to Mum and she could hold me and I could go to sleep. . . [but] in this family, they simply did not touch each other."

Julie admits that she has been trying to ignore the pain she caused her parents, noting "she had been making things easier for herself by saying, they won't care I'm not there. They probably won't even notice. Now she could see how much they had been grieving for her."

Although she "soaped and rubbed, getting rid of the birth," in her shower, desperately trying to get rid of the memory of what she had done, later, while watching the news, "hot waves of jealousy went through Julie when she saw how the nurse smiled down at the little face seen briefly by Julie in torchlight."

When her parents admit that her aunt had gotten pregnant and kept the baby at home, Julie becomes "numbed and confused," recognizing that "she, Julie, could have . . . she could be sitting here now, with her baby Rosie, they wouldn't have thrown her out." At this point "she didn't know what to think, or to feel," or what she wants, and so calls out "oh, Debbie . . . what am I to do?"

Finally she resolves to finish school, go back to London and get her baby, but then the reality of her situation hits her. She acknowledges "what things cost" and so tells herself "stop it, stop it, you know better." She understands that Rosie, her daughter, "could not come here, because she, Julie, could not stand it." The price for Julie's survival is the loss of her daughter.

Lessing closes the story with Julie's focus on herself and her needs. Julie drifts off to sleep determining, "I've got to get out of here. . . . I've got to," and "I'm all right. . . . I can do anything I want to do, I've proved that."

In her interview with Lessing, Florence Howe admits that Lessing's stories do not make her "feel comfortable. They're tough-minded, thoroughly unsentimental, sometimes cruel, often pessimistic, at least about personal relations." This conclusion becomes an apt description for "Debbie and Julie" as Lessing tests the limits of conscience and endurance in the face of overwhelming loss.

Source: Wendy Perkins, Critical Essay on "Debbie and Julie," in *Short Stories for Students*, Gale Group, 2001.

Sources

Bemrose, John, of *The Real Thing*, in *Maclean's*, Vol. 105, No. 34, August 24, 1992, p. 62.

Howe, Florence, "A Conversation with Doris Lessing (1966)," in *Doris Lessing: Critical Studies*, edited by Annis Pratt and L. S. Dembo, University of Wisconsin, 1974, pp. 1–19.

Knapp, Mona, *Doris Lessing*, Frederick Ungar, 1984.

Lotozo, Eils, "In Short," in *New York Times Book Review*, July 26, 1992, p. 14.

Pratt, Annis, and L. S. Dembo, eds., *Doris Lessing: Critical Studies*, University of Wisconsin, 1974, pp. 1–19.

Review in *Kirkus Reviews* March 1, 1992.

Review in *Publishers Weekly*, Vol. 239, No. 17, April 6, 1992, p. 51.

Further Reading

Englander, Annrenee, and Corinne M. Wilks, eds., *Dear Diary, I'm Pregnant*, Annick Press, 1997.
    The editors non-judgmentally present first-person accounts of the experiences of ten teenagers who became pregnant and explored the options and consequences of abortion, adoption, and motherhood.

Lessing, Doris, *Doris Lessing: Conversations*, with an introduction by Earl G. Ingersoll, Ontario Review Press, 2000.
    Interviews dated from the 1960s to the 1990s shed light on Lessing's provocative and changing views on literature, gender relations, and social justice.

———, *Under My Skin: Volume One of My Autobiography*, HarperCollins, 1994.
    The first part of Lessing's two-part autobiography tells of her childhood and upbringing in colonial Southern Rhodesia, her developing political beliefs, and her marriages, leaving off before her move to London.

Rowe, Margaret Moan, and Simon P. Sibelman, *Doris Lessing*, St. Martin's Press, 1994.
    One of the more recent studies of Lessing's long writing career, this volume is concerned primarily with Lessing's novels. The authors discuss her as being both maverick and mainstream in her approach to literature.

The Erlking

Angela Carter

1979

After first appearing in the periodical *Bananas*, Angela Carter's ''The Erlking'' was published in her 1979 collection of short stories *The Bloody Chamber*. Throughout this collection, Carter revises classic European fairy tales, exploring provocative variations on their underlying themes of the bestiality within human nature and the power dynamics of sexual desire. This was the first book that brought the lyrical and iconoclastic British writer's fiction to the attention of people in the United States. Controversial for its gender politics as well as its ornately descriptive writing style, the collection garnered mixed reviews. In the years since her 1992 death, Carter's reputation has soared, and *The Bloody Chamber* remains one of her most highly esteemed and frequently discussed works.

In ''The Erlking,'' an innocent young woman walking through a deserted wood is seduced by a wild man who lives there. Like the animals that surround him, she falls subject to the Erlking's strange power. She learns that he is planning to transform her into a bird—many of which he keeps in cages in his cottage to sing for him—but she nevertheless remains compelled to submit to his will. However, an alternate fate for the woman is imagined when, at the story's close, it is conjectured that she will strangle him with his own hair and set free all the birds, which will then turn back into the form of other young virgins the Erlking has seduced. ''The Erlking'' is one of the collection's more experimental stories. Through a series of

sudden and disorienting shifts in point of view, Carter creates an intimate sense of the protagonist's experience of losing herself. The story addresses contemporary issues of female psychology and sexuality, making the ancient literary form of the fairy tale freshly relevant.

Author Biography

Carter was born in Eastborne, England, in 1940, the daughter of Hugh and Olive Stalker. It was the beginning of World War II and, fearing Hitler's approach, the family soon moved to South Yorkshire, where Carter was raised by her mother and maternal grandmother. After the war the family returned to the London area. Carter reports a close relationship with her father, a journalist originally from Scotland, but also claims that he was overprotective of her. In adolescence she suffered from anorexia, which she attributes to her family's sexual conservatism. Nevertheless, writes Alison Lee in her study *Angela Carter*, "the picture she paints of her family life is generally affectionate and her depiction of her childhood home highlights its dreamlike aura." She hated school and, against her mother's wishes, did not apply to university. Her father helped Carter secure a job as a journalist.

In 1960 she married Paul Carter, an industrial chemist, and moved to Bristol. Soon bored with life as a housewife, she began a degree in English at Bristol University. She graduated in 1965 with a specialization in medieval literature. Over one summer vacation, she wrote her first novel, *Shadow Dance*, which was published in 1966. She quickly wrote several other novels that were very well received. In 1968, separating from her husband, she took the prize money from a literary award and moved to Japan. It was there, she wrote in *Nothing Sacred*, "I learned what it is to be a woman and became radicalized." For the rest of her career, Carter remained an outspoken, if iconoclastic, leftist and feminist.

Carter returned to England and supported herself teaching and writing political commentary for several newspapers. A small but highly literate and enthusiastic readership, including well-known authors such as Robert Coover and Salman Rushdie, embraced her fiction. But Carter's work was experimental and hard to categorize, and literary glory eluded her. Nevertheless, she wrote prolifically. In the 1970s, in addition to writing nonfiction, several novels, and the stories in *The Bloody Chamber*, she also translated a volume of fairy tales and wrote a controversial tract on famed French pornographer the Marquis de Sade, entitled *The Sadeian Woman*. In the late 1970s, she married Mark Pearce, with whom she had a son in 1983, at age 43.

In her last years, Carter wrote her most highly acclaimed novels, *Nights at the Circus* (recipient of the James Tait Black Memorial Prize) and *Wise Children* (Carter's own favorite). In 1991 she was diagnosed with lung cancer. Carter died at home the following year at age fifty-one.

Plot Summary

The story opens with a long descriptive passage depicting the stark and gloomy atmosphere of the woods in late October. These woods are characterized as entrapping and menacing, not so much because of any physical danger they present as because of their ability to undermine human identity: "It is easy to lose yourself in these woods." This point is further emphasized though disorienting shifts from second- to third- to first-person narration.

When a clear first-person narrator's voice does emerge, she describes hearing a bird song that expresses her own "girlish and delicious loneliness" as she walks through the woods. She believes that she is alone. She then comes upon a clearing where animals have gathered. The Erlking enters playing a pipe that sounds like a birdsong and reaches out to the narrator. She is immediately subject to his strange charisma. She states that he has the power to do "grievous harm."

The story goes on to describe the Erlking's way of life. He lives alone in an orderly one-room house, surviving on the wild foods he gathers in the woods and the milk of a white goat. The Erlking tells the narrator about the ways of the strange woodland animals and teaches her to weave reeds and twigs into baskets, which he uses to cage the wild birds he keeps trapped in his cottage. He laughs at her when she accuses him of cruelty for doing this. In his house, full of the music of birdsong, there is an old fiddle, silent because it has no strings.

The narrator relates that, when she goes out for walks, she now feels compelled to go to the Erlking and have sex with him, which she describes ambivalently as both tender and violent. She claims that she is not afraid of him, though she is afraid of how he makes her feel. She describes this feeling as vertigo, a dizzying loss of orientation. Like the birds he calls with his pipe, the narrator is pulled toward him again and again, despite the danger he evokes.

The narrator describes one such encounter with the Erlking: She finds him playing his pipe, surrounded by birds, at one with the natural environment. It begins to rain and they retreat to his cottage. They embrace and he bites her neck. As they have sex, she reflects on her innocence before meeting him and his magical attraction. She imagines stringing the silent fiddle with his long wild hair, making music she would prefer to that of the caged birds that surround them in the room. She describes her feeling of being stripped by him and then clothed by his body. She wishes to grow small so that he could swallow her and then give birth to her.

As winter draws nearer, there is less to eat in the woods, and the wild birds are dependent on the Erlking for food. They flock to him and cover his body. Like a bird, the narrator accepts the "goblin feast of fruit" he has set out for her. Looking into his eyes makes her feel as if she has become small as a bird. The Erlking has the power to contain her. She realizes his plan to keep her in a cage, another singing bird, but says that she will remain silent out of spite. She doesn't think the Erlking means any harm, despite the fact that he has captured her psychically with his strange powers.

The first-person narrator describes lying with the Erlking and combing the dead leaves out of his long hair. She says that, as he sleeps in her lap, she will take his hair and wind it into two ropes to strangle him with. There is a sudden shift to third-person narration. This narrator states that the protagonist will next open all the of cages and set free the birds, each of which will turn into a young girl with the mark of the Erlking's red love bite on her neck. Then she will cut off his hair and string the silent fiddle with five strands of it, and the fiddle will play magically without a human hand. The strings will cry out a discordant music, saying "Mother, Mother you have murdered me!"

Characters

Erlking

The Erlking is the main subject of the story. The narrator, an innocent young woman, comes upon

Angela Carter

him while walking through the woods one October day. She immediately becomes subject to his magical attraction, which he also uses to charm and tame the woodland animals around him. The Erlking lives in a cottage alone in the woods and lives off the bounty of nature. While he seems in some ways to be at one with nature, he also exerts a certain tyranny over it. Most significantly, he draws the birds to him with the beautiful songs of his pipe playing; then he traps them in cages, which he keeps in his house.

Like the natural environment around him, the Erlking is both alluring and menacing. The narrator is drawn into a sexual relationship with him that she describes as both tender and brutal. While he seems to represent a model of masculine dominance, his power transcends gender boundaries. His young lover depicts him alternately as an overpowering mother figure that would swallow her and then give birth to her and as a butcher who skins her like a rabbit. She describes him as kind but also states that he intends to do her "grievous harm," and she realizes that he can cage her, along with his other bird-women. She feels trapped by him but ascribes to him no malice, as if he were a force of nature or an animal merely following its instincts.

Narrator

The young woman, who narrates most of the story in the first person, meets the Erlking and, under his power, loses her grip on her own identity. Readers learn little about her except how she feels as subject to the Erlking's strange allure. She is an innocent when she first drifts into the Erlking's enchanted clearing, but she abruptly enters a sexual relationship with him to which she is compelled to return, despite the danger it poses to her freedom and sense of self. His eyes ''eat'' her and his love-making ''skins'' her, both ''consol[ing] and devastat[ing]'' her.

The songbirds that the Erlking keeps in cages in his house reflect the narrator's plight. Like her, they are drawn to the Erlking and then entrapped by him. She sees how her relationship to him makes her small, and she anticipates that he will cage her like his other birds. This has a psychological dimension to it—suggesting the extent to which her will and sense of identity are overwhelmed by him—as well as a magical one—suggesting that he has the power to actually transform her into a bird. At the end of the story, in a passage narrated in the third person, the young woman frees all of the birds, which turn back into young women who, like her, were seduced by the Erlking. Thus, despite her enchantment by the Erlking, the young woman does see an alternative: she projects strangling the Erlking and replacing the music of caged birds with that of his hair, strung on a violin.

Themes

Nature and Its Meaning

The deep woods where the story is set is a lonely, melancholy place, giving in to the creeping coldness of the oncoming winter. It is also a truly wild place; it has ''reverted to its original privacy.'' It has a disorienting effect on any human passerby, as indicated by the second-person address: ''It is easy to lose yourself in these woods.'' The unsettling power of the wood is soon ascribed to the Erlking, whose presence permeates it. The Erlking is a wild man. He lives among animals, surviving off the land, and has dried leaves in his long, wild hair. He is a symbol of nature's power but also transcends nature with his magical control. He is destructive in the same way that nature is destructive—merely by following who he is, with no malicious intent. Yet he tames fierce and independent beasts like the fox and draws all the wild animals to him with his charming pipe-playing and offers of food. He rules nature, not through the human power of civilization but through the supernatural powers of charisma and transformation. The story addresses the wild nature within human beings, including its attraction and power as well as its danger. Nature is associated with the loss of individual identity and with sexuality.

Freedom and Entrapment

The story pivots on the relationship between the Erlking—a figure of freedom—and the narrator—a figure of entrapment. The narrator feels trapped as soon as she enters the wood, a place where the Erlking lives free from the rules and judgments of human society. The story takes up the theme of freedom and entrapment most explicitly through the treatment of the caged birds that the Erlking keeps in his cottage. Birds—especially birds in flight—are a conventional symbol of freedom. The Erlking lures these wild creatures with his pipe-playing and selects the ones with the most beautiful songs to sing for him, depriving them of their ability to fly. More broadly, wild animals, free from the strictures of civilization, represent a special kind of freedom. But the Erlking, who is in some ways a creature of nature himself, commands the animals of the wood with his magical and controlling presence.

The plight of the caged birds closely reflects that of the narrator. At the end of the story it is revealed that the Erlking has transformed his earlier lovers into birds and that he is preparing a similar fate for the narrator. This magical plot twist reflects the psychological state of the narrator, a previously virginal young woman who has become ensnared in a powerful sexual bond with the Erlking. As his lover, she feels small, incapable of flight, and afraid of falling down. ''Falling as a bird would fall through the air if the Erlking tied up the winds in his handkerchief and knotted the ends together so they could not get out. Then the moving currents of the air would no longer sustain them and all the birds would fall at the imperative of gravity, as I fall down for him.'' Though she senses his danger to her, she seems to have lost her free will. She is compelled to return to him and submit herself to his power. The story suggests the extent to which she—and, more broadly, women—participate in their own psychological entrapment. Only through the narrator's

Topics for Further Study

- List some of the adjectives that Carter uses to describe the woods and natural environment in "The Erlking." What is Carter's attitude toward nature? How does this differ from your ideas about nature?

- The narrator feels entrapped and diminished by the Erlking, but she is also drawn to him. Do you think she would have preferred to remain innocent, a "perfect child of the meadows of summer," as she had been before she met him? Describe what benefits she may have derived from her relationship with him.

- Carter was an outspoken but unconventional feminist. What does "The Erlking" suggest about the relations between men and women? What possible feminist messages may be within the story?

- Discuss the symbolism of the silent violin. Why, when strung with the Erlking's hair, does it cry out, "Mother, mother you have murdered me!"?

- Research one or more of the fairy tales from which "The Erlking" derives. What are some of the most significant changes that Carter has made to the original stories?

---

murder of him—narrated ambiguously in the future tense—will she regain freedom, for herself and the other entranced and entrapped bird-women.

Sex and Sex Roles

Sexuality can be understood as a natural and animalistic aspect of the human self, a wilderness territory of the human soul. Therefore, this fairy tale can be read as a parable about the psychological impact of sexual awakening. The narrator is innocent, virginal as Little Red Ridinghood, when she enters the wood. After becoming initiated into sex by the wild Erlking, she cannot ever truly leave the wood. She is trapped, compelled to return and to lose herself in the woods and in the Erlking's powerful attraction again and again.

Carter represents sexuality as dark and dangerous in ways that are tied to gender roles. The Erlking, a man, experiences the wilderness of sexuality as its master, its king. The narrator, a woman, experiences it as a loss of self. She feels herself becoming smaller as they make love. There is a combination of violence and tenderness in her experience of their encounters. "He is the tender butcher who showed me how the price of flesh is love; skin the rabbit, he says! Off come all my clothes." Their power relations seem very fixed according to gen-

der roles, but the end of the story suggests the possibility of reversal, when the narrator twists the Erlking's hair into ropes and strangles him from a posture of lovers' tenderness.

Style

Setting

The story takes place at a time and in a place that is not historically specific. It is set, like a classic fairy tale "once upon a time," in a timeless, magical anyplace. Yet, unlike a traditional fairy tale, the concrete, sensual elements of the setting are very important to the story, as indicated by the highly specific and descriptive opening paragraphs. The story takes place in a wood whose dangerous and seductive ambience seems almost like a character itself. It opens with a long passage describing the natural environment. The wood is invested with a powerful and menacing atmosphere, one connected to the passing of the seasons and the inevitable death that winter brings. The wood has the power to enclose: "once you are inside it, you must stay there until it lets you out." It robs human passersby of their sense of self, obliterating their identities.

Point of View

Carter's manipulation of point of view is the most difficult stylistic element of "The Erlking." It is therefore helpful to review the shifts in point of view throughout the story. It opens with a third-person description of the wood, seemingly described by an outside observer: "The lucidity, the clarity of light that afternoon was sufficient to itself." Then it drifts into a more immediate and intimate second-person address, with the "you" addressed being the reader: "There is not much in the autumn wood to make you smile." Not until the fifth paragraph of the story is the identity of the speaker revealed to be that of a first-person narrator who has, until then, spoken of the woods only in general descriptive terms. She goes on to describe meeting the Erlking and her strange and dangerous relationship with him in the first person, occasionally returning to address the reader in the second person ("Erlking will do you grievous harm") and occasionally addressing the Erlking himself in this same voice ("You sink your teeth into my throat and make me scream"). Finally, at the story's close, the first-person narration abruptly ceases, replaced by a third-person narrator who describes the former narrator as "she."

"The Erlking" begins with statements that the wood undermines human identity. The story concerns the primary, first-person narrator's frightening experience of losing her direction, will, and sense of self. The abrupt and disorienting shifts in narrative point of view create a similar effect on the reader. Upon entering the world conjured in the story, like entering the wood itself, one frequently loses one's bearings. It becomes hard to keep track of who "you" is, and the "I" who speaks appears and recedes mysteriously. Thus the shifts in point of view create a more immediate sense of the disorientation that the protagonist describes experiencing.

Symbolism

The story is highly symbolic, with most of its meaning suggested through metaphors rather than descriptive statements. Before the narration of the narrator's experience of becoming lost in the Erlking's power is even initiated, the woods are described with a simile foreshadowing this experience: "The trees stir with a noise like taffeta skirts of women who have lost themselves in the woods and hunt around hopelessly for the way out."

The narrator loses herself, but she also sees herself in all that is around her. Her subjective experience is expressed through the wood itself and the animals that surround the Erlking, particularly the birds that he keeps caged in his cottage. Like a bird, she is drawn to him, and he chooses her because of her charms. He takes the wild, innocent things and harnesses their power of song for his own pleasure. These birds reflect her ambivalent feelings in his presence—they are small, dependent, charmed, and hopelessly trapped. In the end, in a magical twist, it is revealed that the Erlking is in fact building a cage for the narrator and plans to actually transform her, through his lovemaking, into a bird. It is the logic of fairy tales that symbolic connections are enacted as literal ones; a woman who feels like a caged bird is threatened to be transformed into one, and the birds that remind her so much of herself are revealed as the Erlking's former lovers, young innocents like herself who fell subject to his transformational power.

The fiddle that sits silent in the Erlking's cottage offers a symbolic contrast to caged birds. A musical instrument, the fiddle represents culture and civilization. The Erlking silences these realms, finding music in nature instead. After the narrator strangles the Erlking and strings his long wild hair on the fiddle, the tables are turned, and he symbolically sings for her.

Historical Context

Fairy Tales

The genre of stories known as fairy tales is very diverse but shares certain important qualities. Fairy tales derive from oral culture. That is, they were told and retold by generations of people around the world before they were ever committed to print. They are not set at a specific time in history, but they are set in places that are (or at least were) familiar to the stories' listeners and tellers. Despite their everyday settings, in fairy tales normal rules of reality do not apply. Fairy tales contain an element of the supernatural—typically, objects and characters that change form, animals that speak, and figures both good and evil who have magical powers.

"The Erlking" is one of Carter's modern interpretations of the ancient fairy tale form. Carter sees classic fairy tales—often discounted as lowly or juvenile—as an important, even crucial, part of literary history. She places particular value on the original, oral forms of the tales that flourished before the rise of literacy and the publication of books for wide consumption that spread through

Europe in the mid-nineteenth century. She writes in her introduction to *The Old Wives' Fairy Tale Book*, "Fairy tales, folk tales stories from the oral tradition, are all of them the most vital connection we have with the imaginations of ordinary men and women who labored to create our world." When fairy tales were set down in print, a popular form of entertainment for the poor was transformed, as Carter writes in the same introduction, into "the refined pastime of the middle-classes, and especially the middle-class nursery." In her revisions in *The Bloody Chamber*, part of Carter's intent is to restore to the fairy tale the vitality, maturity, and frankness of its earlier oral form.

"The Erlking" employs various fairy tale devices—a wild man, a speaking instrument, and humans that are transformed into animals. "The Erlking" also makes two specific references to the classic fairy tale "Little Red Ridinghood" and shares several of its features. At the beginning of "The Erlking," the narrator is compared to the familiar fairy tale figure: "A young girl would go into the wood as trustingly as Red Ridinghood to her granny's house." Like the protagonist in the classic fairy tale, the innocent narrator is charmed by a man/beast whom she meets deep in the wilderness. Later, a famous line from the classic tale is repeated in reference to the Erlking: "What big eyes you have." In "The Erlking" Carter makes explicit the fairy tale's subtle sexual subtext—a warning against seduction by strange men.

Feminism

In all of the stories included in *The Bloody Chamber*, Carter writes about the pleasure and fear that women experience in their relationships with men. Using fairy tales as a starting point, she explores issues of sexuality, power, and identity. This focus must be understood in the context of Carter's unconventional feminism. She was part of a generation of feminists who came of age in the 1960s and 1970s who strove not only for legal and economic equality with men but also for a fundamental change in interpersonal relations. The bedroom was a battleground in this political struggle, with conventional forms of masculine and feminine sexuality seen as a root of gender inequality. Pornography became one of the movement's targets, blamed for reinforcing unequal sexual power dynamics.

Carter was often criticized by fellow feminists for her acceptance of female sexual submissiveness and masochism—which might be illustrated in "The Erlking" through the narrator's consent to and partial enjoyment of the Erlking's power over her. Other feminists, including Carter, saw the denial of the element of power relations in sex as a form of censorship that itself hampered female liberation. Shortly before coming out with *The Bloody Chamber*, Carter published a nonfiction tract entitled *The Sadeian Woman* that was a feminist defense of the notorious French pornographer the Marquis de Sade. Carter was fascinated with psychological questions surrounding sexuality and was interested in the freedom that the genre of pornographic writing allowed for exploring this issue.

In her study *Angela Carter*, Alison Lee suggests that criticism by some feminists of Carter's representations of female suffering "must be balanced against the extraordinary complexity with which she viewed relations between men and women. She called herself a feminist, but her feminism is no more monolithic than her representations of female sexuality. As is clear from her fairy tales, women can not only run with wolves but be wolves and even seduce wolves."

Critical Overview

Carter began to publish novels when she was in her mid-twenties, and her early works brought her an unusual degree of recognition for a young writer. Her first two novels, *Shadow Dance* and *The Magic Toyshop*, were received warmly by reviewers, and her third, *Several Perceptions*, won a Somerset Maugham Award. After such an auspicious start, however, Carter's literary career became more of a struggle. Taking her prize money, she left her first husband and moved to Japan, where she became politically radicalized and began to identify herself as a feminist. Her writing developed in important ways during this period, becoming less realistic and more speculative and intellectual. Upon returning to England several years later, she found herself without a secure relationship with a publisher and marginal to the British literary scene. In the 1970s, when Carter was in her thirties, she considered herself deeply unsuccessful. "At that time," wrote Joseph Bristow and Trev Lynn Broughton in their preface to *The Infernal Desires of Angela Carter: Fiction, Femininity, Feminism*, "hardly anyone seemed to understand what she was trying to prove in her increasingly experimental work."

Carter's writing, which incorporated and revised various popular genres, such as gothic, romance, science fiction, fairy tales, and pornography, clearly did not fit in with the prevailing literary vogue of realism. In a 1977 *New Review* essay, Lorna Sage applauded Carter's works for the way they "prowl around the fringes of the proper English novel like dream-monsters, nasty, exotic, brilliant creatures that feed off cultural crisis." But for the most part, Carter received little positive attention in the press in this period. Particularly controversial was her use of eroticism. "It is not a particularly English trait, nor a conventionally feminine one, for a writer to be brazenly concerned with sexuality. So it is unsurprising that Carter was not always favored by a literary establishment that sometimes found her message and her methods troubling," write Bristow and Broughton.

With the publication of a pair of books—the nonfiction study of pornographer Marquis de Sade, *The Sadeian Woman*, and the collection of revised fairy tales, *The Bloody Chamber*—in the late 1970s, Carter began to attract a wider audience, if not a friendlier one. Both books drew fire from establishment critics for their sexual explicitness and from fellow feminists for their nonjudgmental portrayal of female masochism. Alan Friedman of the *New York Times Book Review* criticized *The Bloody Chamber* on stylistic grounds, accusing Carter of "comical overwriting" and describing the stories' "whipped passion as full of cold air as whipped butter." Patricia Duncker, writing for *Literature History*, objected to the collection's erotic descriptions of female victimization. "Heterosexual feminists have not yet invented an alternative, anti-sexist language of the erotic. Carter envisages women's sensuality simply as a response to male arousal. She has no conception of women's sexuality as autonomous desire." But others saw more of value in these representations. Praising the stories' rich symbolism, Patricia Craig of the *New Statesman* wrote that "hints, connections and associations proliferate. . . . Ms. Carter's stories are too rich and heady for casual consumption, but they do provide, at a very high level, romantic nourishment for the imagination." Despite, or perhaps because of, the controversy it generated, *The Bloody Chamber* was widely reviewed and sold relatively well.

In the 1980s Carter wrote novels highly commended by a small group of literary figures but little known in the mainstream. However, since her untimely death in 1992—when she was widely considered to be at the height of her creative powers—her reputation has grown. She is now a part of the contemporary British canon and has become especially popular in university curricula and scholarship. Despite the criticism at the time of its publication, *The Bloody Chamber*, as well as Carter's other works, became increasingly recognized as visionary in both style—anticipating movements such as magical realism and postmodernism—and politics—anticipating feminist debates about pornography and gender identity. In her 1997 study *Angela Carter*, Alison Lee posits that "one consistent interest [throughout Carter's works] is the position of women in literature, in history, and in the world, and her corpus provides a large number of perspectives from which to see women and from which women may see themselves." Bristow and Broughton declare that the stories in *The Bloody Chamber* "have never ceased to engage—and enrage—their readers, who continue to debate whether Carter's revisionary handling of European legends contests or colludes with patriarchal values." Scholars agree that Carter was ahead of her time and that her fiction has only begun to be understood and appreciated.

Criticism

Sarah Madsen Hardy

Madsen Hardy has a doctorate in English literature and is a freelance writer and editor. In the following essay, she discusses how Carter both borrows and diverges from the traditional fairy tale "Little Red Ridinghood" in her story "The Erlking."

All of the stories in *The Bloody Chamber* re-imagine the plots and revisit the themes of traditional fairy tales, making explicit their sexual subtexts. For example, Carter offers several different versions of "Little Red Ridinghood" and "Beauty and the Beast" that focus on innocent young girls' seduction by animalistic men. Carter observes in her introduction to *The Old Wives' Fairy Tale Book*, that "most fairy tales are structured around the relations between men and women," thus offering an opportunity to look at these relations in all of their complexities and variations. But Carter laments how fairy tales have been simplified and sanitized in their transition from a popular oral tradition to books published for an audience of middle-class children. Carter sets out to candidly tell the morally ambiguous truths of gender dynam-

What Do I Read Next?

- *Wise Children* (1991), Carter's last novel, is also considered one of her best. Telling the story of twin sisters who are showgirls, the novel is an ironic and comic comment on family, theater, and the place of Shakespeare in Western culture.

- *Old Wives' Fairy Tale Book* (1987), a set of classic, folkloric fairy tales from around the world, collected and edited by Carter, centers on the struggles and triumphs of female protagonists.

- *Spells of Enchantment* (1991), edited by Jack Zipes, is an extensive collection of fairy tales from the Western tradition, spanning the contributions of Ancient Greek antecedents and contemporary revisions.

- *The Tales of Hoffman* (1990), a recent anthology of nineteenth-century German writer E. T. A. Hoffmann's bizarre and grotesque tales, was translated by R. J. Hollingdale. Hoffmann's in-

fluential and unsettling stories inspired psychoanalyst Sigmund Freud's theory of ''The Uncanny.''

- *Red as Blood, or Tales from the Grimmer Sisters* (1983), by science fiction and fantasy writer Tanith Lee, is a morbid and macabre collection of classic fairy tales that have been revised from a feminist perspective.

- *The Djinn in the Nightingale's Eye: Five Fairy Tales* (1997) is a sophisticated take on the fairy tale genre by British writer A. S. Byatt. It narrates the enchanted events that transform a middle-aged linguistics professor's life.

- *The Robber Bride* (1993), by Canadian novelist Margaret Atwood, is a gender-reversing story of revenge inspired by Grimm's fairy tale ''The Robber Bridegroom.''

---

ics in her own time by restoring frank sexuality and violence to the ancient fairy tale form.

While many of the stories in *The Bloody Chamber* are immediately recognizable as modern adaptations of classic fairy tales, ''The Erlking'' is not so easy to place. It borrows images and figures from various fairy tales and makes an explicit reference to one of the best-known European fairy tales, ''Little Red Ridinghood.'' In this essay, some of the connections between ''The Erlking'' and ''Little Red Ridinghood'' will be explored, as well as ways in which the two stories differ.

In the most familiar version of ''Little Red Ridinghood,'' published by the German brothers Jakob and Wilhelm Grimm in the mid-nineteenth century, an innocent and much-beloved young girl sets out into the woods to bring her ailing grandmother, who lives there, a basket of treats. She is waylaid by a wolf who—humanlike in his ability to talk—encourages her to dally in the woods and enjoy herself. She is naïve to any danger he poses

and trustingly takes his suggestion, pausing to gather a bouquet of flowers for her grandmother. Meanwhile, the wolf goes to the grandmother's house, devours her, dresses in her clothes, and lies in her bed in wait of the girl's arrival. When she gets there, she feels that something is wrong but nevertheless speaks to the wolf as if he were her granny, at which point he devours her as well. Luckily, a huntsman comes to the rescue, cutting open the wolf's stomach, from which both grandmother and Red Ridinghood emerge safe and sound. They kill the wolf by placing stones in his stomach.

The Grimm version is an example of what Carter would consider a sanitized and simplified fairy tale. The moral conflicts that arise are completely resolved; there is a clear distinction between good and evil. In the end, Little Red Ridinghood's innocence remains intact and the wolf's deception and violence are punished. In an interview with John Haffenden in his *Novelists in Interview*, Carter recounts her first encounter with the story. She says

> The oral versions of
> the original fairy tales were
> not intended especially for
> children; thus they were
> often not only frightening
> but also risqué."

that her grandmother "had no truck with that sentimental nonsense about a friendly woodcutter carefully slitting open the wolf's belly and letting out the grandmother." At the frightening climax of the tale, when the wolf eats Little Red Ridinghood, "she used to jump on me and pretend to eat me. Like all small children, I loved being tickled and nuzzled; I found it bliss, and I'd beg her to relate the story to me just for the sake of the ecstatic moment when she jumped on me." She goes on to say that, as a traditional oral tale, "the acting out of the story has always been part of the story," which turns it into "something completely different—a rough kind of game." It is a game that combines fear with pleasure. In Carter's case, since it was her grandmother who told the tale, the confusion between benevolent and malevolent figures is particularly thorough: Carter's (real, good) grandmother pretends to be the (evil) wolf who is, in the story, pretending to be the (fictional, good) grandmother. Maternal, caring, playful features are combined with masculine, threatening, deceptive features. The complexity of the emotions this evokes is apparent nowhere in the Grimm version but everywhere in *The Bloody Chamber*.

The oral versions of the original fairy tales were not intended especially for children; thus they were often not only frightening but also risqué. In *The Old Wives' Fairy Tale Book*, Carter explains that, starting with fairy tales' print publication in the nineteenth century, "the excision of references to sexual and excremental functions, the toning down of sexual situations and the reluctance to include 'indelicate' material—that is, dirty jokes—helped to denaturize the fairy tale and, indeed, helped to denaturize its vision of everyday life." The happy ending to the Grimm version of "Little Red Ridinghood" is one example of such expurgation. Another is the toning down of the story's erotic

subtext. This remains in Grimm only residually, for example, in the fact that the wolf lies in wait for Little Red Ridinghood in bed. Oral versions of "Little Red Ridinghood," derived from werewolf tales, were likely to have Little Red Ridinghood a girl poised on the verge of womanhood and the wolf taking human form during their first encounter in the woods. This allows the story to stand as a warning against seduction and rape as much as against the danger of wild animals. Carter tells John Haffenden that it was her intent in *The Bloody Chamber* to "extract the latent content from the traditional stories and use it as the beginnings of new stories."

"The Company of Wolves," which also appears in *The Bloody Chamber*, retells the "Little Red Ridinghood" story quite faithfully, sticking to the events and even the language of the classic tale. A young girl, just beginning to become a woman, departs for her grandmother's house deep in the woods, carrying a basket of treats and wearing a brilliant red shawl. She meets a werewolf in the human form of a charming hunter who finds out where she is heading, goes there ahead of her, eats her grandmother, and lies in wait for her. When he reveals himself as a wolf, intending to eat her, she—as if in response to the story's subtext warning young girls against seductive strangers—takes off her clothes and submits to him sexually. The story ends with a tender embrace between girl and beast. While this ending may seem perverse, Carter explains it in terms of a change in power dynamics between the wolf and the girl, with Little Red Ridinghood taking control. "She 'eats' the wolf," Carter explains to Haffenden.

"The Erlking" is a much looser interpretation of "Little Red Ridinghood," borrowing from other tales as well. However, like "The Company of Wolves," it treats the latent erotic content of the traditional tale as a starting point and shares an unflinching interest in a young girl's ambivalent experience of losing her sexual innocence. It diverges significantly from the plot of the classic "Little Red Ridinghood," though it loosely follows the events of a virginal protagonist's perils as she sets out in the wilderness, meets a beast-like man, and loses herself in him. Carter makes this parallel specific in one of two explicit references to "Little Red Ridinghood": "A young girl would go into the wood as trustingly as Red Ridinghood to her granny's house, but this light admits of no ambiguities and, here, she will be trapped in her own illusions because everything in the wood is exactly as it seems.'' This statement both sets up the story's parallel to the classic tale and suggests how it will reinterpret it.

Some of the imagery in ''The Erlking'' also refers to ''Little Red Ridinghood.'' The wolf's most salient features are his hair (in the earlier werewolf version, hairiness is the first thing that distinguishes the beast from a man), his eyes (''the better to see you with!''), and his teeth (''the better to eat you with!''). These are also the physical features of the Erlking that Carter emphasizes. His long hair, the color of dead leaves and tangled with them, signals the Erlking as a bestial creature of nature. His eyes, ''quite green, as if from too much looking at the wood'' also represent his wildness and his danger. ''What big eyes you have,'' Carter writes, again referring explicitly to ''Little Red Ridinghood.'' ''Eyes of an incomparable luminosity, the numinous phosphorescence of the eyes of lycanthropes [werewolves].'' When he laughs, he ''shows his white, pointed teeth with the spittle gleaming on them,'' and in one sexual encounter he actually bites the narrator's neck.

Furthermore, the Erlking's unsettling charisma is described through imagery of eating: ''There are some eyes that can eat you.'' Eating is, indeed, the most prominent metaphor used to describe the girl's sexual encounters with him. However, as in ''The Company of Wolves,'' Carter re-imagines the original girl-beast dynamic in ''Little Red Ridinghood'' through imagery of eating that goes both ways. He is a ''tender butcher'' who skins her like a rabbit, but he also offers her food, and his own body is described in erotic terms as edible: ''His skin is the tint and texture of sour cream, he has stiff, russet nipples ripe as berries.'' Thus he combines nurturing and threatening qualities, ones that reflect back on the grandmotherly guise the wolf takes in the classic tale.

The Erlking also takes on maternal characteristics even more explicitly in other passages. ''I should like to grow enormously small, so that you could swallow me, like those queens in fairy tales who conceive when they swallow a grain of corn or a sesame seed. Then I could lodge inside of your body and you would bear me.'' The combination of pleasure and fear, of warning against strange seductive beasts and loving ''rough play'' that Carter encountered hearing the story on her grandmother's lap are evidenced in her characterization of the Erlking himself. To be eaten by this ''wolf'' is, on some level, a tenderly nurturing experience.

In the traditional tale, the wolf charms Little Red Ridinghood, then pretends to be her grandmother, then, finally revealing himself as the true beast that he is, ravages her. In ''The Erlking'' there are ''no such ambiguities . . . everything in the wood is exactly as it seems.'' The animal-man figure, the Erlking, doesn't trick her. He doesn't change form or pretend to be anything other than what he is—a beastly and sexual man who is also compellingly attractive. It is only the young narrator's own illusions that allow her to become entrapped by him, if she is indeed entrapped. The story's ambiguously narrated ending—where the protagonist's revenge and liberation are narrated in the future tense—leaves open the question of who ultimately gains the upper hand.

Though ''Little Red Ridinghood'' is doubtless one of ''The Erlking's'' imaginative underpinnings, Carter transforms the tale to an almost unrecognizable degree and, in the process, transforms the way female ''innocence'' and its loss are represented. While some feminists have criticized Carter for portraying women who enjoy their own victimization, it clearly could be argued that Carter, instead, redefines the deflowered Little Red Ridinghood figure as ultimately responsible for her own fate and, therefore, not a victim. She is not tricked by a wolf; at worst she is ''trapped in her own illusions.'' And even before the story's ambiguous close, there is evidence that the protagonist is capable of acting in her own interest, motivated by pleasure as well as fear.

Source: Sarah Madsen Hardy, Critical Essay on ''The Erlking,'' in *Short Stories for Students*, The Gale Group, 2001.

Rena Korb

Korb has a master's degree in English literature and creative writing and has written for a wide variety of educational publishers. In the following essay, she analyzes the young girl's attraction for and fear of the Erlking.

In 1782 Johannes von Goethe wrote his lyrical poem ''The Erl King'' about a young boy riding through a dark, cold forest with his father. He is scared as he hears the entreating calls of the king of the elves, but the father refuses to validate his son's fears. The Erl King continues fruitlessly to tempt the boy with promises of games, colorful flowers, and attentive stepsisters, but the boy will not willingly join the Erl King. By the time the father and son have arrived home, the boy is dead, the Erl King having taken him through force. Almost 200 years later, Carter evoked the eeriness of this earlier work with her own ''Erlking,'' which depicts a young girl drawn into the ''heart of the wood'' by a green-eyed man. Though powerfully drawn to him, both sexually and emotionally, the girl eventually will trick her seducer through his murder and her own escape.

''The Erlking'' is included in *The Bloody Chamber*, Carter's collection of reworked, feminist fairy tales. Alison Lurie comments on the tale in a *New York Times* article:

> A recurring scenario [in Carter's fairy tales] is that of a beautiful young girl imprisoned in a remote castle by a rich, powerful, animalistic-or part-animal-man. Sometimes the heroine is destroyed; at other times she is rescued; but often she turns the tables by proving to be as passionately animal as the hero or villain.

This generalization can be further extended to apply to ''The Erlking,'' in which the young girl is imprisoned by her own desire for her ''tender butcher.'' In order to emerge unharmed from their relationship, she has no choice but to ruthlessly murder him. ''I shall take two huge handfuls of his rustling hair,'' she plans, ''as he lies half dreaming, half waking, and wind them into ropes, very softly, so he will not wake up, and, softly, with hands as gentle as rain, I shall strangle him with them.''

Goethe's ''Erl King,'' explains Marina Warner in *No Go the Bogeyman*, ''personifies death as a danger above all to the young, who are credited with a more intense perception of the other world in the first place; this intimacy with the supernatural makes them vulnerable to its charms and its desires.'' Similarly, in Carter's ''Erlking,'' the narrator is attuned to a whole underworld of the forest. The Erlking, who calls the girl to him by means of a bird whistle, is at the center of this world that is far away from civilized, safe society, even though the girl can easily walk the distance. As the story opens, ominous hints abound. On this day, the day the narrator will first meet the Erlking, the late fall sunlight ''struck the wood with nicotine-stained fingers.'' She walks among ''stark elders [that] have an anorexic look'' into wood so dense it quickly ''swallows you up.'' The ground below is carpeted with the ''russet slime of dead bracken where the rains . . . had so soaked the earth that the cold oozed up through the soles of the shoes.'' A ''haunting sense of the imminent cessation of being'' fills the air, as does ''a sickroom hush.''

The narrator feels ''the cold wind that always heralds your presence'' but as the air ''blew gentle around me, I thought that nobody was in the wood but me.'' It is only later, after she has become deeply involved with the Erlking, that she likens this wind to ''the cold air that blows over graveyards.'' Despite these cues, the scene that she observes on her first meeting with the Erlking evokes innocent pleasures. He rests in a garden of beasts and birds. Animals flock to him; the ''little brown bunnies with their ears laid together along their backs like spoons, crouching at his feet''; ''the rusty fox . . . laid its head upon his knee''; a watching squirrel; an observant rooster; ''a goat of uncanny whiteness, gleaming like a goat of snow, who turned her mild eyes towards me and bleated softly, so that he knew I had arrived.'' Before meeting the Erlking, the narrator was innocent and ''girlish.'' She recalls, ''How sweet I roamed, or, rather, used to roam; once I was the perfect child of the meadows of summer, but then the year turned, the light clarified and I saw the gaunt Erlking.'' She thus likens her attraction to the Erlking as the very perversion of her innocence as she continues to answer his call ''like any other trusting thing that perches on the crook of his wrist.'' But, she later writes, ''I knew from the first moment I saw him how Erlking would do me grievous harm.'' Despite her intuition, she allows him to lure her to him. In stripping her of her clothes and teaching her of desire, he also opens her eyes to the possibility of deceit, to the formidable melding of love, desire, and danger. As she admits, ''[H]is touch both consoles and devastates me.''

In a real sense, the danger is attractive to the girl, who relishes in her sexual subjugation to him. His larger body almost completely covers hers. The imagery she employs also shows how she prefers to conceive of herself in relationship to her seducer. More than once, she compares her nakedness to the body of a skinned rabbit. Against the Erlking and his seductive power, she becomes helpless. ''Desire is dangerous because you may create out of it the cage of your own entrapment, like the young girls trapped as birds in the Erlking's cages,'' writes Avis Lewallen in an examination of *The Bloody Chamber* that appeared in *Perspectives on Pornography*. Because the girl does not want to become trapped by the Erlking and her own desire for him, the narrator must kill him.

The theme of entrapment is woven throughout the story, and the girl always knows just how troublesome it is. ''How cruel it is, to keep wild birds in cages!'' she says without realizing the enormity of that statement; these birds were once girls who had fallen under the mercy of the Erlking.

His laughter at her exclamation emphasizes "his white, pointed teeth with the spittle gleaming on them." The wood that leads to the Erlking also serves as cage. "Once you are inside it, you must stay there until it lets you out again for there is no clue to guide you through in perfect safety." His arms become bonds, even "his embraces were his enticements and yet, oh yet! they were the branches of which the trap itself was wove."

The Erlking's eyes also become objects of entrapment that will figuratively devour the girl and steal her away from herself. "There are some eyes can eat you," she succinctly notes. Later, she rhapsodizes on the power of these eyes:

> If I look into it long enough, I will become as small as my own reflection. I will diminish to a point and vanish. I will be drawn down into that black whirlpool and be consumed by you. I shall become so small you can keep me in one of your osier cages and mock my loss of liberty.

The idea of being physically and symbolically eaten up by the Erlking is emphasized elsewhere as well. The teeth appear again as she muses, "I feel your sharp teeth in the subaqueous depths of your kisses. . . you sink your teeth into my throat and make me scream." The girls who have come before, such as the baker's daughter who is now an owl, have been similarly treated. When the Erlking's death will allow the birds to go free, "they will change back into young girls, every one, each with the crimson imprint of his love-bite on their throats."

The narrator, however, is powerfully attracted to being so consumed. "I should like to grow enormously small," she says, "so that you could swallow me." The metaphor that the girl invokes immediately thereafter, however, drastically changes the tone. She says she would like the Erlking to swallow her "like those queens in fairy tales who conceive when they swallow a grain of corn or a sesame seed." Then the narrator "could lodge inside your body and you would bear me out." This imagery of the Erlking becoming impregnated by the girl is powerful and disturbing. Though this fantasy arises from her desire to be enclosed in the same skin as the Erlking, in essence, he is her lover and yet she longs for him to be her father too. This paragraph raises the specter of incest, which re-emerges in the story's closing line, the violin with strings fashioned out of the Erlking's hair, giving voice to his final thoughts: "Mother, mother, you have murdered me!" As Lewallen writes, "[W]e deduce from the punch-line . . . that the Erlking is

> " The Erlking, who calls the girl to him by means of a bird whistle, is at the center of this world that is far away from civilized, safe society, even though the girl can easily walk the distance."

also the created child of desire in an Oedipal configuration."

By the end of the story, despite the abundance of imagery implying cruelty and destruction, the narrator has again bestowed purity upon the Erlking. "But in his innocence," she says, "he never knew he might be the death of me." Indeed, the description that follows most resembles maternal tenderness.

> Sometimes he lays his head on my lap and lets me comb his lovely hair for him . . . His hair falls down over my knees. Silence like a dream in front of the spitting fire while he lies at my feet and I comb the dead leaves out of his languorous hair.

The extreme quickness with which this scene turns violent only underscores the fragile but very real connection that the girl has been expressing throughout the story: the coupling of danger and desire.

In her discussion of Carter's fairy tales, Lurie makes this assessment: "Violence is always a possibility; beauty and courage and passion may prevail, but the weak and the timid go to the wall." The narrator in "The Erlking" knows that only one person can emerge from this relationship unharmed, either she or the Erlking but never both. Though she acknowledges that "I loved him with all my heart," her desire to survive is far stronger, and she rises, deceitfully, against him. In this depiction, Carter remains true to one of the basic tenets of fairy tales: there is always someone who is evil and must be vanquished. Carter's message is not surprising. As Lurie concludes, "After all, one reason the old fairy tales have survived for hundreds of years is that they do not try to disguise what the world is really like."

Source: Rena Korb, Critical Essay on "The Erlking," in *Short Stories for Students*, The Gale Group, 2001.

Joyce Hart

Hart has degrees in English literature and creative writing and is a copyeditor and published writer. In this essay, she looks at the feminist twists in Carter's fairytale parody of desire, death, and transformation of the virginal female by comparing it to the Brothers Grimm tale, "Little Red Cap."

In an obituary in London's *Guardian* upon Carter's death, Lorna Sage says that Carter had a "founding feminist perception." Carter was, she says, "a writer who always demonstrates how vital counter-cultural impulses are to the very existence of any worthwhile tradition." It is with an eye focused on both Carter's feminist perceptions and her counter-cultural impulses that this essay will examine her short story "The Erlking," with the "worthwhile tradition" being, in this case, the fairytale, a form that many of Carter's stories emulate.

In many of the traditional fairytales, especially those reinterpreted by the Brothers Grimm, some of the more popular moral lessons that are either obviously stated or subtly implied are directed at young, innocent, cute, and sweet little girls, of which the Grimms' tale of "Little Red Cap" is a prime example. "Once there was a dear little girl whom everyone loved," begins this particular tale. Next the fairytale normally posits a warning: the little girl is usually advised not to veer from the traditional path. In the story "Little Red Cap," it is the girl's mother who tells her, "Walk properly like a good little girl, and don't leave the path." Inevitably, in these stories, the little girl disobeys this formidable rule. She does leave the path, and although the consequences of the little girl's actions may vary, depending on the story line, the underlying moral message remains the same. According to feminist readings of these fairytales, the message behind these stories is that if little girls buck the patriarchal rule, they will be punished.

It is upon these sentiments, or rather in ridicule of them, that Carter begins "The Erlking," a fairytale kind of story with a fairytale kind of structure revolving around death, desire, and transformation, much akin to the tale of "Little Red Cap." Carter reinforces the relationship between her story and this traditional fairytale by making reference to it with this phrase in the beginning of her story: "A young girl would go into the wood as trustingly as Red Riding Hood to her granny's house. . . ." ("Red Riding Hood" is the more familiar title of this story.) But there is a big difference between Carter's version and the Grimms' fairytale. The desire, death,

and transformation all come about, but they come about in very dissimilar ways. Although Carter's story is also geared toward sending a chilling moral lesson, the recipient of that lesson is definitely not the little girl.

Similar to the opening of Grimms' fairytale, Carter begins "The Erlking" with a young girl at the edge of a great forest. Carter paints a very gloomy picture of the woods, using words like "dour spooks," "sulphur-yellow interstices," "nicotine-stained fingers," and "russet slime"—not especially enticing images, not ones that would draw a young woman in. In fact, she portrays an environment that a young woman might walk through very quickly, if she had to walk through it at all. "The fairytale genre," states Ruth Bushi in her essay on Carter, "teaches us to be afraid of the woods (the un*man*ned, female space beyond social authority). . . ." Carter, possibly with tongue in cheek or at least duplicating the old formulaic structure of the fairytale, attempts to set up the same fear of the forest. But despite their fears, both Little Red Cap and Carter's young female protagonist enter the woods, though they step carefully, even seriously, with their eyes focused on the forest floor. As the wolf in the Grimms' story puts it to Little Red Cap: "You trudge along as solemnly as if you were going to school."

Ironically, it is the Grimms' wolf who points out the beauty of the woods to Little Red Cap. His motives, however, are not to be trusted. Unbeknownst to the young girl, he is setting a trap, distracting her so he can make it to the grandmother's house before she does. "Little Red Cap, open your eyes," says the Grimms' wolf. "What lovely flowers!" Little Red Cap does not take the subtle hint that the wolf is throwing her way. She is an innocent, trusting the wolf to a fault. She might have opened her eyes, but when she does, all she sees are the flowers, not the wolf's hidden intentions.

Carter's wolf, the Erlking, is also cunning, but he employs a different tactic; and Carter's young girl responds in a more mature way. The Erlking uses a more obvious lure—a whistle that mimics the call of a bird in distress—the sound of which goes directly to the young girl's heart. The mimicked call is "as desolate as if it came from the throat of the last bird left alive." Both Grimms' wolf and Carter's Erlking are successful in tricking their victims, but their lures work on different aspects of the female character. Whereas Little Red Cap is attracted to the flowers for their surface beauty, the young woman in Carter's story is drawn on a much deeper level, to the emotional cry, the "melancholy" of loneliness, and the possibility of a small creature's imminent death. While Little Red Cap gathers the flowers so as to bring pleasure to her grandmother, Carter's young woman senses that she is on a mission to, at the least, commiserate with the lonely bird she hears cry out. Once she sees all the birds that have been lured to the Erlking, she senses that she may have been brought there to save them. "As soon as I saw them I knew at once," states Carter's narrator, "that all its [the wood's] occupants had been waiting for me . . . "

Both Little Red Cap and Carter's protagonist have entered the woods and left the path. By leaving the path and going deeper into the wilder parts of the woods, they have disobeyed the dictates of society and must take the consequences of their actions. The woods into which they wander could be interpreted to stand for many different things. The woods could represent wildness in opposition to the organized and civilized world. On another level, they could represent the emotional as opposed to the rational mind. Whatever they represent, the young women in both of these stories are drawn to that wild space. Something in them desires to wander off the path, and it is this desire that gets them into trouble.

One of the more basic desires of young pubescent females is the sexual desire. In her essay, Bushi points out that not only does the fairytale genre try to warn young women of the dangers of the woods, it also tries to instill a fear of the wolf, "and more particularly, his genitals." There is little insinuation of sexuality in the Grimms' version of the story. Although there are older versions of this story in which the young girl does get into bed with the wolf, in the Grimms' story, the wolf jumps out of bed and consumes the young girl while she stands there in disbelief, so innocent that she thinks that the costumed wolf is her grandmother. "Poor Little Red Cap," says the narrator. The sexuality has been written out of the Grimms' version, but whether she was raped or consumed by the wolf, Little Red Cap is definitely a victim in this story; and she must be rescued by yet another male hunter. So startled is she by all the activities around her, all the consequences of her bad judgment and misbehavior, that she declares at the end of the Grimms' story that "never again will I leave the path and run off into the wood when my mother tells me not to."

Oh, how different is Carter's version! To begin with, sexuality is strongly implicit. And not only is

> **Both Little Red Cap and Carter's protagonist have entered the woods and left the path. By leaving the path and going deeper into the wilder parts of the woods, they have disobeyed the dictates of society and must take the consequences of their actions."**

it implicit but the young protagonist, although possibly under the control of the Erlking's seduction, is an accepting partner. "Now, when I go for walks . . . I always go to the Erlking . . . where I lie at the mercy of his huge hands. . . . Off come all my clothes." It is through the sexual act that the young girl becomes a woman. "Once I was the perfect child of the meadows of summer, but then the year turned . . . and I saw the gaunt Erlking, tall as a tree . . . and he drew me towards him. . . . He strips me to my last nakedness." It is at this point, in the traditional fairytale that the couple lives happily ever after. Once the virgin has lost her hymen, she becomes a possession of the male. Carter illustrates this typical fairytale condition in her story by creating the Erlking's collection of birds trapped in cages. Unlike the innocence of Little Red Cap, Carter's young woman is well aware of the fact that the new cage that the Erlking is making has been earmarked to eventually cage her.

But she cannot resist the Erlking. She goes back and back again. But strangely, in one scene, the narrator declares, "I lie above him," and it is from this point in the story that, despite the tremendous lure of the Erlking, the young woman begins to gain perspective and a sense of self. She begins to realize the power of his gaze and to understand that his eyes are like a "reducing chamber." In other words, she is beginning to comprehend, through the reflection of herself in his eyes, that he sees her as powerless, and it is through this image of herself that she also foresees her destiny of eventually becoming caged. If she does not commit herself to forcing a change, she knows that she will ''become so small you can keep me in one of your osier cages and mock my loss of liberty.'' If she remains submissive and diminutive, as Little Red Cap did, she will become yet another victim.

''Sometimes he lays his head on my lap,'' the narrator says, and a couple of sentences later, the narrator reports that the Erlking ''lies at my feet.'' Lower and lower he drops as the young girl gains more power in herself. There is also the birth of another strong desire in the woman, and it is the desire for revenge. Before the woman is consciously aware of how she will save herself, she knows for a fact that even if the Erlking succeeds in caging her, she will not sing for him. ''I shall sit, hereafter, in my cage among the other singing birds but I—shall be dumb, from spite,'' she says.

But Carter's young woman is not dumb, neither in the colloquial meaning of not being very smart nor in being silent: ''Lay your head on my knee so that I can't see the greenish inward-turning suns of your eyes any more,'' she tells the Erlking. She does not want to be lured by his eyes. She does not want to identify with his definition of her. She wants literally to take matters into her own hands. She needs neither man nor hunter to rescue her. She has discovered that she can be just as cunning as a wolf. She uses what is available—the long hair of the Erlking—and strangles him.

In an interesting twist, the last words of the story have the once-unstrung violin, which the young girl restrings with strands from the Erlking's hair, cry out: ''Mother, mother, you have murdered me!'' Thus the male cries out from beyond his veil of death to his mother, or possibly to matriarchy itself, admonishing her but at the same time acknowledging her power. In her way, Carter may be anticipating a future generation of women singing, ''Patriarchy is dead. Long live the queen.''

Source: Joyce Hart, Critical Essay on ''The Erlking,'' in *Short Stories for Students*, Gale Group, 2001.

Sources

Bristow, Joseph, and Trev Lynn Broughton, *The Infernal Desires of Angela Carter: Fiction, Femininity, Feminism*, Longman, 1997.

Bushi, Ruth, ''Consum[ma/p]tion: Beastly Sex,'' in *The Bloody Chamber*, at http://members.tripod.co.uk/thaz/carter.html (2000).

Carter, Angela, ed., *Old Wives' Fairy Tale Book*, Pantheon Books, 1990.

Craig, Patricia, ''Gory,'' in *New Statesman*, May 25, 1979, p. 726.

Duncker, Patricia, ''Re-Imagining the Fairy Tales: Angela Carter's Bloody Chambers,'' in *Literature and History*, Vol. 10, No. 1, Spring 1984, pp. 3–14.

Friedman, Alan, ''Pleasure and Pain,'' in *New York Times Book Review*, February 17, 1980, pp. 14–15.

Haffenden, John, *Novelists in Interview*, Methuen, 1989.

Lee, Allison, *Angela Carter*, Twayne Publishers, 1997.

Manheim, Ralph, trans., ''Little Red Cap,'' in *Grimms' Tales for Young and Old*, Anchor Press, 1977.

Sage, Lorna, ''The Soaring Imagination,'' in *The Guardian*, February 17, 1992.

Further Reading

Bettelheim, Bruno, *The Uses of Enchantment: The Meaning and Significance of Fairy Tales*, Alfred A. Knopf, 1976.
    Any student interested in fairy tales should be familiar with this influential study of their symbolic meanings and psychological significance. Though Carter often disagreed with Bettelheim's conclusions, they surely influenced her.

Carter, Angela, *Nothing Sacred: Selected Writings*, Virago, 1982.
    A collection of Carter's nonfiction, this volume sheds light on the author's views on feminism, politics, and literature, as well as offering some interesting autobiographical insight.

Lee, Allison, *Angela Carter*, Twayne Publishers, 1997.
    Though it focuses primarily on her novels rather than her short stories, this brief, clearly written study is a helpful introduction to the themes and issues driving Carter's imagination.

Sage, Lorna, *Angela Carter*, Northcote House, 1994.
    This literary biography was written by one of Carter's earliest critics, who was also a close friend. It discusses the relationship between themes in her fiction and events in her life.

Warner, Marina, *From the Beast to the Blonde: Fairy Tales and Their Tellers*, Vintage, 1995.
    While this well-known volume contains only a few specific references to Carter's writing, its comprehensive analysis of fairy tale themes and devices is broadly applicable to her work.

The Feathered Ogre

Italo Calvino

1956

"The Feathered Ogre" was first published in Italo Calvino's collection, *Italian Folk Tales*, in 1956. It is a transcription of a traditional story from the oral tradition in Italian culture. In this fairy tale, a man goes on a quest for a feather plucked from the body of a terrible ogre who lives in a cave on a mountain and eats every human being he sees. In his search for the ogre, the man stops four times and promises each of the people he meets to bring them back a feather from the ogre. When he reaches the ogre's cave, a beautiful girl, the ogre's wife, helps him to trick the ogre, so that they may both flee the cave with the desired feathers. On their way home, they give a feather to each of the parties the man had met along the way, and they share the ogre's solution to the predicament of each. When the man returns with a feather to cure the king, he is doubly rewarded, with a promise to marry the beautiful girl. In transcribing such folk tales, Calvino especially valued brevity, repetition and rhythm in the plot and structure of the tale. "The Feathered Ogre" is written with these stylistic concerns in mind, which lends the story a familiar feel to anyone who has been told fairy tales as a child. It contains familiar themes in which good triumphs over evil, the wicked are punished, and the brave hero is rewarded for his courageous good deeds with wealth and marriage to a beautiful girl.

Author Biography

Italo Calvino was born in Cuba on October 15, 1923, but raised in San Remo, Italy, a town close to France. His father was a professor of tropical agriculture at the University of Turin, and the young Calvino was encouraged to pursue the sciences but preferred literature. He was enrolled at the School of Agriculture at the University of Turin, when the German invasion of Italy during World War II interrupted his studies. At the age of twenty, after his parents were abducted by the Germans, Calvino joined an anti-fascist resistance organization called the Garibaldi Brigade. After the war, he returned to school to study literature, writing his thesis on the writer Joseph Conrad. He began writing in the forties as a journalist for *L'Unita*, a communist newspaper.

In 1947 he published the novel *Il sentiero dei nidi di ragno*, which was translated and published in English as *The Path to the Nest of Spiders* in 1957. In 1949 Calvino published a collection of short stories based on his experiences during the war, entitled *Ultimo viene il corvo* (*The Crow Comes Last*), a selection of which was translated into English in 1957 as *Adam, One Afternoon, and Other Stories*. His 1956 collection and retelling of Italian folktales, entitled *Fiabe italiane*, was translated into English and published as *Italian Fables* in 1961 and later as *Italian Folktales* in 1980. From 1959 to 1966, he worked as co-editor of the Italian journal *Il menabo*.

Calvino moved to Paris in 1964, where he married Esther Singer, an Argentine translator for UNESCO, with whom he had a daughter. His best-known novel among English readers was originally published in Italian in 1979, translated and published in English as *If on a Winter's Night a Traveler* in 1981, an experimental novel which addresses the reader directly as ''You.'' A collection of his essays written between 1955 and 1978, originally published in Italian in 1980, was translated into English and published in 1986. Calvino moved to Rome with his family in 1980, where he stayed until his death of a stroke at the age of sixty-two, on September 19, 1985. Several of his works in progress were published posthumously, such as *Six Memos for the Next Millenium*, which includes five of the six lectures he had been preparing to give at Harvard University. Calvino continues to be widely regarded as one of the greatest writers of the twentieth century.

Plot Summary

A king falls ill and is told by his doctors that the only way he can be cured is by obtaining a feather from the ogre that eats every human being it sees. No one of his subjects is willing to go on a quest for one of the ogre's feathers, until one attendant bravely volunteers to go. The man is told that the ogre lives in a cave on a mountaintop. Along the way, he stops at an inn, where the innkeeper asks if the man will bring back a feather for him, for good luck, and if he will ask the ogre if he knows where the innkeeper's daughter, who disappeared years ago, may be. The man agrees and goes on his way. He then takes a ferry across the river, and the ferryman asks if he will bring back a feather for him and if he will ask the ogre how he can escape from the ferry, as he has not been able to go ashore for years. The man agrees and goes on his way. He then stops to rest by a fountain, and two noblemen ask if he will bring them back a feather and if he will ask the ogre why their fountain, which once spewed silver and gold, has gone dry. The man agrees to do this and goes on his way.

He next stops at a monastery, where the monks ask if he will bring them back a feather as well and if he will ask the ogre why it is that there has been so much discord among the monks for the past ten years. The monks also give the man advice about how to find the ogre. The man agrees to do this, and the next day he climbs the mountain and enters the seventh of seven caves, at the very end of which is the door to the ogre's home.

When the man knocks on the ogre's door, the ogre's wife, a beautiful girl, answers. When he explains that he has come for some of the ogre's feathers, she warns him that the ogre eats every human being he sees. The girl agrees to help him obtain the feathers and to answer the questions he has so that she can escape the ogre, whom she can't stand. When the ogre comes home, the man hides under the bed, and the girl serves the ogre his dinner.

When the girl and the ogre go to bed and the ogre has fallen asleep, the girl plucks one of his feathers and hands it to the man under the bed. When the ogre wakes up with an ''ouch!,'' the girl explains that she had been dreaming that the monks in the monastery had been fighting amongst each other for the past ten years. The ogre responds that the monks have been in discord because the Devil has been living among them, dressed as a priest. When the ogre falls asleep again, the girl plucks another of his feathers and hands it to the man under the bed. When the ogre awakens a second time, she explains that she had been dreaming that the fountain owned by the two noblemen that used to spew silver and gold had dried up. The ogre responds that in fact the fountain has gone dry, because it is blocked up by a snake sleeping curled around a ball. He tells her that the noblemen would have to crush the snake's head under the ball so that the fountain would once again pour silver and gold. When the ogre falls back to sleep, the girl plucks another of his feathers and hands it to the man under the bed. When the ogre awakens a third time, she explains that she had been dreaming that the ferry man had been unable to leave his ferry for years. The ogre responds that this is true, and that he could only be freed from the ferry by jumping to shore before his next passenger gets off the ferry. That way, the passenger would be stuck on the ferry, and the ferry man would be free to go. When the ogre falls back to sleep, the girl plucks a forth feather and hands it to the man under the bed. When the ogre awakens a fourth time, she explains that she had been dreaming that the innkeeper had lost his daughter and had not seen her for years. The ogre responds that she herself is the daughter of the innkeeper.

The next morning, after the ogre leaves for work, the girl and the man flee the ogre's cave together. They first stop at the monastery, where they give the monks a feather and explain that the Devil is living among them, dressed as a priest, and that if all the real priests do good deeds, the Devil will be found out; this they do, and the Devil is sent away. They then stop at the fountain of the noblemen, to whom they give a feather and explain how to unblock their fountain. After they have taken the ferry to the opposite shore and gotten off, they give the ferryman a feather and explain to him how he can be free from the ferry. When they come to the inn, they give the innkeeper a feather, and he is so grateful for his daughter's return that he gives the man her hand in marriage. The man then brings a feather to the king, who recovers from his illness and rewards the man. When the man explains that he is off to be married, the king doubles his reward.

The ogre, meanwhile, upon discovering his wife's absence, goes in search of her and the man, with the intention of eating them both. When he

Italo Calvino

takes the ferry across the river, the ferryman jumps ashore, leaving the ogre trapped on the ferry.

Characters

The Beautiful Girl

The innkeeper's daughter, a ''beautiful girl,'' is first encountered by the protagonist as the wife of the ogre, who has been his captive for years. She comes up with a scheme to take four feathers from the ogre, answer each of the four questions, and escape with the man, without either of them being eaten by the ogre. She tells the man to hide under the bed while she feeds the ogre his dinner, and when she and the ogre go to bed, she plucks one of his feathers, which awakens him, at which point she tells him she has been dreaming, and he explains the significance of her dream. She repeats this four times during the night, handing each feather to the man under the bed as she does so. The fourth dream that she describes to the ogre is about the innkeeper, whose daughter disappeared years ago. The ogre explains that she herself is the daughter of the innkeeper. The next morning, the girl flees with the man, and, when they reach the innkeeper, he is so grateful for the return of his daughter that he immediately gives her hand in marriage to the man.

The Ferry Man

The protagonist first encounters the ferry man on his way to the cave of the ogre. The ferry man asks if the protagonist will bring back one of the feathers of the ogre and if he will ask the ogre why he has been stuck working on the ferry for years and cannot get off. When the girl tells the ogre she has been dreaming of this predicament of the ferry man, the ogre explains that the only way for him to get off the ferry is to jump ashore before his next passenger gets off the ferry; that way he will be free, and the passenger will be stuck working as the ferry man. When the man and the girl take the ferry on their way home, they give him the feather he asked for. Only after they have gotten off on the other side of the river do they explain to him how he can escape the ferry. It so happens that his next passenger is the ogre himself, who has no idea that the ferry man has been informed of this. Before the ogre can step ashore, the ferry man jumps off, and the ogre must stay on the boat.

The Friars

The man first encounters the friars at the monastery on his way to the cave of the ogre. The friars inform him that the ogre lives in the back of the seventh of seven caves, and they give him a candle and matches to light his way. They also ask if he will bring them back a feather from the ogre and if he will ask the ogre why they have had nothing but discord in the monastery for the past ten years. When the girl pretends to be dreaming of the friars, the ogre explains that the Devil has been living among them, disguised as a priest, for the past ten years, and that is why they have not been able to get along. The ogre says that if all of the real priests do good deeds, the Devil will be found out, and they can get rid of him. On their way home, the man and the girl give the friars a feather and tell them what the ogre has said. The true friars all go about doing good deeds, and the Devil is found out and sent away.

The Innkeeper

The innkeeper is the first person encountered by the man on his way to find the ogre. The innkeeper asks if he will bring back one of the ogre's feathers for good luck and if he will ask the ogre where his daughter, who disappeared years

ago, has gone. When the beautiful girl who is the wife of the ogre pretends to have dreamed about the innkeeper's predicament, the ogre tells her that the innkeeper is her own father and that she is the daughter who has disappeared. When the man and the girl reach the innkeeper after escaping the ogre, he is so grateful that he immediately gives her hand in marriage to the man.

The King

The king falls ill and is told by his doctors that he can only be cured with a feather from the ogre. Only one of his attendants, the man who is the protagonist of the story, is brave enough to volunteer to find the ogre and bring back one of his feathers. When the man returns with the feather, the king recovers from his illness and rewards him. When the man tells the king he is going to be married, the king doubles his reward.

The King's Doctors

The king's doctors advise him that the only way for him to recover from his illness is to obtain one of the feathers from the ogre. Their advice turns out to be true, as the king does recover once the man has brought him a feather.

The King's Attendant

The protagonist of the story is one of the king's "most loyal and courageous attendants." He is the only one brave enough to volunteer to obtain a feather from the ogre in order to cure the king's illness. On his way to find the ogre, he stops at four different places, at each of which he is asked if he will also bring back a feather and ask the ogre a question. The man agrees to each request without hesitation. When he reaches the home of the ogre, he is greeted by a beautiful girl, who is the ogre's wife and captive. She instructs him to hide under the ogre's bed, while she plucks his feathers and hands them to the man. The next morning, he and the girl flee the ogre, bringing feathers and answers to each of the four questions. When they reach the innkeeper, whose daughter has been a captive of the ogre, he is given her hand in marriage. When the man brings a feather to the king, which causes the king to recover from his illness, he is rewarded, and, after he tells the king he is going to be married, his reward is doubled.

The Ogre

The feathered ogre lives in the back of the seventh of seven caves on top of a mountain. One of his feathers has the power to cure the king of his illness, and his feathers are also known to be good luck, but he is known for eating every human being he sees. When he comes home for his dinner, he can smell the man hiding under the bed but cannot find him. After he goes to bed, the girl, his wife, tricks him in order to obtain several of his feathers and get him to answer each of the four questions. After he leaves for work the next morning, the girl flees with the man. When the ogre comes home and finds her missing, he goes off in search of them, with the intention of eating them both. But when he takes a ride across the river on the ferry, the ferry man hops ashore before him, and so he cannot leave the boat and is stuck being the ferry man.

The Two Noblemen

The protagonist encounters the two well-dressed noblemen when he sits down to eat at a fountain on his way to find the ogre. The two noblemen ask if he will bring them back one of the ogre's feathers and if he will ask the ogre why their fountain, which once spewed silver and gold, has gone dry. When the girl pretends to be dreaming of the predicament of the two noblemen, the ogre explains that the fountain has been stopped up by a snake that is sleeping curled around a ball at the bottom of the fountain. The ogre tells her that the noblemen must crush the head of the snake with the ball in order for the fountain to flow again. When the girl and the man reach the noblemen on their way home, the noblemen take this advice, and their fountain once again spews silver and gold.

Themes

Heroism

The protagonist of a fairy tale is often a courageous man who risks mortal danger in order to achieve some noble quest. The king's attendant in this story is heroic in every way. He is the only one "loyal and courageous" enough to go in search of a feather from the ogre. Along his journey, he accepts further challenges without hesitation. As a result, he performs many good deeds, helping others out of their predicaments. With the help of the heroine, he effectively prevents the ogre from doing further harm in the world. His heroism is abundantly rewarded in the end with both material wealth from

the king and the hand in marriage of a "beautiful girl."

Good versus Evil

Most fairy tales make clear distinctions between good and evil and generally demonstrate that good always triumphs over evil. The ogre in this story is a clear embodiment of evil. He eats every human being he sees and even kidnaps a girl to hold her hostage and make her his wife. Because the ogre is pure evil, the reader is not expected to have any sympathy for the ogre in the end, when he is tricked into being stuck on the ferry boat. A parallel to the ogre is the presence of the Devil in the monastery, who has disguised himself as a priest and caused discord among them for ten years. Another figure of evil is the snake that has stopped up the fountain of the two noblemen. Based on the Bible, the snake in the Garden of Eden is a symbol of pure evil. In contrast with the ogre, the Devil, and the snake, all of the human beings in this story are helpless victims of these evil forces. The protagonist, the king's attendant, represents the greatest force of good, as he is the only one brave enough to risk death in order to help save everyone else from evil. As a result of his good deeds, the Devil is forced out of the monastery, the snake's head is crushed, and the ogre is trapped on the ferry boat, where he cannot harm anyone again.

Loyalty

Like bravery and courage, this story demonstrates that loyalty brings rewards. The protagonist is described as one of the king's most "loyal" attendants, who is the only one willing to risk his own life in order to cure the king of his illness. It is this man's loyalty to his king that initially leads to his quest for the ogre's feather. In the end, his loyalty is greatly rewarded by the king.

Courage and Bravery

Like many fairy tales, this story is about heroic acts of bravery on the part of the protagonist. The protagonist is one of the king's "most courageous" attendants. None of the king's other subjects are brave enough to go in search of the ogre who eats every human being he sees, but the protagonist shows his bravery by saying, simply, "I will go." When the people he meets on his journey to find the ogre ask if he will bring them back a feather and ask the ogre a question, the man cheerfully agrees to

Topics for Further Study

- Find a book of *Grimm's Fairy Tales* and pick out one story. In what ways is this story similar to, or different from, ''The Feathered Ogre''? In what ways does it contain the elements of brevity, repetition, and rhythm that Calvino valued in the Italian folk tale?

- Write an original fairy tale that includes similar elements to those of ''The Feathered Ogre,'' or other fairy tales with which you are familiar. What elements of a story are necessary in order for it to be considered a fairy tale? Include these in your own fairy tale.

- As well as being a writer, Italo Calvino was once a resistance fighter against fascism in Italy during World War II. Find out more about this period in Italian history and the role of resistance movements during that period.

- Calvino's *Italian Folk Tales*, in which ''The Feathered Ogre'' was first published, is a transcription of stories from the oral tradition in Italian culture. The oral tradition of storytelling still exists today in such forms as family stories that grandparents or parents repeat and pass on to each new generation of the family. Recall stories you've been told that constitute part of the ''oral tradition'' of your own family. ''Transcribe'' one of these stories from the oral to the written form. How does the story change when written on paper? How does the context of the telling of family stories contribute to the effect of the story?

their requests without hesitation, even though each new request makes his mission that much more dangerous. When the man knocks at the ogre's door, the ogre's wife, a beautiful girl, warns him of the danger he is in, as her husband eats every human being he sees. But the man shows his bravery once again with his matter-of-fact attitude in the face of death: '''Since I'm already here, I'll stay and try my luck. If I get eaten, that's that.''' In the end, the man's courage and bravery are abundantly rewarded.

Good Deeds

Each request that the man accepts, starting with the king's need for a feather from the ogre in order to cure his illness, is in the service of selflessly helping others who are in need. He also performs good deeds in promising each of the four parties he meets along his journey to ask the ogre for a solution to their predicament. When he follows through on these promises, the problems of each party are solved. While the hero accepts each challenge without promise of any material reward for his efforts, he is richly rewarded in the end. The message of this tale is that doing good deeds will be rewarded with love and material wealth.

Style

The Folk Tale

''The Feathered Ogre'' was originally published in Calvino's book, *Italian Folktales*, in which he transcribed stories from the oral tradition in Italian culture. However, even read out of this context, this story clearly resembles the familiar folk or fairy tales children are often told. Because they originate in an oral tradition, folk tales are generally not attributable to any particular author but have been passed down through generations of storytellers. Because of this, there are often several versions of any one folk tale, and the writer who chooses to transcribe them must decide which elements of the various versions of the story to include in the written text. Thus, although Calvino gathered this story from other sources, it is also in part his own creation and bears the mark of his own personal writing style in re-telling these traditional tales.

Magic and Fantasy

Fairy tales often include elements of magic and fantasy, which require the reader's ''suspension of disbelief,'' in order to accept the premise of the story. While everyone knows there is no such thing as an ogre, the ogre is a standard character in fairy tales that most readers can imagine with only minimal description. The only feature of this ogre that the narrator specifically describes is that he has feathers. Based only on this one physical aspect, the reader is invited to use her or his imagination in picturing what such a creature would look like. Furthermore, the ogre's feathers have the magical properties to bring people luck and cure the king of his illness. The character of the ferry man also implies that some magical forces are at work in this story, as the ferry boat seems to cast a spell on those so unlucky as to get stuck on it at the wrong juncture. The ferryman is unable to leave the ferry until he tricks the ogre into falling under this spell and getting stuck on the boat instead of the man. Another element of fantasy is the fountain that spews silver and gold; only in the realm of fantasy could such a fountain exist. These elements of magic and fantasy are accepted by the reader in the context of the fairy tale.

The Quest/Journey/Adventure

As do many folk tales, ''The Feathered Ogre'' tells the story of a courageous man who must go on a journey in order to seek out some type of monster or dragon or ogre, obtain some item or items guarded by the evil beast, and return in order to receive a reward, and, usually, a beautiful girl or princess to marry. This type of story is in the form of a quest or journey, requiring bravery, and, often the help of various advisors along the way.

Repetition

In his essay ''Quickness,'' from *Six Memos for the Next Millenium*, Calvino explains that the oral tradition of storytelling ''stresses repetition.'' The predictable repetitions in folk tales create a ''rhythm,'' which structures the entire story: ''Just as in poems and songs the rhymes help to create rhythm, so in prose narrative there are events that rhyme.'' This predictability and repetition, Calvino points out, is part of the pleasure of folk tales: ''A child's pleasure in listening to stories lies partly in waiting for things he expects to be repeated: situations, phrases, formulas.'' ''The Feathered Ogre'' contains many repetitions, or ''events that rhyme.'' For example, the protagonist makes four stops on his way to find the ogre; at each stop, the people he meets ask if he will bring them one of the ogre's feathers, and if he will ask the ogre a question. These questions are repeated when the ogre's wife

tricks him into explaining the solution to each of the four questions by awakening him four times during the night. On their way home, after fleeing the ogre's cave, the man and the girl stop at each of the four places to repeat to the people there the solution to their problem.

Brevity

In recording Italian folk tales, Calvino, as stated in his essay ''Quickness,'' was especially interested in ''the economy, rhythm, and hard logic with which they are told.'' He states that, ''The very first characteristic of a folktale is economy of expression,'' and that he himself ''found most enjoyment when the original text was extremely laconic.'' ''The Feathered Ogre'' is narrated in this type of ''laconic'' style, which does not dwell on ''unnecessary details.'' For example, in the opening of the story, ''Not a word is said about what illness the king was suffering from, or why on earth an ogre should have feathers, or what those caves were like. But everything mentioned has a necessary function to the plot.''

The Happy Ending

Part of the pleasure of folk tales is the predictability of the happy ending. In this story, the protagonist is rewarded for his efforts, both by receiving the hand in marriage of the beautiful girl and by the king's reward, which is doubled. The details of the relationship between the man and the girl are unnecessary in a folk tale, as the elements of the story are reduced to the most basic plot points, implying that the reader (or listener) will assume the ''happily ever after'' status of the romantic couple.

Setting

Like most folk tales, this story is set in an unnamed country during an unspecified period in history, although one can generally assume that it takes place long ago. The non-specificity of the setting is in part what allows for the suspension of disbelief required of the reader in order to accept the unlikely, magical, and unrealistic elements of the story.

Characterization

None of the characters in this story has a specific or proper name. Because it is a folk tale, each character represents a familiar type. This adds to the brevity of the story, as the reader (or listener) is expected to be able to fill in the details based on having heard many such tales before. The characters are named only by their status and occupation, rather than by any indication of individuality or developed character. Note that the characters in the story include the following: the king, the king's attendant, an innkeeper, an ogre, two noblemen, a group of priests, a ''beautiful girl,'' and so on.

Historical Context

Collections of Traditional Folk Tales

''The Feathered Ogre'' was originally published as part of the collection *Italian Folk Tales* (1956), which Calvino transcribed and retold from the oral tradition. The most famous collection of folk tales is probably that of the Brother's Grimm, who wrote a comprehensive collection of traditional German folk tales, which have been republished many times. Less commonly known is Charles Chesnutt's 1899 collection of African-American folk tales, entitled *The Conjure Woman*. In 1935 Zora Neale Hurston published *Mules and Men*, a collection of African-American folk tales she gathered from oral stories during her travels in rural Florida and Louisiana. Leslie Marmon Silko's book, *Storyteller* (1981), translates oral traditions from Native-American culture into a written form.

Mussolini and Fascist Italy

Calvino was a staunch critic of the fascist regime of Benito Mussolini in Italy. Mussolini, an ex-socialist, was the leader of the fascist movement in Italy, which had gained popularity by 1920. In 1921 Mussolini formed the National Fascist Party. After Mussolini organized a ''March on Rome'' by fascist sympathizers, the king of Italy, hoping to curb social unrest, appointed him to form a constitutional government, and in 1923 Mussolini became Prime Minister. In 1939 Mussolini formed an alliance with Hitler's Germany. In 1943 after the Allies had invaded Sicily, the Fascist Grand Council asked the king to depose Mussolini from power, which he did, immediately appointing a new prime minister. Mussolini was arrested shortly thereafter but was eventually rescued from prison by the Germans. Mussolini was shot and killed while fleeing to Switzerland in 1945.

Italian Neorealism

Several of Calvino's works are in the style of Italian neorealism, a literary and cinematic style that emerged in the post-War era. As a response to the traumatic experiences of the War, Italian writers in the post-War period focused on realistic portrayals, often based on their own experiences of life in wartime Italy. Calvino's early novel and short story collection were based on his own experiences during this time. Italian neorealist cinema developed a documentary style of narrative film, which often depicted every day people in their daily lives, in an attempt to capture the experiences of war-torn Italy.

Resistance to Fascism under Mussolini

Communist organizations in Italy were a primary locus of anti-fascist activity. However, Mussolini's crackdown on anti-fascist activity, beginning in 1925, as well as state-sponsored censorship, significantly curbed the strength of any resistance movement. Communist leaders were sent away to remote prisons or executed, and national censorship of the press, radio, and cinema curbed the expression of anti-fascist sentiment and the spread of dissident ideas. The Catholic Church, on the other hand, remained a significant supporter of anti-fascism, despite government attempts to curb such activities. Anti-fascism had gained sympathizers by the late-1930s, and many opposed the institution of anti-Semitic policies in 1938. It was during World War II that Calvino joined the Resistance movement, which he wrote about in his early novel and collection of short stories. The active part the Communists had played in the Resistance during the War made it a popular movement in the post-War era.

Critical Overview

''The Feathered Ogre'' was originally published in *Fiabe Italiane*, Calvino's 1956 collection and retelling of two hundred traditional Italian fables and folktales. It was translated into English by Louis Brigante and published as *Italian Fables* in 1961. In 1980 it was published in a new translation by George Martin, with the title *Italian Folktales*.

The significance of Calvino's collection to the study of international folklore is probably best explained by Calvino himself in his introduction to *Italian Folk Tales*. In tackling the project, Calvino

Compare & Contrast

- **1950s:** When Calvino first begins regularly publishing fiction, during the post-War era, Italian neorealism is the dominant literary style. Neorealism is a reaction to fascism and focuses on the portrayal of personal experiences of World War II and war-torn Italy in the aftermath of the War.

  1990s: Calvino's career spans many developments in literary history over the second half of the twentieth century. By the time of his death in 1985, postmodern and poststructuralist literary styles have become prevalent in literature, in part influenced by the contribution of his own experimental novels.

- **Early Twentieth Century:** During Calvino's youth and early adulthood, Italy is ruled by a king, who eventually institutes a parliament under the fascist Benito Mussolini.

  Late Twentieth Century: After World War II, Mussolini is shot, and the king later deposed in favor of a more democratic parliamentary government, characterized by many parties.

- **1950s:** Although many anthropologists and ethnographers have collected and transcribed stories from the oral tradition of Italian peasants, before Calvino's collection and retelling of Italian folktales—first published in 1956—there are no definitive compilations equivalent to the work of the Brothers Grimm in collecting and retelling traditional German folktales.

  1990s: Calvino's 1956 publication of *Fiabe Italiane* becomes internationally recognized as the definitive text on Italian folktales. Calvino achieves his goal of creating an Italian equivalent of the works of the Brothers Grimm.

- **Nineteenth Century:** Folktales such as "The Feathered Ogre" are originally developed by generations of local peasant storytellers, mostly female and often illiterate, who serve an important role in their town, village or community, with their talent for remembering countless tales and their storytelling skills.

  Twentieth Century: As modern society becomes more literate, the oral tradition fades, and the work of anthropologists, ethnographers, and writers such as Calvino plays a crucial role in preserving cultural texts, which would otherwise have been lost.

wished to produce a definitive volume of Italian folktales and fables equivalent to that of the Brothers Grimm, whose name, since the early nineteenth century, has become synonymous with the German folk tale. Calvino wished to produce a "readable master collection of Italian folktales which would be popular in every sense of the word." In approaching the task, Calvino studied the transcriptions of anthropologists and ethnographers who in the nineteenth century interviewed storytellers in peasant villages throughout Italy, most of whom Calvino describes as "little old women." In choosing which tales, and which version of each tale, to retell, Calvino took into consideration a representative sampling from various regions of Italy; he also translated into a more modern, standardized Italian the many dialects represented by the original storytellers, while maintaining the local flavor of each dialect. Calvino stresses the role of the storyteller in the oral tradition of the folktale: "At the core of the narrative is the storyteller, a prominent figure in every village or hamlet, who has his or her own style and appeal. And it is through this individual that the timeless folktale is linked with the world of its listeners and with history."

Calvino was also a journalist and co-editor for several Italian socialist periodicals, a novelist, short story writer, and essayist. His early published fiction was written during the post-World-War-II period of Italian neorealism in literature, which focused on the experiences of everyday people during

This illustration of ''The Giant of Yewdale'' reflects the time and age of English myths and resembles a traditional folk tale setting for the ogre and the innkeeper's daughter in the ''Feathered Ogre.''

the War and post-War era. His novel *Il sentiero dei nidi di ragno*, first published in 1947, was translated into English and published in 1957 as *The Path to the Nest of Spiders*. His collection of short stories written between 1945 and 1949, *Ultimo viene il corvo* (The Crow Comes Last), first published in 1949—twenty of which were translated into English and published in 1957 as *Adam, One Afternoon,*

and Other Stories —were based on his experiences during the War.

Calvino became a darling of postmodern and post-structuralist literary theorists for his experimental novels, which stretched the boundaries of the novelistic form. *Le citta invisibili*, first published in 1972, translated and published in English in 1974 as *Invisible Cities*, brought his first international recognition as an important writer. In this story, Kublai Khan converses with Marco Polo. *Se una notte d'inverno un viaggiatore*, first published in 1979, translated into English and published in 1981 as *If On a Winter's Night a Traveler*, addresses the reader as ''You'' and consists of ten novels within one frame story, structured by multiple digressions and commentary on the novelistic form, role of the narrator, and expectations of the reader. The meta-narrative level of self-consciousness with which the novel is written is captured in the opening line, ''You are about to begin reading Italo Calvino's new novel, *If on a Winter's Night a Traveler.*''

Franco Ricci, in *Italian Novelists Since World War II*, has summed up the scope of Calvino's work in the context of modern literary history: ''. . . it is a measure of his greatness and uncommon historical awareness that from his early neorealist tales to the meta-narrative modes of his later fiction he can be said to reflect the major literary trends of the past forty years. He is and will continue to be one of the most important writers of the twentieth century.''

Criticism

Liz Brent

Brent has a Ph.D. in American culture, specializing in cinema studies, from the University of Michigan. She is a freelance writer and teaches courses in American cinema. In the following essay, she discusses the allegorical significance of the morals of the story.

One of the elements of the fairy tale that gives it lasting and universal appeal is that the events of the story occur within a universe of clearly defined values, in which good always triumphs over evil and virtues are rewarded with material and personal riches. Calvino's retelling of the Italian folk tale ''The Feathered Ogre,'' in his 1956 collection, *Italian Folk Tales*, demonstrates the values of loyalty, self-sacrifice, bravery, courage, generosity, amiability, cleverness, good deeds, and integrity. In

What Do I Read Next?

- *The Path to the Nest of the Spiders* (1947), by Italo Calvino, is an early collection of his short stories, based on his experiences as a Resistance fighter against fascism in Italy during World War II.

- *Italian Folk Tales* (1956), consisting of transcriptions of Italian folk tales from the oral tradition collected and retold by Italo Calvino, has become a definitive text, equivalent to Grimm's collections of German folktales.

- *If on a Winter's Night a Traveler* (1981), Calvino's well-known novel, experiments with narrative techniques and the art of storytelling.

- *Six Memos for the Next Millenium* (1988), by Italo Calvino, includes five of the six lectures that the author had been preparing at the time of his death. These essays include the topics of lightness, quickness, visibility, and multiplicity.

- *Why Read the Classics?* (1999) by Italo Calvino, published posthumously, provides history and criticism of classic international literature.

- *Understanding Italo Calvino* (1993) by Beno Weiss provides a basic introduction to the complex, experimental narrative techniques developed by Calvino in many of his novels.

- *Calvino: The Writer as Fablemaker* (1979) by Stella Maria Adler, with a preface by Dante Della Terza, provides criticism and interpretation of Calvino's stories, focusing on the role of the narrator in the written folk tale.

---

the following essay, the ways in which the hero of the story embodies these values, which result in the stamping out of evil forces and the rewarding of good deeds, will be discussed. An allegorical interpretation of the story makes it relevant to the modern reader as a lesson in important values.

As in most fairy tales, this story ends with the triumph of good over evil. The ogre is punished in the end, when he is stuck on the ferry boat. Likewise, the Devil is driven out of the monastery. The virtues of the hero, and the heroine, are abundantly rewarded. When the man and the girl reach the innkeeper, he is so grateful for the return of his daughter that he immediately gives her hand in marriage to the man. The man is then doubly rewarded for bringing the king the feather that cures him of his illness. With the ogre safely stuck on the ferry, unable to do further harm in the world, and the hero assured both marriage to a "beautiful girl" and abundant monetary wealth, this story closes with the proverbial "happily ever after" that characterizes the fairy tale ending.

Thus, the values and morals of "The Feathered Ogre" meet the standard expectations a reader (or listener) has of a fairy tale. Yet, to the modern reader, the moral of the story may at first seem outdated and overly simplistic. Unfortunately, evil in the world takes more complex forms than that of an ogre, and monetary wealth is not so easy to come by, nor does it necessarily bring happiness, whereas love and marriage prove greater challenges in real life than is implied by such a story. However, fairy tales, which serve the cultural role of teaching basic values to children, retain their significance in a complex, modern society when interpreted in allegorical terms. An allegory is a tale that is meant to be understood, not literally but in terms of its symbolic significance. For instance, the predicament of the two noblemen is that their fountain, which used to spout gold and silver, is stopped up by a snake sleeping curled around a ball. The snake, based on the story of the Garden of Eden in the Old Testament, is a classic symbol of evil, the Devil in disguise. Therefore, the allegorical implications are that a force of evil (the snake) is the cause of the problem of the noblemen. In order to get their fountain flowing again, they must crush the head of the snake with the ball, an allegory for crushing the forces of evil that have obstructed their lives.

> " All of the virtues of the hero, as well as of the heroine, are in the service of performing 'good deeds' in order to stamp out evil and help others out of their predicaments. . . . The message here is that society as a whole can benefit from good deeds on the part of individuals."

Although the result, that their fountain once again flows gold and silver, is in a literal sense fantastical as well as materialistic, it can be interpreted allegorically as a symbol of the less tangible rewards that result from doing good deeds and counteracting the forces of evil in the world. Likewise, the "evil" embodied by the ogre and the Devil, may be read allegorically as representing a host of more concrete "evils," or problems facing the world, such as poverty, oppression, and so forth.

The man's journey to obtain a feather from the ogre takes the form of a quest. Though most people do not have the opportunity to travel through dangerous territory on a heroic mission, the quest may be interpreted allegorically in terms of goals or ambitions. The quest for the ogre's feather and the hero's willingness to risk death and to persevere in the face of danger is an allegory for setting and pursuing an ambitious goal that, in order to reach it, requires persistence and the willingness to take risks or to overcome obstacles.

The protagonist of the story, one of the king's attendants, is notable for his loyalty, bravery, and self-sacrifice in volunteering to seek out the ogre. When the king falls ill and is told by his doctors that he can only be cured by obtaining a feather from the ogre who eats every human being he sees, no one of his subjects is willing to risk death in order to save the king's life: "the king passed the word on to everybody, but no one was willing to go to the ogre." The hero, however, described as "one of the king's most loyal and courageous attendants," dem-onstrates his loyalty and courage by volunteering to seek out the deadly ogre for no other reason than out of allegiance to the king. There is no obvious personal gain to be derived from this deed, and he is promised no reward for his efforts. Nevertheless, his bravery and courage are demonstrated by the simple and straightforward words with which he agrees to the quest: "I will go."

The hero's willingness to risk self-sacrifice, as well as his generosity and amiability, are further demonstrated at each of his four stops along the way to the cave of the ogre. Upon his first stop at the inn, the innkeeper asks to be brought back a feather from the ogre, "since they are so beneficial," but offers the man no reward or compensation in return, although he is well aware that it is a dangerous mission. The man's simple and amiable response, "I'll be glad to," again demonstrates both his courage and his willingness to risk danger for the benefit of others. When the ferry man asks him to bring back a feather, he again answers simply and amiably, "Yes, of course I'll bring you one." And, when the well-dressed noblemen, who are obviously men of great wealth, ask to be brought a feather without mention of reward or compensation, the man replies, "I certainly will."

The danger faced by the hero in accepting such a mission is reinforced by the prior of the monastery, who warns him, "My poor man. . . if you are unmindful of all the danger, you'll certainly lose your life. This is no laughing matter." But the hero is undaunted by such warnings and graciously thanks the prior for this information, replying simply, "How good of you to tell me all these things I didn't know." When he reaches the door of the ogre, he is once more warned of the mortal danger he faces, as the ogre's wife with great alarm exclaims, "You don't know my husband! He eats every human being he sees!" Yet the hero demonstrates his dedication to his quest, as well as his courage and bravery in the face of death, with the matter-of-fact statement that, "I came for some feathers. Since I'm already here, I'll stay and try my luck. If I get eaten, that's that."

The hero's loyalty to his king, his bravery in volunteering to obtain a feather from the deadly ogre, and his courage in facing the challenges of such a quest can be read as symbolic of values relevant to the individual in modern society. Loyalty to the king in accepting his dangerous task may be read in terms of the loyalty one may have to a friend or family member who may be ill or in need of aid. Though few people have the opportunity to go on a quest for the feather of an ogre in order to save the life of an ailing king, the hero's act of bravery teaches a life lesson in self-sacrifice— whether of time or of money or of life itself—in order to help others in need. His "loyalty" to his king may be an allegory for loyalty to a community in volunteering one's resources toward some goal for the greater good of society. The hero's generosity in unquestioningly agreeing to help each party he meets as he makes his journey can be interpreted in modern terms as the willingness to respond with compassion to the needs and problems of other people.

In addition to loyalty, bravery, courage, generosity, self-sacrifice, and dedication, "The Feathered Ogre," as do many fairy tales, places a high value on cleverness. Protagonists often overcome great odds through their cleverness in devising schemes to trick evil creatures. In this story it is the beautiful girl, the wife of the ogre and daughter of the innkeeper, who possesses the quality of cleverness, which, in effect, results in a happy ending for all of the good characters and a speedy demise for all of the evil characters. Before the hero even meets the girl, the prior at the monastery describes her as "a bright girl." Indeed, her intelligence is demonstrated by the scheme she devises in order to ensure the safety of the hero, to obtain several of the ogre's feathers, to draw out answers to each of the four questions, and to flee successfully from the ogre's cave with both her own life and the hero's.

The cleverness of the innkeeper's daughter in tricking the ogre may be translated into the value of well-thought-out solutions to a variety of problems one faces throughout life. While the ogre has the physical ability to devour both the girl and the man, it is her intelligence that triumphs over the ogre's brute power. Whereas the ogre's only resource seems to be the threat of eating every human being he sees, the girl and the man enjoy the benefits of intelligent, thoughtful problem-solving skills.

All of the virtues of the hero, as well as of the heroine, are in the service of performing "good deeds" in order to stamp out evil and help others out of their predicaments. The hero's initial act of volunteering to obtain a feather from the ogre is a good deed in itself, as it is for the purpose of curing the king of his illness. Obtaining the solutions to each of the four problems posed by the innkeeper, the ferry man, the two noblemen, and the friars is a good deed, which benefits each of these characters. The value placed on "good deeds" in this story is further emphasized in the solution to the problem of the friars in the monastery. In order to expose the Devil, who lives among them disguised as a priest, the friars must all do "good deeds" so that the Devil will be found out as the only one not doing good deeds and can then be expelled from the monastery; "the friars all did one good deed after another until the Devil finally fled." The message here is that society as a whole can benefit from good deeds on the part of individuals.

Finally, while material wealth and marriage to a "beautiful girl" are oversimplified images of what constitutes happiness in life, the reward from the king and the impending marriage can be read allegorically as representing the rewards of a virtuous life, which, in reality, may come in more abstract, subtle, or complex forms than the concrete rewards of a fairy tale. Thus, while the specific elements of a fairy tale such as "The Feathered Ogre" may on the surface seem to have little relevance to the conditions of modern life, an allegorical perspective allows the reader to take away lessons in basic values, which remain timeless and universal. The function of the allegorical effect of the fairy tale is to provide a concise, shorthand narrative which may have applications to greater, more complex concerns facing the individual in society.

Source: Liz Brent, Critical Essay on "The Feathered Ogre," in *Short Stories for Students*, The Gale Group, 2001.

Rena Korb

Korb has a master's degree in English literature and creative writing and has written for a wide variety of educational publishers. In the following essay, she discusses how the various elements of "The Feathered Ogre" are representative of the archetypal hero's journey.

In his introduction to his collection *Italian Folktales*, Calvino describes the typical folktale:

[T]hey offer, in their oft-repeated and constantly varying examinations of human vicissitudes, a general explanation of life preserved in the slow ripening of rustic consciences; these folk stories are the catalog of the potential destinies of men and women, especially for that stage in life when destiny is formed, i.e., youth, beginning with birth, which itself often foreshadows the future; then the departure from home,

" The attendant is willing to leave the security of the familiar and challenge the unknown. This setting out on adventure marks the hero's--in metaphoric terms, the child's--initial departure from the home."

and finally, through the trials of growing up, the attainment of maturity and the proof of one's humanity.

The trajectory of ''The Feathered Ogre'' closely follows this pattern, but inspiredly so. As Calvino points out, ''[a] regard for conventions and a free inventiveness are equally necessary in constructing a folktale. Once the theme is laid out there are certain steps required to reach a solution; [but] they are interchangeable ingredients.'' ''The Feathered Ogre'' includes both the quintessential fairy tale journey toward adulthood, as well as its own mystical elements in the fountain that once spewed gold and silver, and primarily in the overall power of the feathers to bring luck and good fortune to those who possess them.

The nameless hero of ''The Feathered Ogre'' is a young man who must leave the safety of his home and face danger in pursuit of an important quest. The man is an attendant to a king who has fallen ill. All that can save the king is the feather of an ogre who lives in a seven-chambered cave. The ogre ''eats every human he sees,'' so everyone refuses to go and get a feather. Finally, the king—who represents the parental authority figure—asks ''one of his most loyal and courageous attendants'' and finds success. The attendant is willing to leave the security of the familiar and challenge the unknown. This setting out on adventure marks the hero's—in metaphoric terms, the child's—initial departure from the home.

Along the journey to the ogre's cave, the attendant meets several different people. Most of them ask him to bring them back a feather, and all of them ask him to find the answer to a perplexing

problem. An innkeeper is curious about what happened to his daughter who ''disappeared years ago.'' A ferry man needs to find out what he can do to finally get off the ferry. Two noblemen want to know why the fountain has dried up and no longer spews gold and silver. Each of these people can be seen as representative of different stages of a person's life. The innkeeper represents a person's essential need for food and shelter. His daughter's disappearance, with the potential lack of continuation of the business and the lack of his progeny, threatens the obtainment of these basics. If a man cannot even keep his own daughter safe, how can he be expected to provide security for others? The ferry man stands for life's journey. He brings people from one side of the river to the other side, or from one stage of life to the succeeding stage. The noblemen represent the successful attainment of adulthood. They have time for leisure, for instance, meeting the attendant when they sit down to relax by the fountain. However, their interest in getting the fountain to continue to provide gold and silver also shows their desire for greater wealth and material comfort, which often is a part of adulthood.

By the time the attendant reaches the monastery, the last stop before facing the ogre, he is almost—metaphorically—grown. The monastery and the friars within clearly represent the power and civilizing force of faith and religion. Significantly, and unlike the other people the attendant has met, the friars lend him critical help. When the hero knocks on their door and tells his story, the friars are uncertain that he knows what perils lie ahead. The attendant *thinks* he is prepared: ''I was told there are seven caves,'' he answers simply. ''At the back of one of them is a door I'm to knock on and be greeted by the ogre.'' The prior immediately points out the attendant's naivete. ''If you are unmindful of all the danger,'' he says, ''you'll certainly lose your life.'' Only with the help of the friars will the attendant survive the ogre's lair. Only with the power of faith will the hero take the final steps to true adulthood. Like the other people the attendant has met along the journey, the friars ask him to find something out for them: why their monastery has been filled with strife for the last ten years when before that they had ''lived here in peace for no telling how many years.'' Unlike the others, however, the friars do not ask the attendant to bring them a feather. The power of the feather, it would seem, applies only to earthly matters, not to spiritual ones.

With the advice of the friars, the attendant is able to complete the last leg of his journey to attain adulthood. The attendant ''scaled a mountain'' to reach the ogre's home, and this type of movement signifies the colossal difficulty of the task. After he makes his way into the seventh cave, he lights the candle the friars gave him—the tool by which he will illuminate his path and make the discoveries that will bring him to true maturity. With this tool, he finds the ogre's door. There he is met by the ogre's wife.

The ogre's wife, who turns out to be the innkeeper's missing daughter, is anything but a monster. This ''bright'' and ''beautiful'' girl lives in fear of her husband. Like the friars, she offers the hero lifesaving assistance by hiding him under the bed, obtaining the ogre's feathers, and getting the ogre to supply the answers to the hero's questions. Similar to the actions of the hero, the girl's appearance into the fairy tale is preordained, as is her flight to safety with the hero after his goals have been accomplished. According to Calvino, the fairy tale's summary includes ''the persecution of the innocent and their subsequent vindication, which are the terms inherent in every life.''

With the favorable completion of the quest, the hero has become an adult. Through effort and brave actions, he has acquired both the maturity and the humanity that are imperative to a successful society. As proof of his humanity, he imparts his solutions to those who requested his help. Once he had explained to the noblemen how to kill the snake that lived underground, ''it wasn't long before the fountain was again spewing gold and silver.'' The feather that he carries causes the king to get well again. The attendant's solution to the friars is perhaps most meaningful because of the actions it inspires, however.

> ''One of you is the Devil. You must start doing all the good you can, and he will flee.''
>
> The friars all did one good deed after another until the Devil finally fled.

Further proof of the attendant's maturity comes. The innkeeper, enormously pleased at the safe return of his daughter, offers her hand in marriage to the attendant. Thus, as Calvino writes in the Introduction, ''love [is] unrecognized when first encountered.'' The attendant, however, doesn't immediately accept. His reaction, ''Let me first take the king his feather and ask his permission,'' demonstrates the difficulty a newly mature person may have in renouncing the authority of the family homestead and accepting the responsibilities of

adulthood. However, the king approves of the wedding. When he demonstrates this approval by doubling the attendant's reward, the attendant allows himself to fully embrace his new adult life. The attendant ''took leave of him and returned to the inn.'' The hero's happy ending, intrinsically linked with that of the innkeeper's daughter, demonstrates the conclusion of Calvino's summary of the fairy tale:

> The common fate of subjection to spells, or having one's existence predetermined by complex and unknown forces. This complexity pervades one's entire existence and forces one to struggle to free oneself, to determine one's own fate; at the same time we can liberate ourselves only if we can liberate other people, for this is *sine qua non* of one's own liberation.

With the hero's return to his betrothed, the archetypal fairy tale journey ends. However, Calvino chooses to continue the story. The ogre, who had set out in pursuit of his wife ''fully intending to devour her and whoever was involved in her escape,'' gets his punishment. The ferry man learned from the attendant that in order to leave the ferry all he had to do was disembark before his passenger. The ogre boards the ferry and then is trapped as ''off jumped the ferryman, and the ogre could no longer leave the boat.'' In his Note to the tale, Calvino acknowledges that ''the ending with the retention of the ogre on the ferry is mine, but it does not strike me as arbitrary since the same happens in [a Brother Grimms' tale].'' Indeed, the Calvino-imposed conclusion onto ''The Feathered Ogre'' is in accordance with the Italian folktale tradition of movement toward a ''healing solution, a part of which is a quick and pitiless punishment of the malefactor.'' Calvino's ending is also symbolically congruent. Whereas earlier in the tale the ferry man had represented part of the hero's childhood journey to adulthood, now the new ferryman—the ogre—takes on an entirely new meaning. In ancient Greek mythology, the ferryman, Charon, was the person responsible for bringing the spirits of the dead across the River Styx to the gates of the Underworld. Similarly, the ogre ferryman now represents the end of life's journey, or death.

Source: Rena Korb, Critical Essay on ''The Feathered Ogre,'' in *Short Stories for Students*, The Gale Group, 2001.

Carole Hamilton

Hamilton is an English teacher at Cary Academy, an innovative private school in Cary, North Carolina. In this essay she postulates that Calvino's post-structuralist fascination with the structural elements of short stories can be detected in his collection of Italian oral tales, Italian Folktales *(1956), years before he began to experiment more radically in his writing. His interest is especially evident in one of the shortest of the tales, ''The Feathered Ogre.''*

In 1927, when Italo Calvino was a young child, Vladimir Propp published his ''Morphology of the Folktale,'' which outlines thirty-one possible stages, or elements, of the folktale. His discovery was groundbreaking and convincing, supported as it was with numerous examples from Russian folklore. Propp compared these story elements to the Russian formalist notion of the ''morpheme,'' the smallest meaningful element of the sentence, on the level of the syllable. The formalists, in turn, had based their concept on the linguistic term for the smallest vocal unit, the ''phoneme.'' Russian formalism valued form over content and prompted a movement to study linguistic form as an end in itself. Correspondingly, Propp focused on the smallest analyzable narrative element of the folktale, which he dubbed the ''narrateme.'' All thirty-one folktale elements, or narratemes, that Propp identified do not appear in every Russian folktale, but those that do are always in sequence. In the second half of Propp's list, he includes the various stages of the hero's journey made popular by the late anthropological scholar Joseph Campbell.

Italo Calvino mentions Propp's contribution to the scholarship of the folktale in his introduction to *Italian Folktales*. And, not surprisingly, the narrative stages of the folktale ''The Feathered Ogre'' that Calvino includes in his anthology match at least eleven of Propp's later stages, those of the hero's journey. The tale begins with Propp's narrateme #9, when the hero learns of a ''misfortune or lack''—in this case, the doctor's advise to obtain an ogre's feather to cure the sick king. The tale then proceeds through eleven more narratemes, as the hero leaves home (#11), gains advice and help along the way (#12), reacts to the advice (#13), reaches the place where he can find the needed object (#15), engages the villain in combat (#16, in this case via the ogre's wife), defeats the villain (#17), obtains the object (#19, the feathers), returns (#20), but is pursued by the villain (#21), gets rescued (#22, the ogre becomes trapped on the ferry), and then marries and is rewarded (#31). Altogether, this, as well as most of the other Italian tales Calvino collected, corresponds with Propp's narrateme cycle, despite any

intention on Calvino's part: he was simply reporting variants of common folk tales. Nevertheless, Calvino noticed the patterns that emerged as he collected and studied the stories, and, in a 1967 essay called ''Cybernetics and Ghosts,'' he mentions Propp again and states that in Italian folktales, as in Russian ones, all ''tales were like variants of a single tale, and could be broken down into a limited number of narrative functions'' like Propp's narratemes.

In this essay, Calvino compares the ''fixed structures'' or ''prefabricated elements'' of stories to mental processes, which could, like computer functions, lead to infinite combinatorial groupings, though the number of discrete, separate elements was finite in number. In 1956 when he published the anthology of tales, Calvino recognized that narratemes were ''interchangeable ingredients'' and that it was the narrator's job ''to pile them up like bricks in a wall'' to form a story that will ''reach a solution.'' Did Calvino have any inkling then that he would depart radically from this prescribed form of the tale in his own fiction? Is there evidence, even as early as 1956, in a story ostensibly not even his own, that Calvino would push the concept of interchangeable narratemes to an extreme that Propp could not have foreseen?

Certainly the idea of ''story units'' was germinating at the time Calvino was working on his collection of Italian tales. The French structuralists were building upon the ideas of the Russian formalists regarding sentence structural units (morphemes) and Propp's narrative units (narratemes). One of them, anthropologist Claude Levi-Strauss, identified the elemental structure of myth, which he termed ''mythemes.'' Ultimately, he devised a new field of study that he called ''structural anthropology,'' which applies structuralist precepts to myth. He outlined the basis of what would become French structuralism in his landmark 1955 article ''The Structural Study of Myth,'' published just months before Calvino's anthology of Italian Folktales. In ''Cybernetics and Ghosts,'' Calvino acknowledges the influence on his later work of anthropologist Claude Levi-Strauss's writings.

According to Levi-Strauss, myth, like language, comprises ''gross constituent units'' that are organized in ritual ways. In myth, the units often appear in symmetrical relationships, consisting of binary pairs, or opposites, and other common structures. Claude Levi-Strauss illustrated his theory with the example of the *Oedipus* myth, which he breaks down into mythemes, such as ''Oedipus marries his mother Jocasta'' and ''Antigone buries her brother, Polynices.'' Levi-Strauss strips away the sequence of narrative progression and isolates these mythemes as discrete units in order to reveal the essential relations or ideas being portrayed by the myth. These two units of *Oedipus* express, according to Levi-Strauss, the mytheme or idea of ''overrating blood relations.'' Had Calvino applied similar analysis to the story ''The Feathered Ogre,'' he might have identified such mythemes as the hero agreeing to bring a feather to the noblemen, the ferryman, and the king, and the friars' offer of advice on how to obtain the help of the ogre's wife to get the feathers. He then might have discovered their common theme of ''spontaneous generosity,'' using Levi-Strauss's methods. Whether or not Calvino applied the anthropological structuralist approach to derive common themes in specific stories, it is apparent from his introduction to the anthology that Calvino had an affinity for recognizing the building blocks of story, or narratemes.

Levi-Strauss also advocated comparing variants of myths to obtain greater confidence in determining the universal social significance of a given mytheme. Italo Calvino accepted this challenge when he undertook to create his anthology of Italian folktales. He searched exhaustively for new variants, becoming, as he said, ''gradually possessed by a kind of mania, an insatiable hunger for more and more versions and variants'' and ultimately he accumulated ''mountains of narratives (always basically the same ones and amounting altogether to some fifty types).'' He compared the many versions he found in order to choose the most ''unusual, beautiful, and original texts'' for his anthology. ''The Feathered Ogre'' is one of his finest choices, especially in regard to its unusual narratemes.

In compiling his tales, however, Calvino committed a crime in the eyes of cultural anthropologists: like the Brothers Grimm, he could not refrain from modifying the folktales he retold, embellishing them to meet his own literary standards. In the introduction to the anthology of tales, he justifies his action by saying that he was ''guided by the Tuscan proverb . . . 'The tale is not beautiful if nothing is added to it.''' As Calvino ''touched up'' or ''enriched'' the texts and tried to make them more ''plastic,'' he did not feel constrained to use any particular version; rather, he merged the variants and then polished the resulting tale to make it better. He asserts that he did so with the aim of ''restoring its lost originality;'' he sought to preserve the original character. His emendations were

> ''The Feathered Ogre' attests to Calvino's appreciation of balanced story elements in carefully crafted narrative structures. Like the artist who learns to dissect a body in order to better understand its skeletal system and musculature, the writer, too, serves an apprenticeship with the morphology of the folktales.''

not appreciated by later folklorists, such as Max Luöthi, who complained that in revising the stories, Calvino ''often takes liberties by adding poetic embellishments and insertions and thereby exceeds the limits of the permissible.'' For his part, Calvino did not regret his alterations, for, as he points out in the introduction, he considers his authorial role as simply another ''link in the anonymous chain without end by which folktales are handed down.''

Perhaps Calvino derived his communal sense of authorship from another of the French structuralists, Roland Barthes, who, like Levi-Strauss, was not yet renowned but whose work Calvino had read as early as 1953. Barthes at that time was beginning to conceive his theory of the ''death of the author.'' In *Writing Degree Zero* (1953), Barthes avowed that ''no one can . . . pretend to insert his freedom as a writer into the resistant medium of language because, behind the latter, the whole of history stands unified and complete in the manner of a natural order.'' According to Barthes, the author's message is molded by history and can only find expression through words and phrases already in use. The author, then, merely expounds on contemporary ideas, using contemporary language, and does not really invent anything new. Only through style can the writer express his or her own personal contribution to writing, since style comes from personal history. The author's style, Barthes explains, ''rises up from the writer's myth-laden depths and unfolds beyond his area of control.'' Although it would not be until 1968 that Barthes would literally announce the ''death of the author,'' his earlier works de-emphasize the importance of the writer, in favor of language, ''the corpus of prescriptions and habits common to all the writers of a period.'' Calvino's comment that he is part of ''an anonymous chain'' of storytellers is consistent with Barthes' concept of the author as linked to an era, an ideology, and a mode of speaking. In that ''great chain'' of writers, Calvino represents the link where literary works entered a new era, that of the formalist, whose primary interest is in form, not content.

In the same interview Calvino admits that he is ''not attracted to psychology,'' but rather to ''the whole mosaic in which man is set, the interplay of relationships, the design that emerges from the squiggles on the carpet.'' Certainly Calvino's interest at the time of the interview lay in the interplay and design of story structure, as evident in works such as *Cosmicomics* (1965), where characters are derived from mathematical formulae; *The Castle of Crossed Destinies* (1969), where characters speak using Tarot cards; and *Invisible Cities* (1972), an elaborate allegory of the architectural nature of narrative. *If on a Winter's Night a Traveler* (1979), a brilliant novella that pursues multiple, coinciding narrative paths, would come another decade later. In these and other Calvino novels and stories, ''narratemes'' are liberated from narrow, linear narrative straits and sent to play in a fantasyland governed by a bizarre new physics of narrative form.

Calvino's interest in narrative form is most evident in the starkly symmetrical narrative structure of ''The Feathered Ogre.'' In that folktale, the ''loyal and courageous attendant'' (not the smallest or youngest one, as is often the case in folktales) has four meetings on his way with people who give him advice for his mission: the innkeeper, the ferryman, two noblemen, and the friars. As the ogre's wife plucks feathers off her husband for the interloper, she gets advice back from the ogre, in reverse order: the friars, the noblemen, the ferryman, and then the innkeeper. The escaping pair visit them in reverse order as well. Whether or not this structure originates with the folktale or in Calvino's modifications, the story's fine balance attracted his attention and merited inclusion in his anthology. ''The Feathered Ogre'' attests to Calvino's appreciation of balanced story elements in carefully crafted narrative structures. Like the artist who learns to dissect a

body in order to better understand its skeletal system and musculature, the writer, too, serves an apprenticeship with the morphology of the folktales. As his artistic scalpel moved along the sinews and joints of folktales, Calvino developed a literary surgeon's intuition that would find fuller expression in his post-structuralist novels and stories.

Calvino's writing eventually would epitomize the belief he expressed in ''Cybernetics and Ghosts'' that ''[l]iterature is a combinatorial game that pursues the possibilities implicit in its own material.'' In other words, Calvino values the ''play'' of literary forms. Although he could not fully explore this interest when he compiled the anthology, his ''architectural'' approach can be seen in his choice of stories with unusual structural elements. To this end, ''The Feathered Ogre'' is a prime example, for not only are the elements balanced chronologically but certain of them are inverted, demonstrating the opposite form expected in the typical folktale. Calvino was familiar with the Stith Thompson motif index (1955–1958), which he mentions in his introduction. From this exhaustive compilation of known story lines and motifs, Calvino would have known that, for example, the hero is usually the youngest, weakest, least likely candidate, and not the ''most loyal and courageous'' as it is in ''The Feathered Ogre.'' In addition, in each case the people he meets along the way ask for an ogre's feather for no particular reason, before casually mentioning a real problem. Usually, it's the other way around: the hero meets someone with a problem, and he promises to help in return for advice or a magic talisman from the stranger. In this story, the people do not seem to recognize that they have a problem: the innkeeper is nonchalant about his daughter's disappearance, and the nobles do not urgently need to get the fountain of gold and silver repaired. ''The Feathered Ogre'' is a structural anomaly in this regard, which accounts for the reason Calvino included it. This is one more instance in which a particular folktale rendered by Calvino offers evidence of his fascination with narrative anatomy.

Although he would not align himself with the structuralists for about another decade, Calvino's rendering of the traditional Italian folk tale ''The Feathered Ogre'' attests to his fascination with story structure. This fascination would lead him down the path of the kind of narrative experimentation that typifies his later works. For Calvino, the folklore collection project proved as important in terms of studying the inner workings of myth and tale as it was in terms of representing Italy in the annals of folklore collections and in recording an important aspect of Italian cultural history. It was the start of a trajectory of syntactic development that has its beginnings in a humble folktale with auspicious features.

Source: Carole Hamilton, Critical Essay on ''The Feathered Ogre,'' in *Short Stories for Students*, The Gale Group, 2001.

Sources

Calvino, Italo, ''Cybernetics and Ghosts,'' in *The Uses of Literature*, Harcourt Brace, Inc., 1982, pp. 3–27.

———, Introduction to *Italian Folktales*, Harcourt Brace, Inc., 1956, 1980, pp. xv–xxxii.

———, ''Quickness,'' from *Six Memos for the Next Millenium*, Harvard University Press, 1988, pp. 35–37.

———, ''Two Interviews on Science and Literature,'' in *The Uses of Literature*, Harcourt Brace, Inc., 1982, pp. 28–38.

Luöthi, Max, *The European Folktales: Form and Nature*, Institute for the Study of Human Issues, Inc., 1982.

Ricci, Franco, ''Italo Calvino,'' in *Dictionary of Literary Biography*, Volume 196: *Italian Novelists Since World War II, 1965–1990*, Gale Research, 1999, pp. 50–67.

Sontag, Susan, ed., *A Barthes Reader*, Hill and Wang, 1982.

Further Reading

Brink, Andre Philippus, *The Novel: Language and Narrative from Cervantes to Calvino*, New York University Press, 1998.
   This work is a history of narration in the novel from Miguel de Cervantes' *Don Quixote de la Mancha* (often considered the first novel) through Calvino's *If on a Winter's Night a Traveler.*

Calvino, Italo, ed., *Fantastic Tales: Visionary and Everyday*, Pantheon Books, 1997.
   This collection of international short stories of the fantastic, or supernatural, has an introduction by Calvino, and includes such authors as Edgar Allan Poe, Ambrose Bierce, Nathaniel Hawthorne, Hans Christian Anderson, and many others.

Grimm, Jacob, *Grimm's Tales for Young and Old: The Complete Stories*, Doubleday, 1977.
   This is a modern translation by Ralph Manheim of the German folk tales originally collected by the Brothers Grimm.

Hague, Michael, *The Book of Dragons*, Morrow Junior Books, 1995.
   This collection of short stories about dragons includes ''The Dragon and the Enchanted Filly,'' an Italian folktale retold by Calvino.

Rottensteiner, Franz, ed., *The Slaying of the Dragon: Modern Tales of the Playful Imagination*, Harcourt Brace Jovanovich, 1984.
   This collection of modern short stories of the fantastic, by such authors as Jorge Luis Borges, Carlos Fuentes, Donald Barthelme, and Joyce Carol Oates, includes ''Adam, One Afternoon'' by Calvino.

Slonim, Marc, *Modern Italian Short Stories*, Simon and Schuster, 1954.
   This collection of short stories by modern Italian writers in translation includes ''Adam, One Afternoon'' by Calvino.

Fountains in the Rain

Yukio Mishima

1963

"More than two decades after his death," writes Susan J. Napier in the *Dictionary of Literary Biography*, "Mishima Yukio is arguably still the most famous writer modern Japan has produced." Mishima's admirers point to "the brilliance of his style, the power of his imagination, and the fascination and variety of his themes. . . all of which are in marked contrast to much of postwar Japanese fiction." Mishima's work is probably better known to English-speaking readers than any other Japanese writer's work.

Several collections of Mishima's short stories were translated while he was still alive, but in 1989 seven stories that had never before been translated were collected in *Acts of Worship*. In reviewing this volume, Roy Starrs wrote, "This present sampling . . . will provide a tantalizing glimpse for the Western reader of some of these still undiscovered riches. For in no art did Mishima perform better than in the art of the short story. In fact, he achieved the kind of mature mastery, even perfection, in his short stories that always seems to elude him in his novels."

Despite such kudos and despite inclusion in anthologies and college syllabi, Mishima's "Fountains in the Rain" has elicited little critical attention in English. Its most in-depth analysis comes from Mishima's translator, John Bester, who wrote the preface to *Acts of Worship*. "Fountains in the Rain," with a hero so like many of Mishima's male characters, invites further investigation.

Author Biography

Yukio Mishima was born as Hiroka Kimitake in Tokyo, Japan, in 1925. His ancestors were of the upper samurai class, and his grandmother encouraged his interest in Kabuki theater and in the notion of an aristocratic past. Mishima attended an elite school, but his early literary inclinations were not encouraged at his school, which emphasized physical activity over intellectual activity, and Mishima was often made to feel like an outsider by his classmates. Mishima began writing stories in middle school. When he was sixteen, his first piece of short fiction, ''Hanazakari no mori'' (''The Forest in Full Flower'') was published in nationalist literary magazine. It quickly sold out its first edition. It focuses on the narrator's aristocratic ancestors. Mishima's teachers encouraged his involvement with the Nihon Romanha, a group of Japanese romantics who insisted on the uniqueness of the Japanese people and their history and culture. Mishima avoided military service in World War II because he was misdiagnosed as having tuberculosis.

In 1947 Mishima received his law degree from Tokyo University. He took a position with the Finance Ministry but resigned less than a year later in order to devote himself full-time to his writing. In 1948 his first novel, *Tozoku* was published. Soon thereafter he was invited to join the group that published a literary magazine. In 1949 the autobiographical novel *Confessions of a Mask* was published, and it became a best seller and established Mishima's reputation as an important voice in Japanese fiction.

In 1952 Mishima traveled abroad, which inspired his next writings. Throughout the decade he continued to publish novels, essays, No (also known as ''Noh'') plays, and stories. His work also began to be translated into other languages for foreign readers.

By the early 1960s, some people thought that Mishima had passed the peak of his literary career, but he became more of a public figure than ever. In 1967 he spent a month training with the Self Defense Forces, and the following year, he formed a private army called the Shield Society. It was sworn to defend the emperor. By the late 1960s, Mishima had become increasingly consumed by the desire to revive the traditional values and morals of Japan's imperialistic past. He believed that his country was being corrupted by Westernization. His subsequent works, which include novels, short stories, and an essay collection, reflect this political belief as well as his belief in self-sacrifice in order to achieve spiritual fulfillment. His final tetrology, *The Sea of Fertility*, was published in monthly installments from 1965 until the day of Mishima's death in 1970. He believed that this tetrology was the product of all he had learned as a writer. He told friends that when he finished, there would be nothing left for him to do but kill himself.

On November 25, 1970, Mishima and members of the Shield Society took over headquarters of the Japanese Self-Defense Forces in Tokyo in what he called an attempted ''Showa Restoration.'' After unsuccessfully trying to get the soldiers to listen to him, Mishima committed seppuku, or the ritual suicide of the samurai warrior.

Plot Summary

The story opens with a young man and a young woman walking through the rain. The girl, Masako, is crying incessantly. The boy, Akio, has recently broken off their relationship while they were having tea. Akio had pursued the relationship only in order to break up with her. Once he did so, however, Masako began to cry. She cried soundlessly, with the tears gushing forth in a continuous flow. Akio assumed that the tears would stop, but when they didn't, Akio felt self-conscious under the curious stares of the tea room's other patrons. Abruptly, Akio stood up to leave, but Masako followed him because she had no umbrella. Now the pair find themselves wandering through the streets.

Akio decides to head toward a public garden that has three fountains. He thinks that by bringing Masako's tears and the fountains together, she will stop crying. He thinks that Masako will surely see that her tears—which all go to waste—cannot compete with the fountain, and this will make her stop crying. Akio feels elated by his decision.

The pair walk in silence through the empty streets. Akio thinks that Masako is waiting for him to say something about their relationship. Out of pride, he will not speak.

When they reach the garden, they are alone. Akio and Masako sit down, but Akio becomes angry, though he does not know why. He is no longer amused or happy. In his anger, Akio runs toward the fountains. Masako follows him. She asks

Yukio Mishima

where he is going. Akio replies by telling her to look at the fountains and points out that her tears are no match for them. The pair turns to look at the fountains, but it is Akio who becomes entranced by them. Fascinated, he intently watches the jets of water rushing upward into the sky. He thinks about the futility of the column of water to reach the sky, though it seems to be trying hard to do so. He raises his gaze to the sky and gets rain in his eye.

Immediately, the image of the fountains is gone from his mind. Suddenly, the fountains represent only endless, pointless repetition. He forgets his former elation and also his former anger. He starts walking.

Masako falls into step beside him and asks where he is going. He tells her that it is his business. "I told you quite plainly," he says, but she asks what it was that he thinks he told her. He looks at her in horror and repeats what he had said about breaking up. In a completely normal tone of voice, she responds that she had not heard him. In shock, he asks her why she started crying if she had not heard what he said. She says that there was no reason, that the tears just came. Akio gets furious and wants to shout at her. He opens his mouth but sneezes instead. He thinks that if he is not careful, he will get a cold.

Characters

Akio

Akio is the main character of the story. He has set out this afternoon to break up with his girlfriend, whom he claims to have previously wooed simply in order to be able to break up with her. Akio desperately needs to control Masako because he senses his inability to control himself. His lack of self-control is exhibited through his fascination with the fountains; he had come to the fountains to humiliate Masako and ended up surprising himself. At the end, he seems to acknowledge how viewing the fountains arouses a sexuality that he had earlier denied. By the end of the story, Akio's ineffectual manner of controlling himself and any situation in which he finds himself is apparent. He reverts back to the boy he once was, willing to accept the mundaneness of life.

Masako

Masako is Akio's girlfriend. She is a student. She seems to react badly to the news of the break-up, but it turns out that she was simply crying for no reason at all. When she does learn what Akio has to say, she is unaffected and unimpressed by his news. She also does not let go of his umbrella, which may indicate her unwillingness to break up.

Themes

Love

Although love is not what Akio feels for Masako, it is still a theme in the story since Akio used the promise of love to woo Masako. He did so only in order to form a relationship with her so he could break up with her. Akio has no emotional ties to Masako, but he believes she has them to him, which is what he attributes her tears to. At the end of the story, however, he discovers that Masako is not in love with him either. She responds to his words calmly and reasonably and appears to be affected very little by the ending of the love affair.

Sexuality

A strong current of sexuality runs through the story. Akio clearly believes that sleeping with Masako will make her love him and will reinforce his claims of love for her. Thus Akio shows that he equates sex

Topics for Further Study

- Read one of Mishima's more political or philosophical stories, such as "Patriotism" or "Death in Midsummer." Then contrast the story you have chosen and "Fountains in the Rain" in terms of characters, action, and message. Which story do you prefer, and why?

- Little criticism is available on "Fountains in the Rain." If you had to present an original talk on the story, what would you say? Create an outline for your speech.

- Japanese society changed greatly in the post–World War II years. Find out what changes took place, particularly in regard to the relationships between young men and women. Then decide if you think "Fountains in the Rain" accurately portrays these societal changes.

- One explanation of the imagery of the fountains has been discussed in this entry. John Bester also suggests that the fountains symbolize aggression and ambition in addition to sexuality. What do you think the fountains most closely symbolize? Explain your answer.

- Do you think the boy's claims not to care for the girl are true? Explain your answer.

- Though the young woman says and does very little in the story, her presence is integral to its unraveling. What can you say about the character of Masako? What is she like as a person?

- What image does Mishima present of Japan in the 1960s through the story? Does this image coincide with what you may have learned about Japan in the 1960s?

---

and love, even though he acknowledges to himself that he does not love Masako. Akio also takes pride in his ability to control his sexuality, falsely seeing himself as "free from the dominance of desire." When faced with the fountains, however, the truth emerges: Akio is fascinated by the rushing water, which takes on ambiguous sexual symbolism under his gaze.

Deception

The art of deception is critical to the success of Akio's scheme, but he is not good at it. He pretends to love Masako, but he does not; and he believes that he has made Masako fall in love with him, but she does not love him. Not only does he deceive himself by repressing feelings of sexual desire, he also deceives himself by focusing his sexual energy on women, though he is, in fact, also aroused by images suggesting male sexuality. Throughout most of the story, Akio exists in some state of self-deception. At the end, however, he does think one purely natural thought, yet it is quite mundane: "If I'm not careful I'm going to get a cold." Such an ending demonstrates the great depth to which Akio's

deception has drawn him as well as the grandiosity that he finds in this false way of looking at life.

Emotional Transformation

Akio experiences many different emotions throughout the course of this brief story. When he first sits down in the tea room with Masako, he is feeling great anticipation and excitement at breaking off their relationship. He thinks this action will bring him greater maturity. When Masako does not stop crying, however, he begins to feel embarrassed. He wants to get away from her, but he is thwarted in this desire, for she has no umbrella and he must let her share his. When he settles on the plan of bringing her to the fountains, Akio feels elated. He thinks it is a joke on Masako, and he wants to humiliate her. When they arrive at the fountains, however, Akio feels unaccountably angry. He no longer draws pleasure from his plan. He tries to escape from Masako, and he runs toward the fountains, but she follows. Next Akio becomes fascinated with the movement of the water. After that moment passes, however, Akio falls into a state best characterized by a certain vacancy. He wanders away with no thought of Masako. That is when he discovers that she never even heard him breaking up with her, and he is left in a state of shock.

Control and Self-Control

Above all else, Akio values self-control. He prefers to think of himself as a young man who has self-control, but his actions show otherwise. In order to make himself feel like he does have control over himself, Akio tries to assert control over others; it is for this that he wanted to break up with a woman. The elements of the story—first, Akio's insistence on what a hard person he is, even beyond the boundaries of sexual desire, and later, Akio's fascination with the fountains—clearly show that Akio has very little control over himself. Masako's reaction to the news of the end of relationship also shows that Akio's actions have little effect—thus little control—on her.

Style

Point of View

The story is told from the third-person point of view. Everything that happens in the story is filtered through Akio. The reader only learns his thoughts and ideas. Because Akio is so unperceptive and so uninterested in Masako, the reader learns very little about her. The only indications of what she is thinking come through her brief opportunities for dialogue and the few times that Akio describes what she is doing. For instance, in her most important moment, Masako responds to the news (redelivered) that Akio is breaking up with her: "Really? Did you say that? I didn't hear you," she says in a "normal" voice. This moment undercuts all the feelings that Akio has been going through and turns the joke—both of them, in fact: wooing Masako in order to break up with her and making her confront the fountain—on himself.

Symbolism

The fountains are the story's primary symbols. They are described in sexual terms. The main columns of the fountains, which "shot upward from the center of each basin," are phallic symbols representing the male genitalia. The basins that surround the fountains, with their "radiating curves" are representative of the female genitalia. Akio's fascination with the fountains belies his stated indifference to sex. His ambivalence is further revealed

to be in sexual orientation as well. He first describes the columns of water but then claims to be "less taken" with them than with the surrounding waters. Watching all the water's "untiring rushing," Akio goes into a sexual reverie, "being taken over by the water, carried away on its rushing, cast far away." That reverie continues when the big central column captures his attention. He sees within the column the water rushing upward. Unlike the male genitalia, however, this phallus experiences a "kind of perpetual replenishment." Despite this, the column will be "frustrated." However, the column has something that Akio wants: "unwaning power."

Setting

The story is set in Tokyo, even though the location is not named. By not labeling the city, Mishima shows that this story could take place anywhere, and, indeed, in nearly any culture.

The anonymous setting is also important because it underscores Akio's isolation in relation to himself and to others. In the tea house, the setting is amid overwhelming noise and bustling activity. The sounds produced inside the tea house—the customers' voices, the clattering dishes, the cash register—"clashed with each other all the more violently . . . to create a single, mind-fuddling commotion." These sounds—and this emotion—reflect Akio's feelings at the moment. He is overwrought and excited by his ending of the relationship, yet he is not as at ease with his actions as he would like to be. The setting is also important because the noise created in the tea house provides the reason that Masako doesn't hear Akio's words.

When the pair leave the tea room, the setting changes. Outside, Masako follows Akio "silently"; he himself walks "in silence." The sidewalks are empty; thus at this moment Akio and Masako exist in complete isolation. When they reach the garden, "not a soul" is around, but "beyond the garden, there was a constant procession of wet truck hoods and bus roofs in red, white, or yellow." Akio is aware that the world goes on, but at this moment he is not part of it.

Historical Context

The Japanese Economy

After World War II, Japan made a rapid and impressive economic recovery. Many factors contributed to the country's success. Instead of concen-

Compare & Contrast

- **1960s:** In 1960, the population of Japan is 93,419,000.

  1990s: In 1998, the population of Japan is 126,486,000.

- **1960s:** By 1970, seventy-nine percent of students continue to attend school past the compulsory level, and twenty-four percent of students go to college.

  1990s: In 1998, 96.9 percent of students continue to attend upper secondary school, and 44.2 percent of students go to university.

- **1960s:** In 1960, 32.6 percent of the Japanese labor force are employed in primary industries, such as farming or forestry.

1990s: By the 1990s, less than ten percent of the Japanese labor force are employed in primary industries, and more than half of the labor force is employed in tertiary industries, such as research or management.

- **1960s:** Most Japanese women enter the labor force early, work for a few years, and then retire by their mid-twenties to marry and have children. For many companies, retirement upon childbearing is mandatory.

  1990s: Many married women re-enter the workforce when they are in their mid-thirties, after their children are of school age. Women make up nearly forty percent of the workforce.

---

trating on producing inexpensive textiles sold to other Asian countries, Japan began to produce advanced technology for a world market. Japan's workforce was skilled and highly motivated. The government also cooperated and supported industry.

By 1960 Japan had become the fifth-largest among the world's market economies; by 1968 it was second only to the United States. Also by the middle of the decade, Japan was exporting more goods to the United States than it was importing. While a brief depression took place mid-decade, between 1965 and 1970, the economy saw an average growth of over eleven percent per year.

Society and Wealth

The distribution of individual income moved toward greater equality in the 1960s. Post-war land and labor reforms and the dissolution of the *zaibatsu* (a Japanese conglomerate or cartel) all worked to bring this greater equality in income distribution. During this period, Japan, among all the advanced industrialized nations, became the country with the most equal income distribution. Indeed, nearly ninety percent of Japanese felt that they enjoyed a middle-class standard of living. Along with this rise of

middle-class consciousness came a rise in school and university enrollment, personal savings, desire for home ownership, and the purchase of consumer goods, such as televisions.

Japanese Lifestyle

The Japanese population did see some downsides to the economic growth. The Japanese worked longer hours than workers holding similar jobs in Western countries. The cost of living in Japan was also much higher than it was in other industrialized nations.

Rapid industrialization and population growth emerged as a major issue in Japan in the 1960s. In the early 1960s, many rural residents began to migrate to the cities. Urban areas grew overcrowded. Space and housing were scarce, and prices began to rise dramatically in the 1960s. In the six largest cities, the price index for urban land increased more than twenty times between 1955 and 1970.

As thousands of people flocked to the cities, rural municipalities sought ways to increase their tax base and revenue. To this effect, they encouraged industries, through monetary incentives, to move into their areas. Rural Japan thus underwent a period of industrialization. Pollution became commonplace, and the government took no measures to prevent it. By the mid-1960s, citizens had begun to form grassroots organizations to put a stop to potentially deadly polluting of the environment.

The U.S.-Japan Mutual Security Treaty

The United States organized the reconstruction of the Japanese government after Japan's surrender in World War II and maintained military troops there as provided by the U.S.-Japan Mutual Security Treaty. In 1960, however, Japan and the United States sought to revise the treaty. Some of the terms were changed, and the objective of economic cooperation between the two countries was added. Political leftists were opposed to the treaty on the grounds that Japan, which would continue to allow the United States to maintain military bases in Japan, would be forced to follow whatever military action the United States might want to take in Asia. The administration of Prime Minister Nobusuke Kishi, however, supported the amended treaty in order to appease American wishes. In his desire to ratify the treaty when U.S. President Dwight Eisenhower visited the following month, Japan's prime minister pushed the treaty through without consulting the opposition parties. Tens of thousands of students and workers joined in protest, and rioting broke out in the streets. Eisenhower cancelled his visit because his security could not be assured. The prime minister flew to Washington, where the treaty was ratified. Upon his return, Kishi resigned.

Critical Overview

Since childhood, Mishima was drawn to the history and cultural traditions of Japan. As a young writer, he became acquainted with the Japanese romantics, a group of writers and intellectuals who rejected literary modernism—including the genres of naturalism and realism—and advocated the reading of Japanese classics. Mishima supported their literary theories, for example, expressing a decided disinterest in realistic, banal dialogue. Mishima's early stories and his first novel demonstrate elements typical of this school of literature, such as beautiful young lovers who die a romantic death, and the sea. Such elements would be seen again in Mishima's later works but more often as ironic symbols. Mishima's early work also lacked his later re-

nowned contemporary social vision, drawing more deeply on Japan's past.

With his second novel, *Confessions of a Mask* (1949), Mishima first raised some of the themes that he would continue to explore over the next few decades, such as homosexuality, explicit sexuality, and societal hypocrisy. Short stories, such as those included in *Death in Midsummer*, also explore Mishima's preoccupation with death as well as the traditional character of Japan and the loss of Japanese tradition. Critics have characterized Mishima's work from the 1950s as nihilistic, a school of writing that was popular in post-War Japan.

In the 1960s, however, Mishima turned to the exploration of political and philosophical themes. The story ''Patriotism,'' perhaps Mishima's most well-known work, is based on a 1936 rebellion in which a group of young officers attempt to restore the emperor. Culminating in the ritual suicide of a married couple, the story alludes to Mishima's belief in the interconnectedness of love and death. Mishima's glorification of the emperor is also first noted in this work, as is his personal obsession with violent and beautiful death.

Throughout the decade, Mishima was growing increasingly unhappy with contemporary Japan. He saw the country becoming more and more corrupt as a result of Westernization and wanted a return to more traditional values. In the last four years of his life, Mishima focused all of his creative efforts on his tetralogy, *The Sea of Fertility*, in which he attempted to sum up his philosophy of life and his view of the history of modern Japan. The day its final installment appeared, Mishima committed suicide.

The story ''Fountains in the Rain'' was not available to English-speaking audiences until almost two decades after Mishima's death and close to thirty years after the story was first published in Japan. *Acts of Worship* included seven stories that spanned Mishima's career. There has been very little criticism in English on the story; the variety of opinion on it demonstrates the fact that no main consensus exists. John Bester, Mishima's translator who introduced *Acts of Worship*, referred to it as a ''slight, humorous account of a tiff between a very ordinary young man and his girl.'' Roy Starrs, who reviewed the collection for *The Journal of Asian Studies*, called it a ''cynical study'' about a ''heartless but stupid young man's attempts to ditch his girlfriend.'' Paul Anderer, a reviewer for the *Los Angeles Times*, wrote that Akio ''whips himself into a romantic frenzy, not his girlfriend—which would be a banal and predictable romance—but for the chance to walk out on her.''

In their discussion of the collection as a whole, however, many critics touched upon certain themes common to much of Mishima's work, such as male dominance. J. M. Ditsky pointed out in *Choice*, ''If there is a striking common theme running through all seven stories, it is the attempt of the male ego to control its environment—including, of course, other persons.''

Today, Mishima still enjoys a secure reputation, and many critics believe him to be the finest writer of modern Japan. Due to the spectacular nature of his death, however, many people tend to focus on that instead of his body of work. They are intertwined.

Criticism

Rena Korb

Korb has a master's degree in English literature and creative writing and has written for a wide variety of educational publishers. In the following essay, she discusses Akio's efforts to prove his self-control.

Yukio Mishima became a rising star in the Japanese literary field when he was only in his mid-twenties, and he remains today one of that country's most internationally renowned contemporary writers. Susan J. Napier writes in the *Dictionary of Literary Biography* that Mishima is a ''writer who has helped mold the Western imagination of Japan at the same time as one who continues to haunt the contemporary Japanese mind.'' Aside from his numerous writings, Mishima achieved notoriety for his ritual suicide, performed while still at the pinnacle of his career.

Stories like ''Patriotism'' glorify traditional aspects of Japanese society, such as imperialism and the nobility of the samurai. In contrast to such works dealing with abstract social ideals, a story like ''Fountains in the Rain,'' which was not made accessible to the English-speaking public until 1989, has often been called a story about the end of a love affair. Indeed, its most in-depth commentary comes from John Bester, Mishima's translator. In his preface to the 1989 collection, *Acts of Worship*, Bester writes,

The ability to organize a small form is very evident in 'Fountains in the Rain.' A slight, humorous account of a tiff between a very ordinary young man and his girl, it skillfully portrays the instability, lack of confidence, and above all the self-centeredness that often characterize youth. With great skill, the imagery set forth in the title is worked into the fabric of the story; in a central set piece of description, the fountains reveal themselves as a symbol of the shifting impulses—ambition, aggression, sexuality—to which the hero is prey, and which are liable at any moment to be negated by the monotony of everyday life—the rain—and its obligations. The girl is barely sketched in, but the suggestion of a firmer grasp of immediate realities provides a good foil to the boy's instability.

Though readers may disagree with such simplistic reductions of ''Fountains in the Rain,'' many of Bester's points hold up. The story is rich in imagery, the boy does rebel against the obligations of everyday life, the boy is extremely self centered—but the boy is hardly a ''very ordinary young man.'' The character Akio actually obliquely references Mishima's aesthetic beliefs in the celebration of rigidity and self-control, as well as the necessity for it, which are far from aspects of the average person.

Akio, the main character of the story, has previously set himself the task of making a young woman fall in love with him simply so he can end the relationship. He apparently has accomplished this goal, for as the story begins he has recently told Masako that they must break up, which was ''something he had long dreamed of'' doing. The impetus for this action, though not explicated by the young man, is Akio's desire to demonstrate control over another human. As indicated by the grandiosity of his description of what he imagined would happen, Akio believes himself to hold Masako in his thrall: '''It's time to break it off!' Those words, the mere enunciation of which would be enough to rend the sky asunder. . . . That phrase, more heroic, more glorious than any other in the world.'' Akio further ascribes the ability to manipulate a woman as something belonging to only ''the most manly of men.''

His need to prove that he can achieve this ''height of masculinity'' stems from Akio's insecurity. As hinted at early in the story and again indicated closer to its end, Akio fears losing control of himself. His subconscious recognizes this truth, and he takes great pains to shore up his self-image. He seeks to strengthen himself by gaining control of others. He assigns personality traits to himself that he would like to possess; for instance, he maintains that his nature is ''cut-and-dried,'' a blatant misrepresentation. Akio's nature is actually quite muta-

What Do I Read Next?

- ''Patriotism'' is Mishima's most well-known short story. Mishima portrays a married couple unable to participate in the attempted reinstatement of the Japanese emperor. The couple commit ritual suicide, and the story delineates the connection between death and sexual ecstasy.

- Kazuo Ishiguro's novel *The Remains of the Day* depicts through the eyes of the butler the events of an English manor house in the 1930s and 1940s.

- Kenzaburo Oe is a Japanese novelist whose work epitomizes the rebellion of the post-World War II generation. *The Silent Cry* is a novel that explores the issues of personal identity, self-knowledge, and the ability to relate to the truth.

- *House of Sleeping Beauties and Other Stories* includes three stories by the Japanese writer Yasunari Kawabata. Mishima wrote the introduction to this collection.

- Haruki Murikami's novel *The Wind-Up Bird Chronicles* is about a man whose wife disappears; in his efforts to find her, he discovers the bizarre underworld of Tokyo.

---

ble—simply note the myriad emotions that he undergoes throughout the course of the afternoon—and beyond his ability to control. Even the moment of his greatest triumph—breaking off with Masako—is undercut by his weakness. Instead of speaking firmly and forcefully, he had spoken ''with such a deplorable lack of clarity, with a rattling noise in the throat.'' His fear is evident, yet he continues and thus accomplishes this ''splendid achievement.'' Evincing such power over another human draws Akio to what he calls a ''newfound sense of maturity.''

Akio feels oppressed by Masako's tears, for they represent his inability to shake her free. Despite his claims at being able to simply end the relationship, he feels an obligation to her. Even after he tells her his news, he still spends the afternoon with her, for it is raining and Masako has no umbrella of her own. The sense of freedom he had hoped to achieve through his actions cannot come as long as she is crying. He feels ''absolute frustration . . . at the rain, the tears, the leaden sky that hung like a barrier before him.'' Angry at the usurpation of his superiority, ''the boy gave in to a simple desire to hurt.''

Bringing Masako into confrontation with the fountains only ends in Akio's fascination with the fountains. He even finds greater truths there, though he hides them from himself, unwilling to face what they reveal about him. His wonderment as he gazes at the fountains reveals a sublimated sexual desire for both men and women. Akio had earlier denied any true sexuality, claiming ''that he had made love to Masako'' even though he ''had always been free from the dominance of desire,'' but his perception of the fountains utterly disproves that claim. The columns with water that ''shot upward'' and ''spouted vertically and undisturbed'' represent the male sexual organ, while the ''jets from the big central fountain'' with the ''untiring rushing'' arcs of water represent the female sexual organ.

Although Akio begins his contemplation by focusing on the columns, he still is ''less taken with three main columns of water than with the water that shot out in radiating curves all around.'' At this point, he forces himself to be drawn to the representation of a woman's sexuality. As he watches the arcs of water surrounding the columns, his mind is ''taken over by the water, carried away on its rushing, cast far away. . . .'' Akio's rapture can be likened to one that would emerge from a sexual encounter. He feels the same way, however, while watching the central column. He is fascinated by the ''furious speed'' of the water climbing within it, ''steadily filling a slender cycle of space from base to summit, replacing each moment what had been lost the moment before, in a kind of perpetual replenishment.'' Here Akio describes his fantasy of the ultimate, ongoing orgasm. Although he seems to take pleasure in this idea, as he has done previously, he counters what he has said by adding, ''It was plain that at heaven's height it would be finally frustrated; yet the unwaning power that supported unceasing failure was magnificent.'' Here Akio unconsciously expresses his own image of himself as a sexually frustrated creature, yet one who longs to achieve true fulfillment.

As abruptly as Akio falls into this sexual reverie, he is brought out of it: ''suddenly, fountains in the rain seemed to represent no more than the endless repetition of a stupid and pointless process.'' With this perception, Akio again denies his sexuality, casting himself back into that person he claimed to be at the beginning of the story—one who has complete control over himself. The reader, however, knows this to be untrue. Not only does Akio have true sexual desires, he has them for men as well as women. His subconscious understanding of this is demonstrated when he starts to walk away from the fountains, having completely forgotten Masako; she is no longer important to his maintenance of the belief that he can control others, for he knows that he cannot even control himself.

The story further exposes Akio as he discovers that Masako never even heard his words breaking up with her. She was crying for no special reason; the ''tears just came.'' The shock of learning the truth is so great that Akio is ''[A]lmost bowled over.'' When he speaks to her again, he has reverted back to the unsure self who first met Masako at the tea house. He stammers out a reply that is desperate in its attempt to regain the upper hand: ''he wanted to shout something at her,'' but he is foiled again in this effort as ''at the crucial moment'' he let forth an ''enormous sneeze.'' Akio thinks, ''If I'm not careful I'm going to get a cold.'' As the story's final sentence, it sums up Akio's release of his whole fantasy of controlling himself and others, at least for the moment. His acceptance of himself as a fallible human, even a mundane one at that instant, shows the utter failure of his plan toward Masako and his plan to shore up his own ego.

Source: Rena Korb, Critical Essay on ''Fountains in the Rain,'' in *Short Stories for Students*, The Gale Group, 2001.

Doreen Piano

Piano is a Ph.D. candidate in English at Bowling Green State University. In the following essay, she explores the vain and egocentric attempt of a young man to achieve manhood by intentionally

> **"** Angry at the usurpation of his superiority, 'the boy gave in to a simple desire to hurt.'"

seducing and abandoning a young woman in ''Fountains in the Rain.''

Written in 1963, the short story ''Fountains in the Rain'' by Japanese writer Yukio Mishima reveals the calculated intentions of a young man who breaks up with the woman he is dating because ''it was something he had long dreamed of.'' His motivation for the breakup is not that he no longer loves or desires her, but that he thinks his action will bring him a maturity that he has not yet experienced. Although the young man Akio claims that breaking up with Masako will usher in an elevated stage of emotional and mental development, in fact, it does not. Ironically, the situation engenders not confidence but doubt when the breakup does not go as planned. Despite his initial feelings of intense relief and pleasure, eventually Akio finds himself bereft, confronting feelings of inadequacy, aggression, frustrated passion, and doubt at the core of his being as he realizes the emptiness and futility of his gesture. The heroic, manly act that Akio imagines will initiate him into manhood is actually a desperately shallow and irresponsible one that has no meaning or relevance either to Masako, the young woman whom Akio intends to hurt, or himself. Throughout the story, Mishima uses point of view, imagery, irony, and setting to evoke Akio's imaginative yet futile attempt at achieving manhood.

Told from a third person point of view, ''Fountains in the Rain'' focuses primarily on the internal reactions of Akio to his breakup with Masako in a teahouse in Tokyo. From this point of view, the reader gains an understanding of Akio as a self-absorbed and naïve young man who thinks that becoming a man depends on carrying out certain kinds of acts that establish one's authority and credibility. In this case, it is breaking up with a girl. From the very beginning of the story, Akio's self-centeredness is apparent as he drags Masako along the streets of Tokyo, recounting in his mind what he has just done. Mishima's use of an extended flash-

> " The heroic, manly act
> that Akio imagines will
> initiate him into manhood is
> actually a desperately
> shallow and irresponsible one
> that has no meaning or
> relevance either to Masako,
> the young woman whom Akio
> intends to hurt, or himself."

back as an organizing structure reveals the depth of Akio's self-absorption as well as his self-congratulatory amazement that he has gotten the reaction he wanted from Masako: she is crying uncontrollably.

> . . . he marveled at the peppermint freshness of mind with which he contemplated the phenomenon. This was precisely what he had planned, worked to encompass and brought to reality: a splendid achievement, though admittedly somewhat mechanical.

By intentionally breaking up with Masako—a woman whom, it can be argued, he still loves—and seeing her cry, Akio imagines that his action will change his very being from that of a boy to a man: "Under his own steam, Akio had crossed the pass over the mountains that he'd gazed at for so long in the distance." Yet Akio's initial confidence quickly wears thin as Masako's profuse weeping thwarts Akio's plan. It is because of Masako's crying that Akio goes to the fountains in the park where he eventually confronts the myth of masculinity that he has dreamed up.

Although Masako is presented to the reader only through Akio's eyes, she has a central role in the story in terms of how she affects and undermines Akio's vision of achieving manhood. As the translator of *Acts of Worship*, John Bester remarks, "The girl is barely sketched in, but the suggestion of a firmer grasp of immediate realities provides a good foil to the boy's instability." It seems that the more Akio attempts to emotionally detach himself from Masako, the more he is overwhelmed by what he thinks is her reaction to the break up. "The abundance of Masako's tears was a genuine cause for astonishment. Not for a moment did their volume

diminish." Her capacity for crying and its effect on the people in the teahouse who looked at them "with stares of a kind calculated to disturb Akio's newfound sense of maturity" lead him to take drastic and cruel measures. But what starts out to be a cruel joke, bringing Masako to the fountains in the park to confront a mightier force than her own tears, only ends up backfiring.

> . . . the only trouble was the absolute frustration he felt at the rain, the tears, the leaden sky that hung like a barrier before him. They pressed down on him on all sides, reducing his freedom to a kind of damp rag.

Because of the oppressive setting, Akio finds he can no longer maintain the elation he felt moments before when telling Masako that he wanted to break it off. Everything he tries to do to regain that preliminary feeling falls to the wayside. Masako seems impervious to anything he does, which leads the reader to believe that Akio is creating an image of himself that exists only in his imagination. For example, Akio prides himself on particular behaviors that reveal his newfound restraint and maturity such as "being cut-and-dried about things. Yes: to be cut-and-dried . . . suited Akio's nature. . . ."; however, in actuality he is quick to anger and acts childishly toward Masako. His unpredictable manner contrasts sharply to Masako's, whose crying is as constant as the pouring rain and the fountains. Thus Masako, though a dimly outlined figure in the story, serves as a steady emotional gauge compared to the flighty, self-absorbed, and emotionally unstable Akio.

Despite the story being told from Akio's point of view, readers are not provided with many direct statements about what motivates the roiling emotions he experiences. Akio is obviously dissatisfied, disaffected, and peevish, yet the reader is not told why. Instead, Mishima subtly evokes Akio's dissatisfaction with himself and his life through the use of specific images such as the fountain, Masako's tears, and the evocative rainy, monochromatic Tokyo setting. In an interview in the *Paris Review* with Donald Keene, translator and professor of Japanese literature, Mishima notes that "the methods of description followed by some Western novelists seems unnecessarily detailed to Japanese readers, who are accustomed to make the intuitive leap necessary to understand a haiku." Therefore, the concise images Mishima uses are often a key to the underlying meaning of his stories. Moreover, the spare yet monumental details he provides allow readers to fill in the blanks so as to fully comprehend the story's emotional complexity. As a testimony to the compact beauty of Mishima's images and his powerful evocation of atmosphere, translator John Bestler, in his introduction to *Acts of Worship: Seven Stories*, writes that in "Fountains in the Rain" "the imagery set forth in the title is worked into the fabric of the story."

In particular, water, as found in the girl's tears, the pouring rain, and the fountains, becomes an overriding trope that connects the boy's emotional world to the external world around him. For example, the fountains that Akio becomes transfixed by in the park are contrasted with the steady downpour of a Tokyo summer day as well as Masako's tears that at times seem to be just as powerful a force on Akio's psyche. Although Akio appears dismissive of Masako's tears, in fact he is deeply affected by her emotional outpouring. At first, he seems pleased by her reaction, yet this quickly turns to dismay and anger as he contemplates the situation. "What with the rain and the tears, Akio felt as if his whole body was getting wet." The wetness begins to drag him down, diminishing his feelings of power and success at dumping Masako. Moreover, Masako's tears are so powerful that Akio at first gleefully and then later angrily equates them with the fountains that which never cease, even in the rain. "A human being was scarcely a match for a reflex fountain; almost certainly, she'd give up and stop crying." Ironically, Masako's tears continue to flow while Akio's attention is drawn to the fountains.

Mesmerized by the fountains, Akio's dreams of achieving manhood are at first elevated by observing the fountains' power and then dashed to the ground. In his confrontation with the fountains, Akio realizes that he cannot take action except through his imagination. At first his fixation with the fountains seems to temporarily soothe his dismay and frustration over the situation with Masako, as he attempts to restore his masculinity by perceiving the fountains as what John Bester claims in his introduction to *Acts of Worship*, "a symbol of the shifting impulses—ambition, aggression, sexuality—to which the hero is prey. . . ." The water spouting forth from the fountains reveals an omnipotent force, both sexual and emotional, that the young man identifies with as he contemplates its ability to rejuvenate itself; ". . . the unwaning power that supported unceasing failure was magnificent." Yet unlike the fountain, Akio cannot continually replenish his feelings of confidence. He is too fickle and unreliable, too young and self-absorbed. Rather than living life, Akio seems doomed to dream about it. This becomes most clear when he realizes that the

fountains he previously found so powerful and fascinating are suddenly "no more than the endless repetition of a stupid and pointless process." Akio suffers from a lack of self that is too easily influenced by his environment, such as the dull rain that not only permeates his clothes and shoes but also his consciousness.

Finally, the rain, another powerful image Mishima uses to evoke certain feelings in Akio, seems to bring Akio to his senses, making him realize how futile his plan was to break up with Masako. His act is diminished by the rain's utter pervasiveness, its banality and everydayness. As he contemplates the intensity of the rain as it hits various surfaces such as city roofs and hotels, Akio realizes that he has not done anything spectacular in breaking up with Masako; his life, in fact, is quite ordinary. "From the rain's point of view, his cheeks and the dirty concrete roof were quite identical." This insight causes him to lose interest in the fountains as well as Masako. Mishima's use of irony at the end of the story reveals how delusional Akio is when he discovers to his dismay that Masako is not crying because of Akio's words; she is crying for no special reason. At this point, Akio is so undone by the overwhelming banality of his life as reflected in the rainy, dull atmosphere of contemporary Tokyo that the anger he feels at Masako's statement comes out as a sneeze. Akio's vision of manhood, what he has imagined achieving throughout the story, is no longer a pressing issue as he contemplates the possibility of getting a cold from standing in the rain. Although this last line reveals Akio's limitations, both emotionally and physically, to become the man he desires, the sneeze also makes him aware that he is part of his surroundings and not outside of it.

There is much to criticize about the character of Akio, who appears desperately self-centered and irresponsible, yet, despite Akio's representation as a callow, self-absorbed youth, his imaginative flights of fancy touch on a feature of Mishima's work that is common in some of his novels: the role of the artist in contemporary Japanese society. In her book *Escape from the Wasteland: Romanticism and Realism in the Fiction of Mishima Yukio and Oe Kenzaburo*, Susan Napier suggests that Mishima's fiction often depicts characters who are unlikable and egocentric, yet their willful denial of reality "is also allied to a more positive figure, the artist, for the visions of these violent youthful protagonists have a creative function equivalent to the artist." Viewed in this way, Akio can be seen as an artist who attempts to effect change in the monotonous urban environment through acts of imagination. Unfortunately, these flights of fancy may serve momentarily to alleviate the artist's frustration at the world, but they do not change his or her environment. As an artist figure, Akio is completely divorced from the world of things; thus his imaginative capabilities isolate rather than connect him to the external world. This is seen most acutely in the discussion between Masako and Akio where he realizes that Masako's crying has nothing to do with his actions. Similar to Akio, Masako also is engrossed in her own imaginative world, one that has little to do with external reality, or even with Akio. However, having said that, the ending of the story holds out a shred of hope in terms of transcending such a monotonous existence in its image of the blooming crimson azalea bushes that Akio notices. These bushes may hint at possibilities for creating a world more colorful and vibrant than the one in which both Akio and Masako currently live.

Source: Doreen Piano, Critical Essay on ''Fountains in the Rain,'' in *Short Stories for Students*, The Gale Group, 2001.

Joyce Hart

Hart has degrees in English literature and creative writing and is a copyeditor and published writer. In this essay, she looks at Mishima's concepts of the disparity in power between the natural and the mechanical world as portrayed in his story.

Akio, the protagonist in Mishima's short story ''Fountains in the Rain,'' is a very calculating young man. He has contrived a plan much like an engineer might plot the dimensions of a proposed building. But there is a major flaw in Akio's calculations, a blind spot brought on by his own obsessions. Akio has failed to see the difference between the mathematical precision of the mechanical world and the emotional ambiguity of nature.

Most of Mishima's protagonists are ''anti-heroes, physically or psychologically wounded,'' states Philip Shabecoff for the *New York Times*. They are ''tormented by obsessions with beauty or sex or mutilation and martyrdom.'' Shabecoff describes Mishima as being ''fascinated by blood and pain and terror.'' Somewhere in these elements, the reader will be able to find Akio, a not too likeable character who has been somehow psychologically wounded and has become obsessed with wanting to inflict pain. The target of his obsession is his girl friend, Masako. What emotions trigger his obsession are not clear. However, what is clear is that he

has plotted his way through this relationship with a very clear purpose. And that purpose is met when Akio sees the pain in Masako's tears. But these characteristics or quirks in Akio's personality only color the story. They pull the reader in, make the reader want to stay long enough to find out where Akio's obsessions will take him. The real story lies somewhere underneath Akio's obsessions—in that place where there is at least a hint of recognition that life is not quite as mechanical as Akio had originally thought.

Akio starts out very confidently. He has been scheming for what appears to be an extended period of time. He has ''pretended to love'' Masako, and with his false love he has ''undermined her defenses.'' He believes himself to be the actor, the director, and the producer of his own show. He has even written what he anticipates to be the entire script for his little drama, which will include only six words: ''It's time to break it off!'' Having spoken his solitary line, he waits for a pre-calculated response: an affirmation from Masako that she has heard him. So far, so good. Masako delivers her reaction ''in a flash, like chewing gum ejected from a vending machine.'' Everything appears to be running smoothly, just like a well-oiled and meticulously maintained machine.

Out of Masako's eyes, which were ''no longer eyes,'' rush streams of tears that are ''expressing nothing.'' Of course this is Akio's slanted take on the events. He sees the tears as a plumber sees a leak in a pipe. Masako's tears are merely ''waters.'' His play is still on course. ''This was precisely what he had planned.'' It was a ''splendid achievement, though admittedly somewhat mechanical.'' Akio rejoices in this event. He has divorced himself from feeling, from the ''dominance of desire.'' What power he has created, like a mechanic who has built an automobile and for the first time has placed the key into the ignition and turned it. Akio hears the equivalent of the sound of that car's engine as he watches his own creation, Masako, cry. After months of faking a relationship with this woman, faking an emotional connection with her, Akio exclaims that ''this was reality!''

Unfortunately, immediately following this statement, Akio sees the first sign of trouble. Masako is crying far longer than he had anticipated. It is also at this moment that Akio notices the color red, the color of passion and emotions. It is a color noticed in passing—''the collar of a red blouse showed at the neck of the [Masako's] coat.'' It is only a brief encounter with the color, barely noticed, but it is coupled with the words ''a tremendous force'' in her hands, making the encounter a bit more significant. On first reading, the mention of this color appears unimportant, just as it might have appeared inconsequential to Akio when he first notices it. Only later does this color blossom, and it does so at the further expense of Akio's carefully planned calculations. Maybe emotions are not as mechanical as Akio had anticipated. The color red at this point is located on Masako's body. Are these Masako's emotions, or are they Akio's emotions for her?

Akio tries to shake this small glimpse, this tiny reminder that he might be acting less than mechanically in reference to his relationship with Masako. He needs to get back to his preconceived scheme, his script, his unemotional stance. He watches Masako, listening to her breath, then compares her cries to the ''wheeze of new shoes.'' Later he refers to her as a ''tearbag,'' and ''unwanted baggage.'' When he accidentally bumps against her under the umbrella, Masako's raincoat has the feel of ''a reptile.'' These are the ways that Akio keeps his distance from Masako, turning her into some inanimate object or, at best, turning her into a cold-blooded snake.

Akio reminds himself that he must remain remote and unfeeling, and he focuses on his sudden urge to take Masako to the water fountain. He believes that it is for Masako's sake that the fountain must be seen, dismissing his own initial curiosity that made him think of the fountains in the first place. He will show Masako that those emotional tears that are streaming down her face are no match for the clever, mechanical fountain. After all, the mechanical fountain reuses its waters, whereas Masako's ''tears all ran to waste.'' The mechanical fountain is utilitarian and efficient. In comparison, Masako would see that her own tears (and presumably all the emotions behind them) are useless. ''A human being was scarcely a match for a reflex fountain.''

It is at this point in the story that another flaw appears in Akio's overall plan. The reader is given a glimpse of a slight deterioration in Akio's effort to remain aloof, to maintain his original contention that his calculated drama will unfold mechanically. ''What with the rain and the tears, Akio felt as if his whole body was getting wet.'' This is the first mention of Akio's feelings. Not only is he feeling drenched by the rain but Masako's tears are also

> **The real story lies somewhere underneath Akio's obsessions--in that place where there is at least a hint of recognition that life is not quite as mechanical as Akio had originally thought."**

starting to get to him. And coincidentally, it is at this moment in the story that Akio sees the color red, again. This time it is the ''red chairs of a hotel dining room, dimly visible. . . .'' It is also at this point in the story that things begin to look different from the way Akio had once imagined they would. For instance, the rain looks like ''fine white dew'' in Masako's hair. The water spouts of the fountain look like ''curved glass tubes.'' Something is changing inside of Akio, but he's not sure what it is.

A flurry of colors follow. There is a brilliant green in the shrubs and the multiple colors of the cars and trucks in the distant traffic; and it is at this point that Akio senses an anger building up inside of him. He is filled with an ''obscure sense of dissatisfaction,'' which he cannot totally blame on Masako's crying. There is something bigger here. Something is tearing away at his scheme. That slick vending machine metaphor that the narrator used to mark the beginning of Masako's tears at the start of this story is suddenly out of order. The dysfunction of Akio's mechanical metaphor is causing him frustration. He senses a barrier that reduces ''his freedom to a kind of damp rag.'' In other words, he is losing control. His calculated scheme is going awry.

To regain his power as the director and creator of his plan, Akio has a craving to cause new pain. And how does he propose to do this? His concentration seems to be slipping. The only idea that he comes up with falls short of the sharpness of his original plan that caused Masako to cry. But it's better than nothing. If he can't inflict pain, he can at least try to make Masako more miserable. He will get her to run out into the rain, again, and get even wetter. This will also force her to take an even closer and fuller view of the water fountain. So he runs, knowing that Masako will follow. This renews his confidence, renews his sense of being in control. Akio is still trying to engineer his plot. He is still trying to prove that his relationship with Masako is mechanically based. When he runs, Masako does follow.

However, there is another turn in the story at this point. Although Masako runs to Akio, when she gets there, she takes a ''firm grip'' of the umbrella. This is the first time that Masako has played an active role in this little calculated play of Akio's. It is also the first time she speaks. Akio is caught off guard with Masako's question: ''Where are you going?'' she asks. Akio had not planned other lines past his initial statement that had set this story in motion. And yet in spite of himself, he finds himself speaking ''effortlessly.'' He responds to her with nothing really new, only pointing out once again that Masako's tears are ''no match'' for the waters of the fountains. But what is new is that the narrator describes the couple at this point as displaying a change in body language: ''And the two of them tilted the umbrella and, freed from the need to keep their eyes on each other, stared for awhile at the three fountains. . . .'' This is the first time in the story that Akio and Masako act in unison. They have come together and for the moment have stopped reacting to Akio's scheme that has been attempting to pull them apart. It is also at this point that the narrator points out that the water of the fountains and the water of the rain are ''almost indistinguishable.'' They, too, have come together.

Once again, the narrator points out that things are not what they seem. The mechanical drone of the traffic and the mechanical noise of the fountain weave ''so closely into the surrounding air'' that the couple appears to be ''enclosed in perfect silence.'' The water at the top of the fountain is ''almost too powdery-looking for real water,'' and the water around the lip of the basin becomes ''white manes.'' These visions, these things that are not what they seem, disturb Akio. His thoughts are being ''taken over by the water. . . .'' To his surprise, the fountains that he had wanted to teach Masako a lesson, were now teaching him.

As Akio stands near the fountain, staring up at the highest point of the water flow, he realizes that the fountain will never reach its goal of ''heaven's height.'' It is at this point that his gaze is ''lifted higher.'' When he tilts his face fully to the rain, he becomes fascinated with the natural world, and the image of the fountain fades from his thoughts. ''Quite suddenly, fountains in the rain seemed to represent no more than the endless repetition of a stupid and pointless process.'' With this realization, Akio not only forgets the fountain, he forgets his anger, his frustration, and all his silly, calculated schemes.

With Akio walking ''aimlessly'' and Masako ''keeping a firm hold on the handle of the umbrella,'' the story moves closer to an end. But not before Masako denies that she ever heard Akio's dramatically rehearsed words: ''It's time to break it off!'' All that planning and scheming; all the false emotions; the setting of the traps: Akio is horrified that his carefully engineered calculations have been totally obliterated by Masako's denial, just as all traces of Masako's tears have been washed away from her face by the rain. He stammers a bit and then restates his famous line, but he says them with weakened sentiments. He even adds a questioning tone to them: ''I told you a while back, didn't I— that we'd better split up.''

Things are changing fast, and they are changing in ways that Akio had not calculated. Masako is not playing out her role as he had planned. But it is not only Masako who has surprised him; it appears that Akio's own calculating mind has turned on him. Just as Akio finishes his last words to Masako, he sees azalea bushes blooming ''grudgingly, here and there on the lawn.'' The color of the blossoms is crimson, a very deep red. The color red has moved to the natural world, and with this movement, the steam and fury is removed from Akio's plan. He thinks he is angry about his plan falling apart, but when he tries to shout, all that comes out is a sneeze. And it is this sneeze that reminds Akio of his vulnerability: ''If I am not careful, I'm going to get a cold, he thought.'' His perspective of himself has changed, much like his perspective of the fountains, which he once thought were grander than Masako's tears and the rain. It is with these sentiments that Mishima ends his story. There are no clues that the young couple will stay together or break up, but there is hope that Akio has learned that there is more power in the natural world than he had initially conceived. Perhhaps by allowing his natural self to come out, as opposed to playing out a calculated, mechanical role, he will break out of ''the endless repetition of a stupid and pointless process.''

Source: Joyce Hart, Critical Essay on ''Fountains in the Rain,'' in *Short Stories for Students*, Gale Group, 2001.

Sources

Anderer, Paul, Review in *Los Angles Times*, December 17, 1989, p. 2.

Bester, John, Preface to *Acts of Worship*, Kodansha International, 1989, pp. vii–xii.

Ditsky, J. M., Review in *Choice*, April 1990, p. 1329.

Mishima, Yukio, ''Fountains in the Rain,'' in *Acts of Worship: Seven Stories*, translated by John Bester, Kodansha International, 1989.

Napier, Susan J., *Escape from the Wasteland: Romanticism and Realism in the Fiction of Mishima Yukio and Oe Kenzaburo*, Harvard University Press, 1995.

———, ''Mishima Yukio,'' in *Dictionary of Literary Biography*, Vol. 182: *Japanese Fiction Writers Since World War II*, Gale Research, Detroit, 1997, pp. 121–34.

Shabecoff, Philip, ''Everyone in Japan Has Heard of Him,'' in *New York Times*, August 2, 1970.

Starrs, Roy, Review of *Acts of Worship*, in *The Journal of Asian Studies*, August 1990, p. 659.

Further Reading

Scott-Stokes, Henry, *The Life and Death of Yukio Mishima*, Farrar, Strauss and Giroux, New York, 1974.
    This is the first biography of Mishima published in the west, and it was written by a friend of the author's.

Yourcenar, Marguerite, *Mishima: A Vision of the Void*, translated by Alberto Manguel, Farrar, Strauss and Giroux, New York, 1986.
    In this essay, the noted French writer discusses Mishima's work and life and the often blurred boundary between them.

Goodbye, Columbus

Philip Roth

1959

The novella "Goodbye, Columbus" was first published in Roth's 1959 collection, *Goodbye, Columbus, and Five Short Stories*, which won the National Book Award. Other stories in the collection include "The Conversion of the Jews," "Epstein," "Defender of the Faith," "You Can't Tell a Man by the Song He Sings," and "Eli, the Fanatic." "Goodbye, Columbus" was adapted to the screen in the 1969 movie by the same title, produced by Paramount, directed by Larry Peerce and starring Ali McGraw and Richard Benjamin.

"Goodbye, Columbus" is narrated from the point of view of Neil Klugman, a twenty-three-year-old Jewish man who lives with his aunt and uncle in a lower-middle-class neighborhood in Newark, New Jersey, and works at a public library. It concerns his relationship over the course of one summer with Brenda Patimkin, an upper-middle-class Jewish college student staying with her family in the suburbs. Their relationship is characterized by the stark contrast of their socioeconomic differences, despite the fact that they are both Jewish. The summer ends with Brenda's brother Ron's wedding, after which Brenda returns to Radcliffe College in Massachusetts. When the two arrange to meet at a hotel over the Jewish holidays, she tells him that her parents have discovered her diaphragm and have both written her letters expressing their dismay *and* their disdain for Neil as a result. As Brenda feels she can no longer continue the relationship, Neil leaves the hotel, ultimately achieving

a new sense of self-knowledge, which is expressed by the dawning of the Jewish New Year as he arrives back in Newark.

"Goodbye, Columbus" explores themes of Jewish identity, class divisions within the Jewish community, spiritual crisis over Judaism, love, sex and relationships, and the struggle for self-knowledge in a young man. Despite its serious subject matter and themes, the novella is characterized by humor, as expressed through the narrator's finely tuned sense of irony in his observations of both his own and his girlfriend's families.

which, at the age of twenty-six, he received the National Book Award. His third novel, *Portnoy's Complaint*, which became a bestseller, is his most well-known, as well as his most controversial. This novel is written in a stream-of-consciousness style narrated by Alexander Portnoy, the protagonist, who speaks to his silent psychoanalyst. Subsequent novels have followed the character of Nathan Zuckerman, a Jewish writer generally regarded as an autobiographical stand-in for Roth himself. Roth's actual autobiography, *The Facts: A Novelist's Autobiography,* was published in 1988.

Author Biography

Philip Roth was born on March 19, 1933, in Newark, New Jersey, into a lower-middle-class Jewish family. He attended Rutgers University in Newark from 1950 to 1951, then transferred to Bucknell University, from which he graduated Phi Beta Kappa and magna cum laud, with a major in English, in 1954. Roth earned a Master of Arts from the University of Chicago in 1955, and from 1955 to 1956 he served in the U.S. Army, from which he was honorably discharged due to a back injury. He briefly enrolled in a Ph.D. program in English at the University of Chicago, but left in 1957 to pursue a career in writing. Roth has worked as an instructor at University of Chicago (1956–1958), University of Iowa (1960–1962), State University of New York at Stony Brook (1967–1968), and Hunter City College University of New York (1989–1992). He was writer-in-residence at Princeton University from 1962 to 1964 and at University of Pennsylvania from 1965 to 1980. Roth has been married twice, to Margaret Martinson, from 1959 until her death in 1968, and then to Claire Bloom, the noted British Shakespearean actress, from 1990 until their divorce in 1994. Roth's 1998 novel, *I Married a Communist*, is based on the aftermath of this messy divorce, perhaps in response to Bloom's 1996 memoir, *Leaving a Doll's House*, which focuses on their relationship, depicting Roth in an unflattering light.

Because his protagonists and their experiences usually closely resemble Roth and his experiences, Roth's fiction is generally considered to be based largely on his own life, although the author himself remains equivocal on this matter. His first major literary publication was the collection *Goodbye, Columbus, and Five Short Stories* in 1959, for

Plot Summary

Neil Klugman is twenty-three and Jewish. He works at a public library and lives with his Aunt Gladys and Uncle Max, as his parents have moved to Arizona because of their asthma. Neil first meets Brenda Patimkin, also Jewish, a student at Radcliffe College in Boston, Massachusetts, at a country club swimming pool, to which he has been invited by his cousin. Brenda asks him to hold her glasses while she dives into the pool. He later calls her, and they arrange to meet at the tennis courts. She invites him to dinner with her parents the next day. Neil meets Brenda's parents, Mr. and Mrs. Patimkin, her brother Ron, and her ten-year-old sister Julie. Neil lives in a working class section of Newark, New Jersey, whereas the Patimkins live in a large home in an upper-middle-class suburb. Except for Mrs. Patimkin, every member of the family is almost constantly preoccupied with sports, such as golf, basketball, ping pong, and so on. Neil and Brenda go out every night together for two weeks, and she later invites him to stay at her house for a week during his summer vacation. Whereas Neil officially stays in the guest room, he and Brenda secretly sleep together every night in her bedroom. Brenda invites Neil to stay a second week, during which the family is preoccupied with making plans for her brother Ron's imminent wedding. One day, Neil suggests to Brenda that she get a diaphragm. She does not want to, but eventually agrees. At the end of the second week, Neil attends the wedding, where he meets Mr. Patimkin's half-brother, Leo, who drunkenly talks to Neil about his family and their financial situation. Soon after the wedding, Neil drives Brenda to the train station to go back to college in Boston. For several weeks, they communicate by letter and phone, until she invites him up to Boston for the

Philip Roth

Jewish holiday of Rosh Hashanah, the Jewish New Year. Neil's Aunt Gladys cries at the news that he will not be with his family for the holiday. Neil meets up with Brenda, and the two check into a hotel under the names "Mr. and Mrs. Klugman." But, as soon as they enter the hotel room, Brenda tells Neil that her mother has found her diaphragm in a drawer under a pile of sweaters. She shows Neil two letters she has received, one from her father and one from her mother, expressing their dismay at this discovery. Brenda insists that she can barely face her parents after this, let alone continue to see Neil. Neil picks up his bag and leaves the hotel. He wanders around the Harvard campus and stops outside the library, where he contemplates his own image in the mirror of the darkened window. He catches the train back to Newark, "just as the sun was rising on the first day of the Jewish New Year," and in time to make it to work.

Characters

Carlota

Carlotta is the Patimkin's maid. That the Patimkins have a maid is an indication of their wealth.

Harriet Ehrlich

Harriet Ehrlich is the fiancée of Brenda's brother Ron. Harriet arrives at the Patimkin household several days before the wedding. Neil describes her as "a young lady singularly unconscious of a motive in others or herself. All was all surfaces, and she seemed a perfect match for Ron, and too for the Patimkins."

Aunt Gladys

Gladys is Neil's aunt, and Neil lives at her house. She is indirectly critical of his relationship with Brenda, based on her awareness of the vast socioeconomic class differences between the families.

Doris Klugman

Doris Klugman is Neil's cousin, who first invited him to the country club swimming pool where he met Brenda.

Neil Klugman

Neil Klugman is the protagonist and narrator of the story. Neil's first-person narration tells the story of his relationship with Brenda from his own perspective. The story is one of self-discovery for Neil, as their relationship is characterized by their difference in socioeconomic status. Neil, who is twenty-three, lives with his Aunt Gladys and Uncle Max in Newark, New Jersey, and works at a library. He first meets Brenda at a country club swimming pool, to which his cousin Doris has invited him. He later calls Brenda and meets her at a tennis court. The next day, he is invited to dinner at her parents' house. Brenda's upper-middle-class suburban Jewish family is in stark contrast to the Neil's lower-middle-class Jewish family. After several weeks of dating, Brenda invites Neil to stay a week at her parents' house. While he is there, he and Brenda secretly spend the night together in her room. She invites him to stay another week, at the end of which she goes back to college for the fall. After several weeks without seeing one another, they arrange to spend a weekend together at a hotel, but, when they meet, Brenda tells him that her parents have discovered the diaphragm she had been using with him. As Brenda feels that, because of her parents' reaction, they cannot continue their relationship, Neil leaves the hotel and heads back home and to his job.

The Little Boy

This is the little African-American boy, described by the outdated term "colored," who daily visits the library to look at the book of Gauguin paintings of native women in Tahiti. He appears in Neil's dream, as they both drift away from Tahiti on a ship. Neil identifies with the boy because they are both preoccupied with a fantasy of inhabiting a paradise which in reality they cannot reach—for the boy it's Tahiti, for Neil it is the upper-middle-class world of Brenda's family.

Uncle Max

Max is Neil's uncle, and Neil lives at his house. Uncle Max does not appear in the story, except as Neil and Neil's aunt refer to him.

John McKee

John McKee is Neil's co-worker at the library, whom Neil doesn't like. Neil also refers to him as John McRubberhands.

Ben Patimkin

Ben Patimkin is Brenda Patimkin's father. Described as ''tall, strong and ungrammatical,'' Mr. Patimkin is a wealthy businessman, who owns Patimkin Kitchen and Bathroom Sinks. Mr. Patimkin is a man of few words, and who spends his time with his family primarily in playing various sports in their yard. He comments that Neil ''eats like a sparrow,'' which Neil interprets as a slight against his masculinity. Toward the end of the story, Mr. Patimkin seems willing to accept Neil as a potential son-in-law, hinting that there would be room for him in the family business. After Brenda's mother, Mrs. Patimkin, discovers Brenda's diaphragm, Mr. Patimkin writes Brenda a letter, intended to soften the impact of her mother's harsher letter. His primary response to the situation is to insist that he buy her a new coat, which reflects his ability to treat family matters mostly in terms of business and material possessions.

Brenda Patimkin

Brenda is Neil's lover. Neil first meets Brenda at a country club swimming pool, where she asks him to hold her glasses while she dives into the pool. Neil later calls her, and she invites him to meet her at the tennis court. The next day, she invites him to dinner with her family, and, eventually, to spend two weeks at their house, during which the two secretly spend the night together. Neil's relationship with Brenda is characterized by their socioeconomic class differences. Although they are both Jewish, everything about their family lives is in stark contrast. Brenda, like the rest of her family, is preoccupied with sports, competition, and athletics.

Media Adaptations

- ''Goodbye, Columbus'' was adapted to the screen and made into a movie by the same title directed by Larry Peerce and released in 1969. It stars Ali McGraw as Brenda Patimkin and Richard Benjamin as Neil Klugman.

She attends Radcliffe College in Cambridge, Massachusetts, to which she returns at the end of the summer. She and Neil do not see each other again until they check into a hotel together for a weekend. When they arrive at the hotel room, however, Brenda tells him that her parents have discovered the diaphragm she had been using with Neil over the summer. Her mother and father have written her separate letters, expressing their dismay at this discovery. She makes it clear to Neil that, due to her family's disapproval, she cannot continue their relationship.

Julie Patimkin

Julie Patimkin is Brenda's little sister. Described as ''ten, round-faced, bright,'' Julie is as preoccupied with sports and competition as the rest of the Patimkin family. After Neil insists on beating her at a game of ping pong one day when he is left to baby sit her, Julie becomes upset and cools toward him from then on.

Leo Patimkin

Leo Patimkin is Mr. Patimkin's half-brother, whom Neil meets at the wedding. Leo Patimkin gets drunk and talks extensively to Neil about his family and financial circumstances.

Mrs. Patimkin

Mrs. Patimkin is Brenda's mother. Neil describes her in the following way: ''with her purple eyes, her dark hair, and large, persuasive frame, she gave me the feeling of some captive beauty, some wild princess, who has been tamed and made the servant to the king's daughter—who was Brenda.''

Mrs. Patimkin is cold toward Brenda, her own daughter, and clearly skeptical of Neil, based on his humble class origins. When, toward the end of the story, Mrs. Patimkin finds Brenda's diaphragm under a pile of sweaters in a drawer, she writes a distraught letter, which she sends via air mail to Brenda at college. It is primarily Mrs. Patimkin's response to the situation which seems to influence Brenda to end the relationship with Neil.

Ron Patimkin

Ron Patimkin is Brenda's brother. Ron was an athlete at Ohio State University, in Columbus, Ohio, and shares the Patimkin family preoccupation with sports, competition, and athletic activities. He marries Harriet in a big wedding, which Neil attends. Ron invites Neil to listen to his "Columbus" record, which is a sort of college yearbook narrated through such events as the last basketball game of the season, in which Ron played. The record ends with the singing of "Goodbye, Columbus . . . ," a nostalgic farewell to college life for graduating seniors. It is this line from which the story takes its title, and which expresses Neil's eventual sense of nostalgia for his brief relationship with Brenda.

Mr. Scapello

Mr. Scapello is Neil's boss at the library. He gives Neil a promotion, with the implication that Neil can expect to work his way up the library hierarchy, should he continue his job there.

Laura Simpson Stolowitch

Laura Stolowitch is Brenda's friend, with whom Brenda plays tennis the first time she and Neil arrange to meet. Brenda calls her "Simp."

Susan

Susan is Neil's cousin, the daughter of his Aunt Gladys and Uncle Max, with whom Neil lives.

Themes

Love, Sex and Relationships

The story centers around the development of Neil's relationship with Brenda, from their first meeting to their final breakup. The first person narration portrays the relationship from Neil's perspective, highlighting the class differences between the two of them. A significant element of their relationship is their sexual encounters, first in her

family TV room, and later, while he is staying at her house, in her bedroom at night. Neil describes his first sexual encounter with Brenda in terms of "winning," using the metaphor of the competitive game to describe the experience of making love to her; due to their class differences, having Brenda as a girlfriend represents a symbolic socioeconomic rise for him. Their first quarrel revolves around his suggestion that she get a diaphragm, her initial negative response to the idea, and eventual conciliation. For Neil, the issue of the diaphragm represents a gesture of commitment on Brenda's part. It also becomes a nexus of the power dynamics between the two of them: Neil, in part, wants her to take his suggestion because he feels that she has all the power in the relationship; he wants her to do what he says for once, rather than their usual dynamic, in which he does everything she tells him to do. The diaphragm becomes a key element of their relationship after her parents find it and are dismayed at the discovery. As a result, Brenda chooses loyalty to her family over her commitment to Neil.

Families

Family dynamics are a central focus of this story. Neil's working class family is portrayed in stark contrast to Brenda's wealthy family. Much of the narration is taken up with Neil's perceptions of Brenda's family members, her household, and their family dynamics. His own family situation, living with his aunt and uncle, since his parents have moved to Arizona, serves as a backdrop for the foreignness of Brenda's household. Neil gains further insight into Brenda's father's perceptions of his work and family when he sees Mr. Patimkin at his place of business. Brenda's brother Ron's wedding to Harriet Ehrlich is described in terms of a characterization of the relatives and Neil's interactions with some of them. Throughout these interactions and observations, Neil attempts both to compensate for his "lower" class standing and to envision himself becoming a member of the Patimkin family.

Class Divisions

The central dynamic of Neil's relationship with Brenda is based on their differences in socioeconomic class. Although they are both Jewish, the fact that Brenda's family is wealthy and Neil's is not means that they come from completely different worlds. Brenda's family started out in Newark, New Jersey, where Neil currently resides, thus indicating the Patimkins' rise in class as they moved out of Newark. Neil's insecurity in the presence of Brenda's family is primarily due to his painful awareness of his ''lower'' class standing. This class division is central to the power dynamic in his relationship with Brenda, as she seems to determine almost everything they do together. Neil's interactions with Brenda's uncle Leo, at the wedding, further expand upon the class dynamic between them; Leo blatantly congratulates Neil on his luck in the prospect of marrying ''up'' into the financial abundance of the Patimkin family. Ultimately, the class divisions between Neil and Brenda contribute to tearing them apart, but it is left unclear if it is primarily Neil's insecurities about their differences which negatively affect their relationship, or if Brenda genuinely looks down on him.

Self-knowledge

This is a story of self-examination and self-discovery for Neil. In his involvement with Brenda, Neil attempts to fit into her upper-middle-class Jewish family, remaining continually aware that it is not an easy or a comfortable fit. At the end of the story, after he and Brenda have in effect broken up, Neil experiences a symbolic epiphany in his sense of self and personal identity. This renewed sense of self, in the wake of his breakup with Brenda, is further symbolized by the dawning of the Jewish New Year, which implies a new beginning for Neil.

Nostalgia

The title of the story refers to Brenda's brother Ron's yearbook record album, which ends with the song lyrics, ''Goodbye, Columbus.'' The lyric literally refers to the nostalgia of the graduating college senior who must say ''goodbye'' to his college years spent at Ohio State University in Columbus, Ohio. But this ''truckload of nostalgia'' symbolically represents the sense of nostalgia Neil feels for his relationship with Brenda, which lasted only half a summer. Like the years spent in college, Neil, as narrator of the story, knows that his time spent with Brenda can never be recaptured. As Neil tells the story of their relationship in retrospect, it is infused with this sense of nostalgia for a bittersweet youthful experience.

Fantasy

Neil ultimately comes to identify with the little boy who comes to the library every day to look at the book of Gauguin paintings of Tahiti. The boy's preoccupation with these images of a foreign land functions as a form of fantasy, in which the locations in the paintings seem to him a sort of paradise, compared to his own life. The world of wealth and abundance in which Brenda lives functions for Neil as a similar fantasy life. He comes to realize that his own foray into her world is similar to engaging in a fantasy life through looking at pictures in a book. It seems to be a paradise of abundance that he can never realistically inhabit. The fact that the book is finally taken off the shelf and borrowed by another library patron symbolizes Neil's realization that Brenda could never really be ''his,'' but only a temporary excursion into a fantasy world.

Competition and Games

Brenda's family is completely preoccupied with sports, athletics, games, and competition. Neil carries these themes throughout the narrative as meta-

Topics for Further Study

- The little boy who comes to the library every day in ''Goodbye, Columbus'' spends his time looking only at a book of paintings of native women in Tahiti by Paul Gauguin. Roth uses the imagery of the paintings to symbolize a world of escapist fantasy. Find a book of paintings by Gauguin. In what ways are these paintings especially suited to the story's theme of fantasy and escapism?

- The novella ''Goodbye, Columbus'' was made into a movie by the same title in 1969. Watch the movie and compare and contrast the ways in which the themes of the novella are treated in the cinematic form.

- Roth's stories are usually about Jewish characters and include themes of Jewish culture and identity. Read another short story or novella by Roth. In what ways does it treat these themes similar to or different from the ways they are handled in the story ''Goodbye, Columbus''?

- Roth intersperses Yiddish words throughout his story. While Yiddish is rooted in Jewish culture, it has also become a part of the idiom of American English. Compile a list of Yiddish words you know or have heard, and what they mean.

phors for his relationship with Brenda and his interactions with her family. Neil continually feels that he is being challenged to compete with Brenda and her family, which symbolizes his feelings of inadequacy in the face of their upper-middle-class lifestyle.

Style

Point of View and Narration

This story is narrated from the first person restricted point of view. Neil Klugman is both the narrator and the protagonist and everything is portrayed from his perspective. This is effective because this is a story about identity and self-discovery; what is important is how Neil perceives himself and his relationships with others, particularly Brenda, and how these perceptions change over the course of the story.

Setting

This story is set during the 1950s in Newark, New Jersey, the New York City metropolitan area, and Cambridge, Massachusetts. The settings are important in establishing the class divisions between Neil's family and Brenda's family. The geography of the city becomes a map of socioeconomic divisions. For instance, Brenda's family used to live in Newark, where Neil now lives with his aunt and uncle. This information indicates that the Patimkins once shared the socioeconomic standing that Neil's family holds but moved their way up the socioeconomic ladder, as indicated by their current residence in the suburbs. Areas of New Jersey and New York are also described in terms of the flow of particular ethnic populations throughout the century in and out of particular neighborhoods and socioeconomic strata within the city.

Yiddish

Roth's story is smattered with Yiddish words and expressions, which capture the flavor of Jewish culture. The use or non-use of Yiddish words by various characters in the story is significant in indicating their relationship to Jewish identity. For instance, Mr. Patimkin uses the Yiddish word ''gonif,'' which Neil knows means ''thief.'' Mr. Patimkin comments that his own children do not

know Yiddish; they are so assimilated into mainstream American society that he refers to them as ''goyim''—a Yiddish term which is a derogatory expression for non-Jewish people. Other Yiddish words that appear in the story are ''jahrzeit,'' ''schmuck,'' ''mazel tov,'' ''shtarke,'' ''poilishehs,'' and ''schmaltz.''

Allegory and Symbolism

An allegory is a use of figurative language in which the literal elements are meant to be interpreted symbolically. A central allegory of this story is indicated by the title ''Goodbye, Columbus,'' which refers to the *Columbus* album which Brenda's brother Ron plays for Neil. The album is a narrated yearbook account of Ron's senior year in college at Ohio State in Columbus, Ohio, which ends with the nostalgic song lyric, ''Goodbye, Columbus.'' Although the song and the album narration are about the nostalgia of the college graduate for his alma mater, it takes on an allegorical meaning in speaking to Neil's sense of loss and nostalgia at the ending of his relationship with Brenda.

The Novella

This story is in the form of the novella—sometimes referred to as a novelette—meaning that it is shorter than a novel but longer than a short story. The form of the novella originated in medieval Italy, where it was characterized by tales based on local occurrences. In England, Geoffrey Chaucer is credited with having introduced the novella form through his *Canterbury Tales*. The novella is often characterized by a ''frame narrative,'' in which the narrator is a character who is telling the story or series of stories. The development of both the modern novel and the modern short story was in part influenced by the novella form.

Historical Context

Jewish Holidays

Toward the end of the story, Neil and Brenda agree to spend the weekend of the Jewish holidays together. Specifically, it is during the Jewish High Holy Day of Rosh Hashanah, which is the Jewish New Year and usually occurs in mid to late September. As the end of summer had indicated the end of

Compare & Contrast

- **1950s:** Radcliffe College, which Brenda attends, is a women's college and sister school to Harvard, a men's college.

  1999: Radcliffe College merges with Harvard University; both are now completely co-ed.

- **1950s:** Conservative Judaism, which originated in the 1840s, largely adheres to traditional Jewish religious practices, while allowing for some modernizing of these traditions. Less modernized than Reform Judaism, Conservative Judaism holds closer to the practices of Orthodoxy.

  1990s: In 1985 the Conservative Jewish movement makes a significant change in policy when it begins to allow for the ordaining of female rabbis. This change increases the differences between Reform and Orthodox Jewish practices.

- **Pre-World-War-II era:** There are approximately 11 million Yiddish-speaking people in the world.

  Post-World-War-II era: Approximately half the world's population of Yiddish-speaking people have perished in the Holocaust.

- **1950s:** Although the diaphragm is available to married women, access to birth control is limited for young, unmarried women, and abortions are performed only illegally and often under conditions hazardous to the pregnant woman.

  1990s: Women have greater access to birth control options, after the birth control pill became readily available to American women in the 1960s, and abortion was made legal in the early 1970s.

---

their relationship, the story's end on the dawn of the Jewish New Year indicates a sense of rebirth and a fresh, new beginning for Neil.

Movie: **Ma and Pa Kettle in the City**

Neil mentions that he and Brenda sneak into the drive-in movies to see the last fifteen minutes of whatever show is playing that night. They agree that their favorite last fifteen minutes of a movie is *Ma and Pa Kettle in the City*. This refers to a series of movies released between 1949 and 1955, featuring Ma and Pa Kettle, "hillbillies" from Washington state, in various encounters with more urban, sophisticated elements of American culture. The series is similar in theme to the later TV series, *The Beverly Hillbillies*, which is about members of a poor, rural family who move to Beverly Hills, California, after discovering oil on their land. The earlier series included *Ma and Pa Kettle* (1949), *Ma and Pa Kettle Go to Town* (1950), *Ma and Pa Kettle at the Fair* (1951), *Ma and Pa Kettle Back on the Farm* (1951), *Ma and Pa Kettle on Vacation* (1953), *Ma and Pa Kettle at Home* (1954), and *Ma and Pa Kettle at Waikiki* (1955). The mention of this series

in the story is significant in that it emphasizes the theme of encounter between two socioeconomic classes, such as the one between Neil and Brenda.

Mary McCarthy

When Neil first asks Brenda to get a diaphragm, her response is negative. After he suggests she go to "Margaret Sanger, in New York" to get fitted for one, Brenda asks if this is something he's done before. Neil responds, "'I read Mary McCarthy.'" When, toward the end of the story, they check into a hotel room together, and Neil asks if she's done this before, she responds, "'I read Mary McCarthy.'" Mary McCarthy (1912–1989) was a novelist, critic, and editor, known, as stated in *Encyclopaedia Britannica Online*, for "bitingly satiric commentaries on marriage, sexual expression, the impotence of intellectuals, and the role of women in contemporary urban America." At the time of this story's publication in 1959, McCarthy had published three novels: *The Company She Keeps* (1942), *The Oasis* (1949), and *The Groves of the Academe* (1952). Her first autobiography, *Memories of a Catholic Girlhood*, was published in 1957.

Paul Gauguin

At his job in the library, Neil encounters a little boy who comes in every day to look at a large book of paintings by Paul Gauguin. Gauguin (1848–1903) was a French artist known for his colorful paintings of native women in Tahiti, an island in the Pacific Ocean where he lived from 1891 to 1893 and from 1895 to 1901. Gauguin was influential in the art world for breaking with the impressionist movement and becoming a master of the symbolist movement in artistic style. His most famous painting, one of his masterpieces, is entitled *Where Do We Come From? What Are We? Where Are We Going?* Gauguin valued what he saw as ''primitive'' life among the native Tahitians above the bourgeois materialism of Western culture. His paintings in the story represent an escapist fantasy in a ''resort''-like foreign paradise for the little boy, just as Brenda's upper-middle-class world represents an escapist fantasy for Neil, as remote and unreachable as Tahiti is for the little boy.

Margaret Sanger

When Neil first asks Brenda that she get fitted for a diaphragm, he suggests she go to ''Margaret Sanger, in New York.'' Margaret Sanger (1879–1966) is known as a pioneer in making birth control readily available to women in the United States and elsewhere. It was Sanger, a nurse, who first coined the term ''birth control.'' She opened the first birth control clinic in the United States in Brooklyn in 1916, for which she was arrested in 1917. Sanger influenced legal changes that allowed physicians to give women advice about birth control and succeeded in altering the Comstock Act of 1873, according to which pamphlets on birth control and contraceptive devises were considered obscene materials and therefore illegal to distribute. Sanger founded the American Birth Control League in 1921, which became the Birth Control Federation of America, renamed the Planned Parenthood Organization of America in 1942.

Martin Buber

During a conversation with Mrs. Patimkin, in which she attempts to determine his Jewish affiliations, Neil asks if she is familiar with the work of Martin Buber, which she is clearly not. Martin Buber (1878–1965) was one of the most renowned, as well as controversial, modern Jewish philosophers. He was born in Vienna but eventually settled in Palestine, where he was influential in teaching and in establishing educational institutions. Buber was raised in a family of assimilated, secular Jews, but in adulthood he became interested in Judaism. The fundamental concept of Buber's modern Jewish philosophy is the I-Thou relationship, as explained in his most famous work, *I and Thou* (1923). Buber was less concerned with maintaining the observant practices of Judaism than with the relationship between the individual and God, nature, and other men.

Yiddish

The characters in Roth's story occasionally include Yiddish words in their dialogue. The Yiddish language, associated with Ashkenazie Jews, originated in the tenth century from Hebrew and Aramaic roots but later developed through the influence of Germanic and Slavic languages, although it is written in the Hebrew alphabet. Before World War II there were over ten million Yiddish-speaking people in the world, but some half of them perished in the Holocaust. Many Yiddish words are still used by English-speaking Jews; others have made their way into the mainstream of the English language.

Critical Overview

The novella ''Goodbye, Columbus,'' was first published in the 1959 collection, *Goodbye, Columbus, and Five Short Stories*, by Philip Roth, for which he received the National Book Award. Other stories in the collection include ''The Conversion of the Jews,'' ''Epstein,'' ''Defender of the Faith,'' ''You Can't Tell a Man by the Song he Sings,'' and ''Eli, the Fanatic.'' ''Goodbye, Columbus'' was adapted to the screen in the 1969 movie by the same title, produced by Paramount, directed by Larry Peerce and starring Ali McGraw as Brenda Patimkin and Richard Benjamin as Neil Klugman.

Upon its publication, *Goodbye, Columbus, and Five Short Stories* received immediate and vehement condemnation by rabbis across the country, who considered Roth's portrayal of Jews and Judaism to be anti-Semitic, a viewpoint which they expressed in letters and sermons. As stated in the Gale Group's *Contemporary Authors Online*, it was to be ''the first of many Roth books to be castigated from the synagogue pulpits.'' John N. McDaniel explains Roth's point of view and his response to his critics:

Richard Ellmann, flanked by Robert Lowell (left) and Philip Roth (right) holding the book "Goodbye, Columbus" at the National Book Awards in New York City. Roth's "Goodbye, Columbus" won the National Book Award for fiction in 1960.

Roth has repeatedly answered his critics from the Jewish community by insisting that as a writer he has no obligation to write Jewish "propaganda.". . . Jewish critics, Roth maintains, confuse the purpose of the writer with the purpose of the public relations man. Jews feel that Roth is "informing" on Jews when he should be providing a picture of the positive aspects of Jewish life; Roth argues that he is indeed an informer, but all that he has told the gentiles is that "the perils of human nature afflict the members of our minority."

McDaniel defends Roth's work against charges of anti-Semitism on the grounds that his stories address more generalized human concerns in the literary mode of "social realism":

> If we would understand Roth's intentions and achievements as a writer of fiction, we must look at his central characters not as Jews in an ideological, traditional, or metaphysical sense, but as men yearning to discover themselves by swimming into dangerous waters beyond social and familial structures: beyond the last rope. Only by so approaching Roth's fiction are we likely to see what it is that the stories are really about.

Goodbye, Columbus, and Five Short Stories remained popular despite censures from Jewish religious leaders. Its defenders praise the use of humor, the use of Jewish-American dialect, and the representation of the feelings of alienation of many post-War American Jews, caught between the guilt and trauma of the Holocaust and the forces of assimilation that came with post-War prosperity. Critics recognized Roth as a fresh, new voice in literature. As Irving Howe has observed, "His stories were immediately recognizable as his own, distinctive in voice, attitude, and subject. . . ." McDaniel describes the stories in *Goodbye, Columbus, and Five Short Stories* as "sharp-edged and well-crafted." Critics also praised Roth's use of humor. According to Joseph Epstein, this first volume by the young author demonstrated that "[Roth] is famously funny, dangerously funny, as Mel Brooks once characterized the kind of humor that can cause strokes from laughter." Roth is also noted for his portrayal and commentary on American life. Categorizing Roth as a "social realist," McDaniel claims that his works "illustrate important insights into America's cultural predicament as Roth sees it from his own vantage point: up close and personal. . . . No other living writer has so rigorously and actively attempted to describe the destructive element of experience in American life. . . ."

Roth's third novel, *Portnoy's Complaint* (1969), is his most well known, most popular, and most controversial. The book immediately became highly controversial for its use of scatological language, bordering on the pornographic, and, as with *Goodbye, Columbus, and Five Short Stories*, for its depiction of Jews, for which it was also banned by rabbis across the country. However, the novel is also credited with catapulting Jewish-American literature into the realm of popular culture. *Portnoy's Complaint* was adapted to the screen in a 1972 Warner Brothers production, written and directed by Ernest Lehman.

Many subsequent novels by Roth feature the protagonist Nathan Zuckerman, a Jewish writer, generally considered to be a stand-in for Roth himself, in what critics assume to be autobiographical works disguised as fiction. The Zuckerman trilogy includes *The Ghost Writer*, *Zuckerman Unbound*, and *The Anatomy Lesson*, which were collected into one volume entitled *Zuckerman Bound: A Trilogy and Epilogue*, in 1984. Roth won the 1987 National Book Critics Circle Award for *The Counter Life*, a fourth installment in the Zuckerman series.

Criticism

Liz Brent

Brent has a Ph.D. in American culture, specializing in cinema studies, from the University of Michigan. She is a freelance writer and teaches courses in American cinema. In the following essay, Brent discusses Neil's identity crisis.

"Goodbye, Columbus" is a coming-of-age story, in which the twenty-three-year-old protagonist, Neil Klugman, grapples with his sense of self, particularly in relation to his Jewish identity. The event that that precipitates this identity crisis is meeting Brenda Patimkin, with whom he has a relationship over the course of a summer. While Brenda and Neil are both Jewish, their differences in socioeconomic class create the central tensions of their relationship. Neil lives with his aunt and uncle in a lower-middle-class area of Newark, New Jersey, and works in a public library. Brenda is a college student at Radcliff College in Boston, Massachusetts, spending her summer vacation at her upper-middle-class family's house in the suburbs outside of New York City.

The class differences between Neil and Brenda are intertwined with their vast differences in Jewish identity. Brenda's family is assimilationist, in that their wealth leads them to de-emphasize their Jew-

ish cultural heritage. For instance, Brenda tells Neil that she has gotten a "nose job," plastic surgery on her nose, in order to remove the "bump" in her nose structure, which is considered a Jewish facial characteristic. She tells him it cost a thousand dollars to have it done, a sign both of her family's wealth in being able to afford cosmetic surgery, and of the value they place on shedding their Jewish features so as to assimilate more easily into mainstream, non-Jewish American culture. Neil's disdain for Brenda's "nose job" is expressed later in the narration, when he meets Brenda's father, Mr. Patimkin, and sees the natural nose feature, which Brenda had inherited from him. Neil regards the bump in Mr. Patimkin's nose in positive terms, describing it as a "diamond," which suggests the symbolic value Neil himself places on this sign of Jewish identity: "Brenda's old nose fitted him well. There was a bump in it, all right; up at the bridge it seemed as though a small eight-sided diamond had been squeezed in under the skin." He describes the removal of this "diamond" from Brenda's nose in terms that imply that getting a "nose job" is equivalent to flushing a beautiful and valuable diamond down the toilet: "I knew Mr. Patimkin would never bother to have that stone cut from his face, and yet, with joy and pride, no doubt, had paid to have Brenda's diamond removed and dropped down some toilet in Fifth Avenue Hospital." Later, Mr. Patimkin expresses some sense of ambivalence about the degree to which his children have lost their Jewish heritage in their efforts toward assimilation, even disdainfully describing them at as non-Jewish. When Brenda's father uses a Yiddish word, based in Jewish cultural heritage, he is surprised that Neil knows what it means, as his own children, he claims, are "goyim," a derogatory term for non-Jewish people.

Yet the Patimkin's are not simply or unequivocally assimilationist. Neil has an uncomfortable interaction with Mrs. Patimkin in discussing Jewish religious affiliations and organizations. Just as Neil is painfully aware of his class differences with the Patimkins, he is also defensive and insecure in discussing his Jewish identity with Mrs. Patimkin. Their conversation, which Neil regards from an antagonistic perspective, highlights the differences in their Jewish cultural identities. Mrs. Patimkin is checking a mailing list for Hadassah, a Jewish women's organization. Hadassah was founded in 1912 as the Women's Zionist Organization of America, known for its efforts in the areas of health care, education, and the needs of Jewish children. When

What Do I Read Next?

- *Portnoy's Complaint* (1969) is Roth's third novel, and is his most famous, most popular, and most controversial. This novel is a stream-of-consciousness narrative by the protagonist, a young Jewish man, speaking to his psychoanalyst, who says nothing.

- *Goodbye, Columbus and Five Short Stories* (1959) is Roth's first published collection, which won him the 1959 Book Critics Award. It includes the novella ''Goodbye, Columbus'' and the short stories ''The Conversion of the Jews,'' ''Epstein,'' ''Defender of the Faith,'' ''You Can't Tell a Man by the Song he Sings,'' and ''Eli, the Fanatic.''

- *The Oxford Book of Jewish Stories* (1998), edited and with an introduction by Ilan Stavans, is a collection and translation into English of international Jewish short stories. It includes ''The Conversion of the Jews'' by Philip Roth. The Introduction covers language and tradition in Jewish short stories.

- *God: Stories* (1998), edited by C. Michael Curtis, is a collection of short stories on themes of God, faith, spirituality, belief, and doubt. This collection includes ''Defender of the Faith'' by Philip Roth.

- *First Sightings: Stories of American Youth* (1993), edited by John Loughery, is a collection of short stories featuring protagonists from three to eighteen years old. It includes ''The Conversion of the Jews'' by Philip Roth.

Mrs. Patimkin asks if Neil's mother belongs to Hadassah, he nervously says that she did, he's not sure if she does now, but that his Aunt Sylvia is also in Hadassah. Mrs. Patimkin then asks Neil if he belongs to B'nai Brith, a Jewish men's organization, which he is not a member of. Mrs. Patimkin, who is active in an Orthodox temple, the most strictly observant Jewish religious affiliation, then questions Neil about his religious affiliations, inquiring if he belongs to a temple. Neil attempts to hide the fact that he is not affiliated with a synagogue or Jewish organization, for fear that Mrs. Patimkin will disapprove of his ''pagan'' tendencies. When Mrs. Patimkin invites him to attend Friday night services at their temple, he stammers, and says, '''I'm just Jewish.''' With this simple statement Neil attempts to reconcile his sense of his Jewish identity with his religious ''paganism,'' evidenced by his lack of religious affiliation or observance. Yet, he still wishes ''desperately'' to ''convince her I wasn't an infidel.'' When he attempts to gain some legitimacy in her eyes by asking if she's heard of Martin Buber, her response indicates her complete ignorance of this modern Jewish philosopher. Martin Buber is one of the most renowned, if controversial, Jewish philosophers of the twentieth century. While Buber felt that strict observance of Jewish religious laws was not necessary or important, his central tenet, expressed in his 1923 book, *I and Thou*, stresses the importance of the relationship between man and fellow man, man and nature, and man and God. Neil's mention of Buber in this context is ironic in that the entire story revolves around Neil's attempt to establish a genuine relationship with Brenda, which ultimately seems impossible, given their cultural differences.

Mrs. Patimkin tells Neil that she is Orthodox, while her husband is Conservative. Conservative Judaism, while adhering to observance of traditional Jewish religious law, is less strict than Orthodox. Reform Judaism is the least concerned with observing traditional Jewish religious law, in favor of modernizing religious observance practices. Mrs. Patimkin then states that '''Brenda is nothing,''' meaning that Brenda is not religious. Neil, however, attempts to make a joke of this statement by punning on the terms ''conservative'' and ''reform.'' '''I'd say Brenda is conservative. Maybe a little re-

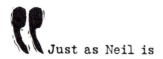Just as Neil is painfully aware of his class differences with the Patimkins, he is also defensive and insecure in discussing his Jewish identity with Mrs. Patimkin. Their conversation, which Neil regards from an antagonistic perspective, highlights the differences in their Jewish cultural identities."

formed. . . .'" Neil realizes that joking about Judaism with Mrs. Patimkin will not go over well, and so, when the phone rings, "rescuing" him from the conversation, he says "a silent Orthodox prayer to the Lord." The humor in this lies in the irony of a non-religious Jewish man saying an "Orthodox prayer to the Lord," in thanks for "rescuing" him from being found out as a "pagan" and an "infidel" by Mrs. Patimkin, who is genuinely Orthodox.

Later in the story, however, Neil's internal thoughts about God take on a more serious tone, as they are an expression of a genuine desire for insight and self-knowledge, albeit with a strong edge of irony, cynicism, and skepticism. While he is waiting for Brenda to get fitted for a diaphragm, Neil wanders into a Catholic church and sits down in a pew. Holding his hands together, he leans forward and closes his eyes. In this praying posture, Neil makes "a little speech" to himself: "Can I call the self-conscious words I spoke a prayer? At any rate, I called my audience God." Neil's "prayer" takes the form of his first concentrated attempt to understand his relationship with Brenda, asking, "What is it I love, Lord? Why have I chosen? Who is Brenda? The race is to the swift. Should I have stopped to think?" Neil goes on to question his "carnality" and his "acquisitiveness," maintaining in a blatantly sacrilegious assertion that such

pleasures of the flesh are a part of God: "If we meet You at all, God, it's that we're carnal, and acquisitive, and thereby partake of You. I am carnal, and I know You approve, I just know it. But how carnal can I get? I am acquisitive. Where do I turn now in my acquisitiveness? Where do we meet? Which prize is You?" Neil expresses some awareness that his "love" for Brenda is in part a love for the wealth and assimilation she represents; he cynically suggests that the "prize" that is "You" (God) is in fact these material luxuries and the assimilation they enable: "Gold dinnerware, sporting-goods trees, nectarines, garbage disposals, bumpless noses, Patimkin Sink, Bonwit Teller—." Neil concludes that "damn it, God, that *is* You!" that God is the materialism and consumerism made possible by wealth. This line of thinking on Neil's part indicates a complete crisis in faith. He indicates that he is aware of his own foolishness and wrong-headedness, by concluding, "God only laughed, that clown." (One can easily see why rabbis were outraged by Roth's representations of Jewish faith!) Roth does not provide the reader with a moral compass by which to chart Neil's bizarre rumination on God. Rather, the reader is drawn into the sense of crisis experienced by Neil himself, who waivers between worshipping a God of material goods and carnal pleasures, and mocking his own lack of faith.

Neil's identity crisis reaches an epiphany at the end of the story, after he leaves Brenda and the relationship behind him. While wandering around the Harvard campus, he stops to look at his reflection in the darkened window of the library. The "mirror" of the window symbolizes Neil's mental self-reflection. Seeing his external form reflected in the window, Neil wishes for some sense of self-knowledge of his internal self. Neil seriously questions the nature of his "love" for Brenda, and what that love has to do with who he really is: "What was it inside me that had turned pursuit and clutching into love, and then turned it inside out again? What was it that had turned winning into losing, and losing—who knows—into winning? I was sure I had loved Brenda, though standing there, I knew I couldn't any longer." The identity crisis which had been sparked by Neil's entry into Brenda's world of luxury and Brenda's family's concept of Jewish identity is in part resolved for Neil by his realization that, whoever he is, he is certainly not *that*.

Although no definite conclusions are drawn in Neil's mind, a self-knowledge is symbolically achieved: "I looked hard at the image of me, at that darkening of the glass, and then my gaze pushed through it, over the cool floor, to a broken wall of books, imperfectly shelved.'' The image of the ''broken wall'' and the books ''imperfectly shelved'' symbolizes Neil's acceptance of himself as ''imperfect.'' It is highly significant that Neil reaches home ''just as the sun was rising on the first day of the Jewish New Year.'' This closing image provides multiple symbols of renewal, both in the rising sun, and the first day of a New Year. Further, it is not a secular New Year, but a ''Jewish'' New Year. Neil's renewed sense of himself as a Jew, while not clearly defined, is expressed in an image full of hope.

Source: Liz Brent, Critical Essay on ''Goodbye, Columbus,'' in *Short Stories for Students*, The Gale Group, 2001.

Jay L. Halio

In the following essay, Halio presents an overview of ''Goodbye, Columbus,'' and examines the character development of Neil Klugman.

Roth's most famous protagonist, Alexander Portnoy, complains that he is living inside a Jewish joke and pleads with his psychiatrist, Dr. Spielvogel, to help get him out of it. Though at first he seems oblivious of it, Neil Klugman in ''Goodbye, Columbus'' lives inside a burlesque-show joke—a sexual tease that from the opening paragraph sets his hormones pumping wildly. He describes his first sight of Brenda Patimkin at the country club swimming pool, when she asks him to hold her glasses. After her dive, as Neil returns her glasses he gazes after her. ''I watched her move off. Her hands suddenly appeared behind her. She caught the bottom of her suit between her thumb and index finger and flicked what flesh had been showing back where it belonged. My blood jumped.'' Without any kind of formal introduction, Neil calls her that very evening for a date. Thus their affair begins.

That Neil is a ''nice Jewish boy'' who quickly captures the reader's sympathy is manifest from his background, his education, his current job, and his warm family relationships. Educated at the Newark Colleges of Rutgers University with a degree in philosophy, he makes no apologies for not having gone to an Ivy League school or anything so prestigious (Brenda is a Radcliffe undergraduate). An only child, he lives with his aunt and uncle and their daughter in a Jewish neighborhood of Newark, because his mother and father, afflicted with asthma, have immigrated to the aridity of Arizona. Neil is devoted to his surrogate family, especially his Aunt Gladys who, like any Jewish mama, worries about his food, his social behavior, and anything else that

> "That Neil is a 'nice Jewish boy' who quickly captures the reader's sympathy is manifest from his background, his education, his current job, and his warm family relationships. . . . But nice Jewish boys also have strong masculine glands, and Neil is no exception."

affects her loved ones. Like many nice Jewish boys, Neil is often impatient of her concern and desperately, sometimes bluntly, tries to reassure her so that she will leave him alone. He works at the Newark Public Library in a respectable position that promises early promotion to the kind of industrious, conscientious young man Neil appears to his immediate superiors to be.

But nice Jewish boys also have strong masculine glands, and Neil is no exception. When he first sees Brenda, no wonder his heart jumps. Although this is not an attraction Roth often deals with later (Neil is not enticed by the forbidden fruit a shiksa, or gentile woman, represents to an older generation of Jews), in its way the situation is still typical. Brenda is Jewish; it is at a Jewish country club that Neil meets her. But Jewish American Princess that she is (Neil, as narrator, never uses the phrase himself), Brenda is rich, spoiled, and smart, if somewhat shortsighted (literally and perhaps figuratively). She knows her attractions, and she knows how to use them.

And so when Neil calls her, Brenda does not put him off. Evidently without a current boyfriend (though she has had her share in the past), she allows Neil to meet her at tennis with her girlfriend, Laura Simpson (''Simp'') Stolowitch. The game Brenda plays is another good initial indication of her character. Cocky, confident, she wins the set from Simp, but not in the ''one more game'' she tells Neil it will take when he arrives. Though dusk is falling, and falls, the two battle on into the dark, giving Neil a further chance to size Brenda up. He is struck by her ferocious play, her unwillingness to let the set end in a tie, and her reluctance to rush the net and put herself in physical jeopardy: "Her passion for winning a point seemed outmatched by an even stronger passion for maintaining her beauty as it was." After the game is over, as they walk off the court together Neil falls a step behind Brenda, giving him another opportunity to "appreciate" her: "Her hands did not twitch at her bottom, but the form revealed itself, covered or not, under the closeness of her khaki Bermudas. There were two wet triangles on the back of her tiny-collared white polo shirt, right where her wings would have been if she'd had a pair. She wore, to complete the picture, a tartan belt, white sock, and white tennis sneakers."

The suggestion of wings may be deliberately misleading, for Brenda is no angel, no more than Neil is, though to all outward appearances they are a nice Jewish couple. Moreover, in Neil's romantic/erotic gaze the wings image may be justified. Falling under a spell, he ignores warnings against the temptation Brenda represents. Although he registers her eagerness to win, which later will have important consequences for them—or him—and is irritated by her flip reply to where she goes to school, he perseveres in his pursuit of her. Further warnings, such as Brenda's comments on living in Newark or on the nose job she has had ("I was pretty. Now I'm prettier"), are also registered—and ignored.

Neil counters her responses with sarcastic wit, which Brenda either doesn't get or criticizes as being "nasty." Intent on the relationship, which he finds challenging, he tries to recover "civility," more or less successfully. When he asks for a closer look at her nose, Brenda takes the gambit, on which she too seems intent, and says, as he peers at her, "If I let you kiss me would you stop being nasty?" Whether or not this is another tease, or something more, Neil thinks he feels "a faint fluttering, as though something stirred so deep in her breasts, so far back it could make itself felt through her shirt. It was like the fluttering of wings." That the wings were so small, smaller than her breasts, does not bother him: "it would not take an eagle to carry me up those lousy hundred and eighty feet that make summer nights so much cooler in Short Hills [where Brenda lives] than they are in Newark."

That is how it all starts; the few pages that constitute the first chapter of the novella present the basic contours of the story and its theme. About halfway through the book, however, the story takes a different twist, as the burlesque-show joke deepens into something else. As often happens to nice Jewish boys, what starts out as an affair turns into love—with all its attendant complications. As this aspect of the story unfolds, Neil's true character reveals itself, also involving complications, for the writer as well as the narrator. From this earliest stage in his career, Roth shows that he cannot resist the urge to develop the character of a *schlemiel*. That is what Neil Klugman, despite his surname (which means "clever fellow"), turns out to be, though about this aspect of his protagonist's character Roth seems to be somewhat ambivalent or uncertain. On the one hand, he has developed and seems reluctant to surrender the sympathy Neil has earned; on the other hand, he finds all but irresistible the comedy latent in the predicament Neil gets himself into by falling in love with a girl like Brenda. But we are getting ahead of the story. Neil has still to meet Brenda's family, the Patimkins.

Mr. and Mrs. Patimkin are among the nouveau riche Jewish families that years earlier moved out of the city and into the suburbs. The fortune Mr. Patimkin made in the war by supplying sinks to army barracks is partly responsible for that; the rest is the result of his continuing hard work and shrewdness as a businessman who knows how to make a buck—lots of them. The Patimkin household thus comes in for the kind of satire that has since become a rich source for Roth's wit and humor—and his trademark, as viewed by many critics. When Brenda invites Neil to dinner for the first time, we see what lies ahead for him—and the Patimkins. The invitation comes after another day at the country club pool, where Brenda and Neil have disported themselves in the water and engaged in further erotic play. The invitation is spontaneous and, for Neil, unexpected, as he tries to explain to his naturally worried Aunt Gladys why he will not be home for dinner that night.

Neil has already met Brenda's older brother, Ron, at the pool. He is built on the lines of a Greek god, as Neil describes him: "suddenly, like a crew-cut Proteus rising from the sea, Ron Patimkin emerged from the lower depths we'd just inhabited and his immensity was before us." Ron is a playful, harmless Proteus, not very bright, but amiable and, like all the Patimkins, athletic. The comic juxtapositions Roth uses to describe Ron he also uses to describe Mr. Patimkin at the dinner table: "He was tall, strong, ungrammatical, and a ferocious eater." Brenda's kid sister is rather less amiable, not yet a princess but certainly a princess-in-training. Julie is "ten, round-faced, bright, who before dinner, while the other little girls on the street had been playing with jacks and boys and each other, had been on the back lawn putting golf balls with her father." Though she is the handsomest of them all, Mrs. Patimkin appears ominous and arouses an immediate dislike, or fear, in Neil: "She was disastrously polite to me, and with her purple eyes, her dark hair, and large, persuasive frame, she gave me the feeling of some captive beauty, some wild princess, who has been tamed and made the servant of the king's daughter—who was Brenda."

The comic potential of such a cast is great, and Roth exploits it fully and economically. Instead of transcribing the fragmented or garbled talk interrupting the Patimkins' energetic eating, he consolidates dialogue and description and presents them both in "one fell swoop." The result is just as funny as—perhaps funnier than—the actual talk, which the reader can easily imagine. Eating among these Brobdingnagians seems to reduce their guest, even to diminish him physically (or so he thinks), and gives early indications of the schlemiel that will emerge. The conflict between Mrs. Patimkin and Brenda also emerges, ever so subtly. In the midst of everything the erotic play continues, as Neil feels Brenda's fingers fondling his calf under the table.

After dinner the comedy continues, with somewhat darker overtones. Brenda describes her feelings about her mother and the jealousy between the two women, mother and daughter, which she calls "practically a case study." An excellent tennis player in her youth, Mrs. Patimkin arouses Brenda's admiration for what she was—then. Now the two constantly battle about money, about clothes, about everything. Brenda's snobbery again shows itself, but Neil chooses to ignore it, afraid to "lift the cover and reveal that hideous emotion I always felt for her, and is the underside of love." If Neil is falling in love with Brenda, he is nevertheless aware of the lust that has drawn him to her and keeps him by her side.

At this moment Julie interrupts, and another indication of Neil the schlemiel emerges, as he lets a basketball thrown at him bounce off his chest. Like Mr. Patimkin, Neil allows the child to win a game of "five and two," though a part of him desperately wants "to run little Julie into the ground." Extremely self-conscious, he feels the gaze of the Patimkins and even Carlota, the black maid who served dinner. Feeling humiliated, Neil is reassured when

Brenda says that even Ron, a star basketball player, lets Julie win.

The next morning Neil, at work in the library, has an experience that seems to comment on his involvement with Brenda and her family. As he goes to work he sees a little black boy in front of the library growling and snarling at the cement lions that guard the building. "Man, you's a coward," the boy says to one of them, and then growls again. Shortly afterward the boy enters the library and asks Neil where the "heart" section is. He means the *art* section, and Neil later finds him absorbed in a folio of Gauguin reproductions. The boy is struck by the serenity and beauty of the Tahitian women in the paintings: "These people, man, they sure does look cool," he says. "They ain't no yelling or shouting here, you could just see it." Turning the pages, he shows Neil another picture and says, "Man, that's the f—n' life."

The boy's rapture is not quite what Neil feels about Brenda and Short Hills, but it's close. In fact, Neil makes an explicit comparison, as he daydreams about meeting Brenda that evening in Short Hills, "which I could see now, in my mind's eye, at dusk, rose-colored, like a Gauguin stream." His rose-colored expectations are disappointed, however, for when he arrives Brenda and her family drive Ron to the airport, leaving Neil at home to baby-sit Julie. Angered by the imposition, he sends Julie off to watch television alone. His impulse is to leave quietly and return to Newark, where he feels he belongs, among his own humble people. But he doesn't leave. Instead, he explores the house, or rather the basement, where among other things he finds an unused bar with two dozen unopened bottles of Jack Daniels—"the bar of a wealthy man who never entertains drinking people, who himself does not drink, who, in fact, gets a fishy look from his wife when every several months he takes a shot of schnapps before dinner"—further comic commentary on the middle-class Jewish household the Patimkins' represents. Wanting a drink now himself, Neil is afraid to break the seal of one of the unopened bottles. He muses that the bar had not seen a dirty glass since Ron's bar mitzvah and probably wouldn't see another until one of the children was married or engaged. He then finds an old refrigerator full of fruit, to which he helps himself until discovered by Julie, who surprises him in the act of eating a nectarine. The handful of cherries he has also taken he drops into his pocket, afraid of further discovery.

Neil gets his revenge against Julie for the interruption and the game of five and two when he unmercifully beats her at Ping-Pong in the basement recreation room. Actually, Julie quits in hysterics before he is able to score the final point. She is outraged that Neil, no longer under the gaze of the family, will not make concessions and let her win, as he and the others had always done before. He completes his revenge after the family has gone to bed that night, when he makes love to Brenda for the first time: ''How can I describe loving Brenda?'' he muses. ''It was so sweet, as though I'd finally scored that twenty-first point.'' The juxtaposition of events is deliberate and reveals what the love affair is truly about: winning. The question is, Who is winning what?

In the episodes that follow Roth reemphasizes that the affair is a game—another aspect of the burlesque-show joke, or tease—and not truly love, despite Neil's longings and self-deceptions. First Neil plays games with an elderly, jowly gentleman who tries to check out the Gauguin book the little boy has been looking at during his daily trips to the library. Neil explains that the book has a ''hold'' on it and cannot be taken out. Later Neil and Brenda are at the country club; it is late evening, and they are alone. As the lights go out around the pool, Neil thinks they should be going home, but reassuring him it's all right to stay, Brenda starts asking him questions about himself—for the first time since they met. Although initially these are questions her mother wants answered, soon Brenda admits to her own curiosity, and then asks Neil if he loves her. He hesitates, and she says she will sleep with him anyway, whether he loves her or not. When he says he does not, she answers, ''I want you to.'' He refers to his library job, but she seems untroubled by his humble occupation, and continues: ''When you love me, there'll be nothing to worry about.'' Then they begin playing pool games, hiding from each other for longer and longer intervals, until Neil, anxious, confesses, ''I love you . . . I do.''

Gamesome, manipulative Brenda wins that one as she wins others. By now fully aware of what is happening, Neil seems not to care. They see each other every evening, make love whenever possible, and finally Brenda invites Neil to spend a week of his vacation at her house. Then they make love every night in her room. The day Neil arrives is the day Ron announces his engagement to Harriet, his girlfriend in Milwaukee, and the house plunges into turmoil preparing for a Labor Day wedding. Why the wedding is so rushed is not clear, though there are hints that Harriet may be pregnant. Neither is an explanation offered as to why the wedding is arranged by the groom's parents and not the bride's, following tradition. Perhaps no explanation is needed. Mr. Patimkin, the equivalent of a *nogid* (rich Jew of the shtetl) enjoys showing off what his money can buy, and in any event Roth wants Neil to be a wedding guest.

Roth's introduction of these events, however, is not simply to find yet another opportunity for satiric comedy, which first Harriet's arrival and then the wedding celebration afford. He means to juxtapose Neil's affair with Brenda against Ron's wedding to Harriet so that the issue of marriage between Neil and Brenda can come to the fore, as it does. Rather than proposing marriage to Brenda, which is the way their relationship seems to be heading, Neil instead proposes that she get a diaphragm, thereby forcing quite a different kind of issue.

Brenda rejects Neil's proposal, claiming that they are OK as they are, but Neil presses her. Although the best argument he can offer is that a diaphragm will make sex more pleasurable for him as well as safer for her, he ultimately admits that he wants her to get one simply to please him, to yield to his desire. It is another contest of wills between them, another attempt by Neil to assert his manhood against Brenda's domineering spirit. In many other respects she has successfully led him around by the nose, so that by the time he is living in her house he has actually begun to look like her, not only in dress—sneakers, sweat socks, khaki Bermudas, and all—but in manner and deportment; he has begun to look the way she wants him to. He has started to fit into the Patimkin family, much to his Aunt Gladys's disgust but precisely as Brenda wants. It is time for Neil either to assert himself or to lose his manhood altogether.

Why, then, doesn't Neil ask Brenda to marry him? He is sure he loves her, and she him, but somehow things don't seem quite right, as she promised him they would be the night at the pool. Fearing that anything other than a resounding ''Hallelujah!'' to a marriage proposal would utterly daunt him, he proposes the diaphragm instead, hardly realizing how much more daring the latter would actually be. More evidence of the kind of schlemiel Neil is occurs in a scene at Patimkin Kitchen and Bathroom Sinks. There Neil watches in amazement as men load sinks onto a truck, tossing them to one another, oblivious of the danger of dropping them. Suddenly Neil imagines himself directing them and hears himself screaming warnings. His reverie continues: ''Suppose Mr. Patimkin should come up to me and say, 'Okay, boy, you want to marry my daughter, let's see what you can do.' Well, he would see: in a moment that floor would be a shattered mosaic, a crunchy path of enamel. 'Klugman, what kind of worker are you? You work like you eat!' 'That's right, that's right, I'm a sparrow, let me go.' 'Don't you even know how to load and unload?' 'Mr. Patimkin, even breathing gives me trouble, sleep tires me out, let me go, let me go.''' Is this the real Neil Klugman? Where is the sensitive, clever young fellow Roth has been presenting to us? Where is the assertive, masculine chap who orders his lover to get fitted with a diaphragm? Is he capable only of stealing fruit and beating little Julie at Ping-Pong so long as no one is looking? or of telling transparent lies so that the black boy can enjoy his book in the library a little longer?

Obviously Neil is both men, and therein lies Roth's ambivalence toward his character and the source—conscious or otherwise—of both subterranean and surface comedy. While Neil's wit can puncture the pretentiousness of the Patimkins and other social-climbing middle-class Jews, he is also vulnerable within himself. He lacks the *cojones* of a real man. Arguing vehemently with Brenda about the diaphragm, he eventually agrees not to force her to get one. Whereupon she does.

The victory that should have been Neil's therefore becomes Brenda's. She even makes him accompany her to New York to the doctor's office, though she does not force him to go in with her. And when she comes out and Neil does not see her carrying a package, he thinks she may have changed her mind. Actually, he is relieved, but then his emotion turns completely around when Brenda tells him she's wearing the device. ''He said shall I wrap it up,'' she explains, ''or will you take it with you?'' Whereupon Neil cries, ''Oh Brenda, I love you.''

Roth's ambivalence toward Neil is matched by Neil's toward Brenda and leads to further indications of his schlemielhood. Even as Brenda apparently yields to Neil's wishes and is fitted with the diaphragm, Neil wanders away to St. Patrick's Cathedral and indulges in a kind of prayer: ''God, I said, I am twenty-three years old. I want to make the best of things. Now the doctor is about to wed Brenda to me, and I am not entirely certain this is all for the best. What is it I love, Lord? Why have I chosen? Who is Brenda? The race is to the swift.

Should I have stopped to think?'' Getting no answers, he perseveres, confessing his carnal and acquisitive nature and identifying it with God: ''I am carnal, and I know You approve, I just know it. But how carnal can I get? I am acquisitive. Where do I turn now in my acquisitiveness? Where do we meet? Which prize is You?'' Suddenly he feels ashamed and, still without an answer, walks out into the hubbub of Fifth Avenue, and hears, ''Which prize do you think, *schmuck?* Gold dinnerware, sporting-goods trees, nectarines, garbage disposals, bumpless noses, Patimkin Sink, Bonwit Teller—.'' The answer, which in his imagination Neil again insistently identifies with God, gets only a celestial belly laugh.

In later novels, preeminently in *Portnoy's Complaint* but also in *My Life as a Man* and in others, Roth develops ambivalence toward his protagonists for comic effect. His attitude can be related to the typical kind of Jewish humor in which Jews make fun of their own inconsistencies and contradictions, while frowning on anyone else's doing so. But Roth has other sources of humor. His excellent eye and ear capture, and his typewriter accurately transcribes, observations that not only are funny in themselves but serve as social commentary and as commentary too on the observer, in this instance Neil Klugman. Aunt Gladys is an excellent case in point, and though a minor character, she is surely a contender for the real heroine of the novella.

As against Neil's false sense of superiority and the Patimkin women's wealth and pretentiousness, Aunt Gladys stands as a model of common sense, hard work, wry humor, and shrewd perception. An early version of the typical Jewish mother in Roth's fiction, she partly eludes the stereotype by knowing how and when to stop nagging Neil, by her reduced role in the fiction (compare Sophie Portnoy later on), and by her innate stature as above all a decent, caring woman. Forever complaining about the work she has to do—for example, the four different meals she has to prepare at four different times for the members of her household, including herself—she simply gives vent to her feelings in a harmless, usually humorous way. Neil does not try to explain her odd dinnertime routine except to say that his aunt is ''crazy.'' From his rationalist viewpoint it certainly seems that way, but underlying the ''craziness'' is a firm resolve to serve the needs of her loved ones. Neil's flip comment thus boomerangs. Witty as he is, her wit matches his but, more important, Aunt Gladys differs from Neil in the depths and strengths of her commitments. Funny in her remarks and her fractured syntax—''I'll see it I'll believe it''—she is not merely a figure of fun but a standard of humanity against which others in the novella, including Neil, pale.

Roth wisely does not sentimentalize Aunt Gladys; in fact, he strongly opposes sentimentality, as he shows in his satiric portrait of Ron Patimkin. Large and amiable, Ron is devoted to the ''light classics'' of André Kostelanetz and Mantovani but above all to the album that gives this story its title and theme. Lying on his bed after a basketball game in the evening, Ron enjoys listening to the graduation record narrated by ''a Voice, bowel-deep and historic, the kind one associates with documentaries about the rise of Fascism.'' Nostalgia for the Class of '57 lulls Ron to sleep as he hums along with the band and the Voice intones ''goodbye, Ohio State, goodbye, red and white, goodbye, Columbus . . . goodbye, Columbus . . . goodbye.'' The perfect ending to a perfect day.

Source: Jay L. Halio, ''Nice Jewish Boys: The Comedy of 'Goodbye, Columbus' and the Early Stories,'' in *Philip Roth Revisited*, Twayne, 1992, pp. 13–22.

Helge Normann Nilsen

In the following essay, Nilsen examines Neil Klugman's attempts to establish an individual identity amidst various societal pressures.

In this novella by Philip Roth the protagonist, Neil Klugman, is involved in a struggle to develop and preserve an identity of his own amid different environments and conflicting impulses within himself. Throughout the story he makes love to Brenda Patimkin and tries to find a role in society that corresponds to what he regards as his own, unique self. In the process he loses Brenda, but he refuses to compromise and surrender what he regards as his integrity. As a result of this he remains mainly a detached observer in relation to the various settings and role models that make up the social universe of the story. Brenda is the only one that he seeks an intimate relationship with. However, Neil does not choose this outsider role solely for its own sake, as an expression of wilfulness. As a modern, liberal intellectual living in the conservative and repressive American society of the nineteen fifties, he identifies with a set of secular and rationalistic values that are bound to bring him into conflict with the world around him.

Neil's struggle to establish his own identity is highly understandable in view of his circumstances. He represents the third generation of a Jewish immigrant group that has experienced great changes and transitions. His milieu is basically working class or lower middle class and strongly colored by traditional Jewish ethnic attitudes and customs, but he himself is a librarian with a bachelor's degree in philosophy and a modern, assimilationist approach to American society. Neil finds it impossible to accept the narrow-minded concept of life of his relatives, especially his aunt Gladys. He is ready to break away from the lifestyle of the parental generation, and when he meets Brenda, he is attracted both to her beauty and her manners. A resident of the wealthy suburb of Short Hills, she seems to represent a different and better world. Newark and Short Hills constitute two sharply contrasted regions in the symbolic geography of the story, and Neil tries to define his own self mainly in relation to these two extremes, though the library where he works seems to represent a third alternative.

In the Patimkin household Neil is regarded as an outsider and he responds with acerbic inner comments to the various absurdities of this family. They are affluent, but crudely materialistic and snobbish, devoted to appearances, material wealth, social position and athletic prowess. Neil does not hesitate to characterize the whole clan as 'Brobdingnags' who make him feel small and insignificant at their overfilled dinner table. Everything about them and the class that they represent reinforces his conviction that this lifestyle does not correspond to the identity that he seeks for himself.

The library is disappointing to Neil because he cannot identify with the others there and worries that he may end up like one of them, a dusty librarian with a pale skin whose life becomes a bloodless devotion to his duties. Always alert and aware of the imperfections of his surroundings, Neil creates a distance between himself and his colleagues and wants to define himself in terms of his opposition to them, just as he does in relation to his own family and that of Brenda. In the library he achieves such a separation by sympathizing with a black boy who spends hours in the art book section looking at pictures of Gauguin's Tahiti paintings. Another librarian, John McKee, is worried about this little black intruder and what he may be up to in the stacks looking at pictures of nudes. But this racism and sexual anxiety and prudery are repellent to Neil, who has experienced and rejected such attitudes already in his own environment.

Neil appreciates the longings of the black boy for a better world, a freer and more sensuous life, which is so powerfully expressed in Gauguin's colorful scenes and figures. In the story, these pictures are part of a chain of images of an exotic setting which includes Neil's vision of Brenda as a Polynesian maiden and his later dream of a South Sea island. This imagery symbolizes an alternative lifestyle and a happiness which Neil also longs for. Though he is frustrated by the Patimkins, he is not yet ready to given up his dream of a different and more satisfying life which may lie in store for Brenda and himself. Short Hills is the same kind of dream for him that Tahiti is for the black boy, and he envisages the suburb 'at dusk, rose-colored, like a Gauguin stream.'

Neil tries to fulfil his dream by creating a separate realm of love between himself and Brenda which assumes a subversive function in relation to the respectable Puritanism of the Patimkin family. The young couple's erotic activities in the television room are a kind of conspiracy and a parallel to the black boy's hiding in the library to look at pictures. Gauguin himself lived in Tahiti, in voluntary exile from his native French bourgeoisie. Neil's conquest of Brenda and their surreptitious lovemaking are the means by which he not only bolsters his sense of masculinity, but also supports a part of his identity which he feels is threatened by his new situation. His efforts to help the black boy are also an element of this self-protective mechanism.

However, Brenda soon begins to reveal her insecurity and dependence on her parents' approval. They want to know more about Neil and his prospects, and she starts to question him in order to determine his social acceptability or lack of it. She also asks him if he loves her and tells him that she intends to go on sleeping with him whether he does or not. This declaration suggests that she regards her affair with Neil, up to this point, mainly as a sexual fling. She also reveals that she attributes the same motives to himself, something which he finds 'crude' because he has greater hopes for their relationship than that. Thus he is pained by her inability to understand the real nature of his feelings. From the start, it seems that the two of them have different concepts of love. Unable to appreciate Neil's motives for approaching her, Brenda believes that he does not love her yet, telling him that she wants him to do so and that when he does, 'there'll be nothing to worry about.' She has a superficial concept of love which has little relation to the actual process which is going on between them. He does love her,

> " He returns to the library with a new and greater awareness of its attractions and limitations. It is, after all, an institution where culture, art and dreams are allowed a kind of existence which is impossible in the other environments that he has known. . . ."

and that is the problem, since he wants to aid her in her tentative efforts to liberate herself from her parents' influence.

Brenda is a willing partner for Neil in the physical sense, but in reality she is much less independent than he. She attempts to cover up the whole issue by asserting that everything will be all right once he loves her, but this turns out to be an illusion. However, Neil is not in a position to foresee that this will be the case, and he commits himself to her and declares his love for her. According to one critic, however, the relationship between these two is 'nothing more than a means of escape,' and Neil 'remains without the values of commitment which could take escape beyond itself.' Here, Neil's love for Brenda is seen as pure escapism, whereas he in fact is engaged in a search for something and someone that he can commit himself to in a genuine fashion because they correspond to his real self. This commentator sees no difference between Neil and Brenda and argues that 'neither is willing to face the problems that any involvement entails.' It would rather seem that it is mainly Brenda who shies away from contemplating the deeper challenge that is inherent in Neil's courting of her.

The approaching marriage of Ron Patimkin and his fiancée Harriet is an indication of the kind of life that is expected of a member of the clan, and Neil has a hard time hiding his dislike of the completely unimaginative sort of marriage and life that Ron seems to contemplate quite happily. Neil is aware that Ron is quite nice to him, but the fact remains that the latter's mental horizon does not extend to anything beyond sports and the music of Mantovani or Kostelanetz. As for Brenda, she quarrels with her mother and reveals that she is jealous of Harriet. She complains that Mrs. Patimkin will forget that she exists once Harriet arrives, and Neil suggests that this ought not to be a problem, but rather an advantage. He would like for both himself and Brenda to be as free of parental influence as possible, but Brenda is more hesitant about this. She is very upset about her mother and tells Neil that she would have torn up some of her own hundred dollar bills if she had found them and then put the pieces in her mother's purse. She is crying as she says this, and the whole idea seems to be an expression of her childish need to revenge herself upon her mother for not giving her the love and attention that will now be bestowed upon Harriet, the bride to be. Brenda then throws herself at Neil, demanding that he make love to her on the old sofa in the storage room where she had hidden her money. But this, like some of her later actions, is an immature rather than a truly self-assertive rebellion against her parents.

When Brenda asks Neil to take up running with her, he realizes that this is a way in which she tries to make him more acceptable to her by changing his identity so that it becomes less threatening to her and the family. She tells him that he looks like her, and they are wearing similar clothes for the occasion, but Neil feels that 'She meant, I was sure, that I was somehow beginning to look the way she wanted me to. Like herself.' Neil enjoys the running and feels happy afterwards, but this is because both he and Brenda are having a fine time together as young and healthy people in love, not because he has decided to change his attitudes to suit her needs. This, however, is probably what she believes while they are exercising, and hence she gives him the love and attention that contribute to his happiness. In fact, it is only after they have been running for a while on a regular basis that she feels free to tell him that she loves him. Thus their relationship is fraught with misunderstandings and conflicts that come to a head at the end of the story.

The content of Neil's dream about a Pacific island suggests that he is beginning to fear that the affair with Brenda cannot last, that the realities of their situation, the power of the Patimkin environment, may destroy his goal of love and freedom. In the dream, he and the black boy, his fellow conspirator, as it were, are on a boat in the harbor of the island, but soon they drift away from the naked Negro women on the shore and have to watch their island paradise disappear. The natives sing 'Goodbye, Columbus,' the refrain of Ron's college record, as the two of them go, suggesting that they will not possess their dream, their America. The historical parallel is fitting, inasmuch as the real Columbus also became disillusioned in his quest for a better world. Thus Neil is spurred on by his fear that the affair will be over once Brenda returns to Radcliffe, and he begins to contemplate a marriage proposal as a way of securing her for himself. He is, however, afraid to propose since he is not sure of Brenda's reaction and suspects that there are still unresolved issues between them. Instead he decides to ask her to wear a diaphragm both to increase his sexual pleasure and as a symbol of their defiantly intimate relationship out of wedlock.

This diaphragm hardly represents what has been called Neil's dream of a 'classless, creedless hedonism.' It is true that he aims to break down the barriers of class and religious conventions, but hedonism is not a purpose in itself for him, but rather a means by which he affirms his dissenting values and identity. Brenda does not feel mature enough to commit herself to such a deliberate action, but for Neil it is imperative that they are both conscious of what they are doing and that they use the opportunity of their love to define themselves in opposition to the outside pressures that bear upon them. By sustaining their conspiracy, so to speak, they will be changed together and in a direction which Neil finds is right and stimulating. But Brenda rejects the suggestion, making him feel that she also rejects him and what he stands for. The core of the problem is his actual self, which she cannot accommodate herself to.

Neil is offered a new identity, in a manner of speaking, as an employee in Mr. Patimkin's firm, where Ron already works. Mr. Patimkin suggests to Neil that he, too, would be able to learn the business, but the latter recognizes that he is unsuited for such a life. He is not robust enough for the work, but, on the other hand, he is attracted to the neighborhood where the company is located, the black section of Newark that once was peopled by immigrant Jews of his grandparents' generation. This and other parts of Newark are the only locations that Neil feels continuously drawn to throughout the novella. There is an authenticity and vitality in life as it was and as it is lived in these neighborhoods, and the colorful scenes and pungent smells suggest this. The ways of the old Jews as well as those of the blacks of the present are chaotic and poverty-ridden yet more suited to real human needs than the middle-class lifestyle that is replacing them. The old blacks, for example, are not segregated from the community, but are placed in 'screenless windows' where they can watch the throbbing life in the streets. Here, in spite of many problems, there is a freedom and zest for life that Neil appreciates and will not entirely surrender in his own existence either.

Brenda is sufficiently influenced by Neil to finally accede to his request that she obtain a diaphragm. She seems to do this because she wants to act like an adult, but also because she is affected by Ron's marriage and begins to want the same thing for herself. For example, she acquires a new dress which makes her look as attractive as the bride, or even more so. Deep down, it seems, Brenda sees herself in the role that Harriet plays, as a lovely bride with a successful husband, being led to the altar on her father's arm and being protected and cared for by her mother. But for the time being she carries on with Neil Klugman and goes to New York with him to get the diaphragm. For Neil, however, this development is very serious and fraught with consequences. He is both enthusiastic about what he sees as Brenda's affirmation of their rebellious bond and anxious about the responsibilities that lie ahead of him now that their union is about to assume a more permanent aspect.

Neil's uncertainty emerges in his reflections in St. Patrick's Cathedral, where he seeks refuge while Brenda is in the doctor's office: 'Now the doctor is about to wed Brenda to me, and I am not entirely certain that this is all for the best. What is it I love, Lord? Why have I chosen? Who is Brenda?' One crucial question is the first one, concerning the nature of his love. The answer that suggests itself is that Neil loves the possibilities he sees in Brenda, apart from her physical attractiveness, and that he is haunted by a sense that he may be mistaken, that he does not really know her.

Continuing his meditation in the church, Neil addresses God, but his 'prayer' is hardly meant to be serious. In fact, the God he talks to seems to be a pantheistic one who is present in everything: 'If we meet You at all, God, it's that we're carnal, and acquisitive, and thereby partake of You. I am carnal, and I know You approve. I just know it. But how carnal can I get? I am acquisitive. Where do I turn now in my acquisitiveness? Where do we meet? Which prize is You?'

Neil is hardly a philosophic pantheist, but he makes some good points in this strange inner monologue. If God is identical with a universal process of creation and life, our sexual urges must be manifestations of the divine will. Moreover, if God made us acquisitive, he himself must share that trait in some sense. Neil has no problems with his carnal nature and welcomes it, and he also admits to being acquisitive. He is, however, less certain of the strength of this particular trait in himself and is overwhelmed by the power of the answer that Fifth Avenue gives to his question about the importance of the desire for possessions: 'Which prize do you think, *Schmuck?* Gold dinnerware, sporting goods trees, nectarines, garbage disposals, bumpless noses, Patimkin Sink, Bonwit Teller.'

Neil's concept of God is jocular, but it also embodies his satirical view of religion as an integrated part of the whole bourgeois value system of an acquisitive middle class. To join this class and its gods means joining in the race for wealth and position, and it is here that Neil draws the line as far as he himself is concerned and insists on another self-definition. But he knows that it is difficult to preserve one's identity in the face of society's demands and that it will not be any easier together with Brenda Patimkin. Accordingly, he is momentarily relieved when he sees her coming from the doctor without carrying anything. He thinks that she has broken their agreement, which means that their relationship will be less binding, as he sees it, thus letting him off the hook. However, this relief is only a passing 'levity,' as Neil calls it. He is still committed to Brenda, with or without the diaphragm. But when she tells him that she is actually wearing the device, he is overjoyed and takes it as a sign that she is joining forces with him in their defiance of traditional norms.

But back in the Patimkin house there is no relief for Neil. The wedding of Ron and Harriet offers an array of middle-aged couples that can only serve to confirm Neil's worst expectations of what the Jewish bourgeois lifestyle amounts to. Many of these people are affluent, but they have paid dearly for their success with emotional frustration, physical decay and spiritual emptiness. They are locked into their tradition of hard work, materialism and puritanism coupled with a narrow-minded outlook on everything outside their own circles, and they also suffer from rigid sex roles where the male is the provider and the female the excessively proper housewife. There is no room in their lives for joy, passion or any individualism except mere eccentricity.

Brenda's uncle Leo is the only one who seems to have an inkling of what has happened to him and is aware that only two good things have occurred in his life: finding an apartment in New York and having oral sex with a certain Hannah Schreiber. Otherwise, he has sacrificed all joy and spontaneity as a result of his struggle to survive as a bulb salesman, and his many frustrations have turned into a settled melancholy that is the only emotional content that is left in his life. Neil is touched by the older man's confessions and regards his story as further confirmation that he, Neil, is on the right track in refusing to let his life be controlled by such misery and renunciation. The older generation may have been victims of circumstances, of economic and social necessity, but for modern Jews the situation is different and offers more options.

The end of the novella is ripe with imagery suggesting loss of love as well as of illusions. Leo and his wife leave the wedding, looking like people 'fleeing a captured city,' and to Neil, driving on the New Jersey Turnpike, the desolate landscape looks like 'an oversight of God,' a phrase that echoes the image of the valley of ashes in *The Great Gatsby*. When Brenda leaves for Boston, 'the wind was blowing the fall in and the branches of the weeping willow were fingering at the Patimkin front lawn.' At the library things are also changing, the black boy disappears and Neil is charged with discourtesy by an old gentleman who had wanted to borrow the Gauguin book which Neil had put on reserve, against the regulations, for the boy.

However, by now Neil has also changed his attitude towards his job and his colleagues. He becomes more assertive and sure of himself and invents a story to cover up his manipulations with the book. He is beginning to feel that he belongs in the library as much as the others, but on his own terms and according to his own definition, and he even has Mr. Scapello, the boss, apologizing to him as he is led to his new post and actually receives a promotion. He is aware of the change in himself and half-ironically attributes his newfound strength to the lesson he has learnt in the Patimkin family, where there is a premium on aggressive behavior in the workplace. However, Neil's renewed attachment to the library does not bode well for his relationship with Brenda, who has never shown any appreciation of the job he has chosen for himself and the meaning it may have for him.

The last meeting between Brenda and Neil takes place in a Cambridge hotel where she has reserved a room, pretending that they are married and wearing a fake wedding ring. At this point, Neil, with his strengthened sense of identity as a result of his experiences in the Patimkin family and the library, realizes that he has come to visit her because he wants to ask her to marry him: '. . . it had been long enough. It was time to stop kidding about marriage.' Her registering in the hotel also encourages him, since he sees it as a sign that she is getting more liberated and ready to subvert social conventions. However, she tells him that her parents have discovered her diaphragm at home and that she has received two letters from them, an angry one from her mother and a more conciliatory one from her father, who is all too willing to forgive and forget if she will only stop seeing Neil any more. The letters themselves are marvelous examples of the crippling conventionalism in the sexual area on the part of the parents.

Brenda's revelation comes as a shock to Neil, and he feels that her carelessness in leaving the diaphragm indicates her half-conscious wish to prevent their relationship from becoming serious and permanent. She is scared by the prospect, which would force her to take a stand against her parents and risk their enmity. Her decision to take a hotel room with Neil does not suggest any liberation, but rather that she wants him as a casual lover. Again, she indulges in what can be called a pseudo-rebellious act. But Neil is acutely aware of the significance of her forgetting the diaphragm and suspects that this means that they are incompatible. She denies having left it on purpose, and there is no way to prove that this has been the case. However, the fact that she has done it is enough. It clearly reveals her insecurity and insincerity to Neil and makes him desperate, since it suggests that she has never really freed herself from the moral viewpoint of her parents. When he asks her if she thinks that their sleeping together was wrong, she does not answer for herself but refers to her parents' opinion. In other words, she accepts their verdict by refusing to declare herself against it.

Brenda tells Neil that she cannot bring him home for Thanksgiving, once more indicating her compliance with her parents' decisions and attitudes. Without saying so, she seems to agree with them, which is suggested by the 'solid and decisive' look on her face. Her expression reveals the internalized norms that Neil will not stop fighting against, and he tries hard to make Brenda see what she is doing to herself and their relationship. Their dialogue demonstrates the conflict: 'Who can I bring home, Neil? I don't know, who can you? Can I bring you home? "I don't know," I said, "can you?" Stop repeating the question! I sure as hell can't give you the answer.'

Brenda continues to evade responsibility for herself by referring to her family's standards instead of her own opinions, and Neil tries vainly to make her realize that she alone is responsible for what she does with her life, whether she chooses to ally herself with him or not. Neil also suggests that she can stay away from home if she likes, but her only answer is that she has to go home and that 'Families are different.' He is forced to conclude that she prefers her family to him and the challenge he represents, and that they have more or less misunderstood each other all along. She complains about his criticism of her, failing to perceive that he was critical because he wanted her to be true to herself instead of to her family. As he sees it, he had offered his opinions because he cared for her.

During this final confrontation the issues between them become clear. Neil declares his willingness to continue the relationship and defy her family, but Brenda chooses the security of the known instead of the uncertainties that she feels that he represents. There is no doubt that Neil is ready to go with Brenda to the Patimkin house for the Thanksgiving feast and defy her parents along with her. To argue that 'To oppose Brenda's parents would have required a decisive commitment which neither is capable or really desirous of making' is to misread the ending of the story. It is only Brenda who shies away from this confrontation. Considering that the story takes place during the fifties, Brenda's choice is understandable, but the fact remains that she puts a stop to a relationship that has a basis in love and that contains the promise of increasing depth and development.

It is likely that Neil would have been accepted by the Patimkins, including Brenda, if he had recanted and followed a path similar to that of Ron, but this is never an option for him. The whole point of the story is to render a protagonist who is determined to retain his own identity and not surrender to outside pressures. It is misleading to interpret Neil mainly as a confused and 'uncoordinated soul' who cannot maintain any sense of selfhood at all and whose life is 'aimless.' Such a view leads to the statement that 'Neil does not know how to be true to himself,' which is the opposite of what the story demonstrates. It is exactly Neil's feeling that he has an inner self that is different and oppositional that

makes him act in accordance with his convictions. Both he and Brenda finally realize that there is an unbridgeable gap between them, and he leaves the hotel room, walking into the yard of Harvard University. He stops before the Lamont Library, where he can see himself in a window as if it was a mirror. Frustrated and disappointed as he is, he has an impulse to pick up a rock and throw it through the glass, but instead he gives way to a profound meditation: 'I looked, but the outside of me gave up little information about the inside of me. . . . What was it inside me that had turned pursuit and clutching into love, and then turned it inside out again? What was it that had turned winning into losing, and losing—who knows—into winning? I was sure I had loved Brenda, though standing there, I knew I couldn't any longer.'

To become aware of one's real identity, or that of others, is difficult. Ultimately, personal identity is a mystery that can only be partly unveiled, and Neil had felt this also when looking at the sleeping Brenda at the end of the wedding party, wondering if he knew 'no more of her than what I could see in a photograph.' But though he admits to a sense of confusion regarding the enigma of his own self, certain answers to his questions do suggest themselves. He has lost Brenda by winning her, since she did not turn out to be what he thought, but by relinquishing, or losing, her, he was won in the only real sense that exists for him, that is, by remaining true to himself.

The final paragraph of the story has a promising ring: 'I did not look very much longer, but took a train that got me into Newark just as the sun was rising on the first day of the Jewish New Year. I was back in plenty of time for work.' The image of the rising sun suggests that Neil is doing to make a new start in life, and that Newark, as indicated earlier, is his real home after all. It is not the region associated with the parental generation of Jews, but his own Newark, as it were, a place where he can maintain the self that he has struggled toward during his hectic summer of lovemaking and measuring himself against various temptations and illusions. He returns to the library with a new and greater awareness of its attractions and limitations. It is, after all, an institution where culture, art and dreams are allowed a kind of existence which is impossible in the other environments that he has known, and it is located in a neighborhood that has preserved a certain room for individuality and a measure of freedom. In the library, one must assume that Neil will steer a course of his own, between the pedantry of his colleagues and the anti-social attitudes of the black boy that had spent so much time among the book stacks. If Roth's later novels are anything to go by, it may well be the role of the artist or writer that lies in store for Neil Klugman and which he is preparing for by remaining faithful to his outsider status and to his talent for observing and analysing people and places with such unerring critical accuracy.

Source: Helge Normann Nilsen, ''Love and Identity: Neil Klugman's Quest in 'Goodbye, Columbus,''' in *English Studies*, Vol. 68, No. 1, 1987, pp. 79–88.

Norman Macleod

In the following essay, Macleod examines parallels between ''Goodbye, Columbus'' and F. Scott Fitzgerald's The Great Gatsby.

In his monograph on the writings of Philip Roth, Bernard F. Rodgers, Jr., draws a useful comparison between Roth's first novella, ''Goodbye, Columbus,'' and Fitzgerald's *The Great Gatsby*. Rodgers notes that Neil Klugman's final ruminations, at the end of ''Goodbye, Columbus,'' remind us of Nick Carraway's observation about Jay Gatsby having lost something of himself in loving Daisy. Rodgers goes on to suggest that, given their typological similarity, any links between these novels are best seen as inevitable structural similarities which should not get in the way of more tangible differences. Nevertheless, several kinds of intriguing correspondences can be pointed to between these novels, some of them close enough to seem, not typological at all, but a conscious part of the artistic design of the later story.

Brenda Patimkin, the heroine of ''Columbus'' is—as Jeffrey Helterman has called her—the ''archetypal Jewish American princess.'' The fairy-tale title is more than descriptively apt—it is exactly how Neil himself sees Brenda. In what is Roth's most 'explicit allusion' to *The Great Gatsby*, Neil at one point sees the relationship between Brenda and her mother as one where the mother is ''some captive beauty, some wild princess, who has been tamed and made the servant to the King's daughter—who was Brenda.'' Daisy Fay was seen by Nick as being, for Gatsby, ''High in a white palace the King's daughter, the golden girl. . . . ''

Certain very specific features of ''Columbus'' and *Gatsby* march in parallel. Thus, both novels tell of the crowded events of a single summer, the passage of time related in both books to significant conventional or seasonal dates—the Fourth of July, Labor Day, the longest day of the year, Rosh Hashana. In both cases, the heroes are imaginative orphans—Gatsby has abandoned his parents, hinting or letting people believe that they are dead: '' . . . his imagination had never really accepted them as his parents at all,'' Neil too sees himself as something of an orphan, left to be provided for by his aunt and uncle, while his parents—''those penniless deserters''—have retired to Arizona. Both stories start when a major protagonist is introduced to an alien social milieu through a cousin—Neil by his cousin Doris, a member of the same country club as Brenda; and Nick Carraway reminds us, as he drives over to dinner with the Buchanans, that Daisy is his ''second cousin once removed.''

Significant events in both stories involve letters delivered and read while the heroes are briefly in unaccustomed academic surroundings. Gatsby received his ''Dear John'' letter from Daisy, announcing her betrothal to Tom Buchanan, while he was at Oxford for five months in 1919, an opportunity available after the armistice for Allied officers when they could go to any of the universities in England or France. The letter from Brenda's mother—the event which precipitates the end of Neil's and Brenda's affair—is received by Brenda (and shown by her to Neil) on the very day when Neil arrives at Radcliffe to spend the holiday weekend of Rosh Hashana in Boston with Brenda.

Both Gatsby and Neil contravene a fundamental canon of old-fashioned hospitality. Neither the Fays nor the Patimkins, it seems, were entertaining what they would regard as angels when they each gave hospitality to strangers. Gatsby, who ''knew that he was in Daisy's house by a colossal accident . . . made the most of his time. He took what he could get, ravenously and unscrupulously—eventually he took Daisy one still October night. . . .'' Neil similarly transgresses the old-fashioned houseguest's code, and Brenda's mother's letter, after she has found out, complains with dismissive irony—''Certainly that was a fine way to repay us for the hospitality we were nice enough to show him, a perfect stranger.''

Correspondences between both novels involve not only themes and motifs, but also details of style, characterization and setting. Both novels make jokes about noses—concerning their injury, loss, absence, size, shape, or alteration. In both novels there are characters who refer (following the habits of their social strata) to universities by the names of the places where they are situated: Tom Buchanan and Nick talk about ''New Haven'' (hardly noticing that Jordan Baker talks about ''Yale''), and Neil, who pointedly describes his own college as ''Newark College of Rutgers University,'' is irritated by Brenda's and other people's various references to ''Bennington,'' ''Boston,'' (not Radcliffe), ''New Haven,'' ''Northampton'' (not Smith College), and so on. In both novels socially distinct areas exist side by side. Across the bay on Long Island Sound from where ''the white palaces of fashionable East Egg glittered along the water,'' Nick Carraway lives at West Egg, ''the less fashionable of the two.'' Neil and Brenda are similarly separated by the social division between neighboring areas, Neil living in Newark, in the older suburb of Livingston, Brenda in affluent and fashionable Short Hills.

Sometimes a reference in ''Columbus'' seems an ironic counterpoint to a corresponding feature in *Gatsby*. In his bedroom, Gatsby takes a simple delight in showing Nick and Daisy ''his shirts, piled like bricks in stacks a dozen high'' showing them off by throwing them into careless disarray. Gatsby's flamboyant pleasure in his collection of luxurious shirts contrasts with Neil's impoverished self-consciousness and his strained, insecure gesture of ostentation when he unpacks on arrival at the Patimkin house, watched by Brenda's brother, Ron: ''I have one shirt with a Brook Brothers label and I let it linger on the bed a while; the Arrows I heaped in the drawer.''

References to the same sports crop up in both *Gatsby* and ''Columbus.'' Each novel has its shadowy champions—Brenda's mother was the best at tennis in her state, Jordan is a golf champion and tournament finalist, Brenda has been a teen-age champion horserider. Ron Patimkin and Tom Buchanan have both been university football stars (Ron for Ohio State, Tom for Yale) and both are similar characters—clumsily physical, culturally unsophisticated, mentally commonplace, verbally inarticulate or platitudinous, neither intellectual nor reflective. Ron's and Tom's mature lives are desolate after their youthful sporting *floruit*. Ron, who, like Tom, is ''a great, big, hulking physical specimen,'' is someone who—also like Tom—will ''drift on forever seeking, a little wistfully, for the dramatic turbulence of some irrecoverable football game.''

Jordan Baker plays the same games—tennis and golf—as Brenda, and her appearance is one that strongly recalls Brenda: ''. . . she was a slender,

> In 'Goodbye Columbus,' Philip Roth has intercalated allusions to, and recollection of, The Great Gatsby in a new, kaleidoscopically shifted pattern. This allusive sub-text appropriately links novels which explore, from different standpoints and in different settings, complementary themes."

small-breasted girl, with an erect carriage.'' But in her character Jordan Baker is more clearly called to mind by Brenda Patimkin's little ten-year-old sister, Julie. Jordan is hollow and selfish, and a liar—Nick calls her ''incurably dishonest.'' She is interested only in her own satisfaction, and shows a jaunty defiance towards those who cross her or act against her interests. Jordan shares her spoilt, selfish nature with Julie Patimkin—a nature exemplified in each case by the fact that they are bad sports and cheats. Jordan is reputed to have cheated by moving a ball from a bad lie in her first big golf tournament. In Nick's estimate, ''She wasn't able to endure being at a disadvantage and, given this unwillingness, I suppose she had begun dealing in subterfuges when she was very young in order to keep that cool, insolent smile turned to the world . . .'' These words would apply exactly to the young Julie. Julie is indulged by all her family (''Even Ron lets her win,'' says Brenda) who allow her to take basketball and golf shots over again when they go astray: ''. . . over the years Mr. Patimkin had taught his daughters that free throws were theirs for the asking.'' Only Neil, playing table tennis with her, fails to comply with Julie's expectations, instead ignoring her constant pleas, supported by got-up excuses, to take points over again.

The story of ''Goodbye Columbus'' reminds us of the story of Gatsby's sojourn with Daisy in Louisville. Indeed, ''Columbus'' is in many ways structured like a ''prequel'' to *Gatsby*, to use the modish cinematic term for a later, ''follow on'' production set at an earlier stage than the predecessor. ''Goodbye, Columbus'' shows us the early stages of the story of Gatsby and Daisy being repeated in the story of Neil and Brenda. Julie and Brenda Patimkin are like younger, still formative versions of Jordan Baker and Daisy: Ron Patimkin is still near that ''acute limited excellence at twenty-one'' before everything ''savors of anticlimax'' as it has done for Tom Buchanan. Neil's disappointment from which he looks forward to a future after the loss of Brenda where ''I knew it would be a long while before I made love to anyone the way I made love to her'' previews exactly the sense of loss which motivates Gatsby's dream of recovering ''the freshest and the best.''

In ''Goodbye Columbus,'' Philip Roth has intercalated allusions to, and recollection of, *The Great Gatsby* in a new, kaleidoscopically shifted pattern. This allusive sub-text appropriately links novels which explore, from different standpoints and in different settings, complementary themes.

Source: Norman Macleod, ''A Note on Philip Roth's 'Goodbye, Columbus' and Fitzgerald's *The Great Gatsby*,'' in *The International Fiction Review*, Vol. 12. No. 2, Summer 1985, pp. 104–07.

Sources

Epstein, Joseph, ''What Does Philip Roth Want?,'' in *Commentary*, Vol. 77, No. 1, January 1984, pp. 620–27.

Howe, Irving, ''Philip Roth Reconsidered,'' in *Commentary*, December 1972, pp. 69–77.

''McCarthy, Mary (Therese),'' in *Encyclopaedia Britannica Online*, http://www.eb.com (November 22, 1999).

McDaniel, John N., ''The Fiction of Philip Roth,'' in *The Fiction of Philip Roth*, Haddenfield House, 1974, p. 243.

''Roth, Phillip (Milton),'' in *Contemporary Authors Online*, Gale Group, 1999.

Further Reading

Buber, Martin, *I and Thou*, Scribner, 1958.
In this central text from one of the foremost modern Jewish philosophers, Buber's main concern is with the relationships of man to God, to nature, and to his fellow man.

Maney, J. P., and Tom Hazuka, eds., *A Celestial Omnibus: Short Fiction on Faith*, Beacon Press, 1997.
This collection of American short stories on the theme of faith includes ''The Conversion of the Jews'' by Philip Roth.

Shapiro, Gerald, ed., *American Jewish Fiction: A Century of Stories*, University of Nebraska Press, 1998.
This collection of short stories by Jewish-American authors includes ''On the Air'' by Philip Roth.

Updike, John, and Katrina Kenison, eds., *The Best American Short Stories of the Century*, Houghton Mifflin, 1999.
This collection of short stories from the series *The Best American Short Stories*, published every year from 1915 through 1998, includes an introduction by John Updike and ''Defender of the Faith'' by Philip Roth.

Heart of Darkness

Joseph Conrad
1899

Joseph Conrad's long short story, "Heart of Darkness" (1899), is considered to be his greatest literary achievement, as well as his most controversial. It was first published in *Blackwood's Magazine* in 1899, in three monthly installments. In 1902, it was republished in a book entitled *Youth: A Narrative, and Two Other Stories*.

The story is partly based on Conrad's personal experiences as the captain of a riverboat on the Congo River, and was immediately interpreted as an indictment of the colonial rule of the Belgian government in the Congo. The story is characterized by a narrative embedded in a narrative; the "frame" narrator relates a story told him by the sailor Charlie Marlow, Conrad's famous character who appears as a storyteller in much of his fiction. Marlow relates his experiences as the captain of a steamboat, sent down the Congo River in the employ of an unnamed ivory company, to retrieve Kurtz, a company manager whose "methods" had become "unsound."

The central symbolism of the "heart of darkness" has been interpreted in several ways. On one level, it represents the "darkness" at the "heart" of men's souls—the descent into an evil that lurks in the hearts of all men. In this sense, it is a psychological journey into the unconscious. On a somewhat more literal level, the journey represents a descent into the "darkness" or evil of imperialism—the

greed for ivory and other resources that character-ized the exploitation of African people by European colonialism. African writer Chinua Achebe has interpreted the story's central symbolism in terms of a racist perception of Africa and African people as representative of more "primitive" or "savage," less evolved society, representing the repressed desires of European society. Achebe interprets Con-rad's story in these terms as thoroughly racist. Other critics have countered Achebe's interpretation in terms that defend Conrad as a critic of racist imperialism.

Author Biography

Novelist and short story writer Joseph Conrad was born Jozef Teodor Konrad Korzeniowski on Decem-ber 3, 1857, in Berdiczew, Podolia, then part of the Russian Empire (now Poland). His father, Apollo Nalecz Korzeniowski, was a resistance organizer against Russian rule in Poland; in 1861, he was arrested for these activities, and sentenced to exile in Vologda in northern Russia, accompanied by his wife and son. Conrad's mother, whose tuberculosis was worsened by the harsh weather, died in 1865, when Conrad was eight years old.

At this time, Conrad was introduced to litera-ture and to the English language by his father, a poet and translator. In 1869, his father died, also of tuberculosis. Conrad was left in the care of relatives, eventually under the guardianship of his uncle, Tadeusz Bobrowski, a lawyer, who supported and encouraged Conrad financially, professionally, and emotionally, throughout his life.

Yearning from an early age to be a sailor, Conrad went to Marseilles in 1874, and eventually served for sixteen years in the British merchant navy. In 1886, he became a British citizen, and earned a master mariner's certificate. In 1889, he had the opportunity to command a Congo river boat, realizing a childhood dream of going to Africa. His most famous and most critically acclaimed story, "Heart of Darkness," was based on his experiences in Africa.

In 1894, his beloved uncle died. By this time, Conrad had retired from sea travel and settled in England, becoming a full-time writer. His first novel, *Almayer's Folly*, was published in 1895 under the newly assumed name, Joseph Conrad. Also in 1895, at the age of thirty-eight, he married twenty-two-year old Jessie George, with whom he had two sons. His second novel, *An Outcast of the Islands*, was published in 1896.

Conrad became known as a novelist of sea adventures, but his literary style and thematic con-cerns as expressed through these stories were of a more serious nature. Among his works which take place at sea are *The Nigger of the "Narcis-sus"* (1897), *Lord Jim* (1900), *Youth* (1902), and *Typhoon* (1902). He died of a heart attack on August 3, 1924.

Plot Summary

"Heart of Darkness" begins with the "frame" narrator's description of a group of men relaxing on a private yacht one evening. One of the men, Charlie Marlow, a sailor, commences to tell his friends a tale of one of his adventures as the captain of a steamboat going down the Congo River. The rest of the narrative consists of Marlow's tale, with only occasional interruptions by the "frame" narrator to describe Marlow and his storytelling style.

Marlow's tale is about his assignment to work for "the Company," an ivory trading company in what was then the Free State of the Congo, a colony of the Belgian government. Marlow is assigned to retrieve a certain Kurtz, a company manager operat-ing deep in the Congo to retrieve ivory whose "methods" were reported to be "unsound." Marlow initially stops at one of the Company sites, where he is appalled by the brutal, inhumane, slavery-like conditions of the African people made to work for the Company. He comes upon a grove where those who have been worked nearly to starvation and death lie in wait for death. Marlow is equally appalled, although ironically impressed, with the callousness of the company management and bu-reaucracy toward the suffering Africans. Making several stops at company sites, Marlow hears intri-guing reference to the enigmatic Kurtz, to the point that he himself becomes eager to meet and converse with the man.

As Marlow's boat moves closer to Kurtz's compound, the small steamboat crew are barraged with deadly arrows, even as they are blinded by a thick fog. Marlow watches in sympathy as one of the Africans on his boat dies from an arrow wound. He is struck by his sense of identification with the black man. Arriving at Kurtz's compound, Marlow meets with a man he refers to as the Russian Harlequin soldier, who maniacally and obsessively worships Kurtz. Marlow observes decapitated human heads stuck on poles throughout the compound. He then finds Kurtz himself, a shriveled up man dying of malarial fever. As he takes the dying Kurtz aboard his boat, Marlow observes a woman who seems to have been Kurtz's companion, mourning his departure. As they make their way back up the river, Kurtz soon dies, with the enigmatic and haunting words ''The horror! The horror!'' on his lips. Marlow is then taken up with fever and illness, which renders him delirious. Upon recovering, Marlow returns to England, where he goes to visit Kurtz's ''Intended,'' the woman Kurtz was engaged to marry. Marlow has come to give her the packet of letters and writings Kurtz had entrusted with him. Although he abhors liars and lying, Marlow withholds from her Kurtz's haunting final words, telling her instead that he had died with her own name on his lips.

Joseph Conrad

Characters

The Harlequin Russian Soldier

The Harlequin Russian soldier greets Marlow upon his arrival at Kurtz's compound. A Westerner, he seems half-crazed and maniacally obsessed with the worship of Kurtz as an exceptional being.

Kurtz

Kurtz is a Company employee of ''unsound methods,'' whom Marlow has been charged with retrieving from the depths of the Congo. Marlow becomes increasingly intrigued by the enigmatic Kurtz, eventually craving above all else to converse with him. What Marlow finds at the end of his journey is a man dying of malaria. However, it becomes clear that Kurtz has become an object of some dread and worship among the local inhabi-

tants, and that his ruthless ''methods'' of obtaining vast quantities of ivory have become brutal and inhumane. Kurtz represents the greed and cruelty of the imperialist exploitation of the Congo by the Belgian government that had colonized it.

Kurtz's Intended

Upon his death, Kurtz refers to his ''Intended,'' his fiancée, a white woman living in London. At the end of the story, Marlow goes to visit her in her lavish home. The story ends with Marlow's lie, that Kurtz had died with her name upon his lips. There is some sense that she knows Marlow is lying.

Charlie Marlow

Marlow is the narrator of the central ''framed'' narrative of the story. The character of Marlow appears in a number of Conrad's stories, often in the role of observer and narrator of the central events of the story. Marlow is a sailor whose narrative relates his experiences under hire by an unnamed ivory company to take a riverboat down the Congo River in order to retrieve Kurtz, a maverick company manager. Marlow is appalled at the treatment of the African people by the Company; but he is also

Media Adaptations

- The 1978 movie *Apocalypse Now*, directed by Francis Ford Coppola, is adapted from Conrad's "Heart of Darkness." The film is set during the Vietnam War. Martin Sheen plays Captain Willard, a stand-in for Conrad's narrator Charlie Marlow; Kurtz is played by Marlon Brando. There was a 1994 adaptation directed by Nicolas Roeg and starring John Malkovich as Kurtz and Tim Roth as Marlowe.

disturbed by the behavior of the Africans, which seem to him "mysterious." Marlow eventually finds Kurtz, who is dying of malaria, and brings him aboard the steamboat. Kurtz dies shortly thereafter, and then Marlow himself is stricken with fever and illness. When he returns to England, he visits Kurtz's "Intended," his fiancée, to give her some of Kurtz's personal writings. Although Kurtz's enigmatic dying words were "The horror! The horror!" Marlow, who abhors liars, himself lies to the Intended, telling her that Kurtz's final words had been her name. Marlow's perspective on what he witnesses in the Congo is somewhat ambivalent, and is the source of much critical debate among literary scholars, particularly in terms of his perspective on the African people; the matter of whether or not Marlow's, or Conrad's, perspective is racist has been argued persuasively on both sides, and is a subject of ongoing debate.

The Narrator

The narrator of the story is a character only insofar as he relates to the reader a story told him by Marlow. He is therefore referred to as the "frame narrator," because his narrative merely frames the central narrative, which is related by Marlow. For this reason, most of the seventy-five page story is written as a direct quotation from Marlow. The frame narrator only occasionally pauses to describe Marlow's character and the small group of men listening to his story.

Themes

Civilization and the Primitive

The central theme around which this story revolves is civilization versus wilderness. The symbolism that represents this theme is the opposition of light versus darkness. As in much of European art and literature, the imagery of "light" is associated with Western culture, civilization, knowledge, and the conscious mind. The imagery of "darkness," on the other hand, is associated with Third World cultures (such as Africa), the "primitive" or "savage," the unknown or mysterious, and the psychological unconscious. Many of the themes in Conrad's story are based on this set of oppositions. Thus, European culture is contrasted with African culture, where African culture is seen to represent the primitive, unconscious mind of the white European man. Marlow's narrative of his journey down the Congo River, and his encounter with Kurtz, expresses the anxiety of the white man who is tempted by his foray into the "wilderness" to "go native," lose the trappings of civilization, and revert to a more "primitive" state of mind. As writer Chinua Achebe has pointed out, this conceptual construct on the part of Western cultures in their perceptions and representations of African culture is thoroughly racist. Other critics have argued, however, that Conrad's story is a critique of the racist colonial mentality of the Europeans in Africa.

Capitalist Exploitation

Conrad's story is critical of the "methods" of the white European "Company" that, motivated by pure greed, exploits African resources and labor. Conrad's commentary is in part based on his own experiences with the ivory business in the Congo, and is supported by historical records that make it clear that the ivory trade in Africa was brutal on a par with the slave trade. Conrad mocks such European trade practices through his ironic representation of the generically named "Company," which clearly stands in for the presence of European companies in Africa. The Company management is also portrayed ironically, such as the manager who maintains a high starched white collar in spite of the signs of suffering and cruelty that he perpetuates in the treatment of the Africans. Conrad also satirizes the values of "efficiency" practiced by the Company as both irrational and inhumane. The character

Topics for Further Study

- The movie *Apocalypse Now*, directed by Francis Ford Coppola, is based on Conrad's "Heart of Darkness." Compare and contrast it to Conrad's story. What elements of the original story are preserved in the film? Conrad's story is a commentary on the conditions of imperialism in the Congo in the late nineteenth century; Coppola's film is a commentary on the involvement of the United States in the Vietnam War. What, in your opinion, makes Conrad's story appropriate to the situation of the Vietnam War? How would you describe Coppola's vision of the Vietnam war, and what perspective does he present? In what ways is the character of Kurtz different in the story and in the movie?

- Writer Chinua Achebe has criticized Conrad's "Heart of Darkness" as a racist depiction of Africa. Achebe's well-known novel, *Things Fall Apart*, is a very different representation of Africa. In what ways are Africa and Africans depicted differently in Achebe's novel as compared to Conrad's story?

- "Heart of Darkness" is based on Conrad's experiences in the Congo in the 1890s. Learn more about the history of the Congo in the nineteenth and twentieth centuries. What social, political, and economic changes has it gone through during the century since Conrad's story was published?

- Conrad's father was a resistance organizer in the Polish rebellion against the rule of the Russian empire in the nineteenth century. Learn more about the history of Poland under the Russian empire. What are the major events, and changes in Poland over the past century?

- Conrad's novel *Lord Jim*, another sea story, was adapted to the screen in a 1965 film directed by Richard Brooks, and starring Peter O'Toole and James Mason. What themes does it address? In what ways is the story concerned with similar elements of human nature and character to those in "Heart of Darkness?" What elements of story does the film provide that are not possible in the written medium of the novel?

---

of Kurtz, whose "methods" are "unsound," represents the height of hypocrisy—the "methods" of the Company seem to be thoroughly "unsound," from a moral perspective.

Race and Racism

Whether or not one concludes that Conrad's story is racist, it is clear that the issue of race and racism in the European colonies is a central theme of the story. Marlow links colonial conquest directly to racism in the often-quoted passage: "The conquest of the earth, which mostly means the taking it away from those who have a different complexion or slightly flatter noses than ourselves, is not a pretty thing when you look into it too much." At the same time, however, the modern reader is struck by Conrad's nonchalant use of the term "nigger," which is now considered thoroughly racist.

Lies

Marlow's narrative includes an underlying theme regarding lies and lying. Marlow explains to his listeners his disdain for lies and lying:

> There is a taint of death, a flavour of mortality in lies—which is exactly what I hate and detest in the world—what I want to forget. It makes me miserable and sick like biting something rotten would do.

And yet, when faced with Kurtz's "Intended," at the end of the story, Marlow deliberately defies his own values in choosing to lie to her about Kurtz's final words. Unable to bring himself to do "justice" to Kurtz's dying wish that he be properly represented, Marlow refrains from repeating those haunting words, ''The horror! The horror!'' telling her instead that Kurtz had died with her name on his lips. Feeling that he has sinned in telling this lie, Marlow half expects ''that the heavens would fall upon my head,'' but concludes that ''the heavens do not fall for such a trifle.'' Aware that he has betrayed Kurtz through his lie, Marlow's justification seems to be a desire to protect the white woman from the truth of the true evil that lurks in the soul of man: ''I could not tell her. It would have been too dark—too dark altogether.''

Style

Narration

Narrative technique is an important element of Conrad's literary style. This story is structured as an ''embedded narrative.'' This means that the central story, narrated by the fictional character Charlie Marlow, is ''embedded'' in a ''frame'' narrative, whereby the ''frame'' narrator introduces Marlow's character, and presents the central story as a direct quotation from Marlow. For this reason, nearly every paragraph of the story begins with a quotation mark, indicating that it is a continuation of the frame narrator's direct quotation of Marlow's narration. This type of ''embedded'' narrative constitutes the structure of several of Conrad's stories, as the character of Marlow is the ''embedded'' narrator. This narrative structure focuses the reader's attention as much on the art of storytelling, and the character of the storyteller, as it does on the central story itself. Conrad's ''frame'' narrator calls attention to the significance of the frame narrator in describing Marlow's storytelling style. The narrator uses the metaphor of a ''nut''—indicating that, for Marlow, the meaning of the story lies more in the ''shell'' (the narration) than in the ''nut'' (the central story) it contains:

> The yarns of seamen have a direct simplicity, the whole meaning of which lies within the shell of a cracked nut. But Marlow was not typical (if his propensity to spin yarns be excepted) and to him the meaning of an episode was not inside like a kernel but outside, enveloping the tale which brought it out only as a glow brings out a haze, in the likeness of one of these misty halos that, sometimes, are made visible by the spectral illumination of moonshine.

Setting

The setting of the frame narrative is in England, as a group of men relax on a private yacht. The central story, narrated by the sailor Marlow, takes place on the Congo River, in an area of Africa then colonized by the Belgian King Leopold II, who deceptively named it the Free State of the Congo. The story takes place in the 1890s. The setting is significant because the tale is based in part on Conrad's own personal experiences as the captain of a riverboat on the Congo in the 1890s. Conrad's character of Marlow relates the brutal, slave-like conditions under which the native Africans were treated by their Belgian colonizers, and the story was interpreted upon initial publication in 1899 as an indictment of Belgian imperialism. The ivory company for which Marlow works represents the historical circumstances of the ivory trade in Africa, by which European colonizers greedily exploited both the African people for their labor and the resources of the continent. Conrad paints an unflattering picture of the European presence in Africa during the colonial period.

Imagery: Light and Darkness

The central imagery of the story revolves around the binary oppositions suggested in the title: light and darkness. This imagery sets up a contrast between the ''light'' white Europeans in Africa, and the ''dark'' native Africans. Likewise, the ''light'' is suggestive of European ''civilization,'' while the ''darkness'' refers to the culture of the African people, which Europeans perceived as ''primitive'' and ''savage.'' The imagery of light and darkness also refers metaphorically to the ''light'' of what is now referred to as the ''conscious'' self, which the Europeans associated with their own society, as opposed to the ''darkness'' of the unconscious, which the Europeans associated with African society. The ''light'' also represents the realm of that which is known and understandable to the Europeans (their own culture and native land), as opposed to the unknown (darkness), ''mysterious'' land, peoples and cultures of the African continent. How one interprets the story generally revolves around this central axis of light/dark imagery, and the variety of metaphorical and symbolic implications of this imagery.

Historical Context

Apocalypse Now

The 1978 film *Apocalypse Now*, directed by Francis Ford Coppola, is based on Conrad's story ''Heart of Darkness.'' While Conrad's story is set in the Congo in the 1890s, and is a commentary on

Compare & Contrast

- **Nineteenth Century:** The deceptively named Free State of the Congo is under the rule of the Belgian King Leopold II, who exploits the natural resources of the region, as well as its people in slavery-like conditions.

  Twentieth Century: The Free State of the Congo is renamed the Belgian Congo in 1908. It wins its independence from Belgium in 1960, and in 1965 Mobutu becomes president, renaming the nation Zaire in 1971. In 1997, Zaire is renamed the Democratic Republic of the Congo.

- **Nineteenth Century:** Under the rule of France and Holland before 1830, Belgium attains national independence in 1831 through the Belgian Revolution. In 1831, King Leopold I becomes the first king of the newly established nation. On his death in 1865 he is succeeded by his son, Leopold II, who rules until his own death in 1909.

  Twentieth Century: Leopold II is succeeded by his nephew King Albert I, who rules from 1909 to 1934. From 1914 to 1918, during the first World War, Belgium is occupied by Germany. When Belgium is liberated from the Germans and the king is restored to power in 1918, universal male suffrage (for those over age 21) is instituted (women do not get the right to vote in Belgium until 1948). In 1934, King Leopold III succeeds his father Albert. In 1940, during World War II, Belgium is once again invaded and occupied by Germany. After refusing to flee the country, King Leopold III is held prisoner by the Germans until 1945. In 1951, Leopold III abdicates in favor of his son, Baudouin, who reigns until 1993. Between 1971 and 1992, Belgium goes through the process of becoming a federal state made up of several autonomous regions, including the Flemish region, the Walloon region, and Brussels. In 1993, the second son of Leopold III, now Albert II, succeeds to the throne.

- **Nineteenth Century:** During Conrad's lifetime, his native Poland is under the rule of the Russian Empire. Conrad's father is a member of a resistance organization, which fights unsuccessfully for Polish independence from Russia.

  Twentieth Century: Poland gains national independence in the years following World War I. During World War II, Poland is occupied by Nazi Germany and Russia, and after the war it comes under Communist control. With the 1989 collapse of communism in Eastern Europe, Poland begins the process of converting to a democratic government with a free-market economy.

---

imperialism in the form of Belgian colonization, Coppola's film is set during the Vietnam War in the 1960s, and is a commentary on U.S. involvement in the Vietnam conflict. Coppola retained the central narrative trajectory, in which a Captain Willard (played by Martin Sheen), substituted for Conrad's character Marlow, is sent on a mission to retrieve a renegade Colonel Kurtz (played by Marlon Brando), whose "unsound methods" in Cambodia have caused alarm among military leaders. *Apocalypse Now* includes a notable performance by Dennis Hopper as the character equivalent to Conrad's Harlequin Russian soldier, who maniacally worships Kurtz. While critics agree that Coppola's film is an impressive achievement in cinematic style, they disagree on the political implications of the film. It is clearly an indictment of U.S. involvement in Vietnam, but is full of ambiguity in its greater implications. The documentary, *Hearts of Darkness* (1992), chronicles the making of the film.

The Congo

"Heart of Darkness" is based on Conrad's experiences as the captain of a steamboat in the Congo River (the second longest river in Africa, after the Nile) during the 1890s. At that time, the Congo was under the rule of King Leopold II of Belgium. Although he "gave" what was then called

The Free State of the Congo to the Belgian people in 1895, his rule over the region effectively remained until his death in 1909. Under Leopold's rule, the African people were exploited for their work, and treated as badly and brutally as slaves. Upon Leopold's death, it became the Belgian Congo, and was ruled by Belgium until 1960, when it won independence. Between 1960 and 1965, the region suffered from the political upheaval of formulating a new government. In 1965, Joseph-Desire Mobutu became president of the Congo. In 1971, Mobutu changed the country's name to Zaire, and his own name to Mobutu Sese Seko, as well as changing the names of other places within the nation. In 1997, it became the Democratic Republic of the Congo.

Ford Madox Ford

Conrad became a personal friend and co-author of the novelist Ford Madox Ford, with whom he wrote two books. Ford, considered among the greatest of novelists, is best known for *The Good Soldier* (1915). Other important works include *Parade's End*, a four-part series made up of: *Some Do Not* (1924), *No More Parades* (1925), *A Man Could Stand Up* (1926), and *Last Post* (1928). Ford was known for his close association with many of the great writers of his day, and for his encouragement of younger writers.

Blackwood's Magazine

"Heart of Darkness" was first published in three monthly installment's in *Blackwood's Magazine*. *Blackwood's Magazine* was an important literary influence in nineteenth-century Britain. It was originally founded by William Blackwood, a Scottish bookseller, in 1817, originally entitled *Edinburgh Monthly Magazine*, and later *Blackwood's Edinburgh Magazine*; in 1905 it became *Blackwood's Magazine*. Originally focusing on political satire, it was also a literary journal publishing poems, short stories, and novels in serial form. Eventually, it became less political and more literary, publishing works of such renowned authors as George Eliot and Anthony Trollope as well as Joseph Conrad.

Critical Overview

"Heart of Darkness" is widely considered to be Conrad's masterpiece. It was first published in *Blackwood's Magazine* in a series of three installments, in February, March, and April of 1899. In

1902, it was published in the book, *Youth: A Narrative, and Two Other Stories.*

"Heart of Darkness" was understood by critics at the time of its initial publication as an indictment of Belgian colonial rule in the Free State of the Congo (now the Democratic Republic of the Congo). According to Robert F. Haugh, in *Joseph Conrad*, "The story was taken by some as an attack upon Belgian colonial methods in the Congo; as a moral tract; and as a study of race relationships." Haugh goes on to say that, "Most contemporary reviewers read it as a criticism of Belgian colonialism, an issue that remained alive until Conrad's death and got attention in his obituary notices." Other reviewers interpreted the story in terms of Christian religious iconography. As Haugh explains, "Paul Wiley, in his *Conrad's Measure of Man* . . . finds the myth of the fall from innocence throughout Conrad, and . . . makes of Kurtz the man driven from the Garden of Eden."

More recent critical debate on "Heart of Darkness" has focused on the issue of whether the story is actually a critique of racism, or if the story is based on a fundamentally racist perspective. In a lecture first given in 1975, entitled "An Image of Africa," African novelist Chinua Achebe made the argument that, based on this story, "Joseph Conrad was a thoroughgoing racist." Achebe argues that the story is structured on a common racist conception in Western thought, which perceives African people as uncivilized and white people as civilized, and that Conrad, rather than challenging racist conceptions, "chose the role of purveyor of comforting myths. 'Heart of Darkness' projects the image of Africa as 'the other world,' the antithesis of Europe and therefore of civilization, a place where man's vaunted intelligence and refinement are finally mocked by triumphant bestiality." Achebe goes on to explain that this story continues the racist conception that conceives "Africa as setting and backdrop which eliminates the African as human factor. Africa as a metaphysical battlefield devoid of all recognizable humanity. . . ." Achebe goes on to criticize the body of Western criticism of Conrad's story, which continues to overlook these racist assumptions. "That this simple truth is glossed over in criticisms of his work is due to the fact that white racism against Africa is such a normal way of thinking that its manifestations go completely unremarked." Achebe posits that "the question is whether a novel which celebrates this dehumanization, which depersonalizes a portion of the human race, can be called a great work of art. My answer is:

Tim Roth, as Marlow, in the 1994 television movie, "Heart of Darkness."

No, it cannot." He concludes that Conrad's "obvious racism has, however, not been addressed. And it is high time it was!"

Francis B. Singh, in a 1978 essay entitled "The Colonialistic Bias of 'Heart of Darkness,'" on the other hand, states that "it is a truth universally acknowledged that 'Heart of Darkness' is one of the most powerful indictments of colonialism ever written." He qualifies this statement, however, by concluding that "ambivalent, in fact, is probably the most accurate way to sum up Conrad's attitude toward colonialism." Singh goes on to explain that "the compromises that Marlow makes, as when he fights off identification with the blacks or when he tells lies about Kurtz to prevent the civilized Western world from collapsing, stem from Conrad's own inability to face unflinchingly the nature of colonialism." C. P. Saravan, in a 1980 article entitled "Racism and the 'Heart of Darkness,'" makes the claim that Conrad was not necessarily in agreement with his fictional character of Marlow on his perceptions of Africa and Africans. Saravan claims that "it is not correct to say that Marlow has Conrad's complete confidence," and that the "ironic distance between Marlow and Conrad should not be overlooked." He asserts that, through this story, "Conrad suggests that Europe's claim to be civi-

lized and therefore superior, needs earnest reexamination." Saravan concludes that "Conrad was not entirely immune to the infection of the beliefs and attitudes of his age, but he was ahead of most in trying to break free."

Criticism

Liz Brent

Brent has a Ph.D. in American culture, specializing in cinema studies, from the University of Michigan. She is a freelance writer and teaches courses in history of American cinema at the University of Michigan. In the following essay, Brent discusses the minor female characters in Conrad's story.

Many of Conrad's stories take place primarily in the all-male environment of the sailing ship, or other all-male social or work settings. Yet, the female characters in "Heart of Darkness" play an important role in the central themes and symbolism of the story. Female characters here include: Marlow's aunt, who helps him to get the job on the steamboat; the two knitting women in the office of the Company, in France; the African woman who seems to

What Do I Read Next?

- *Lord Jim* (1900) is Conrad's other "masterpiece." This story focuses on a young sailor, Jim, who belongs to a crew that abandons their ship during a wreck, leaving hundreds of passengers to drown. It is narrated by Conrad's character Marlow.

- *The Secret Agent: A Simple Tale* (1907) by Joseph Conrad is a novel from Conrad's later period.

- *The Good Soldier* (1915) by Ford Madox Ford is a masterpiece by Conrad's friend, contemporary novelist, and sometime co-author. It concerns the intrigues of two couples.

- *Conrad on Film* (1997), edited by Gene M. Moore, is a collection of articles regarding adap-

tations of Conrad's stories to the screen. Several articles focus on Francis Ford Coppola's *Apocalypse Now*, based on "Heart of Darkness."

- *The Mirror of the Sea and A Personal Record* (1988) by Joseph Conrad consists of reissues of Conrad's earlier autobiographical books.

- *The Complete Short Fiction of Joseph Conrad* (1992), edited by Samuel Hynes, is a four-volume set of the collected works of Conrad: *Volumes I and II: The Stories; Volumes III and IV: The Tales.*

- *Joseph Conrad: Selected Works* (1994), writings by Joseph Conrad, is a collection that contains Conrad's most famous and most critically acclaimed stories.

---

be Kurtz's companion; and, Kurtz's "Intended," the white woman Kurtz is engaged to marry at the time of his death. The following essay examines the roles of minor female characters—Marlow's aunt and the two knitting women—in terms of their significance to central themes of the story.

> Then—would you believe it—I tried the women. I, Charlie Marlow, set the women to work—to get a job! Heavens!

The first woman to be mentioned in the story is Charlie Marlow's aunt, who, through various social connections, secures him the job with the Company as captain of a steamboat in the Congo. Marlow's attitude toward his aunt is based on his sense of himself as a sailor, a man's man, independent of any woman. It is with a tone of self-mockery that Marlow marvels at the phenomenon that he, of all people, would allow himself to seek out the aid of a woman in his own affairs.

Marlow describes his aunt's response to his request for help in getting a job in the Congo in terms that imply he finds it somewhat infantile—in the sense that he seems uncomfortable with having such a "fuss" made over him by a woman. Along

the same lines, Marlow finds his aunt's attentions to him somewhat emasculating, in the sense that the flowery enthusiasm of a society woman is alien to the all-male world of seafaring men in which he is at home. Calling her "a dear enthusiastic soul," he explains that,

> She wrote: "It would be delightful. I am ready to do anything, anything for you. It is a glorious idea. I know the wife of a very high personage in the Administration and also a man who has lots of influence with," etc., etc. She was determined to make no end of fuss to get me appointed skipper of a river steamboat, if such was my fancy.

Marlow explains his motivation for stooping to seek out the help of a woman as based on the fervor of his desire to find work that would take him to Africa. He excuses his willingness to succumb to his aunt's "fuss," by explaining "Well, you see, the notion drove me."

The next women Marlow encounters are the two women who greet him at the Company offices in France. Upon entering the office, he is greeted by two women, dressed rather austerely, who sit silently knitting. "Two women, one fat and the other slim, sat on straw-bottomed chairs knitting black wool.'' These women strike Marlow as enigmatic, and he describes one as a ''somnambulist''—a sleepwalker.

> The slim one got up and walked straight at me—still knitting with downcast eyes—and only just as I began to think of getting out of her way, as you would for a somnambulist, stood still, and looked up. Her dress was as plain as an umbrella cover, and she turned round without a word and preceded me into a waiting-room.

These women pose a picture of stark feminine domesticity—with their continual knitting, austere clothing, and plain countenance—and yet, they strike Marlow as ''ominous.''

> In the outer room the two women knitted black wool feverishly. . . . The old one sat on her chair. Her flat cloth slippers were propped up on a foot-warmer and a cast reposed on her lap. She wore a stretched white affair on her head, had a wart on her cheek, and silver-rimmed spectacles hung on the tip of her nose. She glanced at me above the glasses. The swift and indifferent placidity of that look troubled me. . . . An eerie feeling came over me. She seemed uncanny and fateful.

The significance of Marlow's description of these two women, which contrasts a ''placid'' domestic picture with an ''uncanny'' and ''ominous'' atmosphere, gains greater significance and meaning when contrasted with the ''horror'' of the Company's activities, which Marlow eventually discovers in Africa. Once in Africa, Marlow perceives the two women as ''guarding the door of Darkness''; in other words, their role of greeting the men who enter the office of the Company on their way to Africa—men who generally never return—imbues them with both the foreknowledge of the fate of each man, and suggests the dark, evil underbelly of the Company's exploitation of the African people—a trade in ivory, which, from the vantage point of the Company offices in France, appears to be a ''placid'' business, but which is, in fact, brutal and inhumane to the point of ''horror.''

> Often far away there I thought of these two, guarding the door of Darkness, knitting black wool as for a warm pall, one introducing, introducing continuously to the unknown, the other scrutinising the cheery and foolish faces with unconcerned old eyes.

The continual knitting of black wool, and the black dresses worn by the women, resonate with the story's central imagery of ''darkness''—darkness is associated with death, with the unknown, and with evil. Thus, the ''door of Darkness'' that the women ''guard'' is a passage to death for the men who naively sign on with the Company. Marlow's description of the women takes on a tone of grim irony

> " Likewise, as the two women who wear black dresses and knit black wool are strongly associated with death and darkness, the aunt's perception of the Company's role in Africa is naïvely associated with efforts at Christian enlightenment of the native Africans."

with the use of a Latin phrase: ''*Ave!* Old knitter of black wool. *Morituri te salutant*,''—meaning, ''Hail! Old knitter of black wool. Those who are about to die salute you.'' The use of this Latin phrase (similar to the phrase used by gladiators in the Roman arena) ironically elevates the impending death of each man whom the women greet to the level of a proud battle cry.

Marlow's subsequent goodbye visit to the aunt who got him the job with the Company acquires greater depth in comparison to his encounter with the two knitting women. Marlow continues the characterization of his aunt as excessive in her feminine enthusiasm regarding his imminent travels. Marlow's description of her suggests an affectionate indulgence of her good-hearted ''fuss'' over him:

> One more thing remained to do—say good-bye to my excellent aunt. I found her triumphant. . . . it became quite plain to me I had been represented to the wife of the high dignitary and goodness knows to how many more people besides as an exceptional and gifted creature—a piece of good fortune for the Company—a man you don't get hold of every day. Good Heavens!

The domestic setting of tea and a chat by the fireside echoes the ''ominous'' domestic setting of the two women knitting.

> I had a cup of tea—the last decent cup of tea for many days—and in a room that most soothingly looked just as you would expect a lady's drawing-room to look, we had a long quiet chat by the fireside.

But the aunt's fireside is described as "soothing" in contrast with the Company's fireside, which is "ominous." The "ominous" air of the two knitting women—who seem to know that the fate of each man who enters the office is horror and death—is contrasted with the aunt's complete innocence of the danger and horrors that await Marlow in Africa. Likewise, as the two women who wear black dresses and knit black wool are strongly associated with death and darkness, the aunt's perception of the Company's role in Africa is naïvely associated with efforts at Christian enlightenment of the native Africans. In other words, she imagines Marlow to be a sort of Christian missionary.

> It appears however I was also one of the Workers, with a capital—you know. Something like an emissary of light, something like a lower sort of apostle. There had been a lot of such rot let loose in print and talk just about that time, and the excellent woman living right in the rush of all that humbug got carried off her feet. She talked about "weaning those ignorant millions from their horrid ways," till, upon my word, she made me quite uncomfortable.

Unlike his aunt, Marlow knows, even before leaving for Africa, that "the Company was run for profit"—and that its mission was nothing more than extracting the greatest possible profit from the sources of ivory in Africa.

His aunt's naïve delusions about the nature of the Company's mission in Africa leads Marlow to make a generalization about women that is key to the central themes of the story. He concludes that women live in a fantasy world that denies the brutal realities of human thoughts and deeds—the "horror" that Marlow is forced to face head-on in his encounter with Kurtz.

> It's queer how out of touch with truth women are! They live in a world of their own and there had never been anything like it and can never be. It is too beautiful altogether, and if they were to set it up it would go to pieces before sunset. Some confounded fact we men have been living with ever since the day of Creation, would start up and knock the whole thing over.

Conrad's treatment of these minor female characters—who seem only incidental upon first reading of the story—take on greater depth with closer examination. They function to set up a contrast of the "placid" world of female domesticity in Europe with Marlow's experience of "horror" on the part of Europeans in Africa. A central irony of the story is the idea that European "civilization" rests upon the "horrors" of colonialism in Africa. Furthermore, Marlow's affectionate, yet indulgent, descriptions of his aunt add a note of playful irony to the "dark" ironies that characterize the story as a whole.

Source: Liz Brent, Critical Essay on ''Heart of Darkness,'' in *Short Stories for Students*, The Gale Group, 2001.

Ted Billy

In the following essay, Billy focuses on Conrad's "critical attitude toward verbal expressions of truth" in "Heart of Darkness" and its parallels to Friedrich Nietzsche's philosophies of language.

Conrad drew attention to the last pages of ''Heart of Darkness'' in his letter of 31 May 1902 to William Blackwood, in which he says that ''the interview of the man and the girl *locks* in—as it were—the whole 30000 words of narrative description into one suggestive view of a whole phase of life, and makes of that story something quite on another plane than an anecdote of a man who went mad in the Centre of Africa'' (. . . emphasis added). Instead of concluding in the heart of the Congo, the tale comes full circle to its point of origin, the Thames, by way of Marlow's return to the sepulchral city and subsequent encounter with Kurtz's Intended.

Conrad's impressionistic depiction of Brussels, both early and late in the narrative, externalizes the sham and hypocrisy he sees at the heart of Western civilization. On the second visit, Marlow takes offense at the ''irritating pretense'' of perfect security reflected in the faces of the insignificant citizens. Yet here, in the heart of the city of untruth, Marlow lies to conceal the horror of Kurtz's degradation and, apparently, to reinforce the Intended's ''saving illusion.'' True, Marlow does admit his contempt for lies early in the narrative, but his African nightmare transcends conventional polarities such as truth and falsehood, good and evil, appearance and reality. He finally recognizes truths as convenient fictions, useful in matters of survival, but totally invalid in terms of understanding the nature of life. Marlow lies (at least, so he tells us) to preserve the Intended's opportunity for affirmation and survival. He also lies because he perceives something of Kurtz in himself as well as in the Intended. The melodramatic interview ends with Marlow bowing before the inscrutable enigma of existence. Conrad insinuates throughout this crucial locking, or summarizing, scene that in order to sustain life one must project one's own illusions for living. Self-deception, the essential condition for happiness, becomes a kind of existential higher understanding, and thus Conrad invalidates all conventional truths and moralities in his iconoclastic narrative of the truth of fiction and the fiction of truth.

Conrad's critical attitude toward verbal expressions of truth in ''Heart of Darkness'' closely parallels Nietzsche's skeptical outlook. As critics have noted, Conrad and Nietzsche adopted similar attitudes toward language. Conrad views language as an imprecise—if not deceptive—means of communication, as does Nietzsche in his essays ''On Truth and Lie in an Extra-Moral Sense'' and ''On the Prejudices of Philosophers.'' In the former essay, Nietzsche argues that the mind is an arbitrary instrument of knowledge more concerned with flattering deceptions than with perceiving the truth beyond appearances. Defining man as an assemblage of masks, roles, poses, and postures, he sees the vanity of the human race as dependent on the capacity for self-deceit. External reality mystifies the modern individual, who remains imprisoned within a self-deceiving consciousness that decrees, in accordance with ''linguistic legislation,'' that truth must be always agreeable and never damaging to the ego: ''And, moreover, what about these conventions of language? Are they really the products of knowledge, of the sense of truth? Do the designations and the things coincide? Is language the adequate expression of all realities?'' Language is general and conceptual, but each experience is particular and unique, and therefore words fail to communicate without equivocation: ''[T]ruths are illusions about which one has forgotten that this is what they are; metaphors which are worn out and without sensuous power; coins which have lost their pictures and now matter only as metal, no longer as coins.'' Truth, debased and defrauded into surface truths, no longer functions as anything but an agent for conditioning and conformity: ''[T]o be truthful means using the customary metaphors—in moral terms: the obligation to lie according to fixed convention, to lie herd-like in a style obligatory for all.''

In his essay ''On the Prejudices of Philosophers,'' he further contends that since reality is unknowable through conventional means, primarily logic and language, existence would be impossible without a consistent falsification of the world as it is. Recognizing ''untruth as a condition of life,'' one can no longer seriously entertain questions of truth or falsehood; instead, what really matters is the affirmation or denial of life. If illusions are necessary to preserve and promote life, Nietzsche maintains, the human ego will abandon the search for true judgments and explanations of existence in favor of conventional fictions, that is, the specious

> **Truth remains elusive, and any effort to package it in linguistic wrapping seems doomed to failure. So why speak at all?"**

consolations of language, logic, and other formulaic systems of reference.

Although I am not arguing that Nietzsche's linguistic skepticism directly influenced Conrad, some of Nietzsche's works may have been available to Conrad before he began writing ''Heart of Darkness.'' But what Nietzsche was propounding in theoretical terms Conrad expressed in the fabric of his fiction, becoming one of the first major twentieth-century authors to challenge the efficacy of language as a vehicle for transmitting meaningful communication. More specifically, Conrad targets the deleterious effects of the labeling function of language. Words and things are not synonymous. Or, as Djuna Barnes puts it, writing almost four decades after the publication of ''Heart of Darkness'' : ''Life is not to be told, call it as loud as you like, it will not tell itself. . . . There is no truth, . . . you have been unwise enough to make a formula; you have dressed the unknowable in the garments of the known.''

Yet Conrad's ending involves more than Marlow's lie and its motivation. In particular, Marlow's saving falsehood gains new significance in light of the intricate series of corresponding words and phrases that pervade the final pages of the novella. These correspondences are sometimes superficial, as when Marlow compares Kurtz's ''ebbing'' life to the swiftly running ''brown current.'' In the last paragraph, Conrad's narrator reports the Director's announcement ''We have lost the first of the ebb,'' and states that ''the tranquil waterway . . . seemed to lead into the heart of an immense darkness.'' This takes us back to the opening of the narrative, when the *Nellie* waits ''for the turn of the tide'' at ''the beginning of an interminable waterway.'' Conrad's nautical imagery suggests that Marlow and his auditors must share Kurtz's fate, an implication that seems substantiated by the name of their cruising yawl, the *Nellie*, perhaps a comic diminutive of death *knell*, as the geographical reference to ''Gravesend'' may corroborate. Employing death as a metaphor for disillusionment, or spiritual extinction, Conrad chronicles the failure of human intentions and lofty aspirations. At the heart of darkness, Marlow, who has been linked to Kurtz as one of the new breed of agents, finds himself ''numbered with the dead.'' Conrad again identifies Marlow with Kurtz in the final scene when Marlow rationalizes his visit to the Intended as an attempt to give up everything that remains of Kurtz. But the meeting does not unfold as Marlow imagines, and he finally accepts the burden of insight as a permanent part of his psyche. Marlow must live with the memory of Kurtz's horror for the rest of his life.

Kurtz dies before the locking scene begins, but he reappears as a phantom to haunt Marlow in the sepulchral city, speaking through the mouthpiece of the Intended to dumbfound him once again. Conrad hints at the correspondence of Kurtz and the Intended by punning on the word *expression*. In Marlow's estimation, Kurtz's greatest attribute is his ''gift of noble and lofty expression,'' and while admiring the Intended's portrait, Marlow remarks that ''she had a beautiful expression.'' Kurtz's eloquent rhetoric corresponds to the beauty of his fiancée's countenance. But we must also keep in mind that Marlow interprets Kurtz's cry ''The horror'' as ''the expression of some sort of belief; it had candor, it had conviction, it had the appalling face of a glimpsed truth.'' Much earlier, Marlow had digressed to discuss the ''flavour of mortality in lies''; however, Conrad asserts that truth can also be appalling, as in Kurtz's shock of recognition (''The horror!'') preceding his death. The ''flavour of mortality'' also becomes manifest in the final scene, when Marlow begins a sentence and the Intended finishes it, substituting her own words and feelings for Marlow's:

> Then before the appealing fixity of her gaze that seemed to watch for more words on my lips I went on, ''It was impossible not to . . .''

> ''Love him,'' she finished eagerly, silencing me into an appalled dumbness. ''How true! How true!''

Truth can be appalling more often than appealing whenever it negates life. The example of misunderstanding above suggests that knowing the truth about Kurtz might destroy the Intended's sentimental cocoon. Marlow seems no more capable of enlightening her than he was with Kurtz when he attempted to speak common sense to him at the Inner Station. Conrad's linking of Marlow with Kurtz and Kurtz with the Intended implies that we are prisoners of our own preconceptions about life.

Truth and falsehood have little to do with the affirmations and negations that render existence purposeful or pointless.

Conrad also links Kurtz to the Intended by emphasizing their mutual capacity for belief. In Europe, a journalist tells Marlow that Kurtz ''had the faith. He could get himself to believe anything—anything.'' Marlow echoes this assessment in much the same language when he describes the Intended: ''She had a mature capacity for fidelity, for belief, for suffering. The room seemed to have grown darker as if all the sad light of the cloudy evening had taken refuge on her forehead.'' Here, light and darkness do not correspond to truth and falsehood. Rather, the ''sad light'' represents a diminishing beacon of faith in a devouring chaos of darkness. Moreover, Conrad often calls attention to the Intended's ''ashy halo'' (an arresting oxymoron) in this scene: ''[W]ith every word spoken the room was growing darker, and only her forehead, smooth and white, remained illumined by the unextinguishable light of belief and love.'' Fidelity, whether well-founded or unfounded, seems the sole alternative to the psychological paralysis of unmitigated despair. Conrad transmutes the metaphysics of despair into a poetics of immobility and blindness when he immerses Kurtz in ''impenetrable darkness'' on his deathbed to contemplate the harrowing thought of his own emptiness. In similar fashion, Conrad stages the interview with the Intended in a room that gradually succumbs to dusk and darkness. As the room grows darker, Marlow realizes he must keep secret Kurtz's withering words: ''The dusk was repeating them in a persistent whisper all around us, in a whisper that seemed to swell menacingly like the first whisper of a rising wind. 'The horror! The horror!''' By lying, Marlow does not give Kurtz the justice he had requested: ''I could not tell her. It would have been too dark—too dark altogether. . . .'' Yet, by attempting to save the Intended from the despair that consumed Kurtz, Marlow affirms Kurtz's original intentions, rather than the actual consequences of those intentions. Marlow keeps the darkness within himself, refusing to extinguish the Intended's dim light of belief. His lie functions as a surface truth that preserves life at the price of deceit.

There is also the question of how Marlow can be convinced that he knows the truth about Kurtz. The Intended asks for Kurtz's last words, but Marlow was dining in the mess room at the time of his death. It is possible that in his delirium Kurtz could have spoken almost anything without being overheard.

Marlow cannot be sure that Kurtz's *last* words were "The horror! The horror!" And even if they were, what do they really mean? The secret lies with Kurtz, not with Marlow, who expatiates on the topic ad nauseum without providing a clear-cut explanation. Does Kurtz's cry "The horror!" signify his recognition of the abominable evil he has committed? Or is it an acknowledgment of his inner emptiness? Like Ahab's doubloon in *Moby-Dick*, Kurtz's outburst has as many meanings as interpreters. Ultimately, the meaning of this stirring exclamation must be determined subjectively, and individually, by each reader and on each reading of the novella.

Throughout the locking scene, the Intended represents the image of light threatened by darkness, of order besieged by chaos. In the dusk, her "pale head" seems to float toward Marlow, as if disembodied from her black garments. Conrad calls attention to "the last gleams of twilight," the "glitter of her eyes," and the "glimmer of gold" hair that "seemed to catch all the remaining light." When the Intended assumes a posture of supplication that reminds Marlow of Kurtz's other woman, his native mistress of inextinguishable faith, he describes her as "stretching bare brown arms over the glitter of the infernal stream, the stream of darkness." Conrad's light and darkness correspond to affirmation and negation, not to truth and falsehood, for "Heart of Darkness" unfolds as a journey to the brink of cosmic nihilism and back again to a broken world of dim beliefs. Marlow ultimately views the Intended's delusion as a sanctuary from the snares of experience, as he finds himself "bowing my head before the faith that was in her, before that great and saving illusion that shone with an unearthly glow in the darkness, in the triumphant darkness from which I could not have defended her—from which I could not even defend myself." His lie forges a solidarity of belief among himself, Kurtz, and the Intended. Marlow's compassionate act may serve as a temporary triumph for life set against the backdrop of the inevitable triumph of darkness. A case can even be made for the view that Marlow's real lie is his attempt to rid himself of the burden of Kurtz at the Intended's doorstep. Marlow realizes that he cannot dispose of the memory so easily, and he departs with the "truth" and the trauma still within him. He confesses to a "feeling of infinite pity" for the woman who had more faith in Kurtz than Kurtz had in himself. Given a "choice of nightmares," Marlow ultimately selects the lesser of two negations—the appalling "lie" instead of the annihilating "truth."

Conrad presents Marlow's visit to the Intended as a ghostly reunion with Kurtz; every detail gives the impression of a posthumous existence. Even her street resembles a "well-kept alley in a cemetery." Unable to cast off his memories, Marlow envisions Kurtz "on the stretcher opening his mouth voraciously as if to devour all the earth with all its mankind." The voice that Conrad accentuates throughout the tale intimidates Marlow even long after Kurtz's death. Marlow imagines Kurtz staring at him from the panel of the door "with that wide and immense stare embracing, condemning, loathing all the universe." The white and black piano keys suggest the disparity of Kurtz's idealistic rhetoric and his rapacious lust for ivory.

But Conrad also employs more subtle tactics in this scene. The Intended suddenly materializes, dressed in black, as if Kurtz had died only the day before. Catching sight of her, Marlow also feels that time has stopped since the death of Kurtz:

> I saw her and him in the same instant of time—his death and her sorrow—I saw her sorrow in the very moment of his death. Do you understand? I saw them together—I heard them together. She had said with a deep catch of the breath, "I have survived"—while my strained ears seemed to hear distinctly, mingled with her tone of despairing regret, the summing-up whisper of his eternal condemnation.

Beneath the rhetoric of late-Victorian melodrama, Conrad implies that the Intended embodies Kurtz's short-lived intentions as an apostle of idealism and that the phantom whisper represents Kurtz's well-deserved damnation, his total psychological inversion in the heart of Africa. Marlow apprehends this duality as the general condition of mankind, not as an isolated eccentricity of human nature. Earlier, he had remarked that the human mind is capable of anything. Marlow even perceives this duality within his own identity, when he faces the failure of his misguided mission as an emissary of light and realizes that company officials have lumped him with Kurtz as practitioners of advanced methods of colonialism. But Marlow most distinctly hears this judgment against the hollowness of humanity in the disconsolate words of the Intended: "[T]he sound of her low voice seemed to have the accompaniment of all the other sounds full of mystery, desolation, and sorrow I had ever heard . . . the faint ring of incomprehensible words cried from afar, the whisper of a voice speaking from beyond the threshold of an eternal darkness." Seeing Kurtz in the glowing face of the ever-faithful Intended, hearing Kurtz's insane whisper in her trembling voice, Marlow recognizes once again the inescapable phantom he had earlier called the ''initiated wraith from the back of Nowhere.'' It dwells within him, within all humankind. Kurtz literally is the nowhere man; his ancestry stems from all over Europe, and his corpse lies *somewhere* in a muddy hole. His shade is everyone's shadow. Marlow understands this implicitly and realizes the futility of all ego-oriented actions. His lie temporarily preserves his integrity and the Intended's illusion, but like the ''life-lie'' in Ibsen's *The Wild Duck* the deception does not ensure salvation but merely survival.

Marlow does survive. He survives what Kurtz failed to endure in the heart of the wilderness. Marlow affirms that like ancient explorers in the great age of navigation modern individuals must learn ''to live in the midst of the incomprehensible which is also detestable.'' The language of ''Heart of Darkness'' amplifies ''the incomprehensible'' with acute exaggerations of Conrad's own account of his journey to the inner recesses of Africa. Conrad's rhetoric, with its preponderance of superlative and indefinite abstractions, consistently dramatizes the gulf between human experiences and the imprecise linguistic representations of those events. ''Heart of Darkness'' unfolds as an excursion into the absurd, a penetrating scrutiny of nothingness, and a dramatic example of Conrad's evolving articulation of humanity's perennially frustrated search for meaning. The very novella itself, according to Peter Brooks, calls into question the ''epistemology of narrative'' and demonstrates ''the inadequacy of the inherited orders of meaning.'' Truth remains elusive, and any effort to package it in linguistic wrapping seems doomed to failure. So why speak at all?

In the final paragraph, Marlow returns to his original posture, silent and detached ''in the pose of a meditating Buddha.'' This ultimate parallel, Marlow as Buddha, actually conceals Marlow's role as mediator between the benevolence of Buddha and the rapacity of Kurtz. Marlow plays the part of the man of action who turns to a life of contemplation, even though, paradoxically, he ''still followed the sea.'' The external narrator's reference to Marlow's ''pose'' as Buddha may suggest that he is mocking Marlow's pontificating wisdom, yet Conrad's unnamed external narrator does conclude the story with the image of the Thames, the civilized counterpart of the primeval Congo, leading to ''the heart of an immense darkness.'' If the external narrator has any awareness of Marlow's grim revelation, then he is certainly unique, for the other auditors never respond to Marlow's interpretation of his experi-

ence, except by way of petty objections or stupefied silence. Enveloped in their own little word-worlds, invisible cocoons of catch phrases and slogans, they consider Marlow's ''inconclusive'' narration a usurpation of their right to fritter away the hours playing dominoes. They function, in the more sophisticated ''jungle'' of progressive London, as counterparts to the worthless pilgrims who litter the deck of Marlow's steamboat in the Congo. Like Kurtz, they exist on the fringe of egomania, fitting inheritors of Kurtz's I-me-mine sensibility: ''My Intended, my station, my career, my ideas—these were the subjects for the occasional utterances of elevated sentiments.'' The Managing Director's utterance in the last paragraph—''We have lost the first of the ebb''—rings with the same hollowness. Even the Intended's turn-of-the-century sentimentality is expressed in reflexive language. Each character speaks in the idiom of his or her cultural conditioning, from the minor figures to the Intended, Kurtz, and Marlow himself. None of them breaks down the barriers prohibiting authentic communication.

By happenstance or design, Conrad has fashioned in ''Heart of Darkness'' a logomachy, or battle of words. On one level, he constructs a semiotic framework whereby concrete signs stand for abstract symbols (e.g., the river is the inexorable stream of time; the wilderness, the irrationality of life; and the darkness, the vacuous heart of mankind). In juxtaposition to this scheme, he establishes a semantic pattern that undermines much of the particularity of the narrative. For example, most of the characters either have no name, like the external narrator and Kurtz's African mistress, or are identified only by occupation: the Director of Companies, the Lawyer, the Accountant, the manager, the brickmaker, and so on. Or else Conrad links the character to a verbal tag, as in the case of the Intended, the Harlequin, and Marlow's pose as a modern European Buddha. Conrad's rhetoric, replete with superlatives and indefinite abstractions, consistently dramatizes the gulf between human experiences and the imprecise linguistic formulations that allegedly correspond to them. Conrad's verbal tactics tend to render the whole narrative of Marlow's journey as an amorphous cloud of moonmist and to alchemize abstractions such as ''immense,'' ''unspeakable,'' and ''unknowable'' into concrete form. The great fecundity of scholarly commentaries on ''Heart of Darkness'' testifies to Conrad's genius in crafting such a multifaceted jewel for meticulous appraisal. Critics, like early explorers, must write ''in the midst of the incomprehensible.'' And every attempt at a definitive interpretation of the narrative ultimately falls short of a full disclosure. By taking us to the heart of darkness, Conrad paradoxically uses words to demonstrate the inability of language to encompass the unfathomability of human existence.

Source: Ted Billy, ''The Clash of Nebulous Ideas,'' in *A Wilderness of Words: Closure and Disclosure in Conrad's Short Fiction*, Texas Tech University Press, 1997, pp. 69–77.

Adam Gillon

In the following essay, Gillon examines some of the complex moral issues in ''Heart of Darkness,'' including white exploitation of Africa as symbolized by the ivory trade.

The transformation of this narrator into the Marlow of ''Heart of Darkness'' represents a great artistic stride forward. Once again there is the familiar group of listeners whose common bond is the sea, seated on the deck of the *Nellie*, a cruising yawl: the Director of Companies, the Lawyer, the Accountant, Marlow, and the initial storyteller who provides the description of the Thames, the four men, and sets the mood for the journey that will lead into the ''heart of darkness,'' starting Marlow on his long discourse. But this time it is not a straightforward tale of adventure. From the first Conrad gives warning of his serious purpose, and later in the story Marlow takes great pains to assure himself that his audience is following him:

> Do you see him? Do you see the story? Do you see anything? It seems to me I am trying to tell you a dream—making a vain attempt, because no relation of a dream can convey the dream-sensation, that commingling of absurdity, surprise, and bewilderment in a tremor of struggling revolt, that notion of being captured by the incredible which is of the very essence of dreams.

Perhaps Conrad is straining a bit this device of creating an air of verisimilitude, but he succeeds splendidly with the story as a whole. For ''Heart of Darkness'' is not really a tale about a man called Kurtz, told by Marlow to a group of his friends. It is about Marlow and, no doubt, about Conrad himself. The story, as one of Conrad's letters to William Blackwood indicates, is about ''the criminality of inefficiency and pure selfishness when tackling the civilizing work in Africa. . . . It turned out to be much more—an illuminating personal confession, a profound discussion of man's moral complexity, and, last but not least, a remarkable short novel whose literary merit is not lessened by its being at once an adventure story and a psychological thriller.

> Thus, in discovering the horrors of exploitation, the brutality and hypocrisy of the Belgian colonists, Conrad also discovered (as Marlow did) a terrifying feeling of affinity with the savagery of the jungle."

Once more Conrad examines the plight of the white man in the wilderness of the jungle. As in ''Karain'' and the first two novels, the images of light and darkness, of sound and stillness, abound, but their function is more effective here; they are not only more numerous and varied, but they are used on three different levels: literary, intellectual, and psychological. The jungle becomes the symbol of the savage in man and a symbol of man's isolation. The white man in the darkness of the primeval forest wages a double battle against the destructive powers that prey on his body, and also against the forces that undermine his moral integrity. People who live in an organized, civilized community, protected by law and police, cannot understand the powers of darkness.

Neither did Marlow—*before* he went to the Congo, and his search for Kurtz began in the depths of the primeval forest symbolically representing man's quest for self-knowledge. This quest, which appears in almost all of Conrad's works, is the core of his literary method, and especially so in the two stories and two novels featuring Marlow, the spinner of yarns engaging the attention of his audiences. In each case the reader is drawn not merely into Marlow's narrative about other people but also into an exploration of Marlow's own personality. Of course, this happens also in other tales, e.g., in ''The Secret Sharer,'' where the Captain reaches a measure of self-knowledge only after he has totally identified himself with the problem of the confessed murderer, Leggatt, whom he shelters from punishment. In *Lord Jim* Marlow is joined by Brierly and Stein in his painstaking and painful efforts to understand Jim's motives, and each of them ends up with self-examination. Similarly, Marlow's unflagging pursuit of Kurtz is an attempt to fathom his own soul, conducted with accents of self-mockery.

The tone of Marlow's narrative is easy to understand when one recalls Conrad's own experiences in the Congo and his comments on his interest in geography and the strange fascination exercised upon his boyish mind by Sir Leopold McClintock's *The Voyage of the "Fox" in the Arctic Seas*:

> The great spirit of the realities of the story sent me off on the romantic explorations of my inner self; to the discovery of the taste of poring over maps. . . . Only once did that enthusiasm [geographical] expose me to the derision of my schoolboy chums. One day, putting my finger on a spot in the very middle of the then white heart of Africa, I declared that some day I would go there.

What Conrad discovered when he did go to Africa some eighteen years later was no romantic dream or exalted adventure but "the distasteful *knowledge* of the vilest scramble for loot that ever disfigured the history of human conscience and geographical exploration." Little wonder Conrad was melancholy and lonely there in the heart of the African continent, and was prompted to observe with considerable bitterness: "What an end to the idealized realities of a boy's daydreams!"

Yet the Congo journey was valuable to Conrad beyond supplying him with material for his fiction. Before it, he said, he was a mere animal. After it, he lost his illusions, perhaps, but not love of humanity in general. Thus, in discovering the horrors of exploitation, the brutality and hypocrisy of the Belgian colonists, Conrad also discovered (as Marlow did) a terrifying feeling of affinity with the savagery of the jungle.

Marlow alone, among the members of the expedition, can understand the nature of Kurtz's fall *because* he has experienced the same temptation. But though the wilderness, to use his own phrase, has patted him on the head, he does not succumb to its momentary spell. He may feel alienated from his fellow men, both in the jungle and upon his return to the civilized world, but he has not cut himself off from the whole world, as Kurtz did.

The potent suggestiveness and the dreamlike quality of Kurtz's words shake Marlow profoundly, but he keeps his head, though not his soberness. The fate of Kurtz is a symbolic warning to Marlow to beware of the danger of extreme isolation. Kurtz ". . . had kicked himself loose of the earth . . . he had kicked the very earth to pieces. . . . He was alone. . . ." This is the penalty he must pay for

having yielded to the dark powers of the forest *and* to the darkness of his own soul.

Kurtz had arrived in the Congo with a notion of being considerably more than a mere producer of ivory. He believed that the whites were regarded by the savage natives as superior beings, and he meant to reform them. Instead of overcoming the savages' ignorance, however, Kurtz became one of them—as their demigod, to be true. He submitted to adulation and rites in his own honor (probably involving cannibalism and therefore not described but merely suggested); he resorted to violence in extorting ivory for his company. Yet he came to hate the natives. The paper for the International Society for the Suppression of Savage Customs, which the idealistic Kurtz had once written, bore a scrawled note, "Exterminate all the brutes!" obviously jotted down much later.

For all his degradation, Kurtz stands, morally speaking, one notch above the manager of the company, who never wanted anything but financial gain for himself. In comparison with the manager Kurt's corruption is rather attractive, for it lacks the manager's hollowness; and because of Kurtz's eloquence it is dramatic, so much so, in fact, that it casts a spell on the young bepatched Russian trader and on Marlow, for whom Kurtz's lot becomes "the nightmare of [my] choice." Marlow is fascinated but not overcome by the power emanating from the face of the dying Kurtz. It seems to him that a veil had been lifted from Kurtz's ivory face. Having glanced over the edge of the precipice, Marlow knows the meaning of Kurtz's stare on his deathbed.

"Droll thing life is," Marlow declares, "that mysterious arrangement of merciless logic for a futile purpose. The most you can hope from it is some knowledge of yourself—that comes too late—a crop of *unextinguishable regrets*." Yet Marlow considers Kurtz a remarkable man because his cry "The horror!" was ". . . the expression of some sort of *belief*; it had candor, it had *conviction* . . . it had the appalling face of a *glimpsed truth*. . . ." That is why Marlow remains loyal to Kurtz; the latter "had stepped over the edge" while he, Marlow, was "permitted to draw back [my] hesitating foot." Therein, he observes, lies the whole difference. Kurtz's cry represents a revulsion against his darker self, a sign that he has not been lost completely. In fact, Marlow believes, "It was an affirmation, a moral victory. . . ."

After he recovers from his illness Marlow comes to Brussels, full of disgust for its people, who are intruders because they cannot possibly understand his state of mind. He walks about the city, bitterly grinning at people, haunted by the vision of Kurtz on the stretcher. The gloom of the jungle and the beating of the drums are still vivid in his imagination. When he brings this vision with him to Kurtz's "Intended," he realizes that he can never stop seeing that eloquent phantom as long as he lives. The memory of Kurtz is like a dream (or rather like a nightmare) he can share with nobody else. Kurtz's "Intended" is isolated by her grief and her illusion of Kurtz's integrity and greatness, as the Russian youth was cut off from the rest of the white colonizers by his fervent belief in Kurtz's eminence. This woman is endowed with a "... mature capacity for *fidelity*, for *belief*, for *suffering*."

Marlow's efforts to find Kurtz and to understand him represent, essentially, his search for truth. It is natural, therefore, that he cannot abide falsehood. Seeking the truth about himself, too, and a true way to tell his story, he concludes that it is impossible

> to convey the life-sensation of any given epoch of one's existence—that which makes its truth, its meaning—its subtle and penetrating essence.

It is one of the major ironies of the story that Marlow, for all his dedication to truth, must stoop to a lie. Kurtz's fiancée asks what the dying man's last words were, and Marlow cannot tell her the truth, that Kurtz's last cryptic message to the world was an agonizing cry, "The horror! The horror!" He cannot because "It would have been too dark—too dark altogether. . . ." Marlow caustically observes that the heavens didn't fall upon his head when he uttered the lie. Truth has become a rather ambiguous thing, and so has the notion of darkness. For, while Kurtz's voice reaches Marlow ". . . from the threshold of an eternal darkness," he bows his head before the faith that was in Kurtz's Intended, ". . . before that *great and saving illusion* that shone with an unearthly glow in the darkness, in the *triumphant darkness* from which I could not have defended her—from which [I] could not even defend [myself]. . . ." Marlow gives the young woman what she wants, something to treasure for the rest of her life; he tells her that the last word Kurtz pronounced was her name. Conrad belabors the irony of the situation. The woman's ". . . cry of inconceivable triumph and of unspeakable pain" indicates that "She knew. She was sure. . . ."

Marlow was not; having proven his loyalty to the darkness of Kurtz does he thereby prove that her illusion is true light? After all (to continue the symbolism of dark and light), she remains in the dark about her beloved Kurtz. Conrad does not give a clear answer. Despite the light of her belief, the "ashy halo" about her head, the room of the Intended has grown darker, and she is "all in black . . . floating . . . in the dusk."

Marlow has emerged from the depths of the jungle a wiser and a sadder man. The contact with Kurtz has given him something valuable, a heightened perception of life's complexity. He no longer takes things for granted; nothing is either black or white, for the two merge into each other. The supreme lesson he has learned is to respect man's faith, any faith or sincere conviction. He harbors a secret he cannot divulge to other people. Man must forever remain shut within the shell of his own personality. Like the captain in "The Secret Sharer," whose special knowledge sets him apart from his crew, Marlow is unable to communicate with others. He doubts whether his experience can ever be conveyed to his listeners. He has come to believe that ". . . we live as we dream—alone."

Marlow is right in expressing this doubt, for many a reader of Conrad occasionally fails to distinguish between the literal and the symbolic aspects of his fiction. Yet the symbolic level is a most essential feature of the writer's method. As Conrad's use of the central narrator enables the author to remove himself from his subject matter, so his symbolism and his images convey and enhance the doubts, ambiguities, and moral predicaments of his heroes.

Ivory is *white* and it is craved by the white man but it also represents moral darkness; the two white women in the Company's offices knit *black* wool; ". . . It seems to me," Marlow says, "I had stepped into the gloomy circle of some Inferno." As he proceeds to fathom Kurtz's mystery, he perceives that its essentials ". . . lay deep under the surface, beyond [my] reach. . . ." Because Marlow's story goes beyond the obvious it carries an abundance of suggestive words or images, e.g., silence, stillness, blazing heat, immobility, somber trees, decay, somber and brooding ferocity, skulls on posts, blind whiteness of a fog, overcast sky, impenetrable darkness. Thus, the memory of an actual experience is transformed into a symbolic and deeply ironic account of a modern descent into Hell.

We see, therefore, that "Heart of Darkness" is not a simple story. The symbolic journeys of Kurtz and Marlow are one theme. Another, perhaps no less important, is the political issue of Belgian colonialism. Conrad, his own conservatism notwithstanding, indignantly condemns Belgian imperialism in the Congo.

The first narrator connects the story that is to come from Marlow with some comments on the history of the Thames and the conquerors who had gone out on that river. He paves the way to Marlow's opening words, spoken against the setting of a falling dusk and the lights of moving ships, ''And this also . . . has been one of the dark places of the earth.'' Marlow takes up the theme of man's conquest, briefly mentions the Romans, the fascination of the mystery in the wilderness, and then, before he makes the most significant observation, he assumes ''the pose of a Buddha preaching in European clothes and without a lotus flower.'' Marlow speaks of the ancient conquerors:

> They grabbed what they could get for the sake of what was to be got. It was just robbery with violence, aggravated murder on a great scale, and men going at it blind—as is very proper for *those who tackle a darkness.* The conquest of the earth, which mostly means the taking it away from those who have a different complexion or slightly flatter noses than ourselves, is not a pretty thing when you look into it too much. What *redeems it is the idea only.* An *idea* at the back of it; not sentimental pretense but an *idea;* and an *unselfish belief in the idea*—something you can set up, and bow down before, and offer *a sacrifice to. . . .*

This is a fitting prelude to the picture of the Belgian exploitation of the Congo Marlow paints later on, as he plunges into his narrative. With biting irony he describes the activities of a French man-of-war, anchored off the coast, and shelling the bush although there was not a shed in sight. This was indeed a passage into places which had a deadly but also a farcical aspect. During this nightmarish pilgrimage Marlow comes upon a chain-gang of native slaves and then a group of black shapes crouching among the trees and dying. This is one of the most powerful and shocking evocations of man's brutality, an indignant indictment of the white man's inhumanity to the black man in the Congo.

> They were dying slowly—it was very clear. They were nothing earthly now, nothing but black shadows of disease and starvation, lying confusedly in the greenish gloom. Brought from all the recesses of the coast in all the legality of time contracts, lost in uncongenial surroundings, fed on unfamiliar food, they sickened, became inefficient, and were then allowed to crawl away and rest. These moribund shapes were as free as air—and nearly as thin.

Little wonder Marlow has some strong words for the so-called Eldorado Exploring Expedition.

These explorers were merely buccaneers who lacked the idea, the only redeeming quality of the necessary brutality. They only wanted to wrest the treasure from the land with ''. . . no more moral purpose at the back of it than there is in burglars breaking into a safe.''

''Heart of Darkness'' can thus be regarded as a study of Belgian colonialism, and not a very complimentary one at that. Like *The Nigger of the ''Narcissus,''* however, it has provoked ire among some more extreme black writers of our age. For example, Chinua Achebe, the African novelist (*A Man of the People* and *Things Fall Apart*), in a paper entitled ''An Image of Africa,'' presents a central and strident thesis ''that Conrad was a bloody racist.'' He fails to see anything else in ''Heart of Darkness'' and does not mention any other works of Joseph Conrad. Achebe's parochial and rather simplistic view of Conrad's achievement in this short novel is underscored by the recent avalanche of references to ''Heart of Darkness'' in the media, following the disastrous war in Vietnam and the macabre events in the jungle of Guyana which ended with the mass murder-suicide of the followers of Rev. Jim Jones. The popular appeal of the story is further shown in Francis Ford Coppola's film *Apocalypse Now*, which uses Kurtz's name and the metaphor of the boat going up the river and draws on several other motifs of the novella, whose title has entered the language as a term for the drama of fanaticism, the dark mystery of the bush, and the darkness of the human soul.

Yet it is a great deal more. Its many-leveled ambiguities and apparently inexhaustible literary allusiveness (conscious or unconscious) have inspired or baffled numerous critics questing for an explanation of its symbolic design and significance. Some, like E. M. Forster (in *Abinger Harvest*), assailed Conrad for his mistiness. The secret task of Conrad's genius, Forster asserted, contained a vapor rather than a jewel. There was no point discussing the philosophy of Conrad in this work or in other works of Conrad, for they had no creed worth discussion. Others, like F. R. Leavis (in *The Great Tradition*), while agreeing with some tenets of Forster, considered ''Heart of Darkness'' one of Conrad's best performances. T. S. Eliot found in it a fitting epigraph for his ''The Hollow Men''— ''Mistah Kurtz, he dead.'' One could argue its appropriateness, for Kurtz is anything but hollow. It is people like the Manager, or Kayerts and Carlier (in ''An Outpost of Progress'') who qualify for the epithet.

Like any good work of art, this novel affords many interpretations, so many, in fact, that they would fill several thick volumes. I shall mention a few only, to illustrate some critical possibilities. Lilian Feder suggests an analogy of Marlow's journey with Vergil's [also spelled ''Virgil''] visit to Hades in the sixth book of the *Aeneid*. Robert O. Evans calls it a ''descent into the underworld.'' Paul Wiley compares Kurtz's lot with the Christian myth of man's fall from innocence, Kurtz being the man expelled from the Garden of Eden. Zdzislaw Najder detects allusions to the legends about Alexander the Great. Feder's view may offend some as being too forced a literary exercise, and Wiley's as not quite in keeping with Conrad's own attitude to Christianity or the conventional understanding of the Christian dogma. Marlow is no Christ-like figure, nor is Kurtz the Christian Satan. Najder's parallel with the death of a great military leader is fascinating, but it is treated almost parenthetically in a note and thus never fully developed. Cedric Watts (in *Conrad's ''Heart of Darkness'': A Critical and Contextual Discussion*) attempts a definitive answer to all other critics of the novel, as he weaves into his argument ''references to Dr. Johnson, T. S. Eliot, Vergil, Darwin, T. H. Exile, Shakespeare, Bucket, Berkeley, UNESCO, Pound *et al.* (for this is only a partial list). . . . He rejects 'allegorizing a non-allegoric work' as Robert O. Evans's treatment of Dantean illusion. He rejects Hillis Miller's whole approach as being 'so vehement a tribute to Conrad's nihilism that his ingenuity was strenuously exercised by the fact that Conrad had put pen to paper at all'; this has led to Miller's neglect of 'the nobility of Marlow's humanity and of Conrad's moral and political indignation.' He rejects Guerard's 'night-journey' theory, 'the prime weakness' of which is that we lose more by it than we gain.'' Watts's credo is simple enough but, like all other theories that preceded it, it hardly offers an end to the continued exegesis of this work: ''The better the interpretation of a text, the larger the number of salient narrative facts that interpretation will (in principle or in demonstration) accommodate, and the fewer it will contravene.''

Perhaps the familiarity with Conrad's biographical background of this novel and the existence of his *Congo Diary* are partly responsible for the elaborate aesthetic and psychological interpretations which may obscure the author's basic preoccupation with man's guilt (as in ''Karain'' and ''The Lagoon''), and thereby man's moral stance tested in the darkness of a jungle. Conrad did not *choose* vagueness or mistiness in order to confuse or mystify his readers or critics. Such mistiness, if one agrees with Forster, as there is results from Conrad's narrative method (which makes the narrator a major protagonist of the story, thus placing a distance between him and the author) and his symbolic language. In a sense, it is precisely this sense of mistiness, which I prefer to call mystery, that is one of Conrad's stylistic traits. The author cannot reveal the mystery without the reader's participation. Conrad's heroes (in this and in other novels) include both the Marlows who tortuously seek self-knowledge and the Kurtzes who leap into moral darkness and are swallowed by it. The contact between the two, sometimes the conflict, must be shared by the reader who is asked to experience a kind of moral and aesthetic ephiphany: the revelation of his own affinity with the nether regions of the human soul or an identification with the tragic triumphs of heroes who assert their elusive glory by exalted idealism or misguided conviction.

Source: Adam Gillon, ''The Appalling Face of a Glimpsed Truth: 'Heart of Darkness,''' in *Joseph Conrad*, Twayne, 1982, pp. 68–77.

Sources

Achebe, Chinua, ''An Image of Africa: Racism in Conrad's 'Heart of Darkness,''' in *Heart of Darkness*, 3d ed., Norton, 1988, pp. 251–53, 256–59.

Haugh, Robert F., '''Heart of Darkness': Problem for Critics,'' in *Heart of Darkness*, 3d ed., Norton, 1988, pp. 239, 241.

Saravan, C. P., ''Racism and the 'Heart of Darkness,''' in *Heart of Darkness*, 3d ed., Norton, 1988, pp. 282, 283, 285.

Singh, Frances B., ''The Colonialistic Bias of 'Heart of Darkness,''' in *Heart of Darkness*, 3d ed., Norton, 1988, pp. 268, 269, 279.

Further Reading

Batchelor, John, *The Life of Joseph Conrad: A Critical Biography*, Blackwell, 1994.
    Batchelor's book is a recent biography of Conrad, published by Blackwell press, which originally published many of Conrad's stories and novels.

Hammer, Robert D., ed., *Joseph Conrad: Third World Perspectives*, Three Continents Press, 1990.
    Conrad has been criticized for his Eurocentric depictions of Africa and other ''Third World'' cultures; this collection of critical essays presents a variety of Third World perspectives on Conrad's work.

Hochschild, Adam, *King Leopold's Ghost: A Story of Greed, Terror, and Heroism in Colonial Africa*, Houghton Mifflin, 1998.

This work is a history of Colonial Africa under Belgian King Leopold II, during the period in which several of Conrad's stories take place.

Moore, Gene M., ed., *Conrad on Film*, Cambridge University Press, 1997.

Moore's collection of critical essays on film adaptations of Conrad stories includes several essays on *Apocalypse Now*, which was based on ''Heart of Darkness.''

Nelson, Samuel H., *Colonialism in the Congo Basin, 1880–1940*, Ohio University Center for International Studies, 1994.

This work is a history of European conquest and colonization of the Congo during the period in which several of Conrad's stories take place.

Roberts, Andrew Michael, ed., *Conrad and Gender*, Rodopi, 1993.

This text is a collection of critical essays on Conrad's representations of sex, gender, and sexuality in his fictional work.

Wilson, Derek, and Peter Ayerst, *White Gold: The Story of African Ivory*, Heinemann, 1976.

Wilson's and Ayerst's book provides a history of the ivory trade in Africa.

Kew Gardens

Virginia Woolf
1919

The story was published on May 12, 1919, by Hogarth Press, a publishing enterprise cofounded by Woolf and her husband Leonard in 1917. For the first edition, Woolf's sister Vanessa Bell fashioned two woodcut illustrations to accompany the text. When the third edition was printed in 1927, Bell's illustrations appeared on each page throughout the text.

The story was also reprinted in Woolf's *Monday or Tuesday* (1921) and in *A Haunted House and Other Short Stories* (1944), edited by Leonard Woolf. In the past decades it has been anthologized many times, representing a slice of Woolf's artistic mastery and reflection of her keen insight into what it means to be human.

Author Biography

Virginia Woolf is one of the most admired authors of the twentieth century. She was born on January 25, 1882, to Julie and Leslie Stephens in London, England. Sir Leslie Stephens was a very influential writer and critic who sternly and methodically published volume after volume of the *Dictionary of Literary Biography*, of which he was the first editor. Growing up, Woolf met many famous writers including George Meredith and Henry James.

Woolf's parents had each been married before; her mother Julia brought three children with her and Leslie two children to their marriage. Woolf's family was large and she later lamented growing up with a lack of privacy and of time to spend with her mother. The Stephens family was financially well situated and employed servants who helped keep the family running in their London home. Woolf remembered her mother working nonstop to raise her three children, the stepchildren from Stephen's previous marriage, and her four children with Leslie. In her fiction, Woolf often concentrates on the pain, sacrifice, and beauty of mothers, probing the quiet agony of a solitude seemly ironic in a world of children, society, and fast-paced innovation. Julia died when Woolf was thirteen, precipitating Woolf's first major breakdown. Her father was increasingly morose and detached after the death of his wife and died himself in 1904 when Virginia was twenty-two. After Sir Leslie Stephen's death, she and her older brother Thoby lived in London and started the Bloomsbury Group discussions. The Bloomsbury group was a collection of young people in London who met to discuss art, politics, and literature. During this time, Woolf taught at Morley College and wrote literary reviews.

Woolf's older brother Thoby died of typhoid in 1906 after returning from a vacation in Greece. The same year, Woolf's sister agreed to marry Clive Bell. In this time of loneliness and depression, Woolf struggled to write. In 1912, Virginia Stephens married Leonard Woolf who had been a friend of older brother Thoby and had participated in the Bloomsbury conversations. While they continued to write, the Woolfs also started their own publishing company. From modest beginnings in 1917, Hogarth Press would eventually publish works by Sigmund Freud, T. S. Eliot, and Katherine Mansfield and enable Virginia Woolf to publish any of her own work without any interference.

Woolf's major literary production began with her novel *A Voyage Out* (1915). It and her next novel, *Night and Day* (1919), were long novels with more conventional plot patterns. Later more experimental prose works include *Jacob's Room* (1922), *Mrs. Dalloway* (1925), *To the Lighthouse* (1927), *Orlando* (1928), and, perhaps the most challenging of Woolf's novels, *The Waves* (1931). While Woolf's novels were masterpieces of subtlety, manner, and insight, her nonfiction, such as *Three Guineas* and *A Room of One's Own*, powerfully advocate for women's rights and critique structures of patriarchy.

Woolf eventually took her life in the middle of World War II. Overwhelmed with the hatred of war, she and her husband, who was Jewish, had signed a suicide pact that would ensure they not be taken prisoner if Hitler invaded England. After suffering from depression for most of her life and enduring many nervous breakdowns, Woolf had had enough. After a morning of writing on March 28, 1941, she walked down to the river, loaded her pockets with stones and drowned herself.

Woolf's career responds to the contradictions of her youth and of a larger Victorian society in which men of the proper English class where shuttled into positions of authority while women stayed at home, bound by sexual mores and domestic, family duties that isolated them. But, to reduce Woolf merely to restating the conventional terms of gendered double standards or to her bouts with depression is to miss the vibrancy, energy, and resistant force of her writing and her mind.

Plot Summary

The story begins by setting the garden scene: a mild, breezy, summer day in July with "perhaps a hundred stalks" of colorful flowers, petals unfurled to meet the sunlight. The light hits not only the flowers in an "oval-shaped flower-bed" but the brown earth from which they spring and across which a small snail is slowly making its way. As human characters saunter thoughtfully or chattily through the garden and through the story, the narrator returns again and again to descriptions of the garden and the snail's slow progression.

Men and women meander down the garden paths, zigzagging like butterflies, as the narrator hones in on particular conversations. The first group the reader meets is a husband and wife walking just ahead of their children. The husband, Simon, privately reminisces about asking a former girlfriend to marry him. As he waited for her answer, he hoped that the dragonfly buzzing around them would land on a leaf and that Lily would then say yes. The dragonfly never settled and Lily never said yes. Now, as he turns to his wife Eleanor, he wistfully remembers dragonflies and silver shoe buckles.

Simon then asks his wife if she ever thinks of the past; she replies, "'Doesn't one always think of the past, in a garden with men and women lying under trees?''' She tells her husband that when she was just six years old she received '''the mother of all my kisses all my life.''' When painting in the garden, a grey-haired old woman suddenly and quietly kissed the back of her neck. The family vanishes as the mother calls to Caroline and Hubert and the narrator tells of the snail beginning to move, his antennae quivering as he navigates a leaf that has fallen in its path.

The second set of feet walking by the flower bed belong to an elder and younger man. The younger man, William, walks steadily with an ''expression of perhaps unnatural calm'' as his companion talks ''incessantly'' and walks erratically, smiling and murmuring as if holding a conversation with himself. His speech is cryptic and sporadic, but he believes himself to be talking to ''the spirits of the dead'' now in ''Heaven.''

The old man tells William that Heaven was '''known to the ancients''' and with the war the spirits are restless, '''rolling between the hills like thunder.''' William listens as the older man proposes to record and collect the voices of dead husbands by putting an electrical device at the head of widows' beds. He then suddenly catches sight of a woman who appears to be dressed in ''purple black'' and exclaims '''Women! Widows! Women in black.''' William catches his older friend, perhaps his father or patient, by the sleeve and distracts him by pointing to a flower. The old man looks confused and then proceeds to bend his ear to the flower, to listen and to begin a mysterious conversation as if the flower were a telephone. The old man then begins to speak of having visited the ''tropical roses, nightingales'' and mermaids of Uruguay, hundreds of years ago with the ''most beautiful young woman in Europe.'' William moves him along through the garden with increasingly ''stoical patience.''

Two elderly women ''of the lower middle class'' curiously follow the odd old man who listens to flowers. One of the women is ''stout and ponderous'' and the other ''rosy-cheeked and nimble.'' They are fascinated by his eccentricity especially because they think the man to be of an upper ''well-to-do'' class but wonder if he might indeed be mad. After scrutinizing the old man, they give each other a ''queer, sly look'' and continue with their conversation.

Their conversation is filled with names ''Nell, Bert, Lot, Cess, Phil'' and with ''he says, I says, she says, I says, I says, I says—''; the ''ponderous

Virginia Woolf

woman'' stops listening, letting the words fall over her as she stares at the flowers and rocks back and forth, hypnotized by their light and their color. Abruptly she suggests to her companion that they find a seat and have their tea.

As these two women walk away, the snail begins to traverse the leaf in his path by crawling under it. As he moves under the leaf, a fourth pair of feet come by the oval flower bed.

A young man and woman, Trissie, in the ''season'' just before ''the prime of their youth'' stand in front of the flower bed, each with a hand on Trissie's parasol, pushing it into the earth. Their conversation is commonplace—about the price of admission to the garden on Fridays—and filled with long pauses and spoken with monotonous voices. Despite this seeming simplicity, each seems to look with wonder at the ordinary objects around them. The parasol, the coin in the young man's pocket with which he will pay for their tea, and the flowers around seem to mean something inexplicably important. The young couple stands with eager anticipation and speaks ''words with short wings for their heavy body of meaning.'' Suddenly, the young man declares to Trissie that it is time they had their tea and he steers her onward as she ''turns her head this way and that'' thinking about ''orchids and cranes among wild flowers'' and wondering what is down each garden path.

The story ends with a final reflection on the garden in which people, like butterflies and flowers, color the vast, orchestral scene. Bodies of people and plants dissolve into a misty atmosphere, punctuated by brilliant flashes of light out of which arise ''Voices, yes, voices, wordless voices, breaking the silence suddenly with such depth of contentment, such passion of desire, or, in the voices of children, such freshness of surprise.'' But the final note of the story places this garden scene in an ominous context of droning city life, of immense industry, and of world war outside the garden—''a vast nest of Chinese boxes all of wrought steel turning ceaselessly one within another.''

Characters

Eleanor

The wife of Simon and the mother of two children (Caroline and Hubert), Eleanor walks through the garden chatting with her husband who tells her of his failed marriage proposal to Lily years before in Kew Garden. Eleanor remembers herself as a little girl, painting by the lake with five other girls. As Eleanor painted, a ''grey haired woman with a wart on her nose'' suddenly kissed her on the back of the neck, a precious kiss that became Eleanor's ''mother of all [her] kisses all [her] life.'' When her husband asks whether she minds if he talks about the past, she responds that she does not mind and asks, '''Doesn't one always think of the past, in a garden with men and women lying under the trees? Aren't they one's past, all that remains of it, those men and women, those ghosts lying under the trees . . . one's happiness, one's reality?'''

Narrator

The narrator seems able to notice almost anything but only slightly interprets the various interactions, conversation, and details. The focus of narration is the flowerbed and those who walk by it or, like the snail, move unnoticed by any character in the story. The story moves from depicting small, telling details of specific interactions to a more general reflection on the wide network of life in which the garden, its flowers, snails, and patrons all coexist.

Older Man Who Listens to Flowers

Accompanied by William who steers him through a garden course, this older man smiles and talks ''almost incessantly'' to himself. To William he speaks of ''spirits of the dead'' and their experience in Heaven. He tells William of an electrical contraption that would allow a widowed woman to talk to the spirits in Heaven; the older man then gets distracted by the ''purple black'' dress of a woman who he seemingly mistakes as a widow. William distracts the older man by drawing attention to a flower, to which the confused older man listens momentarily before changing the subject to the ''forests of Uruguay, which he had visited hundreds of years ago in company with the most beautiful woman in Europe.''

Simon

The husband of Eleanor and father of Caroline and Hubert, Simon walks just six inches in front of his family in Kew Gardens, reminiscing about a failed proposal to a past love named Lily. He tells Eleanor about his reflection, asking Eleanor if she minds his thinking about the past. When she replies that she does not mind, Simon explains that his feelings about Lily and her rejection of his proposal can be symbolized by ''a square silver shoe-buckle and a dragon-fly'' in Kew Garden.

The Snail

The snail with a shell of ''brown circular veins'' makes its way slowly across the floor of a flowerbed as the human characters saunter by, lost in their own thoughts and conversation. While the characters have no occasion to even notice the snail, the narrator comments on its progress throughout the story.

Trissie

A young man and woman (Trissie) on the verge of youth's prime, walk by the snail's flowerbed. The young man talks of the price of admission on Friday while Trissie asks about belief in ''luck'' and the experience of walking through Kew Gardens. Nervously, she stands with him, looking at the flowerbed as they express themselves in ''words with short wings for their heavy body of meaning'' and lean together on Trissie's parasol, hands slightly touching as the parasol sinks into the earth. Abruptly, the young man suggests they have tea and Trissie excitedly responds ''Where does one have one's tea?''

Two Elderly Women of the Lower Middle Class

These unnamed characters are lower middle-class women who follow curiously the erratic movements of the older man whom William directs. One of them is "stout and ponderous" and the other "rosy-cheeked and nimble." After their fascination with the older man fades, they "energetically" resume a "complicated dialogue" that the stories narrator records as a mere lists of names, of "I says" and "she says" as well as "Sugar, flour, kippers, greens" and "Sugar, sugar sugar." As the "nimble" woman talks, the "stout woman's" thoughts wander as she stares into the oval flower bed before suggesting that they find a seat and have tea.

William

The younger of two men walking together in Kew Gardens, William wears "an expression of perhaps unnatural calm." He steers his companion through the garden with care, listening to the older man prattle on almost nonsensically about Heaven and Uruguay. William directs the older man's attention to a flower to keep him from approaching a woman that seems to remind the old man of a widow dressed in black.

Young Man with Trissie

As the young man accompanies Trissie on their walk through Kew Gardens, he touches the two shilling piece in his pocket with which he will pay for tea. He nervously tries to grasp the reality of his new experience as a man in a garden with a woman.

Topics for Further Study

- Compare the four different groups of people who stroll through Kew Gardens. Do you see any similarities among them? How do Eleanor and Trissie compare? How do Simon and the young man compare with Trissie?

- Why is so much attention paid to a snail walking across the garden floor?

- What is unique about this story? Can you formulate a plot? What is the story trying to do by skipping around from group to group and why doesn't the story tell the reader more about what happens to each of its characters?

- Analyze in detail the scene of Trissie and the young man standing by the flower bed. What does the umbrella symbolize? What does the two-shilling piece in the young man's pocket symbolize? Why does Woolf expect the reader to figure out the details?

- After meandering through the garden, several of the people decide to go have their tea. Why? What are the literal reasons and what are some possible figurative interpretations?

Themes

Loneliness and Alienation

Each human character in the story seems lost in his or her own reminiscences. Despite walking with someone in Kew Gardens, the narrator emphasizes ways in which their thoughts are their own. Some of the characters are merely alone with their thoughts, like the first couple who remember by themselves and then talk with each other about their memories. Other characters, like William and the "ponderous woman," seem lonely. They walk with a companion who does not seem to notice them. In the end, the man and the "ponderous woman" are perhaps not merely lonely but alienated from those around them. The old man's strange behavior seems to keep him locked into a world all his own, unable to connect with anyone around him.

By making a garden the focal point of this rumination on ideas of aloneness, loneliness, and alienation, Woolf evokes the biblical image of the garden of Eden from which the Adam and Eve were cast out. Woolf's story seems to suggest that the very language that humans beings use to connect to other human beings is not only filled with misunderstanding but can itself be a wall that prevents communication.

The Modern World

The final paragraph of the story situates "Kew Gardens" in an ominously vast and overbearing world of the machinery and systems of industrial production that undergirded World War I. The old man seeking to hear the voices of dead husbands might be a picture of a more general experience in which war and industry link to destroy peoples' families. The contraption he stutters on about is an ambivalent symbol, serving to denote a way in which he can reconnect to those who have been lost and ironically connoting his own isolation from William who walks beside him.

Gender Roles

Each couple that passes through the garden seems to represent ideas regarding what men and women are supposed to do in society. The husband and wife operate in an understated harmony even as they reflect with a hint of melancholy on youthful days when the world seemed full of unlimited potential. The old man and William imply the inability of men to connect with one another, even about things as devastating as death in war. The ''lower middle class women'' illustrate the seeming futility and emptiness of working as servants; their conversation is but an inadequate distraction from the fact they seem to have little to love in life. The final couple is a young man and woman who are just learning the roles that they are expected to play. As the young man takes charge of Trissie, steering her toward tea for which he will pay with the coin in his pocket, one is left hoping she or they will find a way of straying down those curious garden paths.

Generally, Woolf seems to point out the way women depend on complementing men. Marriage, however, does not seem to grant happiness or connection. Rather, it seems to imply a certain loneliness of motherhood, the eventual alienation of widowhood, or the reputation of being a lower-class spinster. Woolf also seems to emphasize the way young men are pushed into taking charge, stifling attempts at openness and honesty with women or other men. As the machinery of life drones on outside the garden, the men seem called to take their place in a system that will use them up.

The Natural World

Although the idea of a garden might imply the vibrancy, life, and innocence of nature, Kew Gardens is described in terms that emphasize the more formal effect of color and angular play of light. The narrative tone emphasizes geometric shapes, discrete objects, and characters' trajectories as they advance through the garden. This emphasis seems to implicate the garden in the ''vast nest of Chinese boxes all of wrought steel turning ceaselessly'' outside the garden in the city. It is important that

Kew Gardens is not a spontaneous expression of natural forces but a space whose construction was engineered and constructed and whose flowers, trees, and grass were meticulously planted and cultivated. While inviting the reader to consider the garden as a touchstone of natural force, the garden seems to offer a formalistic screen across which peoples' lives fleetingly cast their shadows as the snail methodically proceeds in his arduous trek across the fertilized floor of the flower bed.

Style

Point of View and Narration

The narrator is an omniscient third person. The narrator sets the scene and is able to delve into each character's private thoughts. The true narrative insight appears not so much in what is said or illustrated but in the demonstrated inadequacy of the characters' conversations.

The narrator illustrates the garden scene in a fashion that deflects emphasis from an individual person or group of persons. People appear in a series that is implicitly continuous and repetitive. The snail offers the only consistent character and even ''his'' progress is not only mundane, but it is not narrated to completion; the story ends with the snail in the act of tentative progression. The descriptions of the garden are omniscient about the visual impression of the garden—the play of light, the shape, angle, and placement of garden objects, and the diffusion of color. As a result of these narrative emphases, the story deflects attention from a human-centered narrative to a more detached suggestion of how humans fit in a larger formal structure.

Setting

The story takes place in Kew Gardens, the Royal Botanical Gardens near London. Presumably, it unfolds near the time Woolf wrote the story in 1917. The gardens provide a public space that people of different classes share, even if they do not directly associate. Similarly, the practice of having tea denotes a continuity in these Londoners.

Symbol and Images

Kew Gardens is the story's title and central image. The narrative development of Kew Gardens overrides any specific characterization and challenges what readers normally expect in a story. While one normally thinks of a garden as providing a backdrop to the plot of human drama, be it comedy or tragedy, here the garden overwhelms any singular human persona.

The image of the garden, then, operates as a symbol on at least two different levels. First, the garden implies the idea of nature in which humans are at harmony with organic growth processes. The biblical garden of Eden is perhaps the most forceful manifestation of this harmony. To people living in the modern era of machinery and urbanity, is the idea of nature just another invention? By rendering images of the garden with emphasis on geometry, light, and perspective, the story uses the garden as an ironic symbol of humanity's distance from nature and the ensuing manufacture of natural spaces.

This ironic "garden" echoes the ironic companionship in the story. Each set of those promenading Kew Gardens seems to offer a deceptive picture of understanding and solidarity. The narrative perspective lights on each pair to demonstrate the ways in which they are actually walking the grounds quite alone.

Historical Context

World War I

Before World War II, the First World War was simply known as the Great War. As the twentieth century began, Germany, France, England, Russia, and Austria-Hungary intensely guarded their international territorial and economic interests, even to the point of threatening war. The assassination of Archduke Ferdinand by a Serbian nationalist in 1914 sparked a shooting war between the major power alliances (the Triple Alliance and the Triple Entente) of Europe. After four years of war, approximately ten million people were killed and over twenty million were wounded.

Death of Queen Victoria

In 1901, Queen Victoria died. She had become queen in 1837, succeeding William IV, and had enjoyed the longest reign of any British monarch. In her old age she was very popular. Throughout her reign, she fought hard to maintain England's colonial control throughout the world. She also was opposed to granting women the legal right to vote.

Industrial Age

The beginning of the twentieth century seemed both a time of immense promise and a chilling reminder of the cost of "progress." Cities were places of international commerce and culture where artists and writers lived and associated. Cities were also the space of factories; and in a time before governmental standards that regulated workplace safety, the age of workers, and the length of the working day, trade unions fought for humane conditions. Gardens and parks had long provided a space for people to mingle, now they took on an added role of providing a space of natural beauty in an industrial environment.

As the world headed for the political domino reactions that triggered world war, the industrial age seemed less of a promise and more of a deadly mechanism with an uncontrollable force. Factories produced immense amounts of artillery and other implements of war, and people questioned the value of an industrial capability that could so easily be harnessed and directed for the destruction of other human beings.

Impressionism and Narrative Perspective

As the legacy of nineteenth-century imperialism laid the groundwork for the economic state of affairs in the twentieth century, traditional ideas of what was literature and how to tell a story also changed. Painters like Seurat, Monet, Picasso, and Chirico challenged traditional notions of perspective in the visual arts; instead of assuming that art would present a cohesive vision of the world, artists proposed exploring the ways in which all perspective was partial, fractured, and even violently dissonant.

Women's Rights

Woolf's story presents at least three types of women. First, there is the dutiful wife walking a step behind her husband with an eye on her children. Second are the lower middle-class women who seem lost and lonely. Third and finally is the curious young woman who stifles her inquisitive enthusiasm to follow her boyfriend to tea. In these slight pictures are different visions of women's roles in the aftermath of a Victorian era in which conventional morality scripted women to be self-sacrificing domestic angels, lonely old spinsters, and virginal, innocent young girls in need of male direction. As devastating as World War I had been to young men of her generation, Woolf considered the insti-

Compare & Contrast

- **1915:** There are 4,300,330 visitors to Kew Gardens. In 1916, the number falls to 713,922 after the institution of an entrance fee.

  1990s: About one million people visit Kew Gardens annually.

- **1918:** The fourth Reform Act increases the electorate from eight to twenty-one million. The Reform Act gives all men over the age of twenty-

one the right to vote, while women over thirty are granted voting rights. In the United States, women's suffrage is guaranteed by the nineteenth amendment to the Constitution, ratified in 1920. In 1928, all men and women over twenty-one who meet the residency requirement are entitled to vote.

  1990s: All men and women eighteen and older can vote in England and the United States.

---

tution of marriage a similar devastation as young girls were disciplined to march into the role of a good wife.

At the turn of the century, participants in the women's movement became more and more militant in their demand for political enfranchisement. "Kew Gardens" was published in the year after the fourth Reform Bill was finally passed in 1918. The Reform Bill gave all women over the age of thirty the right to vote. Not until 1928 were voting rights in England the same for men and women.

Throughout her career, Woolf addressed the stereotypes that limited and oppressed women, not only by denying them the same opportunities as men, but also by limiting their sphere of influence to a stifling and small domestic space. She would urge women to kill the "angel in the house," that is to self-reflect and combat the unreasonable and stagnant expectations placed on women regarding their intellectual, sexual, and public lives. Killing the angel required not only facing the public force of sexism but examining the ways sexism was internalized by women themselves.

Critical Overview

Upon its publication, "Kew Gardens" enjoyed modest praise. In 1919, the *Times Literary Supple-*

ment published an unsigned review of "Kew Gardens," praising the story for its strange beauty and atmosphere. Since then, the story has remained a favorite of Woolf's short fiction. In the 1970s, literary attention on Woolf revived and intensified. In 1985, Susan Dick edited *The Complete Shorter Fiction of Virginia Woolf*, which includes "Kew Gardens."

The general critical attention paid to Woolf has produced articles dedicated to "Kew Gardens." In "Pursuing 'It' Through 'Kew Gardens'" of 1982, Edward Bishop addresses what he calls Woolf's capture of "the essence of the natural and the human world of the garden." Bishop's essay provides a clear summary of the story's critical history, from the *Times Literary Supplement* through subsequent critics who attempted to account for the story's atmospheric quality by exploring how language relates to life experience, to sight, to expectations of narrative progression, and to the vital forces driving human experiences into narrative formulas of forward progression.

In 1997, Alice Staveley's "Visualizing the Feminine: Fashion, Flowers and Other Fine Arts," considers the genesis of "Kew Gardens," arguing that it represents a dialogue that Woolf was having with Katherine Mansfield in 1917 while Woolf was simultaneously writing the long novel, *Night and Day*. This connection to Mansfield anticipates the story's republication in 1927, just as Woolf begins writing *Orlando*, a novel about Vita Sackville-West with whom Woolf enjoyed a meaningful and intense relationship.

In *The Sisters' Arts* (1988), Diane Gillespie discusses Vanessa Bell's Illustrations to ''Kew Gardens.'' Gillespie uses the short story to demonstrate the process of negotiation with Woolf through which Bell created the cover design, the other illustrations, and the sustained marginal illustration of the 1927 edition published by Hogarth Press.

Criticism

Kendall Johnson

Johnson teaches in the English Department at the University of Pennsylvania. In this essay, he examines how Woolf uses nuances of light and form to reflect national disharmonies that culminated at the end of the Victorian era.

In naming her story ''Kew Gardens,'' Woolf chose a specific space to present the melancholy scenes of the characters' conversation. While the garden might connote an Edenic space in which human beings realize a natural completeness or contentment, Woolf's Kew Gardens transforms, as the story progresses, into a mere screen across which pass the transient presences of individuals. By understanding the local Kew history, one better understands the thematic irony of Woolf's garden.

Kew Gardens is outside London on the south bank of the Thames, covering over two hundred and eighty acres. It was established in the late seventeenth century and its history parallels changes in England's status as an empire. Before 1841, the garden was a retreat for royalty. In response to general public criticism that the garden had fallen into a state of neglect and to a national inquiry into the management of royal gardens, Queen Victoria transferred responsibility for maintaining Kew Gardens to national administration by the Office of Woods and Forest. Sir William Hooker became the first official director of the gardens.

Under Hooker, the garden developed into a national project that not only invited visitors to its grounds but also collected, assembled, and displayed specimens of plant-life that had been gathered from England's colonial possessions around the world. After 1885, Hooker retired and William Thiselton-Dyer became director. He developed Kew more aggressively into an arm of colonial enter-

prise. As Ray Desmond noted in *Kew: The History of the Royal Botanic Garden*, he even once commented to the governor of Madras (a seaport in India, then a colonial possession of England) that, ''we at Kew feel individual[ly] the weight of the Empire as a whole, more than they do in Downing Street.'' Botanical experiments refined more efficient ways of cultivating lucrative plant life, such as rubber plants, which would then be distributed to England's territorial colonies throughout the world.

In 1905, Sir David Prane became director. Three years later he ushered in the first subway posters that advertised Kew Gardens as a temporary escape from the urban life. The advertisements marked a new stage at Kew, foreshadowing the entrance fee instituted in 1916. The admission fee drastically reduced the number of visitors: in 1915, attendance figures record over 4.3 million people visiting the garden; the following year the number dropped to just under 714,000 people. Tuesday and Friday were reserved as student days for observing and sketching the garden's vast collection of specimen plants. Sundays remained free. In Woolf's story, when the young man ''in that season which precedes the prime of youth'' comments that ''they make you pay sixpence on Fridays,'' he may be announcing his adulthood by implying that he is no longer a student.

In the years just before the story's publication, the world had become dominated by the demands of an industrial economy in which the manufacture of war materials played a fundamental role. In the years before the war, Kew maintained a double mission of attracting the public to its grounds and assembling an imperial collection of botanical specimens. The tumult of World War I had a direct effect on Kew Gardens. Many more women become gardeners, replacing men who had been sent to the continent to fight. Additionally, beginning in 1914, Kew's grounds were put to a more practical purpose, cultivating onions. In 1918 the Palace lawn at Kew was converted to a potato field, yielding twenty-seven tons of potatoes to help alleviate the food supply shortage.

Given its publication date, it is difficult not to read ''Kew Gardens'' as an attempt to come to terms with the First World War. The war was devastating to Woolf, who like the rest of England, struggled to make sense out of casualties numbering 8.9 million men. How can one come to terms with the enormity of a world conflict that leads young men into trenches? What of the industrial power,

What Do I Read Next?

- *Dubliners* (1914), by James Joyce, includes short pieces that shed light on different people living in Dublin. Many stories focus on seemingly ordinary experiences that the characters struggle ineffectively to idealize. Joyce challenges his reader to read subtle cues to understand the implications of his characters' observations.

- *The Garden Party and Other Stories* (1922), by Katherine Mansfield, includes stories that utilize varied tones to illustrate people in their daily lives. Sketching the different impressions and perspectives of family members or solitary characters, Mansfield's prose can be fresh, stark, and haunting.

- *Jacob's Room* (1922), by Virginia Woolf, tells the story of Jacob Flanders who, like Woolf's beloved older brother, Thoby, died as a young man. Jacob is killed in World War I and the story is told through the perspective of those who interact with Jacob as family, friends, lovers, or mere acquaintances. Like ''Kew Gardens,'' the novel employs innovative writing techniques.

- *To the Lighthouse* (1927), by Virginia Woolf, tells the story of the Ramsay family's yearly retreat to their summer house. Mr. Ramsay is a philosopher and Mrs. Ramsay is a mother devoted to her children. The novel records the dynamics of family life and the touching effects of time's passage on human relationships. Like *Jacob's Room*, the novel employs innovative techniques and a network of subtle details.

---

technological advancement, and cultivated artistic production of which the Victorian age had been so proud?

Initially the story's garden seems to promise a space of therapeutic reflection. People strolling on the grounds move with curious irregularity, like ''white and blue butterflies who crossed the turf in zig-zag flights from bed to bed.'' But this space of repose is belied by the increasingly empty conversations between characters that substitute for intimacy. In a story, one expects character development and a plot in which the characters do something; instead, the reader of ''Kew Gardens'' notices a fundamental shift that relegates human activity to a mere visual feature in the final paragraph. Snails and people equivalently set the stage. Instead of a backdrop for character-driven plot, the garden becomes a formal centerpiece, composed of patches of color, angles of perspective, and rays of light.

The story's final paragraph flattens characters into visual components of an expanding horizon. Instead of a separate place of peace, the garden becomes ''so hot that even the thrush chose to hop, like a mechanical bird, in the shadow of the flow-ers.'' The people strolling the garden are reduced to instances in general pattern as they move: ''one couple after another with much the same irregular and aimless movement passed the flower-bed and were enveloped in layer after layer of green-blue vapour, in which at first their bodies had substance and a dash of color.'' They become shades of ''yellow and black, pink and snow white.'' And further, ''shapes of all these colors, men women and children,'' wavering and then seeking ''shade beneath the trees, dissolving like drops of water in the yellow and green atmosphere, staining it faintly with red and blue.'' In this reduction to abstract visual effect, humanity become as fragile as an erratic ''white and blue butterflies,'' floating in a careless and even malevolent machine world.

As people dissolve into the visual structure of the garden, the narrator links the garden to the machinery of the urban world outside of it. The children's voices no longer rupture a pastoral silence but instead are drowned by the incessant drone of ''motor omnibuses . . . turning their wheels and changing their gears; like a vast nest of Chinese boxes all of wrought steel turning ceaselessly one within another.'' Overlapping each other in this vast ''nest,'' the garden's flowers can merely flash their colors into the air. The different meanings of the word ''shade'' reflects the story's loss of human center: the protective shade of a garden tree is juxtaposed with the dead spirits or ''shades'' of those both lost to war or the inexorable progression of history. As Simon's wife observes, '''Doesn't one always think of the past, in a garden with men and women lying under the trees? Aren't they one's past, all that remains of it, those men and women, those ghosts lying under the trees, . . . one's happiness, one's reality?'''

The seemingly crazy old man's behavior explains the story's relation to the trauma of the war. He searches for the ''sprits of the dead'' whom he hears ''rolling between the hills like thunder.'' In his disorientation there is a reflection of each of the other characters' isolation from each other. The old man may be the spectacle of lunacy for the women following him, but the conversation between these sane women is superficial and lonely, consisting of a mere iteration of disconnected names and food items.

As the old man's eyes search the garden for spirits of the dead brought on by ''the war,'' he first proposes to hook up a machine through which widows can summon the dead spirits of their husbands. Distracted by the sight of a ''woman's dress . . . which in the shade looked a purple black,'' he tries to approach her but is caught by the supervising William, who diverts his attention with a flower. The old man bends his ear to the flower and begins speaking about ''the forest of Uruguay which he had visited hundreds of years ago in company with the most beautiful woman in Europe.''

There is a logic to the old man's words and actions that reflect the social tensions pervasive in England and evident in the specific history of Kew. In referencing Uruguay, the old man draws attention to the imperial design of the Kew grounds. During the nineteenth century, the garden collected specimens from around the world to complement England's imperial pride in building an empire worthy of ''the ancients.'' Plant collectors gathered ''specimens'' from all over the world—Brazil, Canada, United States, Nepal, Congo, India, Ceylon, Trinidad, Jamaica, Australia, China, Japan, and Timor, to name but a small number. The old man's quest for dead spirits may violate conventions of sanity—of sequential time and ordered space—but in doing so he emphasizes the symbolic pretension

> **Instead of a backdrop for character-driven plot, the garden becomes a formal centerpiece, composed of patches of color, angles of perspective, and rays of light."**

of the garden's imperial collection and implies the general breakdown of the imperial social order.

His preoccupation with women and his exclamation of ''Women! Widows! Women in black'' points to another aspect of the story's reflection on the effect of the war. Women in the story—the wife, the maids and the young girl—seem to share a stifling dependence on men. While widows are obvious victims of the war, the story implies a broader cost to being a woman; and the social conventions that brought on the war also limited women to specific domestic roles while disenfranchising them both economically and politically. In the years before the war, women were violently contesting these limitations and the social prejudice that motivated them.

At Kew Gardens, the fight for women's rights erupted in violence just before the war. In February of 1913, suffragettes destroyed a large quantity of plants and nearly two weeks later burned down the Refreshment Pavilion. At the end of the eighteenth and throughout the nineteenth century, the right for women to vote was a key demand in the movement for women's rights in England. It is perhaps ironic that Queen Victoria remained consistently opposed to enfranchising women to vote. After years of lobbying Parliament, the suffrage movement was dealt a crucial defeat when Prime Minister Gladstone frustrated the inclusion of women's suffrage in the Reform Bill of 1884. The women's movement became increasingly militant in their efforts to win voting rights. By 1913 when Kew Gardens was attacked, the suffrage movement had won strong public support and mustered the financial means to fund the many demonstrations; yet, many suffrage bills were defeated. When the World War I began in 1914, the question of suffrage was suspended, even as women worked in jobs now vacated by men in uniform. As the war ended in 1918, Prime Minister David Lloyd George's Reform Bill recognized the right of women to vote and to hold public office. This was the fourth in a series of reform acts that, over almost one hundred years, slowly reorganized government and extended suffrage. By 1928, voting requirements for men and women of England were finally uniform.

The garden at Kew, then, is not just an "innocent" space. Rather, it is a reflection of national imperial history. In 1919, the inherited social order of the Victorian age had seemingly betrayed both men and women, expending the former in senseless carnage and systematically limiting the latter into nearly total dependence on an ideal husband. Woolf's story punctures the symbol of this inheritance with a narrative that poses a new perspective. In her displacement of human character, Woolf echoes the dehumanization of her time and suggests a role for art that dares to challenge the conventional structure of meaning and perspective.

Source: Kendall Johnson, Critical Essay on "Kew Gardens," in *Short Stories for Students*, The Gale Group, 2001.

Deborah Kelly Kloepfer

In the following essay, Kloepfer presents an overview of "Kew Gardens" through its characters.

"Kew Gardens" was first published as a small book by Leonard and Virginia Woolf's Hogarth Press (1919) and later included in the volume *Monday or Tuesday* (1921). Woolf herself judged it "slight and short" and wrote in her diary, "the worst of writing is that one depends so much upon praise. I feel rather sure that I shall get none for this story; & I shall mind a little." Later, however, she was consoled by numerous orders for copies, "a surfeit of praise" from influential friends, and a favorable review in the *Times Literary Supplement*.

More recent critics find "Kew Gardens" an important transitional piece in which Woolf "worked out the lyrical, oblique approach in which her best later works would be written." The story, which on one level is simply about "the men and women who talk in Kew Gardens in July," is highly descriptive and visually charged with a sensuous, almost microscopic vision: describing the "heart-shaped or tongue-shaped leaves" on "perhaps a hundred stalks" rising from a flower-bed, Woolf writes, "The petals were voluminous enough to be stirred by the summer breeze, and when they moved, their red, blue and yellow lights passed one over the other, staining an inch of the brown earth beneath with a spot of the most intricate colour." Four couples pass across the field of vision: a middle-aged married couple with their two children; a confused old man, accompanied by a young male companion, who hears voices; two "elderly women of the lower middle class . . . frankly fascinated by any signs of eccentricity betokening a disordered brain, especially in the well-to-do"; and a young man and woman "in the prime of youth, or even in that season which precedes the prime of youth"— awkward, inexperienced, excited.

One of the curious features of the story is that it is narrated in the third person from the point of view of a snail in the garden, "a unique but ultimately disappointing vantage point," according to one critic, "from which to observe the flow of life. Woolf has not yet found a fictional body to inhabit."

While not entirely successful, "Kew Gardens" does lay the groundwork for many of the strategies and concerns developed in Woolf's later work.

The older couple evokes Woolf's preoccupation with the passage of time and the ghosts of the past. The old man embodies the thin line between eccentricity and genuine madness, an issue of particular interest to Woolf, who was prone to episodes of debilitating depression throughout her life, finally committing suicide in 1941. The young couple are caught in another space compelling to Woolf where the function and efficacy of language itself are called into question, a space punctuated with "words with short wings for their heavy body of meaning, inadequate to carry them far." In the section involving the two old women "piecing together their very complicated dialogue," Woolf examines the "pattern of falling words" and begins to experiment textually: "Nell, Bert, Lot, Cess, Phil, Pa, he says, I says, she says, I says, I says—" This scene later troubled Woolf, and she worried that it "discredited" the story a little.

She is nonetheless at the beginning here of her lifelong literary project to explore language, substance, human intercourse, consciousness, and, ultimately, reality. "Stylistically, formally," the critic Phyllis Rose finds the story "exciting" but "ultimately unsatisfying," in part because although "Kew Gardens" represents "daring innovations in technique," the author "had not yet found a subject which would allow her to express her humane experience of life." And yet finally Woolf is not simply experimenting with form but writing about "depth of contentment," "passion of desire," and "freshness of surprise" as she attempts to catch, according to Rose, "the fragmentary, transient nature of what *is* real, people passing, wisps of conversation, nature in motion, the wafting of life."

The story ends with a long paragraph of dissolving "substance and color" as all life in the garden—"yellow and black, pink and snow white, shapes of all these colours, men, women, and children"—appears and then seems to evanesce. But if one truly listens, Woolf maintains, "there was no silence; . . . like a vast nest of Chinese boxes all of wrought steel turning ceaselessly one within another the city murmured; on the top of which the voices cried aloud and the petals of myriads of flowers flashed their colours into the air."

Source: Deborah Kelly Kloepfer, "'Kew Gardens': Overview," in *Reference Guide to Short Fiction*, edited by Noelle Watson, St. James Press, 1994.

John Oakland

In the following excerpt, Oakland examines "Kew Gardens," revealing a progression of formal and thematic patterns in which "randomly individual activity has been given coherence, order, and optimism."

[It] is salutary to re-examine, against a background of Woolf's literary principles, what is actually being said in ["Kew Gardens"], as well as how it is being said. For "Kew Gardens" is more than atmosphere, insubstantial impressionism or an experiment. Arguably, it is not an expression of meaningless life but, on the contrary, reveals a harmonious, organic optimism. The choice of such a short piece for close reading is appropriate, since it is perhaps more central to Woolf's fiction than has been generally accepted, and contains in embryo many of the issues of form, theme, content, character, plot and action which occupied her in all her work.

While these are, unfortunately, loaded terms in contemporary criticism, they are all symbiotically subsumed in Woolf's design under 'form,' to include both technical and thematic concerns. So that theme was not merely the subject matter of a story, but more appropriately the essential significance of the total work revealed through its organisation. Although it has been frequently argued that Woolf's fiction lacks the traditional ideas of plot, action and character, "Kew Gardens" can be very adequately analysed in these terms, while accepting that here they are minimal and couched in special ways.

> One of the curious features of the story is that it is narrated in the third person from the point of view of a snail in the garden. . . ."

Indeed, Woolf's creative method is perhaps more conventional than has been granted, and within it the old categories still operate.

Woolf herself was conscious of their inherent value in her attempts to organise all the various aspects of form. Writing of the proposed composition of *Jacob's Room* (1922) in words which reflect the already completed "Kew Gardens," she remarks that:

> I'm a great deal happier . . . today than I was yesterday having this afternoon arrived at some idea of a new form for a new novel. Suppose that one thing should open out of another—as in an unwritten novel—only not for 10 pages, but 200 or so—doesn't that give the looseness and lightness that I want; doesn't that get closer and yet keep form and speed, and enclose everything, everything? . . . but conceive (?) "Mark on the Wall," "K. G." ["Kew Gardens"], and "Unwritten Novel" taking hands and dancing in unity. What the unity shall be I have yet to discover; the theme is a blank to me; but I see immense possibilities in the form I hit upon more or less by chance two weeks ago.

These views show that Woolf did deliberately work in terms of theme and form, that she was concerned to show one thing opening out of another in good narrative fashion, and that this creative process should demonstrate a thematic unity in the work, culminating in a final resolution. . . .

Woolf's search for a fictional form which would allow her to communicate her particular view of life and the modern consciousness was mainly expressed in her famous comments about the conventions of Edwardian literature. Life was not 'a series of gig-lamps symmetrically arranged,' but a 'luminous halo' allowing the mind to receive 'an incessant shower of innumerable atoms,' each differing in intensity, quality and duration, which created a particular identification at a specific moment in time. Once glimpsed, this fleeting impression passes to be replaced by a succession of others. While such

> "The snail, insects, butterflies, water-drops, flowers, buses, an aeroplane, a thrush and the final voices are included within an all-embracing thematic perspective."

views may seem inadequate psychology and involve a too passive conception of perception, they do nevertheless reflect the framework in which Woolf's fiction is set.

Although this emphasis upon the fragmented temporary rendered by impressions and associations superficially suggests passivity, many of Woolf's characters, even in a short piece like "Kew Gardens," do respond to stimuli and assert themselves. Such reactions are part of a movement towards a unified meaning, and also have an identifying quality in the presentation of character over a period of time. Terms such as space, perception, time, relativity and subjectivity have been frequently used by critics to identify Woolf's immediate fictional world, with a warning that the vision is only transient. But "Kew Gardens" invites us beyond the surface impressions to a larger, growing reality. It is significant that Woolf was very aware of December 1910 (the first London Exhibition of Post-Impressionist Paintings) as being the date for a new consciousness. The Exhibition proclaimed that the earlier Impressionism was dead, and that Post-Impressionism would rescue the object from mere light and air by concentrating upon firmer pictorial construction and interconnected form. In its translation to fiction, this emphasis obviously implied both an organic structure and a thematic centre beyond impressions. These were the means to the end, not ends in themselves, so that painting's representation in space would be echoed in fiction's arrangement over time. . . .

[Woolf's] fiction initially focuses upon the characters' interior responses to associations. Implicit in this process, as it is actually conveyed in works such as "Kew Gardens," is both an acceptance of the temporariness and fragmentation of the initial

impressions, but also, in a time-lapse continuum, a realisation of a continuing character identification composed collectively of these moments and the reactions to them, so that a wider version of life and selfhood is promoted.

The initial impressions constitute the primary texture of experience and awareness. The organisational function then creates formal coherence and harmonious themes out of the moments. "Kew Gardens" is structured to present a series of points of view, authorial comment and descriptions, progressing from one experience to another by interlocking devices of association. The various stages of the story appear to be very consciously planned in a formal and thematic attempt to create order despite (or because of) the fluid nature of the initial impressions.

In this process, the presentation of character through an examination of individual consciousness is central to Woolf's design. The characters in "Kew Gardens" may be sketchy, but the story demonstrate that even the minimal is composed of revelation in action, and that the apparently ordinary has significance. The characters do confront experience in their individual ways, and are engaged in the problems of choice, self-awareness and self-definition that such a confrontation forces. There is enough information in the character-presentation for the reader to analyse personality and theme. Surfaces are penetrated to reveal a newer view of the characters' realities, as well as suggesting, in the unfolding plot, a shared experience and fate.

For, although Woolf is clearly the third person omniscient narrator who reveals as much (or as little) as she wishes, there is beyond her no one dominant character in terms of point of view. Rather, the individual characters after their various exposures (together with the narrator) make up a collective theme-voice, which is progressively expanded through the episodes. The story additionally focuses on the natural background and non-human creatures to such an extent that they anthropomorphically become characters with lives and points of view of their own. The snail, insects, butterflies, water-drops, flowers, buses, an aeroplane, a thrush and the final voices are included within an all-embracing thematic perspective. The cumulative theme-voice of "Kew Gardens" is composed of descriptions, fragmented conversations and interior monologues which all generalise character in a dramatically creative way that eventually leads to the universality of the voices in the final paragraph.

This technique demonstrates the major process of ''Kew Gardens,'' that of the gradual fusion of the human and the non-human into an organic whole. Formally and thematically, one thing opens out of another and all experience is fused into one reality. This theme, as some critics have suggested, indicates that behind the diversity of people and things there lies an essential oneness. More importantly for Woolf's later work, such an awareness represents the kind of organicism which would be examined at greater length in *Jacob's Room*, *Mrs. Dalloway* (1925) and *The Waves* (1931). . . . This particular kind of organicism, however, does not so much indicate pantheism with its postulation of a God, but rather a non-specific form of vitalism which, in spite of its vagueness, is nevertheless illustrated as the main thrust of ''Kew Gardens.''

While the initial revelations of the characters are shown in fragmented isolation, the episodic structure demonstrates the growing commonality of these experiences and develops significant patterns in the movement towards fusion. All the events share common elements such as the flower bed and Kew Gardens, but also references to relationships, restrictions, desires, purpose, introspection, consciousness and unconsciousness. From these roots rise larger interconnected themes such as the nature and perception of time, memory and space, death, the quality of understanding, the nature of love and personal relationships, the attraction and mystery of the unknown, linear and lateral movement, and the urge to freedom beyond restraints. All the characters, human and non-human, share to some degree in aspects of these various concerns.

There is nothing in the text to suggest that this qualitative movement towards unity is anything but harmonious and optimistic, and the tone is joyful rather than despairing. The story does not show the meaninglessness and horror of life, but a progress towards meaning, in much the same way as the snail, far from being victimised, demonstrates purpose and achievement. Each revelatory experience is part of and contributes to a unified reality, and the fusing processes, particularly that of human with non-human, break down differentiation in the establishment of interrelated harmonies. . . .

The story's associational structures, changing and deepening in each episode, provide constant transitions from the natural to the human and back again The catalysts for the individual revelations in this linear progression are the flower bed and Kew Gardens itself. All these experiences and move-ments occur between the first and last paragraphs which form the 'book-ends' or the lyrical prose-poetry of the events.

The description of the flower bed in the first paragraph, with its erotic stalk imagery, references to 'heart-shaped or tongue-shaped leaves,' and the 'throats' of the flowers, immediately connects the human and the natural worlds. Within the latter there is an active aggressiveness of a quasi-human type, with the conditioning influences of the summer breeze, sun and light upon petals, the earth, pebbles, leaves and raindrops. The snail is similarly coloured by the setting, and operates within the natural world in terms of the problems it faces from lateral and linear choices of movement. . . .

The shifting mixture of a linear plot and lateral experiences, together with the circling of the dragonfly in this episode and the continuing struggles of the snail, bring together, both formally and thematically, the two worlds. Such descriptions do not serve merely for decorative or experimental effect, but indicate very conscious designs. Significantly, the fluctuating themes of purpose, introspection, consciousness and unconsciousness are also introduced at this stage. For, while Simon strolls carelessly and Eleanor bears on with greater determination, he '. . . kept this distance in front of the woman purposely, though perhaps unconsciously, for he wished to go on with his thoughts.'

In spite of its brevity, much happens to Simon and Eleanor in this first human episode. They connect the past with the present through associations of love and relationships, which are additionally reflected by natural objects such as the dragonfly and the waterlilies, by humans such as Lily and the old grey-haired woman, and by inanimate objects such as the silver shoe buckle and shoes. Fusion of these elements is natural for Simon since '. . . the whole of her seemed to be in her shoe. And my love, my desire, were in the dragonfly. . . .' Furthermore, the dragonfly in its refusal to settle and confirm Lily's choice, maintains a sense of perennial flux, just as Eleanor's marking the time of the kiss with her watch is a continuous present and a universal referent, '. . . the mother of all my kisses in my life.' Similarly, for Eleanor, past and present are joined in common experiences and in the collection of other human beings in Kew Gardens. 'Doesn't one always think of the past, in a garden with men and women lying under the trees? Aren't they one's past, all that remains of it, those men and women, those ghosts lying under the trees . . . one's happiness, one's reality?' Such time and space references scattered throughout the story have structural and thematic parts to play in the unfolding theme of fusion, and are not simply superfluous. The consciousness of past and present, the dead and the living, in this first episode becomes more confused as the story progresses, when similar processes are repeated by other characters. This illustrates not only the gradual blurring sense of objective reality as against the power of association, but also the movements towards a fusion of elements in time and space.

The human interlude of Simon and Eleanor eventually shifts again into the natural world, as they walk past the flower bed '. . . now walking four abreast, and soon diminished in size among the trees and looked half-transparent as the sunlight and shade swam over their backs in large trembling irregular patches.' The family's earlier haphazard progress has become almost military, and the irregularity passes to the natural world, under whose conditioning the human characters now fall in partial fusion. Their reduction in size and significance illustrates the joining of the two worlds, and also invites comparison with the snail's scene, to which the transition structure now returns.

In this episode, the snail is a link between human and natural, and possesses a linear identity which is different to that of 'the singular high stepping angular green insect,' which is able to change direction at will. The snail is again briefly, like the family earlier, stained by the flowers before moving on, significantly now appearing to have a definite goal in front of it. It is faced by obstacles in its movement until its attempts are interrupted by the human. 'Before he had decided whether to circumvent the arched tent of a dead leaf or to breast it there came past the bed the feet of other human beings.' This episode illustrates not the snail's victim-status but its gradual immersion in the two worlds, its purposive manoeuvres, and its discovered possibility of choice between lateral and linear progression. . . .

[The] final paragraph of the story shows the apparent fusion of all in the common experience of Kew Gardens. The natural and the human worlds coincide in a unity which resolves all previous tentative approaches and haphazard movements. 'Thus one couple after another with much the same irregular and aimless movement passed the flower-bed and were enveloped in layer after layer of green blue vapour, in which at first their bodies had

substance and a dash of colour, but later both substance and colour dissolved in the green-blue atmosphere.' Under the influence of the heat the irregular movements of the thrush and butterflies are conditioned into more orderly patterns, and eventually all the colours of the human and natural worlds are unified. 'Yellow and black, pink and snow white, shapes of all these colours, men, women, and children were spotted for a second upon the horizon, and then, seeing the breadth of yellow that lay upon the grass they wavered and sought shade beneath the trees, dissolving like drops of water in the yellow and green atmosphere, staining it faintly with red and blue.'

From this immersion voices rise, expressing contentment, desire and freshness of surprise, reaching beyond the purely material. But Kew Gardens is now only a microcosm of this process, for the fusing image is also applied to the adjacent city of London and its buses, '. . . like a vast nest of Chinese boxes all of wrought steel turning ceaselessly one within another the city murmured; on the top of which the voices cried aloud and the petals of myriads of flowers flashed their colours into the air.' Beyond, '. . . in the drone of the aeroplane the voice of the summer sky murmured its fierce soul,' so that all the elements of the story, animate and inanimate, have been fused, and their sounds stretch beyond the earth to a further universal fusion and identification.

The Chinese box reference demonstrates precisely the main theme of "Kew Gardens" by showing the interconnection of object, or a complex of boxes within boxes, the opening of which are presumably infinite. The story's progressive uncoverings have illustrated a greater reality and fusion at each step, so that, formally and thematically, random individual activity has been given coherence, order and optimism. . . .

Source: John Oakland, "Virginia Woolf's 'Kew Gardens,'" in *English Studies*, Vol. 68, No. 3, June 1987, pp. 264–73.

Edward L. Bishop

In the following essay, Bishop explores Woolf's relationship between "language and reality," which is seen through her use of characters and techniques.

"Lucky it isn't Friday," he observed. "Why? D'you believe in luck?" "They make you pay sixpence on Friday." "What's sixpence anyway? Isn't it worth sixpence?" "What's 'it'—what do you mean by 'it'?" "O, anything—I mean—you know what I mean."

The reader knows what the young woman means because the conversation occurs near the close of ''Kew Gardens'' and Virginia Woolf has already captured ''it'': the essence of the natural and the human world of the garden. From the beginning of her career Woolf had been pursuing the ''uncircumscribed spirit'' of life, but she had been frustrated by the methods of conventional fiction. Now, she makes no attempt to deal with ''it'' discursively—she does not, as she might have done in *The Voyage Out*, have a pair of sensitive individuals discuss the ''whatness'' of Kew. Neither does she offer straightforward description. The sketch represents the artistic application of Woolf's famous manifesto published only the month before in her essay ''Modern Fiction'': ''Life is not a series of gig-lamps symmetrically arranged: life is a luminous halo, a semi-transparent envelope surrounding us from the beginning of consciousness to the end.'' In ''Kew Gardens'' Woolf does not document the physical scene, she immerses the reader in the atmosphere of the garden.

Her success in the piece was immediately recognized. Harold Child, writing in *TLS* [*Times Literary Supplement*] on the first appearance of ''Kew Gardens'' (1919) lauded this ''new proof of the complete unimportance in art of the *hyle*, the subject matter'':

> Titian paints Bacchus and Ariadne; and Rembrandt paints a hideous old woman. . . . And Mrs. Woolf writes about Kew Gardens and a snail and some stupid people. But here is ''Kew Gardens''—a work of art, made, ''created,'' as we say, finished, four-square; a thing of original and therefore strange beauty, with its own ''atmosphere,'' its own vital force.

Subsequent writers have agreed with Child, notice that the source of the sketch's vitality lies in the linguistic strategies of the narrating consciousness. In an early study (1942), David Daiches writes, ''The author's reverie is what organizes the images and the characters; and an intellectual play uses the images as starting points for meditation.'' James Hafley, in his exploration of the Bergsonian concepts in Woolf's fiction (1954), argues that the sketch is about ''life'' in the Bergsonian sense, a ''vital impetus'' that is not logically explicable, and which must be ''first directly apprehended and then crippled into words.'' But what is contradictory in Bergson is, Hafley claims, ''supremely consistent and translucent'' in Woolf. In the next decade (1965) Guiget focussed on the method of the piece, observing that ''as the eye traces an imagined arabesque through this mosaic, the mind regroups fresh wholes in this atomized universe, breaks ha-

bitual links and associations to form others, hitherto unnoticed or neglected.'' In a recent consideration of Woolf's narrators (1980) Hafley returns to ''Kew Gardens,'' locating the ''vital force'' in the language itself, not in any specific quality of imagery but in the action of the voice. In the sketch narration becomes ''creation rather than transmission.'' Yet precisely *how* this is achieved, how the mind is led to ''regroup fresh wholes,'' how the ''luminous halo'' is generated, has never been adequately demonstrated. And it is only by looking very closely at the way the language operates that we can see how Woolf simultaneously creates and engages the reader with something as nebulous as an ''atmosphere.''

To glance first at the most obvious strategies of narration, in ''Kew Gardens'' Woolf dispenses with the carefully articulated structures of *Night and Day,* the ''scaffolding'' as she calls it. There is very little external action here—a series of couples strolls past a flower bed in which a snail is struggling to get past a leaf—and the development seems as ''aimless and irregular'' as the movements of the people in the gardens. On closer examination it becomes obvious that the sketch is carefully constructed: there are four couples and among them they constitute a cross-section of social class (middle, upper, and lower), age (maturity, old age, and youth) and relation (husband and wife, male companions, female friends, lovers); and their appearances are neatly interspersed among four passages which describe the action in the flower bed. Yet this pattern is not insisted upon; the juxtapositions are not abrupt or pointed. As in her later works, the progression of events (the ''series of gig-lamps'') has been subordinated to the modulation of emotion, and the ending conveys a sense of resolution more than of narrative conclusion. In the human encounters too a similarly understated order obtains. The pleasantly elegiac mood created by the married couple, Eleanor and Simon, gives way to uneasy tension as the old man exhibits a senility that borders on madness. The glimpse of something darker merely hints at the turmoil underlying the tranquil scene (a conjunction of beauty and terror that remains constant in Woolf's writings) before the coarse curiosity of the two women restores the lighter tone. Finally the emotions that the lovers now feel echo those evoked in Eleanor and Simon only by their memories. Thus Woolf quietly comes full circle to end with love, before shifting to a more encompassing vision of unity—the entelechy of all her works—of human beings integrated not just with each other but with the phenomenal world:

''they wavered and sought shade beneath the trees, dissolving like drops of water in the yellow and green atmosphere, staining it faintly with red and blue. . . .''

The achieved effect of the sketch, the sense that it is an atmosphere into which one moves, follows in part from the fluid overall structure, but the reader's immersion begins at the outset with the smoothly shifting point of view. Woolf does more than set the scene in the opening paragraph, she smoothly dislocates the reader's accustomed perspective of a landscape. The first sentence, ''From the oval-shaped flower-bed there rose perhaps a hundred stalks. . .,'' begins with a description from a middle distance; the narrator sees the shape of the bed as a whole, but also sees the flowers as individual entities, not as a solid mass. Yet by the end of the sentence the narrator has moved much closer, to the ''yellow gloom of the throat,'' from which emerges ''a straight bar, rough with gold dust and slightly clubbed at the end.'' And, as the light ''move[s] on and spread[s] its illumination in the *vast* green spaces'' (my italics) beneath the dome of leaves, the reader has been placed among the flowers and given a correspondingly different sense of scale. As the paragraph closes, the breeze ''over-head'' is above him in the petals, not in the trees: ''Then the breeze stirred rather more briskly overhead and the colour was flashed into the air above, into the eyes of the men and women. . . .'' The reader now finds himself viewing the bed from within—his angle of vision is in fact that of the snail—rather than admiring the floral designs as a more distant observer.

Just as the initial description begins with and then moves beyond a conventional perspective on the scene, so the first exchange between Eleanor and Simon (''Fifteen years ago I came here with Lily,' he thought. . . . 'Tell me, Eleanor. D'you ever think of the past?''') moves out of interior monologue and then, with ''For me, a square silver shoe buckle and a dragonfly—' 'For me, a kiss . . .''' into a new mode, one that seems to combine qualities of both thought and speech. Again, Woolf is gently forcing the reader out of his established perceptual habits, raising questions about the nature of discourse and the conventions used to render it. And, just as she has placed the reader within the garden, so with each successive dialogue she moves deeper, below the flat surface of words, to reveal that, like the apparently flat flower-bed, language too has cliffs and hollows. In doing so she dramatizes the way in which one often perceives words less as units of information than as physical sensation. Indeed, as

the two women talk, their words finally cease to have more than vestigial denotative meaning for the ''stout'' member of the pair; they become as palpable, and as non-cognitive, as a rain shower: ''The ponderous women looked through the pattern of falling words at the flowers. . . . She stood there letting the words fall over her, swaying the top part of her body slowly backwards and forwards, looking at the flowers.'' The image prepares the reader for the final encounter, that between Trissie and her young man. For after the brief discussion on the cost of admission (quoted at the beginning of this essay) Woolf moves into their minds, exploring the unvoiced reactions to their colloquy. It is here that the alternation between description and dialogue becomes a fusion, as the words become not merely a ''pattern'' but a contoured landscape, and one whose features echo those of the terrain through which the snail has been moving.

In this episode Woolf displays what will become the defining characteristic of her later prose: a flexible narrative style which allows her to move without obvious transition from an external point of view to one within the mind of a character, and back again, thus fusing the physical setting with the perceiving consciousness. Further, it is a mode which invites the reader's participation in the process, so that the reality Woolf conveys is apprehended through the experience of reading. In the passage quoted below, the reader becomes conscious of moving *among* words, just as the characters do.

> Long pauses came between each of these remarks; they were uttered in toneless and monotonous voices. The couple stood still on the edge of the flower bed, and together pressed the end of her parasol deep down into the soft earth. The action and the fact that his hand rested on the top of hers expressed their feelings in a strange way, as these short insignificant words also expressed something, words with short wings for their heavy body of meaning, inadequate to carry *them* far and thus alighting awkwardly upon the very common objects that surrounded *them*, and were to *their* inexperienced touch so massive; but who knows (so they thought as they pressed the parasol into the earth) what precipices aren't concealed in *them*, or what slopes of ice don't shine in the sun on the other side? Who knows? Who has ever seen this before? Even when she wondered what sort of tea they gave you at Kew, he felt that something loomed up behind her words, and stood vast and solid behind them; and the mist very slowly rose and uncovered—O, Heavens, what were those shapes?—little white tables, and waitresses. . . . (my italics). . . .

The passage begins straightforwardly enough: the narrator notes the pauses, the tone of the remarks, the posture of the couple. But in the third sentence, as she explores the relation of the words to the feelings they are meant to convey, the narrator draws the reader into the emotions of the couple. The initial image describing the words evolves into an extended metaphor that communicates more exactly the ''something'' the young couple feels, and the metaphor works in part through deliberately ambiguous pronouns which both enforce the reader's engagement and unite the disparate elements of the scene.

The words ''with short wings for their heavy body . . .'' suggest bees—appropriate both to the garden and to the drone of the ''toneless and monotonous voices'' of the speakers. As the passage develops, it sustains this dual reference: ''inadequate to carry them far'' seems to refer as easily to the words being inadequate to carry the couple far as it does to the wings being inadequate to carry the words far. The latter proves to be the primary meaning, for the words alight on the ''common objects.'' But with ''common objects that surrounded *them*'' the pronoun can refer to either the couple or the words. The latter would appear to be the logical choice, yet in the next clause, ''and were to *their* inexperienced touch so massive,'' the pronoun obviously refers to the couple.

''Massive,'' however, seems to modify the ''common objects''—in which case ''their'' should refer to the words-as-bees—unless the words from the couple's point of view are massive. This seems unlikely (they have been described as ''short, insignificant''), and the following clause ''but who knows . . . what precipices aren't concealed in them'' perpetuates the confusion over the pronoun referent, for the reader knows that there are precipices in these common objects; he has already encountered the ''brown cliffs and deep green lakes'' that block the snail's path. Nevertheless, the precipices do reside in the words. The image of the bee has somehow fallen by the way, and the young man and woman now look through the words, as the older woman earlier ''looked through the pattern of falling words at the flowers,'' to the something ''vast and solid'' behind the words.

I spoke of confusion, and the passage is confusing if one insists on pinning down all the referents. But through an alert and unprejudiced attention to the syntax, one can more firmly apprehend the action of the figures: what is being fostered is identification, not confusion. The reader does not find the passage muddled; rather he experiences the sense of one thing merging with another—the couple with the words, the words with the surrounding objects. And he easily makes the transition from bees to precipices, for the one expresses the activity of the conversation, while the other conveys the young man's perception of the meaning behind the words; the massiveness and solidity express the intensity of their emotions. Indeed, the image of the bee, from ''words with short wings . . .'' to ''. . . that surrounded them,'' can be regarded as a parenthetical aside by the narrator, after which she returns to the consciousness of the young couple. In any case, Woolf's supple prose ensures that while the reader is invited to attend closely he is not forced to pause. The impression of a cloudiness or ''mist'' that she creates derives from extreme precision, not vagueness, and it conveys exactly that sense lovers have of the world dissolving into soft focus as they become for a moment oblivious of all except each other. Further, the reader experiences the wonder at ordinary objects which follows such intense moments: ''O, Heavens, what were those shapes— little white tables. . . .'' Yet by using the most bathetic object available to satisfy that portentous anticipation, Woolf gently puts the event in perspective; the reader feels a sympathetic amusement toward the infatuated couple. He continues to identify with them, however, for the shock of wonder is not described, rather it is conveyed through the prose as the reader emerges from the mist of the passage.

In fact the reader is not yet fully out of the mist, for the tables and waitresses, he gradually discerns, have not been observed—they are just now taking shape in the young man's mind:

> O, Heavens, what were those shapes?—little white tables, and waitresses who looked first at her and then at him; and there was a bill that he would pay with a real two shilling piece, and it was real, all real, he assured himself, fingering the coin in his pocket, real to everyone except to him and to her; even to him it began to seem real; and then—but it was too exciting to stand and think any longer, and he pulled the parasol out of the earth with a jerk and was impatient to find the place where one had tea with other people, like other people. . . .

The touch of the coin brings him back by degrees to the external world—''even to him it began to seem real''—and the reader too must struggle to regain the conventional sense of the reality of the park. For Woolf has convinced him of what she had so firmly stated in ''Modern Fiction,'' that life ''is a little other than custom would have us believe it.'' In any case, Woolf does not follow them to tea; the sketch closes with a vision of the human bodies, the flowers, the voices and the traffic noises all dissolving in the heat of the afternoon. The tables, the shilling, the parasol, elements she called ''the alien and external,'' finally have far less immediacy than what Trissie could only describe as ''it'': the ''yellow and green atmosphere'' that is both ethos and ambience of the garden.

In her fiction Woolf continued to explore the relation between language and reality—both dramatically, through the experience and conscious probing of her characters, and formally, through the experimental techniques of her works. But with ''Kew Gardens'' she had discovered her voice, one that would remain more or less constant through the varied narrative structures she employed from *Jacob's Room* to *Between the Acts*. The quality she called ''life'' or the ''essential thing'' refused to be fixed by a phrase, but it could be arrested, briefly, by a net of words: words that evoke as well as indicate, that conspire to produce their own luminous halo, rendering (by inducing) a process of consciousness rather than a concrete picture. Thus it is that the value of her fiction derives less from the specific insights it imparts (one finds it difficult to remember the particulars of her works) than from the fact that the experience of reading initiates, in the sensitive reader, a growth of perception. We too come closer to apprehending ''it'' through our sojourn in ''Kew Gardens.''

Source: Edward L. Bishop, ''Pursuing 'It' Through 'Kew Gardens,''' in *Studies in Short Fiction*, Vol. 19, No. 3, Summer 1982, pp. 269–75.

Avrom Fleishman

In the following excerpt, Fleishman provides an analysis of Woolf's ''Kew Gardens,'' which he categorizes as a linear tale.

The standard format for a critical study of Virginia Woolf is a series of chapters on the nine longer fictions, one after the other. The body of her short stories tends to be neglected, except as quarry for the longer works. In contributing to a revaluation of Woolf's achievement, I take up these stories to discover what is distinctive in their form and, by implication, their innovations within the development of the modern short story. . . .

From the inception of critical discussion of the short story, the theory of its form has not moved much beyond Poe's notion of the unity of effect to be realized in a genre of limited means. While

problems of subject (plot or no plot?), theme (point or no point?), and narrative (telescoping . . . exposition . . . development) still persist, the question of form has never approached resolution. The usual byway down which this trail leads is epiphany; since the most prominent of modern stories come accompanied by the theory of epiphany, it was inevitable that Joyce's term has been used in lieu of a concept of form. A recent study of epiphany recognizes the laxity of such usage; despite Joyce's emphasis on the suddenness of the epiphanic moment, ''it has been fashionable to speak of one or another of his entire works as 'an' epiphany . . . If an epiphany is 'sudden,' as it is, then works as long as the average short story—and certainly any novel— simply cannot 'be' epiphanies, for they cannot be 'experienced' or apprehended immediately.'' The story, short or long, is not a single event but a form extended in time and, conceptually, in space as well.

If short stories are not unitary events but extended forms, they involve sequences of phenomena, verbal or representational. Morris Beja's definitions of epiphany are useful in defining story form, for he goes on to discriminate another frequent element of short fiction, the leitmotif. In the epiphany, Beja writes,

> [T]here has to be some such revelation—and it is here that we must beware a common misconception that confuses Joyce's epiphany with the leitmotif, the obsessive image which keeps coming back into the consciousness of a character or into the work as a whole but which at no single time involves any special, sudden illumination.

This apt distinction between a series of repetitions and a salient event unfortunately avoids stating a possible relationship between the two: the epiphany may appear at the end of a sequence, either as a term that stands outside the ''obsessive'' chain and suddenly emerges to cap it, or as the final and crowning instance of the repetition itself—that is, either a new motif, like the coin of success and betrayal in Joyce's ''Two Gallants,'' or a definitive statement of an established one, as in the protagonist's return to isolation in his ''A Painful Case.''

In this way, one can better appreciate the repetitiveness that appears so widely in modern literature—witness Pound, Eliot, Faulkner, Proust— but nowhere more strikingly than in the short story. What Frank O'Connor somewhat facetiously calls Hemingway's ''elegant repetition'' (on the model of ''elegant variation'') may be only a mannered extension of the repetitive patterns that mark the stories of Joyce, Mansfield, and Woolf. . . .

Virginia Woolf's short stories can be broadly divided into those that are formally linear and those that are formally circular. Another word on terminology here: the adjectives "linear" and "circular" are obviously metaphoric and, just as obviously, spatial. The use of these terms implies no exclusive disposition toward "spatial form" in Woolf: one might just as easily use the terms "progressive" and "returning," though these would emphasize the ongoing temporal flow of the narrative. *Linear* or *progressive* forms are those that start at one place or time or motif or verbal cluster and move through a number of others, arriving at a place, time, motif, or verbal cluster distinct from those with which they begin; while *circular* or *returning* forms are those which begin and end with the same or similar elements. . . .

A related group of stories takes a form similar to this gradual expansion or emergent creation, but in such a group there is no single term which moves through a sequence. Instead, a *series* of items is set out, the final item emerging as the key one. The most famous instance of such an organization is the well-known "Kew Gardens," in which eight beings or kinds of being are observed as they saunter through the botanical gardens. First comes the general class: "men and women." There follow a married couple remembering the past; a snail (who appears three times in all); a mystical and somewhat disturbed old man and his younger companion; "two elderly women of the lower middle class," looking for their tea; a young couple, also thinking of tea amid the glow of their romance; a group of aerial beings, including a thrush, butterflies, and an airplane; and finally, the voices. After lulling us with what seems a random and casual series of passers-by, the story reaches a new level of intensity at its final paragraph:

> It seemed as if all gross and heavy bodies had sunk down in the heat motionless and lay huddled upon the ground, but their voices went wavering from them as if they were flames lolling from the thick waxen bodies of candles. Voices. Yes, voices. Wordless voices, breaking the silence suddenly with such depth of contentment, such passion of desire, or, in the voices of children, such freshness of surprise; breaking the silence? But there was no silence; all the time the motor omnibuses were turning their wheels and changing their gear; like a vast nest of Chinese boxes all of wrought steel turning ceaselessly one within another the city murmured; on the top of which the voices cried aloud and the petals of myriads of flowers flashed their colours into the air.

This crescendo of the repeated word "voices" emerges as the final and triumphant term in the

> This crescendo of the repeated word 'voices' emerges as the final and triumphant term in the series of elements presented by the story. The voices are, indeed, a chorus of all the beings who have trooped through Kew Gardens, those named and all the others that might have been listed--come at last to expression and united in a common life."

series of elements presented by the story. The voices are, indeed, a chorus of all the beings who have trooped through Kew Gardens, those named and all the others that might have been listed—come at last to expression and united in a common life. It is difficult to distinguish form and content in this beautiful piece; even the simplest description of the form verges on an interpretation of the content, and I must content myself on this occasion with singling out the linear progression by which "Kew Gardens" reaches its heights at the close.

Source: Avrom Fleishman, "Forms of the Woolfian Short Story," in *Virginia Woolf: Revaluation and Continuity*, edited by Ralph Freedman, University of California Press, 1980, pp. 44–70.

Sources

Bishop, Edward, "Pursuing 'It' Through 'Kew Gardens,'" in *Studies in Short Fiction*, Vol. 19, No. 3, Summer 1982, pp. 269–76.

Desmond, Ray, *Kew: The History of the Royal Botanic Garden*, The Harvill Press, 1995.

Gillespie, Diane Filby, *The Sisters' Arts: The Writing and Painting of Virginia Woolf and Vanessa Bell*, Syracuse University Press, 1988.

Staveley, Alice, ''Visualizing the Feminine: Fashion, Flowers, and Other Fine Arts,'' in *Virginia Woolf and the Arts: Selected Papers from the Sixth Annual Conference on Virginia Woolf*, edited by Diane F. Gillespie and Leslie K. Hankins, Pace University Press, 1997.

Further Reading

Gillespie, Diane Filby, *The Sisters' Arts: The Writing and Painting of Virginia Woolf and Vanessa Bell*, Syracuse University Press, 1988.

    This work examines the relationship of Virginia Woolf to her sister Vanessa Bell. Bell was an artist who collaborated with Woolf in illustrating her stories and providing frontispieces for some of her novels. Gillespie discusses how ''Kew Gardens'' became an important collaborative project between the two sisters.

Lee, Hermione, *Virginia Woolf*, Knopf, 1997.

    This highly readable biography traces the life of Woolf not only as an author, a feminist, and a public figure but also as a private person.

Woolf, Virginia, *Moments of Being*, edited by Jean Schulkind, Harcourt Brace Jovanovich, 1976.

    This is a collection of Woolf's autobiographical essays. Not published in her lifetime, they lend insight on her childhood and relationships with her family, her fight with depression, and her decision to marry Leonard Woolf.

Leaving the Yellow House

Saul Bellow

1957

Saul Bellow's story "Leaving the Yellow House" is atypical of his body of work, which usually features urban settings and intellectual explorers. Still, yet it remains one of his most well-known and discussed stories. "Leaving the Yellow House" presents a protagonist who seems almost the antithesis of the Bellow searcher. Hattie Wagonner, seventy-two years old and alone, has lived most of her life under a cloud of self-deception. After an accident threatens her independent way of life, Hattie finds herself forced to look back on the past. Viewing her life as if it were a movie reel, Hattie is able to stop and examine the most important periods and events. Yet, such scrutiny seems to have little effect on her mindset. The resolution Hattie makes at the end of the story resides as firmly in her habit of denying the truth as any of the actions she has taken in the decades of her adult life.

This resolution has captivated scholars and critics. Many disagree on how to interpret the ending, Hattie's actions, and Hattie's character. Indeed, criticism of the story has been varied since its publication in the collection *Mosby's Memoirs and Other Stories* in 1968. Such a variety of ways to read the story only exemplifies its complexity and richness.

Author Biography

Saul Bellow was born in 1915 to Russian parents who had emigrated to Quebec, Canada. Solomon Bellows, as the child was called, spent the first years of his life in a poor, ethnic neighborhood in the suburbs of Montreal. When Bellow was nine, the family moved to Chicago, Illinois. A childhood illness led to a year-long confinement in a hospital, and during this time Bellow developed his interest in literature. His high school friends were also interested in writing as well as discussion of politics, religions, and ideas in general, and Bellow and his friends read their stories and writings aloud to one another. When he was only seventeen, Bellow and a friend ran away to New York City, where both boys attempted unsuccessfully to sell their first novels.

Bellow eventually returned to Chicago, studying literature at the University of Chicago. He switched his academic interests to anthropology and transferred to Northwestern University in 1935. After graduation, he began a program of graduate study in anthropology at the University of Wisconsin, but he quickly abandoned his studies because he was more interested in writing fiction than writing his thesis. After dropping out of school, Bellow obtained work with the WPA Writers' Project, preparing short biographies of midwestern writers. His ensuing jobs were all related to his literary interests. In 1938, Bellow began to work as a teacher. His first story was published in 1941.

During World War II, Bellow served as a merchant marine but was stationed stateside. This experience led to the writing of his first published novel, 1944's *The Dangling Man*. This novel established him as a spokesperson for his contemporaries. Until publication of his next novel, *The Victim*, published in 1947, Bellow worked as a teacher and a freelancer. *The Victim* helped earn him a Guggenheim Fellow, which enabled him to travel in Europe. Upon his return to the United States, Bellow settled in New York.

In 1953, Bellow published another promising novel, *The Adventures of Augie March*. While many critics negatively reviewed this book, it won for Bellow a number of impressive awards. It was his 1956 novella, *Seize the Day*, however, that attracted widespread critical acclaim. Today, this piece of work is considered a masterpiece of modern American fiction. "Leaving the Yellow House," another of Bellow's important works, was published two years later, but it was not incorporated into a short fiction collection until 1968. Throughout the 1960s and 1970s, Bellow continued a steady stream of publishing, including novels, lectures, a memoir, short stories, and a play. He was also co-editor of a journal.

Bellow has won numerous awards and made significant achievements throughout his career. His importance as a writer is recognized on an international level as well. For instance, French President Francois Mitterand made Bellow a commander of the Legion of Honour, and he was elected a fellow by the Scottish Arts Council. Most importantly perhaps, he also won the Nobel Prize for literature in 1976. Since the mid-1980s, he has primarily concentrated on writing novellas.

Plot Summary

As the story opens, seventy-two-year-old Hattie has lived in the old yellow house in the practically deserted community of Sego Desert Lake, Utah, for years. Born and bred on the East Coast, Hattie came out West after a failed marriage to a Philadelphia blueblood. She used to have a lover named Wicks. He was a cowboy, but Hattie, unable to overcome her inherent snobbery, refused to marry him and eventually rejected him. She also lived with another elderly woman, India, who left the house to her after her death.

Hattie is a likeable old woman, though she is difficult. She drinks too much and smokes too much, and is often mean-spirited. She also has a problem with self-deception. Although she lives alone, she maintains a routine that includes weekly trips to the nearest town to buy groceries, visit with friends, and get her hair done.

One day, returning from her neighboring friends' house, Hattie has an accident. Hattie explains away her loss of control of the car as due to a sneeze, but everyone knows that she was drunk at the time. Whatever its cause, the accident leaves Hattie's car stranded on the railway tracks, and a train is due along soon. Hattie hurries to the nearby Pace dude ranch for help. Darly, the elderly ranch hand, returns with her to the car. Darly wraps a chain around the car's bumper and tries to tow it off the tracks with his truck, but Hattie, near the chain, gets knocked down. The fall breaks her arm. Darly eventually gets the car off the tracks, and then he takes Hattie to the neighbor's house, the Rolfes. The couple take her home, put her to bed, and say they will call the doctor in the morning.

Hattie spends the next several weeks in the hospital, but she worries about how she is going to pay off her bill. Hattie has little money; her only asset is her house and its tattered furnishings. She thinks she will have to sell or rent her house in order to get the money, but when she speaks of her plan to Jerry Rolfe, he tells her she is expecting too high a price for the house.

After leaving the hospital, Hattie stays with the Rolfes. Jerry Rolfe thinks she should go back East to live with her brother, because she cannot (even before her accident) take care of herself. Hattie herself worries about what she will do. Once she returns to her own house, the Rolfes continue to help her, bringing her groceries and supplies back from town. Still unable to drive her car, Hattie must rely on their aid. She knows, however, that they will be vacationing soon. She resents their defection and she also wonders who will help her get by in their absence.

The Rolfes explore different options for Hattie's care. Jerry Rolfe talks to another neighbor, an elderly but tough woman named Amy Walters. When he suggests the two women live together, however, Amy says no because she and Hattie are too different. Amy, however, agrees to take care of Hattie if Hattie wills her the yellow house. Rolfe, knowing Hattie would refuse this offer, never even mentions Amy's proposition to Hattie. Another neighbor, Pace, also offers to give Hattie a monthly stipend if she leaves the house to him. Hattie refuses angrily.

Meanwhile, despite the doctor's warnings, Hattie is drinking and smoking as much as ever. In her solitude, she thinks back over her life, playing it back like a film. She remembers how she had to kill her dog, when he turned mean and attacked her. She had publicly blamed Pace for the disappearance of the dog, and this memory makes her acknowledge the way she has lied to herself and others throughout her life.

She decides to take greater responsibility of herself and her actions by making a will, but she can think of no one who is deserving of her only asset, the house. She discounts her relatives and her friends. In the end, knowing that it is unreasonable, she wills the house to herself. Yet, she promises herself that

Saul Bellow

she will think about her problem and work it out the next day.

Characters

Darly

Darly is Pace's sixty-eight-year-old ranch hand. Like Hattie, he comes from the East Coast. Darly inadvertently causes Hattie to break her arm, but he never apologizes for his mistake. Throughout the story, he and Hattie are seen as behaving antagonistically toward each other, each annoyed by the others' tacit accusations of being a drunk. In reality, they are uncomfortable with the mirror image each presents to the other.

Pace

Pace, one of Hattie's neighbors, runs a dude ranch. He offers to help Hattie out by giving her a monthly stipend, but only in return for her leaving the house to him after her death.

Helen Rolfe

Helen Rolfe is a neighbor of Hattie's. She and her retired husband live comfortably, able to afford such luxuries as new cars and vacations. She is Hattie's friend, but Hattie also harbors resentment toward her for her life of relative ease.

Jerry Rolfe

Jerry Rolfe is Hattie's neighbor and perhaps her only real friend. Hattie respects what Jerry says and confides her problems to him, as much as she is able. Jerry also is the only person who truly seems to understand Hattie's pride and circumstance. He makes significant efforts to help Hattie out after she breaks her arm, but he is unable to find someone who will look after her the same way he and his wife do.

Hattie Wagonner

Hattie is the protagonist of the story. Originally from the East Coast and a city woman, Hattie came out West decades ago. She wants to be a "rough, experienced" western woman, but in reality, Hattie cannot take care of herself. She has no close friends; indeed, her only friends in the story are a neighbor couple, the Rolfes, but Hattie demands too much from them. She has already chased away or been chased away by her family, including a husband and a lover. Now, at the age of seventy-two, with a broken arm, Hattie finds herself essentially alone and isolated from any sort of community. In her helplessness, she grows to understand both the precariousness of her own situation and her relationships with others in her community. Despite this realization, Hattie does little to repair these relationships. Instead, her search within herself leads to an affirmation that her identity is intrinsically linked to the house itself. The story's final action—Hattie's willing of her house to herself—seems to further reiterate her self-imposed isolation.

Amy Walters

Amy Walters is a self-sufficient miner's widow. She lives about twenty miles away from Hattie, and Jerry Rolfe approaches her with the suggestion that she and Hattie live together. Amy, however, can well take care of herself, and she will only help Hattie out in return for inheritance of her house.

Themes

Identity

The theme of identity is important in "Leaving the Yellow House" as Hattie strives toward some sort of self-understanding. Hattie has lived for decades under a cloud of self-deception. For instance, she pretends that her drinking is not as problematic as it is, and she pretends to care for India when she really feels that the other woman treats her like a servant. She blames her neighbor Pace for the disappearance of her dog when she killed the dog herself. After breaking her arm, Hattie realizes the extent of her reliance on other people, but she also realizes there are very few people, if any, whose assistance and love she can count on. This epiphany contributes to her attempts at self-exploration.

In reality, Hattie's striving toward self-understanding makes little progress. She concludes that the house is her only meaningful possession and indeed the best part of her. Though she reflects on the people she has chased out of her life, such as Wick, she does not explore the inherent sadness of life mostly lived at odds with others. When Hattie writes her will, which is her attempt to take some kind of responsibility for herself, she deems none of her estranged family as good enough to inherit her house. Her true feeling about the house, and the life she has led, are revealed when she writes "[b]ecause I only lately received what I have to give away, I can't bear it." With these words, Hattie demonstrates that only she is worthy of the house; thus, it is clear that she derives self-worth from the house.

Alienation and Loneliness

Hattie's alienation from any sort of community and her loneliness form the essential elements of her character. Hattie lives alone in the yellow house. She used to share the house with India, another aging alcoholic, but it is clear from Hattie's reflections that the relationship between the two women was not based on close ties but rather on mutual need: India needed someone to look after her, and Hattie needed someone to support her. The only neighbors with whom Hattie is on good terms are the Rolfes, yet she turns on them when she feels they are deserting her in her time of need; she believes they are selfish for vacationing when she needs their assistance. Hattie antagonizes Darly, the Pace's ranch hand, to such an extent that he cannot even bring himself to apologize for the role he played in her accident. Amy Walters and Pace both agree to help her after her accident only if they will receive financial remuneration after her death, i.e., the deed to her house. Hattie has turned away Wick, her lover, for inconsequential reasons, but primarily because he is not as good as her former husband, who himself turned her away.

Topics for Further Study

- How do you think Hattie will react to her situation the following day? Write a scene that could come at the end of the story, showing Hattie's reaction.

- Read Bellow's novella *Seize the Day*, and draw your own comparisons between its protagonist, Tommy Wilhelm, and Hattie Waggoner.

- Do you think Hattie is representative of the adventurous, self-sufficient Westerner? Why or why not? Do you think anyone in the story is representative of the West? Explain your answer.

- The narrator states that "you couldn't help being fond of Hattie." Do you agree with this statement? Why or why not?

- Bellow scholar Robert Kiernan stated that Hattie's "alienation from her own emotions . . . borders on schizophrenia." Conduct research on schizophrenia and then assess the validity of Kiernan's statement.

- Bellow's fiction generally takes place in urban settings. Imagine that Hattie lived in New York City. Would she experience the same problems as she does in Utah? Why do you think as you do? Imagine the course of Hattie's life if she lived in a city and write a paragraph about it.

This irony underscores Hattie's tenacious ability to cling to what has little worth even if she is left with nothing. Hattie had always dreamed of coming out west, but all she has sown in this land of adventure is loneliness and isolation. By the time she writes her will, Hattie recognizes her own state, referring to herself as "cast off and lonely." Hattie's inability to will her house to anyone demonstrates her extreme isolation, for she feels that no one is worthy of it because there is no one in her life whom she loves or respects.

Poverty

The poverty Hattie experiences is both monetary and spiritual. Hattie has very little money in the form of a small pension. Her primary asset is the yellow house, however, even the house does not truly represent much worth because she cannot sell it or rent it for a reasonable price. Hattie's anxiety after she leaves the hospital is exacerbated by her inability to pay her medical bill and the knowledge that she has no way to raise the money. When both Amy Walters and Pace volunteer to take care of Hattie in return for ownership of her house after she dies, the instability that Hattie experiences because of her poverty is clearly demonstrated. These actions also underscore Hattie's spiritual poverty. She is a woman whom people, with the exception of the Rolfes, will only help if they are getting something in return for it. In truth, this is only fair, for Hattie herself offers little to anyone else. She is judgmental, deceitful, and self-absorbed to the point of pettiness and clearly has been this way for some time. Hattie's spiritual poverty is also apparent in her loneliness.

Style

Narration

"Leaving the Yellow House" is told chronologically. The beginning of the story gives relevant background about Hattie, and then the story shifts to an unfolding of the plot—Hattie's breaking her arm, her need for assistance, and her feelings of isolation. At the end of the story, Hattie seems about to embark on a crucial decision—who will inherit the yellow house—but she cannot follow through with completing this action; the decision she does make—to leave the house to herself—emphasizes that the story resides in the character's development rather than in any plot development. Indeed, in his study of

Saul Bellow, Robert F. Kiernan called ''Leaving the Yellow House'' ''[m]ore portrait than story.''

Hattie also spends a significant amount of time reflecting on her past. She envisions her life as playing before her as if on a movie screen. Thus the past intertwines with the present narrative, a technique that shows the importance of former experiences to Hattie. The ''film'' also demonstrates how events and people from days gone by have influenced the situation in which Hattie finds herself at the present time. One memory—when she killed her dog Richie after he attacked her—is particularly significant, for it leads to her self-examination about the life she has led. She has lied to others, and perhaps more importantly, she has been dishonest with herself about the life she has chosen for herself.

Point of View

''Leaving the Yellow House'' is told in the third-person omniscient point of view. The narrator reflects objectively on people, places, events, and thoughts. This point of view is effective for several reasons: first, the detached point of view negates Hattie's overenthusiastic perceptions of her life and surroundings; second, it allows readers to understand Hattie's situation through a variety of people.

The point of view focuses primarily on Hattie's thoughts and observations, particularly after she breaks her arm and experiences a crisis of identity. The narrative focuses on Hattie's psyche as she is in the process of increasingly pondering her options and the fabric of her life.

Setting

The setting of the story is Sego Desert Lake, Utah, where a tiny community of people—whites, Mexicans, African Americans, and Native Americans—live. The white people live in houses by the lake, while the minorities live in boxcars and shacks. The nearest town is forty miles away, through the mountainous desert, and supplies all must be purchased from there. The narrator describes the region as ''barren,'' which sharply contrasts with Hattie's insistence on the beauty of the place.

The idea of the West played prominently in Hattie's mind. Drawn to the seeming allure of the rough-and-tumble life, Hattie, like Darly, wanted to experience adventure. At times, Hattie glorifies her life out West; for instance, she recalls living on the range with Wick, but the clearest memory that emerges from this time is of her disturbed feelings as Wick trapped and killed a pure white coyote.

Symbolism

Many symbolic elements are present in ''Leaving the Yellow House,'' particularly the house itself. Like Hattie, the house is run-down, aging, and a mass of contradictions. It is filled both with fine china and with decrepit furniture. The library walls are lined, not with books, but with canned goods. The house serves as a kind of prison for Hattie. She spends most of her time in it asleep, but she also feels that she cannot live without the house; this seeming contradiction shows that Hattie has come to embrace her place of confinement. By the end of the story, Hattie identifies herself with the house itself, seeing it as the best part of her.

Other elements of the story have symbolic value. The landscape reflects Hattie's demeanor; on the surface it is barren but underneath lie volcanic eruptions. Hattie keeps up a pretension of politeness to her friends and neighbors, but secretly she berates them and sometimes she even can't keep from exploding, as when she verbally attacks Pace. The white coyote killed by Wick can be seen as symbolic of the innocence of the West, corrupted by people, like Hattie, who don't belong there. Hattie's car stalled on the railroad tracks symbolizes the course of Hattie's own life; as she later admits, ''I have stalled. And now what shall I do?'' Like Hattie's broken-down car, Hattie's life and body are in states of disrepair and inactivity.

Historical Context

A Prosperous Nation?

For many Americans, the 1950s was a decade of economic prosperity. Unemployment and inflation remained low, usually below five percent. By the middle of the decade, more than sixty percent of Americans earned a middle-class income, which at that time was a salary between $3,000 and $10,000 a year. The number of homeowners increased by more than twenty-one million during this decade, and people enjoyed material comforts and the benefits of household inventions and improvements. Government programs benefited many Americans. Social security and unemployment benefits also expanded in the mid-1950s, and the minimum wage increased. President Dwight D. Eisenhower also supported the largest increase in educational spending up to that time.

Nearly forty million Americans, however, lived near or below the poverty line of $3,000 for a family

Compare & Contrast

- **1950s:** An annual middle-class income ranges between $3,000 and $10,000 annually. More than 60 percent of Americans fall into the middle class.

  1990s: The annual median income of all U.S. households is $35,492. Americans aged 65 and older have a lower median income: $28,983.

- **1950s:** Utah experiences a population gain of between 20 and 30 percent. By 1955, Utah's population is 781,000.

  1990s: The population of Utah is 2,059,000, with 8.7 percent more than 65 years of age. Utah is one of the ten fastest-growing states in the country. The population rises by 19.5 percent from 1990 to 1997.

- **1950s:** In 1955, 71 percent of American households own an automobile and 76 percent own a television set.

  1990s: In 1996, more than 129 million automobiles are registered in the United States. In 1997, 98.7 percent of all American households own at least one color television.

- **1950s:** An average of 21.3 per 100,000 deaths are caused by car accidents annually.

  1990s: In 1995, 56,155 fatal car crashes, out of around 6.8 million total reported, involve alcohol. Of these, 6,238 of the cars are driven by women.

- **1950s:** The median price for a single-family home is $10,050. Throughout the decade, increasing numbers of Americans buy their own home, many of which are located in the suburbs.

  1990s: The median sales price of homes in the United States is $95,500. Close to seventy-three percent of all Americans live in an owner-occupied home. A slightly higher percentage of Americans aged 65 and over own their own homes: just more than seventy-nine percent.

- **1950s:** Of a total U.S. population of close to 164.3 million in 1955, around 7.4 million are aged between 65 and 79, or 4.5 percent.

  1990s: Of a total U.S. population of 273.9 million in 1998, just more than 18 million are aged between 65 and 79, or 6.6 percent.

---

of four, as determined by a 1957 study. Poor Americans were more often earning a lesser portion of the nation's wealth. Almost one half lived in rural areas and suffered from inadequate health care and a lack of education. City dwellers also saw their conditions worsen as urban slums deteriorated. In response, the federal government began a program of urban renewal to replace run-down inner-city buildings with new ones. When older urban neighborhoods were bulldozed to make way for low-income public housing projects, however, many residents felt this transformation ruined the fabric of their community.

A Changing American Population

During the 1950s, increasing numbers of Americans relocated. Millions of prosperous whites moved to the suburbs, while many poor rural citizens traveled to the cities to look for a better life. The construction of interstate highways contributed to the relocation of Americans, particularly to the Western states. Additionally, many Mexican immigrants settled in Western cities. Overall as well, the American population grew, particularly because many Americans had waited until after the end of World War II to marry or start families. Throughout the decade, the American population saw an increase of nearly 30 million, from 150 million to 179 million.

Many women in the 1950s stayed at home and took care of their families and households, though a larger percentage worked outside of the home, often part-time. In general, women often faced discrimination and exploitation both at home and at work.

Minorities also experienced prejudice, and many were denied the same educational and employment opportunities as whites enjoyed.

The Beginning of the Civil Rights Movement

Protest movements took place in the 1950s to try and change these discriminatory practices. In 1955, African-American citizens in Montgomery, Alabama, began a bus boycott in an attempt to end segregation on public transportation. For almost a year, thousands of African Americans stopped riding the buses. In 1956, the U.S. Supreme Court declared Alabama's segregation laws unconstitutional. This struggle not only integrated the bus system, but it also brought a new civil rights leader to the forefront: Martin Luther King, Jr. Two years earlier, in 1954, the U.S. Supreme Court had ruled in the monumental decision known as *Brown v. The Board of Education of Topeka* that the segregation of school by race was unconstitutional. As a result of this decision, states throughout the South moved to desegregate their schools—most unwillingly, however. Central High School in Little Rock, Arkansas, was the first school to comply with *Brown*. Although angry whites and Arkansas' National Guard, sent by the governor, tried to keep nine African-American teenagers out of Central High, in 1957, African-American students began to attend what had been an all-white school.

A Society of Conformity

Despite these racial struggles, society of the 1950s was generally dominated by the idea of conformity. For instance, in the suburbs, houses looked the same and had the same floorplans. Some teenagers challenged this conformity through literature that mocked the hypocritical adult world, as well as through rock 'n' roll, which many parents disliked. Adults also challenged the conformity of American life. John Kenneth Galbraith argued in his 1958 book *An Affluent Society* that Americans were ignoring pressing social issues in their pursuit of material possessions and comfort. A group of writers and poets known as the Beats challenged literary and lifestyle conventions of the middle class. Jack Kerouac's *On the Road*, one of the best-known Beat works, celebrated the search for individual identity. Other novelists such as Ralph Ellison discussed the experiences of those Americans who faced poverty and discrimination.

Critical Overview

"Leaving the Yellow House" was first published in *Esquire* magazine in 1957. Eleven years later, along with five other stories, it was collected in *Mosby's Memoirs and Other Stories*. This collection reflected work written over a period of seventeen years; the first story was published only a few years after Bellow emerged onto America's literary scene with the publication of his earliest novels. *Mosby's Memoirs* included three stories that had been previously published with the novella *Seize the Day*.

"Leaving the Yellow House" was one of the stories that was not brought to the public attention since its original publication. Since the 1960s, however, it has become one of Bellow's most anthologized pieces of fiction, however, it is uncharacteristic of his work. Unlike most of Bellow's work, "Leaving the Yellow House" focuses on uneducated rural characters in a southwestern setting rather than the more typical urban intellectuals.

In considering the story and the collection as a whole, contemporary reviewers discussed such elements as plot, themes, and character. In *Library Journal*, Bill Katz categorized all the stories as being "about people who by design or by fate try to make it alone." Hattie, Katz writes, is "memorable" and she "well deserves a place with [other noted Bellow protagonists] Herzog and Henderson as classic characterization." Katz believed that four of the six stories, including "Leaving the Yellow House," were written in the "best Bellow style." C. T. Samuels, writing for the *Atlantic*, however, believed that "Leaving the Yellow House" was "more sentimental" than some of the others in the collection. Other reviewers focused on issues of aging and death in the story.

Contemporary criticism and discussion of the story has tended to regard it more in light of Bellow's body of work. Critics have compared Hattie with some of Bellow's most well-known and well-drawn male protagonists, such as Tommy Wilhelm of Seize the Day. Like Bellow's men, Hattie agonizes over the meaning of her existence. Most critics agree, however, that Bellow does not allow Hattie an intellectual resolution, as he does his men. Robert F. Kiernan wrote in his chapter on the volume in *Saul Bellow* that Hattie is "without the mental and spiritual resources that allow [Bellow's male characters] . . . to meet the world head-on." Constance Rooke further noted Bellow's particular strain of sexism and stereotyping in "Leaving the

Yellow House." "While Bellow can grant Hattie certain of the characteristics which he has parcelled out from his own riches for the male protagonists," she wrote, "and can accord her the sympathy which is due to her participation in such qualities, he is obliged because she is a woman to withhold the Bellowesque *sina qua non* of a genuine intellectual life. He cannot in a single leap make of her a woman, a sympathetic character, and an intellectual." Noriko M. Lippit is one Bellow scholar who contended that Hattie, like Bellow's male characters, achieves salvation and recovers from self-imposed alienation through her confrontation of death at the end of the story.

Critics also disagree on how to perceive Hattie's final actions. Samuels, for instance, found Hattie's decision to "affirm existence at its lowest ebb." Others find her merely to be putting off the idea of death without drawing any truly positive elements from her mental agitation. Other critics make note of the note on which the story ends, with Hattie's thoughts: "Only tonight I can't give the house away. I'm drunk and so I need it. And tomorrow, she promised herself, I'll think again. I'll work it out for sure." These thoughts echo the words of the southern belle, Scarlett O'Hara of *Gone with the Wind*. While Rooke sees these thoughts as further evidence of Hattie's avoidance of the reality of her advancing death, Eusebio L. Rodriguez analyzes this snippet in a laudatory fashion: "The parody proclaims that Hattie Waggoner is not Scarlett O'Hara but a gnarled, weather-beaten representative of contemporary man hurling forth a cry of protest against this place and this condition."

Criticism

Rena Korb

Korb has a master's degree in English literature and creative writing and has written for a wide variety of educational publishers. In the following essay, she explores the dual nature of Hattie Waggoner and other characters and elements of "Leaving the Yellow House."

Saul Bellow's "Leaving the Yellow House" is one of his most frequently anthologized and discussed pieces of fiction, yet in many ways it is atypical of his body of work. It is set in the western desert, not the city, and its protagonist is a woman disinclined to intellectual or spiritual matters. However, the story is as complex as any of Bellow's other works. In Hattie Waggoner, Bellow creates a character with an unintentional duplicitous nature. Hattie's tendency toward prevarication—to herself as well as to others—leads her to create an unstable and disinterested world in which her way of life becomes threatened.

Many elements of the story manifest this dual nature. Hattie claims that Sego Desert Lake is "'one of the most beautiful places in the world,'" but in reality it is "barren" and decrepit with "very few trees" and fewer "good houses." Jerry Rolfe, one of the few characters who epitomizes good sense, points out some of Sego Desert Lake's deficiencies: for one thing, it is located hundreds of miles away from any major city. "'Who wants to live way out here but a few eccentrics?'" he asks Hattie, not shying away from labeling both of them thusly.

Many of the other people who populate Sego Desert Lake are eccentric and double natured. Darly is "not a genuine cowboy." Like Hattie, he is a "late-comer from the East," but he has taken on the necessary accoutrements of Western life, such as boots, and works at a dude ranch where women go to bed with him because they think he is a real cowboy. India, Hattie's former companion, was a cultured woman who claimed to be interested in intellectual discussions of religion and literature, but in reality, she generally spent her time, like Hattie, wandering around the house, drunk, clad only in her slip. India's double nature further revealed itself along with the development of her temper: "the worse her temper the more British her accent became." Amy Walters, another elderly resident, lives at what she calls Fort Walters, but the structure is really only a shack-like building made out of tar paper that sits over a deserted mine shaft.

Hattie's existence is truly based on her self-imposed network of false premises. The very presentation of the woman underscores her double nature. Although Hattie is an aging alcoholic who lives a life of sloth and procrastination, the narrator nevertheless asserts, "You couldn't help being fond of Hattie." For while Hattie is lazy and mean-spirited, she is also "big and cheerful, puffy, comic." Once a week, Hattie dresses up in her girdle, high heels, and lipstick to make the forty-mile trip to the nearest town. Hattie's past also indicates a fall from grace, thus a change from what she once was; she once attended finishing school and studied the organ in Paris, and she had been married to a member of a fine, old Philadelphia family. This social shift is

What Do I Read Next?

- Saul Bellow's 1956 novella *Seize the Day* tells of a significant day in the life of down-and-out Tommy Wilhelm. Like Hattie Waggoner, Wilhelm reflects on his past and searches for resolution.

- *Mrs. Bridge*, by Evan S. Connell (1959), presents a portrait of a woman's life, from her childhood to her old age. Its companion book, *Mr. Bridge*, treats her husband's life in a similar fashion. Both novels have as their genesis the short story, ''Mr. and Mrs. Bridge.''

- Mary Gordon's 1989 novel, *The Other Side*, narrates the story of an elderly couple as they reflect back on their lives.

- ''Timothy's Birthday,'' a short story by William

Trevor in his 1996 collection *After Rain*, tells of an old couple who await their adult son's birthday visit.

- Bellow is best known for his portrayals of modern urban dwellers. Henry Roth's novel *Call It Sleep*, first published in 1934, is the story of Jewish immigrants in a New York City ghetto. Largely forgotten until the late 1950s, today it stands as a classic of Jewish-American literature.

- Wallace Stegner's prizewinning novel *Angle of Repose* (1971) switches between present-time, in which an older man is stricken with a paralyzing disease, and the past, in which the man's ancestors make their way in the rugged, nineteenth-century West.

---

epitomized by her home, which has canned goods stacked on the library shelves but also ''good silver and good china and engraved stationery.'' More important to the understanding of Hattie's complex characterization, though, is that although ''she wanted to be thought of as a rough, experienced woman of the West,'' she can't even take care of herself.

The most significant evidence of Hattie's double nature, however, is her habit of self-deception. For instance, Hattie claims to be a Christian, thus she can '''never bear a grudge,''' but the text points out that only by repeating these words to herself does she succeed in not holding a grudge against the people who have wronged her. She also thinks unkind things about the Rolfes though they are the only people who truly go out of their way—and with no other motivation than genuine concern—to help her. When the Rolfes tell her not to be stingy and leave the heating pad on her arm even though it will use up her butane gas, Hattie thinks, '''Stingy! Why you're the stingy ones. I haven't got anything. You and Helen are ready to hit each other over two bits in canasta.''' But she immediately acknowledges to herself that ''the Rolfes were good to her; they were

her only real friends here.'' Such comprehension, however, does not keep her from silently calling Helen Rolfe such names as ''*B—h-eyes*.'' She even believes that the Rolfes should not take a vacation because they will be leaving her alone: ''But there was no reason to go to Seattle—'' Hattie thinks of the Rolfes' upcoming trip, ''no genuine business. . . . It was only idleness, only a holiday.'' Not only does Hattie fail to realize that her own life has also turned into one of idleness, she also extends her self-alienation when she concludes that the Rolfes are vacationing as a way of telling her that ''there was a limit to what she could expect them to do for her.'' Hattie, who considers herself a nice person, only knows how to react to this supposed slight with cruelty; to get back at the Rolfes, she tells Helen, ''if I have to leave the lake you'll be ten times more lonely than before.''

Hattie also lies to herself, both about her own character and actions. She perceives of herself as ''one of the pioneers'' of the West, though she only arrived a few decades back, a ''city woman'' who could never make it on her own. Though she ''had lived on the range like an old-timer,'' the story makes clear that it was her lover, Wick, who enabled the couple to survive thusly. In fact, though Wick wants to marry her, she refuses because she was a ''snob about her Philadelphia connections. Give up the name of Waggoner? How could she?'' But she is so deceptive that she never even tells Wick the real reason that she turns down his proposal. She further deceives herself by rejecting Wick, who truly cared for her.

Also significant in the story is the way Hattie lies to herself about her drinking. She maintains that she had the car accident because she sneezed, but it is clear that she was drunk and lost control of her car—just as she has lost control of steering her life on any proper course. As the car is stuck on the railroad tracks, so Hattie's life is stuck in Sego Desert Lake—primarily because of the choices she has made and her refusal to deal with life honestly.

A turning point comes for Hattie when she admits to herself that she killed her own dog, Richie, and buried him in the yard, though she has long accused a neighbor of the animal's disappearance. She had no choice but to kill Richie when he turned ''evil'' and physically attacked her. The human characters in the story, however, also have a habit of turning evil and figuratively attacking those who are closest to them: India attacks Hattie and then begs for forgiveness; Hattie, in turn, attacks Wick and shuns his love. The cyclical nature of this mean spirit is demonstrated as Hattie reiterates India's words when she mentally asks Wick for his forgiveness; '''I hurt myself in my evil,''' she says, as did India. The revelation that she has lied to others about the dog, and to herself, shocks Hattie: *''God what shall I do?''* she thinks. *''I have taken life. I have lied. I have borne false witness. I have stalled.''*

Her realization that her life is not progressing toward any goal makes her do what she has been putting off for weeks now: seeing if she can drive her car, which symbolizes her independence and her capacity to care for herself. But she is unable to shift the gears and steer. This inability makes her understand the frailty of her own life. Determined to do, at long last, something responsible, Hattie sits down to write her will. Though she has already ''wept over the ruin of her life,'' reflecting on who to give the house to makes her think even more deeply. She acknowledges that she has waited for India to die and that she considered Wick to be inferior to her. Through her ruminations, Hattie comes to define herself by ownership of the house even more. Though she tries to tell herself that she should not give the

> The most significant evidence of Hattie's double nature, however, is her habit of self-deception. For instance, Hattie claims to be a Christian, thus she can 'never bear a grudge,' but the text points out that only by repeating these words to herself does she succeed in not holding a grudge against the people who have wronged her."

house to her cousin's daughter Joyce because she does not want to ''doom a younger person to the same life'' that she had, in reality, Hattie believes that ''[O]nly I fit here.'' Indeed, owning the house is all that she has ever had—her car no longer functions for her, and the house now is her only evidence of having achieved any kind of successful life. *''I was never one single thing anyway,''* she thinks. *''Never my own. I was only loaned to myself.''* By the end of the story, in her seventy-second year, Hattie has come to equate herself with the house—it is her only worthy quality. Thus, she does the impossible—knowing full well that '''this is bad and wrong,''' she wills the house and its property to herself. In so doing, Hattie continues her lifelong habit of denying reality. Just as Hattie refuses to think that there is a beginning, a middle, and an end to life—choosing instead to divide time into the ''early middle, then middle middle, late middle middle, quite late middle''—she arrives, not at the end of life where she doesn't want to be, but at the conclusion that ''the middle is all I know.'' Such rationalizations not only justify her decision to leave the house to herself—if she isn't going to die, she doesn't need to will her house to someone—just negate self-knowledge of her inevitable death.

Source: Rena Korb, Critical Essay on ''Leaving the Yellow House,'' in *Short Stories for Students*, The Gale Group, 2001.

Wendy Perkins

Perkins is an associate professor of English at Prince George's Community College in Maryland. In the following essay, she examines Bellow's study in "Leaving the Yellow House" of how one woman copes with feelings of displacement.

Nobody truly occupies a station in life any more. There are mostly people who feel that they occupy the place that belongs to another by rights. There are displaced persons everywhere.

Earl Rovit in his article on Saul Bellow in *American Writers* determines that these words spoken by Eugene Henderson in Bellow's highly acclaimed novel, *Henderson the Rain King*, "could have been spoken by almost any of Bellow's characters, or, for that matter, by Bellow himself." Rovit finds that a major theme in Bellow's fiction is how we cope with a sense of alienation and displacement. This is also the case with Hattie Simms Waggoner, the heroine of Bellow's short story, "Leaving the Yellow House." Throughout the story, Hattie experiences sometimes overwhelming feelings of disconnection. Yet she endures through her strength of spirit.

At the beginning of the story, the other characters determine that Hattie "could no longer make it on her own." Since her arm has not healed from its break, and she has trouble taking care of herself, they urge her to sell her house so that she will have enough money for someone to look after her. Hattie had lived in the yellow house independently for more than twenty years, struggling to establish it and the surrounding area as her home. During this time she often experienced feelings of dislocation. Although she has had important relationships in her life, none has endured.

This sense expresses itself through Hattie's feeling that all of her memories appear to her as if they were on film in disconnected bits and pieces. She imagines that when she dies "she would see the film shown. Then she would know how she had appeared from the back" and that the pieces would come together, giving her a clearer sense of who she was and how she was connected to her world.

One of the main reasons Hattie has had such a difficult time creating a sense of place is due to her lack of family. All she has left are two older brothers and cousins' children, none of whom she is close to. The husband she had loved divorced her and left her with no money. Her painful memory of that broken relationship surfaces when Hattie wonders how her husband could "fling a wife away." She wonders whether she drank too much or bored him. She acknowledges that one of the reasons her husband left her was her inability to bear children but concludes, "There were no kids in me. . . . Not that I wouldn't have loved them, but such my nature was. And who can blame me for having . . . my nature?"

Rovit notes the important role family plays in Bellow's work. He comments that the idea of family "intrudes itself on the present as an ironically unusable past. It compels the memory of a way of life in which personality seemed not to be fragmented and isolated." His characters were happy in the past when they were "integral parts of a congenial whole, able to share their griefs and joys spontaneously and directly, instead of carrying them onerously on their own shoulders." As is typical of Bellow's characters, Hattie suffers her burdens more acutely since she has no familial support.

Hattie did establish a relationship with Wicks, an itinerant cowboy, but her pride kept her from making a more permanent commitment to him. She never married Wicks because she didn't want to give up her name and all that it represented. Hattie acknowledges that Wicks was a good man, but, according to her, he was a cowboy and therefore, "socially nothing." She had gone to finishing school and studied the organ in Paris and so could not give up her upper class connections, represented by her "good silver and good china and engraved stationery." After an argument, she threw him out, admitting later, "I couldn't bear to fall so low . . . to be slave to a shiftless cowboy."

Hattie's relationship with India, who had owned the yellow house, compounded her feelings of displacement. India was more educated than she and so acted as her superior. While Hattie suggested to others that they were true equals, India left "many small scars" on Hattie's pride and treated her "like a servant."

Rovit explains that Bellow's heroes do not resign themselves to their suffering. Instead, they continually climb out of "the craters of the spirit," determined to shield themselves against future, inevitable onslaughts. Hattie exhibits this strength when she decides, "it's looked bad many a time before, but when push came to shove I made it. Somehow I got by." Her vision of her relationship to her surroundings helps sustain her. She sees herself as "one of the pioneers" in her ability to successfully live off the land. Often she can convince herself that others see her "as a rough, experienced woman of the West" as well as "a lady."

Hattie also endures through her devotion to routine. Once a week ''in the same cheerful, plugging but absent way,'' she squeezes into a clean dress and high heels and travels forty miles across the desert into town where she shops and later drinks with her friends. There she tells of her time with Wicks, reminiscing sadly ''but also gloatingly, and with many trimmings.'' Hattie often embellishes the truth as a way to ease the painful reality of her life.

Her accident, however, threatens to prevent her from falling back on her old survival skills. While she tries to fool herself into thinking that a sneeze caused her to get stuck on the railroad tracks, eventually, she must face the truth that ''she was not fit to live in this place. She had never made the grade at all, only seemed to have made it.'' As the pain in her arm grows worse, she admits, ''she couldn't take much more'' and wonders, ''how many more twists and angles had life to show her yet?''

Initially, she is confident that her friends will come to her aid, but when she acknowledges the fact that she must fend for herself, she worries about her future. When she considers moving in with her brother and his wife, she realizes he is ''too crabby'' and that he and his wife ''were not her kind.'' If she lived with them, she would not be able to drink or smoke or, in essence, be herself.

Her sense of displacement is intensified by her response to her aging process. As her body has aged, it has become alien to her and, as a result, she feels that it has betrayed her as others have. She admits she has taken the shape of an ''old jug, wider and wider toward the top,'' swollen ''with tears and fat'' and that ''she no longer even smelled to herself like a woman. Her face with its much-slept-upon skin was only faintly like her own.'' It became a ball of yarn, drifting open and ''scattered.''

Bellow's descriptions of the barren atmosphere of the desert landscape symbolize Hattie's deteriorating state. The narrator notes at one point that at the back of the house ''the soil had caved in a little over the cesspool and a few of the old railroad ties over the top had rotted.'' Yet, the sego lilies spring up everywhere through the parched land, even on the burnt granite. Hattie's indistinguishable desire to live gives her the strength to endure. Another symbol Bellow employs to suggest Hattie's resilience is reflected in the state of her car. After her accident, she tests the engine and determines, ''yes, the old pot would still go.'' Even though at that

> As the pain in her arm grows worse, she admits, 'she couldn't take much more' and wonders, 'how many more twists and angles had life to show her yet?''

point, she could not work the shift, she was confident that she would soon be able to, which to her, suggests her need for control over her environment.

After she recovers from her surgery, ''with joyous eyes, the cigarette in her mouth and her hair newly frizzed and overhanging her forehead,'' her spirit has been renewed. Although still pale and shaky, she is in high spirits and full of confidence. At one point she admits to Jerry that she feels ''wrung out,'' but ''she was not one to be miserable for long; she had the expression of a perennial survivor.''

When the doctor tells her she might need another operation because she has not been exercising her arm enough, she panics, but immediately suppresses it. She decides, ''night and day . . . I was in the Valley of the Shadow. But I'm alive.'' The narrator notes, ''she was weak, she was old, she couldn't follow a train of thought very easily, she felt faint in the head. But she was still here.'' Her body ''filled space,'' and it was ''a great body.'' Though she was often in pain, she drank in life and reveled in the attention of others. She convinces herself her friends would eventually help her, explaining, ''It never did me any good to worry. At the last minute something turned up, when I wasn't looking for it.''

Her occasional bursts of anger over her predicament never last long, since they are ''reabsorbed into the feeling of golden pleasure that enveloped her. She had little strength, but all that she had was a pleasure to her.'' She finds strength in the beauty of her world—from the fragrant flowers, from ''the mares, naked and gentle,'' walking through them. The beauty she finds in the world touches ''a deep place in Hattie's nature.'' Her philosophy is to ''take what God brings'' understanding ''He gives no gifts unmixed.''

Her strength of spirit ebbs, however, after she is forced to admit that she no longer can drive her car. Urged by all to sell her house, Hattie feels ''disillusioned'' deciding, ''everybody wants to push me out.'' She insists, ''this is my only home in all the world, this is where my friends are.''

Again, though, Hattie rises up out of her despair, deciding that giving her house up would mean doing ''right by her family.'' Her ownership of the house proves her value, a fact she is convinced her family will recognize when she wills the house to one of them. As a result of this decision, ''her heart experienced a childish glory, not yet tired of it after seventy-two years. She, too, had amounted to something.'' She too could contribute.

Robert R. Dutton, in his article on Saul Bellow for *Twayne's United States Authors Series Online*, notes that at the end of the story, ''[i]n spite of a life seemingly not worth living'' and ''one that cannot last much longer, Hattie refuses to call it quits, and she can no more give up her house than she can give up on life.'' She insists, ''even though by my own fault I have put myself into this position, I am not ready to give up on this.'' As a result, she decides, ''I leave this property, land, house, garden, and water rights, to Hattie Simms Waggoner.'' Although she claims her decision is wrong, she notes that it is the only possible one she can make, at least at that moment. She admits, ''tonight I can't give the house away. I'm drunk and so I need it. And tomorrow . . . I'll think again. I'll work it out, for sure.''

Rovit comments that through his work, Bellow reveals ''a single-minded attention toward defining what is viably *human* in modern life—what is creatively and morally possible for the displaced person that modern man feels himself to be.'' Rovit argues that Bellow tries to ''define habitable limits'' within which people ''can rest secure and still seize hold of the day with a partial power and the responsibility for [their] employment of that power.'' In ''Leaving the Yellow House,'' Hattie embodies this sense of displacement as well as the desire to retain a measure of power over her life. For Hattie, the house becomes a metaphor for her commitment to survive her bleak world and to retain a measure of personal dignity. Through his characterization of this resilient woman, Bellow reaffirms our faith in the endurance of the human spirit.

Source: Wendy Perkins, Critical Essay on ''Leaving the Yellow House,'' in *Short Stories for Students*, The Gale Group, 2001.

Noriko M. Lippit

In the following essay on ''Leaving the Yellow House,'' Lippit proposes that the character Hattie is the one exception to Bellows's treatment of female characters in his fiction.

Charles Newman asserts that ''there is not a single woman in all of Saul Bellow's work whose active search for identity is viewed compassionately, while every vice of his male introspectives is given some genuine imperative.'' While I agree, in the final analysis, with Mr. Newman's remark and with his subsequent comment that ''this attitude is generally indicative of serious writing since the war,'' I believe that Bellow's ''Leaving the Yellow House'' (1957) provides an exception; Hattie, the protagonist of this work, is a female searcher. ''Leaving the Yellow House'' is also exceptional in its desert setting, for Bellow has consistently presented dramas of people living in the modern metropolis. Despite the difference in sex and setting, however, ''Leaving the Yellow House'' deals with one of the main themes of Saul Bellow, that of recovery from the narrow confinement of the self through inner search.

The yellow house where the heroine Hattie lives stands near Sego Desert Lake—some several hundred miles from San Francisco and Salt Lake City. The house, which Hattie inherited from her ''friend'' India, is one of the three structures around there that could be called a house. The story is about the aging Hattie, deprived of physical mobility because of an accident, who worries seriously about whom she should leave the yellow house to after her death.

Sego Desert Lake is a sterile nowhere, the end of the world. Its residents include an idle retired couple who move from place to place according to their convenience, alcoholic divorcées, the owner of a ranch that exploits rare tourists, a ''cowboy'' from the East who rode on a horse for the first time at the age of forty, and so forth: they are all drop-outs from life, floaters who settled at Sego Desert after wandering toward the West in search of their dream of ''making it.'' Hattie herself, once married to a man from an old Philadelphia family, floated from the East; and India, whom she looked after, was once a ''lady'' who travelled in the world and talked of philosophy and literature at parties. Not one of them is a genuine Westerner; these modern frontiersmen are city-born failures, and the wilderness is a skid row akin to the Bowery in New York.

Among them, Hattie's corruption is particularly pathetic. She is a born sloth, a professional loser who has not accomplished a single thing in her life. In this respect, Hattie is a female version of Tommy Wilhelm in *Seize the Day*. Tommy, still pursuing the dream of "making it" while taking pills and alcohol in a shabby hotel-room in downtown New York, feels that the metropolis is not the place for him, yet finds there some mysterious, attractive and cruel force rendering him incapable of escaping. It is the same force that Hattie senses in the desert. Watching the lake in the desert, Hattie reflects: "They drew you from yourself. But after they had drawn you, what did they do with you? It was too late to find out. I'll never know. I wasn't meant to. I'm not the type, Hattie reflected. Maybe something too cruel for women, young or old." The cruel attractive force that Tommy and Hattie see in New York and the desert respectively is the gigantic, unregulated energy of America, the energy that created American material civilization. Controlled by the force, both the metropolis and the desert are "giant raw places." American pastoral reality and urban reality are the same; to live in either is more terrifying than a nightmare.

"Leaving the Yellow House" depicts the wreck of the American dream comically and pathetically. Sego Desert Lake is a sarcastic symbol of America's Eden. The lake is mysteriously tempting and diabolic. It is bottomless and its surface as smooth as if it contained milk. White pelicans fly over the lake spreading their large white wings like angels. Hattie, watching the lake in a stupor brought by drink, feels as if she were in heaven. Yet she senses simultaneously the sterile and destructive force surrounding the lake. She feels the desert embodying this force is like a man who exposes his masculine chest covered with hair.

The greediness, loneliness, and sense of emptiness of the inhabitants of Sego Desert Lake are expressed in Amy, "a gold miner's widow," a miser who plays waltzes on her piano and reads murder-stories late into the night. India, who was also caught by the destructive power of the desert, completed the final touch of her self-destruction with alcohol, and Hattie steadily follows the pattern of her mistress. Sego Desert Lake is seemingly a virgin land, yet it is a ghost-town haunted by the unquiet shadows of the American dream. The sterile, deserted gold mine symbolizes this. The land is a virgin wilderness, a source of the American dream of earthly paradise, yet it is also an American junkyard; it is Eden and hell simultaneously.

> "'Leaving the Yellow House' depicts the wreck of the American dream comically and pathetically. Sego Desert Lake is a sarcastic symbol of America's Eden. The lake is mysteriously tempting and diabolic. It is bottomless and its surface as smooth as if it contained milk."

This horrifying yet comical story of human ruin, however, does not remain as a mere comical grotesquerie. Although Hattie is an anti-heroine, she is a masochistic self-searcher, a proud loser with dignity, one typical of Saul Bellow's male protagonists. Hattie, like Tommy Wilhelm and Moses Herzog, gains salvation through confronting death and mental crisis. While Tommy and Moses arrive at a reconciliation with life and the universe through the dissolution of narrow self-identity, Hattie recognizes, in her confrontation with death, a greedy and idle self, unreligious, unloved and luckless, yet still wanting to live. Her writing a will leaving the house to herself is here way—absurd yet audacious—of insisting on her American ego. It is also her way of sublimating her frustration and of accepting life as she experiences it. Yet Hattie, like Tommy and Moses, arrives at self-recognition after losing everything and exposing her naked self. Recognizing herself as a failure and victim and admitting her guilt for not loving enable Hattie to accept her present state and to reconcile herself with her fate.

To the question "Who are you?" Hattie can only answer "I am I." It is, within the Judaic context of Bellow's literature, the only possible answer for secular Jews, who are unable to reply "I am the son of my father." In "Leaving the Yellow House," it is also the only answer that modern Americans can give. As Leslie Fiedler points out, America, after completing the great Westward expansion, lost its innocence as well as its Puritan-colored cultural tradition. It is America's new generation, which must improvise its own history and determine its own fate, that inhabits Sego Desert Lake and struggles vainly to maintain its integrity in the desert.

Although Hattie is a loser, she is also, like Tommy Wilhelm and Moses Herzog, a ''perennial survivor.'' She is a perennial sego lily, a dainty yet vital little wildflower that blooms among the rocks in a sterile desert. As her favorite joke tells, she had been caught in the mud many times, but each time she ''came out of everything.'' After reviewing her whole life as if watching a movie film and experiencing a catharsis of anger and remorse, this prisoner of Sego Desert Lake arrives at a state of accepting her life, the equilibrium of a person who has confronted and survived destruction once again. Although this peaceful state (a delirious state of stupor, too) can by no means be called the silence of inward knowledge, Hattie reaches it through her own inner search, the inner drama of one who experiences a crisis of identity. ''Then she thought that there was a beginning, and a middle. She shrank from the last term. She began once more—a beginning. After that, there was the early middle, then middle middle, late middle middle, quite late middle. In fact the middle is all I know. The rest is just a rumor. Only tonight I can't give the house away. I'm drunk and so I need it. And tomorrow, she promised herself, I'll think again. I'll work it out, for sure.'' The attaining of this tragicomical state of peace and reconciliation with humanity appears later, more fully developed, as a major theme of *Herzog*. Treating an archetypal American theme in ''Leaving the Yellow House,'' Saul Bellow presents a unique drama of man's (woman's!) struggle for recovery from modern alienation.

Source: Noriko M. Lippit, ''A Perennial Survivor: Saul Bellow's Heroine in the Desert,'' in *Studies in Short Fiction*, Vol. XIII, No. 3, Summer 1975, pp. 281–83.

Sources

Katz, Bill, Review in *Library Journal*, October 15, 1968, p. 3797.

Kiernan, Robert F., *Saul Bellow*, Continuum, 1989.

Lippit, Noriko M., ''A Perennial Survivor: Saul Bellow's Heroine in the Desert,'' in *Short Studies in Fiction*, Vol. XII, No. 3, Summer 1975, pp. 281–83.

Rodrigues, Eusebio L., ''A Rough Hewed Heroine of Our Time: Saul Bellow's 'Leaving the Yellow House,''' in *Saul Bellow Newsletter*, Vol. 1, No. 1, Spring 1981, pp. 11–7.

Rooke, Constance, ''Saul Bellow's 'Leaving the Yellow House': The Trouble with Women,'' in *Studies in Short Fiction*, Vol. 14, No. 2, Spring 1977, pp. 184–87.

Samuels, C. T., Review in *Atlantic*, November, 1968, p. 126.

Further Reading

Fuchs, Daniel, *Saul Bellow: Vision and Revision*, Duke University Press, 1984.
This discussion of Bellow's writings draws on previously unpublished letters and manuscripts.

Halberstam, David, *The Fifties*, Villard Books, 1993.
This work provides an in-depth look at the major issues, both political and social, of the 1950s.

Malin, Irving, *Saul Bellow's Fiction*, Southern Illinois University Press, 1969.
This work provides a discussion of Bellow's writings.

Trachtenberg, Stanley, ed., *Critical Essays on Saul Bellow*, G. K. Hall & Co., 1979.
This collection consists of book reviews and essays about Bellow's work.

The Lesson

Toni Cade Bambara

1972

The stories in Toni Cade Bambara's first collection, *Gorilla, My Love*, celebrate African-American culture and community, sometimes in juxtaposition against white society. Bambara challenges her characters to rethink ideas of accepted social values and norms at the same time that she challenges her readers to do the same. Many of her stories also feature a young, intelligent female narrator living in a world that she questions and examines. The narrator's discoveries, again, mirror the discovery of the reader.

"The Lesson" examines the realization of economic inequity in 1960s America through the eyes of a young girl. In Sylvia, Bambara creates a proud, sensitive, tough girl who is far too smart to ignore the realities around her, even though she knows it might be easier to do so. At the same time, Bambara creates a host of characters, all of whom help Sylvia explore and demonstrate the issues that face poor people and minorities in the United States.

Throughout her career, Bambara used her fiction writing as a forum for teaching people how to better their lives and how to demand more for themselves. Critics at the time of *Gorilla, My Love*'s publication saw in her fiction a true voice. At the same time that Bambara aptly drew the African-American community, she also taught about what it could become. With stories such as "The Lesson," she indeed, imparts a lesson without sacrificing her art form to didactic thought or morals.

Author Biography

Toni Cade Bambara was born March 25, 1939, in New York City in Harlem. Her family moved frequently, and Bambara spent her childhood in different neighborhoods of New York and New Jersey. She was drawn to the arts and learning, and her childhood included the following: trips to the influential Apollo Theater to hear music; Speaker's Corner, where she listened to political debates and was exposed to many different ways of thinking; and the public library.

She attended Queens College in New York, and she studied English and theater arts. In 1959, her first published work of fiction, "Sweet Town," appeared in *Vendome* magazine. She also earned her Bachelor of Arts degree that year, as well as a fiction award from her college.

Bambara enrolled for graduate work in modern American fiction at City College of New York. While attending classes, she also worked as a social worker for the Harlem Welfare Center. In 1961, she studied in Milan, Italy. Over the next few years, she completed her master's degree while doing social and therapy work. She also coordinated and directed several neighborhood programs.

After receiving her master's degree, Bambara taught at City College from 1965 to 1969. She also served as director/advisor for an African-American theater group and with several City College literary publications. During this period, more and more of her stories began to appear in national journals and magazines.

Bambara always put her community work at the forefront, and in 1970 she merged her sociopolitical and literary interests when she edited and published an anthology entitled *The Black Woman*. It featured works by African-American women who were involved in both the civil rights and women's movements.

From 1969 to 1974, Bambara taught in the English department at Livingstone College in New Jersey. She continued to work with the African-American community, and the students and faculty honored her efforts. Also during this time, Bambara edited her second anthology, *Tales and Stories for Black Folks*.

From 1959 to 1970, Bambara continued to work on her own fiction. In 1972 she published *Gorilla, My Love*, which became her most widely read collection. Its fifteen stories focus on the relationships in African-American communities and includes the story "The Lesson."

In the 1970s, Bambara visited Cuba and Vietnam, travels that spurred her continued involvement with fighting traditional gender and racial roles. Her 1977 collection *The Sea Birds Are Still Alive* was influenced by these travels and her continuing sociopolitical involvement. Bambara settled in Georgia, where she became a founding member of the Southern Collective of African-American Writers.

Bambara published two novels and one work of juvenile fiction in addition to her short story collections. She also worked on scriptwriting and conducted workshops to train community organizations on how to use videos to enact social changes. Bambara died of colon cancer in December, 1995. A collection of her fiction, essays, and interviews, edited by Toni Morrison, was published the year after her death.

Plot Summary

In "The Lesson," Miss Moore has moved into the narrator's—Sylvia's—neighborhood recently. Miss Moore is unlike the other African Americans in the neighborhood. She wears her hair in its natural curls, she speaks proper English, she goes by her last name, she has attended college, and she wants to teach the neighborhood children about the world around them.

One day Miss Moore takes the children on a field trip. She starts off by talking about how much things cost, what the children's parents earn, and the unequal division of wealth in the United States. She makes Sylvia angry when she says that they are poor and live in the slums.

Miss Moore hails two cabs, and she gives Sylvia five dollars to pay their driver. Sylvia suggests that they jump out of the cab and go get barbecue, but no one, including Sylvia's friend and cohort Sugar, agrees. When they get to their destination, Sylvia keeps the four dollars change.

Their destination is the famous Fifth Avenue toy store, F. A. O. Schwarz. Before the group enters, they look in the store windows. They see very expensive toys—a microscope that costs $300, a paperweight that costs $480, and a sailboat that costs $1,195. While they look at these items, they talk about what they see. Miss Moore explains what a paperweight is for. Most of the children don't see the need for it—only Mercedes has a desk at home. It is the sailboat that surprises them the most, however. Even Sylvia speaks: "Unbelievable," she says. The children discuss the sailboat in the window and the sailboats that they make from kits. Sylvia wonders what a real boat costs, but Miss Moore won't tell her; she says that Sylvia should check it out and report back to the group later.

The group then goes into the store. Sylvia hangs back, feeling funny and a bit ashamed, though she doesn't know why. The children walk quietly through the store, hardly touching anything at all. Sugar reaches out to touch the sailboat, and Sylvia feels jealous and angry; she feels like punching someone. She asks Miss Moore why she brought them here, and Miss Moore asks if she is mad about something.

They take the subway home. On the train, Sylvia thinks about a clown that she saw that cost $35. In her world, $35 buys a lot: bunk beds, a visit to Grandpa for the entire family, the rent, and the piano bill. She wonders who are the people who have so much money to spend on toys. She wonders why they have so much money, and she and her family and friends have none. She thinks how Miss Moore says that poor people don't have to remain poor, that they need to rebel against the status quo. Sylvia thinks that Miss Moore isn't so smart after all, because she won't get back her change from the taxi. Sylvia is unhappy with Miss Moore for unsettling her day with such thoughts.

Back in the building, Miss Moore asks what the children thought of the toy store. One of the children says that white people are crazy, and another girl says that she wants to go there when she gets her birthday money. Sugar surprises Sylvia by speaking up. She notes that the sailboat costs more than the cost of feeding all the children in a year. Miss Moore gets excited by what Sugar says and encourages her to continue. Sugar does, despite Sylvia stepping on her feet to quiet her. Sugar says that she doesn't think the country is much of a democracy if people do not have equal opportunity to wealth. Miss Moore is pleased with Sugar's answer, but Sylvia is disgusted by her treachery. She stands on Sugar's foot again, and this time Sugar is quiet. Miss Moore looks at Sylvia and asks if she learned anything, but Sylvia walks away. Sugar follows. Sylvia mentions the money they have, but Sylvia doesn't really answer. Sylvia suggests going to

Toni Cade Bambara

Hascombs and getting junk food, and then she suggests that they race. Sylvia lets Sugar run out ahead of her. Sylvia plans on going off to be alone to think about the day.

Characters

Big Butt

Big Butt most likely derives his nickname from his eating habits. Before the group leaves for the toy store, he is "already wasting his peanut-butter-and-jelly sandwich like the pig he is." His response to the toys also reflects this rapaciousness. He wants things without knowing what they are.

Fat Butt

See Big Butt

Flyboy

Flyboy demonstrates the crafty sophistication of a ghetto child. He knows how to extract pity and financial assistance from whites. In his clear-eyed understanding of how to play the monetary game, he appears older than he really is.

Junebug

Junebug is relatively quiet at the store. He sees the expensive sailboat, which launches the children on the success and failure of the fifty-cent sailboats they sail in the parks.

Mercedes

Mercedes is unlike the other children because she wants to be like the rich, white Americans. She has her own desk at home for doing her homework. She is at home in F. A. O. Schwarz and wants to come back with her birthday money to buy herself a toy. Mercedes, alone of the children, is unperturbed by the price tags on the toys or what they represent about America.

Miss Moore

Miss Moore is a college-educated woman who has come to live in a poor, African-American neighborhood of New York. She takes upon herself the responsibility to teach the neighborhood children about the larger community and the problems that African Americans and poor people face in the world. She takes the neighborhood children on field trips and exposes them to various issues and ways of life. She challenges the children to think about what they see—like the prices on the toys in F. A. O. Schwarz—to question the status quo, and to find out more about the world around them. Miss Moore also imparts her belief in the need for the poor people to step up and demand their fair share of America's wealth.

Q. T.

Q. T. is the youngest and quietest child in the group. His major contribution to the discussion is to openly long for the expensive sailboat and declare the unspoken—that F. A. O. Schwarz is a store for "rich people."

Sugar

Sugar is Sylvia's closest friend and her cohort. Despite the friendship, Sylvia feels an element of competition with Sugar. When Sugar gets up the nerve to touch the $1,000-dollar sailboat, Sylvia is so jealous that she wants to hit her friend. Sugar is the only child who tells Miss Moore exactly what she wants to hear—that the toys at F. A. O. Schwarz are indicative of the inequity of American society and do not aptly reflect the democratic principles on which the country was founded. She does, however, run off with Sylvia to spend the money left over from the cab.

Sylvia

Sylvia is the narrator of the story. She is a young, tough, smart girl. She is strongly affected by her surroundings and has the capacity to see the truth in things, for example, in the way her family treats Aunt Gretchen. Despite her ability to see the truth in things, she also acts in a dishonest manner; she speaks of wanting to steal hair ribbons and money from the West Indian kids; she doesn't give the cab driver a tip, preferring to keep the money for herself; and she doesn't give the change from the cab ride back to Miss Moore.

Sylvia gets very angry during the trip to F. A. O. Schwarz, even though she claims not to know why. This anger that people could spend so much money on useless items leads her to speak to Miss Moore about her feelings, which surprises even her.

Themes

Poverty and Wealth

The children in "The Lesson" all come from poor families. They live in apartment buildings where drunks live in the hallways that reek of urine; they live in what Miss Moore terms the "slums." The children's families, however, exhibit somewhat varying degrees of monetary security. Mercedes, for instance, has a desk at home with a box of stationary on it—gifts from her godmother—while Flyboy claims he does not even have a home.

The children, however, surely understand the value of money, and they easily comprehend that the amount of money charged for the toys at F. A. O. Schwarz is astronomical. They compare the handcrafted fiberglass sailboat, which costs $1,195, to the ones they make from a kit, which cost about 50 cents. Sylvia further thinks about what her family could buy with the $35 a clown costs: bunk beds, a family visit to Grandaddy out in the country, even the rent, and the piano bills. The disparity between the way the rich people live and the way Sylvia and her neighbors live is the lesson that Miss Moore wants to impart.

The children internalize this lesson in different ways. Sugar questions whether a nation in which

Topics for Further Study

- This story aptly reflects thoughts that were prevalent in the 1960s, which was a decade of great social change. Could it take place now? Explain your answer.

- Compare Sylvia and Sugar. How are they alike? How are they different? Which child do you think is most affected by the events of the day? Why do you think as you do?

- Conduct research to find out more about the Black Power movement. Do you think Miss Moore ascribes to the beliefs of this movement? Why or why not?

- Think about present-day society and the inequalities inherent in it. What groups of people do you think suffer from economic inequities? From social inequities?

- Miss Moore proposes one solution to the economic unfairness that existed in the 1960s: poor people should demand their piece of the pie. Do you think her solution would work? What are other solutions that could have helped poor people?

- For the children in "The Lesson," F. A. O. Schwarz is a blatant symbolism of the failure of capitalism. What other symbols can you think of that might symbolize both the failures and successes of the capitalist system?

- Sylvia briefly describes the physical environment in which she lives. Conduct research to find out more about ghetto life in the 1960s in northern cities. Write a few paragraphs about your findings.

some people have so much but others have so little is truly a democracy. Sylvia grows angry at the disparity that she sees, and she also recognizes the potential showiness of wealth, as represented by the woman who wears a fur coat despite the hot weather. Mercedes, in contrast, aspires more to be like the white people who spend so much money on toys.

The poverty in which the children live is further emphasized by Sylvia's constant attention to money and what *she* can use it to buy. Even before the group arrives at the toy store, she acknowledges what she uses money for, such as the grocer, presumably to buy groceries for the family. Barbeque, which she suggests purchasing with Miss Moore's cab fare, is a luxury, as is the chocolate layer cake and the movie tickets and junk food on which Sugar suggests they spend the remaining money.

Race

Although race is hardly specifically mentioned, it is the undercurrent of the story. That race is not made a point is not surprising; in Sylvia's world, everyone is African American. The only person who inhabits the exterior is Miss Moore, who actually is "black as hell." Miss Moore's otherness stems not from race, but from the way she is different from the African Americans who predominate in the neighborhood. She has a college education, she wears her hair in its natural curls instead of straightening it, as many African-American women of the era did, and she insists on being called by her last name.

Two important ideas—that wealth and race are intrinsically linked and that white people and African-American people are different—are revealed in one brief sentence: when Sylvia sees a woman wearing a fur coat even though it is summer, she says "White folks crazy." Skin color is mentioned only a few other times, when Sylvia relates that Flyboy tries to get the white people at school "off his back and sorry for him" and when Rosa Giraffe reiterates Sylvia's belief that white people are crazy. By the time the children leave the store, it is clear to the reader that they believe that only white people have so much money to spend—and to spend so foolishly.

Resistance

Bambara has used her writing as an attempt to empower the African-American community; she believed that African Americans needed to pursue a policy of resistance against the racism inherent in American society. Such a policy is evident in ''The Lesson'' as Miss Moore encourages the children and her neighbors to question the inequality in the world around them. On the way to the toy store she tells the children that ''money ain't divided up right in this country.'' After the children leave the toy store she urges them to think about their society ''in which some people can spend on a toy what it would cost to feed a family of six or seven.'' She is encouraging them to think about the world in order to resist it. She has already told the children that they live in a slum, and as Sylvia recalls,

> Where we are is who we are, Miss Moore always pointin out. But it don't necessarily have to be that way, she always adds, then waits for somebody to say that poor people have to wake up and demand their share of the pie.

Miss Moore's task of promoting resistance is formidable, for Sylvia questions ''none of us know what kind of pie she talking about in the first damn place.'' However, her tactics do have some effect on the children. She raises anger in Sylvia, though Sylvia can't articulate why she is mad. She also has gotten Sylvia, and several of the other children, thinking about these inequities. At the end of the day, Sylvia goes off alone to ponder the day—and thinking about something is often the first step to taking action to change it.

Style

Point of View

''The Lesson'' is told from Sylvia's first-person point of view. This means that all the events are perceived through Sylvia. Despite this potentially restrictive viewpoint, Sylvia is able to present a wider view of her community. She compares Miss Moore to the rest of the adults. Not only does this show how different Miss Moore is, she also indicates certain cultural standards of the time, such as Miss Moore's wearing her hair ''nappy,'' or curly, at a time when many African-American women straightened their hair, or that the adults dislike that Miss Moore does not go to church, indicating the importance of religion to the community. Sylvia also presents the different types of people who inhabit her community through the children in the group. Mercedes wants to be like the white people who shop at F. A. O. Schwarz; Flyboy seeks pity and charity as a result of his poverty and unstable homelife; Sugar, Sylvia's cohort, surprisingly shows both a desire to please Miss Moore and a clear-headed understanding of the inequities of American society. Sylvia's inner musings, her obvious intelligence, and her sudden feelings of anger when she is at the toy store show that she could very well grow up to be the kind of person that Miss Moore wants them all to be: one who resists and who invokes change.

Setting

The story takes place in New York City. The children live in an African-American neighborhood, most likely Harlem. The store they visit is on Fifth Avenue in midtown, which is a much more expensive part of New York. For much of its history, New York has been a place where the wealthy and the poor live, sometimes within only blocks of each other. It has also been seen as a land of opportunity. Starting in the 1910s, many southern African Americans migrated to the North—as did Sylvia's family—generally to find better employment and less racial prejudice.

Dialect

The characters in the story, with the exception of Miss Moore, speak in a non-standard form of English. They do not always speak with standard grammar or inflection. They say words like *ain't*, drop the final *g* off words like *pointing*, and leave words out of sentences, as in ''she not even related by marriage'' or ''white people crazy.'' This aptly reflects how the people in Sylvia's African-American community talked. One of the first details that Sylvia relates about Miss Moore is that she has ''proper speech,'' indicating how unique she is. The speech of Sylvia and her friends—though non-standard—is more common in their world.

Black Aesthetic Movement

The Black Aesthetic Movement, which is also known as the Black Arts Movement, was a period of artistic and literary development among African Americans in the 1960s and early 1970s. It was the first major African-American movement since the

Harlem Renaissance, and the civil rights and Black Power movements closely paralleled it. Black aesthetic writers attempted to produce works of art that would be meaningful to the African-American mass audience. The movement sought to use art to promote the idea of African-American separatism. Typical literature of the movement was generally written in African-American English vernacular, was confrontational in tone, and addressed such issues as interracial tension, sociopolitical awareness, and the relevance of African history and culture to African Americans. Alice A. Deck wrote in the *Dictionary of Literary Biography*, ''In many ways Toni Cade Bambara is one of the best representatives of [this] group.''

''The Lesson'' demonstrates many attributes of this movement. Bambara draws on typical African-American urban culture in creating her characters and dialogue, and in focusing attention on issues of real concern. Miss Moore clearly advocates taking a strong position to achieve equality; she wants the poor African Americans to ''demand'' their fair share of American prosperity. The children demonstrate the racial tension they feel daily; they openly speak of how ''crazy'' white folks are. By the end of the story, Sylvia and Sugar have clearly internalized Miss Moore's lesson.

Historical Context

The Civil Rights Movement in the 1950s

African Americans began taking a more active stance in the 1950s to end discrimination in the United States. The 1952 Supreme Court case, *Brown v. Board of Education of Topeka* successfully challenged segregation in public schools. Then civil rights leaders launched the Montgomery bus boycott to end segregation on southern transportation systems. For close to a year African Americans in Montgomery, Alabama, refused to ride the public bus system, and in November 1956, the Supreme Court declared such segregation laws unconstitutional. Meanwhile, despite the earlier court ruling, school desegregation was slow in coming. In 1957, when nine African Americans attempted to attend Central High in Little Rock, Arkansas, the governor sent the National Guard to prevent them from doing so. The students were not able to enter the school until three weeks later and under protection from federal troops. Despite angry whites who resented this integration, most of the students graduated from Central High. In the midst of this crisis, President Dwight Eisenhower signed the Civil Rights Act of 1957. The first civil rights law passed since Reconstruction, this act made it a federal crime to prevent any qualified person from voting. Also that year, southern civil rights leaders formed the Southern Christian Leadership Conference (SLCC), led by the Reverend Martin Luther King Jr. to end discrimination.

The Civil Rights Movement in the 1960s

The SLCC advocated nonviolent resistance to achieve its goals, and many non-SLCC members took up nonviolent protests of their own. In February 1960, four African-American college students staged a sit-in at a lunch counter in Greensboro, North Carolina. Within weeks, similar demonstrations had spread throughout the South. White racists responded angrily to these demonstrators, and sometimes their harassment escalated into physical attacks, but the demonstrators remained impassive. By the end of the year, many restaurants throughout the South had been integrated.

In May 1961, a northern-based, integrated civil rights group launched the Freedom Rides to protest segregation in interstate transportation. These young activists set off by bus from Washington, D.C., with the intention of traveling through the South, but when the buses stopped, riders were attacked by white mobs. In Jackson, Mississippi, state officials arrested the riders. Outraged, more than 300 additional Freedom Riders traveled the South to protest segregation. Their numbers pressured the Interstate Commerce Commission to strengthen its desegregation regulations. Additionally, the white mob violence led to increased national support for the civil rights movement.

In 1963, more than 200,000 people gathered in Washington, D.C., to encourage support for a new civil rights act designed to end segregation. The Civil Rights Act of 1964 was passed the following year. It barred discrimination in employment, public accommodations, and gave the Justice Department the power to enforce school desegregation.

In June 1964, activists turned their attention to voter registration, launching Freedom Summer, a

Compare
&
Contrast

- **1970s:** In 1970, of the 25.4 million Americans who live in poverty, 7.5 million, or 33.5 percent, are African American. The average income cutoff level for a family of four at the poverty level is $3,968.

  1990s: In 1995, 36.4 million Americans, including 27.5 million families, live in poverty. Almost 10 million individuals, or 29.3 percent of the population, are African American. At the beginning of the decade, 44 percent of poor children are African American, while 15 percent are white. The average income cutoff level for a family of four at the poverty level is $15,569.

- **1970s:** In 1970, Americans in the lowest 5 percent have a mean income of $7,281, and the top 5 percent have a mean income of $119,432, in 1996 dollars.

  1990s: In 1994, Americans in the lowest fifth have a mean income of $7,762. The top five percent have a mean income of $183,044.

- **1970s:** There are 9.7 million Americans who receive some form of welfare. In New York City in 1968, one million people, or one in eight residents, receive welfare, and one in five New York children depend on welfare payments. One quarter of the city's budget is spent on welfare. A family of four receives $278 per month, which still places them below the poverty line.

- **1990s:** In 1995, the United States spends just over $22 million on Aid to Families with Dependent Children. An average of 13.7 million people receive this form of welfare each month.

- **1960s:** In 1968, African Americans earn sixty-three percent as much as whites. The median household income for African Americans is $22,000 as compared to $38,000 for whites (in 1998 dollars).

  1990s: In 1998, the median household income for African Americans is $25,500 and for whites it is $42,000.

- **1960s and 1970s:** In 1968, 57 percent of non-whites complete high school. In 1972, 27.2 percent of African Americans who complete high school go to college, as compared to a national percentage for all races of 31.9 percent.

  1990s: In 1995, 356,000 African Americans graduate from high school, and 183,000 enroll in college. In 1997, 39.3 percent of African Americans who graduate from high school go to college as compared to a national percentage for all races of 44.9 percent. Also, 13.4 percent of African-American students drop out of high school, compared to a national percentage for all students of 8.6 percent.

---

campaign to register African-American voters in the South. They focused on Mississippi, a state where only five percent of African Americans were registered to vote. Violence quickly struck when two white northerners and one African American were abducted and killed. Many African Americans, fearing reprisal, refused to register to vote. After a similar registration drive in Selma, Alabama, ended in a fierce attack on marchers, President Lyndon Johnson asked Congress to pass a voting rights bill. Five months later, Congress passed the Voting Rights Act of 1965, which put the voter registration process under federal control. Within three years, over half of all eligible African Americans in the South had registered to vote.

Black Power

Despite these successes, many African Americans grew to question the effectiveness of nonviolent protest. Some felt they should use violence for self-defense, while others did not want to integrate into white society. These African Americans adopted the slogan "Black Power," which became widely used by the late 1960s. They argued for mobilization to gain economic and political power and even complete separation from white society.

Malcolm X was one of the Black Power leaders. He championed black separatism and believed African Americans should use any means necessary to achieve freedom. He was assassinated in 1965, but other activists carried out his ideas. In 1966 two college students founded the Black Panther party to promote self-determination in the African-American community. The Black Panthers armed themselves and patrolled the streets of their communities.

In August 1965, a riot broke out in an African-American neighborhood of Watts after an arrest. The riot lasted for six days and spurred more than one hundred riots around the country over the next two years. A federal report charged that white racism was largely responsible for the tensions that led to the riots. This report stated that "our nation is moving toward two societies, one black, one white—separate and unequal."

The War on Poverty and the Great Society

In 1962, Michael Harrington published his book *The Other America*, a well-documented study of poverty in the United States. It stated that more than 42 million Americans lived on less than $1,000 per year and shattered the widespread belief that most Americans had benefited from the post-war prosperity of the 1950s. The book also noted that racism kept many ethnic groups, especially African Americans, in poverty. Responding to such concerns, President Johnson launched the War on Poverty. In 1964, Congress passed a bill that authorized $1 billion to coordinate a series of antipoverty programs, including work-training and education programs.

Johnson also announced his desire to build a Great Society in which poverty and racial injustice would not exist. To this effect, Johnson persuaded Congress to establish national health insurance programs for elderly and low-income Americans. In 1965, Congress also passed an education act that allocated $1.3 billion to schools in impoverished areas. Other acts set aside billions of dollars for urban renewal and housing assistance for low-income families.

Critical Overview

Before publication of her first book, Bambara had already made a reputation for herself as a short story writer, as an editor of anthologies of works by African-American writers, and as an activist in the New York African-American community. The impetus for publishing *Gorilla, My Love* came from a friend of Bambara's, who suggested that Bambara collect her stories, and indicated that Toni Morrison (then an editor at Random House) was interested in working toward its publication. With her first collection, Bambara established herself as a vital voice in the growing Black Aesthetic movement. Elliot Butler-Evans analyzed the collection in his *Race, Gender, and Desire: Narrative Strategies in the Fiction on Toni Cade Bambara, Toni Morrison, and Alice Walker*:

> The stories in *Gorilla* clearly locate the collection in the broad context of Black nationalist fiction of the 1960s. Employing classic realism as their dominant narrative form, Bambara constructed organic Black communities in which intra-racial strife was minimal, the White world remained on the periphery, and the pervasive "realities" of Black life were presented.

Published in 1972, *Gorilla, My Love* includes fifteen stories, mostly written between 1959 and 1970. They focus on the relationships among African Americans, primarily in the urban North of Bambara's childhood. They celebrate sassy and tough narrators—usually young girls—and explore the developmental experiences of young people as they learn about identity, self-worth, and belonging.

The backdrop for Bambara's tales is the African-American community. Martha Vertreace wrote the following in her chapter in *American Women Writing Fiction: Memory, Identity, Family, Space*:

> For Bambara the community becomes essential as a locus for growth, not simply as a source of narrative tension . . . her characters and community do a circle dance around and with each other as learning and growth occur.

The collection drew immediate praise, both from the white and African-American audience, and for a variety of reasons. Bell Gale Chevigny of *The Village Voice*, appreciated the stories both for their artform and for what they had to say:

> I find much of the writing here wonderful and well worth anyone's attention. . . . The stories are often sketchy as to plot, but always lavish in their strokes. . . . The black life she draws on . . . is so vividly particularized you don't feel the wisdom or bite till later.

Some critics also responded to the Bambara's message, which they felt was delivered in a more positive manner than similar ones given by other African-American writers of the time. C. D. B. Bryan expressed this idea in his review in *The New York Times Book Review*:

> Toni Cade Bambara tells me more about being black through her quiet, proud, silly, tender, hip, acute, loving stories than any amount of literary polemicizing could hope to do. She writes about love: a love for one's family, one's friends, one's race, one's neighborhood, and it is the sort of love that comes with maturity and inner peace.

Many critics, both at the time of publication and since, have commented on Bambara's accurate portrayal of the African-American community and the relationships within it. The *Saturday Review* called *Gorilla, My Love* "among the best portraits of black life to have appeared in some time."

Several contemporary reviewers and literary scholars since have found "The Lesson" to be one of Bambara's finest stories. Nancy D. Hargrove suggested in an essay in *The Southern Quarterly* that it was "perhaps the best of the fifteen stories."

Bambara went on the publish another short fiction collection, as well as two novels, a juvenile book, and a collection of essays, interviews, and fiction, but she is still best known for *Gorilla, My Love*.

Criticism

Rena Korb

Korb has a master's degree in English literature and creative writing and has written for a wide variety of educational publishers. In the following essay, she discusses the different reactions of the children in "The Lesson."

According to Teri Ann Doerksen writing in *The Dictionary of Literary Biography*, Toni Cade Bambara's first short story collection, *Gorilla, My Love*, "celebrates urban African-American life, black English, and a spirit of hopefulness inspired by the Civil Rights movement." By 1972, when the collection was published, Bambara had already established herself as an advocate for African-American and women's rights, and many of her stories were a literary call to arms; Bambara saw in her writing the opportunity to initiate resistance to the cultural—

and racist—norms of her day. Toni Morrison wrote of Bambara in *Deep Sightings and Rescue Missions: Fiction, Essays, and Conversations*

> There was no doubt whatsoever that the work she did had work to do. She always knew what her work was for. Any hint that art was over there and politics over here would break her up into tears of laughter, or elicit a look so withering it made silence the only intelligent response.

"The Lesson" is one of several stories in *Gorilla, My Love* that feature a strong-willed adolescent female narrator. Over the course of one afternoon, Sylvia is forced to an unpleasant awareness of the unfairness of the social and economic system that prevails in the United States of the 1960s. Sylvia lives in a "slum" neighborhood. Her family has moved from the South—presumably to better their financial circumstances, as did so many southern African Americans throughout the twentieth century—but they find themselves living in the ghetto. Only one person in the neighborhood distinguishes herself—Miss Moore, a symbol of changing times. Unlike the other African Americans, Miss Moore is college educated and speaks in standard English. She disdains to go to church. Her physical appearance alone denotes her differences. She has "nappy hair" and wears "no makeup." Most crucial for the neighborhood children, she takes upon herself the "responsibility for the young ones' education" and exposes them to the world outside of their neighborhood and the truths it holds. On the afternoon the story takes place, she takes a group of children, including Sylvia, to F. A. O. Schwarz, an expensive toy store. The lesson she wants to impart is the economic inequity that exists in the United States, and for the most part, she succeeds admirably in her goal.

One unusual aspect in a story of this brevity is the number of characters included. Miss Moore brings eight children to the store, and all of these children have a different perspective on the events of the day. The children are alike in that all of them recognize the exorbitant cost of the toys, particularly a sailboat that costs $1,195. (Remember that "The Lesson" takes place within a decade after a study revealed that 42 million American families lived on less than $1,000 per year.) The children, however, can be broken into three categories: those who acknowledge the outrageous prices of the toys (Big Butt, Rosie Giraffe, Junebug, Q. T., and Flyboy); those who show no understanding of the greater significance of these toys (Mercedes); and those who openly or tacitly acknowledge the economic injustice the toys demonstrate (Sylvia and Sugar).

What Do I Read Next?

- Toni Cade Bambara's *Gorilla, My Love* collects fifteen stories written between 1959 and 1972. Many of the stories have a child narrator, as does ''The Lesson,'' and they raise issues significant to the African-American community.

- *Black Fire: An Anthology of Afro-American Writing* (1968), edited by LeRoi Jones and Larry Neal, collects creative works that are part of the Black Aesthetic Movement.

- Madhubuti's verse collection *Don't Cry, Scream* (1969) is representative of poetry produced during the Black Aesthetic Movement. His work is characterized by use of dialect and slang and the author's anger at social and economic injustice as well as his joy in African-American culture.

- The play *Dutchman* (1964), by Amiri Baraka, is one of the writer's most well-known works. It illustrates the hatred between African Americans and white Americans through the chance encounter of a middle-class African-American man and a white woman. It also explores the political and psychological conflicts facing the African-American man in the 1960s.

- *The Black Woman* (1970), edited by Toni Cade Bambara, is a collection of poetry, short stories, and essays by well-known African-American women writers. It was the first anthology of its kind published in the United States.

- James Baldwin's essay book, *The Fire Next Time* (1963), warned white Americans of the violence that would result if attitudes and policies towards African Americans did not change. The first essay attacks the notion of African-American inferiority, and the second essay recounts Baldwin's coming-of-age in Harlem and his involvement with the Black Power movement.

- Kaye Gibson's novel *Ellen Foster* is told from the point of view of the child narrator. Ellen, a young, impoverished southern girl, grows up in an abusive home. This brief yet powerful novel chronicles her attempts to find a real family.

Of the larger group of children, each child does react to the expensive toys in a somewhat distinctive manner. Big Butt reacts on a visceral level. He sees the microscope and declares ''I'm going to buy that there,'' when he is not even sure what a person uses a microscope to look at. Junebug reflects a more simplistic approach. When Miss Moore explains what a paperweight is, he figures she ''crazy or lyin''' because ''we don't keep paper on top of the desk in my class.'' When she explains that people might use a paperweight on their desks at home, he says, ''I don't even have a desk,'' but then turns to his older brother Big Butt for confirmation: ''Do we?'' Rosie Giraffe, vulnerable as a recent immigrant from the South, asks the pointed questions that the more hard-boiled northern children will not deign to ask, such as what is a paperweight. Q. T., the quietest and the youngest, says little but he stares ''hard at the sailboat and you could see he

wanted it bad.'' Q. T. also voices the obvious: ''Must be rich people shop here.''

Of this group of children, Flyboy is the most outspoken. The ''wise man from the East'' plays the know-it-all. He announces that a paperweight is ''To weigh paper with, dumbbell,'' and Miss Moore is forced to correct him. Flyboy knows how to use his poverty and deprivation to make people, especially ''white folks,'' feel pity for him; ''Send this poor kid to camp posters, is his specialty.'' It is also Flyboy who firsts notices the sailboat that shocks all the children. His ultimate reaction to the afternoon, and to Miss Moore's final question, also chillingly echoes an adult's—''I'd like a shower,'' he says. ''Tiring day.''—the words of a child too soon exposed to the harsh realities of the world.

At the far end of the spectrum is Mercedes. From the beginning of the story, she is presented as

> "The lesson she wants to impart is the economic inequity that exists in the United States, and for the most part, she succeeds admirably in her goal."

outside the circle of children, the butt of their irritation. As the story continues, differences between Mercedes and the others are continually raised. For instance, she is the only child who has a desk at home. "I have a box of stationery on my desk and a picture of my cat. My godmother bought the stationery and the desk. There's a big rose on each sheet and the envelopes smell like roses," she says in a statement that draws the anger of the other children; "'Who wants to know about your smelly—stationery,' says Rosie Giraffe fore I can get my two cents in." Mercedes aspires to these symbols of the "white" world, *because* they are the symbols of success. Her interest in education and her more articulated speech liken her to Miss Moore, but unlike Miss Moore, Mercedes does not see the signifiers of the white world as pointing out problems within the African-American world. She would emulate Miss Moore *in order* to be like whites, not to improve the circumstance of the African-American community.

Only Mercedes expresses no shock at the prices of the toys. She enters the store first, moving primly and properly, "smoothing out her jumper and walking right down the aisle." The other children, in contrast, do not belong. Their entrance is marked by chaos; they "tumble in like a glued-together jigsaw done all wrong." When the other children exclaim over the expensive sailboat, acknowledging that they buy sailboat sets that cost fifty cents, Mercedes attempts to deflate their pride: "But will it take water?" At the end of the day, when the group has returned to the neighborhood, Miss Moore asks what they thought of the store. Mercedes' only response is "I'd like to go there again when I get my birthday money." She has taken no greater lesson from the day than to learn to want to be more like the white people who can so recklessly and carelessly spend their money. Her exclusion from the group is physically symbolized as they "shove her out of the pack so she has to lean on the mailbox by herself."

On the opposite end of the spectrum from Mercedes is Sugar and Sylvia. They are allies before they enter the store. Sugar asks Miss Moore, straight faced, if she can steal, a sassy question that easily could have come from Sylvia. Also, the girls express the initial reaction to the toys in the store; they both scream in one voice, "This is mine, that's mine, I gotta have that, that was made for me, I was born for that." But once the real examination of the toys begins, Sugar is not seen or heard from again until they are in the store. There Sylvia and Sugar split up, signifying their ensuing division. Sugar's actions further anger Sylvia; Sugar "run a finger over the whole boat," something that Sylvia cannot bring herself to do. Once they are on the train returning to the neighborhood, Sugar and Sylvia seem to have regained their solidarity as Sugar motions to Sylvia's pocket where Miss Moore's money is. But Sylvia is again let down by her friend when Miss Moore asks what the children thought of F. A. O. Schwarz. Sugar speaks up with the words that Miss Moore most wants to hear: "I think . . . this is not much of a democracy if you ask me. Equal chance to pursue happiness means an equal crack at the dough, don't it?'" She pleases Miss Moore despite Sylvia's warning nudges.

Sylvia feels betrayed by Sugar's alliance with Miss Moore even though Sugar is verbally expressing the feelings that Sylvia shares, even if she has not yet acknowledged them within herself. It is clear from Sylvia's reactions that she is utterly shocked and appalled by the realization that some people can afford to spend so much money on toys. "'Unbelievable,' I hear myself say and I am really stunned," is her reaction to the sailboat. The word *stunned* has a double meaning. Firstly, Sylvia is stunned by the sheer cost, but she also is stunned that she is so moved that she *voluntarily* responds to Miss Moore's lesson. She attempts to stimulate her intense dislike of Miss Moore. When Sylvia asks how much a real boat costs, Miss Moore won't tell her, instead saying: "Why don't you check that out . . . and report back to the group?" This "really pains" Sylvia. "If you gonna mess up a perfectly good swim day least you could do is have some answers." What is clear, however, as Nancy D. Hargrove writes in *The Southern Quarterly*, is Miss Moore has "touched her deeply, messing up far more than one day."

Miss Moore's field trip also has produced in Sylvia an unwelcome sense of inferiority. The pride that Sylvia wears like shining armor is wounded. Sylvia, accustomed to owning her neighborhood and her own actions, feels out of place in this bastion of white wealth where Sylvia and the children ''all walkin on tiptoe and hardly touchin the games and puzzles and things.'' When she and Sylvia ''bump smack into each other'' these two friends ''don't laugh and go into our fat-lady routine.'' Intimidated by the store and the monstrous price tags, Sylvia grows increasingly angry that Miss Moore has forced this lesson upon her.

Unable to deal with her anger and not truly understanding where it is directed—''And I'm jealous and want to hit her [Sugar],'' Sylvia thinks when Sugar touches the boat. ''Maybe not her, but I sure want to punch somebody in the mouth''—Sylvia reverts back to her tough pose. ''So I slouch around the store being very bored and say, 'Let's go.''' Once on the subway, though she and Sugar reconvene at the back of the train, Sylvia is unable to let go of the afternoon. She mentally compares what essentials her family could purchase with the lowest-priced toy she saw—a $35 birthday clown.

> Who are these people that spend that much for performing clowns and $1000 for toy sailboats? What kinda work they do and how they live and how come we ain't in on it?

She is beginning to channel her anger toward a real focus as she reflects upon Miss Moore's previous lessons as well;

> Where we are is who we are, Miss Moore always pointin out. But it don't necessarily have to be that way, she always adds then waits for somebody to say that poor people have to wake up and demand their share of the pie and don't none of us know what kind of pie she talking about in the first damn place.

Sylvia still cannot acknowledge that she feels the validity of Miss Moore's words. Instead, she congratulates herself on retaining Miss Moore's change from the taxi ride.

After Sugar's exchange with Miss Moore, Sylvia stands on her foot and finally gets her to be quiet. ''Miss Moore looks at me, sorrowfully I'm thinkin. And somethin weird is goin on, I can feel it in my chest.'' Although Sylvia does not name it yet, and although Sugar, despite her previous disclosure, wants to return to their normal activities, Sylvia is unable to do so:

> I'm going to the West End and then over to the Drive to think this day through. She can run if she want to

and run even faster. But ain't nobody gonna beat me at nuthin.

The focus of the story's final sentence reaffirms Sylvia's determination and implies that Miss Moore's lesson, with the ultimate goal of igniting the children's sense of injustice and leading them to enact societal change, may very well have taken hold.

Source: Rena Korb, Critical Essay on ''The Lesson,'' in *Short Stories for Students*, The Gale Group, 2001.

Martha M. Vertreace

In the following excerpt, Vertreace identifies five stages of identity formation in Bambara's fiction and shows how the community plays a role in educating ''beginners'' in ''The Lesson.''

The question of identity—of personal definition within the context of community—emerges as a central motif for Toni Cade Bambara's writing. Her female characters become as strong as they do, not because of some inherent ''eternal feminine'' quality granted at conception, but rather because of the lessons women learn from communal interaction. Identity is achieved, not bestowed. Bambara's short stories focus on such learning. Very careful to present situations in a highly orchestrated manner, Bambara describes the difficulties that her characters must overcome.

Contemporary literature teems with male characters in coming-of-age stories or even female characters coming of age on male typewriters. Additional stories, sometimes written by black authors, indeed portray such concerns but narrowly defined within crushing contexts of city ghettos or rural poverty. Bambara's writing breaks such molds as she branches out, delineating various settings, various economic levels, various characters—both male and female.

Bambara's stories present a decided emphasis on the centrality of community. Many writers concentrate so specifically on character development or plot line that community seems merely a foil against which the characters react. For Bambara the community becomes essential as a locus for growth, not simply as a source of narrative tension. Thus, her characters and community do a circle dance around and within each other as learning and growth occur.

Bambara's women learn how to handle themselves within the divergent, often conflicting, strata that compose their communities. Such learning does not come easily; hard lessons result from hard knocks. Nevertheless, the women do not merely

> For Bambara the community benefits as both 'teacher' and 'student' confront the same problem— that of survival and prospering in hostile settings, without guaranteed outcomes."

endure; they prevail, emerging from these situations more aware of their personal identities and of their potential for further self-actualization. More important, they guide others to achieve such awareness.

Bambara posits learning as purposeful, geared toward personal and societal change. Consequently, the identities into which her characters grow envision change as both necessary and possible, understanding that they themselves play a major part in bringing about that change. This idea approximates the nature of learning described in Paulo Freire's *Pedagogy of the Oppressed*, in which he decries the "banking concept," wherein education becomes "an act of depositing, in which the students are the depositories and the teacher is the depositor." Oppressive situations define the learner as profoundly ignorant, not possessing valuable insights for communal sharing.

Although many of Bambara's stories converge on the school setting as the place of learning in formal patterns, she liberates such settings to admit and encourage community involvement and ownership. Learning then influences societal liberation and self-determination. These stories describe learning as the process of problem solving, which induces a deepening sense of self, Freire's "intentionality."

For Bambara the community benefits as both "teacher" and "student" confront the same problem—that of survival and prospering in hostile settings, without guaranteed outcomes. The commonality of problems, then, encourages a mutual sharing of wisdom and respect for individual difference that transcends age, all too uncommon in a more traditional education context. Bambara's char-

acters encounter learning within situations similar to the older, tribal milieus. The stages of identity formation, vis-à-vis the knowledge base to be mastered, have five segments: (1) beginner, (2) apprentice, (3) journeyman, (4) artisan, and (5) expert.

Traditional societies employed these stages to pass on to their youth that information necessary to ensure the survival of the tribe, such as farming techniques, and that information needed to inculcate tribal mores, such as songs and stories. Because of Bambara's interest in cultural transmission of values, her characters experience these stages in their maturational quest. In her stories these levels do not correlate with age but rather connote degrees of experience in community. . . .

The movement from beginner to apprentice occurs when the beginner confronts a situation not explained by known rules. Someone steps in who breaks open the situation so that learning can occur. For Sylvia, in "The Lesson," Miss Moore was that person. Sylvia was an unwilling apprentice, resenting Miss Moore's teaching.

Miss Moore wants to radicalize the young, explaining the nature of poverty by taking her charges from their slums to visit Fifth Avenue stores, providing cutting-edge experiences for the children, making them question their acceptance of their lot. When asked what they learned, various ideas surfaced. "I don't think all of us here put together eat in a year what that sailboat costs"; "I think that this is not much of a democracy if you ask me. Equal chance to pursue happiness means an equal crack at the dough, don't it?"

The children, encouraged by Miss Moore, coalesce into a community of support that encourages such questions. For these children these questions represent rules that no longer work, assumptions that are no longer valid.

The adult Miss Moore has stepped out of the adult world to act as guide to the children. Sylvia, for her part, profoundly affected by the day, concludes, "She can run if she want to and even run faster. But ain't nobody gonna beat me at nuthin.'"

Sylvia's determination to defeat her poverty represents movement to the next level, that of journeyman. No longer hampered by a strict adherence to established rules, the journeyman feels confident enough to trust instinct. Risk becomes possible as the journeyman extrapolates from numerous past experiences to stand alone, even if shakily. At this point the community must provide support without heavy-handed restraint or control as the journeyman ventures forth. . . .

Toni Cade Bambara's stories do more than paint a picture of black life in contemporary black settings. Many writers have done that, more or less successfully. Her stories portray women who struggle with issues and learn from them. Sometimes the lessons taste bitter and the women must accumulate more experience in order to gain perspective. By centering community in her stories, Bambara displays both the supportive and the destructive aspects of communal interaction. Her stories do not describe a predictable, linear plot line; rather, the cyclic enfolding of characters and community produces the kind of tension missing in stories with a more episodic emphasis.

Her characters achieve a personal identity as a result of their participation in the human quest for knowledge, which brings power. Bambara's skill as a writer saves her characters from being stereotypic cutouts. Although her themes are universal, communities that Bambara describes rise above the generic. More fully delineated than her male characters, the women come across as specific people living in specific places. Bambara's best stories show her characters interacting within a political framework wherein the personal becomes political.

Source: Martha M. Vertreace, ''The Dance of Character and Community,'' in *American Women Writing Fiction: Memory, Identity, Family, Space*, edited by Mickey Pearlman, University Press of Kentucky, 1989, pp. 155–71.

Nancy D. Hargrove

In the following essay, Hargrove traces the painful process Sylvia undergoes as ''she is forced to realize the unfairness of life.''

[A] painful experience of disillusionment appears in what is perhaps the best of the fifteen stories, ''The Lesson.'' Again, the story centers on and owes much of its vitality to its first-person narrator, a young girl named Sylvia. Arrogant, sassy, and tough, with a vocabulary that might shock a sailor, Sylvia is also witty, bright, and vulnerable. In the course of the story she learns a lesson which disillusions her about the world in which she lives, about the society of which she is a part. Against her will, she is forced to realize the unfairness of life and, as a black girl, her often low position in the scheme of things. Although she fights against this realization and indeed refuses adamantly even to acknowledge it, it is clear to the reader that the young girl is irrevocably affected by the events of the day.

> Her shame arises from her sense of inferiority, of not belonging in such an expensive store, communicated indirectly and subtly by her comparison of the children's chaotic entrance to 'a glued-together jigsaw done all wrong.'

In the opening paragraph, Sylvia sets the stage for the action to follow by introducing her antagonist, Miss Moore, while revealing some facets of her own personality as well as the kind of environment in which she lives. Having a college degree, Miss Moore has taken upon herself ''responsibility for the young ones' education.'' Accordingly, from time to time she takes them on ''field trips,'' during which they learn a great deal about life. Sylvia clearly does not like Miss Moore or her lessons: ''And quite naturally we laughed at her. . . . And we kinda hated her too. . . . [She] was always planning these boring-ass things for us to do.'' In describing Miss Moore, Sylvia reveals her own toughness, which she communicates largely through strong language (''sorry-a–s horse,'' ''g–d–n gas mask,'' ''some ole dumb s–t foolishness''), as well as her own pride and sense of superiority (''[M]e and Sugar were the only ones just right''), both of which will be seriously damaged in the course of the story. Finally, she indirectly indicates the type of urban environment in which she lives: ''And we kinda hated [Miss Moore] . . . the way we did the winos who cluttered up our parks and pissed on our handball walls and stank up our hallways and stairs so you couldn't halfway play hide-and-seek without a g–d–n gas mask.'' She also reveals that she and her cousin live with their aunt, who is ''saddled'' with them while ''our mothers [are] in a la-de-da apartment up the block having a good ole time.''

The action begins on a hot summer day when Miss Moore ''rounds us all up at the mailbox'' for one of her outings. This one will be on the subject of money, although the implications are much wider by the story's end: "... Miss Moore asking us do we know what money is, like we a bunch of retards." Even though Sylvia affects boredom with the subject, it is clear that the mention of their condition of poverty is unpleasant to her, apparently because it causes her to feel inferior: "So we heading down the street and she's boring us silly about what things cost and what our parents make and how much goes for rent and how money ain't divided up right in this country. And then she gets to the part about *we all poor and live in the slums, which I don't feature*" (italics mine).

To illustrate her point in a striking manner, Miss Moore takes the children to an expensive store on Fifth Avenue where they can see for themselves the extravagant prices and then realize the difference between their lives and those of the very wealthy. A skillful teacher who provides the opportunity for the children to have their own flashes of insight, Miss Moore simply leads them from window to window, casually asking or answering questions. They are amazed at a $300 microscope, at a $480 paperweight (an object with which they are not even familiar), and finally at a $1,195 toy sailboat. Even Sylvia, as superior and untouched as she has tried to be, is astonished at the latter, whose price seems beyond all reason: "'Unbelievable,' I hear myself say and am really stunned." Although she herself does not realize the cause of her anger ("*For some reason* this pisses me off"), the reader understands that it lies in the injustice of things in general, but more specifically in Sylvia's frustration at being unable to purchase and possess even one of the toys displayed tantalizingly before her.

Another unpleasant, and in this case unfamiliar, emotion overcomes her as Miss Moore tells the children to go into the store. Ordinarily aggressive and daring, Sylvia now hangs back: "Not that I'm scared, what's there to be afraid of, just a toy store. But I feel funny, shame. But what I got to be shamed about? Got as much right to go in as anybody. But somehow I can't seem to get hold of the door...." Her shame arises from her sense of inferiority, of not belonging in such an expensive store, communicated indirectly and subtly by her comparison of the children's chaotic entrance to "a glued-together jigsaw done all wrong." Once inside, her painful feelings become intense: "Then Sugar run a finger over the whole boat. And I'm jealous and want to hit her. Maybe not her, but I sure want to punch somebody in the mouth." Angry not only at her own deprivation but also at Miss Moore for making her aware of it, Sylvia bitterly lashes out at the older

woman: "Watcha bring us here for, Miss Moore?" Attempting to help Sylvia acknowledge her anger, Miss Moore responds, "You sound angry, Sylvia. Are you mad about something?"

Although too proud to admit her emotions to Miss Moore, Sylvia on the way home reveals her longing for one of the toys, her realization that what it costs would buy many items desperately needed by her family, and her anguish at the injustice endured by the poor:

> Thirty-five dollars could buy new bunk beds for Junior and Gretchen's boy. Thirty-five dollars and the whole household could go visit Granddaddy Nelson in the country. Thirty-five dollars would pay for the rent and the piano bill too. Who are these people that spend that much for performing clowns and $1,000 for toy sailboats? What kind of work they do and how they live and how come we ain't in on it?

When she seems toughly to dismiss the painful lessons of the day, "Messin' up my day with this s–t," the reader is aware that they have in truth touched her deeply, messing up far more than that one day. When she returns home, the overwhelming effects of her disillusionment are confirmed through her description of time (she seems years older than she had been that morning) and her revelation that she has a headache: "Miss Moore lines us up in front of the mailbox where we started from, seem like years ago, and I got a headache for thinkin' so hard."

Her only protection against further pain and humiliation seems to be in not acknowledging formally, aloud, what has been so powerfully demonstrated to her. Yet, when Miss Moore urges the children to express what they have learned, her cousin Sugar blurts out the harsh facts in what is to Sylvia a bitter betrayal, an admission of the injustice, inferiority, imperfection of her world. Responding to Miss Moore's question, "Well, what do you think of F. A. O. Schwartz?" Sugar surprises Sylvia by saying, "You know, Miss Moore, I don't think all of us here put together eat in a year what that sailboat costs." The older woman urges her on to further exploration of the subject by commenting, "Imagine for a minute what kind of society it is in which some people can spend on a toy what it would cost to feed a family of six or seven. What do you think?" (This is a rather blunt and heavy-handed statement of the theme). When Sugar, rejecting Sylvia's desperate attempts to silence her, asserts, "I think ... that this is not much of a democracy if you ask me," Sylvia is "disgusted with Sugar's treachery." However, as the story ends, she is going "to think this day through," even though she still appears determined to maintain her former arrogance and superiority: "But ain't nobody gonna beat me at nuthin."

"The Lesson" is especially fine in its sensitive portrayal of Sylvia, in its realistic use of black dialect, and in the view of American society it offers from the vantage point of the poor.

Source: Nancy D. Hargrove, "Youth in Toni Cade Bambara's *Gorilla, My Love*," in *Women Writers of the Contemporary South*, edited by Peggy Whitman Prenshaw, University Press of Mississippi, 1984, pp. 215–32.

Sources

Bryan, C. D. B., Review in the *New York Times Book Review*, October 15, 1972, p. 31.

Butler-Evans, Elliot, *Race, Gender, and Desire: Narrative Strategies in the Fiction of Toni Cade Bambara, Toni Morrison, and Alice Walker*, Temple University Press, 1989, pp. 91–122.

Chevigny, Bell Gale, Review in the *Village Voice*, April 12, 1973, pp. 39–40.

Deck, Alice A., "Toni Cade Bambara," in *The Dictionary of Literary Biography*, Vol. 38: *Afro-American Writers After 1955: Dramatists and Prose Writers*, edited by Thadious M. Davis and Trudier Harris, Gale Research, 1985.

Doerkson, Teri Ann, "Toni Cade Bambara." in *The Dictionary of Literary Biography*, Vol. 218: *American Short Story Writers since World War II*, Second Series, edited by Patrick Meanor and Gwen Crane, Gale Group, 2000.

Hargrove, Nancy D., "Youth in Toni Cade Bambara's *Gorilla, My Love*," in *The Southern Quarterly*, Vol. 22, No.1, Fall 1983, pp. 81–99.

Vertreace, Martha M., "The Dance of Character and Community," in *American Women Writing Fiction: Memory, Identity, Family, Space*, edited by Mickey Pearlman, University Press of Kentucky, 1989, pp. 155–71.

Further Reading

Cone, James H., *Martin and Malcolm and America: A Dream or a Nightmare?*, Orbis Books, 1992.
This book examines the two most influential African-American leaders of the twentieth century and reveals that the visions of these two men were moving toward convergence.

Morrison, Toni, ed., "Bambara, Toni Cade," in *Deep Sightings and Rescue Missions: Fiction, Essays, and Conversations*, Random House, 1996.
This work is Bambara's final collection, including short stories, essays, and interviews.

Tate, Claudia, ed., "Interview with Toni Cade Bambara," in *Black Women Writers at Work*, Continuum, 1983.
This interview is a lengthy dialogue with Bambara in which she discusses her writing, creativity, and personal history.

The Metamorphosis

Franz Kafka

1915

"The Metamorphosis" is probably the best-known story written by the Czech-born German-Jewish writer Franz Kafka, ranking with his two novel-length masterpieces, *The Trial* and *The Castle*.

First published in 1915 in German (under the title "Die Verwandlung"), "The Metamorphosis" was written over the course of three weeks in November and December 1912. Kafka at one point contemplated publishing it along with two other stories about father-son relations in a collection to be called *Sons*, but later decided to issue it on its own. It was first translated into English in 1936, and has been translated several times since.

The haunting story of a man transformed into an insect has attracted numerous commentators, who while agreeing on the high quality and importance of the story disagree strongly about what it means. Freudian, Marxist, existentialist, and religious interpretations have all been proposed, and there has been debate over whether Gregor Samsa, the man-turned-insect, symbolizes the human condition.

It is generally agreed, however, that the story portrays a world that is hostile and perhaps absurd and that major themes in the story include father-son antagonism (perhaps reflecting Kafka's difficult relationship with his own father), alienation at work, isolation, and self-sacrifice.

The story is sometimes praised for its symmetrical, three-part structure and its use of black humor, and its symbols (such as the lady in furs and the music played by Gregor's sister) are sometimes puzzled over, but what makes the story memorable is the central situation of the transformation of a man into an insect and the image of the man-insect lying on his back helplessly waving his little insect legs in the air.

Author Biography

Born in Prague in 1883 into a Jewish family, Kafka lived the life of an isolated loner. He never married, though he was engaged several times, and he lived most of his life in his parents' house. He had a difficult relationship with his businessman father, which he described at length in ''Letter to His Father,'' and had difficulty writing at home amidst the noise and distractions of a household that included three younger sisters and servants.

After graduating from university, Kafka took a job in an insurance company, which he hated; he later found a more congenial position in the Workmen's Accident Insurance Institute, but still felt that his full-time job interfered with his writing. He eventually had to give up his full-time job because of illness: throughout his life he was prone to a variety of real and imaginary illnesses, and became a vegetarian in an attempt to improve his constitution. He died of tuberculosis a month before his forty-first birthday, June 3, 1924.

Although Prague was a Czech city, it had a sizable German minority, and the Jews of Prague tended to identify with the Germans. The Kafka family was no exception, and Kafka's first language, and the language he wrote in, was German. He began writing at an early age, but destroyed most of his childhood works and remained very critical of his writings all his life. He had to be encouraged, most notably by his friend and fellow writer Max Brod, to keep on writing and publishing. ''The Metamorphosis'' was one work that he did think worth publishing, though he was critical even of it when he first completed it.

At the end of his life, Kafka felt so negative about his works that he instructed Brod to burn his unpublished manuscripts and make sure that his published works were never republished. Brod, however, ignored these instructions and brought out posthumous editions of two of Kafka's previously unknown masterpieces: *The Trial* and *The Castle*.

Plot Summary

Part I

As the story opens, Gregor Samsa has already turned into a gigantic insect. He notices this, but does not seem to find it horrifying or even that unusual, merely an inconvenience or perhaps a delusion. He worries mainly that he has overslept and will be late for work. He also thinks to himself about how unpleasant his job is and how he would have quit long before now if not for having to earn money to pay off his parents' debts.

Gregor's parents and his sister knock at his locked bedroom door and ask if something is the matter. Gregor tries to answer, but his voice sounds strange, like a ''horrible twittering squeak.'' He is also unable at first to control his new insect body well enough to get out of bed; his little insect legs wave helplessly as he lies on his back.

The chief clerk from Gregor's job arrives, demanding to know why Gregor has not shown up for work. This irritates Gregor, who thinks it is excessive of his firm to send such a high-level person to inquire into such a minor deviation from duty. When the chief clerk, speaking through the door to the still unseen Gregor, criticizes him and hints that he may lose his job, Gregor becomes even more upset and makes a long speech in his defense which none of the listeners can understand. ''That was no human voice,'' says the chief clerk. Gregor's mother thinks he must be ill and sends his sister, Grete, for a doctor. Gregor's father sends the servant girl for a locksmith.

Gregor meanwhile has decided that the best thing will be to show himself. With great difficulty, using his toothless insect jaws, he turns the key in the lock and then pulls the door open. At the sight of him, the chief clerk backs away, Gregor's mother falls to the floor, and his father first shakes his fist and then begins to cry.

Gregor is anxious to keep the chief clerk from leaving and spreading bad reports about him—Gregor's main concern is still the possible loss of

Franz Kafka

his job—but the clerk rushes out, yelling ''Ugh!'' and his father shoos Gregor back into his room.

Part II

Gregor in this section of the story becomes more and more insect-like. He discovers that he is most comfortable under the sofa and comes to enjoy crawling up the walls and hanging from the ceiling. He also learns that he no longer likes fresh food, but prefers the half-decayed scraps that his sister leaves for him. His sister is now the only one who takes care of him, but even she seems disgusted by him. Realizing this, Gregor arranges a sheet in front of the sofa to hide himself from her.

Thinking that it might be best for Gregor if he had more room in which to crawl, Gregor's sister decides to remove his furniture and gets her mother to help. Gregor thinks this is a good idea too until he hears his mother say that perhaps after all it is wrong: it is signaling to Gregor that the family has given up all hope that he will return to human form. Suddenly feeling very attached to the symbols of his human past, Gregor rushes out from his hiding place under the sofa and decides to defend his belongings, especially the picture on his wall of a lady in furs, which he climbs on top of. When his mother sees him, she faints, and the ensuing confusion ends with

Gregor's father attacking Gregor by bombarding him with apples, one of which seriously wounds him. It is Gregor who now faints, but before he loses consciousness he sees his half-undressed mother rush into his father's arms.

Part III

Without Gregor's income to support them, the other family members, who formerly did not work, now all take jobs and as a result complain of being overworked and tired as well as of being uniquely afflicted—presumably referring to their having to take care of Gregor. Gregor meanwhile is still suffering from being struck by the apple; in fact, the apple has lodged in his back, no one has bothered to remove it, and the area around it has become inflamed. Gregor also feels neglected and loses his appetite, and has to put up with having his room turned into a dumping area after the family takes in three lodgers. As well, he is tormented by the new charwoman the family hires to replace the live-in servant they could no longer afford.

One evening Gregor's sister plays the violin for her parents and the lodgers. Gregor is greatly affected by the music and thinks it is opening a path for him to some unknown sort of nourishment. He ventures out of his room, intending to reach his sister, all the while fantasizing about getting her to move into his room with her violin, where he would protect her from all intruders and kiss her on the neck.

When the lodgers see Gregor and for the first time realize that they are sharing a house with such a creature, they instantly give notice and say they will sue for damages. Gregor's sister says it is time they got rid of Gregor; he is driving away their lodgers and generally persecuting his family, and he is not really Gregor anymore, just a creature.

Gregor retreats to his room, feeling weak and thinking that he must disappear as his sister wanted. He dies that night and is disposed of the next day by the charwoman. His death seems to energize the family, especially Mr. Samsa, who stops being deferential to the three lodgers and instead orders them out of the house.

The story ends with the three surviving Samsas on an excursion into the countryside thinking about their prospects. They decide that things are not so bad: their jobs are actually promising, and Grete has blossomed into an attractive young woman for whom her parents will soon find a husband.

Characters

Charwoman

Hired by the Samsas to replace their live-in servant, the charwoman is a tough old woman who, unlike the other characters, is neither horrified nor frightened by Gregor's insect form. She even refers to Gregor affectionately as ''the old dung beetle'' and less affectionately threatens him with a chair. She is the one who discovers that Gregor has died and who cheerfully disposes of his body.

Chief Clerk

The chief clerk from Gregor's firm comes to the Samsa house to find out why Gregor has not shown up for work. When Gregor delays coming out of his room, the clerk criticizes him for poor work performance and reports that the head of the firm suspects Gregor of embezzling funds. When Gregor finally emerges, the clerk flees in horror.

Gregor's father

See Mr. Samsa

Gregor's mother

See Mrs. Samsa

Gregor's sister

See Grete Samsa

Gregor Samsa

Gregor Samsa, the protagonist of the story, is a self-sacrificing, dutiful young man who is mysteriously transformed into a giant insect as the story begins. He lives with his parents and his sister, whom he has been supporting by working as a travelling salesman, a job he very much dislikes, but which he devotes his life to: he seems to have no close friends and no social life. There are hints of repressed resentment in Gregor's attitude toward his family; he seems to feel that his sacrifices for them have not been properly appreciated. And despite his dutiful nature, he does not seem very close to his family, except for his sister, whose musical studies he has been planning to finance.

After his transformation, Gregor's character changes somewhat: on two occasions, he puts his own desires ahead of what others want, first when he tries to defend his belongings in opposition to his sister's plan to remove them, and second when he seeks to obtain the mysterious nourishment associated with his sister's violin playing. In the end,

however, he reverts to his self-sacrificing ways by willingly going to his death because his family wants to be rid of him.

Grete Samsa

Grete Samsa, usually referred to in the story as Gregor's sister, is the family member Gregor seems closest to and is the one who takes care of him after his transformation. Even she seems disgusted by his new form, however, and she is the one who at the end demands that he be got rid of.

Before the transformation, the seventeen-year-old Grete leads an idle life and is regarded by her parents as ''a somewhat useless daughter.'' After the transformation, she becomes a sales clerk as well as taking on the responsibility of caring for Gregor. Tired out by all these new duties, she begins to neglect Gregor, but is furious when her mother cleans Gregor's room, seeing this action as an invasion of her domain.

Twice Grete does things that lead Gregor to leave his room, for which he suffers serious consequences. First, her decision to remove Gregor's furniture leads to a confrontation in the living room that ends with Gregor being seriously injured. Later her violin playing lures Gregor into the living room again, provoking the conflict that leads to his death. She is also the one who argues the most strongly for getting rid of Gregor. After Gregor's death, Grete blooms, and her parents think she is ready for a husband.

Mr. Samsa

Mr. Samsa, referred to only as Gregor's father until Gregor's death, is a failed businessman who has been idle for five years, living off what Gregor earns. He seems quite antagonistic to his son, fierce toward him, though at the same time weak: when he first sees the transformed Gregor, he shakes a fist at him, but then breaks down and cries.

It is the fierceness that dominates, however. The first two times Gregor ventures out of his room, his father forces him back in, the first time brandishing a walking stick and a newspaper at him, the second time bombarding him with apples. He does injury to Gregor both times.

After Gregor's transformation, Mr. Samsa is also transformed; before, he was a sluggish man who hardly ever got dressed and who could barely walk; now he is a bank messenger in a smart uniform who is reluctant ever to take it off. He

Media Adaptations

- In 1987, there was a British television adaptation of "The Metamorphosis." Called *Metamorphosis* and starring Tim Roth as Gregor Samsa, it was written by Steven Berkoff and directed by Jim Goddard.

- Steven Berkoff also wrote a stage adaptation of the story, which was first performed at the Round House in London in 1969 with him in the role of Gregor Samsa. Between 1969 and 1992, there were nine productions of Berkoff's adaptation, including ones in 1986 at the Mermaid in London with Tim Roth, in 1988 in Paris with Roman Polanski, in 1989 in New York with Mikhail Baryshnikov, and in 1992 in Tokyo. The text of the adaptation can be found in *"The Trial"; "Metamorphosis"; "In the Penal Colony": Three Theatre Adaptations from Franz Kafka* by Berkoff (Oxford, 1988). Berkoff discusses the various theatre productions in his book, *Meditations on "Metamorphosis"* (Faber, 1995).

- In 1976, a Swedish film directed by Ivo Dvorák was made of "The Metamorphosis" under the title *Förvandlingen*. There have also been two short animated versions of the story, one a 1977 Canadian film directed by Caroline Leaf and called *The Metamorphosis of Mr. Samsa*, and the other an eight-minute-long 1999 Spanish production directed by Charlie Ramos.

- There is a 1993 British short film called *Franz Kafka's It's a Wonderful Life*. This odd production is not an adaptation of "The Metamorphosis," but it does provide a fanciful, fictional account of how Kafka supposedly wrote the story, showing him as being constantly interrupted while he tries to decide what sort of creature Gregor Samsa will be transformed into. Written and directed by Peter Capaldi, it stars Richard E. Grant as Kafka and Crispin Letts as Gregor Samsa.

- Another odd production is the 1989 film called *Nabokov On Kafka: "The Metamorphosis,"* directed by Peter Medak, in which Christopher Plummer plays the author Vladimir Nabokov giving a lecture on "The Metamorphosis."

- "The Metamorphosis" was recorded on audiocassette in 1994. Read by Alan Hewitt, the cassette version, on two tapes, is three hours long and is unabridged.

---

is still weak in some ways, though, waiting cap in hand on the lodgers, for instance, until Gregor's death, at which point he becomes invigorated and is able to stand up to both the lodgers and the charwoman.

Mrs. Samsa

Mrs. Samsa, who is referred to as Gregor's mother throughout except after Gregor dies, is perhaps the character most sympathetic to Gregor, and the most willing to come to his defense. When something first seems wrong with Gregor, she assumes he is ill and wants to send for the doctor. When the chief clerk is being critical of Gregor, she assures him that Gregor is a very hard worker.

When Mr. Samsa throws apples at Gregor, Mrs. Samsa rushes to intervene.

On the other hand, Mrs. Samsa cannot really stand to look at her son in his transformed state: the first two times she does so she screams and faints. She is also not strong enough to defend Gregor successfully: she allows Grete to overrule her on whether to remove Gregor's furniture; and when Grete and Mr. Samsa begin to discuss getting rid of Gregor, Mrs. Samsa has an asthmatic fit and is unable to intervene.

The Three Lodgers

Arriving in the Samsa household near the end of the story, the three lodgers are serious gentlemen who acquire power over the household. They always act together, as if they were a single character, though they do have a leader ("the middle lodger"). It is their request that leads to Grete's violin concert in the living room. When they discover Gregor, they give notice and threaten to sue, but when Mr. Samsa orders them out they leave quietly.

Themes

Alienation at Work

One of the themes of the story is the unpleasantness of work. Gregor Samsa hates his job as a travelling salesman, but must continue doing it to pay off his parents' debts. There is no suggestion that he gets any job satisfaction; all he talks about is how exhausting the job is, how irritating it is to be always travelling: making train connections, sleeping in strange beds, always dealing with new people and thus never getting the chance to make good friends, and so forth. Moreover, it turns out that Gregor works for a firm that does not trust its employees at all: because he is late this one day, the chief clerk shows up to check on him and begins hinting that he is suspected of embezzling funds and may very well be fired. It also seems that Gregor's co-workers dislike him because he is on the road so often; they gossip about him and the other travelling salesmen, making unfounded complaints such as that they make lots of money and just enjoy themselves. Work is hell, the story seems to suggest.

Father-Son Antagonism

Life at home, according to the story, is no paradise either. In particular, Gregor seems to have a difficult relationship with his father. The very first time Gregor's father is seen he is making a fist, albeit just to knock on Gregor's door. Soon after, however, he makes a fist more in earnest: when he first sees Gregor in his insect form, he shakes his fist at him and glares at him fiercely. Later he attacks him with a newspaper and a walking stick, and, later still, bombards him with apples, causing him serious injury. He is also not above making sarcastic comments, suggesting for instance that Gregor's room is untidy. And it turns out that he has deceived Gregor about the family finances, thus needlessly extending the length of Gregor's employment at the hateful travelling salesman's job. Finally, he does not seem particularly appreciative of the money Gregor has been bringing in; he is content to live off

his son's labor, but Gregor feels there was "no special uprush of warm feeling" about it.

Gregor's disappointment over the lack of appreciation is one of the few critical thoughts he thinks about his father. He also thinks briefly that the money his father hid from him could have been used to free him from his job sooner, but he quickly dismisses the thought by saying that no doubt his father knew best. In short, the antagonism as portrayed in the story is mostly one-way: the father abuses the son, but the son suppresses his angry responses and accepts his downtrodden state.

Betrayal

The one person Gregor feels close to is his sister, and she at first seems like the one most attentive to his needs. She brings him his food and

---

Topics for Further Study

- Depending on the translation and the commentator, Gregor is described variously as an insect, a bug, a beetle, a cockroach, a louse, and a piece of vermin. Is it possible to say precisely what sort of creature he turns into?

- What are the advantages and disadvantages of turning into a bug the way Gregor does?

- Music is sometimes identified with the spiritual realm. On the other hand, it is sometimes linked to the animal kingdom as something that appeals even to nonhuman species. How does music, especially Grete's violin playing, function in this story?

- To what extent is "The Metamorphosis" part of the existentialist tradition in literature exemplified by the works of such writers as Jean-Paul Sartre, Albert Camus, and Eugene Ionesco?

- What does Gregor die of? His wound? Starvation? Self-starvation? A broken heart? A desire to die? Who is responsible for his death? Is Kakfa being deliberately ambiguous on this issue? If so, why?

cleans his room, and even her plan to remove Gregor's furniture, which he objects to, seems well-meant: she thinks he needs more room in his insect state to crawl around. After a while, she begins neglecting Gregor. When he tries to approach her one last time, she turns on him viciously, falsely accusing him of wanting to kick the rest of the family out of the house, saying that he is not really Gregor but a creature that must be got rid of. The story seems to be suggesting that no one is to be trusted.

Isolation and Self-Sacrifice

Gregor seems to have no close friends at work or elsewhere, and no romantic attachments; he is not very close with his family, except for his sister who it turns out cannot be trusted; he seems to lead a lonely, isolated life even before his transformation, and the transformation reinforces his situation. As an insect, he cannot communicate at all, and he is forced to stay in his room; he is cut off almost entirely from the rest of humanity.

As an insect, he can still hear, however, so he knows what others want, but they cannot know what he wants. This seems an apt situation for Gregor to end up in, because his life even before his transformation seems to have been one of catering to others' needs while suppressing his own.

Escaping

Although in some ways the transformation re-inforces Gregor's situation, in other ways becoming an insect is a way for him to escape his unhappy life. No longer will he have to work at his burdensome job; instead, he can spend his days scurrying around his room, something he seems to enjoy. One of the themes is the joy of escaping from one's responsibilities.

Seizing Power

Although this is not a route Gregor is able to pursue successfully, the story does indicate that some people are able to reverse the power relations in their lives. Gregor seems able only to remain downtrodden or to escape to insectdom; but his father is able to overthrow the domination of the three lodgers and recapture the authority in his house.

Interestingly, he can only do this after Gregor himself, the self-sacrificing, downtrodden one, is

dead, perhaps suggesting that the presence of a self-sacrificing person drains those around him.

Style

Point of View

The story is told in the third person but is for the most part limited to Gregor's point of view. Only his thoughts and feelings are presented, and most of the events are seen through his eyes. The point seems to be to present a picture of Gregor and the world as he understands it, both before and after his metamorphosis. This does not necessarily mean that all of Gregor's judgements are to be accepted; on the contrary, Kafka uses irony and black comedy to indicate that Gregor is at times misled, for instance in thinking he can still go to the office even after becoming an insect and, more sadly, in thinking his family is putting his interests first.

Of course, after Gregor's death, the point of view has to shift; it becomes simply impersonal third-person narration, remaining on the outside of the surviving characters, not revealing their thoughts and feelings the way Gregor's were revealed earlier. Interestingly, Gregor's parents are now referred to impersonally as Mr. and Mrs. Samsa; earlier, when the story was being told from Gregor's point of view, they were invariably referred to as Gregor's father and Gregor's mother. The point of this shift seems to be to emphasize that Gregor is not just gone but forgotten.

Setting

The story has a very constricted setting; almost all the events take place within the Samsa house, mostly in Gregor's room, reflecting the fact that Gregor is essentially a prisoner. The room itself is small and, by the end, unclean. Gregor can see outside, but mostly what he sees is an overcast sky, rain, fog, and a gray hospital building; when his eyesight fades, he cannot even see the hospital, and the world beyond his room appears to him to be a gray desert.

The gloominess of this setting begins to change near the end. There is heavy rain, but the narrator suggests it might be a sign of spring. This is when Gregor is still alive. However, the truly decisive change in the setting occurs only after Gregor's death. For the first time, the story leaves the house, following the surviving Samsas into the countryside, where the sun shines on them as they cheerfully plan their future.

Structure

The story is divided into three parts, each one culminating in a foray by Gregor outside his room. The first two parts end when Gregor is forced back into his room. In part three, Gregor is again forced to return to his room; however, this part differs from the other two in that it does not end with Gregor's return, but contains a coda describing events of the next day.

Flashbacks and other Narrative Devices

Most of the story consists of extended scenes. All of part one is the scene that unfolds when Gregor awakes to find himself an insect; the last section of part two is the extended scene that begins when Gregor's sister and mother enter Gregor's room to remove his furniture; and the bulk of part three consists of two linked scenes: the violin concert that leads to Gregor's death and the scene that begins the next day with the discovery of his body, and that ends with the excursion to the countryside.

Only a small part of the story consists of summaries: most notably the passages near the beginning of each of the last two parts, which recount Gregor's typical activities, explain how he gets fed and informed, and report on how the family copes with the loss of Gregor's income.

Kafka also uses brief flashbacks to explain how Gregor came to be supporting his family and to contrast the current behavior of Gregor's father with how he behaved in the past.

Symbols

Kafka uses some obvious and not-so-obvious symbols in the story. Some symbols even the characters recognize as such: for instance, the furniture in Gregor's room, which his mother is reluctant to remove because of its association with Gregor's human past; to remove the furniture is to declare symbolically that Gregor is no longer human and will never be human again.

Other symbols are less easy to understand. The recurrent use of the number three, for instance (three parts to the story, three doors to Gregor's room, three lodgers, three other family members), seems significant, but of what it is not clear. The fact that Gregor's father insists on wearing his uniform so long that it becomes greasy also seems significant but unclear; to wear a smart uniform instead of a bathrobe seems at first an indication of the father's increasing strength, but to wear it so long that it becomes greasy seems to indicate weakness again. It is also not entirely clear what the significance is of the picture of a carefree Gregor in a lieutenant's uniform: does it suggest that he once had a more satisfying existence, before becoming stuck in his boring job?

The picture of the lady in furs, which Gregor presses against when his belongings are taken away, seems to be some sort of romantic or sexual symbol, representing the limited nature of Gregor's romantic life. The music that draws Gregor seems to have a spiritual significance—or does it, on the contrary, suggest (as Gregor himself says) something animal-like? The appearance of the butcher's boy at the end could be a symbol of returning life—or is it death? And the sunshine at the end also speaks of life, though it is a life dependent on Gregor's death, a life open to the Samsas only because they have got rid of Gregor.

Of course, the central symbol of the story is Gregor's insect form itself. What does it signify for a man to be turned into a giant bug? Is Kafka suggesting that this is the human condition? Is it the condition of only some humans? And what is that condition? Disgusting and ineffectual, or somehow positive?

Historical Context

Socio-Economic Background

For most of Kafka's lifetime, his home town of Prague was a Czech city within a German-speaking empire, the Austro-Hungarian Empire. Only at the end of World War I did that Empire disappear, leading to the creation of an independent Czechoslovakia. But in 1912, when Kafka was writing ''The Metamorphosis,'' the Czechs had not yet won their independence, and despite its Czech majority, Prague was dominated by a German-speaking elite. Recognizing where the power lay in the city, the Jews of Prague tended to identify with the German minority rather than with the Czech majority; the Czechs therefore considered the Jews to be part of the German community, but the Germans themselves did not. As a result, it was easy for the Jews to feel that they did not fit in anywhere.

In general, Prague was a city of ethnic tensions, primarily between Czechs and Germans and be-

Compare
&
Contrast

- **1840–1920s:** Kafka writes at a time when the drudgery of work is becoming a serious issue. Long hours at boring jobs create alienation. And tyrannical employers like Gregor's are the norm.

  Twentieth Century: Computers and other advances have allowed for more flexibility for employees, including flex time and telecommuting. Since computers can handle some of the more tedious and repetitive aspects of work, work for some may also be more intellectually stimulating. Also, the trend now is to promote friendlier employer-employee interactions. However, there are new employment problems today, and it is doubtful that the sort of work alienation depicted in Kafka's story has been eliminated altogether.

- **1840–1920s:** In Kafka's day, it is common for reasonably well-off families to employ full-time live-in servants to cook and clean and do other menial chores.

  Twentieth Century: Full-time servants are almost unheard of now, replaced primarily by labor-saving devices.

- **1840–1920s:** Kafka's ''The Metamorphosis'' depicts a troubled father-son relationship that seems to reflect Kafka's own relationship with his father. Such troubled relationships may be widespread, inasmuch as during this time Sigmund Freud develops his theory of the Oedipus complex, which takes as its starting point the existence of a fundamental antagonism between fathers and sons.

  Twentieth Century: The theory of the Oedipus complex has come under criticism, and the relationship of fathers and sons is often celebrated today. However, it would be hard to argue that the antagonisms described by Freud and Kafka do not exist.

- **1840–1920s:** Kafka's ''The Metamorphosis'' assumes that the insect is repulsive, suggesting that in Kafka's day it would be hard to have any positive feelings towards a bug.

  Twentieth Century: Perhaps in an era that produces movies that glamorize insects, like *A Bug's Life*, and which prides itself on ecological awareness and understanding of the importance of all orders of creatures, there is a more positive attitude towards bugs. However, it is hard to imagine that there would be much less horror today than a century ago at the idea of a man being changed into a cockroach.

---

tween Czechs and Jews. In 1897, when Kafka was fourteen, the tensions erupted into anti-Semitic riots started by the Czechs. Thus Kafka would have grown up knowing hatred and hostility as well as the difficulty of fitting in.

Economically, the late nineteenth century marked the culmination of the Industrial Revolution in Europe. Industrial development was not as advanced in the Austro-Hungarian Empire as elsewhere in Europe, but within the Empire, Prague was one of the most advanced and prosperous cities. However, along with the prosperity created by the new industrialism came dislocation and disruption of the old ways, largely as a result of the shift of large numbers of people from the countryside to the city. Industrialization also meant the appearance of large numbers of jobs, for both factory and office workers, which were pure drudgery. And as if recognizing the need to train people for such jobs, the school system enforced a system of rote learning that seemed relentlessly joyless—at least it seemed joyless to young Kafka, who hated school, just as he hated his first full-time job.

Cultural Background

Prague was a cultured city, full of newspapers, theatres, and coffeehouses where avant-garde literary types could discuss the latest intellectual fashions. Kafka was a regular at two of these coffeehouses, the Arco and the Louvre, and through the discussions there may have been introduced to new philosophical ideas. He was certainly familiar with the newly published works of Sigmund Freud, referring to Freud in his diary not long before writing ''The Metamorphosis.'' However, he was no Freudian disciple and wrote negatively of psychoanalytic theory. He was perhaps more in tune with the major nineteenth-century writers (such as Fyodor Dostoevsky, Friedrich Nietzsche, and Sören Kierkegaard) who wrote pessimistically of life in a meaningless or hostile universe, anticipating twentieth-century existentialism, a movement with which Kafka is sometimes associated.

In the year before writing ''The Metamorphosis,'' Kafka became familiar with a Jewish theatre troupe that visited Prague and put on performances in Yiddish. He even became friendly with one of the troupe's members and tried to promote the troupe by securing introductions for it and writing favorable reviews of its work. It has been suggested that both the tragicomic tone of the Yiddish plays Kafka saw at this time and also the story in one play of an outcast son may have influenced him in writing ''The Metamorphosis.''

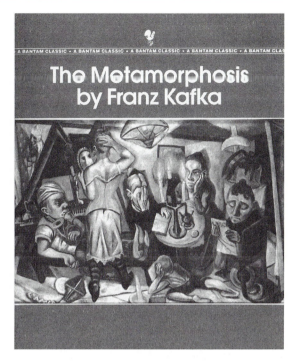

Cover page from ''Metamorphosis'' by Franz Kafka, featuring the 1920 painting Family Picture *by Max Beckmann.*

Critical Overview

Kafka today is a household word around the world, one of the few writers to have an adjective named after him (''Kafkaesque''), describing the dreamlike yet oppressive atmosphere characteristic of his works. When his writings first appeared, however, some reviewers found them baffling, tedious, or exasperating; and the two extreme ideological movements of the twentieth century both found his message unacceptable. The Nazis banned him, and Communist critics denounced him as decadent and despairing.

But fairly quickly Kafka began to be praised by a host of influential writers and intellectuals. The English poet W. H. Auden compared him to Dante, Shakespeare, and Goethe. The German writer Thomas Mann, quoted by Ronald Gray in his book *Franz Kafka*, said that Kafka's works are ''among the worthiest things to be read in German literature.'' And the philosopher Hannah Arendt, writing during World War II, said (also as quoted by Gray) that ''Kafka's nightmare of a world . . . has actually come to pass.''

Kafka's friend Max Brod, one of the earliest commentators on Kafka, saw his works as essentially religious and Jewish, but later commentators have situated Kafka more in the existential, modernist tradition of the first half of the twentieth century, associating him with writers such as Albert Camus and Jean-Paul Sartre, whose works suggest the absurdity and futility of existence.

Among Kafka's works, ''The Metamorphosis'' is generally considered one of his most representative and also one of his best, along with the novels *The Trial* and *The Castle*. Kafka himself was not always happy with his work, however. In his diary (as quoted in Nahum Glatzer's edition of his stories), he wrote on one occasion that he had ''great antipathy'' to ''The Metamorphosis,'' calling its ending unreadable. However, ''The Metamorphosis'' was one of the few works that Kafka made a concerted effort to get published, so he could not have been entirely dissatisfied with it.

In any case, commentators since Kafka have been drawn to the story. By 1973, Stanley Corngold was able to publish a book of summaries of essays on ''The Metamorphosis'' containing accounts of well over a hundred articles, beginning as early as

1916, when one Robert Müller described the story as ingenious but implausible. In subsequent years, commentators have generally taken for granted the quality and importance of the story, and have focused on trying to interpret it.

There have been many different and contradictory interpretations. Freudian critics have seen in it a working out of the Oedipal struggle between a father and a son who are rivals for Gregor's mother. Marxist critics, those not simply denouncing Kafka as reactionary, have seen the story as depicting the exploitation of the proletariat. Gregor Samsa has also been seen as a Christ figure who dies so that his family can live.

Critics interested in language and form have seen the story as the working out of a metaphor, an elaboration on the common comparison of a man to an insect. Some critics have emphasized the autobiographical elements in the story, pointing out the similarities between the Samsa household and the Kafkas' while also noting the similarity of the names "Samsa" and "Kafka," a similarity that Kafka himself was aware of, though he said—in a conversation cited in Nahum Glatzer's edition of his stories—that Samsa was not merely Kafka and nothing else.

Other critics have traced the story's sources back to Fyodor Dostoevsky, Charles Dickens, the Jewish plays that Kafka saw in Prague, and Leopold Von Sacher-Masoch's novel about sado-masochism, *Venus in Furs*. Some have become caught up in taking sides for or against Gregor Samsa. And some have argued that the story is impossible to interpret, which is perhaps why Corngold called his book on the story *The Commentators' Despair*.

But however it is interpreted, the fact that the story has drawn so much attention indicates that it is, as Corngold puts it, "the most haunting and universal of all his stories."

Criticism

Sheldon Goldfarb

Goldfarb has a Ph.D. in English and has published two books on the Victorian author William Makepeace Thackeray. In the following essay, he discusses the significance of the insect symbol in "The Metamorphosis."

Probably the two most memorable images in "The Metamorphosis" occur in its first section: first the picture of Gregor Samsa transformed into an insect, lying on his back in bed and unable to get up, with all his little legs fluttering helplessly in the air; and second the picture of Gregor the giant insect stuck on his side in his bedroom doorway, injured and bleeding and again helplessly unable to move until his father shoves him into the bedroom.

If this were all there were to the story, it would be easy to conclude, as some have done, that "The Metamorphosis" is a depiction of the helplessness and disgusting nature of the human race; here is what people really are, these two images seem to say: revolting pieces of vermin unable to do anything.

But there are two problems with this interpretation: first, not everyone in the story becomes a piece of revolting vermin, only Gregor Samsa does; and second, there is more to Gregor Samsa's life as a bug than being disgusting and helpless. That may be the dominant impression left by Part I of the story, when Gregor is first transformed, but in Part II the situation is different.

In fact, even near the end of Part I, when Gregor begins to adjust to life as a multi-legged insect, he has a sudden "sense of physical comfort"; once he is right side up, his legs become "completely obedient," as he noted with joy:

> they even strove to carry him forward in whatever direction he chose; and he was inclined to believe that a final relief from all his sufferings was at hand.

In Part II, there is more of this sense of joy and escape from suffering. For "mere recreation," Gregor begins crawling across the walls and ceiling, as only an insect could. Moreover:

> He especially enjoyed hanging suspended from the ceiling; it was much better than lying on the floor; one could breathe more freely; one's body swung and rocked lightly; and in the almost blissful absorption induced by this suspension it could happen to his own surprise that he let go and fell plump on the floor. Yet he now had his body much better under control than formerly, and even such a big fall did him no harm.

Gregor the insect is having fun. Is it good after all to be a bug?

Certainly, Gregor's life as a bug seems in some ways better than his life as a human being. As a human being, he is stuck in a job he immensely dislikes and has the burden of supporting a family to whom he does not even feel close. He has no friends or lovers or social life; in the evenings he stays

What Do I Read Next?

- *The Trial* (1925) is Kafka's novel about a man arrested and put through nightmarish court proceedings for a crime that is never explained to him.

- *The Castle* (1926) is a Kafka novel about a man who seeks in vain to be allowed into a nearby but frustratingly inaccessible castle.

- *The Strange Case of Dr. Jekyll and Mr. Hyde* (1886) by Robert Louis Stevenson is an early transformation story about a physician who uses a potion to change himself into an evil, repulsive man.

- *Frankenstein* (1818) by Mary Shelley is a classic novel about a monster who is frustrated in his attempts to connect with human beings.

- ''The Fly'' (1957) by George Langelaan is a story that focuses on a scientist who transforms himself into a fly. The story was reprinted in *Wolf's Complete Book of Terror*, edited by Leo-nard Wolf (Potter, 1979) and was made into movies under the same name in 1958 and 1986.

- *Rhinoceros* (1959) by Eugene Ionesco is a play about people turning into rhinoceroses. The play is a study of conformity and the dangers of totalitarianism.

- *The Stranger* (1942) by Albert Camus, also translated as *The Outsider*, is a novel concerning an alienated outsider who inexplicably commits a murder.

- ''The Death of Ivan Ilyich'' (1886) by Leo Tolstoy follows a man without close personal ties whose family does little for him when he contracts a fatal illness.

- *Notes from Underground* (1864) by Fyodor Dostoevsky is a novel-length monologue by an alienated anti-hero who stays indoors and denounces the world outside.

---

home, and during the day he is off to his alienating job.

As an insect, Gregor is free of his job and his family responsibilities. Instead of rushing off to work, he can stay home and play. Instead of taking care of his family, they take care of him. In some ways, his life as a bug is the life of the carefree child. He even heals faster than he used to, as a child would.

Still, there is something repulsive about being a bug. Even Gregor realizes this, and tries to hide his repulsiveness from his mother and his sister when they enter his room. He spends hours arranging a sheet to cover himself so they will not have to see him. And Gregor also realizes at one point, even after he has discovered the joys of climbing the walls, that he does not want to stay a bug forever. When his mother and sister start removing his furniture, his mother's second thoughts provoke him to resist: he does not want to give up his human past and the possibility of returning to it.

Now, perhaps Gregor is simply mistaken to fight for his human past; perhaps Kafka means for the reader to see his life as a bug as something so superior to his human past that he should want to stay a bug forever. But if Kafka were creating an ideal escape from adult responsibilities, surely he would have created a more appealing one than becoming a giant insect; he could have transformed Gregor into a cute little puppy or a young child instead of a repulsive vermin.

And there are distinct disadvantages to being a bug. For one thing, Gregor's repulsive appearance means he has to remain in his room, a prisoner, completely isolated. His existence was always a fairly lonely one, but this is worse: as far as friendship and intimacy are concerned, Gregor's transformation is not an escape from his past loneliness but an intensification of it.

Moreover, for all Gregor's ability to climb walls, as an insect he is fairly helpless: he depends

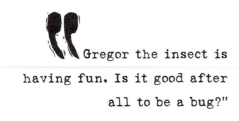

"Gregor the insect is having fun. Is it good after all to be a bug?"

on others now for food and for keeping his room clean; and his inability to talk means he cannot express his needs clearly.

Not that Gregor seems to have expressed his needs clearly even before his transformation. He seems to have been a classic self-sacrificer and martyr, devoting his entire life to paying off his family's debts, worrying about wasting even an hour of his employer's time, spending very little time developing his own life.

It is true that there are hints in the story that he feels resentment over this situation: for instance, he allows himself to think for a moment that his father might have used some of the money he saved to help Gregor escape sooner from his oppressive job; he also seems to think there could have been more appreciation for his efforts to bring in the money his family needed. Then, when he is first transformed and is struggling to open the door, he thinks the family might be more encouraging. And when he hears his sister sobbing that first morning, he seems irritated with her.

But these are fleeting moments. It is more typical of him to think, concerning the money his father has held back, that his father must know best. It is also typical of him that the thing he worries about, if he crashes out of bed, is that the noise may alarm the others. And his laborious effort to hide himself with a sheet is done completely to serve others' needs. Finally, when his mother makes a rare entrance into his room, to avoid upsetting her "he renounced the pleasure of seeing [her]." Gregor seems to have led a life of renouncing pleasures.

Now, it is true that as a bug he is finally able to have some pleasure; he also, as a bug, makes two attempts to fight for what he wants: first, when he resists the removal of his furniture, and second when he seeks to obtain the mysterious nourishment associated with his sister's violin playing. He fails in both attempts, however, and thus to a certain

extent being a bug is just like being a human being for Gregor: he cannot get his needs met in either form.

In short, Gregor's transformation has a double meaning: it is both an escape from his oppressive life and a representation or even an intensification of it. But even as an escape, it is not very successful, for to maintain his life as a carefree, wall-climbing insect, he needs others to care for him: to bring him his food and to clean his room. Eventually, his sister, who has been doing this, loses interest; his room becomes dirty; and he becomes despondent and angry over being neglected.

And of course he is more than neglected; he is attacked. Attacked twice by his father, the second time seriously enough to cause a perhaps life-threatening wound. Gregor is unable to prevent this injury and also unable to obtain treatment for it; the family does not seem to care, and he is at their mercy.

There thus seems to be a problem with escaping as a response to an oppressive life: the escapist idyll cannot be maintained; it is too dependent on others. And perhaps, just like childhood, it cannot be expected to last forever.

Now, if Gregor Samsa were the only character in the story, one might still say that Kafka is painting a gloomy picture of the whole human condition. The only options open to Gregor Samsa seem to be life as a downtrodden martyr at work and at home or the purely temporary escape he finds as a bug.

It is true that there are two other options he seeks to pursue. One is associated with the music played by his sister. The music makes him think he can obtain some "unknown nourishment"—perhaps something spiritual, though that is unclear. It also makes him fantasize about his sister moving into his room with him and about kissing her on the neck, indicating perhaps a closer sort of relationship as a way out of his troubles.

However, he is repulsed when he tries to follow this option involving his sister and her music, just as he is repulsed when he pursues the option of resistance, of fighting back when his belongings are taken from him.

Not everyone in the story is similarly repulsed, however. Gregor's father, in contrast to Gregor, is able to succeed by pursuing the path of resistance.

Much like Gregor, Gregor's father finds himself in a downtrodden, self-sacrificing state in Part III of the story, with the arrival of the three lodgers, who somehow seize control in the household. Even before the arrival of the lodgers, the elder Samsa has seemed like a curiously weak figure, except when attacking Gregor. With Gregor as the breadwinner, Gregor's father becomes the dependent one and spends his days lying almost comatose in a chair, wearing his bathrobe, almost unable to walk. After Gregor's transformation, he goes back to work and regains some of his strength, but he and the rest of the family at first feel tired and overworked as a result of taking on jobs, and Gregor sees in them a sense of "complete hopelessness."

When the lodgers arrive, things become even worse. Mr. Samsa and the others dote on them, Mr. Samsa with cap in hand; they yield the best seats at the dinner table to the lodgers, and in general are overly anxious to please, having "an exaggerated idea of the courtesy due to lodgers."

But when Gregor dies, suddenly Mr. Samsa finds new strength and orders the lodgers out. He is also suddenly able to stand up to the intimidating charwoman, stopping her from talking "with a decisive hand." The result of this newfound strength is that Mr. Samsa and his family are suddenly able to contemplate a happy and fulfilling life: their jobs will lead to better things, and their daughter will get married.

For some people, then, there is a way out. People may be living in a hostile universe, the story suggests, and some people are like Gregor: they cannot stand up to it; at best they can run away for some temporary respite. But others can rise up against the universe and seize control of their destiny.

This is perhaps a more optimistic message to take from the story than seeing it as portraying a universally gloomy existence—or perhaps not. Throughout the story the reader has been drawn to identify with Gregor; the story is told from his point of view, and he seems appealing in his self-sacrificing way. But he is defeated. And who is it that triumphs? His bullying father and the sister who betrayed him. Not everyone is doomed to be crushed like a bug, the story is saying; not everyone, just you and I, while other people somehow get ahead at our expense. It is a despairing conclusion.

Source: Sheldon Goldfarb, Critical Essay on "The Metamorphosis," in *Short Stories for Students*, The Gale Group, 2001.

Meno Spann

The following essay explores Kafka's presentation of various characters and their traits as "vermin" in "The Metamorphosis."

While the young businessman Georg Bendemann is condemned to death in Kafka's metaphorical world, the young commercial traveler Gregor Samsa in "Die Verwandlung" ("The Metamorphosis") must live out the last months of his life in the same world changed as a giant bug, which resembles a cockroach.

Compared with "Die Verwandlung," the little prose piece "Grosser Larm" appears like a first sketch for the larger story. The characterization of father and son is the same: the father is the mighty master of the family, and the son, living helplessly in their midst, frightens them in his monstrous shape. "Grosser Larm" appeared in October, 1912, in a Prague magazine; and on November 11 Kafka sent a copy to Felice. The little prose piece was fresh in his mind when, six days later, waiting in bed for a letter from her, the idea for "Die Verwandlung" came to him in his "wretchedness." As in "Das Urteil," which preceded it, the inspiration for "Die Verwandlung" was his unhappy family life, which was only eased somewhat by his sister Ottla, who also defied the father and tried to help her unfortunate brother.

"Die Verwandlung" opens with the sentence: "As Gregor Samsa awoke one morning from uneasy dreams he found himself transformed in his bed into a gigantic insect." The dependent clause tells us of the real world, and—such is Kafka's subtle style—something important about the hero's previous life. The main clause shifts immediately to Gregor's metaphorical state. During the last night, in which he had fallen asleep in bed as a man, Gregor had "uneasy dreams," the result of an inner unrest; and his thoughts upon awakening reveal what caused them. He complains about the physical discomfort of the commercial traveler, but also about something much more important, about the dehumanizing effect of his job due to the always changing human contacts, which never lead to close personal relations. Worst of all, he feels humiliated by the head of the firm, who has the disgusting habit of sitting on a high desk, so he can talk down to his employees. Although by ordinary literary and human standards a miserable creature, this man shares with many another authoritative character the divine honors bestowed upon him by an allegorizer: "The description of Gregor's boss has breadth enough to apply not just to a petty office tyrant, but

> " The assertion that 'one really had to admit that possibility' that the manager would some day awaken as a bug is typical of Kafka's wry humor; at the same time, it hints at the possibility that a human being may awaken to the insight that he is a 'bug,' a person without character and, consequently, without human dignity."

even to an [*sic*] Old Testament God. Indeed, the reference to the high desk echoes the Old Testament metaphor of the God 'most high' who yet can 'hear' us.'' This ''petty office tyrant'' would fulminate against Gregor should he be late for work. Since, as Gregor firmly believes, his parents owe his employer money he has to stay with the despised job for five or six more years.

Such reflections have occupied Gregor's mind for some while before the catastrophe and have made him lose faith in himself and in the rightness of his life, as had also happened to Georg Bendemann. In the author's fictitious world, Gregor has become what he had metaphorically been for a long time: an insect.

As if to ward off subsequent critical misinterpretation of the events described in this story as nightmares of a neurotic, the narrator explains in the second sentence: ''It was no dream: his room, a regular bedroom, only rather too small, lay quiet between the four familiar walls.'' Gregor had his breakthrough to self-recognition, and the implied metaphor—something like ''I am really a spineless bug''—is at once fused with the realistically described life he leads between the four walls of his room.

On one of these hangs Gregor's ''pinup,'' a testimony to his sense of inferiority. It is a cutout from some illustrated magazine, representing a lady

of wealth, high above his rank, wearing a fur stole and ''holding out to the spectator a huge fur muff, in which the whole of her forearm had vanished.'' Fur stoles, it should be noted, were considered by some in prewar Europe to be ostentatious status symbols, and Kafka detested them. He once informed Grete Bloch: ''One has some convictions that are so deepseated and true that one doesn't have to worry about a detailed justification. . . . I don't have many convictions of this kind,'' and then he mentions two of them: ''the abomination of contemporary medicine, and . . . the ugliness of the fur stole.''

Gregor's fur-clad idol is enclosed in a gilded frame which the young commercial traveler has cut out with a fretsaw, fretwork, a hobby usually associated with boys rather than grown-up men, being the only luxury he allows himself. Otherwise his arid life consists of sitting at home every evening, reading the paper, or studying timetables, so that he may beat the competition by taking earlier trains.

His metamorphosis, of course, makes him miss all the trains on this fateful morning, and the manager, informed by the firm's porter, who spies on the salesmen, arrives at the home of the Samsas. In vain Mrs. Samsa attempts to pacify him. Suspecting that Gregor might be a malingerer, or, still worse, that he was about to make off with some company funds, he displays his art of humiliating his inferiors before the embarrassed family of his employee.

Gregor, still struggling to get out of bed and open the door, is incapable of making himself understood with his beetle mouth, but has kept his human understanding and feeling. At last he succeeds in dropping down on the floor. Lying there for a while helplessly on his back, he has a humorous thought:

> Gregor tried to suppose to himself that something like what had happened to him today might someday happen to the chief clerk; one really could not deny that it was possible. But as if in brusque reply to his supposition the chief clerk took a couple of firm steps in the next-door room and made his patent leather boots creak.

The ''crude answer'' is clear. A man who walks on patent-leather shoes during a work day walks on status symbols and is in no danger of ever losing confidence in himself.

The assertion that ''one really had to admit that possibility'' that the manager would some day awaken as a bug is typical of Kafka's wry humor; at the same time, it hints at the possibility that a human being may awaken to the insight that he is a ''bug,'' a person without character and, consequently, without human dignity. The manager is a malicious, conceited man who, without any knowledge of himself, derives the firmness of his steps solely from the awareness of his patent-leather shoes and all they stand for in his world of spurious values. But Kafka knew that there were people who walked through life with firm steps, and justifiably so. Less than a year after he wrote ''Die Verwandlung,'' the metaphor of such ''authentic'' firm steps appears in his diary, where, as in his letters, he used metaphors occurring in his literary works. The entry reads: ''The unimaginable sadness in the morning. In the evening read Jacobsohn's *Der Fall Jacobsohn*. [Siegfried Jacobsohn was a publicist of about Kafka's age.] This strength to live, to make decisions, joyfully to set one's foot in the right place. He sits in himself the way a practiced rower sits in his boat and would sit in any boat. . . . ''On the same day he reread ''Die Verwandlung.''

Kafka admired men like the author Jacobsohn of the firm steps who is, of course, in firmness and decision the opposite of Gregor and his author. There was, however, a time when Gregor took firm steps like the manager, and though he never wore patent-leather shoes and fine clothes, he wore then something incomparably nobler, a lieutenant's uniform. The beetleman's first excursion out of his room ends in the living room, and there on the wall just opposite him ''hung a photograph of himself in military service, as a lieutenant, hand on sword, a carefree smile on his face, inviting one to respect his uniform and military bearing.''

After the ''fur uniform'' of the proud lady, and lieutenant Gregor Samsa's uniform, a third one appears in this story. As long as Gregor was working, the father had enjoyed a premature dotage, but since Gregor's misfortune he has shaken off his senility and has become the porter of a bank, clad in a uniform with golden buttons, which soon looks soiled since he never takes it off before bedtime. This ''servant-uniform'' strengthens the old man to such a degree that he would have killed the metamorphosed son in a fit of rage by trampling upon him or bombarding him with apples if the mother had not intervened.

''Die Verwandlung'' offers the worst example of the disagreement among Kafka's critics as to the moral qualities of his characters. Strangely enough, nobody mentions the patent fact that the people surrounding the metamorphosed Gregor are the real vermin while he begins to rise even before his misfortune. His ''uneasy dreams'' are the beginning of his development from a timid nothing of a man believing in spurious values to a true human being. There is a gathering of vermin in Gregor's firm: the boss's way of humiliating the employees has been mentioned. The porter, the lowliest creature in the firm, watches at the railroad station, so that he can report to him whether the commercial travelers took the earliest possible train or not. Samsa thinks about him as of an insect: ''He was a creature of the chief's, spineless and stupid.'' The manager well represents the firm, driving Gregor and his family to despair with his false concern and vicious innuendoes. The Italian insurance company had provided Kafka with models for that kind of bug.

The worst insect among the vermin in the story is, however, the parasitical father. Although he knew how his son loathed his employment with the firm to whose principal old Samsa owed money, he never told him that he had saved enough from his bankruptcy and from Gregor's earnings, so that Gregor might have ended his debtor's slave work years earlier than would have been possible under the present conditions.

Among the ''real'' vermin, Gregor's sister is the only exception, at least during the first weeks after his metamorphosis, when she lovingly experiments with food until she knows what her unfortunate brother likes to eat; but then she begins to neglect him more and more. At the same time, Gregor loses his appetite and hardly touches his food any longer. To make his suffering worse, a maid has been hired, an uncouth, rawboned big female who embitters him by addressing him as ''old crap beetle.'' Finally the parents have taken three lodgers into the house, Chaplinesque characters whom he watches while they are eating. '''I'm hungry enough,' said Gregor sadly to himself, 'but not for that kind of food. How these lodgers are stuffing themselves, and here am I dying of starvation!'''

This is no longer the Gregor who admired status symbols, who clung to the cheap picture in his room, fearing it might be removed. The vulgarity of his former life has disappeared, and the food the three roomers are eating with such audible gusto is no longer just food but a symbol of all that pleases and nourishes them as human beings. Gregor can no longer be satisfied with the ''grub'' of their lives and the lives of those like them, as he had been before. The unbridgeable gap between him and people like these becomes clear when his sister plays the violin before them. Since the dullards cannot understand the serious music she has chosen, they boorishly show their contempt for this kind of entertainment, although the young girl reveals all her devotion to music in the way she plays.

This small example of the barbarian's contempt for the language of the arts has provoked, through the ages, many protests like the following one by Goethe, which will help to explain what Gregor is hungering for: "The people do not appreciate us [the artists] if we increase their inner need [Kafka calls it hunger], give them a great ideal for their own selves, if we want to make them feel how glorious a true, noble existence is."

Gregor's inner needs are increased by her playing. His humiliation is approaching its end, his suffering has raised him to a truly human level, and, for the first time since his metamorphosis, he has good reason to doubt the justice of his frightful degradation. The question in which he expresses his doubt is essential to the understanding of the story: "War er ein Tier, da ihn Musik so ergriff?" ("Could he really be an animal since music touched him so?") The use of the conjunction *da* with adversative force is very rare, and most German, and almost all English, critics understood it in its usual causal function, many of them having to rely on the two English translations in which *da* is also rendered as a causal particle. Nevertheless the commentators succeeded to wrest a meaning from the sibylline rhetorical question: "Was he an animal, that music had such an effect upon him?"

One of the four German scholars previously referred to calls Gregor's question fittingly "the decisive sentence," but, tricked by the *da* explains: "As an animal he is at the same time more than an animal." Another German commentator, sensitive to the adversative meaning of *da*, wants nevertheless to save the causal meaning, explaining: "Gregor, about whom we learned earlier that he did not have so intimate a relation to music as his sister, now obtains it on the primitive-emotional basis of his animal organization and in so doing becomes more clearly conscious of being an animal as well." That would make of Gregor, because of his all-encompassing inner life, a superman as well as a superbeetle. One lone commentator gives the correct translation, but then rules out the doubt in Gregor's question and asserts, correcting him: "On the contrary, it is just when he is an animal that music moves him: The totem is the deeper and better self." After these strange metamorphoses of metamorphosed Gregor,

the resigned statement of one critic who interprets *da* in the common, in this case the wrong, way may conclude this strange list: "In Kafka's unfathomable sentence: 'Was he an animal that music could move him so?' paradox echoes jarringly without end." Strangely enough, this paradox, created by interpreters, does not exist in the French, Spanish, and Italian standard translations, where the decisive sentence is rendered correctly.

Gregor, listening, deeply moved, to his sister's violin playing, is now an animal only in his outer form; his inner being reveals a sensitive man, something he was not before, when, as a lieutenant, "he could demand respect for his bearing and uniform," and when later, as a commercial traveler, he stolidly accepted his soul-deadening job. He has reached the highest point in his life which, in its previous form, together with many other human qualities, lacked also interest in music. The violin playing of his sister gives him hope: "He felt as if the way were opening before him to the unknown nourishment he craved."

No longer is the violin-playing sister the middle-class girl discussing with her mother the price of the nextdoor grocer's eggs and the mores of his daughter. While playing the violin, she has left the banality and ugliness of her own and her family's life; she is transfigured. Gregor feels how she is lifted out of this netherworld to which his firm, his parents, the three roomers, and the maid belong, and to which he, too, belonged until he awoke one morning from "uneasy dreams" as a beetle feeding on rotten food. Beginning with this moment of greatest humiliation, he began to rise until the "grub" with which those around him sustained their lives no longer sustained his own, since "his inner needs were increased," as Goethe said.

Having reached this elevated point, his life ends. Dying he thinks "with love and compassion" of his family, just as Georg Bendemann thought of his parents. The maid announces to the older Samsas that the terrible nuisance has "croaked." They all go to Gregor's room, and Grete, as the speaker of this strange chorus surrounding the dead "hero," laments: "Just see how thin he was. It's such a long time since he's eaten anything. The food came out [was taken out] again just as it went in." The parents are too indifferent or too relieved to protect their son from a last ignominy. His body has been left to the maid, who sweeps "the stuff in the next room" away and drops it into the dust bin.

Just as for ''Das Urteil,'' Kafka has provided a Fortinbras end for ''Die Verwandlung.'' Such an end, following the death of the complex, suffering hero is an affirmation of simple life in its brutality, but also in its beauty, which continues unabated by all the tragedies among its ''problem children.'' In ''Das Urteil,'' a mighty stream of traffic across the bridge represents life, drowning out the plop with which unhappy Mr. Bendemann leaves it. In ''Die Verwandlung,'' the parents try to recuperate after Gregor's death from the strains and horrors of the last weeks. Leaving the town by streetcar, they realize that Grete, in spite of the misfortune that had affected them all, has grown up to be a beautiful, nubile girl: ''And it was like a confirmation of their new dreams and excellent intentions that at the end of their journey their daughter sprang to her feet first and stretched her young body.''

Whereas Grete has words of compassion for the dead hero, most commentators who denigrate him dead and alive do not. Obviously misled by the ambiguous translation ''The food came out again just as it went in'' and without paying attention to Grete's compassion, the best-known Kafka critic of the early sixties writing in English misquotes: ''The food came out of him again just as it went in'' and then reflects: ''Grete likens him here to a pipe, a lifeless object. He has not really lived; existence, physical and metaphysical, has moved through him and left no trace. The metamorphosis has failed to change him.'' Others call Gregor a parasite ''that saps the father's and the family's life,'' although as long as he could work he was the opposite. Gregor's rather obvious rise to a level high above his previous state is interpreted by some as a regression to beastliness. His uninteresting pinup lady with the fur accessories is, according to psychoanalyzing critics, dressed in sex symbols and an object of the evil beetle's lust, just as his imagined attempts to show his sister the tenderness he feels for her are considered an incestuous reverie.

We will have further occasion to note that Kafka critics cannot agree on the evaluation of his characters. It seems the misunderstood ''decisive sentence'' has caused many to overlook Gregor's continuous rise toward the level of a truly ''human'' being even though his monstrous shape remains the same. That rise began before the metamorphosis took place, his uneasy dreams were caused by his inner unhappiness, which preceded his misfortune and gradually led him to crave the true food for his inner man. It is hard to see how the villains of the piece, the firm's porter, its president, its manager,

and, most of all, the egotistic father, could have been missed as the true vermin in the story; one critic even praises the vicious manager, for commenting on Gregor's attempt to speak: ''That was an animal's voice.'' The statement is, in that critic's opinion, a word of profoundest wisdom: ''The junior manager, who is in some respects the realist of the story, here utters in four words Kafka's whole criticism both of himself and of mankind.'' In defense of Gregor's rise to human heights it should also be mentioned that Kafka's stories, closely interrelated, usually have a redeeming end. If their heroes die, they do so on a level of being or insight higher than the one on which they lived.

When discussing critics writing before 1967 one should keep in mind that they could not benefit from studying Kafka's letters to Felice, which appeared in that year. Directly and indirectly Kafka speaks repeatedly in these letters about his first publications, before they were written, while they were being written, and after they appeared in print. In his letter and his diaries, Kafka, more than other writers, anticipates the as yet unwritten work in metaphors dealing with its subject matter, mood, and sometimes even the small but revealing details destined to be used, although the author did not know it yet.

Much of ''Die Verwandlung'' is anticipated in a letter to Felice, written on November 1, 1912, sixteen days before the story was begun. In answer to her question about his ''way of life,'' Kafka warns her that he would have to say some ''scabrous things'' about himself. Beginning with the confession that his life consists basically of attempts to write, he uses a strong metaphor which, in the story, was to describe Gregor's burial: ''But when I didn't write, I was at once flat on the floor, fit for the dustbin.'' His general weakness, he continues, made it necessary for him to deprive himself severely to save his strength on all sides, so that he would keep enough strength for this main purpose—writing. ''When I didn't do so, . . . but tried to reach beyond my strength, I was automatically forced back, wounded, humbled, forever weakened.'' He does not mention his father here, but every one of these verbs fits the treatment Kafka received from his father and, in a literary sense, Gregor from old Samsa, who had ''forced back, wounded, and forever weakened'' his monstrous son.

The next paragraph of the letter is an example of ''Kafkaesque'' style, of the smooth shift from reality to a metaphorical plane, applied, in this case, to the metaphors of hunger and becoming thin: "Just as I am thin, and I am the thinnest person I know (and that's saying something, for I am no stranger to sanatoria), there is also otherwise nothing to me which, in relation to writing, one could call superfluous, superfluous in the sense of overflowing." He speaks, first, of his physical thinness and then immediately shifts the concept "thinness" to a metaphorical plane, the word "otherwise" indicating the shift. On the metaphorical plane, his thinness now means that there is no "superfluous" talent or energy or any other positive quality left in him. The double sense of "thinness" forms a parallel to the real and metaphorical sense of food in "Die Verwandlung." First it meant the food Gregor could eat after he was changed, whereas later on it is the life food toward which the violin-playing sister has shown him the way.

And what does this story mean? Of course, like any true work of literary art, it means more than its abstract scheme, that is, the development of a human being from a subhuman level, which is acceptable to the people of his world, to a superior level in a form unacceptable to them and to him, and from which only death can free him. Its meaning is expressed in the words which the author, not the critic, has chosen. The commentator can only help the reader to a closer understanding of motives and images and can clear up philological difficulties. He may do the close reading the works of an author like Kafka require if intellectual obstacles threaten to hinder the understanding of mood and feeling which an older writer like Kafka offers.

The reader himself must feel the humor in the scene where the chief clerk fills the well of the staircase with his shout of fear, while the bug man, rushing toward him on his many thin legs, only wants to excuse his unavoidable tardiness before his superior. The skilled reader, and the one who wants moral edification, will enjoy, each in his own way, the paradox that the "normal" people around Gregor are the vermin while he increasingly becomes a true human being in spite of his monstrous shape. The senile and yet tyrannical father, the Chaplinesque lodgers, the tough maid, the slimy manager as well as the "invisible" characters—the employer at his high desk, the vicious porter, spying at the railroad station—all delight the reader who does not mind enjoying realistically but masterfully presented characters. Gregor's dissatisfaction is indirectly, but for that reason very powerfully, expressed by Kafka. It is not a social or political accusation, but the realization that it is very difficult to find in life the "food"

which lifts the inner man above the banality of existence. The temptation is great to blame our modern times for being particularly hostile to the inner man and his hunger, but such cultural criticism is not Kafka's intention, as he had said himself. Besides, laments about the increasing dehumanization of life, its degeneration due to the utilitarian spirit of the age, were heard as long ago as the later eighteenth and early nineteenth centuries. In Germany, such protests were particularly passionate. There was a writer to whom not music but the Greeks had shown the way to the longed-for, unknown food which this poor Tantalus could never reach: Friedrich Holderlin, the author of a novel with the significant title: *Hyperion*, or *The Solitary in Greece*, expressed Samsa's yearning, although in a totally different tone, in his poem *Der Archipelagus*:

> . . . and much do these barbarians work
> with powerful arms, restlessly, but again and again
> Barren like the Furies are the endeavors of
>   these wretches
> Until awakened, the soul returns to men from their
>   frightening dream
> Youthfully joyful . . .

Source: Meno Spann, "Our Sons," in *Franz Kafka*, Twayne, 1958; reprinted in *Twayne's World Authors Series Online*, 1999.

Norman Hollan

In the following essay, Hollan identifies a balance between unreal and realist elements in "The Metamorphosis," finding that in many cases Kafka has "charged a specific realistic element of the story with a specific non-realistic or spiritual value."

In allegory, symbolism, and surrealism—the three genres are in this respect, at least, indistinguishable—the writer mixes unrealistic elements into a realistic situation. Thus, Kafka, in "Metamorphosis," puts into the realistic, prosaic environment of the Samsa household a situation that is, to put it mildly, unrealistic: "As Gregor Samsa awoke one morning from a troubled dream, he found himself changed in his bed to some monstrous kind of vermin." Kafka's strategy does not in essence differ from the techniques of Spenser and Bunyan: though they used for the unreal elements allegorical names, they, too, set them in realistic or conventional situations. Kafka's method, while rather more overpowering, works the same way: the unreal elements, be they allegorical names or human cockroaches, set up a kind of electric field; the most trite and prosaic detail brought into that field glows with extra meaning. To read allegory is simply to "probe" this field of meaning. We can probe it only if we momentarily put aside the unreality which creates the field and measure the extra values given the realistic elements. By reading them imaginatively, we can understand the nature of the field; only then can we turn back to and understand the unreal element that created the field.

If we look first at the unrealistic elements, there is a danger that we will be dazzled and see no more, as in the usual crude reading of "Metamorphosis:" Samsa is a cockroach, Samsa equals Kafka, Kafka thinks of himself as a cockroach, and so on. Reading Kafka that way is like seeing *The Faerie Queene* as a moralistic tract about Temperance or Justice without realizing the rich, plastic meanings Spenser's realism develops for his allegorical names. Looking first at the realistic elements and their extra values avoids a second danger in reading allegory: substituting abstractions for the realism of the story. Kafka's meaning, as Mr. Eliseo Vivas points out, "is something not to be better stated abstractly in terms of ideas and concepts, to be found beyond the fable, but within it, at the dramatic level, in the interrelationships . . . among the characters and between them and the universe."

If, momentarily, we put aside the unreality of Gregor Samsa's metamorphosis, we can see that the story builds on a commonplace, even a trite, situation: a man feels sick and decides to stay home from work. For fully the first sixth of the story Gregor goes through exactly the kind of internal monologue any of us might if we had caught a discomforting, but not disabling cold. "Nothing is more degrading than always to have to rise so early." "How would it be if I go to sleep again for a while?" "I'd like to see what my boss would say if I tried it; I should be sacked immediately." "What a job I've chosen . . . To hell with it all!" Job, employer, and employee are the core of the realism of "Metamorphosis;" not unnaturally, they form the heart of the allegory as well.

"Metamorphosis" has three parts, each marked by Gregor's emerging from his bedroom into the Samsa's dining-room and then retreating. The first part of the story tells of Gregors' metamorphosis and of his job. In the second part, Gregors' father goes back to work for the first time since the failure of his own business five years before. In the third part, Gregor's mother and sister go to work, al-

> **" "** Once understood, Kafka's method is quite straightforward. In every case, he has charged a specific realistic element of the story with a specific non-realistic or spiritual value."

though Gregor had hoped to send his sister to the conservatory, and the family takes in three lodgers, employers, as it were, in the home. After Gregor's death, in the third part, the lodgers are thrown out, and the Samsas write three letters of excuse to their three employers, and take the day off. Only by reading imaginatively the passages that deal with employers, employees, and jobs, can we see the extra meaning Gregor's metamorphosis gives to these elements.

Gregor, a traveling salesman who sells cloth, says of his boss: "That's a funny thing; to sit on a desk so as to speak to one's employees from such a height, especially when one is hard of hearing and people must come close! Still, all hope is not lost; once I have got together the money my parents owe him—that will be in about five or six years—I shall certainly do it. Then I'll take the big step!" Gregor muses about the firm:

> Why was Gregor, particularly, condemned to work for a firm where the worst was suspected at the slightest inadvertence of the employees? Were the employees, without exception, all scoundrels? Was there among their number not one devoted faithful servant, who, if it did so happen that by chance he missed a few hours work one morning might have found himself so numbed with remorse that he just could not leave his bed?

After Gregor's metamorphosis, his father goes to work for a bank. "By some capricious obstinacy, [he] always refused to take off his uniform even at home . . . as if to keep himself always ready to carry out some order; even in his own home, he seemed to await his superior's voice." Gregor's mother "was killing herself mending the linen of strangers, the sister ran here and there behind her counter at the customers' bidding."

The three lodgers whom the family takes in "were very earnest and serious men; all three had thick beards . . . and they were fanatically tidy; they insisted on order, not only in their own room, but also, now that they were living here, throughout the whole household, and especially in the kitchen." Gregor's mother brings them a plate of meat in the dining room. "The lodgers leaned over it to examine it, and the one who was seated in the middle and who appeared to have some authority over the others, cut a piece of meat as it lay on the dish to ascertain whether it was tender or whether he should send it back to the kitchen. He seemed satisfied, however, and the two women, who had been anxiously watching, gave each other a smile of relief."

These descriptions are ambiguous, even cryptic—but not in themselves unrealistic; the pallor of unreality is cast by the impossible metamorphosis always present, to our minds. The description of Gregor's boss has breadth enough to apply not just to a petty office tyrant, but even to an Old Testament God. Indeed, the reference to the high desk echoes the Old Testament metaphor of the God "most high" who yet can "hear" us: "Though the Lord be high, yet hath he respect unto the lowly"; "The Lord's hand is not shortened, that it cannot save; neither his ear heavy, that it cannot hear: But your iniquities have separated between you and your God, and your sins have hid his face from you, that he will not hear." Read this way, the debt that Gregor assumed for his parents and must pay resembles original sin. Only after he has expiated the sin-debt can he "take the big step" toward freedom.

The description of the "firm," with its atmosphere of universal guilt and punishment, also hints at original sin: "A faithful man who can find?" Gregor and his fellow workers are treated like the evil servant whose lord "shall come in a day when he looketh not for him, and in an hour that he is not aware of, and shall cut him asunder, and appoint him his portion with the hypocrites: there shall be weeping and gnashing of teeth." Gregor is indeed cut off from men; he gets his "portion" of garbage from his hypocritical family, and one evening when he eavesdrops on the three lodgers eating: "It seemed curious to Gregor that he could hear the gnashing of their teeth above all the clatter of cutlery." The lodgers themselves, "very earnest and serious," "fanatically tidy," resemble gods. Frau Samsa's submitting a plate of meat to them is almost like making a burnt offering to some very choosy deities: "Your burnt offerings are not acceptable, nor your sacrifices sweet unto me."

The fact that employers come in threes after the metamorphosis hints at a shift from Old Testament to New like that of "In the Penal Colony"; more immediately, however, it suggests that each member of the family has to take up a share of the burden of subservience that Gregor had borne alone before. Thus, Gregor had proudly brought home cash as a traveling salesman for a cloth concern. His job is now broken into its separate components. His father goes to work for a bank: he now wears the special clothes and acquires Gregor's pride in supporting the family. His mother deals with the cloth, "the linen of strangers." His sister "ran here and there." The fact that there are three lodgers suggests that there is a "god" for each member of the family. The one in the middle, the most important one, corresponds to Gregor's father.

Space does not permit a full development of all the realistic elements in "Metamorphosis" that Gregor's predicament has charged with extra, non-realistic meaning. In every case, however, the same procedure would apply: an imaginative reading of the passages dealing with a particular "realistic" detail. In the few passages I have already quoted, some of these elements emerge. Employers are like gods. Money suggests psychic resources; debts suggest psychic deficits or guilt. Traveling—not only Gregor's normal occupation, but even after his metamorphosis, he learns "to distract himself by walking"—suggests the need to serve an employer, an escape from freedom (sitting still) for *homo viator*. Cloth and clothing are the badges of subservience; it is only in states of nightdress or undress that the inner self can emerge.

Other passages would show many more realistic elements with significance beyond mere physical reality. Food, for example, suggests devotion—reverent offerings demanded by lodgers or communion with one's equals. All the family intercourse of the Samsas seems to take place in the dining room. "Breakfast was the most important meal of the day," because it was the transition from bed, one's private life, to employment. The outdoors, the place where one goes to work, where one travels and wears formal clothing, belongs to the employers. Gregor himself sees his problem as that of getting out of bed: "He would dress, and above all, he would have breakfast; then would come the time to reflect, for he felt that it was not in bed that a reasonable solution could be found. He recalled how often an unusual position adopted in bed had resulted in slight pains which proved imaginary as soon as he arose."

The trifid division of the locale into bedroom (private self), dining room (personal relationships), and outdoors (obligations) hints at that other division into id, ego, and superego. The rooms correspond to areas of experience, the whole apartment upstairs to life on earth and the outdoors downstairs to heaven, with ''some unearthly deliverance . . . at the foot of the stairs.'' Locks and doors, then, symbolize the barriers between these areas of experience. Normally, we break down such barriers by speech, but Gregor can no longer speak intelligibly: he can, however, twist open the lock to his bedroom with his mouth. Locks also symbolize Gregor's imprisonment in the body of an insect. Thus, at first, ''without differentiating between them, he hoped for great and surprising things from the locksmith and the doctor.''

Once understood, Kafka's method is quite straightforward. In every case, he has charged a specific realistic element of the story with a specific non-realistic or spiritual value. Having understood the method and some of the values created in this field of meaning, one can go on to understand the non-realistic element that creates the field. If, in every case, Kafka converts a spiritual concept down to a physical fact, then the transformation of Gregor to dung-beetle, of man to animal, must stand for the transformation of god to man, and, indeed, Kafka has given Gregor a number of Christ-like attributes. At the opening of the story, Gregor had taken on the responsibility of working for the whole family—in particular, he had taken on his parents' debts (guilt or original sin). His metamorphosis takes place around Christmas; he remains a bug for three months and dies at the end of March. What finally kills Gregor is an apple thrown by his father, the apple, presumably, of Eden and mortality. ''One lightly-thrown apple struck Gregor's back and fell off without doing any harm, but the next one literally pierced his flesh [*sic*]. He tried to drag himself a little further away, as if a change of position could relieve the shattering agony he suddenly felt, but he seemed to be nailed fast to the spot.''

Gregor becomes weaker and weaker until he dies. The account of his death parallels the Biblical accounts of Christ's death:

> He lay in this state of peaceful and empty meditation till the clock struck the third morning hour. He saw the landscape grow lighter through the window.

> He realized that he must go. . . . Against his will, his head fell forward and his last feeble breath streamed from his nostrils [*sic*].

> Now from the sixth hour there was darkness over all the land unto the ninth hour

> After this, Jesus knowing that all things were accomplished that the scripture might be fulfilled . . . said, It is finished: and He bowed His head, and gave up the ghost.

> The charwoman arrived early in the morning—and though she had often been forbidden to do so, she always slammed the door so loudly in her vigor and haste that once she was in the house it was impossible to get any sleep.

> Behold, the veil of the temple was rent in twain from the top to the bottom; and the earth did quake, and rocks rent; and the graves were opened; and many bodies of the saints which slept arose.

The Samsas arise from their beds and learn of Gregor's death; they cross themselves. ''Well,'' says Herr Samsa, ''we can thank God for that!'' The charwoman, ''gigantic . . . with bony features and white hair, which stoop up all around her head,'' wearing a ''little ostrich feather which stood upright on her hat,'' which ''now waved lightly in all directions,'' describes Gregor as ''absolutely dead as a doornail,'' ''stone dead.'' ''The angel of the Lord,'' says Matthew, ''descended from heaven, and came and rolled back the stone from the door, and sat upon it. His countenance was like lightning, and his raiment white as snow.'' ''He is not here: for he is risen,'' becomes another kind of divine comedy: '''Well, . . .' she replied, and she laughed so much she could hardly speak for some while. 'Well, you needn't worry about getting rid of that thing in there, I have fixed it already.'''

One question, however, remains: why a cockroach? Several critics have pointed out ''*Metamorphosis's*'' descent from the ''loathly lady'' genre of medieval tales, in which, as in ''Beauty and the Beast,'' someone is transformed into a loathsome animal and can be transformed back only by love. Love, in other words, is tested by disgust, and in *Metamorphosis*, love is found lacking. In at least one such tale which Kafka probably knew, Flaubert's ''The Legend of St. Julian the Hospitaller,'' the loathsome creature turns out to be Christ. Kafka, however, could have used any loathsome animal, a toad, a snake, a spider: why a cockroach? The German word is *Mistkaefer*, applied to Gregor only once—by the charwoman. Technically, the word means a dung-beetle, not a cockroach, and the distinction is important. For one thing, biologically, a cockroach undergoes only a partial metamorphosis, while the beetles go through a total metamorphosis. More important, dung beetles are scarabs. ''The Egyptian scarab,'' says the redoubtable *Bri-*

tannica, "is an image of the sacred dung-beetle . . . which was venerated as a type of the sun-god. Probably the ball of dung, which is rolled along by the beetle in order to place its eggs in it, was regarded as an image of the sun in its course across the heavens, which may have been conceived as a mighty ball rolled by a gigantic beetle." Gregor, we should remember was a travelling salesman; a collection of samples was "entrusted" to him. Samson (Samsa) means in Hebrew "the sun's man." In German, the title of the story, "Die Verwandlung," like the hieroglyphic beetle-sign, means either an insect's metamorphosis or transformation in a general sense. "Die Verwandlung," moreover, is the normal word, for transubstantiation. The dung-beetle, then, was the one animal that gave Kafka everything he needed: *total metamorphosis* from a wingless grub to a hard-working, traveling-salesman-like adult plus the combination of loathsomeness and divinity.

Samson's sacrifice is a traditional analogue to Christ's; in German he is called a *Judenchrist.* Gregor's first name means "vigilant," and so he was when he supported his family. When he is a dim-sighted scarab, though, his first name makes an ironic contrast to his last: Samson was blinded. Samsa, like Samson, rid the chosen people (his family) of the domineering Philistines (the lodgers who didn't like the sister's music) by his own self-destruction, his wished-for death. Gregor, at one point, longs to climb up on his sister's shoulder and kiss her neck; in general, Gregor has a great many incestuous impulses. In this context, his name echoes the medieval legend of Pope Gregory, who in expiating his incestuous birth and marriage became the holiest man in Christendom: chained to a barren rock for seventeen years, the legend says he became an ugly little hedgehog-like creature.

Gregory-Gregor's situation strongly resembles that prophesied by Isaiah: "His visage was so marred more than any man, and his form more than the sons of men . . . he hath no form nor comeliness; and when we shall see him, there is no beauty that we should desire him. He is despised and rejected of men; a man of sorrows, and acquainted with grief: and we hid as it were our faces from him; he was despised, and we esteemed him not. Surely he hath borne our griefs, and carried our sorrows: yet we did esteem him stricken, smitten of God, and afflicted. But he was wounded for our transgressions, he was bruised for our iniquities." In fact, a good deal of the incidental imagery of "*Metamorphosis*" was derived from Isaiah. For example, the statement that

Gregor's sister had worn on her neck "neither collar nor ribbon ever since she had been working in the shop," corresponds to, "Loose thyself from the bands of thy neck, O captive daughter of Zion." The details of Gregor's death are taken from the Passion, and the whole allegorical scheme of employers as gods and money as spiritual resources probably came from the various New Testament parables of lords, stewards, and "talents."

In a crude sense, then, "*Metamorphosis*" satirizes Christians, who are only distressed, angry, and, ultimately, cruel when a second Christ appears. They take gods in times of trouble, even into their own homes, then throw them out when the trouble ends. After Gregor's death, a butcher's boy comes up the stairs, meeting and passing the evicted lodger-gods going down the stairs. Priest-like, he brings the meat that the Samsas will eat themselves, suggesting communion, as opposed to the burnt offerings they had formerly made to the lodgers. At one level, Kafka is parodying Christ's sacrifice, but a merely theological account of the story is far from complete. It neglects the rich sexual symbolism, the double doors, for example, through which Gregor must pass (a birth image) or the phallic symbols associated with his father: indeed, at one point Herr Samsa is described in terms rather more appropriate to a phallus. Kafka is reaching for more than theological allegory.

At the risk of being trite, I would like to suggest that Gregor's transformation dramatizes the human predicament. That is, we are all blind, like Samson, trapped between a set of dark instinctual urges on one hand and an obscure drive to serve "gods" on the other. Like dung-beetles, our lives are defined by the urge to mate and the urge to labor that comes from it. Our only freedom is not to know we are imprisoned. "*Metamorphosis*" represents abstractions physically and charges physical realities with spiritual significance. Gregor's physical transformation, then, stands for a spiritual transformation. Gregor *is* a dung-beetle means he is *spiritually like* one. His back, "hard as armor plate," dramatizes and *substitutes* for his awareness of this human predicament. Similarly, his metamorphosis forces his family to a reluctant awareness of this imprisonment: again, the physical events of the story, taking jobs, for example, dramatize and *substitute* for the awareness itself. Finally, Gregor's metamorphosis forces the reader to an awareness of the cage of id and superego. The reader, so long as he believes in the metamorphosis, by its very unreality is driven to see the realities, Biblical and Freudian, hiding behind the ordinary reality of the story.

The first part of "*Metamorphosis*" forces this understanding on us, but the ending whimsically urges on us the virtues of ignorance. As Gregor's sister says, "You must get the idea out of your head that this is Gregor. We have believed that for too long, and that is the cause of all our unhappiness. How could it be Gregor?" That is, so long as we believe in Gregor's metamorphosis, the realistic details of the story are fraught with significance. If we can forget Gregor's predicament and ours, we can relapse into blissful ignorance. To read "*Metamorphosis,*" one must put aside the "unreal" metamorphosis momentarily; the trouble with the Samsas is that they put it aside forever.

Source: Norman Hollan, "Realism and Unrealism Kafka's 'Metamorphosis,'" in *Modern Fiction Studies*, Vol. 4, No. 2, Summer 1958, pp. 143–50.

Stephen Spender

In the following brief review of the first English translation of "The Metamorphosis," Spender calls it a "strange and terrifying nightmare."

Franz Kafka's great allegorical novels have often been compared to "Pilgrim's Progress." But, in fact, they differ from any allegories written before because they do not set up a system of symbols which can easily be recognized as corresponding to some system existing in the real world, nor do they offer any solution, any "moral," as Bunyan does. I believe the fact is that Kafka saw the world much as he describes it in his novels, just as a man who feels himself to be persecuted sees reality fitting into a system, which is really of a spiritual order, to persecute him. Although we might not agree that the victim of persecution mania was persecuted, we might easily find that his systematization of reality gave us an exceedingly convincing view of reality, a view which at moments penetrated beyond reality itself to another final reality, the persecutors themselves.

We do, indeed, find that Kafka gives us just such a view of reality as would the victim of persecution. However roundabout it may seem, his approach to reality is direct: he is not building up an allegory in order to illustrate a metaphysic, he is penetrating reality in order to discover a system of truth. How often when reading his fantastic accounts of human behavior we find ourselves exclaiming not "how remotely that corresponds to

> "'The Metamorphosis' is a strange and terrifying nightmare, the whole plot of which is contained in the first paragraph."

something in life which we dimly see beyond it," but "how extraordinary, yet how true." For example, the disorderliness, the lack of dignity, the inappropriateness of the officials who are prosecuting K— in "The Trial" have the significance of monumental truth, because it is through these obstructions which are life itself that K— sees the good life, which these very irrelevancies, in being irrelevant, yet imperfectly represent.

What distinguishes K— from the persecution maniac is that he is the least important figure in his own universe, whereas the neurotic is, of course, the center of his universe, and persecution is the means which the world adopts to flatter his ego. In a sublime sense, K— is humble. This traveler whose case in "The Trial," or whose task in "The Castle," is of trifling importance, is a supreme outsider. He is not only ignorant of the way of life which everyone else accepts, he is ignorant of life itself. His love-making is not sexual, it is an innocent attempt to conform, to reach the center of life, a parallel to his spiritual journey. Just because he is an outsider he has the stranger's fresh view of life and the reality beyond life. That truth Kafka never attained: he only knew there was a truth. If he had lived, he might have written novels which started off from a goal, instead of these novels which never attain their goal.

"The Metamorphosis" is a strange and terrifying nightmare, the whole plot of which is contained in the first paragraph. "As Gregor Samsa awoke one morning from a troubled dream, he found himself changed in his bed to some monstrous kind of vermin." The story describes, simply and straightforwardly, Gregor's attempts to adapt himself to this change, the attitude to him of his family and his employer, until finally, neglected by them all, he dies. It contains no metaphysical purpose, it is an account, in Kafka's terms, of a given situation in contemporary life: the situation, say, of a bank clerk, on whom his whole family has depended, who wakes up one morning to discover that he is suffering from an incurable disease.

Source: Stephen Spender, ''Franz Kafka,'' in *The New Republic*, Vol. LXXXXII, No. 1195, October 27, 1937, pp. 347–48.

Sources

Corngold, Stanley, *The Commentators' Despair: The Interpretation of Kafka's Metamorphosis*, Kennikat, 1973.

Gray, Ronald, *Franz Kafka*, Cambridge University Press, 1973.

Kafka, Franz, *The Complete Stories and Parables*, edited by Nahum N. Glatzer, Quality Paperback Book Club, 1983.

Further Reading

Bloom, Harold, ed., *Franz Kafka's ''The Metamorphosis,''* Chelsea House, 1988.
    This text is a collection of essays analyzing the story.

Brod, Max, *Franz Kafka: A Biography*, translated by G. Humphreys Roberts, Schocken, 1947.
    This book of Kafka's life is told by his friend and literary executor.

Hayman, Ronald, *Kafka: A Biography*, Oxford University Press, 1982.
    Hayman's work is a biographical study that relates Kafka's life to his works.

Pawel, Ernst, *The Nightmare of Reason: A Life of Franz Kafka*, Farrar, Straus & Giroux, 1984.
    This text is a biography of Kafka providing psychological analysis and social background.

The Pagan Rabbi

Cynthia Ozick
1971

''The Pagan Rabbi'' was first published in the 1971 collection *The Pagan Rabbi and Other Stories*, which garnered extensive critical acclaim for Cynthia Ozick. The book won the B'nai B'rith Jewish Heritage Award in 1971, The Jewish Book Council Award, and the Edward Lewis Wallant Memorial Award in 1972, and the American Academy of Arts and Letters Award in 1973. It was also nominated for a National Book Award in 1971.

''The Pagan Rabbi'' is told from the point of view of an unnamed narrator, who learns that Isaac Kornfeld, a renowned thirty-six-year-old rabbi with whom the narrator was acquainted, has committed suicide by hanging himself from a tree in a park. The narrator, seeking to understand Isaac's motive, first goes to see the tree from which he hanged himself, and then to see the rabbi's widow, Sheindal Kornfeld. The widow asks him to read the notebook and the letter found in the rabbi's pockets upon his death. The narrator and the widow discuss the meaning of the extensive musings of the rabbi, which address theological and philosophical questions regarding faith and the soul in relation to Nature. They conclude that the rabbi had secretly become a ''pagan,'' seduced by a Creature that seemed to be a goddess of Nature.

This story addresses themes that appear in much of Ozick's short fiction, including the place of Judaism in secular America, idolatry, death, the soul, paganism, and crises in faith. It also addresses

themes of marriage and family in relation to Jewish identity.

Author Biography

Known primarily for her short stories and novellas, Cynthia Ozick is one of the most celebrated Jewish-American writers of the century. She was born in New York, New York, on April 17, 1928. Her mother, born in the town of Hlusk, in the province of Minsk, Belarus, had escaped persecution of Jews there at age nine. Her father was also from Russia. Her parents owned the Park View Pharmacy, where she worked delivering prescriptions. In 1930, the family moved to what was then a rural area in Pelham Bay in the Bronx.

From 1942 to 1946, Ozick attended an all-girls high school at Hunter College in Manhattan. She attended college at New York University, graduating Phi Beta Kappa and cum laude with a major in English in 1949. She earned a master's degree in English from Ohio State University, with a thesis on ''Parable in the Later Novels of Henry James.'' She attended a graduate seminar at Columbia University in 1951. From 1952 to 1953, she worked as an advertising copywriter for Filene's Department Store. Ozick was married in 1952 to an attorney by the name of Bernard Hallote, with whom she lived with her parents in New York City beginning in 1953. From 1964 to 1965, she taught freshman composition at New York University. Her daughter, Rachel, was born in 1965, the same year as the publication of *Trust*, Ozick's first novel, which had taken over six years to write. *Trust* received only lukewarm critical attention.

It was not until 1968 that Ozick began to receive recognition, both nationally and internationally, when she was made a fellow of the National Endowment for the Arts, and then invited to Israel to read one of her essays in 1970. In 1971, publication of *The Pagan Rabbi and Other Stories* brought her work extensive critical acclaim. It won the B'nai B'rith Jewish Heritage Award, the Jewish Book Council Award, the Edward Lewis Wallant Memorial Award, and the American Academy of Arts and Letters Award. Ozick is best known for her short story ''The Shawl'' (1981), in which a woman in a concentration camp hides her baby in a shawl for many months, until it is discovered and thrown against an electrical fence by the Nazis. Ozick has published many books of short stories and essays.

Plot Summary

In ''The Pagan Rabbi,'' The narrator, an unnamed Jewish man in his mid-thirties, hears that Isaac Kornfeld, a childhood friend, has committed suicide at the age of thirty-six. The narrator's father, a rabbi, and Isaac's father, also a rabbi, had been friends as well as professional rivals. The narrator had been in rabbinical school with Isaac but had left while Isaac had gone on to become a renowned rabbi. The narrator had married Jane, a non-Jewish woman, and worked in her father's fur business. He later divorced, and began his own business as a bookseller. His store is called the Book Cellar. When he quit rabbinical school, the narrator's father had declared him dead, observed traditional Jewish mourning practices, and never spoken to him again. His father also had a disease of the throat that made speaking difficult and, eventually, impossible.

Upon hearing of Isaac Kornfeld's suicide, the narrator goes out to see the tree from which Kornfeld hanged himself. Although they were not friends, Isaac had, over the years, ordered all of his books from the narrator's bookstore, during which time they had exchanged brief notes to one another with each book order. Through this means, the narrator had learned that Isaac had seven daughters.

He then goes to see Sheindal, Isaac's widow. Having only met Sheindal once, at her wedding, the narrator finds that he ''loved her at once.'' Sheindal was born in a concentration camp, where, as an infant she had been thrown against an electric barbed-wire fence by the Nazis, to kill her—but had been saved at the last moment when a liberating army cut off the electric current.

Sheindal begins to question the narrator about the type of books Isaac had ordered from him. She asks if he ordered any books having to do with plants or farming or agronomy. Sheindal, who seems bitter about her deceased husband, tells the narrator of the strange behavior Isaac had been exhibiting before his suicide. He read books only about plant life, briefly joined a hiking group, and taken to bringing the family out to the country on picnics. Isaac began to tell the children bizarre and fantastical bedtime stories. He eventually took to leaving the house early in the morning and staying out late.

Sheindal gives the narrator the small notebook that was found in Isaac's pocket after his death. The narrator returns to the tree in the park where Isaac had hung himself to read the contents of the notebook. What is written in it seems unremarkable—the notes of a scholar regarding passages of literature and philosophy. The narrator feels that Sheindal meant to "punish" him for "asking the unaskable"—why Isaac had committed suicide.

Feeling angry and "cheated," the narrator returns to Sheindal's house to give back the notebook. Sheindal asks the narrator to read a "love letter" Isaac left before his death. The letter had been set between the pages of the notebook, but fallen out before the narrator left. The narrator is at first stunned by the idea that Isaac would have been carrying on an affair. He is reluctant to read it, but Sheindal insists upon reading it aloud to him. The letter is addressed to a "Creature," and contains philosophical and theological musings on Nature and the soul. The letter then describes a mythical Creature, Iripomoňoéià, that emerges from Nature in the park by the tree where he eventually hanged himself, and with whom the Rabbi claims that he copulated.

The rabbi's letter expresses a crisis in faith, documenting the struggle between his rabbinical orientation and his discovery of a "pagan" worship of Nature. Sheindal expresses disgust that her husband was secretly a "pagan." The narrator is more sympathetic to the deceased rabbi's philosophical musings upon his "soul." He advises her to forgive Isaac, but she is full of spite and bitterness. While the narrator had at first secretly intended to woo and marry Sheindal, her inability to appreciate the rabbi's crisis in faith leads him to change his mind about her. He leaves, advising her that her "husband's soul is in that park." He goes home and flushes his three houseplants down the toilet.

Cynthia Ozick

Characters

Iripomoňoéià

Iripomoňoéià is the "Creature" Rabbi Isaac Kornfeld addresses in the "love" letter found in his pocket after he hanged himself from a tree in a park. She seems to be a sort of pagan goddess of Nature, who seduces the rabbi into the "pagan" worship of Nature over his Jewish faith.

Isaac and Sheindal's Daughters

Isaac and Sheindal have seven daughters, including Naomi, Esther, Miriam and Ophra. Isaac

announces each new birth to the narrator in brief notes that they exchange with each book the rabbi orders from the bookseller. As the rabbi's preoccupation with Nature becomes more extreme, his bedtime stories to his daughters become more fantastical and disturbing.

Isaac Kornfeld's Father

Isaac Kornfeld's father, a rabbi, was both friends and enemies with the narrator's father, also a rabbi. The two fathers shared a professional competition in their rabbinical work and prestige.

Jane

Jane is the narrator's former wife. As she is non-Jewish, his marriage to her represents a rebellion against his father, who is a rabbi. The narrator worked in Jane's father's fur business while married to her, but left the business when they divorced.

Isaac Kornfeld

Isaac Kornfeld is the "pagan rabbi" of the story's title. He is a renowned rabbi who commits suicide by hanging himself from a tree in a park at the age of thirty-six. The story centers on the narrator's attempts to understand the motivation and meaning of the rabbi's unexpected suicide. He learns, through a letter and a notebook found in the rabbi's pockets at the time of his death, that the rabbi had become preoccupied with philosophical and theological musings on the worship of Nature. The rabbi had written a ''love letter'' to a Creature, which seemed to be some sort of goddess of nature. Seduced by this Creature of Nature, he had become obsessed with nature and plant life, which carried him further and further away from his Jewish faith toward a ''paganism'' based on the worship of Nature.

Sheindal Kornfeld

Sheindal Kornfeld, also addressed as Rebbetzin Kornfeld (wife of the rabbi), is the widow of Rabbi Isaac Kornfeld. The narrator had first met her at her wedding to Isaac, when she was seventeen years old. He was struck by her long, dark, beautiful hair, which would be hidden from the public eye, according to Orthodox Jewish Law, after her marriage. Sheindal is a Holocaust survivor, who was born in a concentration camp and saved by a liberating army at the last minute from death by being thrown against an electrical fence by the Nazis. She retains a scar, shaped like an asterisk, on her cheek where the barbed wire had cut her face. When the narrator goes to visit her upon Isaac's suicide, she is bitter and disdainful of her husband's loss of Jewish faith and foray into the pagan worship of Nature. The narrator falls in love with Sheindal immediately upon seeing her, and plans to woo and marry her. But after she shows him the letter left by the rabbi, the narrator is struck by her inability to forgive her deceased husband for his apostasy. The narrator, reminded of his own father, who refused to forgive him for quitting rabbinical school, leaves Sheindal, no longer interested in marrying her.

The Narrator

The narrator of the story, who is unnamed, is a Jewish man in his mid-thirties. His father was a rabbi. When he left rabbinical school, his father declared him dead and never spoke to him again. As the story opens, he has just learned that Isaac Kornfeld, with whom he had attended rabbinical school, had committed suicide by hanging himself from a tree. In an attempt to understand the meaning of Isaac's death, the narrator first goes to look at the tree from which Isaac hanged himself, then goes to visit Sheindal, Isaac's widow. The narrator learns about Isaac's crisis in faith and turn to the ''pagan'' worship of Nature through Sheindal, who asks him to read both the notebook and the letter left in the rabbi's pockets upon his death. The narrator in-stantly falls in love with Sheindal, having met her only once before, and the two of them discuss Isaac's preoccupation with Nature leading up to his suicide. When the narrator sees that Sheindal is unable to forgive her deceased husband for wander-ing from Jewish faith into paganism, he is reminded of his own father, who was unable to forgive him for leaving rabbinical school. No longer interested in pursuing Sheindal, the narrator leaves her, suggest-ing she go to find her husband's soul in the park where he hung himself. He goes home and flushes the three houseplants he has down the toilet.

The Narrator's Father

The narrator's father, a rabbi, declares his son (the narrator) dead when he leaves rabbinical school. He observes traditional Jewish mourning practices over the loss of his son, and never speaks to him again, even when they are both present at Isaac's wedding to Sheindal. The narrator's father has a disease of the throat, an ''obstruction'' that makes it difficult and, eventually, impossible for him to speak. The narrator explains that ''I was afraid of my father; he had a certain disease of the larynx, and if he even uttered something so trivial as 'Bring the tea' to my mother, it came out splintered, clamor-ous, and vindictive.'' At the present time of the story, the narrator's father is already dead.

Themes

Death and Mourning

This story focuses on the theme of death and mourning. It begins with the death by suicide of Rabbi Isaac Kornfeld. In visiting Sheindal, the rabbi's widow, the narrator implicitly ''asks the unaskable''—what is the meaning of the rabbi's suicide? The narrator's own father, also a rabbi, had declared him dead when he decided to leave rab-binical school and, following traditional Jewish mourning practices, he ''rent his clothes and sat on a stool for eight days.'' The narrator's father never spoke to him again, eventually dying without an-other word to his own son. The narrator declares that ''it is easy to honor a father from afar, but bitter to honor one who is dead.'' In discussing Isaac's suicide with Sheindal, the narrator blurts out, ''What do you want from the dead?'' Isaac's philosophical and theological musings, left in his letter and note-book, also address themes of death, in relation to the

Topics for Further Study

- One of the pagan rabbi's preoccupations, based on the notebook he leaves behind, is with Romantic poetry. Find out more about the literary style, known as Romanticism, which reached its height in the early nineteenth century. The story mentions some of the best-known Romantic poets, such as Byron, Keats and Tennyson. What is the preoccupation of Romantic poetry with nature? How do the poems of these writers portray nature in relation to such spiritual concerns as the soul?

- Sheindal Kornfeld, the wife of the pagan rabbi, is a Holocaust survivor who was born in a concentration camp. Find out more about the experiences of children in concentration camps, and the stories of Holocaust survivors who themselves were children in concentration camps. How did their experiences affect their sense of spirituality and of Jewish identity?

- Rabbi Kornfeld and Sheindal Kornfeld are Ortho-

dox Jews. Learn more about the marriage laws and traditions of Orthodox Judaism. How do they differ from the marital laws and tradition practices by Conservative Judaism? Reform Judaism?

- The god Pan, associated with paganism, comes from Greek mythology. Learn more about Greek mythology and the stories that are derived from Greek mythology. What is the significance of these ancient stories to dilemmas of the modern reader in modern society? What is their enduring appeal to the modern reader?

- In his philosophical musings, the character Rabbi Isaac Kornfeld mentions the philosophers Socrates, Spinoza, Nietzsche, and Hegel. Find out more about one of these philosophers. What are the basic themes and tenets of his philosophy? In what ways do they address concerns similar to those raised in the short story?

---

soul: "There is nothing that is Dead. There is no Non-life. Holy life subsists even in the stone, even in the bones of dead dogs and dead men." In recording his discussion with the Nature goddess, the rabbi reports that she told him, that, in men's praise of Nature, "It is not Nature they love so much as Death they fear."

Marriage and Family

The narrator's quest for the meaning of the rabbi's suicide is in part an attempt to make sense of his own experiences of marriage and family. His father having declared him dead, the narrator married a non-Jewish woman, clearly out of rebellion. At the Orthodox wedding between Isaac and Sheindal, the narrator becomes aware of his non-Jewish wife's negative attitude about Jews and Judaism, and compares their secular wedding in a courthouse to the religious ritual of the Orthodox wedding. The narrator's initial plan to woo and marry Sheindal, after Isaac's suicide, is a swing in

the opposite direction, a desire to reconnect with an Orthodox Jewish life after the failure of his marriage to a non-Jewish woman. In the end, however, the narrator's desire to reconcile his failed relationship with his dead father, a rabbi, by marrying the widow of a rabbi, is negated when he finds that, much as his own father refused to forgive him for leaving rabbinical school, so Sheindal refuses to forgive her dead husband for leaving his Jewish faith in the pursuit of paganism.

Crisis in Faith

This is the story of an Orthodox rabbi's secret crisis in faith, as revealed posthumously through the note and letter he left upon his suicide. The world-renowned rabbi develops a secret life in which he addresses theological and philosophical questions concerning the pagan worship of Nature. The rabbi's extreme crisis in faith, which results in his suicide, parallels the crisis in faith of the narrator, who chose not to pursue his father's rabbinical career. Ozick's writing often addresses crises in faith of Jewish people in secular America. The seduction of the Orthodox rabbi by a pagan goddess of Nature represents the seductiveness of secular, non-Jewish society to many modern Jews.

Nature

The "pagan rabbi" is seduced away from his Jewish faith by a goddess of Nature. He becomes preoccupied with Nature in the form of the plant world, and with literary and philosophical references to Nature. His notebook contains quotes from the Romantic poets of the nineteenth century, whose poetry focuses on Nature as a source of inspiration. Nature is posed in opposition to Jewish theology. Having been exposed to such musing on the part of the rabbi, at the end of the story, the narrator finds himself flushing his three houseplants down the toilet. This is a highly enigmatic ending. Is the narrator negating any evidence in his own home of the worship of Nature? Is he, in effect, liberating the houseplants, by sending them back into nature, via the public sewer system, through which they will end up in the river of sewage by the park where the rabbi hung himself? Is this story a condemnation of paganism? These questions are left for the reader to interpret, without clear guidance from the narrator.

Forgiveness

Forgiveness is an important theme of this story, in terms of the relationships between characters in the context of their Jewish identity. The narrator's father is unable to forgive him for choosing not to become a rabbi. The father's inability to forgive is so extreme that he declares his son dead and never speaks to him again. The narrator's psychology is deeply rooted in the bitterness of being cast out by his own father. When, in the end of the story, the narrator sees that Sheindal is unwilling to forgive her dead husband for his "paganism," he is reminded of his own father's obstinacy, and loses any desire to marry her.

Style

Narrative Point-of-View

This story is told from the first person limited perspective, meaning that the reader is given only information which the narrator, also the protagonist

of the story, also has. This is effective in that, while the story centers on the suicide and religious crisis of Isaac Kornfeld, the "pagan rabbi," it is portrayed as a reflection upon the religious and identity crisis of the narrator himself. The reader is presented with the events and characters only from the perspective of the narrator. Thus, each element of the story further develops the character of the narrator.

Story Framing

As in many of Ozick's stories, this one is built upon multiple types of story framing. The first person narrator begins by narrating the events of the "present" time in the story, which begin when he learns of the suicide of rabbi Kornfeld. The narrator, however, explains the significance of the present events in relation to past events, which are related in a sort of "flashback" mode, jumping between past and present. When he goes to visit Sheindal, the rabbi's widow, she in turn narrates to him the story of her husband's behavior leading up to his suicide. When she gives the narrator the rabbi's notebook, the story unfolds through the narrator's discussion of direct quotes from the rabbi's writings. Later, when Sheindal hands him the letter Isaac left, the narrator is reluctant to read it; instead, Sheindal reads the letter aloud to him. This narrative technique creates a kind of "Chinese box" or Russian tea doll effect, whereby a story is revealed through multiple framing. The narrator is telling a story which is based on Sheindal's story of the rabbi, which is based on her reading aloud the rabbi's letter.

Literary References

Ozick's writing is known to be difficult due in part to the erudite literary references that play a significant role in her stories. In describing Rabbi Isaac Kornfeld's reading habits, the narrator explains that, "One day he was weeping with Dostoyesvski and the next leaping in the air over Thomas Mann." It would be important to know about the great Russian writer Fyodor Dostoyesvski and the great German writer Thomas Mann to appreciate the significance of these references to the themes of the story. In reading Isaac's notebook, the narrator mentions a number of literary references. The rabbi jotted down passages and quotes from various writers, which the narrator describes as "the elegiac favorites of a closeted Romantic." The narrator here is referring specifically to the literary period of Romanticism, which flourished in the early nineteenth century. The narrator cites some of the most renowned romantic poets from the rabbi's notebooks: "He had put down a snatch of Byron, a smudge of Keats . . . "

Greek Mythology

In his pursuit of the worship of Nature, the rabbi turns to Greek mythology. In his notebook the narrator finds the statement, "Great Pan lives." This refers to the Greek god Pan, half goat, half man. The goddess of Nature who seduces the rabbi into paganism is given the Greek-sounding name of Iripomoñoéià.

Character Names

Most of the characters in this story have names taken from the Old Testament. The rabbi's name is Isaac. Isaac is the only son of Abraham and Sarah. God commands Abraham to sacrifice his own son; Abraham demonstrates his faith in God by preparing to carry out this command, but at the last minute, God commands Abraham to spare the boy's life. This biblical tale points to both the unquestioning faith of Abraham and the mercy of God. In Ozick's story, Isaac's daughters also have biblical names such as Naomi, Esther, and Miriam. Each name thus refers to a biblical character and story. Learning more about these biblical references would shed further light on the themes of the story.

Historical Context

The Three Denominations of Judaism

There are three main denominations of Judaism—Orthodox, Conservative, and Reform. Orthodox Judaism maintains the strictest observance of traditional Jewish law and ritual. (Hasidism is an even more traditional practice of Orthodox Judaism.) Conservative Judaism, while maintaining most of these traditions, concedes to some modernization of the observance of Jewish law. Conservative Judaism can be traced back to Germany in the 1840s. In 1985, a significant change in the policy of Conservative Judaism was the decision to ordain women rabbis. Reform Judaism, which dates back to the early 1800s, is the observance most adapted to modern society, and focuses less on the strict observance of traditional Jewish law. Reform Judaism was the first branch to include a girls' Bat Mitzvah confirmation equivalent to the traditional boys' Bar Mitzvah confirmation. A newer and more radical practice of Judaism is Reconstructionism.

The Rabbinical Council of America

The Rabbinical Council of America is a national organization of Orthodox rabbis, founded in 1923. It is a branch of the Union of Orthodox Jewish Congregations of America, founded in 1898. Together, these organizations are devoted to supporting Orthodox Jewish observance and education, as well as supporting the State of Israel. They are also the primary body that overseas the approval of manufactured foods as "kosher," or consistent with Jewish dietary laws.

The Medieval Ghetto

Rabbi Isaac Kornfeld in this story at one point mentions the "medieval ghetto" in the "letter" that the narrator reads. In modern American usage "ghetto" generally refers to low-income areas of a city, often inhabited primarily by minority populations. However, the term "ghetto," first dubbed in the early sixteenth century, referred to areas of many cities in which Jews were legally forced to live, segregated from the rest of the population. A high fence or gate usually enclosed ghettos, and Jews had to observe special rules and precautions when venturing outside of the walls of the ghetto. In Nazi Germany, the practice of the "ghetto" was brought into use as a means of temporarily containing Jews in one area of a city before sending them off to the death camps.

Yeshiva University

A yeshiva is an institution of Jewish learning and scholarship. In the United States, the first yeshiva was established in New York City in 1886. In 1928 it became Yeshiva College, and in 1945 Yeshiva University.

Philip Roth

Philip Roth is a contemporary modern Jewish-American writer, perhaps better known than Ozick. Roth's stories, while very different in style, address many similar themes and concerns as do Ozick's. His first book, *Goodbye, Columbus and Five Short Stories* (1959) addresses themes of Jewish identity and faith in the context of secular American culture, as well as themes of family and sexuality. His most famous, most popular, and most controversial work is *Portnoy's Complaint* (1969), a novel in which Alexander Portnoy, a Jewish man in his thirties, addresses his psychotherapist concerning his preoccupations with his Jewish identity, overbearing mother, and neurotic sexuality.

Compare
&
Contrast

- **1960s:** While Reform Judaism allows the ordaining of female rabbis, Conservative and Orthodox denominations do not.

  1980s–1990s: After 1985, Conservative Judaism begins to ordain female rabbis.

- **1960s:** Ozick's story mentions that the rabbi's parents had traveled to the "Holy Land." This refers to the nation of Israel, established in 1948 as a Jewish state. Ongoing conflict between Israel and surrounding Arab nations lead to several wars, which result in redrawing of boundaries and changes in the balance of power in the Middle East. The Six-Day War of 1967 marks a watershed in Israeli relations with bordering Arab nations, when Israeli acquires control over considerably more territory in the Middle East.

  1980s–1990s: There have been various attempts at peace negotiations throughout the 1980s and 1990s between Israel and the Middle East.

- **1960s:** Before the Six Day War of 1967, Israeli rule over Arab sections of the city of Jerusalem is relatively mild, and resistance on the part of the Arab population is minimal.

  1980s–1990s: After the Six Day War of 1967, the Israeli government begins to institute stricter control over Arab sections of Jerusalem. This eventually leads to acts of terrorism on the part of the Palestinian Liberation Organizations, and such uprisings as the Intifada, which begins in 1987. Attempts at peace negotiations have occurred within this context of terrorist and counterterrorist struggles between Israel and the Palestinians. However, attempts to reach a peace between Israel and the Palestinians have resulted in changes toward self-rule of Palestinians in some areas of Israel.

- **1960s:** Orthodox Jewish interpretations of the Talmud place specific restrictions on issues concerning death and the body. For instance, any activity that may hasten death is forbidden. Mutilation of the body is also forbidden. Such laws are subject to further interpretation by Jewish scholars to accommodate new medical technologies.

  1990s: Advances in medical science and technology over the past thirty years (such as organ transplants, genetic research and advanced methods for, and increased availability of, euthanasia) have raised further challenges to rabbinical scholars in interpreting the significance of the ancient texts of the Talmud. Provisions that make exceptions in the interest of "the preservation of life" can be interpreted by Jewish theologians to be in keeping with various practices of modern medical technology.

Critical Overview

Lawrence S. Friedman refers to "The Pagan Rabbi" as "a quintessential Ozick story." It was first published in *The Hudson Review* in 1966, and then in 1971 as the title piece in the first collection of Ozick's short stories, *The Pagan Rabbi and Other Stories*. Garnering extensive critical acclaim, this collection won the B'nai B'rith Jewish Heritage Award in 1971, The Jewish Book Council Award, and the Edward Lewis Wallant Memorial Award in 1972, and the American Academy of Arts and Letters Award in 1973. It was also nominated for a National Book Award in 1971. "The Pagan Rabbi" is included in the collection *Neurotica: Jewish Writers on Sex* (1999). Critics have consistently praised Ozick as a leading writer of short fiction. Five of Ozick's short stories have been included in the annual anthology, *The Best American Short Stories*, and three of her stories have won the O. Henry Award.

While critics haggle over whether or not Ozick, an Orthodox Jew, can only be understood as a Jewish-American writer, or if she is more accurately categorized in the larger canon of American writers, most agree on the central themes of Ozick's fiction: the place of the Jew in secular American society; the role of the writer in Jewish culture; and the lure of paganism or idolatry in opposition to Judaism. Ozick's first novel *Trust* (1966), which took her over six years to write, received only mild attention and mixed, lukewarm reviews. However, with the publication of *The Pagan Rabbi and Other Stories*, Victor Strandberg asserts that "Ozick makes the transition from being an 'American novelist' to being one of our foremost Jewish American story-tellers." Josephine Z. Knopp states that "Jewishness and Judaism are among Cynthia Ozick's central concerns as a writer." Strandberg states that "a master theme" of Ozick's work is "what, in this time and place, it means to be a Jew."

Gigliola Nocera concurs that Ozick's "main concern as a writer" is "the difficulty of being Jewish today." Sanford Pinkster points to the originality of Ozick's early work as a Jewish writer: "'The Pagan Rabbi' is so unlike any previous Jewish-American story one can think of that its central tension has become Ozick's signature." Pinkster claims that Ozick "has changed radically the way we define Jewish-American writing, and more important, the way Jewish-American writing defines itself." Elaine M. Kuavar, however, makes the case that the stories of Ozick should be understood in a broader context of American literature, claiming that "Cynthia Ozick's art is central to American literature, not peripheral to it."

Friedman states that "with the publication of her first volume of short fiction, Judaism is firmly established as the dominant force in Ozick's work." Friedman sees Ozick's Jewishness as central to her fiction: "Ozick observes the world through the eyes of a deeply committed Jew." He points to a central theme in her work, in which "opposing ideologies clash on the moral battleground of fictions peopled largely by contemporary Jews." These "opposing ideologies" are "conventional Judaism" in conflict with "whatever is not: paganism, Christianity, secularism." The lure of assimilation into mainstream American culture for the contemporary Jew is one focus of this theme. According to Friedman, in Ozick's fiction, "assimilation is anathema, involving as it does the yielding up of Jewish identity, the homogenization of Jewish uniqueness."

One of the most central and recurring conflicts in Ozick's fiction is that between Hellenism (Greek mythology) and Hebraism (Jewish theological doc-

trine). Critics have also referred to this conflict in Ozick's work as "Pan-versus-Moses." Friedman explains that: "In her fiction the Hellenism that spawned pagan gods repeatedly squares off against the Hebraism that invented monotheism. The battle between conflicting values is fought in the hearts and minds of Ozick's Jewish protagonists—all of whom can attain, maintain, or regain moral stature only in fidelity to Judaism." Friedman claims that "The Pagan Rabbi" is one of two of her "most powerful stories" that "illustrate[s] the surrender to pagan temptations associated with the Hellenistic world." Calling "The Pagan Rabbi" Ozick's "most inventive amalgam of the whimsical and the moralistic," Sarah Blacher Cohen concludes that "it stresses the injurious effects of choosing pagan aesthetics over Jewish ethics and spirituality." Closely associated with paganism is the worship of nature; as Friedman claims, "A recurring motif in Ozick's fiction is the opposition of pagan naturalism to Jewish traditional religious practice."

Idolatry, in opposition to the Second Commandment, is one of the most important recurring themes in Ozick's work. Friedman states that "in a typical Ozick story idol worship signifies moral transgression." Quoting from Ozick's essay "The Riddle of the Ordinary," Kuavar explains that, for Ozick "an idol" is "'anything that is allowed to come between ourselves and God. Anything that is *instead* of God.'" Sarah Blacher Cohen points out that "Ozick's characters fall prey to an alluring idolatry, with its false promise of fulfillment." Kuavar points out that "idolatry and idolaters abound" in Ozick's fiction.

Ozick's concern with idolatry has also affected her understanding of the role of the writer in Jewish culture. Friedman explains that "like any Jewish writer, Ozick is subject to the tension created by the sometimes antithetical demands of religion and art. To be a writer is to risk competing with the Creator, thereby drawing perilously close to what the Jew must shun . . . ." Such an act of creation in defiance of God is associated in Ozick's writing with the pagan worship of multiple gods, also a form of idolatry. Friedman states that "the fear that those who make art serve pagan gods instead of the Jewish God threads through Ozick's writing." Joseph Lowin explains that "for many years, Ozick has been asking herself, and us, how it is possible to be both Jewish and a writer. For her, the term 'Jewish writer' is an oxymoron—like 'pagan rabbi'—in which each half of the phrase is antithetical to the other . . ."

Critics agree that an awareness of Jewish history, particularly the Holocaust, is also central to Ozick's stories. Knopp states that:

> As with other Jewish-American writers who merit serious attention, Ozick's work displays an acute historical consciousness, an understanding of the role of Judaism in world history. Her Jewish stories earn that designation by virtue of a perspective shaped by the author's sense of Jewish history. They succeed in placing contemporary Jewish problems within their historical framework, thus illuminating the anomalies of modern Jewish life while at the same time revealing the significance for the present of the link with the Jewish past.

Critics have also made note of the "difficult" nature of Ozick's stories, from the perspective of the reader. Friedman states that "while her stories dealing with what it means to be Jewish understandably fail to achieve broad popular success, they have earned wide critical acclaim." Earl Rovit points out that, because of its "density, allusiveness, intellectual concern, and ambiguity," Ozick's body of work "presents formidable difficulties for its readers." He goes on to explain that "the typical Ozick tale is multilayered, deliberately skewed, and elusive in meaning."

In assessing Ozick's body of fiction as a whole, Strandberg sees her focus on Jewish themes as a strength in her literary achievement as an American writer:

> What matters in the end is the imaginative power to elevate local materials toward universal and timeless significance. By that standard, I judge Ozick's work to be memorably successful. Her variety and consistent mastery of styles; her lengthening caravan of original and unforgettably individualized characters; her eloquent dramatization through these characters of significant themes and issues; her absorbing command of dialogue and narrative structure; her penetrating and independent intellect undergirding all she writes—these characteristics of her art perform a unique service for her subject matter, extracting from her Jewish heritage a vital significance unlike that transmitted by any other writer. In the American tradition, Cynthia Ozick significantly enhances our national literature by so rendering Jewish culture.

Criticism

Liz Brent

Brent has a Ph.D. in American culture, specializing in cinema studies, from the University of Michigan. She is a freelance writer and teaches courses in American cinema. In the following essay, *Brent discusses the Jewish theological texts referred to in this story.*

Critics have noted that Cynthia Ozick's stories are difficult. This assessment is in part due to the erudite character of Ozick's literary style, which makes reference to literary, philosophical, and theological texts not necessarily familiar to the reader. In particular, there are many references to elements of religious doctrine, ritual, and observance practices specific to Judaism. The following essay provides a brief gloss of the key texts of Jewish theology referred to in "The Pagan Rabbi," and their significance to the story.

The narrator mentions that Isaac Kornfeld, the thirty-six year old rabbi whose suicide initiates the story, is a professor of Mishnaic history, who had published a "remarkable collection of responsa." To understand the significance of this, one must have a clear idea of the central texts of Judaism. The Torah refers to the first five books of the Old Testament, also called the Pentateuch (from the root "five"): Genesis, Exodus, Leviticus, Numbers, and Deuteronomy. The Torah is taken to be the text of God's revelation to Moses on Mount Sinai. The Torah in a Jewish synagogue is handwritten on parchment scrolls and kept in a special cabinet called an "ark," removed only for special rituals and holidays. The Mishna was the first written, codified text compiling an authoritative volume of the orally taught Jewish laws, rituals, and traditions to be recorded since the Torah. The Mishna was compiled over the course of two centuries by many scholars, and completed in the early third century, A.D. Two collections of commentary on the Mishna were later compiled in a volume called the Gemara or Talmud, completed in the fourth and fifth centuries, A.D. The Talmud also sometimes refers to the Mishna and Gemara together.

The Mishna is made up of six sections, each of which is divided into tractates (treatises). The first section, Zera'im ("Seeds"), is comprised of eleven tractates, which discuss daily prayer and religious laws regarding agriculture. The second section, Mo'ed ("Festival") is comprised of twelve tractates, which discuss the laws pertaining to ritual observance of the Sabbath and other religious holidays. The third section, Mahim ("Women"), is comprised of seven tractates, which discuss rituals and laws pertaining to marriage and divorce. The fourth section, Neziqin ("Damages") is comprised of ten tractates, which discuss civil and criminal laws.

What Do I Read Next?

- *The Pagan Rabbi and Other Stories* (1971) by Cynthia Ozick is the collection in which "The Pagan Rabbi" first appeared. This collection was the winner of many distinguished literary awards.

- *Fame and Folly: Essays* (1996) is a collection of Ozick's essays on other writers, collected from previous publications.

- *The Shawl* (1991) contains Ozick's most famous short story, "The Shawl," and the novella "Rosa," the sequel to "The Shawl."

- *Goodbye, Columbus and Five Short Stories* (1959) by Philip Roth contains a novella and short stories by one of the most noted Jewish-American writers of the century. It addresses themes of Jewish identity in modern American society.

- *A Cynthia Ozick Reader* (1996), edited by Elaine M. Kuavar, contains selections from previous publications of Ozick's essays and short stories.

- *The Best American Essays* (1998), edited and with an introduction by Cynthia Ozick, is the 1998 edition of the annual series Best American Essays, culled from nationally publicized journals and periodicals.

- *Mythology* (1942), by Edith Hamilton, is a comprehensive collection of ancient Greek mythology.

- *What is Jewish Literature?* (1994), edited and with an introduction by Hana Wirth-Nesher, is a collection of essays on Jewish literature by prominent Jewish writers. It includes the essay "America: Toward Yavneh" by Cynthia Ozick.

- *The God I Believe In* (1994), by Joshua O. Haberman, is a collection of interviews about Judaism by Jewish writers and scholars. It includes an interview with Cynthia Ozick.

Neziqin also includes the important prohibition on Idolatry (the worship of graven images), which is punishable by death. One of these seven tractates, *The Ethics of the Fathers*, provides guidance for a moral life that does not violate these laws. The fifth section, Qodashim ("Holy Things"), is comprised of eleven tractates, and discusses laws and rituals regarding the Temple of Jerusalem. The sixth section of the Mishna, Tohorot ("Purifications"), is divided into twelve tractates, and discusses laws and rituals of purification.

Further written commentary on the Talmud (the Mishna and the Germara), called responsa (written replies), developed in the seventh century. Responsa continue to be written (and published) in modern times, by learned rabbis. The character of rabbi Isaac Kornfeld, the pagan rabbi of Ozick's fictional story, as a scholar of Mishnaic history, has published more than one renowned volume of Responsa at the time of his suicide. The rabbi's apostasy, or moving away from Jewish faith, is all the more drastic in the context of his role as a scholar of Jewish law. For instance, the law against Idolatry, punishable by death, is discussed in the fourth section of the Mishna. The rabbi in the story, however, eventually gives in to "idolatry," as he feels compelled to worship Nature over God. Yet the rabbi's reasoning, as revealed in the letter that Sheindal, his widow, reads to the narrator, concludes that, as God resides in Nature, the worship of Nature is not idolatry at all, but merely an extension of the worship of God. Sheindal reads:

> It is false history, false philosophy and false religion which declare to us human ones that we live among Things. The arts of physics and chemistry begin to teach us differently, but their way of compassion is new, and finds few to carry fidelity to its logical and beautiful end. The molecules dance inside all forms, and within the molecules dance the atoms, and within the atoms dance still profounder sources of divine vitality. There is nothing that is Dead. There is no Non-life. Holy life subsists even in the stone, even in the bones of dead dogs and dead men. Hence in God's fecundating Creation there is no possibility of Idola-

"... it seems that the rabbi, in his thinking, is twisting a Jewish doctrine that clearly emphasizes 'one' god, into a justification for his developing pagan beliefs, which in fact completely violate Jewish doctrine."

try, and therefore no possibility of committing that so-called abomination.

The rabbi thus refers to Jewish doctrine to justify his violation of that very doctrine.

In the notebook found in the pocket of the rabbi after he hanged himself, the narrator finds passages from the Torah, the first five books of the Old Testament. The passages, scrawled in Hebrew, are "drawn mostly from Leviticus and Deuteronomy," the third and fifth books. One quote, which the narrator explains is "not quite verbatim," reads: "And the soul that turneth after familiar spirits to go a-whoring after them, I will cut him off from among his people."

This quote is significant to the story in that the rabbi, in fact, does eventually "turneth after familiar spirits" in the form of the spirit of Nature that he pursues in the park. He can further be said to "go a-whoring after them," as his obsession with the wood nymph takes on a distinctly sexual element. The rabbi, as a result of his direct violation of the laws of his religion, is spiritually "cut off from among his people." The alienation from his own religious community that resulted from the rabbi's foray into the worship of Nature, it is suggested, may have contributed to his eventual suicide.

The rabbi's theological and philosophical foray into the worship of Nature includes reference to Shekhina. Shekhina is a term, which in Jewish theology, refers to the presence of God in the world. It comes from the Hebrew meaning "presence" or "dwelling." Shekhina is sometimes used in place of the word for God in the Talmud. In Ozick's story, the rabbi mentions Shekhina twice. In one passage of the letter that Sheindal reads to the narrator, he mentions Shekhina in relation to the "coupling" of "mortals" with "gods."

An extraordinary thought emerged in me. It was luminous, profound, and practical. More than that, it had innumerable precedents; the mythologies had documented it a dozen times over. It recalled all those mortals reputed to have coupled with gods (a collective word, showing much common sense, signifying what our philosophers more abstrusely call Shekhina), and all that poignant miscegenation represented by centaurs, satyrs, mermaids, fauns, and so forth.

The rabbi's thought process, as recorded, is a process by which he justifies his own act of "coupling" with the Creature, a sort of goddess of Nature. These thoughts, however, represent a complete violation of Jewish theological doctrine, a central tenet of which is the existence of "one" god. The rabbi refers to "gods," which he then relates to Jewish theology, suggesting that Shekhina in fact represents a Jewish notion of multiple gods. One can only assume that there are complex theological discussions in rabbinical scholarship that address the significance of Shekhina, but at least at a fundamental level, it seems that the rabbi, in his thinking, is twisting a Jewish doctrine that clearly emphasizes "one" god, into a justification for his developing pagan beliefs, which in fact completely violate Jewish doctrine. This convoluted reasoning on the part of the rabbi leads up to his attempt to "copulate" with the "Creature" of the Nature goddess. He hopes, by this act, to "free my own soul from my body":

By all these evidences I was emboldened in my confidence that I was surely not the first man to conceive such a desire in the history of our earth. Creature, the thought that took hold of me was this: if only I could couple with one of the free souls, the strength of the connection would likely wrest my own soul from my body—seize it, as if by tongs, draw it out, so to say, to its own freedom. The intensity and force of my desire to capture one of these beings now became prodigious.

The rabbi comes to believe that through sexual union with the pagan Creature, or goddess of Nature, his soul will achieve transcendence. The rabbi successfully calls forth the Creature to satisfy his desire when he evokes the name of Shekhina. "As the sons of God came to copulate with women, so now let a daughter of Shekhina the Emanation reveal herself to me. Nymph, come now, come now." Again, the rabbi uses the term Shekhina, which refers to the Jewish belief in the presence of "one" God, in order to address the purely pagan and multiple spirit of Nature, a concept totally in violation of Jewish doctrine. The rabbi then describes an ecstatic sexual experience, in which he ''couples'' with what seems to be ''some sinewy animal.'' The rabbi is fully aware that this would be a violation of Jewish law, stating that he ''believed I was defiled, as it is written: 'Neither shalt thou lie with any beast.''' But, when he finally sees the Creature, which appears as a form combining features of an adolescent girl and those of a plant or flower, the rabbi justifies his encounter by exclaiming that ''scripture does not forbid sodomy with the plants.''

The rabbi describes a series of nights of passionate copulation with the plant nymph, until, one night, she tells him that his body no longer contains his soul. She points to a man walking on the road, wearing a prayer shawl and carrying ''some huge and terrifying volume, heavy as stone,'' which turns out to be ''a Tractate. A Tractate of the Mishnah.'' (A prayer shawl, also called a talith, is traditionally worn by Jewish men, wrapped around the shoulders, during prayer.) The nymph flees, and the rabbi approaches the man, who admits to being the rabbi's soul. The rabbi's devotion to the study of Jewish theology in books is markedly contrasted to his sexual coupling with the pagan Creature of Nature. The rabbi asks his soul ''if he intended to go with his books through the whole future without change, always with his Tractate in his hand, and he answered that he could do nothing else.'' The rabbi then unwraps the prayer shawl from the man who is his soul, and hangs himself with it from a tree.

The implications of ''The Pagan Rabbi'' for Jewish religious identity cannot be reduced to any one simple or indisputable moral. However one may conclude that the rabbi, through his pagan worship of Nature, loses his Jewish soul. Having strayed from his study of Jewish theology, in the texts of the Tractates of the Mishna, into the pagan realm of Nature, the rabbi is no longer able to turn back to his faith. Abandoning his soul, the rabbi chooses death.

Source: Liz Brent, Critical Essay on ''The Pagan Rabbi,'' in *Short Stories for Students*, The Gale Group, 2001.

Elaine M. Kauvar

In the following essay, Kauvar explores thematic links between Ozick's novel Trust *and the stories in* The Pagan Rabbi. *In particular, Kauvar finds that Ozick continues ''the battle between Hebraism and Hellinism, the artists' dilemma'' in ''The Pagan Rabbi.''*

Faced with divergent paths at the end of her voyage, the narrator of *Trust* follows neither of them; they remain on the same plane of her vision. But they are pursued in *The Pagan Rabbi*, Cynthia Ozick's first collection of stories. Each tale in the volume has its counterpart; each provides a different perspective, records a disparate experience. The dialectical structure of Ozick's first novel shapes not only the individual stories in *The Pagan Rabbi* but the structure of the volume itself. Informed by the storyteller's duplicate vision, the collection revives the themes present in *Trust*, often pairing them within a single tale or else matching them in two separate tales. That juxtaposition of conflicting ideas, like the narrator's reflection in the divided mirror in *Trust*, gives back a dual image of the self, the artist's sense of all identity. The controlling principle for the entire collection, Ozick's penchant for doubling had already evinced itself in the unpublished novel *Mercy, Pity, Peace, and Love* and in the evocative sketch ''The Butterfly and the Traffic Light,'' which grew out of that novel and which was published five years before *Trust*.

History is crucial for the narrator of *Trust*, and history makes an immediate appearance in the first paragraph of ''The Butterfly and the Traffic Light,'' in which Jerusalem serves as a contrast to the places ''where time has not yet deigned to be an inhabitant.'' A ''phoenix city'' with a ''history of histories,'' a city where ''no one is a stranger,'' Jerusalem illuminates the true meaning of the past rather than the fabricated one exemplified in the midwestern American town that is the story's setting. Wanting the college town to have historical allusions, the mayor named one of the town's streets after the ''Bigghe diaries,'' a traveling salesman's forged records. And Big Road, as it came to be spelled, occasions Fishbein's lectures to Isabel. In them are elements bridging *Trust* to *The Pagan Rabbi*, adumbrations of its central thematic concerns, and two of its controlling metaphors.

One metaphor arises from the ''doubleness that clung to the street,'' the doppelgänger every person and every object owns. That ''insistent sense of recognition''—the dawning of the creative process, the birth of metaphor—immediately becomes attached to the Hebraism-and-Hellenism issue in Isabel and Fishbein's ensuing argument. For Fishbein the uniformity of lampposts in America evinces its dreary sameness, the diverse lampposts in Europe its individuality. But Isabel sees them as ''some kind of religious icon'' belonging to an ''advanced religion,'' monotheism. Hers is an opinion Fishbein

> The distinction between Isaac's soul and Isaac's body-- a young body inhabited by an old man, one resembling the rabbi's father--suggests the ambivalence existing between generations and reflects the dissension between the artist and tradition."

disputes: "The index of advancement is flexibility. Human temperaments are so variable, how could one God satisfy them all? The Greeks and Romans had a god for every personality." The Jews' refusal to obey Antiochus IV's decree "to set up a statue of Zeus on the altar of the Temple of Jerusalem" caused the Maccabean War, but that "altogether unintelligible occasion," Fishbein tells Isabel, came "of missing an imagination," of not accommodating "Zeus *and* God under one roof," of forcing icons to be alike. To the Jews' determination to uphold monotheism in the face of severe opposition Fishbein attributes an absence of imagination: he conjures up the argument Enoch Vand and Nick Tilbeck have over personal values and abstractions.

The second metaphor emerges in one of Fishbein's lectures: "Looking at butterflies gives pleasure. Yes, it is a kind of joy . . . but full of poison. It belongs to the knowledge of rapid death. The butterfly lures us not only because he is beautiful, but because he is transitory. The caterpillar is uglier, but in him we can regard the better joy of becoming. The caterpillar's fate is bloom. The butterfly's is waste." An affirmation of process, Fishbein's metaphors recall Baeck's explanation of classical religion and echo Keats's idea of beauty in the "Ode on Melancholy." There the death-moth is linked to Psyche, whose emblem Fishbein adopts. His name and his allusion to Psyche invoke Venus, the role the goddess of love played in the Cupid and Psyche story. As in *Trust*, that goddess is implicated in the creative act. And the story's epigraph—"the moth for the star"—suggests Isabel, whose name resembles that of the American moth Isabella, as the

devotee of "something afar," of Shelley's muse Urania. Yoking these allusions, Ozick proclaims the process of becoming, the "work as it goes," superior to the finality of completion. In the confluence of her references resides the battle between Hebraism and Hellenism, the artist's dilemma and a major conflict in "The Pagan Rabbi."

In that later story Ozick explores the consequences of what Fishbein deems a "harmless affair": bringing Zeus together with God. Whereas in *Trust* and "The Butterfly and the Traffic Light" the dichotomy between Judaism and paganism is represented by two separate characters, in "The Pagan Rabbi" the conflict is an internal one—a rabbi's wrenching struggle to reconcile his attraction to two utterly disparate and discordant ways of life. Rabbi Isaac Kornfeld's predicament, like the narrator's quest in *Trust*, is broadened to include cultural and historical contentions as well. Not only does the tale provide three distinct perspectives on the same situation, not only does it afford a series of ideas and situations which are doubled and divided, it connects the turmoil suffered by the rabbi to the disquiet endured by the artist.

Like *Trust*, "The Pagan Rabbi" has an unnamed first-person narrator who seeks a solution to a mystery, the reason why Isaac Kornfeld hanged himself on a tree in a public park. But as the narrator of Ozick's first novel knows, facts are not enough; they must be judged by history. And it is to history the narrator of "The Pagan Rabbi" turns to recount the events in his life and to describe his relationship with Isaac Kornfeld. Fathers loom as large in this tale as they do in *Trust*, and their presence throughout *The Pagan Rabbi* testifies to their vital and continuing importance to Ozick's fiction. Where in *Trust* Ozick reports the narrator's quest for a father, in *The Pagan Rabbi* she emphasizes the strife between generations. That tension is manifest in "The Pagan Rabbi," in which two sons comply with their fathers' choices of careers and attend a rabbinical seminary but have reactions to their training that diverge from their fathers' expectations. Isaac's experience differed from the narrator's as well, for the seminary that recognized Isaac's "imagination was so remarkable he could concoct holiness out of the fine line of a serif," was the same seminary in which the narrator discovered he had no talent. Neither father regarded Greek philosophy as anything but an "abomination." Judging Socrates a "monotheist," Isaac's father nonetheless believed philosophy to be the corridor to idolatry; the narrator's father vowed philosophy brought his son to atheism and determined him to withdraw from the seminary. His subsequent marriage to a gentile was an occasion for his father to mourn his son as if dead. A lapsed Jew, the narrator furnishes one of the three perspectives on the events in the tale.

Driven to know the entire story of Isaac Kornfeld's suicide, the narrator journeys to Trilham's Inlet to see the tree on which a pious Jew saw fit to end his life. A powerful symbol of both Hebraism and Hellenism, the oak tree revives the tree in *Trust*, and the bay surrounding Trilham's Inlet is reminiscent of the filth at Duneacres: "filled with sickly clams and a bad smell," its water "covered half the city's turds." The cut up pieces of trees, the "deserted monuments" in the park—these recall the dilapidated garden in which the narrator of *Trust* first sees her father. In the garden and in the public park are blasted paradises—the lost idyllic Arcadia, the fallen Garden of Eden. If in *Trust* the daughter's hopes are dashed upon meeting Tilbeck, here the rabbi's crumble in the wake of deviating from a father's established beliefs. The rabbi's name embodies the conflict central to the story: Isaac refers to the trust the biblical son placed in his father and "Kornfeld" alludes to Demeter, the Greek goddess of fertility. But in "The Pagan Rabbi," it is the failure of the son to trust the father's tradition and the rabbi's attraction to Hellenism that ultimately prove destructive. The conjunction of the two names, like the double implications of the oak tree, emphasize the coexistence of two desires which must forever remain embattled. Specifically associated with important biblical events and people, the oak was sacred to Zeus; and linking the tree's roots and the toes of a gryphon Ozick evokes a Greek tree of life, for gryphons function as guardians of immortality, of what is sacred, powerful, or omniscient. Explicitly forbidden in Deuteronomy, however, is the worship of trees: "you shall tear down their altars, and dash in pieces their pillars, and burn their Asherim with fire; you shall hew down the graven images of their gods, and destroy their name out of that place." Serried with allusive and contradictory significance, the oak which the narrator describes at the beginning of the story and on which Isaac hangs himself functions as a hieroglyph of the tale just as the tree in the swamp constitutes an emblem of "Duneacres."

And as the rain, which brings revelation in *Trust*, begins to fall, the narrator of "The Pagan Rabbi" recognizes himself as "a man in a photograph standing next to a gray blur of tree," a man who "would stand through eternity beside Isaac's guilt if [he] did not run." A lapsed Jew whose father died without ever speaking to his son again, the narrator identifies with Isaac's guilt: the photograph, a representation of truth, implies both men have partaken of forbidden fruit. As if to rectify that sin, the narrator runs to the woman he once loved, to the woman Isaac Kornfeld married—the woman born in a concentration camp. About to be thrown against an electrified fence, Sheindel was saved by the vanishing current, a seemingly magical intervention by God. Unlike Isaac and Sheindel's, the narrator's marriage to a gentile was childless and ended in divorce. The histories of the men, their careers as a rabbi and a bookseller, locate one man at the center of Judaism and the other at its fringes. Isaac Kornfeld, an authority on the Mishnah (the oral code of Law), was also a writer who contributed significant responsa answers to questions on halakhic (law) topics. But his was a frenzied path to achievement, as his favorite authors, Saadia Gaon and Nietzsche, attest: one a specialist in biblical study, the other an enthusiast of the ideals of Greece, the two writers represent Isaac's antithetical passions.

The opposition between Sheindel and the narrator, however, is implied by their positions at her dining table "as large as a desert" and "divided . . . into two nations" by a lace cloth. As it does in *Trust*, the division into halves invokes contrary perspectives. Speaking "as if every word emitted a quick white thread of great purity," Sheindel scorns Isaac's reading "about runners with hats made of leaves," the bedtime stories that gave to animals and nature human life, the rabbi's insistence on a "little grove" for the location of their picnics. Her derision of his darkly inventive stories—"stupid and corrupt" fairy tales "full of spirits, nymphs, gods, everything ordinary and old"—adds yet another reference to Isaac's imagination and reveals Sheindel to be, as the narrator observes, "one of those born to dread imagination." One of those born to exalt imagination, Rabbi Isaac Kornfeld writes stories like an artist inspired by a Greek muse.

Of the notebook containing what Sheindel believes is the reason for her husband's suicide, the narrator concludes, "it was all a disappointment." In fact, the notebook affords important and indispensable clues: extracts from Leviticus and Deuteronomy, a "snatch of Byron, a smudge of Keats . . . a pair of truncated lines from Tennyson," and an unidentified quatrain. Passages from the Bible vie with lines from English Romantic poetry and references to the classics, revealing the rabbi's unspoken desire: to reconcile a love of nature with belief in Torah. The very description of the notebook—its "wrinkled leaves," the handwriting that fills it, "oddly formed" like that of a man who is "leaning on a bit of bark"—recall Tilbeck's "wild" handwriting. To determine the tree's age, Isaac thinks of "counting the rings" just as he imagines his age "may be ascertained by counting the rings under his poor myopic eyes." The alliance between the writer of the notebook and the male muse intimates the relationship of writing and paganism. His affiliation of self and tree yokes the Mishnaic scholar to nature. That he has edited the extracts from Deuteronomy and Leviticus in transcribing them indicates a wish to alter their meaning, for they concern the renewal of the Covenant and the penalties for violating its laws. From Deuteronomy Isaac has copied, "He shall utterly destroy all the places of the gods, upon the high mountains, and upon the hills, and under every green tree." His version leaves out the injunction to burn the Asherim, to cut down graven images, to root out their name. An extract from Leviticus follows: "And the soul that turneth after familiar spirits to go awhoring after them, I will cut him off from among his people." Reminding himself of God's commandment, Isaac is then driven to record the penalty for breaking God's commandment.

Unable to penetrate Isaac's preoccupations, the narrator judges the unidentified quatrain in the notebook "cloying and mooning and ridiculous." But the quatrain's last line, "The beauty of the earth is haunted still," precedes the description of the tree, a *Quercus velutina*. An Australian she-oak, it is the spirit with whom Isaac falls in love and from whose branches he hangs himself. Below the passage appears the deliberately legible announcement, "Great Pan lives." Including fragments written in Greek, Hebrew, and English, the tiny notebook presents the "Pan Versus Moses" case in miniature. It begins with the consequences of transgression and ends with a firm declaration; Isaac Kornfeld implies that the Greek cult of nature and beauty should not be reviled by the Hebrew lawgiver, that Moses need not oppose Pan. That idea alludes to one in "The Last of the Valerii" and anticipates the fate of Isaac and Sheindel's marriage: in James's story the Count forsakes his wife for a statue and "communion with the great god Pan." The Count's desires are echoed in Isaac's letter, which is read aloud by Sheindel when the narrator returns the notebook, secretly angry at having been cheated.

Written on "large law-sized paper," the letter of self-explanation contains proofs; it resembles in form Isaac's responsa.

To choose that form to express a powerful attraction to nature is to endeavor to bring what amounts to paganism under the aegis of Judaism. And Judaism impels the rabbi to return to "human history," to his personal history: "At a very young age I understood that a foolish man would not believe in a fish had he not had one enter his experience. Innumerable forms exist and have come to our eyes . . . from this minute perception of what already is, it is easy to conclude that further forms are possible, that all forms are probable." His apprehension of forms precedes his pantheistic celebration of nature, the subsistence of "holy life" in "God's fecundating Creation." Once the immanence of God is acknowledged, the threat of transgressing the Second Commandment vanishes. What Isaac disputes is not the injunction against idolatry but the possibility of committing idolatry: if Divinity resides in nature, worship of its beauty should yield an expanded proclamation of God's glory, not a violation of His Divine fiat. The rabbi's argument is reminiscent of the one propounded by Spinoza, to whom Ozick refers in the story. The immanence of God, that philosopher maintained, was a principle of the law: "It was Spinoza who first dared to cross these boundaries [of tradition], and by the skillful use of weapons accumulated in the arsenals of philosophy itself he succeeded in bringing both God and man under the universal rule of nature and thus establishing its unity." But Spinoza's insistence upon the absolute unity of body and soul is denied by Isaac's assertion: "To see one's soul is to know all, to know all is to own the peace our philosophies futilely envisage. Earth displays two categories of soul: the free and the indwelling. We human ones are cursed with the indwelling." His divergence from talmudic belief and his compulsion to unify discordant ideas is revealed in the revision Isaac attempts of the Platonic theory of Forms and Plato's concept of the soul.

Interested more in humanity than in nature and believing the entire human being was active in history, talmudic Judaism declared body and soul inseparable. That monistic doctrine opposes Platonic dualism, in which the task of philosophy is to liberate the body from the soul. In the *Phaedo*, Socrates tells Simmias that "it is only those who practise philosophy in the right way . . . who always most want to free the soul; and this release and separation of the soul from the body is the preoccupation of the philosophers." But the soul, Socrates contended, belongs to an invisible realm and is imperceptible. That is the realm Isaac proclaims visible, the sight of it divine wisdom. Disputing Spinoza's conviction that Moses was ignorant of nature, Isaac concludes, "Moses never spoke to [our ancestors] of the free souls, lest the people not do God's will and go out from Egypt." Since the existence of free souls was a secret kept from him, Isaac only accidentally discovered a Platonic Form, what Tilbeck called "Sacred Beauty."

It becomes incarnated in "Loveliness," to whom Isaac has addressed his letter and who is its subject. Proof of her existence is the "shape of a girl" whom he saw wading among his seven daughters in a stream and who exemplified, as Sheindel comments bitterly, the "principle" the rabbi habitually found "to cover" his proofs. And the memory of ample precedents for mortals "reputed to have coupled with gods," Isaac explains, emboldened his desire to "couple with one of the free souls" so as to liberate his soul from his body. In an erotic passage that recalls the one in *Trust*, Ozick describes the reaction Isaac has to his union with a dryad: "Meanwhile, though every tissue of my flesh was gratified in its inmost awareness, a marvelous voluptuousness did not leave my body; sensual exultations of a wholly supreme and paradisal order, unlike anything our poets have ever defined, both flared and were intensely satisfied in the same moment." As in *Trust*, the sexual act occurs in a place befouled by filth and decay. But satiety brings in its wake the conviction of having been "defiled," the memory of Leviticus: "Neither shalt thou lie with any beast." But a dryad is not an animal, and the dryad with whom Isaac discovers he has coupled claims she would refuse a man wishing "only to inhabit [her] out of perversity or boastfulness or to indulge a dreamed-of disgust"; to which Isaac responds, "Scripture does not forbid sodomy with plants." The rabbi judges his lust for Nature with his knowledge of the Law: he attempts to bring paganism into accord with Judaism.

But the two are asymptotes and can never meet. That the rabbi's belief in *halakhah* is incompatible with the wish to abandon himself to Nature emerges in the extraordinarily imaginative interchange between Isaac and the dryad. The embodiment of paganism, the dryad Iripomoňoéià, "who shed her own light" and who plays with language, brings back the tree in the swamp at Duneacres and the narrator's dislike of words-in-themselves. As the dryad near the cottage at Brighton augured Tilbeck's disappearance, Iripomoňoéià anticipates Isaac's disappearance. The rabbi, she observes, has "spoiled" himself "with confusions"; in its separation from his soul, his body will become "crumpled and withered and ugly," the very antithesis of Sacred Beauty. It is the very antithesis of everything moral: "'Where you have pain, we have ugliness. Where you profane yourselves by immorality, we are profaned by ugliness.'" By its very nature, the dryad explains, paganism is "all-of-a-sudden"; like Nick's name, "it goes too quick." Of Isaac's soul, the soul of a Jew, Iripomoňoéià complains: "I do not like that soul of yours. It conjures against me. It denies me, it denies every spirit and all my sisters and every nereid of the harbor, it denies all our multiplicity, and all gods diversiform, it spites even Lord Pan, it is an enemy."

Such a soul cannot survive among diversiform gods, nor can it worship Beauty. What the rabbi struggles to bring into consonance must perforce remain asunder, as the confrontation between Isaac Kornfeld and his soul reveals. An ugly old man wrapped in a drooping prayer shawl, his soul trudges along a road reading a tractate of the Mishnah with such absorption that the beauty of the field eludes him. Once desiring to see his own soul, Isaac now rejects it; it cares "only to be bound to the Law." Divided from his body, Isaac's soul declares the dryad has "no real existence," that it was not the soul of Isaac "who clung to her" but his body. In angry despair, Isaac seizes his soul and shakes it, but it confronts him with the truth of his existence: "The sound of the Law . . . is more beautiful than the crickets. The smell of the Law is more radiant than the moss. The taste of the Law exceeds clear water." In contradiction with himself and unable to accept his own soul, Isaac Kornfeld hangs himself with his prayer shawl on the branches of the oak whose spirit he believed would grant him immortality.

This clash between opposing aspects of the self is implicit in the story's title and in the rabbi's name. Worship of Pan cannot subsist alongside obedience to Moses: a rabbi cannot be a pagan. The idea that Form must either retreat or perish at the advance of its opposite is set forth in the *Phaedo*, which Ozick reveals is at odds with Isaac Kornfeld's desire—a reflection of talmudic monism. In her essay on James's *The Sacred Fount*, "The Jamesian Parable," published shortly after she finished *Trust* and three years before "The Pagan Rabbi," Ozick defines the meaning of self-contradiction: "He who desires to change himself, negates the integrity—the entelechy—of his personality." To be in contradiction with oneself is to be "unreal" and unreality leads to "moral self-cancellation." Lured by the beauty of paganism and owning a Jewish soul, Isaac engages in an act of moral self-cancellation; and as the fragment he copied from Leviticus warns, he is "cut off from among his people."

That punishment in Leviticus is the one inflicted on Tithonus. Granted immortality when Eos asked Zeus to bestow it on him, Tithonus was doomed to eternal decrepitude because Eos forgot to ask for everlasting youth; however, he changed himself into a cicada and continued his existence apart from human life. Wanting to couple with Nature, Isaac remembered "Cadmus, Rhoecus, Tithonus, Endymion." But the rabbi forgot that radical isolation results from the negation of entelechy; he turns "after familiar spirits" and is severed from his people. That fate explains why his soul prefers the sound of the Law to that of the cricket. Both Isaac and Tithonus wither, but Tennyson's Tithonus asks:

> Why should a man desire in any way
> To vary from the kindly race of men,
> Or pass beyond the goal of ordinance
> Where all should pause, as is most meet for all.

Ravished by Nature, Isaac wanders outside the Law, and in the process, varies from the ordained source of life—the Torah, Israel's Tree of Life. The epigraph to "The Pagan Rabbi," a maxim from *Pirke Avot*, renders Isaac's story in brief: "Rabbi Jacob said: 'He who is walking along and studying, but then breaks off to remark, "How lovely is that tree" or "How beautiful is that fallow field!"'—Scripture regards such a one as having hurt his own being.'" That following Pan can destroy human existence is evident in the deaths of Isaac Kornfeld and Gustave Nicholas Tilbeck, for both men perish before their lives reach natural completion.

Adherence to Mosaic law in "The Pagan Rabbi" is represented by Sheindel. Contrasting images buttress the conflict between Isaac's notion of Judaism and Sheindel's. The oak tree and the Torah as the Tree of Life, the Fence of the Law and the fence of the concentration camp epitomize the dichotomy between Hebraism and Hellenism, between life and death. And Isaac's reference to the animism that existed as a "historical illumination" within the Fence of the Law alludes to the pantheistic tendencies in the Kabbalah and other forms of Jewish mysticism that were opposed by traditional, rational Judaism—the kind of Judaism to which Sheindel adheres. She has kept pure the Fence Isaac scales. His choice of Sheindel represents his Hebraism, the dryad his Hellenism—the difference between the sacred and the profane. Surrounded by the Fence of the Law, Isaac partakes of God's holy fecundity—his seven children who are reminders of God's creation.

On the other side of that Fence is the sterility of the narrator's life. Unnamed and unattached, the narrator remains as cut off as Isaac becomes from his own people. The men began their journey to that predicament in the same rabbinical seminary from which they followed two paths: one led to God's manifestation everywhere, the other to His absence altogether. Though both Isaac and the narrator loved Sheindel, neither stays with her. The attraction to Nature proves too powerful for the rabbi, and he avoids his wife to capture a dryad. The narrator, however, has divorced his wife and intends to marry Isaac's widow. But her "unforgiving" voice, her pitiless derision of her husband, the "terror of her cough, which was unmistakably laughter"—these determine the narrator not to return to Sheindel, who is as different from him as she was from Isaac. What she deems a superfluity of imagination, a "choking vine on the Fence of the Law," the narrator regards as "possibility," "inspiration," insight. To her claim that her husband was an "illusion," the narrator responds, "'Only the pitiless are illusory,'" and advises her to go to the park to "consult" Isaac's soul. But at home he drops "three green house plants down the toilet" as she had given hers away to rid her house of "little trees." His gesture suggests he shares Sheindel's horror at Isaac's crossing the boundaries of Judaism into paganism even though the narrator has lived outside those boundaries. Where he will go in the future, whether he will climb over the fence to Judaism is a question Ozick characteristically leaves unanswered.

A story that dramatizes the warring drives in a human being, the simultaneous desires to follow Hebraism and Hellenism, the discord between rational mainstream Judaism and its mystical components, "The Pagan Rabbi" itself has a structure that reflects conflict: each character has an opposite, each idea an antithesis. Dividing ideas and characters, Ozick then doubles events by matching them. In her vision of the doubleness that clings to all existence is glimpsed the complexity of human life.

If "The Pagan Rabbi" concerns the cleavage between Pan and Moses, the tale dramatizes the unconscious battle between father and son and the searing conflicts awakened in the Jewish artist. But those conflicts are not confined to Jewish writers. If Isaac Kornfeld "brings to mind I. B. Singer's Yasha Mazur," he also conjures up Henry James's Mark Ambient in "The Author of Beltraffio." In turn, Ambient's wife Beatrice and Sheindel judge their husbands' writing products of paganism. And the description Mark Ambient offers of the rift between him and his wife pertains to Isaac and Sheindel as well:

> The difference between us is simply the opposition between two distinct ways of looking at the world, which have never succeeded in getting on together, or in making any kind of common household, since the beginning of time. They've borne all sorts of names, and my wife would tell you it's the difference between Christi and Pagan. . . . She thinks me at any rate no better than an ancient Greek.

It is also the difference between Jew and Pagan. The inventiveness that produces Isaac Kornfeld's letter of self-explanation, a luminous narrative, establishes the rabbi as a writer who ushers his readers into an unknown world, one he imagines and creates. As the narrator of *Trust* observes, "whether a letter is more substantial than a chapter is moot." Conjuring a realm where all of nature becomes an animated manifestation of God, Isaac Kornfeld fashions Nature into the image of God forbidden to monotheism. The Rabbi becomes the Creator's rival. In opposition with his own soul which embraces Holy Law, Isaac Kornfeld hungers after the beauty of Nature to which he attributes holiness. Two impulses contrast and collide: one impulse wants to maintain the tradition handed to the son by the father at the same time that another impulse seeks revision of that tradition. The distinction between Isaac's soul and Isaac's body—a young body inhabited by an old man, one resembling the rabbi's father—suggests the ambivalence existing between generations and reflects the dissension between the artist and tradition. Whether for a Jew or a Christian, the gulf between Hebraism and Hellenism abides, and as the narrators of Ozick's and James's stories learn, is "well-nigh bottomless." The first in a collection of stories which in their deepest grain concern artists, "The Pagan Rabbi" focuses on the Jewish artist.

Source: Elaine M. Kauvar, "The Insistent Sense of Recognition," in *Cynthia Ozick's Fiction: Tradition and Invention*, Indiana University Press, 1993, pp. 40–49.

Lawrence S. Friedman

In the following essay, Friedman explores Ozick's rendering of Jewish identity and religion in "The Pagan Rabbi."

At the end of *Trust*, Enoch Vand (né Adam Gruenhorn) begins the arduous process of turning himself back into a Jew. Under the tutelage of a bearded Holocaust survivor whose concentration camp number, tattooed on his forearm, "was daily covered by phylacteries" Vand studies Hebrew. After devoting three years to reading the entire Bible in Hebrew, he finishes *The Ethics of the Fathers* in two months and is ready to take up the Talmud when *Trust* ends. Jewish authenticity—embodied in his teacher's beard, tattoo, and prayer implements no less than in Hebrew and holy texts—is Vand's goal as it will eventually prove to be Ozick's dominant theme. Coming as it does at the end of a novel begun "for the Gentiles" and finished for the Jews, Vand's self-willed conversion parallels Ozick's own deliberate transition from an American novelist to a Jewish storyteller. By 1970 she had jettisoned the "religion of Art" for "liturgical" writing in which aesthetic niceties would take a back seat to Jewish values. Fueled by "moral imagination," Ozick's fiction would henceforth resonate with a "communal voice: the echo of the voice of the Lord of History."

While not all of the writing in *The Pagan Rabbi and Other Stories* (1971) satisfies the demands of the "liturgical," Ozick signals her commitment to a predominantly religious point of view by making "The Pagan Rabbi" —the volume's most deeply Jewish fiction—its title story. Anticipating the theme of "The Pagan Rabbi" (1966), however, is "The Butterfly and the Traffic Light" (1961), the earliest story in the collection. Published in the midst of her prodigious labors (1957–63) on *Trust*, this brief sketch rehearses Ozick's fuller treatment of Jewish identity in "The Pagan Rabbi" ever as it testifies to the long gestation of what is to become her dominant theme. The contrast between Jerusalem, where street names "have been forgotten a thousand years," and American cities, where only street names impose centrality upon formlessness, functions as a prelude to the slight main action of "The Butterfly and the Traffic Light." That action consists merely of Fishbein and Isabel conversing in the course of a walk down Big Road, the blandly named main thoroughfare of an unnamed city that could be Anywhere, USA. Fishbein, a Jewish intellectual, is

> " Thus his dropping out of the seminary, marrying and divorcing a Gentile, alienating his father--all conventional indices of apostasy--are writ large in Isaac's definitive transgression. As is often the case in Jewish literature, erudition begets doubt, doubt apostasy."

ill at ease in the society of this midwestern university town. To this "imitation of a city" he opposes the world's ancient and fabled capitals which he vociferously prefers. And because Jerusalem, quintessentially Jewish, is invoked as the epitome of the city hallowed by history and the antithesis of the anonymous American city, invariably Gentile, Fishbein's advocacy seems tantamount to Jewish affiliation.

The first of the story's two central metaphors reinforces Fishbein's apparent Jewishness: although he is attracted to the strolling girls in their summer dresses who sprout "like tapestry blossoms" on the sidewalks, he likens them to the transitory butterfly whose fate is waste. Beautiful but ephemeral, the butterfly compares unfavorably to the uglier caterpillar in which "we can regard the better joy of becoming." If butterfly and caterpillar alike are metaphors for art—the former signifying the finished work, the latter the creative process—then Fishbein may simply be expressing an aesthetic preference. But if the "better joy" relates to the liturgical; if, in other words, butterfly and caterpillar stand respectively for profane and sacred art, then Fishbein's preference is at least as religious (i.e., Jewish) as it is aesthetic. The second metaphor of the title is less ambiguous, and it is in Fishbein's reaction to Isabel's likening of a redundant traffic light over Big Road to "some kind of religious icon with a red and a green eye" that his essential antipathy to Judaism is revealed. Stressing their

sameness, Fishbein denies that traffic lights could ever be icons, since "What kind of religion would it be which had only one version of its deity?." "An advanced religion. I mean a monotheistic one," replies Isabel, symbolically invoking Judaism as the religion which in its transcendent achievement gave birth to monotheism. Fishbein denies the intrinsic superiority of monotheism, arguing for the accommodation of "Zeus *and* God under one roof." Although he is himself a Jew, if only a nominal one, Fishbein maintains that "only the Jews and their imitators . . . insist on a rigid unitarian God." Attracted to the many gods of classical antiquity, he denies the essence of Judaism and his own Jewishness (not "we Jews" but "the Jews" believe inflexibly in one God). In Fishbein, Ozick invokes for the first time the apostate Jew, a recurring figure in her later fiction. "The Butterfly and the Traffic Light" thus foreshadows more exhaustive treatments of her overarching theme—Jewish identity— and hints at her primary strategy—the Hellenism/ Hebraism dichotomy—for expressing it.

The title of "The Pagan Rabbi" rehearses the clash of opposing theologies that the story dramatizes. Just as "pagan" is incompatible with "rabbi," so passion for nature is incompatible with Judaism. That Ozick's rabbi eddies perilously between Jewish and pagan belief is betrayed by his name—an unlikely mingling of the biblical (Isaac) with the pantheistic (Kornfeld). Nor are the oppositions of "The Pagan Rabbi" confined to title or a name: the entire story is grounded in a series of similar contrasts between what is Jewish and what is not. Even before the story opens, its epigraph—about breaking off studying to remark upon the beauty of nature—previews its central dichotomy. Drawn from *The Ethics of the Fathers* (one of the Hebrew texts read by Enoch Vand apropos of reasserting his Jewishness at the end of *Trust*) the epigraph sounds a cautionary note in judging its erring rabbi: "Scripture regards such a one as having hurt his own being." The fathers of Isaac and the narrator, themselves rabbis, echo the epigraph in their belief that philosophy is a "corridor" to the ultimate "abomination"—idolatry. Implicit in the fathers' warnings is their certainty that moral peril lurks just beyond the Jewish pale. Both Isaac's suicide and the narrator's apostasy result from the philosophical waywardness that led them respectively to pantheism and atheism. Jewish literature abounds with stories of sons who stray from the ethics of the fathers, invariably with disastrous results. The Faustian strain—potentially heroic for Gentiles—that manifests itself most often in a fever to enlarge or transgress the boundaries of the traditional—is anathema to pious Jews. A classic account of the wages of intellectual hubris is given by Isaac Bashevis Singer in his massive novel *The Family Moskat*. In the aimless and futile career of Asa Heshel Bannet, another rabbi's son, Singer traces the many dislocations that eventually come to symbolize the breakdown of traditional values and the breakup of the Jewish family and community, and even to foreshadow the ultimate chaos of the Holocaust. While "The Pagan Rabbi" ostensibly focuses on the fate of a single erring Jew, it reverberates with the same fear for the fate of all Jews, the narrator included.

Isaac Kornfeld's suicide—a radical example of the self-destructive action of Rabbi Jacob's nature worshiper in the epigraph—is announced in the first sentence of "The Pagan Rabbi." Thereafter "The Pagan Rabbi" evolves into a kind of detective story: the narrator, in quest of understanding, goes first to Trilham's Inlet, the site of the suicide; then to Sheindel, Isaac's widow. To learn why Isaac hanged himself is to learn what sort of man Isaac had become, and thereby to unlearn what had formerly passed for the truth about Isaac. Not surprisingly, the process of discovery leads the narrator into a series of reappraisals of his friend's life that reveal hitherto unsuspected affinities with his own. Thus his dropping out of the seminary, marrying and divorcing a Gentile, alienating his father—all conventional indices of apostasy—are writ large in Isaac's definitive transgression. As is often the case in Jewish literature, erudition begets doubt, doubt apostasy. From sacred texts Isaac branches out to profane literature, eventually to embrace the Spinozist heresy: that reality is one substance with an infinite number of attributes of which only thought and extension may be apprehended by human intelligence. Redolent of polytheism and therefore anathema to pious Jews, the philosophy of Spinoza is conventionally invoked in opposition to traditional belief. That Asa Heshel Bannet goes nowhere without his copy of Spinoza's *Ethics* immediately signals his flawed Jewishness in *The Family Moskat*. And Isaac Bashevis Singer himself struggled for years to overcome his early attraction to Spinoza, who more than any other secular writer represents the dangers of forbidden knowledge.

For Isaac Kornfeld such knowledge took the form of a deepening fixation with nature. Sheindel's conviction that if her husband "had been faithful to his books he would have lived" seems at first paradoxical in light of the rabbi's scholarly reputation. What Sheindel means, however, is not that Isaac stopped reading but that he no longer read *his* (i.e., holy) books. Instead he began compulsively to devour books on agronomy, horticulture—in short, on anything pertaining to nature. His insistence on picnics, his joining a hiking club, his writing of fairy tales full of "sprites, nymphs, gods"—all manifestations of a sudden passion for nature and the outdoors—prefigure the astonishing last words of his notebook: "Great Pan lives."

It is this apparently deep immersion in paganism that lends credence to Sheindel's no less astonishing remark that Isaac "was never a Jew." An offshoot of the Spinozist heresy of perceiving the one in the many, pantheism nullifies the Second Commandment, the keystone of Judaism. In the transformed Rabbi Kornfeld is the antithesis of one of the classic figures of Jewish literature—the pale and pious scholar buried in holy texts, all but entombed in his study. In the light of traditional Jewish values the narrator's point that "fathers like ours don't know how to love. They live too much indoors" becomes a devastatingly ironic commentary not on the fancied inadequacies of the fathers but on the real shortcomings of the sons. It is the enclosed world of the study rather than the boundless world of external nature that is the proper province for the believing Jew.

Jewish orthodoxy is expressed in Isaac's vision of a bearded old man, bent under the burden of a bag stuffed with holy books, who identifies himself as Isaac's soul. No longer part of Isaac, and therefore lost to him, the old Jew trudges along reading the Law, prayer shawl drooping "on his studious back," oblivious to the beauty of surrounding nature. Significantly, this aged—and age-old—representative of Jewishness appears to Isaac only after the latter has committed the irrevocable sin of coupling with a dryad. In its total abandonment to pagan values this aberrant sexual union triggers the loss of soul signified by the old man's sudden appearance. Whether the dryad's simultaneous disappearance symbolizes the defeat of Pan by Moses—of the ephemerally pagan by the everlastingly Jewish—or merely Isaac's belated awareness that like Dr. Faustus he has lost his soul and gained nothing in return, it seals Isaac's fate. His suicide, the predictable result of this double loss—of pagan nature and Jewish law—is immediately provoked by the old man's reminder of what Isaac should never have forgotten: the Law sounds "more beautiful than the crickets," smells "more radiant than the moss," and tastes better than "clear water." Powerfully expressive of Isaac's failure to resolve theological conflict is his method of suicide: he hangs himself with his soul's prayer shawl from his beloved's body, the young oak tree. Isaac's last words summon the dryad: "For pity of me, come, come." Although her reappearance most probably would have neither alleviated his despair nor averted his suicide, her absence suggests the final inefficacy of the paganism to which Isaac succumbed. Accepting the Jewish Book Council Award for *The Pagan Rabbi and Other Stores* in 1972, Ozick underlined the lesson of her title story: "What is holy is not natural and what is natural is not holy. The God of the Jews must not be conceived of as belonging to nature."

Isaac's long letter, an explanatory confession that fleshes out the implications of his notebook, traces his growing absorption with nature and his foredoomed attempt to reconcile nature worship with Judaism. So desperate was his desire to bridge the gap between pagan and Jewish belief that he imagined a Moses who withheld the "truths" about "the world of Nature" not out of "ignorance" but only because his followers "would have scoffed." Isaac's revisionist estimate of Moses demonstrates the absurd lengths to which he will go to reconcile pagan multiplicity with Jewish monotheism. His many arguments in favor of freeing man's "indwelling" soul from the prison of his body have little to do with Judaism but everything to do with paganism and serve only to foreshadow his total immersion in nature. Not the least of Isaac's transgressions is this desire to detach soul from body, thereby denying the traditional Jewish view that both are inseparable components of a single being and together determine human essence. Again the Hebraic/Hellenic dichotomy is dramatized by an opposition, this time between Sheindel and the dryad with whom Isaac falls in love. Ozick's rabbi forsakes his quintessentially Jewish wife—a Holocaust survivor born in a concentration camp—for a pagan dryad whose girlish form emanates from a tree. An early instance of Ozick's literary strategy of leavening reality with the supernatural as a means of thematic definition, Isaac's coupling with a tree nymph symbolizes his attachment to nature and his detachment from Judaism. Like many fictional Jews who gravitate toward the perceived glitter of external society, he distorts his essential nature by opting for paganism. And Isaac proves no exception to the rule that such Jews self-destruct: "You have spoiled yourself, spoiled yourself with confusions," ex-plains the dryad. Soon thereafter, spoliation finds its most radical expression in suicide.

Seeking in nature to free his imagined soul, Isaac finds in the old man the true (i.e., Jewish) soul he unwittingly abandoned. With the materialization of the old man, signifying the soul detached from and thereby lost to the body, comes the end of Isaac's quest and his symbolic death. Since a soulless man is a contradiction in terms—especially in the moral terms that Judaism espouses and the rabbi cannot escape—Isaac's physical death is but the inevitable culmination of a process that began when he first sighted the old man. Her husband's tragic end elicits only contempt from Sheindel, the embodiment of Jewish orthodoxy. No pity is due the suicide, for "he who takes his own life does an abomination." More sympathetic than Sheindel toward Isaac, the narrator nonetheless flushes down the toilet three green house plants which will eventually make their way to Trilham's Inlet, there to decay "amid the civic excrement." A modest and nearly comic gesture, his disposal of greenery evidences an aversion to nature concomitant with a commitment to Judaism.

Still, the narrator's final position is ambiguous. An atheist whose apostasy at least hastened his father's death if it did not kill him outright, the narrator seems to be turning, however slowly and tentatively, back to Judaism. In his love for Sheindel, and in the section of his bookstore devoted to theological works ("chiefly in Hebrew and Aramaic") which he wishes his father could have seen, no less than in his ridding himself of plants, there are hints of Jewish affiliation. At the time of Isaac's suicide the narrator seems to have come to a crossroads in his own life. Just as Isaac's straying from Sheindel represents a step away from Judaism, the narrator's attraction to Sheindel represents a step toward Judaism. Wanting from Sheindel an explanation of Isaac's suicide, the narrator admits that he wants Sheindel herself. Like many quest stories, "The Pagan Rabbi" counterpoints the search for another with the search for the self. A potential convergence of identities typical in such stories results from the essential Jewishness shared by Isaac and the narrator. In Isaac's case the epiphany of loss triggered by the old man's appearance has a finality about it—it is, after all, a human soul that has been irretrievably lost—that leads him inexorably to suicide. The narrator's ultimate destiny is far less conclusive. Drawn to Sheindel—and symbolically, to Judaism—he nonetheless walks out on her in the end. Shaken by her pitilessness, the narrator intuits the requirements of their prospective union. Too weak in his flickering faith to share with her the uncompromising Jewishness for which she stands, he beats a hasty retreat. In his flight from her—and perhaps from himself—the narrator proves finally unable to shoulder the full burden of Jewish identity.

Source: Lawrence S. Friedman, "*The Pagan Rabbi and Other Stories,*" in *Understanding Cynthia Ozick*, University of South Carolina Press, 1991, pp. 58–67.

Joseph Lowin

In the following essay, Lowin examines the progression from the realistic to the fantastic in "The Pagan Rabbi" and the role of the tree in that progression.

Take, for a first example, the plot of "The Pagan Rabbi." Two young men, sons of prominent rabbis, had been classmates together at a rabbinical seminary. One—the narrator—drops out of school and marries Jane, a gentile girl, an incident which causes his father to sit *shiva* (a seven-day mourning period) on his account. He subsequently goes into his uncle's fur business in upstate New York, is miserable in his marriage because his wife is frigid (he calls her a puritan), gets divorced, moves back to New York City, and, deciding to deal in writers and writing, opens a bookstore. The other—Isaac Kornfeld—continues his rabbinical studies, becomes a professor of "mishnaic history" (whatever that is), publishes brilliant monographs on Jewish subjects, and causes his father to beam broadly with pride. He subsequently marries Sheindel, a *sheitel*-wearing Jewish woman, and together they have seven daughters. Kornfeld winds up committing suicide by hanging himself from a tree with his tallith.

Almost everything about these two parallel lives is ordinary, recognizable, sociologically accurate, and, until the strange, brutal fact and manner of the suicide, utterly realistic. The key, the most important fact in the narrative, is not, however, the tallith. The element that moves the tale from the realistic to the fantastic is the tree from which Isaac Kornfeld hangs himself. He may have been a rabbi, but, as the narrator learns when he goes to pay a condolence call on the widow, he has become a "pagan rabbi," a teller of seemingly supernatural stories and a person who has himself lived inside these stories. Sheindel describes a series of her husband's literary inventions:

> "The element that moves the tale from the realistic to the fantastic is the tree from which Isaac Kornfeld hangs himself. He may have been a rabbi, but, as the narrator learns when he goes to pay a condolence call on the widow, he has become a 'pagan rabbi,' a teller of seemingly supernatural stories and a person who has himself lived inside these stories."

These were the bedtime stories Isaac told Naomi and Esther: about mice that danced and children who laughed. When Miriam came he invented a speaking cloud. With Ophra it was a turtle that married a blade of withered grass. By Leah's time the stones had tears for their leglessness. Rebecca cried because of a tree that turned into a girl and could never grow colors again in autumn. Shiphra, the littlest, believes that a pig has a soul.

A difference between Ozick's fiction and classical nineteenth-century fantastic literature is apparent. Reality is not only social order. It is also natural order, cosmic. The fantastic in Ozick's tale resolves itself into something more than the marvelous, and, despite appearances, into something more than a mere fairy tale. What Ozick is describing in her story about Isaac's stories is the development of the narrative of the family life of Rabbi Isaac and Sheindel Kornfeld into a story belonging to the Jewish fantastic, with its judgment of the world.

Isaac Kornfeld, a Jew, would frequently go out into the field to daydream. This action bursts with significance, places the tale firmly within a certain Jewish textual tradition. The epigraph to Ozick's story, taken from *Mishna Avot*, performs the first step of this function: "He who is walking along and studying but then breaks off to remark, 'How lovely is that tree!' or 'How beautiful is that fallow field!'—Scripture regards such a one has having hurt his own being.'' The connection is clear: there is a danger to one's very Jewishness inherent in an aesthetic appreciation of nature. Ozick has made much of the fundamental opposition between paganism and the Jewish idea.

In this story, the very choice of the name ''Isaac Kornfeld'' places Ozick in the Jewish textual tradition, in the company of no less a Jewish writer than Rashi, the Jewish commentator par excellence. ''Isaac Kornfeld'' clearly alludes to the Scriptural tale of another Isaac, a young Yitzhak, son of Abraham, who, awaiting the arrival of his bride, goes out into the field to daydream. There is, first, the linguistic connection between ''Isaac Kornfeld'' and *''Vayetzeh Yitzhak lasu'ah basadeh.''* And there is a connection between Rashi and Ozick. Rashi recalls a midrash on what Isaac was ''doing'' in the field. Rather than have him daydream on the erotic consequences of a marriage, Rashi reins in the dreamer and has him praying instead ('' *lasuah: leshon tefila* ''). Ozick's midrash tells of what happens when one goes out into nature for nonliturgical purposes.

Isaac Kornfeld, it must be emphasized, was also a writer and not only of scholarly monographs. The story contains, *mise en abyme*, Isaac's text. This text may be interpreted, variously, as the suicide note of a madman (and thus the fantastic story resolves itself into the uncanny), as the description of a supernatural occurrence (in which the story would resolve itself into the marvelous), or as an allegory or parable. Isaac's verbatim text has three ''readers.'' Sheindel, who knows the text by heart, reads the first half to the narrator; the narrator reads the other half out loud. The reader implicit in the text, the reader who knows that he is in the genre of the fantastic, wavers between Sheindel's marvelous reading and the narrator's uncanny one. The ''letter'' is addressed to someone called ''creature,'' and ''loveliness.'' It is a Jewish text and like many Jewish texts, it begins inside the story of the Exodus. It contains a brilliant midrash against diaspora living (based on a highly intuitive, almost pantheistic mysticism). The two philosophical points of Isaac's midrash are that idolatry does not exist—because death does not exist—and that, in the plant world, in the world of trees, in the world of nature, the soul is able to be free.

The next stage in Isaac's *itinerarium mentis* (and in the reader's road to the fantastic) is his ''discovery'' (on the outside as it were, in the field) of wood nymphs: He has seen a nymph save the life of one of his daughters drowning in a stream. He comes to the conclusion that there are only two ways to communicate and commune with these free-floating souls. To experience ecstasy (to stand outside of himself), he must either die or copulate with nature.

He tries the latter first. In what Ozick could only have meant to be the description of an abomination, Isaac Kornfeld fornicates with an oak tree and succeeds in achieving some sort of ecstasy this way. He even conjures up the presence of a nice pagan girl, Iripomoňoéià (the ''apple of his eye''), who informs him that his soul has stepped out of his body and is now visible. Isaac looks at his soul and is mortified by what he sees. Isaac Kornfeld's soul, walking in the field, studying Talmud, is Jewish! The soul does not even notice Iripomoňoéià, denies her, ''passes indifferent through the beauty of the field'' and is faithful to the rabbinic dictum that Ozick had quoted for us in the epigraph of her story. When Isaac Kornfeld confronts his Jewish soul, he learns that to have a Jewish soul is not to be free in nature but to be bound to law. According to Kornfeld's soul, the page of Talmud is a garden, the letters on the page are birds, and the columns of commentary on the page are trees. When Isaac Kornfeld learns that he cannot be a Jew and a writer and teller of stories at the same time, and, moreover, when he learns that he cannot live inside his stories, he decides to die.

If the story ended here, the fantastic would have dissolved into nothing more than allegory, with a clear message: If you want to be a Jew, give up writing and all that enterprise entails. But it does not end here. It ends with the reactions of the narrator and Sheindel to Isaac's tale.

Todorov, for whom the end of a work of art is art itself, and for whom the subject of writing is writing itself, warns against the use of the fantastic genre for allegorical purposes. He sees only two possible resolutions for the fantastic:

> At the story's end the reader makes a decision even if the character does not; he opts for one solution or the other, and thereby emerges from the fantastic. If he decides that the laws of reality remain intact and permit an explanation of the phenomena described, we say that the work belongs to another genre: the uncanny. If, on the contrary, he decides that new laws of nature must be entertained to account for the phenomenon, we enter the genre of the marvelous.

He does recognize, however, that, using a strict definition of allegory, where the double meaning of words is indicated in an *explicit* fashion and does not proceed from the reader's interpretation, whether arbitrary or not, the fantastic lends itself to an allegorical resolution.

Cynthia Ozick, who has called for a liturgical component in Jewish literature, balks, however, at the use of the term *allegory* for her own works:

> Two stories—"The Pagan Rabbi" and "Usurpation"—intend to be representative of certain ideas; but I think of them rather as parables than allegories. In an allegory, the story *stands for* an idea, and the idea can be stated entirely apart from the story, in a parable, story and idea are so inextricably fused that they cannot be torn free of each other. In this sense, I hope I've written an occasional parable. But I would never seek out allegory, which strikes me as a low form.

Whether we use the term *allegory* or *parable*, or indeed neither of these, we can agree with the comment of Ruth R. Wisse about the ending of an Ozick story: "Her reader is expected at the conclusion of her stories to have an insight, to understand the point of events." Ozick's warning against allegory should be heeded in considering the end of this supernatural tale.

Sheindel, it is clear, is on the side of Rashi. There is only one thing a Jew ought to do in a field, and that is to pray. It would be even better to make a fence about the law and not go out into the field at all. The fantastic, she seems to be saying, is not a place for Jewish rabbis. For the narrator, and even more for the reader implicit in the text, the ending is more problematic. The narrator is a product of the Enlightenment and has even failed as a product of the Enlightenment. And yet, when he goes home, the narrator flushes all his house plants down the toilet. He apparently agrees with Sheindel's judgment of the world. Does he thereby also accept Sheindel's reading of the story? Not entirely. When he met Sheindel, in her grief, he was attracted to her. He fell in love with her and even contemplated marrying her and normalizing his life in Judaism. In the end, however, the narrator rejects Sheindel because he cannot accept her severity. He is aware of the dangers of the Enlightenment. But he would rather be normal. The act of consigning the house plants to New York's sewers is a mere gesture, however significant. The narrator will, we are certain, continue to live in the world. And after "The Pagan Rabbi," Cynthia Ozick will continue to write fantastic short stories in which she investigates further the liturgical possibilities of the Jewish fantastic.

Source: Joseph Lowin, "A Jewish Fantastic," in *Cynthia Ozick*, Twayne, 1988, pp. 69–73.

Sources

Cohen, Sarah Blacher, *Cynthia Ozick's Comic Art: From Levity to Liturgy*, Indiana University Press, 1994, pp. 9, 64, 68.

Friedman, Lawrence S., *Understanding Cynthia Ozick*, University of South Carolina Press, 1991, pp. 6, 8, 10, 14, 16.

Kauvar, Elaine M., *Cynthia Ozick's Fiction: Tradition and Invention*, Indiana University Press, 1993.

———, ed., *A Cynthia Ozick Reader*, Indiana University Press, 1996, pp. ix, xix, xxi.

Knopp, Josephine Z., "Ozick's Jewish Stories," in *Cynthia Ozick*, edited by Harold Bloom, Chelsea House, 1986, p. 29.

Lowin, Joseph, *Cynthia Ozick*, Twayne Publishers, 1988, p. 67.

Nocera, Gigliola, "Cynthia Ozick and 'The Pagan Rabbi,'" in *Intertextual Identity: Reflections on Jewish-American Artists*, edited by Franco La Polla and Gabriella Morisco, Patron Editore, 1997, p. 109.

Pinsker, Sanford, *The Uncompromising Fictions of Cynthia Ozick*, University of Missouri Press, 1987, pp. 1, 39.

Rovit, Earl, "The Two Languages of Cynthia Ozick," in *Studies in American Jewish Literature*, Vol. 8, No. 1, Spring 1989, p. 34.

Strandberg, Victor, "The Art of Cynthia Ozick," in *Cynthia Ozick*, edited by Harold Bloom, Chelsea House, 1986, pp. 80, 102, 119.

Further Reading

Block, Gay, and Malka Drucker, *Rescuers: Portraits of Moral Courage in the Holocaust*, Holmes & Meier, 1992.
    This photographic work of pictures by Cynthia Ozick shows people who helped Jews facing persecution in the Holocaust, and contains an afterword by Rabbi Harold M. Schulweis.

Burstein, Janet Handler, *Writing Mothers, Writing Daughters: Tracing the Maternal in Stories by American Jewish Women*, University of Illinois Press, 1996.
    Burstein presents a critical discussion of themes of motherhood in Jewish literature. This work includes a discussion of the work of Cynthia Ozick, in a chapter entitled "Mirroring the Mother: The Ordeal of Narcissism."

Curtis, C. Michael, ed., *God: Stories*, Houghton Mifflin, 1998.
Curtis's book is a collection of short stories on themes of faith, spirituality, and religion, and includes ''Rosa'' by Cynthia Ozick.

Gutkind, Lee, ed., *Surviving Crisis: Twenty Prominent Authors Write about Events that Shaped Their Lives*, Putnam, 1997.
This text includes the essay ''The Break'' by Cynthia Ozick.

Shapiro, Gerald, ed., *American Jewish Fiction: A Century of Stories*, University of Nebraska Press, 1998.
Shapiro presents a collection of international short stories by Jewish writers, which includes ''Envy; or, Yiddish in America'' by Cynthia Ozick.

Stavans, Ilan, ed., *The Oxford Book of Jewish Stories*, Oxford University Press, 1998.
This book is a collection of international short stories by Jewish authors, which includes ''The Shawl'' by Cynthia Ozick.

Updike, John, ed., *The Best American Short Stories of the Century*, Houghton Mifflin, 1999.
This book is a collection of short stories gathered from the series Best American Short Stories, which has been published annually since 1915. It contains an introduction by John Updike and includes ''The Shawl'' by Cynthia Ozick.

The Spinoza of Market Street

Nobel laureate Isaac Bashevis Singer's short story "The Spinoza of Market Street" was first published in *Esquire* magazine in 1961, later anthologized in *The Spinoza of Market Street*, Singer's second collection of short stories. Irving Malin describes the title story as "clearly one of Singer's best," while Paul Kresh observed that this volume, which inspired Irving Howe to declare Singer "a genius," "marked another step in Isaac's acceptance as one of the great short-story writers of our time."

The story is set in the Jewish *shtetl* (a small community of Eastern European Jews) of Warsaw, Poland, against the backdrop of the events leading to the beginning of World War I in August, 1914. It concerns Dr. Fischelson, a scholar of philosophy who has devoted his life to the study of Benedict de Spinoza's masterwork, *Ethics*. Because of his skeptical ideas regarding religion, derived from Spinoza, Dr. Fischelson has been fired from his job at the synagogue library and alienated from the Jewish community due to their perception that he is a "heretic." When Dr. Fischelson falls ill, Black Dobbe, his "old maid" neighbor, nurses him back to health, and the two are soon married in the synagogue. On their wedding night, a "miracle" occurs, by which the old man and the homely woman engage in a surprisingly passionate consummation of their marriage. Dr. Fischelson awakens in the night to gaze up at the stars and murmur, "Divine Spinoza, forgive me. I have become a fool."

Isaac Bashevis Singer

1961

This story concerns many themes typical of Singer's short stories, particularly the conflict of the modern Jewish thinker in the context of traditional orthodox Chassidic Jewish religion and culture. The protagonist's ultimate experience of redemption through physical passion is ironically the event that brings him back into the fold of his Jewish community, having defied the dictates of Spinoza's rationalist philosophy.

Author Biography

Isaac Bashevis Singer, 1978 Nobel Prize laureate, is internationally acclaimed for his short stories and novels, written in Yiddish, but known to readers mostly in translation. He is also a prolific essayist, children's book writer, playwright, journalist, editor, translator and memoirist. Singer was born July 14, 1904, into a Chassidic Jewish family, in Radzymin (or Leoncin), Poland, then part of the Russian Empire. The exact date of his birth is not clear, and has been listed as either July 14, October 26, or November 21. Singer's father and both of his grandfathers were Hassidic rabbis.

In 1908, when Singer was four, the family moved to nearby Warsaw, where he spent most of his childhood. In 1914, Singer read his first non-religious text, *Crime and Punishment*, by the Russian writer Fyodor Dostoyevski. From 1917 to 1921, he and his mother lived with relatives in the rural shtetl of Bilgory, before returning to Warsaw.

He was enrolled in the Warsaw Rabbinical Seminary in 1921, according to the wishes of his parents, but eventually left to pursue a career in writing. From 1923 to 1933, Singer worked as a proofreader and translator for a journal where his elder brother Israel Joshua worked, and as an associate editor of a different journal from 1933–1935. His first short story was published in 1927. In Warsaw, Singer lived with a woman named Runya (or Runia), by whom he had an illegitimate son, Israel Zamir, in 1929.

In 1935, Singer immigrated to the United States, joining his elder brother, Israel Joshua, already an established Yiddish fiction writer. Singer lived in relative poverty in Brooklyn, while working for the renowned Yiddish newspaper, *The Jewish Daily Forward*. His fiction was serialized in *The Jewish Daily Forward* throughout the 1940s. Singer remained a staff writer for the *Daily Forward* until his death.

In 1940, he married Alma Hazmann (or Haimann), a German-Jewish immigrant, and in 1943 became an American citizen. His brother Israel Joshua died the following year. Singer's first novel to be translated into English, *The Family Moskat*, was published in 1950. An important turning point in his career was the publication of his short story "Gimpel the Fool," in an English translation by writer Saul Bellow, in 1953. This was the first high profile introduction of Singer's work to English readers.

Singer's international reputation as the leading Yiddish fiction writer of the century grew steadily throughout the 1950s, as more and more of his works were translated into English and other languages. He won the 1970 National Book Award for children's literature, for *A Day of Pleasure*, and the 1974 National Book Award for fiction for *A Crown of Feathers and Other Stories*. He won the Nobel Prize for literature in 1978.

In later years, he and Alma lived in New York and in Florida. He died after a series of strokes, on July 24, 1991, in Surfside, Florida, and was buried in Beth-El Cemetery in New York. Three of his novels were published posthumously.

Plot Summary

Dr. Nahum Fischelson, a philosopher, has devoted the last thirty years to studying and writing a commentary on the Dutch-German philosopher Benedict de Spinoza's (1632–1677) central text, *Ethics*. Dr. Fischelson has spent years at this task, but has never actually completed his work. Nevertheless, he attempts to live by Spinoza's rationalist philosophy, and often quotes him in making sense of his life and the world. He has severe stomach ailments, which he attempts to abate with various foods. He lives on a meager income, supplied by the Berlin Jewish community by mail every three months.

Fischelson lives in a garret apartment on Market Street, in Warsaw, Poland, and lives economically, with few, if any, physical pleasures. He had once been a minor celebrity in his community, due to his distinguished scholarship, but this attention has completely diminished. He is somewhat outcast from his Chassidic Jewish community, because his "heretical" following of Spinoza's philosophy goes against Jewish theological doctrine. Dr. Fischelson had been the librarian at the synagogue, but has been fired due to his unorthodox views.

This July, Dr. Fischelson does not receive his quarterly pay from the Berlin Jewish community, and begins to go hungry. Meanwhile, rumors of war are leading up to the advent of the Great War (World War I). Dr. Fischelson goes out to buy food with his last remaining funds, but, due to the war, all of the stores are closed. He then goes to see the rabbi for advice, but the rabbi has gone with his family to the spas. He next goes to the café where he once had several acquaintances, but sees no one he knows. While at the café, he begins to feel ill, and is barely able to make it back home to his garret room and fall into bed, where he falls asleep and dreams, wakes up feeling more ill, and falls asleep again.

That night, Black Dobbe the "old maid" who is his neighbor knocks on his door in order to ask him to read a letter for her (she cannot read). She finds him ill in bed, feeling as if he is on the verge of death, and commences to feed him and nurse him back to health. She informs him of the progress of the war, that the Germans are marching toward Warsaw. Eventually, Black Dobbe demonstrates her entire trousseau to Dr. Fischelson, something that a young girl presents to her suitor. The two get married by the rabbi in the synagogue, with members of the community looking on in amusement. On their wedding night, Dr. Fischelson lies down in bed to read Spinoza's *Ethics* but a "miracle" occurs, when Black Dobbe appears adorned in a silk nightgown, and the unlikely couple consummate their union with unexpected passion. Dr. Fischelson awakens to look up at the night sky, amidst the August meteor showers. The story ends with his "murmur": "Divine Spinoza, forgive me. I have become a fool."

Characters

Black Dobbe

Black Dobbe is Dr. Fischelson's only neighbor in his garret apartment. A "spinster," she is described as:

> tall and lean, and as black as a baker's shovel. She had a broken nose and there was a mustache on her upper lip. She spoke with the hoarse voice of a man and she wore men's shoes.

Black Dobbe sells cracked eggs in the market place. She "had no luck with men." Several times,

Issac Bashevis Singer

she had been engaged, but each one was eventually broken off. She has a cousin in America, who writes her promises to send for her, but this seems to be an empty gesture, as he never does. When Black Dobbe knocks on Dr. Fischelson's door to ask him to read a letter to her (she cannot read), she discovers him sick in bed. She nurses him back to health, and encourages their engagement by demonstrating her trousseau. On their wedding night, Black Dobbe unleashes a long-neglected passion on her new husband, which causes him to betray his adherence to Spinozan rational philosophy.

Dr. Nahum Fischelson

Dr Nahum Fischelson is the protagonist of the story. He is a philosophy scholar whose life has been devoted to working on a book about one of the Dutch-Jewish philosopher Benedict de Spinoza's (1632–1677) primary texts, *Ethics*. Dr. Fischelson is described as:

> a short, hunched man with a grayish beard—quite bald except for a few wisps of hair remaining at the nape of his neck. His nose was as crooked as a beak and his eyes were large, dark, and fluttering like those of some huge bird.

He has been outcast from his synagogue because of his philosophical skepticism regarding Judaism. He lives in a garret room on Market Street, a center of Jewish community and commerce, in Warsaw, Poland. As his life has been preoccupied with, and dictated by, the philosophical thinking of Spinoza, his life has been one of social isolation and abstention from physical or material pleasure. When he falls sick one night, his neighbor, Black Dobbe, an "old maid," discovers him and nurses him back to health. The two are soon married by a rabbi in the synagogue, to the surprise and amusement of the community. On their wedding night, the sick old man and the old maid make passionate love, thus causing Dr. Fischelson to renounce his devotion to the teachings of Spinoza, which disdain such indulgences.

Dr. Hildesheimer

Dr. Hildesheimer is a famous scholar with whom Dr. Fischelson corresponds daily. Dr. Hildesheimer influences the Berlin Jewish community to support Dr. Fischelson with a subsidy of five hundred marks per year.

Themes

Philosophy versus Religion

A central theme of this story is the conflict between the ideas put forth in modern philosophy (such as that of Spinoza), and the ancient beliefs held by Orthodox Chassidic Judaism. The protagonist, who considers himself a Jew, is alienated from the Jewish community of the shtetl in which he lives due to his unorthodox ideas derived from modern philosophy. Because of this, Dr. Fischelson is fired from his job as the synagogue librarian, and considered to be a "heretic" or a "convert" by the members of his community. As in many of his stories, Singer explores the theme of the Jew caught between the Enlightenment of the modern secular world and the ancient beliefs of Chassidic Judaism.

Redemption through Passion

Singer's characters often find some sort of solution to their alienation through the experience of sexual passion. Dr. Fischelson attempts to live by the "rational" tenets of Spinoza's philosophy, eschewing the physical world in the pursuit of philosophical scholarship. His marriage to Black Dobbe first brings him back into the fold of his Jewish community, through their traditional wedding ceremony in the synagogue, officiated by the rabbi, and attended by the (albeit snickering) members of the

community. Even on his wedding night, he goes to bed with Spinoza's book of *Ethics* but discovers a long-smothered sexual passion with his new wife. Looking up at the night sky, he declares his apostasy from rationalism and entry into life by his admission to Spinoza that he has become a "fool."

Jewish Culture and History

Many of Singer's stories take place in the now-vanished Jewish shtetl of Warsaw, Poland before the advent of World War II. While the story is centrally concerned with the personal life and thoughts of Dr. Fischelson, it takes place against the backdrop of the very specific historical circumstance of the events leading up to the advent of World War I in August, 1914. Singer's stories address the indirect theme of nostalgia for the Polish Jewish communities desecrated by the Holocaust. Singer is credited with preserving the memory of this rich culture through the settings of his fictional stories in the context of the Jewish world in which he grew up. In addition, Singer's stories, written in Yiddish and meticulously translated into English, in themselves represent an effort to preserve the Yiddish language, also severely devastated by the death of much of the world's Yiddish-speaking population in the Holocaust.

The Cosmic and the Earthly

Dr. Fischelson's only activity, beyond the study and contemplation of Spinoza's philosophy, is looking through his telescope from the roof of his garret room. From this vantage Dr. Fischelson contemplates the cosmic, while below his window the life of the Jewish community occupies Market Street. Dr. Fischelson's alienation from his community, the physical world, and participation in human life is represented by his focus on the cosmic and refusal to participate in the earthly. It is the "miracle" of his newly discovered sexual passion for his new wife that draws Dr. Fischelson down from the realm of the cosmic to the realm of the earthly, thus leading him back into the stream of life, and, almost ironically, a reentry into the Jewish community.

Alienation and Loneliness

Dr. Fischelson's devotion to Spinoza's *Ethics*, and his efforts to live by the rational tenets of the philosopher, have ultimately lead to his complete isolation and loneliness. He has been cast out of his synagogue, regarded with suspicion by the members of his community, and lost all ties with his fellow scholars. In his striving to live a rational life,

Topics for Further Study

- Singer's fiction has been contrasted with that of other prominent twentieth-century Jewish-American writers, such as Cynthia Ozick, Philip Roth, Saul Bellow and Bernard Malmud. Learn more about one of these writers and their short fiction. In what ways does this writer's treatment of issues of Jewish identity and religion compare and contrast with those of Singer?

- Singer's short story takes place in a Jewish shtetl (a small Eastern European Jewish community) in Warsaw, Poland, amidst the backdrop of the beginning of World War I (The Great War). Find out more about the history of Polish Jews in the twentieth century. In what ways did major historical events—such as World War I and World War II—affect the Jewish population in Poland?

- Singer's story takes place in the setting of a Chassidic (or Hassidic) Jewish community. Find out more about the history of Hassidic Judaism, it's beliefs, traditions and customs. How is it different from other denominations of Judaism—such as Conservative, or Reform Judaism?

- The main character's alienation from his community is based on his preoccupation with modern philosophy over Jewish theology. What is modern philosophy? In addition to Spinoza, who are some of the major modern philosophers? Pick one of these to learn more about, including most important works and central tenets of the philosophy.

---

he has cut himself off from human warmth. Black Dobbe, a mannish, homely "old maid," who has been jilted twice, is also a figure of loneliness and isolation. The warmth and human contact she brings to Dr. Fischelson during his illness results in the end of both loneliness and alienation for both of these unlikely bedfellows.

Style

Translation from Yiddish

Throughout his life, Singer wrote almost exclusively in Yiddish. As Yiddish is still spoken by only a relatively small number of people, most readers are acquainted with his work in translation. Later in his life, as he became more comfortable with his own command of English, Singer often translated his Yiddish stories into an English rough draft, and then worked with another translator on the details of the translation. This story retains only one phrase from the original Yiddish; when Black Dobbe appears before Dr. Fischelson in a silk nightgown on

their wedding night, she says, "Mazel tov." This is a Yiddish phrase usually spoken on holidays and celebrations.

Narration

The narration is third person, meaning the narrator is not a character in the story, but is "restricted," rather than "omniscient," meaning that the events of the story are primarily told from the perspective of the protagonist. Only occasionally does the narrative perspective venture outside of Dr. Fischelson's head, to describe some of Dobbe's initial impressions of him.

Intertextual References

Intertextual references are elements of a story that refer to texts, or books, which exist in reality outside of the story. Central to this story is the reference to the philosopher Spinoza's philosophical work, *Ethics*. Dr. Fischelson's life and career have been devoted to the study of *Ethics*, and his thoughts often refer back to the ideas presented in *Ethics*, and even to direct quotes from Spinoza. Full appreciation of this story requires a basic knowledge of Spinoza's life, and a greater familiarity with his philosophy, particularly as set forth in *Ethics*.

Setting—Location

The setting of this story is typical of Singer's fiction. It takes place on Market Street, in a Jewish shtetl of Warsaw, Poland. Singer grew up in such an area in Warsaw, and his stories that take place there depict the conditions of Polish Jews in the early part of the century. Singer is credited with capturing this pocket of Jewish culture, which was lost forever as a result of the Holocaust.

Setting—Time Period

The time period of the story is in July and August of 1914. This is very important because the very personal story of Dr. Fischelson and his marriage takes place in the context of the early part of The Great War (World War I). Dr. Fischelson hears about the coming war when he goes out to buy food, and learns that it has resulted in food shortages and the closing of shops. While he is sick in bed, Black Dobbe further informs him that the Germans are marching toward Warsaw. Dr. Fischelson's philosophical preoccupations prevent him from thinking about the war from other than a very intellectual, distant perspective. Toward the end of the story, as he is looking up at the night sky, he thinks, ''Seen from above even the Great War was nothing but a temporary play of the modes.'' Nevertheless, a historical perspective on the part of the reader leaves no doubt that the war will eventually have an enormous impact on the Jewish population of Poland.

Historical Context

Spinoza

The protagonist of this story has devoted his life to the study of the Dutch-Jewish philosopher, Benedict de Spinoza (1632–1677), particularly his major work, *Ethics*. Although Spinoza finished writing *Ethics* in 1675, it was never published during his lifetime, in part due to its controversial nature and the censure of religious authorities. Spinoza is one of the great modern philosophers, associated with Rationalism. As a Jew, Spinoza's skepticism regarding religion, God, and Judaism was highly controversial within the Jewish community. He was excommunicated from Judaism in 1656 for his radical departure from Jewish doctrine. Unrelated to his philosophical works, Spinoza worked as a lens maker, adept at grinding lenses for telescopes, eyeglasses and microscopes. Dr. Fischelson's telescope in the story is clearly a reference to this connection with Spinoza.

Jewish Daily Forward

The Jewish Daily Forward was founded in New York City in 1897, eventually becoming the leading Yiddish language newspaper in the United States. Singer was a staff writer for the *Forward* from his arrival in the United States in 1935 until his death in 1991. Many of his novels were originally published in serial form in the *Forward*, as were his short stories.

Yiddish Language and Literature

The Yiddish language, associated with populations of the Jewish Diaspora, is rooted in Hebrew and Aramaic, later acquiring the influence of Germanic and Slavic languages. Before World War II, there were approximately eleven million Yiddish speakers, but this number was virtually diminished by half as a result of those who were killed in the Holocaust. Yiddish literature first appeared in the United States as a result of massive migrations of Jews to New York City in the 1880s. Yiddish theater also made its way into U.S. culture in the 1880s, its greatest achievements developing in the 1920s.

World War I

This story takes place in the summer months of 1914, on the eve of the Great War (now referred to as World War I), and its events unfold against the backdrop of the build-up of the war. Dr. Fischelson first hears of the impending war when he goes out to buy food, and learns that ''in Serbia somewhere, an Austrian Prince had been shot and the Austrians had delivered an ultimatum to the Serbs.'' This refers to the event which is considered to have initiated World War I. On June 28, 1914, a Serbian nationalist movement, aiming to ''liberate'' South Slavs from Austria-Hungary, assassinated the heir to the Austrian empire, Archduke Francis Ferdinand, and his wife while they were visiting Serbia on a military inspection. In Singer's short story, a shopkeeper warns Dr. Fischelson that they are on the brink of a ''small war.'' This statement is ironic, given that it was not at all a ''small'' war which ensued, but a World War.

Compare & Contrast

- **Early 1900s:** There are some eleven million speakers of the Yiddish language.

  Late Twentieth Century: Approximately half of the world's population of Yiddish speakers have been killed in the Holocaust.

- **Early 1900s:** Poland is part of the Russian empire under the Tsar (Czar).

  Late Twentieth Century: With the breakup of the Soviet Union, formerly under communist rule, Poland becomes an independent nation.

- **Early 1900s:** The shtetls in Warsaw, Poland, include a high concentration of the Jewish population, and are a locus of Jewish culture.

Late Twentieth Century: Much of the population of Polish Jews has perished in the Holocaust, while others have left Poland to escape such persecution.

- **Early 1900s:** The aborted Russian Revolution of 1905 leaves the empire still under the rule of the Czar. However, the Russian Revolution of 1917 leads to decades of communist rule.

  Late Twentieth Century: The USSR suffers from internal difficulties, signalled, among other things, by the fall of the Berlin Wall in 1989, and eventually ceases to exist in 1991. Russia allows member states to declare their independence.

Warsaw, Poland

Many of Singer's stories take place in the Jewish shtetl of Warsaw, Poland. Poland's defeat in the Russo-Polish War of 1831 resulted in the military occupation of Poland by Russia, ruled by the Tsar. A revolt against Russian rule in 1864 was crushed, solidifying the Poles submission to occupation. A later wave of rebellion between 1905–1907 is mentioned in Singer's story, when Black Dobbe tells Dr. Fischelson "of the battles between the underworld and the revolutionaries in 1905." According to *Encyclopaedia Britannica Online*, Warsaw at the turn of the century "contained the largest urban concentration of Jews in the world." Most of this population perished or emigrated as a result of the Holocaust during World War II.

Critical Overview

Singer's "The Spinoza of Market Street" was first published in *Esquire* magazine in 1961, and later in Singer's 1961 collection of stories written between 1958 and 1961, *The Spinoza of Market Street*. According to Paul Kresh, this collection "marked

another step in Isaac's acceptance as one of the great short-story writers of our time." Irving Malin describes the title story as "clearly one of Singer's best." Although Singer had been living in the United States for over twenty-five years at this point, all of the stories in this collection are set in Jewish communities in Poland. As Kresh states, "the Polish landscape offers plenty of variety and a cast of caricatures as fascinating as any in the Singer gallery." Kresh goes on to claim that, with this collection, "Isaac proved his power to transmute the stuff of provincial folklore and simple faith into works of art of great beauty and universal appeal." Kresh quotes in some detail the response of Irving Howe to the collection:

> This was the collection that prompted Irving Howe in *The New Republic* to call Singer a genius. Howe went on to say that Isaac had "total command of his imagined world; he is original in his use both of traditional Jewish materials and his modernist attitude toward them; he provides a serious if enigmatic moral perspective; and he writes Yiddish prose with a rhythmic and verbal brilliance that can hardly be matched." He added a word of caution: "Singer seems to be mired in his own originality. There are times in some of the lesser stories in *The Spinoza of Market Street*, when he displays a weakness for self-imitation that is disconcerting."

Seventeenth-century philosopher, Benedict de Spinoza. Dr. Fishchelson of "Spinoza of Market Street" has dedicated his life to the study of this great philosopher's masterwork.

Kresh further sums up the central critical responses to *Spinoza of Market Street*:

Herbert Kupterberg, in the *New York Herald Tribune*, said the stories were of the kind that "haunt the memory, for many of them are concerned with the spectral, the occult, and the demonic . . . But it is the everyday life of his people, rather than his demons, that makes Mr. Singer's stories so unforgettable." Milton Hindus, in the *New York Times*, found these stories "very satisfying as entertainment, and provocatively deep in their implications." Eugene Goodheart, in the *Saturday Review*, pronounced Isaac, "perhaps the greatest Jewish writer of all time" and praised his "freedom from parochial pieties." But the most incisive critical appraisal was offered by J. W. Smith in *Commonweal*, who spoke of the "irony and earthiness and wild humor" of these stories, which is where their real strength lies."

While also a novelist, essayist and translator, Singer is most highly acclaimed for his short fiction, of which over one hundred stories have been published in English translation. His five short story collections in English include: *Gimpel the Fool and Other Stories* (1957), *The Spinoza of Market Street* (1961), *Short Friday and Other Stories* (1964),

Passions and Other Stories, and *The Collected Stories* (1982). Irving Malin has observed that "Singer is perhaps more effective as a short story writer than as a novelist. By narrowing his focus even more than he does in the closed novels, he can concentrate upon the intense vision of details. He can give us dream, stylization, and parable."

Singer's best known and most celebrated short story, "Gimpel the Fool," was first published in English in the May 1953 issue of *Partisan Review*. Malin describes it as "probably his finest achievement" of all of his short stories. Edward Alexander asserts that it is "without question Singer's best-known, most frequently anthologized, and most thoroughly studied short story." According to Kresh, this is "the short story that many critics regard as the capstone of his achievement." The "stunningly idiomatic if slightly slangy translation" by Jewish-American author Saul Bellow introduced Singer's work to a wide English-reading audience for the first time. Alexander explains that, with the appearance of Bellow's English translation, "the barrier of parochialism which has kept the American literary world ignorant of even the greatest Yiddish writers in the United States was lowered long enough for Singer to make his escape from the cage of Yiddish into the outside world." Lawrence Friedman concurs that Bellow's translation "won for its author the sort of modernist cachet and mainstream acceptance that no Yiddish writer had hitherto enjoyed."

Following this turning point in Singer's reputation among English readers, many other of his short stories were published throughout the 1950s in periodicals such as *Commentary*, *The Saturday Evening Post*, *Playboy*, *The Reporter*, *Mademoiselle*, *Esquire*, and *Harper's*. His non-fiction essays appeared in such periodicals as the *New York Times* and the *Herald Tribune*.

Describing the wellspring of positive response by the critics to Singer's work, Kresh explains:

Increasingly the critics were praising Isaac's work. Irving Howe called him a genius. *The Times Literary Supplement* said "Gimpel the Fool" was the greatest story ever written about a schlemiel. Milton Hindus praised Isaac as one of the best Yiddish writers in America. Henry Miller, in *Life* magazine, termed him "a writer to drive one crazy if one has the ear for the underlying melody, the meaning behind the meaning." Isaac, he exclaimed, was "afraid of nothing." Miller, the master on the subject, particularly admired Isaac's treatment of sex, "always full-bodied like a rich wine." "Above all," Miller wrote, "there is love, a bigger, broader love than we are accustomed to reading about in books."

One of the most salient features of Singer's work is the frequent setting of stories in the Yiddish speaking world of the Jewish shtetl in Poland, since abolished by the Nazi devastation of Polish Jewry in the Holocaust. Alexander points out that Singer ''has devoted his life to writing about a world that was brutally destroyed, and has done so in a language that is itself on the verge of extinction.'' Friedman concurs that ''Singer has all but single-handedly kept alive a vanished past and a dying language.''

While Singer has been criticized for his unflattering and unorthodox portrayals of Jewish characters, Friedman defends the author's perspective on Judaism:

> Jewish traditionalists who criticize Singer for his many unflattering portraits of, and apparent disloyalty to, his fellow Jews miss the point of his fiction. So relentlessly does Singer define transgression as deviation from Jewish law that his sinners become unwitting allies in preserving Jewish values. Only by doing penance and returning to those values can his sinners find the fulfillment they futilely sought elsewhere. The sexuality, criminality, and demonology which fill his pages and unnerve his orthodox critics are employed to celebrate the pious and humble life style they oppose. Honoring a people and a way of life that are no more but that are worthy of remembrance and emulation, Singer remains faithful to the values traditionally celebrated by Yiddish writers . . . .

Alexander points out Singer's universal appeal, despite his exclusive focus on Jewish characters and culture: ''Singer writes almost always as a Jew, to Jews, for Jews: and yet he is heard by everybody.'' Singer's 1978 Nobel Prize for literature, the first to be awarded a Yiddish writer, speaks to his universal appeal in the culmination of a career comprising one of the greatest literary achievements of the twentieth century.

Criticism

Liz Brent

Brent has a Ph.D. in American culture, specializing in cinema studies, from the University of Michigan. She is a freelance writer and teaches courses in American cinema. In the following essay, Brent discusses the Jewish theological texts referred to in this story.

Critic Lawrence Alexander has pointed out that Isaac Bashevis Singer ''almost always writes as a Jew, to Jews, for Jews: and yet he is heard by everybody.'' Other critics have concurred that it is through Singer's very specific focus on the vanished world of Chassidic Jewry in the *shtetls* (small Eastern European Jewish communities) of Warsaw, Poland, before World War II, the world of his childhood and young adulthood, that Singer's fiction draws its universal appeal. Furthermore, critics generally agree that it is through the skillful translations of Singer's Yiddish stories into English that they successfully maintain the power of his own native language. Given this, many readers will not be familiar with the specific elements of Jewish culture, religion and history referred to in Singer's stories. An explanation of some of these references in Singer's short story ''The Spinoza of Market Street'' will enhance the appreciation of the reader unfamiliar with these references.

A key element of this story is Dr. Fischelson's lifelong devotion to the study of the Dutch-Jewish philosopher Benedict de Spinoza (1632–1677), the leading figure in the philosophy of seventeenth-century rationalism. In order to fully appreciate Singer's story, it is helpful to have some knowledge of Spinoza's relationship to Judaism and the Jewish community in which he lived. Spinoza's non-conformist ideas about religion led to his excommunication by the Jewish authorities in Amsterdam in 1656, for which he was temporarily banished from his native city. While a prolific writer, all but one of Spinoza's philosophical texts were published posthumously, largely because the controversial nature of his ideas prevented publication during his lifetime. His masterpiece, *Ethica* (*Ethics*) was completed in 1675, two years before his death from tuberculosis. Acting against local authority, Spinoza's friends arranged for several of his works to be published after his death.

Dr. Fischelson, in Singer's story, is, like Spinoza, censured by his the Jewish community for his unorthodox ideas (based on his study of Spinoza). Dr. Fischelson had been head librarian of the Warsaw synagogue, but ''because of his heretical ideas he came into conflict with the rabbi and had had to resign his post as librarian.'' The members of the Jewish community on Market Street, where he lives in a garret apartment, regard him with suspicion, considering him a ''heretic'' or a ''convert'' (to Christianity). Black Dobbe, his uneducated neighbor, even associates him with superstitions such as black magic: ''This man made her think of witches, of black mirrors and corpses wandering around at night and terrifying women.'' Dr. Fischelson, how-

What Do I Read Next?

- *The Spinoza of Market Street* (1961) by Isaac Bashevis Singer is a collection of short stories, translated into English from Yiddish.

- *Isaac Bashevis Singer: Children's Stories and Childhood Memoirs* (1996) by Alida Allison is a collection of fictional children's stories as well as excerpts from memoirs of Singer's childhood.

- *Isaac Bashevis Singer: A Life* (1997) by Janet Hadda is a comprehensive biography of Singer.

- *The Pagan Rabbi and Other Stories* (1956) by Cynthia Ozick is a prize-winning collection of short stories written by one of the foremost Jewish-American short fiction writers.

- *Anglish-Yinglish: Yiddish in American Life and Literature* (1989) by Gene Bluestein is about the influence of Yiddish language on American English. Pieces include listings and definitions of common Yiddish words and phrases.

- *Spinoza: A Life* (1999) by Steven Nadler is a biography of the Jewish-Dutch rationalist philosopher who greatly influenced Singer.

- *Benedict de Spinoza: An Introduction* (1987) by Henry E. Allison is an accessible introduction to the basic texts and philosophy of Spinoza.

- *A Treasury of Yiddish Stories* (1954) by Irving Howe and Eliezer Greenberg is a collection of short stories originally written in Yiddish, translated into English. This text includes ''Gimpel the Fool'' by Singer, as well as a story by his brother, Israel Joshua Singer.

---

ever, while clearly a skeptic in the spirit of modern philosophy, considers himself, as he tells Black Dobbe, ''A Jew like any other Jew.''

Dr. Fischelson's character also shares some similarities with that of the author. Like that of Singer, Dr. Fischelson's community is one of Chassidic Judaism. Chassidism (a variation of the term ''Hasidic'') was a movement begun in twelfth-century Germany, which stressed the mystical elements of Jewish theology. Like Singer, Dr. Fischelson's father was a rabbi. Like Singer, Dr. Fischelson had attended a ''yeshiva,'' an institute of rabbinical training. Like Singer, Dr. Fischelson's interests took him in a direction other than that of religious study—for Singer, into literature, for Dr. Fischelson into modern philosophy. Singer has cited his reading of Spinoza as a young man as having had a profound influence on his ideas about Judaism. As Dr. Fischelson has come under censure from the Jewish community for his modern perspectives, so Singer has been criticized by Jewish religious authorities for his literary works, which portray Jewish characters in a less-than-flattering light and express doubt in Jewish theology.

While Dr. Fischelson attempts to live a life in accordance with Spinoza's rationalist philosophy, he also preoccupies himself with contemplation of the cosmic. A few steps up from his garret room, Dr. Fischelson has a telescope, through which he looks out at the night sky. Fischelson's telescope is in part a reference to the fact the Spinoza, unrelated to his philosophical achievements, was a very skilled professional lens crafter, who at times made his living grinding lenses for microscopes, spectacles, and telescopes. For Dr. Fischelson, contemplation of the cosmic is associated with the rationalist philosophy that removes him from the stream of life represented by the lively Jewish community of Market Street below his window. In contemplating the stars and the planets, Dr. Fischelson remains intellectually removed from human companionship, and regards Market Street disdainfully as if it were the depths of Hell.

While Dr. Fischelson's alienation from his Jewish community is in some ways due to his modern ideas, it is in other ways in reaction against the modernization of Jewish culture: ''He began to despise everything associated with the modern Jew

. . ." His perspective on the Hebrew language, for example, is staunchly traditional. Hebrew is the language in which Jewish theological texts are written. But, while Dr. Fischelson "still read a Hebrew magazine occasionally . . . he felt contempt for modern Hebrew which had no roots in the Bible or the Mishnah." The "Bible," refers to the central Jewish theological text, made up of the Pentateuch, the first five books of Moses (Genesis, Exodus, Leviticus, Numbers, and Deuteronomy). Together, they make up the Torah. The Mishna refers to the oral commentary on the Torah that was first written down in a comprehensive volume over a period of about two hundred years, culminating in the third century A.D. Later commentary on the Mishna was collected in a text called the Gemara. The Mishna and Gemara together make up the Talmud. Dr. Fischelson also has contempt for the Zionism of "the modern Jew." Zionism was a movement begun in the nineteenth century that advocated the relocation of members of the Jewish Diaspora to Palestine. Palestine at the time was under British rule, and many European Jews moved there during the first half of the twentieth century, although Israel as a Jewish nation was not founded until 1948.

Dr. Fischelson, an adherent to modern philosophy, who also considers himself a Jew, but who is disdainful of ideas associated with modern Jewry, seems disturbed in part by the co-existence of modern, secular Jewish culture with traditional Jewish religious practice. When he looks down on Market Street, he is disturbed by the existence of Jewish religious observance side by side with the material indulgences of his Jewish community. Dr. Fischelson observes the pious study of Judaism, as "through the window of a Chassidic study house across the way, Dr. Fischelson could see boys with long sidelocks swaying over holy volumes, grimacing and studying aloud in sing-song voices." The "swaying" of the boys in prayer refers to the Jewish practice of "davening," a swaying back and forth while standing in prayer. The "long sidelocks" are the long curls of hair worn by Chassidic men, in accordance with traditional Jewish law.

Yet, alongside this image of piety, Dr. Fischelson observes the pleasure-seeking masses, surrounded by the physical sensations of alcohol, food, music, and sex:

> Butchers, porters, and fruit dealers were drinking beer in the tavern below. Vapor drifted from the tavern's open door like steam from a bathhouse, and there was the sound of loud music. Outside of the tavern,

> **"** The 'Bible,' refers to the central Jewish theological text, made up of the Pentateuch, the first five books of Moses (Genesis, Exodus, Leviticus, Numbers, and Deuteronomy). Together, they make up the Torah."

streetwalkers snatched at drunken soldiers and at workers on their way home from the factories.

To Dr. Fischelson, such activities represent the vices of people destined for Hell:

> Some of the men carried bundles of wood on their shoulders, reminding Dr. Fischelson of the wicked who are condemned to kindle their own fires in Hell.

But, most of all, it is the intermingling of the "sacred" with the "profane" that disturbs the old philosopher:

> Husky record players poured out their raspings through open windows. The liturgy of the high holidays alternated with vulgar vaudeville songs.

Vaudeville was a form of live, on-stage variety show, popular in the late nineteenth and early twentieth centuries, including musical numbers, comedic acts, brief dramatic sketches and other light entertainments. It tends to be associated with the popular entertainment of the most unsophisticated masses of the population. The "high holidays," on the other hand, are the most holy days of the Jewish religious calendar. Yet, while Dr. Fischelson seems disdainful of the intrusion of the "profane" life on Market Street with the "sacred" observance of religious law, he himself does not participate in religious observance, as it is noted that he does not attend prayer.

Dr. Fischelson's alienation from the Jewish community, both its "sacred" and its "secular" elements, is resolved, however, through his marriage to Black Dobbe. Dr. Fischelson is brought back into the fold of Jewish religious observance through his traditional wedding in the synagogue, officiated by the rabbi. The community from which he has been outcast for so long spontaneously comes together for the ceremony. While it is clear that there is a certain perverse interest on the part of these observers, there is also a sense of community expressed through their efforts to dress up and obtain delicacies for the sake of the celebration:

> Although Dr. Fischelson had insisted that the wedding be a small, quiet one, a host of guests assembled in the rabbi's rooms. The baker's apprentices who generally went about barefoot, and in their underwear, with paper bags on the tops of their heads, now put on light-colored suits, straw hats, yellow shoes, gaudy ties, and they brought with them huge cakes and pans filled with cookies. They had even managed to find a bottle of vodka although liquor was forbidden in wartime.

This description brings into the "sacred" space of the rabbi's chambers the "profane" material luxuries that Dr. Fischelson had so disdained: particularly, food and alcohol. The description of the wedding focuses on several specific elements of Jewish wedding ritual. The wedding ceremony itself "proceeded according to law," meaning that the traditional Jewish religious laws of marriage were observed. It is reported that "several porters" had to be brought in from the street to make up the "quorum"; this refers to the Jewish law that at least ten men must be present for prayer. These same porters also served to support the "canopy"—the "hupah" that is a square cloth supported on four poles, under which the bride and groom stand during the wedding ceremony. Next, "Dobbe walked around him seven times as custom required"; in a Jewish wedding the bride circles the groom seven times. Finally, "according to custom, was the smashing of the glass . . . "; in the Jewish wedding tradition, a glass is placed on the floor and the groom smashes it by stepping on it with his foot. After the ceremony, Dobbe's former employer wishes Dr. Fischelson, "Mazel tov" a Yiddish phrase uttered on holidays and special occasions.

The wedding ceremony alleviates Dr. Fischelson's alienation from his community through their participation in the celebration, as well as alleviating his alienation from Judaism through his participation in the traditional religious ritual officiated by the rabbi. It is the "miracle" of the passionate consummation of his marriage to Black Dobbe, however, which ultimately draws Dr. Fischelson down from his removed, cosmic contemplation of the world from a rational perspective, and integrates him back into full participation in both physical and spiritual life. When he awakens in the night to observe the sky from his telescope, Dr. Fischelson, for the first time, sees himself as "a part of this," as

integrated into the "divine substance" of the cosmos: "Yes, the divine substance was extended and had neither beginning nor end; it was absolute, indivisible, eternal, without duration, infinite in its attributes. Its waves and bubbles danced in the universal cauldron, seething with change, following the unbroken chain of causes and effects, and he, Dr. Fischelson, with his unavoidable fate, was part of this."

Source: Liz Brent, Critical Essay on "The Spinoza of Market Street," in *Short Stories for Students*, The Gale Group, 2001.

Lois Kerschen

Kerschen is a writer and public school district administrator. In this essay she considers Singer's conflict with the philosophy of Spinoza as he leads his audience to question the main character's conclusion that he has become a fool.

The first clue to the interpretation of any story lies in its title. "The Spinoza of Market Street" causes the reader to ask "Who or what is Spinoza?" If the reader knows that Spinoza was a seventeenth century Dutch philosopher, then the question might be "What connection does Spinoza have to this street?" Is it significant that the street is named Market rather than Elm or First? The reader learns in the first line of the story that Market Street is the home of Dr. Nahum Fischelson in Warsaw, Poland.

Many of Isaac Bashevis Singer's stories are set in the Jewish ghetto of Warsaw prior to World War II. It was then that the Nazis exterminated the Jews there. Polish Jews and Yiddish, the language of European Jews, became almost extinct. But Singer wrote in Yiddish about the life he knew growing up in Warsaw in an effort to preserve the language and the memories of a unique society. At the same time, his stories prove that, regardless of the time and setting, humans share common feelings and experiences.

Dr. Fischelson is a man who has studied Baruch (aka Benedict) Spinoza for thirty years. He has dedicated his life to this work and to adherence to Spinoza's principles. But Singer identified more with Albert Camus, the twentieth-century French philosopher. As Edwin Gittleman explained in his essay for the *Dictionary of Literary Biography*, Singer was "exasperated by Spinoza's conception of God as infinite intellect but without feelings." Spinoza believed that rationalism, the absence of emotion and the pursuit of purely intellectual thought, led to communion with the mind of God. He proposed that all experience was part of God's plan and was therefore inevitable. Camus, however, taught that the individual cannot make rational sense of his/her experience and that spiritual isolation can have debilitating effects. Singer emphasizes this latter point as he expertly weaves a criticism of Spinozan philosophy into a tale of human foibles and life changes.

Spinoza was expelled from the traditional Jewish community of his time because his teachings were considered heretical. Thereafter, he supported himself as a lens grinder rather than accept any scholarly patronage from others who supported intellectual freedom. In contrast, almost three centuries later, Fischelson earns a doctorate in Spinozan philosophy and is at first heralded by Jewish academia. He is offered many opportunities for personal and professional advancement, but he turns them down because he "wanted to be as independent as Spinoza himself." Then, taking a path similar to Spinoza's, he, too, loses his job because of heretical ideas. He resigns his post as head librarian at the Warsaw synagogue and supports himself "by giving private lessons in Hebrew and German." However, when Fischelson becomes ill, the Berlin Jewish community provides him with a small pension. In all aspects of his life, Fischelson scrupulously tries to follow the teachings of Spinoza according to his own interpretation of Spinoza's writings.

Singer places Fischelson on Market Street to contrast the busy life of the commerce below the scholar's apartment to the isolation of Dr. Fischelson's life. An ordinary residential street would not have provided the obvious difference that Singer wanted to show between Fischelson's eccentricity and the everyday interaction of people. In Part II of the story, the reader is told that Dr. Fischelson "could see into two worlds." He loves to look out his window at the night sky and to peer through a telescope at the celestial bodies. It puts him in a state of euphoria because he believes, as Spinoza taught, that his study of the cosmos brings him in touch with the infinite extension of God. But, when he observes the comings and goings of the people in the street, Fischelson does not appreciate the liveliness and color of human activity. Rather, Fischelson, in his black coat and stiff collar, sees only a "rabble" that is the "very antithesis of reason."

Fischelson's isolation involves not only a separation from people, but also a separation from the times. A man who spends thirty years studying the

> So, just as someone with stage fright or an anxiety attack can experience hyperventilation or nausea, Dr. Fischelson, who prides himself on his rationalism, has irrationally manufactured his own illness in response to his inability to cope with anything beyond his obsession with Spinoza."

same book is not likely to welcome change. Singer points out that the revolt of 1905 "had greatly increased his isolation." Revolution calls for change, and that can be good, but Fischelson feared that it meant the destruction of society. Instead of teaching Spinoza to others and standing up for the preservation of a society he understands, Fischelson withdraws from participation. He no longer reads Hebrew magazines regularly because he "concluded that even the so-called spiritual men had abandoned reason and were doing their utmost to pander to the mob." Although he still occasionally visits a library to check on the latest philosophical writings, he always comes away angry because "the professors did not understand Spinoza, quoted him incorrectly, attributed their own muddled ideas to the philosopher." The astute reader knows that Singer is revealing Dr. Fischelson's own faults through his criticism of others.

Fischelson is so out of touch with the world that, when his pension check is delayed by the crisis that led to World War I, he has to seek out someone to tell him what is happening. The extent to which Fischelson has been in denial about time marching on is illustrated by his inability to find any of his old friends and acquaintances. They have gone on with their lives while he has not; they have moved or they are busy elsewhere. Facing these changes is too much for Dr. Fischelson. He becomes ill and thinks that he is dying. But this ailment, like the stomach trouble he has suffered for years, is a production of his own fears. He has never been truly ill. The doctors have told him that he suffers only from ''nerves.'' So, just as someone with stage fright or an anxiety attack can experience hyperventilation or nausea, Dr. Fischelson, who prides himself on his rationalism, has irrationally manufactured his own illness in response to his inability to cope with anything beyond his obsession with Spinoza. The crippling effect of his malady has given him an excuse for not ever finishing his commentary on Spinoza and to withdraw even further from social contact.

Nili Wachtel, in his article ''Freedom and Slavery in the Fiction of Isaac Bashevis Singer,'' describes those Singer characters who ''lapse into a position which suspects and negates everything, and see vanity and folly everywhere'' as walking a tightrope. In this story, the tightrope is Fischelson's ''garret-room suspended between an orderly heaven above and a chaotic marketplace below. . . . Walking the tightrope means living outside of everything; it means being anchored in nothing more substantial than one's own isolated, 'free' and very precarious self.'' Wachtel explains that

> at issue here is Singer's dualistic perception of reality. As he sees it, reality is fundamentally paradoxical. It does not meet one with a series of neatly separated alternatives, but with a blend in which the contraries exist together. A person, likewise, is a paradox. One dwells a little lower than the angels and a little higher than the beasts; both aspects of one's nature, inextricably intertwined, are at war with each other, and only both together constitute truth. . . . [While] the Enlightenment extolled its rational person, minimizing or altogether ignoring the non-rational aspect of one's nature, Singer labors to show that one does not live by reason alone.

Consequently, Dr. Fischelson must come to a turning point in his life to survive. His intellect cannot will himself to die against a life force he does not even know is still strong within him. To discover this life force requires the introduction of his neighbor Dobbe into Fischelson's life. An expert storyteller, Singer liked to use humor, irony, and the theme of the redemptive power of love. So, he rescues Fischelson through a bride who is his opposite and creates a surprising result that contradicts Spinoza's theories.

Singer saw his primary role in writing as that of an entertainer. Although the richness of Singer's talent still enables one to find depth in ''The Spinoza of Market Street,'' his intent is first a simple human-interest story. The simplicity is emphasized by an easy-to-follow structure of seven sections, each one with a specific function. In Part I, the reader is introduced to Dr. Fischelson, his life's work, and his supposed ailment. In Part II, the obvious contrast between Fischelson's admiration of the mysteries of God in space and his disdain for the real life rabble of the street, i.e., his pursuit of intellectualism to the exclusion of human contact, is established. Part III reveals Fischelson's past and his fear of the future. Part IV introduces the crisis that serves as the catalyst for change in Fischelson's life. Part V introduces the woman who will change Fischelson's life. Part VI develops their relationship, and Part VII describes their wedding and the miracle of their wedding night.

R. V. Cassill, in a criticism of ''The Spinoza of Market Street'' for *The Norton Anthology of Short Fiction* argues that the simplicity of this story is evidence that it is merely a whimsical tale. Thus the reader need not worry about trying to figure out the motivation for the marriage of Fischelson and Dobbe or explain the transformation that occurs on the wedding night. But the answers seem obvious enough. Dr. Fischelson and Dobbe are both unattractive, lonely people who have been forgotten by friends and family. They reach out to each other in their need: Dobbe wants a husband, is attracted to Dr. Fischelson's intellect, and is flattered by his interest in her; Dr. Fischelson needs someone to take care of him, and a wife who has enough money to go to America, but doesn't want to go, fits the bill. In the process, they awaken long dormant emotions in each other. For Fischelson, allowing himself this explosion of repressed feelings seems a failure. He thinks that he has become a fool. But the truth is that he was a fool to lead the life he did before his marriage. Moreover, he will remain a fool if he continues to judge his life by Spinoza's standards and fails to embrace the good fortune that has befallen him.

Cassill further suggests that ''. . . Fischelson is a very unsophisticated man for all his lifelong study of philosophy. He has retained only a few simple precepts of conduct from Spinoza and these seem to do him little good, being at odds with the barrenness of his external life and the weird tumult of his dream. So probably we are supposed to see him as a special sort of fool.'' Wachtel says that Fischelson is one of a number of Singer's ''aging—and often hilarious—Jewish scholars who, having discarded religious traditions and formulations, spend their lives inventing rational equivalents and substitutes.'' Dr. Fischelson no longer goes to prayer and appears to his neighbors to have converted away from

Judaism. When Dobbe asks him why he does not go to synagogue, he gives her a Spinozan answer: ''God is everywhere,'' he replied. ''In the synagogue. In the marketplace. In this very room. We ourselves are parts of God.''

Wachtel goes on to say that Singer argued that ''the world is not rational, it is thoroughly un-Spinozan. Human existence cannot be coerced into an all-rational mold. Dr. Fischelson's rational truths are half-truths; to work, they would need to incorporate—to marry, if Singer's symbolism is borrowed—the realities of the street.'' So, Dr. Fischelson marries Dobbe, a woman who is a product of the streets, and it reminds him that people are complex beings subject to their emotions as well as controlled by their intellect. Perhaps this revelation will free him to live and love, to be just a human again.

Source: Lois Kerschen, Critical Essay on ''The Spinoza of Market Street,'' in *Short Stories for Students*, The Gale Group, 2001.

Edward Alexander

In the following essay, Alexander examines the role Spinoza and his work Ethics *play in ''The Spinoza of Market Street.''*

In several of Singer's stories of courtship leading toward marriage, the woman represents a creative force that can restore vitality to men in whom the springs of life have been dried up by rationalism. These women may distract men from the life of the mind and the dispassionate pursuit of truth seen under the aspect of eternity, but they supply the germinating spirit without which mind remains sterile. One of the most representative of such tales is ''The Spinoza of Market Street'' (*The Spinoza of Market Street*).

Spinoza, recipient of so much uncritical admiration from both Jews and gentiles during the past century and a half, is here bested not by the Judaism against which he set himself but by ignorant, untutored human love. The Spinozistic ideal of detachment from the passions, including love as well as war, is mocked by life. In the story, thirty years of devotion to Spinoza's *Ethics* have made the hero, Dr. Nahum Fischelson of Warsaw, dyspeptic and flatulent, trying without success to sustain himself on the Spinozistic doctrine that morality and happiness are identical. In his detachment, Fischelson sees two worlds: above him, in the infinite space and silence of the heavens, he glimpses ''the *Amor Dei Intellectualis* which is, according to the phi-

> " In the story, thirty years of devotion to Spinoza's **Ethics** have made the hero, Dr. Nahum Fischelson of Warsaw, dyspeptic and flatulent, trying without success to sustain himself on the Spinozistic doctrine that morality and happiness are identical."

losopher of Amsterdam, the highest perfection of the mind''; below, he sees Warsaw's Market Street, the confused multitudinousness of the world, with its thieves, prostitutes, and gamblers, ''the very antithesis of reason . . . immersed in the vainest of passions.'' Fischelson feels an un-Spinozistic anger at nearly all ''modern'' Jewish movements—Zionism, socialism, anarchism, postbiblical Hebrew. In his depression he even thinks of taking his own life, but then remembers that Spinoza—who does, after all, have his uses—disapproved of suicide. This rationalist is plagued by irrational dreams that persuade him of the inescapability of madness.

At this low point, Fischelson is saved by an unprepossessing spinster neighbor named Black Dobbe. This unlettered woman nurses the ailing philosopher, brings him back from the edge of death, and—without the slightest encouragement from him—arranges their marriage. Delicious stabs of satire against Spinozistic intellectualism enliven the account of this bizarre courtship. Why, she wonders, if he is a doctor, can't Fischelson write prescriptions or do much of anything to heal himself? And what, she wonders, can this beloved *Ethics* be but a gentile prayer book? So enfeebled that, at the wedding ceremony, he cannot break the glass goblet, Fischelson is certain he will not be able to consummate the marriage. But Black Dobbe's sensual determination vanquishes Spinoza and snuffs out the Enlightenment. He is saved precisely by that part of the universe which he could not light up with his intellect: ''The *Ethics* dropped from his hands. The candle went out. . . . What happened that night could be called a miracle. . . . Powers long dormant awakened in him. . . . He . . . was again a man as in his youth.'' Under the aspect of eternity, Dr. Fischelson's marriage in old age means little, but, the story says, people do not live entirely under the aspect of eternity; they are not rational beings, but feeling, acting, emotional ones, hence open to miraculous interference. The sterility of Jewish Enlightenment, a frequent theme of Singer's novels, is here expressed through a tale of resurrection wrought by sensuality. After consummating his marriage, Fischelson begs forgiveness: ''Divine Spinoza, forgive me. I have become a fool.'' If so, his new folly is wiser than his old wisdom.

Source: Edward Alexander, ''The Short Fiction,'' in *Isaac Bashevis Singer: A Study of the Short Fiction*, Twayne, 1990, pp. 55–56.

Irving Malin

In the following essay, Malin discusses the stories in The Spinoza of Market Street, *and analyzes the characters of Dr. Nahum Fischelson and Black Dobbe in the title story.*

The Spinoza of Market Street (1961) is another wide-ranging collection of stories.

The title story is clearly one of Singer's best. Dr. Nahum Fischelson is an avid reader of Spinoza—as was the narrator of *In My Father's Court*—and he knows ''every proposition, every proof, every corollary, every note by heart.'' The *Ethics* is his holy text. He attempts to live by its ideas, believing that ''according to Spinoza morality and happiness were identical, and that the most moral deed a man could perform was to indulge in some pleasure which was not contrary to reason.'' Dr. Fischelson is, then, a mature Asa Heschel Bannet or Ezriel; he lives according to a strict moral code (which, of course, has less to do with orthodox Judaism than with rationalism).

But he is a bit obsessive in his life pattern. He has surrendered so completely that he resembles the inhabitants of Goray—he cannot look *ironically* and *playfully* at it. He cannot stop his inflexibility. He gazes at the Milky Way and disregards Market Street below his window. He is between worlds; he is not completely alive on earth. It is, of course, ironic that he condemns the ''vainest of passions'' exhibited by the masses because he is immersed in his own passion for rationalism. He shuns the unpredictable, fearing that ''irrational'' events and people will destroy him. He repeats compulsively:

''All was determined, all necessary, and a man of reason had no right to worry.'' The fears remain: ''Nevertheless, worry invaded his brain, and buzzed about like the flies.''

Singer describes the unpredictable, ''mad'' things surrounding Dr. Fischelson (even as the doctor worships his text). In the very first paragraph we read of a ''variety of insects'' buzzing around the candle flame. These creatures disturb Dr. Fischelson; they are strangely uncontrollable and resemble, without his knowledge, his own confusion over flames. (Fire is again dwelt upon as it was in ''The Gentleman from Cracow.'') A tomcat howls; he calls it ''ignorant savage'' and threatens it with a broom handle. He views the people in the street as noisy, buzzing, agitated animals. He dreams of the burning red sky, of bells ringing. These details undercut the calm rationalism of Dr. Fischelson; they demonstrate that he is on the edge (like Yasha on the balcony?).

Black Dobbe, his neighbor, is a coarse, unpredictable, and illiterate spinster. She is an ''emissary'' from the other world. When she visits him, asking him to read a letter, she finds that he is deathly ill. She proceeds to nurse him back to robust (?) health.

The two are, naturally, frightened of each other. Black Dobbe thinks of ''witches, of black mirrors and corpses wandering around at night and terrifying women . . .'' when she gazes at him. Dr. Fischelson considers her the arch-representative of Market Street. But their differences also attract them. Gradually they think of marriage.

The marriage is presented as a ''miracle.'' It is appropriate because it is perfectly symbolic (and in keeping with the stylized, dream-like tone). Singer is wonderfully ironic. He does not sentimentalize the miracle; he goes so far as to hint that it is black magic. He leaves the outlines fuzzy.

The last paragraph also leaves the matter open; it fails to give a ''final solution'' because it fights such a simple pattern (a pattern which resembles Dr. Fischel son's former life-design). Dr. Fischelson continues to stare at the heavens—he has just discovered his sexual potency—and to think about ''destined courses in unbounded space'': ''Yes, the divine substance was extended and had neither beginning nor end; it was absolute, indivisible, eternal, without duration, infinite in its attributes.'' He sees himself as the product of an ''unbroken chain of causes and effects.'' He is, however, ''shaky'' and unsure. He murmurs: ''Divine Spinoza, forgive me. I have become a fool.'' There is great irony here. It is possible to claim that he is still a fool because he does not realize that his marriage is a divine sign, a life-giving miracle. If only he were truly foolish like Gimpel—that is, wise and vital—he would be less shaky. ''Fool'' means at least two things in the line just quoted—in its ambiguity it defeats the simple-minded ''madness'' of Dr. Fischelson.

''Shiddah and Kuziba'' is only seven pages long, but it creates an extremely powerful impression. The opening sentence introduces the inverted, odd perspective from which the story is told: ''Shiddah and her child, Kuziba, a schoolboy, were sitting nine yards inside the earth at a place where two ledges of rock came together and an underground stream was flowing.'' The juxtaposition of demonic mother and son (no less ''schoolboy'') and subhuman perspective is wonderfully done, especially when we read that Kuziba ''looked like his mother'' (how natural in having wings of a bat and feet like a chicken).

There is a great deal of enlightening play when Singer explains the schooling of Kuziba. Like any child the creature is afraid of the unknown, the ''demonic''; in this case, however, he is afraid of light and humanity. He is comforted when he hears that they are ''safe here—far from light and far from human beings. It's as dark as Egypt here, thank God, and as silent as a cemetery.'' The playfulness suddenly shifts to rage. It is almost as if Singer cannot refrain from attacking humanity for imperfection. Man is said by Shiddah to have ''a white skin but inside he is red. He shouts as if he were strong, but really he is weak and shaky. Throw a stone and he breaks; use a thong and he bleeds.'' Man is condemned for the inability to consider new perspectives (new worlds possibly inhabited by Shiddah and Kuziba) and to escape from pride. It is no wonder that Kuziba is afraid of humanity; he, like us, yields to the graphic, one-sided sermon.

Part Two continues the juxtapositions of natural (that is to say, human) and supernatural elements. Kuziba cries out in his sleep; he is dreaming about a man (horror of horrors!). He has to be reassured by a lullaby which asks God to save them from Light and Words and Man. While he dozes, he is ''cradled'' by his mother.

There is a lengthy theological passage. Shiddah remembers her husband (who does not live at home) and his study of silence. She pursues the idea of

> The two are, naturally, frightened of each other. Black Dobbe thinks of 'witches, of black mirrors and corpses wandering around at night and terrifying women ...' when she gazes at him. Dr. Fischelson considers her the arch-representative of Market Street. But their differences also attract them. Gradually they think of marriage.''

silence: ''He who has reached the final point, the last degree of silence, knows nothing of time and space, of death and lust. There male and female are forever united; will and deed are the same. This last silence is God.'' I think that by his inversion Singer praises the words of men (including, of course, his own fiction). These words may be fuzzy and imprecise—how can they capture the supernatural?—*but they are all we have; they separate us from bats and devils who worship deep silence.* It is beautifully ironic that Shiddah *expounds at length* about silence. Even devils must attempt to shape thoughts in language!

Shiddah also has dreams. She imagines, as any loving mother would, how her boy will grow up (and become a big devil!); how she will take care of her grandchildren (by delousing their heads!); and how her husband will succeed and be offered ''the throne in the Abyss of the Great Female, a thousand miles away from the surface where no one had heard of man and his insanity.''

But her dreams are shattered by a terrible thundering. The holocaust has come! (We expect it from Singer.) There is the noise of a machine—man-made, of course—as it grinds the rock which they inhabit; the noise reduces her dream of silence to dust. She prays to Satan, to Lilith, and ''to all the other powers which maintain creation.'' But her prayer is not answered. Ironically she moves *up-*

ward, to earth, where she will establish a new home, build a new "manor."

The last paragraph is especially chilling (as the playful irony I have mentioned is dropped). Shiddah knows that "the last victory would be to darkness." Then "the remembrance of man and his abominations would be nothing but a bad dream which God had spun out for a while to distract Himself in His eternal night."

Thus "Shiddah and Kuziba," unlike the other stories I have discussed (or, for that matter, most of the novels), ends on a hopeless note—at least for mankind. Although it is possible to claim that Shiddah is an absolutist who cannot see clearly (and dreams of salvation through miracle), it is still difficult to escape the fact that Singer apparently agrees with her denunciations. He is not joking at the end; he is "fiendish" here.

"The Black Wedding" begins with a description of "apathetic" Rabbi Aaron Naphtali. He allows the study house to decay—we are told that "toadstools grew unmolested on the walls"—and he spends his time "practicing miracle—working cabala." He is, obviously, a false spiritual leader (who resembles in part the various ineffectual fathers Singer has portrayed).

Rabbi Aaron Naphtali is so involved with "signs" that he allows the black hosts to destroy him. He hears steps on the roof; he notes candles extinguished suddenly. Is he really able to see vengeful devils? Or does he merely project his madness upon the world? These questions are raised but not answered by Singer (as is true in most of his "demonic" fictions). We are offered facts to support both kinds of explanation; we are free to interpret as we wish. Thus Singer allows our freedom, compelling us to use it and to behave *openly* (unlike Rabbi Aaron).

The madness extends to the Rabbi's daughter, Hindele. She reads esoteric books; she goes into seclusion as does her father. After he dies, she is urged to marry Reb Simon. She cannot stop crying: "She cried at the celebration of the writing of the marriage contract, she cried when the tailors fitted her trousseau, she cried when she was led to the ritual bath." We confront the same ambiguous motivations with Hindele. We do not know how to read her. Perhaps it is best to say that like Dr. Fischelson and the Frampol citizens in "The Gentleman from Cracow," she is an obsessive believer; she wants to fit reality into her design (which was

mysteriously passed on to her by the Rabbi). She creates "miracles"; she shapes visions.

When Hindele stares at her future husband she apparently realizes "what she had suspected long before—that her bridegroom was a demon and that the wedding was nothing but black magic, a satanic hoax." She believes, furthermore, that the wedding is destined to be a Black Wedding. She is alone; she cannot communicate her crazy visions to anyone else. She cannot even tell *us* because we cannot get behind her insights. We see powerfully what she sees; we do not know more than she. We notice, for example, the canopy as "a braid of reptiles," the "hoof" of Reb Simon, a dancing witch, and the "webbed roosters' feet" of the musicians. But we are not sure *why* we (and she) observe these things. In a way we are as unknowledgeable and isolated as Hindele. Singer makes us share in her experience, but he does not completely convince us. He plays a trick.

The story falters after a while because Hindele goes so far in her madness that we cannot assent to it. When she rebels against the child in her womb, calling it "half-frog, half-ape," she oversteps the boundary. She becomes simply another lunatic; she no longer teases us with her great ambiguity.

The story ends ironically. There is a frame effect which demonstrates that the community (like us) can never understand her tortured delusions: "In Tzivkev and in the neighborhood the tidings spread that Hindele had given birth to a male child by Reb Simon of Yampol. The mother had died in childbirth." The previous madness has dissolved; calm objectivity conquers all. I prefer the ending (which is open and playful) to the somewhat easy condition of Hindele before her death.

Source: Irving Malin, "The Short Stories," in *Isaac Bashevis Singer*, Frederick Ungar Publishing Co., 1972, pp. 78–84.

Sources

Alexander, Edward, *Isaac Bashevis Singer*, Twayne Publishers, 1980, pp. 125, 143, 147.

Cassill, R. V., *Instructor's Handbook for the Complete and Shorter Editions, The Norton Anthology of Short Fiction*, 3d ed., W. W. Norton and Company, 1986, p. 219.

Friedman, Lawrence S., *Understanding Isaac Bashevis Singer*, University of South Carolina Press, 1988, pp. 7–8, 230–31.

Gittleman, Edwin, ''Isaac Bashevis Singer,'' in *Dictionary of Literary Biography*, Volume 6: *American Novelists since World War II*, edited by James E. Kibler Jr., Gale Research, 1980, pp. 296–313.

Kresh, Paul, *Isaac Bashevis Singer: The Magician of West 86th Street*, Dial Press, 1979, pp. 203, 206, 230–31, 233–34.

Malin, Irving, *Isaac Bashevis Singer*, Frederick Ungar, 1972, pp. 70, 78.

Wachtel, Nili, ''Freedom and Slavery in the Fiction of Isaac Bashevis Singer,'' in *Judaism*, Vol. 26, No. 2, Spring 1977, pp. 171–86.

''Warsaw,'' in *Encyclopaedia Britannica Online*, 1994.

Further Reading

Farrell, Grace, ed., *Critical Essays on Isaac Bashevis Singer*, Prentice Hall International, 1996.
This collection consists of essays on Singer by such well-known writers and authors as Irving Howe, Susan Sontag, and Leslie Fiedler.

Lifson, David S., *The Yiddish Theater in America*, Yoseloff, 1965.
Lifson's text presents a history of the Yiddish theater in New York City.

Weinreich, Beatrice Silverman, ed., *Yiddish Folktales*, Pantheon, 1988.
This work collects folktales and fairy tales from Eastern European Jewish culture.

Zamir, Israel, *Journey to my Father, Isaac Bashevis Singer*, Arcade Publishers, 1995.
This work contains memoirs about Singer by his son.

Zuckerman, Yitzchak, *A Surplus of Memory: Chronicle of the Warsaw Ghetto Uprising*, University of California Press, 1993.
This history of the uprising of Jews in the Warsaw ghetto during the Holocaust is based on personal narratives of Holocaust survivors

Suspicion

Dorothy L. Sayers
1939

In mystery fiction, Dorothy L. Sayers believed that the writer must play fair with the reader. The solution to the problem must be fathomable to the thoughtful reader. Sayers firmly adhered to this standard both in her novels and her short stories. The detective short story, however, presented challenges, most notably the brevity of the form, which required the writer to propose an interesting complication, an engaging detective, and a believable resolution in a very limited span of pages. Despite these restrictions, Sayers published forty-three short stories between 1925 and 1939.

Sayers cautioned that the detective story must put "all its eggs in one basket; it can turn one trick and one trick only; its detective-interest cannot involve a long investigation—it must be summed up in a single surprise." In her story "Suspicion," Sayers admirably achieves this goal. "Suspicion" was one of the stories in 1939's *In the Teeth of the Evidence* that featured neither of Sayers' stock detectives, Lord Peter Wimsey or Montague Egg. Instead, the main character is the hapless Mr. Mummery, who is convinced that the new cook is out to poison him and his wife. The story seems to be heading toward a solution so obvious that it becomes somewhat unbelievable. Sayers, however, has her "trick" lying in wait, one that turns the entire story around. Because Sayers has so compellingly drawn the reader into Mr. Mummery's web of confusion and suspicion, most readers will

likely feel the effect of the dawning of the truth as keenly as Mr. Mummery does.

Author Biography

Dorothy Sayers was born in Oxford, England, in 1893. Until the age of fifteen, she was tutored at home, and she had a mastery of Latin, French, and German by the time she left home to attend Godolphin School. She was ill at ease among her classmates, but she did participate in debating and in dramatic presentations. She also discovered an interest in and talent for writing while at Godolphin. Her poetry and nonfiction were published in the school magazine.

Sayers won a scholarship to Somerville College, one of the two women's colleges at Oxford University. She earned both bachelor's and master's degrees in 1920, when she graduated among the first group of women to be granted Oxford degrees.

After leaving Oxford, Sayers worked as a teacher and a reader for a publishing house. She also published her own poetry with the house. She worked at a school in Normandy, France, for a year. In 1922, Sayers went to work for a London advertising firm as a copywriter, a job that she held for nine years.

Also that year, Sayers began to write her first detective novel, introducing the recurring character Lord Peter Wimsey. *Whose Body?* was published in 1923 and was followed by several other novels.

In 1928, along with the writer Anthony Berkeley, Sayers founded the London Detection Club, of which she later became president. Members of the club participated in the writing of communal novels, such as *The Floating Admiral*.

By 1931, the financial success of her detective novels allowed her to quit her job and become a full-time writer. She continued work on the Wimsey novels and assorted short stories, edited several mystery anthologies, and introduced a new detective, Montague Egg. She also began experimenting with other types of fiction, most notably the novel of manners—such as the 1935 murderless mystery *Gaudy Night*—and drama.

In 1937, Sayers turned to religious verse drama, which marked the virtual end of her career as a mystery writer. She published one more mystery work, 1939's collection of short stories *In the Teeth of the Evidence*, and several of these stories had previously appeared in magazines. "Suspicion" was among the stories included in *In the Teeth of the Evidence*. Her writing until her death consisted of plays and essays, as well as translations of Dante's poetry. She also gave numerous talks.

Sayers remained well known until her death of a stroke in 1957. She was awarded an honorary doctorate of letters from the University of Durham, and she became a churchwarden at St. Thomas' church in London, where one of her religious dramas was produced.

Plot Summary

"Suspicion" opens with Mr. Mummery, who, on his way to work, increasingly feels a stomachache. He tries to ignore it and continues to browse the paper, reading about, among other items, a cook who poisoned a nearby family. At the office, he works with his partner, Mr. Brookes. At one point, Mr. Brookes asks if Mr. Mummery's wife knows of a good cook. Mr. Mummery says no, in fact, they have just found a new cook themselves. The conversation turns to the arsenic poisoning case, for the still-at-large woman, Mrs. Andrews, may be seeking a situation as a cook.

By the end of the day, Mr. Mummery feels better. When he gets home, Mrs. Sutton, the new cook, tells him that his wife Ethel is not feeling well herself. Mr. Mummery visits her in the bedroom and decides that he will send her supper up. If she doesn't take care of herself, he says, she will not be allowed to go to the Drama Club meetings, and the Welbecks had been asking for her there.

Over the next few days, Mr. Mummery feels better himself, which he ascribes to his home cure of drinking orange juice. One night, however, he gets so violently ill that Ethel calls the doctor, who says his stomach problem is a result of combining orange juice and pork. He is not able to leave his bed for several days. On his first day up again, he must attend to the household accounts. After speaking with his wife, they decide to keep on Mrs. Sutton, who has only been with them a month and came without references.

The next day, Mr. Mummery feels fine. He decides to do some gardening. In the potting shed he finds a tin of weed-killer and notes with some excitement that the brand he uses is the same one that Mrs. Andrews used. He also notices that the

Dorothy Sayers

stopper has been put in quite loosely. When he goes back inside, he finds that Mrs. Welbeck and her son, young Welbeck, have come for a visit. He takes Mrs. Welbeck to the garden to get some cuttings, leaving his wife alone with Welbeck. In the kitchen, where he goes to get newspaper to wrap up the cuttings, he makes another surprising discovery: every mention or picture of Mrs. Andrews and the poisoning case has been cut out of the paper. Mr. Mummery begins to review the past month. He realizes that he has been feeling poorly since Mrs. Sutton came to work for them and that her appearance coincides with the disappearance of Mrs. Andrews. He suspects that Mrs. Sutton may be Mrs. Andrews, but he determines that he must sort this out on his own, without scaring Ethel.

Over the next few days, nothing out of the ordinary occurs, and Mr. Mummery begins to feel foolish for his suspicions. On Thursday evening, he goes out with some men after work, and when he gets home, he finds some cocoa Mrs. Sutton has prepared waiting for him. He takes a sip but the cocoa tastes strange. He pours the cocoa into a medicine bottle. Then he goes out to the potting shed and pulls out the tin of weed-killer. He finds that the stopper is loose again, but he clearly remembers that he had tightened it the last time.

The next morning he brings the cocoa to a chemist friend and explains what he wants it analyzed for and why. At the end of the day, he picks up the sample. The chemist tells him that the cocoa had been laced with a strong dose of arsenic, a main ingredient in the weed-killer. Mr. Mummery rushes to catch the train home, afraid for Ethel, and asks the chemist to call the police. Approaching his house, Mr. Mummery fears he is too late, for he sees a car parked by the door and thinks it must be a doctor. He is quite relieved when a man comes out of the house, followed by Ethel, and drives off. He makes himself calm down and goes in the house, where Ethel is surprised to see him. He asks about the visitor and learns it was young Welbeck come to discuss the Drama Society.

Mr. Mummery tells Ethel he has something unpleasant to tell her. He is about to begin when Mrs. Sutton comes into the room. Among the other news she has to report is that Mrs. Andrews, the poisoner, has been caught. Mr. Mummery feels immediate relief. It had all been a mistake! But then he thinks about the cocoa. If Mrs. Sutton had not poisoned it, who had? He looks at Ethel and notes ''in her eyes . . . something he had never seen before . . .''

Characters

Ethel Mummery

Ethel Mummery is Mr. Mummery's wife. She is younger than her husband, and her actions make her seem childlike and incapable of taking care of herself. In reality, she is manipulative and deceitful, both in her affair with Welbeck and in poisoning her husband. Mr. Mummery, however, treats her as a delicate, fragile creature who must be protected. After having a nervous breakdown the previous summer, she spends most of her time lying down and relaxing. The year before, however, she had participated in the Drama Society, and she intends to do so again. Like her husband, Ethel has not been feeling well lately, but her illness manifests itself through headaches and her general feeling of tiredness. The only time she demonstrates any energy or excitement is with Welbeck.

Harold Mummery

Mr. Mummery is the protagonist of the story. According to the narrator, he has a rather uninteresting life. His hobbies include gardening. He also enjoys reading about the murders committed by Mrs. Andrews, because they give him "an agreeable thrill of vicarious adventure." Mr. Mummery is devoted to his wife, but he treats her less like a wife than a child. When in her presence, he refers to himself in the third person, and he handles all the household affairs. Mr. Mummery's rather dim intellect is challenged when he comes to believe that Mrs. Sutton is poisoning him and his wife. He examines the clues, but instead of informing the police, he decides to investigate the matter himself. He actually takes no action until the cocoa is heavily dosed with arsenic. Although Mr. Mummery eventually "solves" the crime, he does so more through fortunate occurrence than by clever detection.

Mrs. Sutton

Mrs. Sutton is the Mummerys' new cook. She has only been working for them for a month. She came to them without references, for she had previously been caring for her elderly mother. Mr. Mummery comes to suspect that she is poisoning him and his wife.

Welbeck

Welbeck is the son of the Mummerys' neighbor, Mrs. Welbeck. He participates in the Drama Society along with Ethel. He and Ethel have been having an affair.

Topics for Further Study

- Do you think many readers would have suspected Ethel Mummery of the poisoning? Why or why not?

- Does life in the 1930s seem to you to differ greatly from contemporary life? In what ways is it different? In what ways is it alike?

- Read a short story by Agatha Christie, one of Sayers's contemporaries. How does it compare to "Suspicion"? How do the authors' writing styles compare?

- What, if any, generalizations can you make about England in the 1930s from this story?

- Do you agree with the assessment that Sayers plays fair with her reader in "Suspicion"? Why or why not?

- Propose an alternate explanation to the strange events in the Mummery household. Write a paragraph or two explaining your theory.

Themes

Appearances and Reality

The difference between appearances and reality is an important theme in "Suspicion." Mr. Mummery and his wife both have not been feeling well lately. He has been suffering from stomach problems, and she is often tired and sluggish. When Mr. Mummery finds certain suspicious clues, he begins to wonder if their new cook is poisoning them. He finds a can of weed-killer with arsenic in the garage. It is the exact same brand that another cook, Mrs. Andrews, used to poison a family, and it has been opened though he knows he left it capped. He realizes that every article and picture referring to the Andrews poisoning case has been cut out of the newspaper. In addition to the circumstantial evidence against the Mummerys' new cook, Mrs. Sutton, the sequence of events seems to suggest her guilt. The police have been looking for Mrs. Andrews for

about a month, and that is how long Mrs. Sutton has been with the Mummerys. Mrs. Sutton also appears to be acting suspicious and guilty.

Mr. Mummery is on the verge of breaking the frightening news to his wife when Mrs. Sutton announces that Mrs. Andrews has been captured. Mr. Mummery wonders who could have put arsenic in the cocoa. Despite the evidence, which now clearly points to his wife, Mr. Mummery does not suspect her until he turns and sees in Ethel's eyes "something that he had never seen before." This sentence underscores the truth that there is a difference between what something *looks* like and what it really *is*.

The trick ending also immediately reveals that Ethel Mummery has been having an affair with Welbeck. They have been concealing their affair under the guise of friendship, which is yet another example of the confusion, deliberate or otherwise, of appearances and reality.

Deception and Betrayal

By the end of the story, Mr. Mummery is on the brink of the realization that he has been deceived and betrayed. He dearly loves his wife. All this time, however, she has been carrying on an affair with Welbeck. The clues to her affair were available to Mr. Mummery, but he never noticed them. For instance, when the Welbecks come to visit he sees ''a relieved glance pass between Ethel and young Welbeck.'' He ascribes this glance to their mutual understanding of his contrivance to get Mrs. Welbeck to stop talking about the murders in front of Ethel. But in truth, Ethel and Welbeck are pleased because he is going outside with Mrs. Welbeck and leaving them alone. Similarly, when he returns from the garden with Mrs. Welbeck, he finds his wife and young Welbeck holding hands, but he simply makes the assumption that ''their approach to the house had evidently been from the sitting-room window'' and that Welbeck and his wife are ''saying good-bye.'' More importantly, Ethel has been deceiving her husband in her plot to kill him, presumably to free herself to be with Welbeck.

Crime

Mrs. Andrews' crime, which has no actual relation to the events at the Mummery household, nevertheless is very important. The story suggests that reading about the crime may have given Ethel an idea of how she might kill her husband, while throwing suspicion on another party, Mrs. Sutton. There is a strong indication that the poisoning began only with the arrival of Mrs. Sutton, which coincided with the news about the Andrews case.

Mr. Mummery's reaction to the crime is also telling. He gets a ''thrill'' from reading about the Andrews murders, and he worries excessively about discussion of the crimes upsetting his wife. Yet when he suspects that Mrs. Andrews may be in their home masquerading as Mrs. Sutton, he takes no direct action, even when he fears Mrs. Sutton may murder Ethel. He chooses instead to watch carefully how the food is handled, all the while acknowledging that there was little use ''supervising breakfast, when he had to be out of the house every day between half-past nine and six.'' Even though he admits he is ''chary of investigating'' his suspicions, he does so, but not very thoroughly. Instead of reporting his suspicions to the police, he ''must cope with this monstrous suspicion on his own. . . . And he must be sure of his ground. To dismiss the only decent cook they ever had out of sheer unfounded panic would be wanton cruelty.''

Style

Narration and Point of View

The narration of the story is straightforward. It is told chronologically and easily moves in sequence from one event to the next. It does not rely on flashbacks or any other literary devices to add necessary details to the story or to flesh out the characters.

The story is told from a third-person point of view. This means that readers see and hear only what one character sees and hears, and that readers are also privy to that character's thoughts, in this case Mr. Mummery. Because the point of view is so strongly with Mr. Mummery, most readers will only *think* what he thinks. Although an inquisitive reader may question whether Mrs. Sutton is the poisoner— where then is the mystery?—Mr. Mummery's absolute trust in his wife is so complete that many will not even question Ethel's role. Thus, the point of view works extremely well with the story, for it hinges on the reader's—and Mr. Mummery's— utter surprise at the discovery of Ethel's treachery.

Irony

Irony is the use of words to express something other than or, especially, the opposite of the literal meaning. The story contains many instances of irony, which the reader may only fully appreciate *after* the ending is revealed. For instance, the year before, Ethel and Welbeck starred in a Drama Society production of a play called *Romance*. In another example of irony, after Mr. Mummery comes to suspect Mrs. Sutton, he makes it a habit to waken early in the morning and go ''prowling about the kitchen,'' which ''made Ethel nervous, but Mrs. Sutton offered no remark.'' Despite their reactions, Mr. Mummery believes that Mrs. Sutton is watching ''tolerantly,'' even with some ''amusement.'' Even Ethel's seemingly innocent statement, ''Did Mrs. Sutton leave something hot for you? She said she would,'' takes on ironic significance: she is directing him to the cocoa that has been laced with an extremely heavy does of arsenic.

Mr. Mummery's interpretation of his wife's reaction to talk of the Andrews' murders is another example of irony. He describes her as ''quite white and tremulous,'' which he ascribes to the violence of the topic, when really her loss of composure is caused by her own guilt in poisoning her husband. Later that afternoon, she becomes almost hysterical when Mr. Mummery brings up the topic again.

The final instance of irony in the story occurs when Mr. Mummery arrives home after learning conclusively that his cocoa has been poisoned with arsenic. He sees a car by his house and assumes that it belongs to a doctor. "It had happened already. . . . Fool, murderer that he was to have left things so late." The irony here stems from the fact that Mr. Mummery calls himself a murderer, believing that his handling of the poisoning has led to the death of his wife, while in reality his wife is attempting to murder him.

Conclusion

The surprise ending is crucial to the story. It comes at the extreme end of the story, with the story turning drastically and quickly. Mr. Mummery's suspicions transfer to his wife in one brief, open-ended sentence: "He glanced around at his wife, and in her eyes he saw something that he had never seen before. . ." All the clues point to Mrs. Sutton as the poisoner, so a reader, in the act of reading, may very well question where the actual mystery is. The clues, observed through Mr. Mummery, all point to Mrs. Sutton as the guilty party, but they all could just as accurately point to Ethel. Because the plot could just as easily lead in one direction as the other, the ending of the story is a surprise and not a trick ending.

Historical Context

The British Economy

The Great Depression devastated the United Kingdom along with the rest of the industrialized world. In the 1930s, Britain's traditional industrial base began to decline. Coal, shipping, and cotton production were all down significantly from pre-World War I levels. Throughout the inter-war period, unemployment never fell below one million, or one worker in ten. In 1932, unemployment hit a record high of 20 percent of the working population. In that year, more than one third of all miners were unemployed, as were 43 percent of cotton workers, 48 percent of iron and steel workers, and 62 percent of shipyard workers.

Overall, Britain's economy was in a state of change. Despite the mass unemployment, those who had work saw their wages and salaries rise in proportion to the rise in the national product, which averaged 2.1 percent each year between 1920 and 1938. Gross domestic product rose by 2.3 percent between 1924 and 1937, which was a more rapid growth than that of the Victorian era. Also, new economic sectors were emerging, such as electric and electronics manufacturing, the motor vehicles industry, and the production of household equipment. Although England's industrial production in 1938 only accounted for 9 percent of the world's total, that same year, England's share of world trade was 19 percent.

Britain and the World

Great Britain joined the League of Nations after World War I. This organization had set up a system of collective security to stop international aggression. In the 1930s, however, the League of Nations took virtually no action to do so. Japan seized Manchuria, a province in China, in 1931. Within a year, Japan proclaimed Manchuria to be independent and installed a Japanese-controlled government. China appealed to the League of Nations for help, but no member was willing to commit its military forces.

In 1935, Italian forces invaded Ethiopia, Africa's only independent kingdom. Ethiopia, also a member of the League, turned to the organization for help, but the League voted only to condemn the invasion and to impose trade penalties against Italy. By May 1936, Ethiopia had fallen, and its ruler had fled to Britain. In June, Haile Selassie met with the League's Council to reconsider its policy. Despite his pleas, Britain and France, the leading powers, declined to use force in Ethiopia.

Britain and World War II

By the early 1930s, Adolf Hitler ruled Germany with dictatorial powers. In 1936, while Britain and France were occupied with the Ethiopian crisis, Hitler violated the Treaty of Versailles and moved German troops back into the Rhineland. In 1938, Germany annexed Austria and demanded that Czechoslovakia turn over the Sudetenland, a region in the northwest part of the country. Germany's demand threatened war, and the British prime minister, along with the leader of France, met with Hitler and agreed to the annexation of the Sudetenland in return for Hitler's promise to claim no more territory in Europe. In March 1939, however, Germany reneged, taking over most of the rest of Czechoslovakia and then attacking Poland in September. Britain and France demanded an immediate German withdrawal. When Hitler ignored these demands, Britain and France jointly declared war on Germany, beginning World War II.

Compare & Contrast

- **1930s:** The average British household consists of 3.7 persons. For couples married between 1930 and 1934, the average number of children is 2.08.

  1990s: The average British household has less than 2 children.

- **1930s:** The death rate is around 12 people per 1,000.

  1990s: The death rate is 10.7 people per 1,000.

- **1930s:** Britain and France declare war on Germany, which starts World War II.

  1990s: Britain, as a part of the United Nations, fights in the Persian Gulf War. British and American soldiers and troops from many other countries fight against Iraq after that country invades Kuwait.

- **1930s:** The Labour government resigns over budget disputes. The prime minister forms an emergency coalition government comprised of Conservatives and Liberals.

  1990s: The British vote the Conservatives out of office.

- **1930s:** Britain develops into a "social service state." From 1934 onward, legislation is instituted that ensures a social security system that ranks among the most generous of the major western countries.

  1980s: Under Prime Minister Margaret Thatcher, Britain makes cuts in social spending, including the complete elimination of some programs.

Critical Overview

Sayers and other members of the Detection Club vowed "to keep the detective story up to the highest standard that its nature permits, and to free it from the bad legacy of sensationalism, clap-trap and jargon with which it was unhappily burdened in the past." As such, Sayers vowed that the solution to her mysteries would always rely on solid clues and deductive reasoning. In essence, the writer must play fair with the reader. She maintained this literary integrity in both her detective novels and her short stories.

Sayers began to write detective fiction in the 1920s, both novels and short stories. At the time, short stories were the more popular length for the genre. Between 1925 and 1939, Sayers published forty-three short stories, about half of which featured her star detective Lord Peter Wimsey. Another ten featured Montague Egg, and the twelve remaining stories were dubbed by Dawson Gaillard, in his study *Dorothy L. Sayers*, "miscellaneous pieces." Of those, Gaillard writes, "few can properly be called detection stories." "Suspicion" is among these twelve.

In the Teeth of the Evidence, which included "Suspicion," was Sayers' last work of mystery fiction published during her lifetime, in 1939. (One short story was published posthumously.) Reviewers responses to the collection were mixed. Ralph Partridge, writing in the *New Statesman and Nation*, found Sayers to be "supremely competent in everything she touches" and called the stories "lively" and "well-written." Isaac Anderson, a reviewer for the *New York Times*, called the stories "truly remarkable," believing they would "add much to the already great reputation of Dorothy Sayers." Many reviewers also commented on the eagerness that Sayers' fans had for more work by the author. The reviewer for the *Times Literary Supplement* only wanted Sayers' stories to be longer. "The publication of Miss Dorothy Sayers of a collection of her short stories causes one to reflect that many of the best detective stories in the English language are not full-length novels at all. . . . The only complaint to make. . . . is that her tales are a little too short. . . .

Nevertheless—and for this we must be deeply grate-ful—Miss Sayers does make her characters live.''

Some reviewers, however, expressed disap-pointment. The *Saturday Review of Literature* found that the stories, while ''clever enough,'' were ''some-how empty.'' The reviewer for the *Springfield Repub-lican* felt that the stories did not demonstrate enough of Sayers' ''intelligent perception'' and ''vivacity of observation,'' and that in *In the Teeth of the Evidence* Sayers was ''more nearly dependent on mere story telling.'' Rupert Hart-Davis, writing in *The Spectator*, was extremely negative. He found almost all of the new stories to be ''unsatisfying.''

Ten of the seventeen stories in the collection fall into the category of Sayers' ''miscellaneous pieces.'' They do not feature either of Sayers' well-established detectives, or, in fact, any detective at all. The reviewer for the *Times Literary Supplement* found that ''some of the best stories [of the collec-tion] belong to [this] group, notably 'Suspicion.''' Will Cuppy of the *New York Herald Tribune Books* also mentioned ''Suspicion'' for ''high honors.''

In speaking of these ''miscellaneous'' stories, Hart-Davis noted that they ''have little twists in their tails, but one can almost always anticipate them.'' Indeed, enjoyment of ''Suspicion'' depends upon the surprise ending. As Sayers wrote, short detective fiction must put ''all its eggs in one basket; it can turn one trick and one trick only; its detective-interest cannot involve a long investiga-tion—it must be summed up in a single surprise.'' Several critics, however, did find the ending of ''Suspicion'' a surprise. Among them is Mary Brian Durkin, who wrote in her book-length study, *Doro-thy L. Sayers*, that although Mr. Mummery's ''fears deepen into terror, until the last sentence, readers will not guess his horrifying discovery.''

Criticism

Rena Korb

Korb has a master's degree in English litera-ture and creative writing and has written for a wide variety of educational publishers. In the following essay, she discusses how the clues and details in ''Suspicion'' can point to Ethel Mummery's guilt as well as Mrs. Sutton's.

In her introduction to the *The Floating Admiral*, which Dorothy L. Sayers and other members of the Detection Club wrote collaboratively, Sayers set out the rules that the mystery writers were bound to follow:

> Put briefly, it amounts to this: that the author pledges himself to play the game with the public . . . His detectives must detect by their wits, without the help of accident or coincidence; he must not invent impos-sible death-rays and poisons to produce solutions which no living person could expect; he must write as good English as he can.

Sayers abided by these rules in her own detec-tive fiction as well. Her short story *''Suspicion,''* collected in the last volume of mystery writing the author ever published, shows her own dedication to playing the game and playing it fairly.

In *''Suspicion,''* the main character, Mr. Mum-mery, grows to fear that the new cook, Mrs. Sutton, is really Mrs. Andrews, a murderess on the run now trying to poison him and his wife, Ethel. After a bit of bumbling, Mr. Mummery brings a cocoa sample to a chemist and soon finds out that the drink is laced with a heavy dose of arsenic. At the very moment Mr. Mummery is about to share the bad news with his wife, Mrs. Sutton announces that the real Mrs. Andrews has been caught. Mr. Mummery's im-mediate relief is followed up by a more vexing question: ''But there had been the cocoa. . . . Who, then—?''

The story, while exceedingly simple and lack-ing in-depth detection, shows Sayers at her finest. Mr. Mummery indeed uses his wits, even if he seems rather witless from time to time. His discov-ery of the solution is believable, especially as he is forced to the realization of his wife's deceit only by default. Perhaps most interestingly, Sayers' ending is a surprise but never a trick: every clue pointing to Ethel as the poisoner is made clearly available in the text. The story's point of view, however, is so firmly grounded in Mr. Mummery that most readers will likely follow him along in his pursuit of an an-swer, despite his bumbling, timidity, and general ineffectiveness.

Sayers' writing is carefully crafted to build the story to its crescendo while leading the reader to the same conclusion as Mr. Mummery. The latter is a remarkable achievement, for any mystery reader will surely question how Mrs. Sutton can be the murderess given that all the clues so definitely point to her. Again, Sayers' success is grounded in her convincing narration, which is so clearly defined by Mr. Mummery that the reader can hardly entertain an idea that he is not also entertaining. The other major reason for the success of the story is Sayers'

What Do I Read Next?

- Agatha Christie is one of the most popular mystery writers of all times. *The Mysterious Affair at Styles* (1920) was her first detective novel. Her detective Hercule Poirot follows a confounding set of clues to discover who poisoned an old woman.

- G. K. Chesterton, who co-founded the Detection Club with Sayers, created a priest-sleuth in this Father Brown series. Father Brown first appeared in *The Innocence of Father Brown* (1911). On the surface, Father Brown appears to be clumsy and naïve, but his clever mind, penetrating insight, careful observational skills, and deep understanding of human evil allow him to catch the criminal.

- Sayers and thirteen other members of the Detection Club co-wrote *The Floating Admiral* (1932). Each writer wrote one chapter, and in the subsequent chapters, writers had to take into account characters and clues introduced.

- Six members of the Detection Club, including Sayers, participated in *Ask a Policeman* (1933). One member supplied a plot, four members wrote solutions using another member's detective, and another member wrote the conclusion.

- Sayers is well known for her Peter Wimsey mysteries. In 1923, she published her first Wimsey mystery, *Whose Body?*.

- Throughout her career, Sayers became increasingly interested in delving into the psychology of her characters. In 1935, she published *Gaudy Night*, which was in essence a murderless mystery. With this novel, Sayers believed that she had achieved her goal of fusing the mystery with the novel of manners.

---

layering of detail upon detail in a seemingly innocent fashion. Such a technique makes the clues integral parts of the story; once the reader has come to believe that they point to Mrs. Sutton's guilt, the reader is almost bound to stick with that presumption, for diverting from it would be like tearing the very fabric of the story apart.

The story starts out on the train. Mr. Mummery is experiencing stomach pains, which he ascribes to his breakfast not agreeing with him. The narrator then introduces Mr. Mummery's cook, but the careful choice of words—''coffee made as only Mrs. Sutton knew how to make it''—implies that Mrs. Sutton had been with the Mummerys for some time. As the reader gradually learns, however, Mrs. Sutton has only been in their employ for one month—exactly the same amount of time Mrs. Andrews has been on the loose. Her arrival also coincides exactly with the onset of Mr. Mummery's stomach problems. Still later, the reader discovers that Mrs. Sutton came seeking employment without references, a situation that had initially made Mr. Mummery ''uneasy.'' Yet these significant details are revealed slowly, so their effect is one of a gradual build-up. The reader is almost compelled to accept these clues as proof of Mrs. Sutton's guilt, much as Mr. Mummery does.

Sayers' prose also makes Mr. Mummery's suspicions seem utterly natural. In the first scene, Mr. Mummery reads the newspaper, which is how the reader is introduced to the Andrews case: ''The police were still looking for the woman who was supposed to have poisoned a family in Lincoln.'' This tidbit is buried amidst a series of articles on topics including a factory fire and government typewriters. Again, Sayers employs the technique of building detail upon detail to fix the larger picture. Only in a later conversation does the reader learn that, in her last escapade, Mrs. Andrews had been employed as a cook for a husband and wife, and that now police think she may seek another position as a cook. The fate of these last victims of Mrs. Andrews—the husband dies and the wife becomes seriously ill—takes on chilling significance after the story has reached its surprising conclusion.

Sayers' introduction of Mrs. Sutton and Ethel also inflame the reader's suspicions. At first glimpse Mrs. Sutton ''was sitting at the table with her back to him [Mr. Mummery], and started up almost *guiltily* as he approached'' [italics mine]. When Mr. Mummery immediately asks about his wife, the reader finds out that she is ''feeling bad again.'' She has ''a bit of headache,'' so Mrs. Sutton has given her a cup of tea. The juxtaposition of these ideas—Ethel's illness and the tea made by Mrs. Sutton—in subsequent sentences implies a causality that does not actually exist.

After it is revealed that Mrs. Sutton is not Mrs. Andrews—and thus unlikely to be the person who placed arsenic in Mr. Mummery's cocoa—the reader, along with Mr. Mummery, realizes that his poisoner must have been Ethel. A review of the clues shows that Ethel's guilt has been suggested all along, for the clues as easily point to her as they did to Mrs. Sutton. For instance, when Mr. Mummery is sick in bed for several days, his food is ''skillfully prepared by Mrs. Sutton and brought to his bedside by Ethel.'' This detail emphasizes that Ethel has access to all the food that Mr. Mummery eats and could easily poison it. When Mr. Mummery comes home the evening in which a potentially fatal dose of arsenic has been placed in his cocoa, the beverage was made by Mrs. Sutton, but at the instigation of Ethel, who makes a point of asking Mr. Mummery if he drank the cocoa: ''Did Mrs. Sutton leave something hot for you? She said she would.'' Clearly, Ethel wants to know if Mr. Mummery ingested the arsenic.

The clues also suggest Ethel's affair with young Welbeck. The first reference to him comes, innocently enough, from Mr. Mummery's partner, who asks after Ethel's health.

> 'Can't do without her in the drama society, you know,' Mr. Brookes says . . . 'I shan't forget her acting last year in *Romance*. She and young Welbeck positively brought the house down, didn't they? The Welbecks were asking after her only yesterday.'

In re-evaluating this passage, the reader can see the connection between Ethel and Welbeck in a play so aptly titled. But it is also apparent how easily overlooked such a connection might be. The visit they pay to the Mummerys' home shows that Ethel and Welbeck use the acquaintance between the families to disguise their relationship. Further, the Welbecks' visit is revealing: Ethel becomes ''quite white and tremulous'' as Mrs. Welbeck talks on

> "After a bit of bumbling, Mr. Mummery brings a cocoa sample to a chemist and soon finds out that the drink is laced with a heavy dose of arsenic. At the very moment Mr. Mummery is about to share the bad news with his wife, Mrs. Sutton announces that the real Mrs. Andrews has been caught."

about the poisoning case, which Mr. Mummery ascribes to Ethel's delicate nature. Mr. Mummery spies significant glances between Welbeck and Ethel and even catches them with clasped hands, but again, he has a plausible and natural explanation. Ethel grows animated when she finds out that the Welbecks had asked about her, and she speaks with subdued excitement when she reports that young Welbeck had visited to talk about the Drama Society—an excitement both Mummery and the reader could easily attribute to her interest in returning to the stage.

An underlying theme of the story is that things are not always what they appear—nor are people, which is yet another clue to Ethel's treachery. After Mr. Mummery first discovers the loose stopper on the arsenic weed-killer he rams the top in forcefully. ''After that he washed his hands carefully at the scullery tap, for he did not believe in taking risks.'' This statement is blatantly untrue, for even when he suspects Mrs. Sutton of poisoning him and his wife, he takes no action whatsoever with the exception of coming into the kitchen while Mrs. Sutton *and Ethel* are preparing breakfast. He knows, however, that even this precaution is ineffectual, for ''what was the use of supervising the breakfast, when he had to be out of the house every day between half-past nine and six?'' Instead of reporting his suspicions to the police, Mr. Mummery relies on calling home frequently, which would do very little to save Ethel should she be poisoned. In essence, in taking no action, Mr. Mummery is risking his own life and that of his wife.

Mr. Brooke's words, however, which close the opening section of the story, perhaps best demonstrate that a person can live with another person and yet never really *know* them. "She's got a bad mouth," pronounces Mr. Brookes while looking at a newspaper photograph of Mrs. Andrews. "He had a theory that character showed in the mouth. 'I wouldn't trust that woman an inch.'" For Mr. Mummery, however, he has all along been trusting the wrong woman without any suspicion whatsoever.

Source: Rena Korb, Critical Essay on "Suspicion," in *Short Stories for Students*, The Gale Group, 2001.

Wendy Perkins

Perkins is an Associate Professor of English at Prince George's Community College in Maryland. In the following essay she analyzes Sayers' technique in "Suspicion."

Michele Slung, in her overview of Dorothy Sayers' work for *St. James Guide to Crime & Mystery Writers*, notes that in a 1939 essay entitled "Other People's Great Detectives," Sayers compares fictional detectives to their real-life counterparts and determines there is an important difference. Fictional detectives, she claims, are not remembered for their display of "unusual talent and ingenuity" in their methods of detection, nor for their "conspicuous success in bringing criminals to justice." These qualities form the reputation of real-life detectives; however, fictional sleuths are measured by their author's "presentation of the character." Sayers' intricate plotting, nevertheless, keeps the reader guessing about whether or not Mummery is being poisoned and by whom.

Sayers' most famous and celebrated detective is Oxford-educated Lord Peter Wimsey, an amateur sleuth who appears in eleven novels and twenty-one short stories. In his article on Sayers for the *Dictionary of Literary Biography*, Bernard Benstock notes that Sayers created Lord Peter to be "a fascinating if somewhat eccentric charmer, following the Conan Doyle tradition that the character of the detective took precedence over all other facets of the detective fiction."

In the works where Wimsey is absent, Sayers creates other central characters who may not be as charming or as unconventional, yet Sayers' characterizations of them bring them to vivid life. As a result, readers are caught up in the twists and turns of her stories. In "Suspicion," Harold Mummery becomes a reluctant detective after he discovers someone has been trying to poison him. While the story has little thematic import, Sayers' intricate plotting and subtle characterizations of Mummery and his wife make the story memorable.

Mummery is a mild-mannered estate agent who enlivens his dull life by reading about murders in the newspaper, "for, naturally, they were matters quite remote from daily life in the outskirts of Hull." When he notices his weed-killer is the same brand used by Mrs. Andrews, a cook who poisoned the family who employed her, "he was rather pleased about it. It gave him a sensation of being remotely but definitely in touch with important events."

His routine life is governed by a strict attention to decorum, as seen when he becomes upset with Mrs. Welbeck for raising the topic of the poisonings, "a most unsuitable subject for the tea-table." He washes his hands carefully after handling the weed-killer, "for he did not believe in taking risks." His rigid nature allows him only one indulgence—a whisky and soda in the evening—and prompts him to ask his wife to inform their cook, "if she must read the morning paper before I come down, I should be obliged if she would fold it neatly afterwards." The narrator notes, "it was important that the morning paper should come to him fresh and prim, like a virgin." This analogy also suggests his conservative attitude toward women, which emerges in his relationship with his wife.

On the surface, the Mummerys appear to have a happy marriage. Ethel continually asks her husband about his health and speaks to him in terms of endearment. Mummery's devotion is evident in his genuine concern for her health. When he comes home, he brings her flowers to cheer her up, and one evening in bed he clutches her tightly, "as though defying death and hell to take her from him." He admits without hesitation that he "would cheerfully have laid down his rather uninteresting little life to spare Ethel a moment's uneasiness."

Yet a closer look reveals Mummery's extreme paternalistic treatment of his wife. He calls her pet names like "poor child" when she is sick, which suggest his inability to view her as an equal. One afternoon, she looks to him "very small and fragile in the big double bed." He does not trust her with the details of his own ill health because they would, he feels, worry her "terribly." He exercises control over her behavior when he insists she stay in bed and allow the cook to bring her dinner. When she tries to protest, "he was firm with her. If she didn't take care of herself, she wouldn't be allowed to go to the Drama Society meetings." Her doctors forbade her to continue her theatre work after her nervous breakdown the previous summer, insisting "she mustn't over do it," even though each time the subject of the theatre comes up, it cheers her.

One afternoon when their cook tells Mr. Mummery that his wife is not feeling well and concludes that Ethel did too much that day, she notes that Ethel gets restless and "can't bear to be doing nothing." Mummery fails to notice that since he allows his wife little to occupy her time she becomes bored, which Sayers subtly suggests may be one of her motives for trying to poison him.

In much of Sayers' work, she stresses the importance of equality for women, and of men's and women's engagement in meaningful work. She felt that women could often find fulfillment through employment. Sayers criticized society for its treatment of women as almost a separate species from men. This focus becomes evident in "Suspicion," as Sayers implies that if Ethel had been allowed a more active life and had been treated more as an equal, she might have been satisfied with her marriage.

Sayers' intricate plotting, however, keeps the reader guessing about whether or not Mummery is being poisoned and by whom. Since she does not overtly point the finger at Ethel, most readers will be surprised as Mummery solves the mystery. However, subtle hints about who may be trying to kill him become clearer during a second read.

The story opens immediately with its central problem: Mummery's stomach discomfort caused, unbeknownst to him, by his wife's dousing his food with arsenic. His main focus at work is the poisoning case that has been closely followed by the press. Sayers adds a clever touch of ironic foreshadowing when her narrator explains that Mummery takes some pleasure in reading about the murders, since "they gave him an agreeable thrill of vicarious adventure."

Mummery's partner Brookes provides the first clue to the true cause of Mummery's discomfort and to the poisoner's motive when he asks about his wife. He tells Mummery, "I shan't forget her acting last year in *Romance*. She and young Welbeck positively brought the house down." Yet when the two men discuss the Andrews poisoning case, they determine that the perpetrator must be an "arsenic-

> In much of Sayers' work, she stresses the importance of equality for women, and of men's and women's engagement in meaningful work. She felt that women could often find fulfillment through employment. Sayers criticized society for its treatment of women as almost a separate species from men."

maniac" and as "cunning as [a] weasel," a description that does not fit Ethel. Mummery reveals his inability to spot a criminal when as he looks at a picture of Mrs. Andrews and determines her to be "a nice, motherly-looking kind of woman."

Immediately, suspicion is thrown on the Mummery's cook, who might be Mrs. Andrews in disguise and who, in Mummery's opinion, "started up almost guiltily as he approached." Ethel adds to this suspicion when she reminds her husband that the cook came without references.

Mummery misses the most important clues, blinded by his feelings toward his wife. When he asks Mrs. Welbeck to come to the garden with him to get some cuttings after she had been discussing the poison case, he sees "a relieved glance pass between Ethel and young Welbeck." Thinking that Ethel was upset by the mention of such gruesome topics, he concludes that "evidently the boy understood the situation and was chafing at his mother's tactlessness." Later, he again misdiagnoses the interaction between his wife and Welbeck when he returns to the house and discovers them holding hands. He decides that "their approach to the house had evidently been seen from the sitting-room window, for when they entered young Welbeck was already on his feet and holding Ethel's hand in the act of saying goodbye."

Sayers suggests that Mummery may subconsciously suspect his wife but suppresses his feelings. When he discovers that every picture of Mrs. Andrews and every word about the poisoning has been cut out of the paper, "a curious cold lump of something at the pit of his stomach" forms, "something that he was chary of investigating." As a result, he becomes "suddenly very lonely and tired," but reasons that "his illness had taken it out of him." Later he admits to feeling "weak and confused."

When the test on the cocoa comes back positive for arsenic, Mummery rushes home, still convinced his cook is the murderer. One more visit from Welbeck, ostensibly to discuss "arrangements for the Drama Society," does not arouse Mummery's suspicions, even though his wife speaks about their meeting "with an undertone of excitement." It isn't until he discovers that Mrs. Andrews has been caught, and therefore could not have been his cook, that he takes a hard look at his wife and decides that "in her eyes he saw something that he had never seen before. . ."

Sayers's clever plots and well-drawn characters have earned her much critical and popular acclaim. Her skillful technique in "Suspicion" has helped to reinforce her reputation as one of the world's finest writers of detective fiction.

Source: Wendy Perkins, Critical Essay on "Suspicion," in *Short Stories for Students*, The Gale Group, 2001.

Daniel Moran

Moran is a teacher of English and American literature. In this essay he examines the ways in which Sayers' story toys with the suspicions of the reader.

> *Suspicion is not less an enemy to virtue than to happiness; he that is already corrupt is naturally suspicious, and he that becomes suspicious will quickly become corrupt.—Joseph Addison*

All reading is partially motivated by the suspicion of the reader. Anyone reading a work of fiction for the first time automatically raises his or her mental eyebrow when confronted with what seems to be an irregularity or odd occurrence in the fictional world that he or she has entered. In *Hamlet*, for example, the appearance of the Ghost puts the first-time reader in the same predicament as Horatio and the palace guards: Why has "this thing appeared again?" Does it "bode some strange eruption" to the state? Will it speak to them, or Hamlet, or anyone? When Horatio begs the Ghost for guid-

ance, he is trying to satisfy his own curiosity but also working as a stand-in for the reader. "Speak!" he cries, and his pleas are ones which we expect to be answered, since the unfolding of any plot is a process by which our suspicions are provoked, manipulated, and eventually answered. Thus, a reader knows that the Ghost must reveal *something*, but this as-yet-unknown information must be somewhat of a surprise, for if the reader's suspicions are *fully* in line with what is revealed, the plot offers no revelation, the story falls flat and the reader stops turning the pages.

Mystery stories (of which *Hamlet* is, in one sense, an example) rely on this phenomenon more, perhaps, than other kinds of fiction. A reader who begins an Agatha Christie or Dashiell Hammett novel knows that his or her suspicions will be excited and (if the plot is any good) met in unexpected ways. If "the butler did it," the story will be a disappointment; this is why the endings of such books as *Murder on the Orient Express* (where the reader learns that there are actually many killers instead of one) and *The Maltese Falcon* (where the object of the chase turns out to be a fake) are so delightful and memorable. The reader's radar is running at full speed and his or her suspicions are *still* proven to be misguided. If the reader isn't fooled, the writer has failed in one of his or her primary tasks.

"Suspicion" is a story that explores this very process by which the reader's suspicions are deliberately aroused and then exploded at the conclusion. The story can be read not only as a model of the game that is always played between a mystery writers and their readers, but as a dramatization of the mental gymnastics that all readers of fiction perform as they question a character's actions—and the reasons why the writer has revealed them. "Suspicion" is thus both a satisfying mystery with the obligatory twist and a model of the ways that all storytellers rely on their readers' suspicions to keep them interested in the events that they, as writers, unfold.

Consider the story's deceptively simple title as the first tool used by Sayers deliberately to evoke the friendly distrust of her reader. She could have named the story "The New Cook" or "A Touch of Dyspepsia" or "A Chill on the Liver"—all of them decent enough, as far as titles are concerned. However, calling her story "Suspicion" immediately urges the reader to take out his or her magnifying glass. The reader automatically becomes a bloodhound, second-guessing the truth about all kinds of details. The opening sentence—

> As the atmosphere of the railway carriage thickened with tobacco-smoke, Mr. Mummery became increasingly aware that his breakfast had not agreed with him.

—becomes less innocuous than it would in a story with a different title. As the "atmosphere" in Mummery's railway carriage thickens with smoke, so will the reader's mind become clouded in an atmosphere of doubt. Mummery's stomachache becomes an occasion to suspect Sayers herself, whose motives for telling the reader this fact are immediately questioned. Characters in naturalistic and other kinds of fiction get all kinds of illnesses, but a stomachache in a Dorothy Sayers story—and one named "Suspicion" at that—piques her readers' curiosity. "Why am I being told this?" they ask, and as the story proceeds, readers form a suspicion about Mummery's ailment, only to discover (along with Mummery himself) that that suspicion was off the mark.

In this sense, the reader is much like Mummery, who functions as the reader's representative in the world of the story. Although mystery readers are immediately suspicious of everything they are told, while Mummery is not, Mummery eventually becomes as paranoid as they are until, just like his counterpart in the real world, he is forced to confront the fact that his suspicions are well-founded (he *is* being poisoned) yet totally wrong (Mrs. Sutton is *not* the poisoner). He is introduced as an innocent "fuss box" (as his wife later describes him), unaware of the many suspicious details that the reader sees all around him. When he reads the newspaper in the opening scene, for example, the story of the Lincoln poisoning case stands out among the others, and when Mummery examines the photograph of Mrs. Andrews, all he sees is a "harmless enough" and "nice, motherly-looking kind of woman." Like Herman Melville's Billy Budd, Mummery is, initially, incapable of suspecting the ominous details that seem to surround him. When Brookes tells Mummery that Mrs. Andrews has "got a bad mouth" and that he "wouldn't trust that woman an inch," Brookes' suspicion seems empirically ludicrous (there is no such thing as a "bad mouth") yet understandable: he knows that appearances are deceptive, while Mummery does not. The story then proceeds with Mummery's innocence becoming gradually corrupted as his suspicions about the arsenic are confirmed.

Mummery's assumption that one's appearance is indicative of one's inner self is what allows his

> " She could have named the story 'The New Cook' or 'A Touch of Dyspepsia' or 'A Chill on the Liver'--all of them decent enough, as far as titles are concerned. However, calling her story 'Suspicion' immediately urges the reader to take out his or her magnifying glass."

wife to poison him without his knowledge. He is not suspicious of her because he regards her physical health as representative of her character. Until the very end of the story, Mummery—along with the reader—considers Ethel a "poor child," a "small and fragile" woman who "mustn't overdo it," a "precious" and "fastidious" victim of nerves who is "not a business woman" capable of understanding household finances. She is a delicate woman who must be spared "any shock or anxiety" and one who cannot even hear of things as "hateful" and "unsuitable" as a poisoning case. "She had never been a great meat-eater," Mummery thinks at one point, as if even the thought of a dead animal is too much for her to bear. When she asks him why he needs to have the newspaper neatly folded before he reads it, Mummery sighs and thinks, "Women did not feel these things," as if they are too innocent and childlike to understand the importance of the world being ordered in a decorous fashion. When he brings Ethel the chrysanthemums, the reader sees in this gesture what Mummery assumes about her (and women in general): they are weak creatures who need only a bouquet of flowers to be made happy.

This is not to say that Mummery is uncaring or even willfully condescending, for Sayers points out in the opening of the story that Mummery "would cheerfully have laid down his rather uninteresting little life to spare Ethel a moment's uneasiness." What is important to note here is that Mummery's inability to suspect his wife of any wrongdoing (until the end) is a function of his provincial thinking. He enjoys reading about murders in the newspaper because ''naturally, they were matters quite remote from daily life in the outskirts of Hull.'' Ironically, Mummery—not his wife—is the frail and innocent soul who cannot understand the devious and subtle ways in which seemingly innocent people behave. At the end of the story, Mummery and the reader move from the world of innocence to that of experience—where Ethel has been dwelling for some time.

If Mummery is the stand-in for the reader, growing increasingly suspicious as the story progresses, then Ethel is the representative of Sayers herself. The reader is reminded more than once that Ethel is an invaluable member of the local Drama Society, which suits a character so adept at acting that even her husband is completely fooled. (Also note that the name ''Mummery'' suggests ''mummer,'' an actor.) She continually speaks to Mummery with language appropriate to a naive ingénue, calling him ''Tiddley-winks,'' a ''sentimental old thing,'' and her ''old Hubby.'' She feigns concern over her husband's ''tummy-aches'' and, at one point, becomes so ''alarmed'' about his health that she insists on calling a doctor. Like her creator, Ethel must divert Mummery's (and the reader's) suspicions away from the truth, and both women's ability to offer a false, unsuspicious version of reality is what allows them to succeed. As Ethel deceives Mummery, so Sayers dupes the reader. Granted, a reader *might* suspect Ethel of her crime as the story proceeds, but this is only because Ethel is a character in a mystery story, where convention almost demands that some sort of twist occur at the conclusion. Sayers's (and Ethel's) skill lies in the fact that despite the reader's suspicion, only a second examination of the facts reveals the truth: the seemingly innocent Mrs. Mummery is poisoning her husband so that she can carry on her affair with young Welbeck—the man who was her costar in *Romance*, and who Mummery sees leaving his house, and whose presence gives Ethel's speech ''an undertone of excitement.''

At the conclusion of any plot (again, *Hamlet* included), the reader's suspicions must be confirmed or upset, as they are here. However, Sayers cannot resist toying with the reader's suspicions one last time, as seen in the story's final sentences:

> Mr. Mummery clutched the arm of his chair. It had all been a mistake then. He wanted to shout or cry. He wanted to apologize to this foolish, pleasant, excited woman. All a mistake.

> But there had been the cocoa. Mr. Dimthorpe. Marsh's test. Five grains of arsenic. Who, then—?

> He glanced around at his wife, and in her eyes he saw something that he had never seen before . . .

This is Mummery's epiphany, where his desperate attempts to remain in an innocent world free from suspicion prove as futile and weak as he once assumed his wife to be. Sayers does not offer the next scene because what happens next in the Mummery's home is secondary to her artistic concern of dramatizing the moment where a man's previous and off-the-mark suspicions hit the bull's-eye of truth. While readers do not know what Mummery will say (or do) to his wife, they do know that suspicion has affected Mummery to the point where he will never be able to think of Ethel as a ''poor child'' again. Unlike Mummery, however, readers are delighted at Sayers's manipulation of their suspicions, and it is this delight in being manipulated that writers of all genres attempt to elicit in their work.

Source: Daniel Moran, Critical Essay on ''Suspicion,'' in *Short Stories for Students*, The Gale Group, 2001.

Sources

Anderson, Isaac, Review in *New York Times*, February 18, 1940, p. 23.

Cuppy, Will, Review in *New York Times*, February 18, 1940, p. 12.

Durkin, Mary Beth, *Dorothy L. Sayers*, Twayne, 1980, p. 204.

Gaillard, Dawson, *Dorothy L. Sayers*, Frederick Ungar, 1981.

Hart-Davis, Rupert, Review in *The Spectator*, December 15, 1939, p. 878.

Partridge, Ralph, Review in *New Statesman and Nation*, December 23, 1939, p. 936.

Review in *Saturday Review of Literature*, February 17, 1940, p. 18.

Review in *Springfield Republican*, March 31, 1940, p. 7e.

Review in *Times Literary Supplement*, November 18, 1939, p. 675.

Further Reading

Brabazon, James, *Dorothy L. Sayers: A Biography*, Scribner, 1981.
   This comprehensive biography includes a foreword by British mystery writer P. D. James.

Rader, Barbara D., and Howard G. Zettler, eds., *The Sleuth and the Scholar: Origins, Evolutions, and Current Trends in Detective Fiction*, Greenwood Press, 1988.
   This is a collection of historical and critical essays on American and English detective fiction.

That Evening Sun

William Faulkner

1931

William Faulkner's story "That Evening Sun" is the story of three children's reactions to an adult world that they do not fully understand. It is a dark portrait of white Southerners' indifference to the crippling fears of one of their black employees. It is also an exploration of terror, vengeance, and solitude. In the story, the African-American washerwoman Nancy fears that her common-law husband, Jesus, is seeking to murder her because she is pregnant with a white man's child. Published in 1931 in Faulkner's short-story collection *These 13*—the book that also includes Faulkner's most anthologized story, "A Rose For Emily"—"That Evening Sun" has become one of Faulkner's best-known and most popular stories.

Author Biography

William Cuthbert Faulkner (family name originally Falkner) was born in New Albany, Mississippi, on September 25, 1897. He was the oldest of four sons. His family was middle-class and descended from a man who became the model for one of Faulkner's own characters: his great-grandfather, Colonel William Clark Falkner, who commanded a Mississippi unit in the Civil War. Upon returning from the war, Colonel Falkner founded a railroad that his son later took over. His family's colorful history and its intersections with the history of the South pro-

vided Faulkner with models for such families as the Compsons.

Faulkner's family moved to Oxford when he was very young, and in Oxford Faulkner developed a love for the outdoors that comes out in much of his fiction. During World War I, Faulkner enlisted in the Canadian Air Force but never saw combat. Upon his return he began to write in earnest. For much of the 1920s, Faulkner wandered, moving from the University of Mississippi to New York to New Orleans to Europe and back to New Orleans. Faulkner published his first book, *The Marble Faun*, a collection of poems, in 1924. The book was named after one of Nathaniel Hawthorne's books and, like Ha(w)thorne, with its publication, Faulkner added a letter to his last name.

In 1926, Faulkner published his first novel, *Soldiers' Pay*. Although the novel could hardly be called a success either artistically or financially, Faulkner's course was set. In 1929 he published *Sartoris*, his first novel set, like "That Evening Sun," in Yoknapatawpha. Others soon followed, including his masterpieces *The Sound and the Fury*, *As I Lay Dying*, and *Absalom, Absalom!*. Faulkner gained a great deal of critical recognition because of these works but never saw the financial success he craved. To that end he wrote two books, *Sanctuary* and *Requiem for a Nun*, whose sensational subject matter was intended to make them best-sellers and, he hoped, would tempt Hollywood to make movies from them. He also signed on with a Hollywood studio to write screenplays in the 1930s. Two of the famous movies to which he contributed are the film version of Hemingway's *To Have and Have Not* and the film version of Raymond Chandler's *The Big Sleep*, both starring Humphrey Bogart and Lauren Bacall.

Faulkner attempted to get a military commission during the Second World War but was unsuccessful. During the 1940s, Faulkner rededicated himself to the craft of fiction and produced two other masterpieces, *Go Down, Moses* and *The Hamlet*. Also in this decade, critical opinion of Faulkner changed drastically. The prominent critic Malcolm Cowley edited and, in 1946, published *The Portable Faulkner*, an anthology that drew from works throughout Faulkner's career. With the publication of this book, Faulkner quickly became regarded as America's greatest living writer. He was awarded the Nobel Prize for Literature in 1949. In the years following the Nobel Prize, Faulkner continued to write and, in 1957, moved to Charlottesville to become the Writer-in-Residence at the University of Virginia. After completing his final work, the *Huckleberry Finn*-inspired *The Reivers*, Faulkner died of a heart attack in 1962.

Plot Summary

"That Evening Sun" opens as a reminiscence: the narrator, whose identity is unknown at first, reports that in Jefferson, "the streets are paved now, and the telephone and electric companies are cutting down more and more of the shade trees." The time is approximately the turn of the century. The narrator first introduces Nancy, a washerwoman who takes in laundry from white people around Jefferson. The narrator then mentions Jesus, suggests—but does not say—that he is Nancy's husband, and notes that "father told him to stay away from our house."

The story then shifts its focus to Nancy. The narrator tells of how he and his siblings would throw stones at Nancy's house to get her to make breakfast for them and tells the story of how Mr. Stovall refused to pay Nancy and beat her in the street. While in jail for this incident, Nancy attempts suicide by hanging but is cut down the by jailer and beaten again. The story then switches back to the present, and one listens to Jesus and Nancy snipe at each other. She is pregnant, and Jesus suggests that the baby isn't his, but the children do not understand what they are talking about. At this point the identity of the narrator becomes clear: Quentin Compson. As the story progresses, his father, Mr. Compson, forbids Jesus to come in the Compson house, and Nancy tells the children how Jesus left town, perhaps for Memphis. She is still afraid that he plans to attack her, however, suspecting that he may be in hiding.

Mrs. Compson, by Part II of the story, is getting impatient with the time that her family is spending with Nancy and with the extra favors that Nancy is asking. Nancy is feeling very apprehensive, but Caddy and Jason are unaware of why she is feeling this way—to Caddy, the change of routine is welcome, and Jason cares only about what personally affects him. Quentin's reactions to Nancy's plight are unstated—it is unclear whether or not he even understands the causes for the rift between Jesus and Nancy. In Part III, Nancy is visibly terrified and is making sounds of fear to herself; she cannot even swallow coffee from fear. After Mrs. Compson refuses her permission to sleep in the Compson house, Nancy brings the children to her house, hoping that the presence of white children will prevent Jesus from attacking her. The children go home with her, but her attempts to entertain them with stories and popcorn fail. Caddy is interested in the adventure, but Jason is impatient. Mr. Compson comes to the house to fetch the children. In the final part of the story, the children leave Nancy's house accompanied by their father and leave Nancy behind, paralyzed with fear. The narration leaves Nancy entirely as the children leave, and as Nancy prepares for death all the narrator chooses to report is Jason insisting that ''I'm not a nigger'' and Father scolding Caddy.

Characters

Caddy Compson

Caddy is the middle child of the three Compson children of ''That Evening Sun.'' She likes Nancy and can sense Nancy's fear, but is too young to understand what is frightening Nancy.

Candace Compson

See Caddy Compson

Jason Compson

At age five, Jason is the youngest of the Compson children. He is quite childish, and he is also self-centered. He keeps repeating ''I ain't a nigger'' to Nancy, and she is especially worried he is only concerned about such matters as whether Dilsey will make him a chocolate cake. Like his mother, Jason represents the indifference of many white people to the problems of their black employees.

Quentin Compson

Quentin narrates the story. He is nine. We see very little of his personality come out in this story; of the three children, he speaks the least. Yet we do learn that he has the most responsibility of the Compson children, and is a quiet, thoughtful boy. Although he never lets us know this, he seems to understand what Nancy fears, unlike his siblings. He also is a main character in a number of other of Faulkner's works, most notably *Absalom, Absalom!* and *The Sound and the Fury,* in which he kills himself by throwing himself into the Charles River while enrolled at Harvard. In many ways, he is Faulkner's representation of himself.

William Faulkner

Dilsey

Dilsey is the Compson's regular house servant. For much of the story, she is unable to perform her duties, and therefore Nancy must fill in for her.

Father

Mr. Compson, referred to as Father, is the father of the three children and is the patriarch of this important Jefferson family. He seems to have concern for Nancy but is convinced that her fears about Jesus' threat to her are unfounded.

Jesus

Jesus is Nancy's common-law husband. Unlike many of the other washerwomen's husbands, he never helps Nancy get the clothes. He also may be violent, and has a ''razor scar down his face.'' He suspects that she is pregnant with another man's baby. Nancy fears that he wants to kill her, and Mr. Compson forbids his children to have any dealings with him.

Mother

Mrs. Compson, referred to as Mother, is the children's mother. She barely appears in the story, and is utterly unconcerned for Nancy. At one point, a terrified Nancy wants to sleep in the Compson house, perhaps even up in one of the children's rooms, but Mother feels that "I can't have Negroes sleeping in the bedrooms."

Nancy

Nancy is the main character of the story. She is an older African-American woman who makes a living by taking white peoples' laundry in. She is "tall, with a high, sad face sunken where her teeth were missing." Early in the story, while jailed for confronting Mr. Stovall, she attempts suicide but is revived.

Aunt Rachel

Aunt Rachel is a old black woman who lives in Jefferson. She may be Jesus' mother, but she does not always admit this. She is called "Aunt" Rachel because in the South white people often called older black women "Aunt" and older black men "Uncle." The excess familiarity was meant to remind black people of their inferior status.

Mr. Stovall

Mr. Stovall is a cashier in the bank in Jefferson and a deacon of the local Baptist church. He employs Nancy to do his laundry, but has not paid her for some time. When she confronts him, he knocks her down and kicks her in the mouth until the town marshal stops him. He is not punished for his actions; rather, Nancy is jailed.

Themes

Race Relations

The troubled race relations that have characterized the South throughout its history are the backdrop for "That Evening Sun," even if they are not the main concern of the story. Nancy, the main character in the story, is a typical African-American woman of the South in the Jim Crow era. "Jim Crow" was a name given to the system of laws, customs, and ideas by which the white South kept its black Southerners oppressed. In this era, which lasted from the end of Reconstruction in the 1870s until the relative success of the civil rights movement in the late 1960s, black Southerners were denied most basic civil rights—including, but not limited to, the right to vote, to have a fair trial, and to have freedom of expression.

In addition, the Jim Crow system enabled white Southerners to take economic advantage of African Americans. Black Southerners did not have access to higher education, for the most part, but a few entered into the professions or succeeded in business. African Americans whose financial success became too obvious, however, were often the target of attacks by resentful whites.

But it was not only the successful black Southerners who were taken advantage of or attacked by whites. Nancy, in the story, is a washerwoman who takes in white peoples' laundry. Mr. Stovall, who represents both the economic system (he is a cashier at the bank) and the religious institutions (he is a Baptist deacon) of the South, refuses to pay Nancy for her services. When she confronts him, he knocks her down and kicks her repeatedly in the face, causing her to lose her teeth. Mr. Stovall is not punished; rather, it is Nancy who is imprisoned. Quentin does not tell the reader on what charge she is jailed. Faulkner, who was always concerned with race, comments through his maturing narrator on the willing blindness of Southerners to the injustices of their society.

Coming of Age

One of the most familiar themes in Western literature is the "coming of age" or "loss of innocence" theme. In such stories, a young man (or, less frequently, a young woman) moves from childhood to adulthood through vivid and affecting experiences. Such twentieth-century classics as James Joyce's *A Portrait of the Artist as a Young Man*, John Knowles' *A Separate Peace*, and J. D. Salinger's *Catcher in the Rye* are based on this theme. Faulkner also uses this theme, but he generally sets his characters' comings-of-age against a backdrop of declining families and a changing South.

In "That Evening Sun," Quentin Compson, the narrator, moves from childlike innocence toward a sadder but wiser adult experience in the course of the story. Faulkner's narration is quite clever. The story is actually narrated by an older Quentin, a man fifteen years beyond the nine-year-old child who seems to tell the story. But even though the first voice of the narrator is that of an adult, a man with perspective on the events he describes, that voice soon reflects the world of a child, with the short attention span and limited vocabulary characteristic of children. Quentin rarely speaks in the story that dominates the action of "That Evening Sun," the story of Nancy and her fear of Jesus. Instead, the voices one hears the most are those of Jason, Caddy, and Nancy herself.

Topics for Further Study

- Do research about daily life in the South at the turn of the century. The story talks about people having telephones in their houses—when did telephones come into common household use? What appliances and tools do we have now that people did not have then? How do you think this made their lives different?

- Investigate race relations in the South from the end of the Civil War to the start of the civil rights movement in the 1950s. What was "Jim Crow"? What kinds of work did African Americans do? What possibilities did they have for advancement in society?

- Read more work by William Faulkner about his imaginary county in Mississippi. Focus especially on work that involves characters who appear in "That Evening Sun": Quentin, Caddy, and Jason Compson, and Dilsey. Some good sources are the novels *The Sound and the Fury* and *Absalom, Absalom!*. Does reading these works complement or change your understanding of the characters and action of "That Evening Sun"?

- Faulkner uses a line from a famous song, W. C. Handy's "Saint Louis Blues," as the title for his short story. Handy is one of America's most influential musicians. Research the career of W. C. Handy. What musical forms did he pioneer? What musicians were influenced by him?

Caddy, Quentin's younger sister, is excited to play along with the adventures that Nancy promises. Jason, the five-year-old, is utterly and solely concerned with himself. Quentin's feelings about the matters at hand are unexpressed.

It is this lack of expression that represents Quentin's growing maturity. Unlike Caddy and Jason, Quentin can sense that Nancy is feeling a very profound fear—and he has some idea of the source of that fear. Whereas Caddy and Jason see Nancy's troubles only as a sort of game that focuses on them—and Mrs. Compson feels essentially the same way—Quentin can sense a deeper feeling in Nancy, and he recognizes the potential danger that Jesus presents. Quentin's essential silence in this story represents his dawning understanding of evil in the outside world. Unlike Jason, Caddy, and his mother, he refuses to turn Nancy's plight into something that refers to himself. He is not yet old enough to disagree with his father on the right way to handle the problem, nor is he even old enough to explain to himself what is really happening, but the reporter-like tone of the story—one very similar to the tone used by Faulkner's contemporary Ernest Hemingway—belies the deep emotional effect that Nancy's terror is having on him.

Darkness and Violence

"I hate to see that evening sun go down," W. C. Handy's song "St. Louis Blues" says, because the singer's lover is no longer around. In the song, the singer's regret at sunset is because the darkness reminds her of her absent lover; however, for Nancy "that evening sun" represents the danger that her absent lover presents to her. Jesus—whose name is likely an ironic joke on Faulkner's part—represents danger and violence to Nancy, and he will wait until night has fallen to fall upon her. Jesus represents a stock figure in racist Southern folklore. He is the dangerous, violent black man who, after dark, attacks women with a knife or razor. In the Jim Crow era, in order to stir up prejudice against African Americans, newspapers and magazines played up, and often simply made up, crimes committed by black men against white women.

Style

Point of View and Narration

Quentin Compson, one of Faulkner's most memorable characters, narrates the story. In the story, he is a nine-year-old boy, but as a narrator he is twenty-four. Faulkner has Quentin narrate in both voices: the story begins in the voice of the adult Quentin, but soon switches to the voice of the younger Quentin. It is difficult to tell when the narrator reverts to his younger self, because much of the story is simply reported dialogue, but many of the sentences in the first part of the story are long and filled with adjectives and conjunctions. By Part II, the sentences are short, declarative, and often skip around conceptually, suggesting the mind of a young boy.

Later, however, the story begins to revert back, as the older Quentin seems to reflect on what this story has meant to his maturing process. In the sixth section, the voice again becomes more complicated and almost lyrical: "I couldn't see much where the moonlight and the shadows tangled," Quentin says at one point, and also speaks of "the sound that was not singing and not unsinging." Also, his unwillingness to face the real gravity of the situation is indicative of his greater maturity. As an adult narrator, he recognizes that readers will understand the importance of Nancy's fear, whereas a younger narrator would probably feel the need to tell the reader explicitly what was happening. Quentin's silence on the topic of why this story has been so significant to him is, paradoxically, the sign of his maturity.

Irony

Faulkner uses irony in a number of ways in this story. One of the most haunting uses of irony is the name of Nancy's tormentor, Jesus. In the version of the story that was printed in the magazine *The American Mercury* in March 1931, Faulkner had called this character "Jubah," but returned to his original name when the story was printed in the collection *These 13*. "Jesus" refers to the Christian savior, but ironically the Jesus who actually appears in the story poses a threat to Nancy. Faulkner intensifies the irony when the children hear Nancy moaning the name to herself: "'Jesus,' Nancy said. Like this: Jeeeeeeeeesus, until the sound went out, like a match or a candle does." Although the children are too young to realize it, Nancy has "committed a sin" against Jesus, for she is pregnant by another man. But instead of forgiving her, this Jesus may be seeking vengeance against her. Some critics suggest that Nancy is a prostitute, deepening the identification between this Jesus and the Christian Jesus, for Jesus Christ also associated with prostitutes.

The title is also ironic. The phrase "That Evening Sun"—or, as it was titled in the *American Mercury* version, "That Evening Sun Go Down"—is taken from the first line of the well-known song "St. Louis Blues," by W. C. Handy. In this song, the singer dreads the coming of the night because evening reminds her of her absent lover. In Faulkner's story, the darkness reminds Nancy of the same thing, but she is not missing him; rather, she fears that he is waiting to kill her.

Setting

"That Evening Sun" is set in Faulkner's familiar fictional town of Jefferson, in his invented Yoknapatawpha County, at the turn of the century—some critics suggest 1898 or 1899. William Faulkner was from Oxford, in northern Mississippi, and in most of his best-known fiction he constructs an elaborate fictional equivalent for his home. Oxford becomes "Jefferson," and in his works Faulkner traces the history of the town and its county from Indian days to the 1950s. Such families as the Compsons and such black residents as Dilsey recur throughout his work. Jefferson is a small Southern town, dominated by a few families and suffering from the aftereffects of slavery and the Civil War. Few writers have portrayed family life in the South as lovingly and humorously as Faulkner has, but at the same time few writers have examined with a more critical eye the poisonous legacy of slavery. In this story the reader sees the two collide, as the peaceful small town of Jefferson is shown to have a dark, frightening side that emerges after the sun goes down.

Historical Context

New Kinds of Narration

"That Evening Sun" is an example of the different kinds of narration that writers such as Faulkner pioneered. Although very traditional in comparison with some of Faulkner's other experiments—part of *The Sound and the Fury*, for example, is narrated by a mentally retarded boy who has no sense of the passage of time—the story makes use of a narrator whose voice and point of view change in the course of the story. Quentin Compson, the narrator of this story, starts the narration as a grown man (he is presumably twenty-four years old) but in the course of the story reverts back to his identity as the nine-year-old boy in the story. His sentences grow shorter, his vocabulary less devel-

Compare & Contrast

- **1898:** In the South, black people are prevented from voting, and white people can physically attack black people with little fear of punishment.

  1990s: Although some racism persists, the South offers more equal opportunities to African-American citizens than in the past. Southern cities such as Memphis, Atlanta, and Dallas have black mayors, and African Americans represent many Southern districts in Congress.

- **1896:** In *Plessy v. Ferguson*, the United States Supreme Court gives official sanction to racial segregation, ruling that ''separate but equal'' public facilities are Constitutional.

  1990s: President Clinton tells America that racial harmony and understanding should be the nation's greatest priority, and appoints a commission to study ways that the government can promote a more diverse society.

- **1898:** The United States, still recovering from its civil war, is about to enter upon the world stage as an imperialist power by declaring war on Spain. The Spanish-American War will give the United States its first colonies outside of the Western Hemisphere, including Guam and the Philippines.

  1999: After the fall of the Soviet Union, the United States is the world's most important power. In conflicts including those in Iraq, Yugoslavia, and Haiti, the United States leads the world's military forces.

- **1931:** When Faulkner writes his story, America is reeling from the effects of the Great Depression. President Herbert Hoover is blamed for widespread poverty, unemployment, and misery.

  1999: The American economy is as strong as it has ever been, having undergone the largest peacetime expansion in history.

---

oped, and his observations less insightful. The story is just as much about Quentin's growing understanding of the adult world as it is about Nancy's fears, and Quentin's narration presents a man who transports himself back into his own mind as it was fifteen years ago. Because of this, the reader understands Quentin's seeming lack of reaction to the events narrated better than he or she could, had the narrator been outside of Quentin's head.

Jim Crow

After the Civil War, Northern politicians and anti-slavery activists sought to transform the South through a process called Reconstruction. For more than a decade, the Federal government passed laws and Constitutional amendments aimed at giving African Americans in the South all of the rights and privileges of citizenship. In fact, many black lawmakers were elected from Southern districts. (Later, to discredit Reconstruction, white Southerners ridiculed those black lawmakers, and to this day some

American schools teach that Reconstruction went too far and that the idea of competent black lawmakers in the 1870s was ludicrous.) But Reconstruction ended in 1877, and soon after all of the branches of the federal government acted in concert with the Southern states to roll back the gains that African Americans had seen during Reconstruction.

Although after Reconstruction the Constitution guaranteed them the right to vote and receive fair trials, black Southerners soon found that they fell under another, parallel system of legal regulation: Jim Crow. ''Jim Crow'' was the name given to the system of laws, customs, and ideas by which the white South kept black Southerners oppressed in the period after Reconstruction. It included literacy tests for voting, tolerance of lynching, the prevention of African Americans' access to many public facilities, and even the widespread activity of the Ku Klux Klan. Jim Crow persisted well into the 1960s, when the civil rights movement finally made inroads in the South. Yet even in the twenty-first century, in many parts of the South, some vestiges of semi-official racism remained.

Critical Overview

Faulkner is often considered to be America's greatest writer. His fame rests largely on his novels, which examined Southern society more closely than it had ever been examined before, but also relied on radical advances in narrative and fictional techniques. Awarded the Nobel Prize in 1949, Faulkner was a profound influence not only in the United States but also in Latin America, where such writers as Gabriel García Marquez have expressed their feelings that Faulkner is unparalleled.

Although most critical writing on Faulkner is primarily concerned with his novels, Faulkner's short stories are also frequent subjects for analysis. "That Evening Sun," "A Rose for Emily," and "The Bear" are his most famous stories. "That Evening Sun" first appeared in 1931 in the magazine *The American Mercury*, a very important journal that was edited at one time by the critic and writer H. L. Mencken. Its appearance in that journal indicates that Faulkner was already being taken seriously by the critics of his day.

Later that year, Faulkner included the story in his collection *These 13*. Most critics were impressed by the collection. Edward McDonald, in the Philadelphia *Record*, wrote that the stories in the collection display "their author's apparently inexhaustible literary resources . . . his haunting knowledge of the frustrations, the perversions, the imbecilities, in a word, the compulsions of all sorts which drive his men and women into behavior that swings distractedly from the uttermost in heroism to the uttermost in degradation." Robert Cantwell of the *New Republic* felt that the stories were "brilliantly written" and remarked specifically of "That Evening Sun" that "we see that the real story is not the written one of Nancy's foreboding, but the unexplained, unanalyzed condition of strain within the white family, the inner dissension, the battle for prestige that hampers the husband's attempt to help when he first feels that help is needed." But the eminent critic Lionel Trilling, writing in the *Nation*, was less enthusiastic, arguing that "despite the dramatic stress and portentousness of his work its implications are too frequently minor."

In 1950, Faulkner issued a volume of *Collected Stories* in which "That Evening Sun" was included. In the intervening nineteen years, Faulkner's reputation had grown immensely, and critics were largely united in their opinion that he was one of America's major writers. Some felt, however, that Faulkner was too preoccupied by the darker side of the human experience. William Peden, in the *Saturday Review of Literature*, wrote that Faulkner was "the most considerable twentieth-century writer of short fiction" and that "That Evening Sun" was one of his best stories. Peden regretted, however, that many of the stories in the anthology "serve only to illustrate the melancholy fact that even a very great writer can be very bad at times." *Time*, too, reported that Faulkner was "a writer of incomparable talents who has used and misused those talents superbly and recklessly."

Many later critics have read "That Evening Sun" not as a story in its own right, but primarily as an addition to the mythology of Yoknapatawpha County and the saga of the Compson family, whose downfall is told in *The Sound and the Fury*. The man who is perhaps Faulkner's best reader and most prominent critic, Cleanth Brooks, writes that in the story,

> the Compson children have already assumed the personality patterns that we shall find later. Though they are too young to fully understand Nancy's desperation, Caddy and Quentin at least respond to the Negro woman's terror with concerned curiosity and, insofar as they are capable, sympathy. Jason is already a wretched little complainer, interested neither in Nancy nor in his brother and sister." Another critic, James B. Carothers, sees the story in primarily historical and social terms, arguing that Nancy is figured as a "doomed victim of the racial, sexual, and economic matrices by which she is defined.

Other literary scholars have concerned themselves more with the formal aspects of the story, often pointing to Faulkner's use of narration as the heart of what the story is trying to convey. Hans Skei identifies the narration as the central point of the story, writing that "the discrepancy between the limited point of view of the child narrator and an experience beyond his comprehension is modified by the fact that the child has become an adult at the time of narration." Skei appreciates the "great sympathy and empathy" of the story. James Ferguson also notes the narration, writing that "those who argue that Quentin fails to understand the plight of Nancy misread the story. The increasing silence of the boy in the final scenes and his unforgettable culminating question, 'Who will do

H. L. Mencken circa 1920. Mencken was the founder and editor of the prestigious journal, The American Mercury. *"That Evening Sun" was first published in* The American Mercury *in March 1931.*

our washing now, Father?' suggest that Quentin *does* understand that that Jesus will murder Nancy.''

Criticism

Greg Barnhisel

Barnhisel holds a Ph.D. in English and American literature and currently teaches writing at Southwestern University in Georgetown, Texas. He has written a number of entries and critical essays for Gale's Short Stories for Students *series and has published articles on such writers as Ezra Pound and William Carlos Williams. In the following essay he "examines how the pressures of history interact with the darker drives of each individual."*

William Faulkner's fictional world of Yoknapatawpha County, Mississippi, is one of the most familiar locales in all of world literature. The families who inhabit the county—the Sutpens, McCaslins, Snopeses, and Compsons, among others—have family lives more vivid and more well-documented than many real families. As in the South in which Faulkner himself grew up, in Yoknapatawpha the two domi-

nant facts of life, even a century after they ceased to be, are slavery and the Civil War. The relations between black and white inhabitants of the county are always colored by the legacy of slavery, and the values and aspirations of the white citizens of the county are always understood in relation to "the War of Northern Aggression." But the weight of history is not Faulkner's only subject. Rather, Faulkner, perhaps better than any other American writer, examines how the pressures of history interact with the darker drives of each individual—drives for sex, violence, revenge, gain, selfishness.

Faulkner rarely hit upon a more effective combination of the dark side of history and of individual human drives than he did with "That Evening Sun." In this story, the two combine, and a young boy who is rapidly approaching maturity must puzzle together what is happening and what his own place in the impending tragedy might be. Faulkner's choice of narrators is crucial to the theme of the story, for had it been narrated by anyone besides Quentin, a boy on the cusp of understanding, the story would lose its ambiguity and its sense of a maturing awareness. Jason and Caddy simply do not understand the situation; Mr. Compson under-

What Do I Read Next?

- "That Evening Sun" by William Faulkner is included in *The Collected Stories of William Faulkner* (1950), a collection of Faulkner's best and most representative stories. Although Faulkner is best known for his novels, his short stories are some of the best American stories ever written. *Collected Stories* is divided up thematically, into sections about the country, the village, the wilderness, and three sections that take place away from Yoknapatawpha.

- Faulkner's most famous novel is *The Sound and the Fury* (1929). Although sometimes difficult to read and experimental in its narrative techniques, the novel is extremely rewarding. In it the story of the breakup of the Compson family is told from different points of view, including Jason's and Quentin's.

- There have been hundreds of books written about Faulkner's fictional county of Yoknapatawpha. The standard work is Cleanth Brooks' *William Faulkner: The Yoknapatawpha Country* (1963). Brooks exhaustively catalogs every character who appears in Faulkner's world, summarizes and analyzes the novels and stories that take place there, and provides what is probably the best introduction to Faulkner's amazing accomplishment.

- Faulkner's near-contemporary Flannery O'Connor also wrote about the South and often used violence and family conflicts as the backdrops for her stories. O'Connor's characters are often like Quentin Compson, torn between an old South of racial segregation and agrarian values, and a modern South that is becoming more a part of a unified America. Her stories "Everything That Rises Must Converge" (1961) and "A Good Man Is Hard To Find" (1953) both portray middle-aged women who are having trouble accepting the new ways.

- A more modern representation of the South can be found in the writings of the contemporary author Bobbie Ann Mason. In such stories as "Shiloh" (1982), Mason examines the conflict between the old, insular South and the "New South" of office parks, subdivisions, and franchise stores. Like Faulkner before her, Mason draws a vivid portrait of a South in transition.

- Leon Litwack, a historian, has researched the daily lives of black people in the South from the era of slavery to the present. His book *Trouble in Mind: Black Southerners in the Age of Jim Crow* (1998) collects the reactions and recollections of thousands of African Americans who lived in the South at the time that "That Evening Sun" takes place.

---

stands the situation completely; Mrs. Compson dismisses it out of her selfishness and racism; Nancy is fixated on her own terror. But Quentin, from his unique perspective, gives the reader simply information, not interpretation, for the majority of the story. However, he is not the age he seems for most of the story: he is in fact fifteen years older, and although readers forget it quickly after the story begins, he is old enough to have interpretations and explanations for all of the events he narrates.

This ironic disjunction between what Quentin the twenty-four-year-old knows and what Quentin

the nine-year-old narrates is at the heart of the story. In a sense, it is the past—the past's crushing weight, the past's legacy—that is the main theme of the story, as it often is with Faulkner. The weight of the past can be felt from the first words of the story: "Monday is no different from any other week day in Jefferson now." But for the narrator, the past was better. The story begins with a comparison of the dismal present with a happier past. The power lines and poles bear "clusters of bloated and ghostly and bloodless grapes" and the laundry in the city truck "flees apparitionlike behind alert and irritable electric horns.'' The irony here is that the ordinary symbolic resonance of past and present is reversed: in Jefferson today, the accouterments of modern life are like ghosts, and the past is alive and vital.

The story provides more than enough explanation for why the present is viewed in ghostly images, but there is one other reason that few, if any, critics have noted: in Faulkner's carefully constructed chronology of his characters' lives, Quentin is actually dead when he narrates this story. In the appendix to *Absalom, Absalom!*, another novel in which Quentin appears, Faulkner gives Quentin's birth date as 1891. If he is nine in this story, the story takes place in 1899 or 1900. Quentin dies by throwing himself into the Charles River in 1910, but this story must be narrated in 1914 or 1915 if he is looking back to the events of fifteen years before. Of course the present is ghostly, if the narrator himself is a ghost!

Ironic reversals characterize much of the story. Such names as Jesus and Jason are ironic—Jesus is a threatening character, and Jason, rather than being the brave captain of the Argo, is here a selfish child whose only desire is to gratify his desires. Even the title is ironic. ''That Evening Sun'' is part of a line from one of the most famous American songs, W. C. Handy's ''St. Louis Blues.'' In this song, which was published in 1914, presumably the year in which Quentin is narrating, a woman laments that when the sun goes down she begins to feel melancholy because her lover is not around. But in this story, the setting of the sun brings strong emotions to Nancy not because she misses Jesus but because she fears his return. Handy's line ''When that evening sun goes down'' has found its way into any number of blues songs, American standards such as Harold Arlen's ''Stormy Weather,'' and even a song by the Irish soul singer Van Morrison. Faulkner's use of W. C. Handy is even more significant in retrospect, because Handy is a central figure in the history of American music. By inventing ragtime and popularizing the blues form, Handy brought African-American musical traditions to the mainstream of American popular music for the first time. For decades, music has been the most integrated arena of American life; Handy almost singlehandedly brought that into being. Faulkner, writing seventeen years after Handy's song was published, used this symbol of integration to tell his story of profound physical and psychic segregation.

Segregation, the legacy of slavery, is the condition that produces most of the ironies Faulkner uses

> " Yet where Hemingway's narrators are generally stoic men, sometimes shell-shocked, always scarred by experience, this narrator is a nine-year-old boy."

in ''That Evening Sun.'' Segregation's ironies are cruel and bitter: Mr. Stovall's savage beating of Nancy lands her in jail, and when she is cut down from her suicide attempt she is beaten again. The irony of black-white sexual relations in the South always underpins the system of segregation, for sexual contact between white men and black women was common and, if not condoned, certainly tolerated, but sexual contact between black men and white women was a crime even more unspeakable than a black person murdering a white person. Nancy—though it is not clear whether the nine-year-old Quentin knows this—is pregnant by a white man, and this is the reason that Jesus leaves her and the reason she fears his wrath.

The central situation of the story, Nancy's terror at Jesus' threat, a situation that is itself a result of slavery and segregation (what in the South was not?) is treated only slightly ironically. The only real irony of that part of the story is the lack of understanding displayed by Jason and Caddy. Rather, Faulkner introduces the main plot of the story with the very ideology of the South expressed in the clearest terms. After Jesus has left town and Nancy is sitting in the Compson kitchen, having already cleaned up, the Compson family is ready for her to go home. But rather than leaving, Nancy just says, ''I ain't nothing but a nigger . . . it ain't none of my fault.'' It is not immediately clear why she has started to talk this way, but Mrs. Compson does not want to hear it, and once Mr. Compson decides to escort Nancy home she complains that she is really the one at risk.

As the story progresses, Nancy's fear becomes just another part of the Compson children's lives and of the Compson household. Jason separates the fear from himself, considering it an element of being black: ''I ain't a nigger,'' he repeats. The noises she makes to herself—''it was like singing and it wasn't like singing,'' Quentin says—are meant to vent a little of that fear, but it is not enough: she must sleep upstairs with the children. When she is not allowed to do that any longer, she asks the children to come home with her, reasoning that Jesus would not attempt to kill her if there were white children in the house—such an action would merit an immediate lynching, one supposes.

Throughout this section the narration is utterly flat, reporting only what happens and interpreting nothing. Quentin reports every statement and reply of each conversation, just as a boy does. However, that very tone does hearken back to Hemingway's, as does the undertone of experience, understanding, and painful growth, which moves the reader to seek for a greater understanding underneath the flat reportage. Faulkner has provided that source of greater understanding already, however: Quentin's older consciousness.

Quentin's older consciousness comes out again at the end of the story—not in the voice itself, but in the structure, in what the narrator chooses to relate. The Compson family walks back to their house, leaving Nancy sitting by her fire, resigned to her fate. Mr. Compson urges her to put the bar up but she is simply apathetic; she will not even close her door, so sure is she that death will find her that night. The children are agitated: Caddy wants to know what is going to happen, while Jason repeats again that ''I'm not a nigger.'' It is Quentin's voice, however, that echoes in the reader's head as the story ends: ''Who will do our washing now, Father?'' Mr. Compson cannot take any more actions than he has without upsetting the delicate racial balance of the Jim Crow South, and he knows that Nancy is in real danger. Quentin feels that Nancy will die that night, but like his mother his only concern is for the tasks she does for the family. Given the Hemingway-esque tone of the narration, this last line is delivered with a bitter irony—the Quentin of 1914 spits it out, realizing that in retrospect he sounds selfish, like Jason. He wonders what he would have done had he been in his father's place, musing on what remains the same in the South—the brutal reality of a system of segregation, neglect, and enforced racism—even as the outward trappings of his home grow gray and ghostly in the modern day of cars and electricity.

Source: Greg Barnhisel, Critical Essay on ''That Evening Sun,'' in *Short Stories for Students*, The Gale Group, 2001.

Diane Brown Jones

In the following essay, Jones discusses the dubious origin of ''That Evening Sun,'' including changes made for its initial publication in American Mercury.

Circumstances of Composition, Sources, and Influences

The earliest reference to ''That Evening Sun'' is October 1930. Consequently, discussions of its origin frequently assume a 1930 composition date. It is possible, however, that Faulkner wrote this story and ''A Justice'' nearer to the time he began *The Sound and the Fury*—in the first half of 1928, possibly even before he began the novel. David Minter observes that although the evidence for this conclusion is circumstantial, it is compelling.

Many arguments placing ''That Evening Sun'' before *The Sound and the Fury* in chronological order focus on the characterizations of the children. Although Blotner does not claim proof of a pre-novel date for the story, he does say that ''That Evening Sun'' ''is the kind of story of the experiences of the Compson children which WF [William Faulkner] said S & F [*The Sound and the Fury*] developed from.'' In ''That Evening Sun,'' Quentin lives to be older than he does in the novel. Further, the adult Quentin of ''That Evening Sun'' does not reflect his preoccupation with Caddy's virginity, his incessant suicidal thoughts, or his ''obsessive inner voices.'' If composition of the three related texts followed in the order of ''That Evening Sun,'' ''A Justice,'' and *The Sound and the Fury*, then Quentin first appeared as a narrator in ''That Evening Sun.'' Benjy does not appear in the story. Ferguson adds that the Dilsey character in the short story is perhaps ''so passive and ineffectual'' because she had not yet assumed the stronger role she has in *The Sound and the Fury*.

Other similarities also suggest that story and novel might have been written at about the same time. The story's description of the town in present time, including details of telephone poles and laundry trucks, seems more like the present time of *The Sound and the Fury*. The narrative of ''seemingly detached episodes'' is like the episodic narrative of Benjy's section of the novel. According to Ferguson, the earliest version of ''That Evening Sun'' (''Never Done No Weeping When You Wanted to Laugh'') shares ''striking similarities in style, dialogue, and point of view'' with Benjy's section of the novel, and Blotner finds resemblances between the handwriting of ''Never Done No Weeping When

You Wanted to Laugh'' and the manuscript of *The Sound and the Fury*. Minter finds a connection in the image of twilight that appears in both of these texts and ''A Justice.''

Not all critics agree that the short stories came before *The Sound and the Fury*. Although Blotner places the discussion of ''That Evening Sun'' in the chapter entitled ''June, 1927–September, 1928'' in his 1974 biography of Faulkner, in the revised 1984 edition he puts the story in the ''April 1930–January 1931'' chapter, at which time records of the story do exist. Irving Howe believes the story is an ''offshoot'' of *The Sound and the Fury*, and Stephen Whicher finds that it ''bears all the earmarks of an afterthought, whose conclusion the earlier novel could hardly have anticipated.'' Gail Morrison dates the story from the fall of 1928, after *The Sound and the Fury* was completed, and Max Putzel places it in 1930. John Matthews writes of Quentin's older voice in ''That Evening Sun'' as the ''ghostly Quentin who survives through several textual avatars into *Absalom, Absalom!*,'' a statement that presumes Faulkner's intentional use of an already dead Quentin after *The Sound and the Fury*. The arguments on both sides are interesting for what they suggest about the writer's craft during a seminal period. However, Blotner's point in 1974 remains true: there simply is ''no sending schedule, agent's record, or conclusive manuscript evidence which would permit accurate dating of the inception and writing of this story.''

Noel Polk describes the textual history of ''That Evening Sun'' as the ''most complicated of any in *These 13*.'' Nevertheless, critics have been able to make more verifiable observations about the development of the text than about the date of composition. ''That Evening Sun'' exists in several versions, both prepublication and published. The earliest known, undated, holograph manuscript is entitled ''Never Done No Weeping When You Wanted to Laugh.'' Another version, a twenty-six-page, complete ribbon typescript gives the title ''That Evening Sun Go Down,'' but the carbon of that typescript shows the revision in Faulkner's hand to ''That Evening Sun.''

When H. L. Mencken accepted the story for the *American Mercury*, he described it as ''capital,'' but he balked at naming Nancy's husband ''Jesus'' and at referring to her pregnancy so explicitly. Mencken seemed unconcerned that the name change would affect both dialogue and imagery. He wrote,

> Faulkner did not incorporate all of Mencken's requests for revision. Mencken wrote, 'It seems to me that the dialogue about Nancy's pregnancy, on pages four and five, is somewhat loud for a general magazine?'"

''I see no reason why he should be called Jesus—it is, in fact, a very rare name among Negroes, and I fear using it would make most readers believe we were trying to be naughty in a somewhat strained manner.'' Jesus's name became *Jubah* to eliminate Mencken's concern. (In a note to Mencken about the requested changes, Faulkner refers to the character as *Judah* although the magazine version uses *Jubah*.) Faulkner returned to the name *Jesus* in *These 13*. Norman Holmes Pearson correctly observes that the return to ''Jesus'' restores the ''paradoxical tension which was otherwise lost.''

Faulkner did not incorporate all of Mencken's requests for revision. Mencken wrote, ''It seems to me that the dialogue about Nancy's pregnancy, on pages four and five, is somewhat loud for a general magazine? [*sic*] I believe it could be modified without doing the slightest damage to the story.'' Faulkner wrote back that some reference to Nancy's pregnancy needed to be retained in order to maintain her husband ''as a potential factor of the tragedy.'' He did concede to a more subdued reference to Nancy's pregnancy and submitted a revised version of those two pages. The *American Mercury* text explains Nancy's swelling apron as follows:

> ''He [Jubah] said it was a watermelon that Nancy had under her dress. And it was Winter, too. 'Where did you get a watermelon in the Winter?' Caddy said. 'I didn't,' Jubah said. 'It wasn't me that give it to her. But I can cut it down, same as if it was.'''

These 13 reinstates the original imagery:

> ''He [Jesus] said it was a watermelon that Nancy had under her dress. 'It never come off of your vine, though,' Nancy, said. 'Off of what vine?' Caddy said. 'I can cut down the vine it did come off of,' Jesus said.''

Faulkner remarked of his anesthetized revision of Nancy's pregnancy: "I did remove the 'vine' business. I reckon that's what would outrage Boston."

Mencken defended his suggestions to Faulkner as "his best editorial judgment." He made additional changes once Faulkner had returned the revised typescript. The revised typescript page shows the following description of Nancy's belly when she was found hanging struck through: ". . . her belly swelling a little, paling a little as it swelled, like a colored balloon pales with distension." The magazine version reads: ". . . found Nancy hanging from the window, stark naked" and *Collected Stories* text reads: ". . . found Nancy hanging from the window, stark naked, her belly already swelling out a little, like a little balloon." Additional revisions are evident on the ribbon typescript used as setting copy. Some are in Mencken's hand and some are the work of another proofreader. They concern such matters as additional paragraph breaks and section divisions.

When he revised the story for collection, Faulkner restored many of the deletions, but he retained paragraph and section divisions inserted by Mencken, even embellishing the division of the last section by further dividing it into two sections. Leo Manglaviti believes that Faulkner worked on his revisions for *These 13* from the manuscript titled "Never Done No Weeping When You Wanted to Laugh" and the *American Mercury* text. A line present in the typescript describes one of the actions Nancy threatened if Jesus were to take another wife. Among her threats the typescript adds, "Ara hand that touched her, I'd cut it off." This line does not appear in "Never Done No Weeping When You Wanted to Laugh," the magazine version, or the collected version. It was not unusual for Faulkner to agree to revisions to facilitate publication; James Carothers notes that stories such as "Spotted Horses," "Snow," "Knight's Gambit," and "Shall Not Perish" were altered for publication

Although the preceding discussion focuses on the alterations that the story underwent specifically in relation to magazine publication, the extant manuscripts and published versions allow for ample study of the development of the text from the early holograph version to the version in *These 13*. The changes are significant. Pearson's early comparative study of the story at three stages—"Never Done No Weeping When You Wanted to Laugh," the *American Mercury* version, and the *These 13* version—identified the major areas of change.

Pearson regards as particularly significant the substitution of the word *cabin* for *house* when the Compsons describe Nancy's dwelling because it contrasts the Compsons' perspective with that of Nancy and Jesus, who both refer to the dwelling as the "house," and represents Nancy and Jesus's "sense of the personal dignity of what had been invaded." Faulkner's deletion of material from the *Mercury* version to the *These 13* text demonstrates his awareness that direct presentation of action eliminated the need for explanation. Quentin's analysis of the Compsons' leaving Nancy's cabin is omitted; only the dramatic presentation of their exit remains. The primary alteration from the first manuscript version to the final text is the change in the "angle of reference." The point of view shifts from being "essentially Nancy's" to becoming Quentin's; as narrator, he shows the personal growth he experiences.

The Compson family presence increases throughout: the story begins and ends with them. (Pearson justifies Benjy's absence pointing out that Benjy's indifference to time makes him an inappropriate character in this particular story.) Quentin's reaction is crucial and is measured by the other children's lack of understanding: they cannot differentiate between Hallowe'en fright and Nancy's terror. The story becomes Quentin's "story of himself, as he had learned from it." The attempt to forestall the setting sun and inevitable death echo in his suicide. According to Blotner, the early manuscript focuses on Nancy although it employs Quentin as an adult to narrate the story. The "clear implication" is that Nancy returns to her cabin and death. The version entitled "That Evening Sun Go Down" is increased in length with additional description, dialogue, and background information on Nancy. Subsequently, without altering the emphasis on Nancy's story, Faulkner developed the contrast of Quentin's adult perspective with that of his childhood, particularly showing his and Caddy's sensitivity. Ferguson adds that the story is improved by the revised ending, done between magazine publication and inclusion in the collections. The deletion of Quentin's closing observation—"the white people going on, dividing the impinged lives of us and Nancy"—removes a too obvious statement of what the action demonstrates; it also eliminates a breach in the voice of the child narrator found in the inflated style of the phrase "dividing the impinged lives of us and Nancy."

Skei claims that the version in *These 13*, subsequently, used again in *Collected Stories*, is the "final, authoritative one." There are a few differences between the two collected versions, but these involve alterations of spelling, capitalization, and paragraphing. In the critical response to "That Evening Sun," the choice of source text has been irregular. In 1935, Edward O'Brien offered an extended close reading of the story in the *Short Story Case Book* series that depended on the particularities of the text. He used the magazine version, "That Evening Sun Go Down," but cited *These 13* Similarly, Sterling Brown and George Snell cite the *These 13* text, but their references to specifics, such as to Jubah rather than Jesus, indicate their use of the magazine version. Frederick Karl uses "That Evening Sun Go Down" as the operative title for his references to the story unless he is specifically referring to the title in collection.

The popularity of "That Evening Sun" has led to a search for analogues to the story in life and literature. The escapades of the Compson children in this story and other texts are typically linked to the activities of the Falkner boys—Billy, Johncy, and Jack—along with their cousin Sallie Murry. Jackson Benson specifically likens Quentin Compson of "That Evening Sun," and *The Sound and the Fury* to Faulkner as a boy: a "quiet, observant, serious, somewhat introverted, and thoughtful child who had no really close friends outside the family." John Faulkner's remembrances include a woman in the community who he believes served as a model for Nancy. Nancy Snowball, a woman who once cooked and washed for the Falkners, caught the children's interest with her ability to crawl through a barbed wire fence without having to touch the load of laundry balanced on her head. The threat Jesus posed to Nancy may be traced to the murder of a woman by her husband, Dave Bowdry, that took place near the Falkner home. A nearby ditch may have added to the fictional scene that is enhanced by the danger the ditch seems to convey—either by providing Jesus a place to hide or as dividing the safety of the Compson house and the danger of the cabin.

Parallels found in literature and music relate less to characters and action than to the development of dialogue and imagery in the story. "That Evening Sun" is significantly enriched by the influence of blues music on the text. The title comes from the words to "St. Louis Blues." John Hagopian believes the relationship to the song is ironic, citing as an example the song's line "I'll love my baby till the day I die." Ken Bennett traces the story's rich associations with both blues music and black relig-

ious music; his work shows that the story's indebtedness goes much deeper than the mere borrowing of its title from Handy's "St. Louis Blues." The image of the evening sun appears in black religious music, sometimes to represent coming death and judgment. In the blues tradition, the setting sun is linked to despair and also to the "time when the black male proved his masculinity" and the prostitute's time to "shine." The character Jesus is much like the rambler character in the blues tradition who may be a criminal, a misfit, or a promiscuous lover. The language of the story is reminiscent of the double entendre prevalent in blues language, such as the reference to the vine and fruit to mean sexual promiscuity. Also, in blues language sexual acts and organs are referred to through common metaphors. Kitchen images are especially prevalent; frequently the kitchen represents the woman's body. Jesus's complaint ("I can't hang around white man's kitchen") becomes richer in that context. Voodoo also appears in blues lyrics, just as it does in the story. Nancy's discovery of the hog bone, a curse and also a phallic symbol, terrifies her. It implies "that Nancy's 'curse' is her promiscuity."

Comparisons with Hemingway, especially his short story "The Killers," have predominated in the list of important literary antecedents. O'Brien sees resemblances to Ernest Hemingway's style in the "laconic reporting" in the story of Nancy's confinement and attempted suicide in jail and patterns of dialogue in the story. Ray West compares the use of initiation in Hemingway's "The Killers" to Quentin's awakening adult sensibilities in "The Evening Sun"; he also finds similarities between Caddy's and Nick Adams's interest in the nature of evil. Leonard Frey judges Faulkner's story to be "superior" to Hemingway's "The Killers" in that Nancy, the victim of the inevitable violence, remains the dominant character whereas in "The Killers" Nick Adams is the central figure rather than Ole Andreson. Austin Wright makes the point that in both stories a "conflict with a range of possible outcomes" is initiated, but in each, the narrative ends without reaching any of the possible outcomes. The reader then must revise his or her sense of what constitutes the focus of the story. In both these cases, the "issue is precisely the failure of resolution."

A number of other studies have made brief observations of literary links between "The Evening Sun," and a wide variety of texts. Collectively, the list demonstrates more the rich texture of the story than a single dominating influence on the story. O'Brien suggests that a comparison could be made of Balzac's and Faulkner's use of chiaroscuro in the development of atmosphere. Frey likens the irony in the story to ironic presentation in ballads such as ''The Twa Corbies'' and ''The Wife of Usher's Well'': in all these, although an objective presentation of the material is offered, the reader understands more than the narrator does. Frey regards the counterpoint in the mingled conversations of Caddy and Jason with Mr. Compson and Nancy as similar to the remarks of Edgar, Lear, and the Fool in Shakespeare's *King Lear* because in both texts the impact of their comments stems from their ''varying degrees of awareness of their positions.'' Richard Adams finds the phrase ''a long diminishing noise of rubber and asphalt like tearing silk'' to be ''possibly derived from Flaubert.'' The image appears not only in ''That Evening Sun,'' but also in such works as *Mosquitoes*, *The Wild Palms*, and *Intruder in the Dust*. Edward Richardson compares Nancy's terror with the ''driving intensity'' of scenes in *The White Rose of Memphis* by William Clark Faulkner, William's great-grandfather. Mark Coburn considers Tom in Harriet Beecher Stowe's *Uncle Tom's Cabin* a literary analogue to the suffering Nancy.

John Rosenman traces the archetypal pattern of heaven and hell in Faulkner's story and in Ray Bradbury's much later *Dandelion Wine* (1957). Rosenman finds the resemblances striking but does not establish a direct line of influence from Faulkner to Bradbury. Rosenman credits the work of Maud Bodkin in *Archetypal Patterns in Poetry, Psychological Studies of Imagination* as his source for archetypal study.

As other scholars have, Robert Hamb links the title to ''St. Louis Blues,'' but he suggests another possible parallel in William Blake's ''Nurse's Song'' from *Songs of Innocence and Experience*. In the poem, the setting sun is used as an emblem marking the inevitable passage out of childhood. He does not claim with certainty that Faulkner knew this poem, but he confirms the similar use of the image, just as both ''recognized the archetypal initiation pattern in the exposure of children to the realities of time and experience.'' According to John Gerlach, the story bears an inverted relationship to Ephesians. The biblical letter establishes social codes of behavior including the admonition not to let the sun set on one's anger. In ''That Evening Sun'' the children manipulate parents, wives are prostitutes, and the character Jesus remains angry. The story's world is akin to that portrayed in Amos.

Source: Diane Brown Jones, '''That Evening Sun,''' in *A Reader's Guide to the Short Stories of William Faulkner*, G. K. Hall & Co., 1994, pp. 267–74.

Laurence Perrine

In the following essay, Perrine examines unanswered questions in ''That Evening Sun,'' and whether Faulkner implies answers or renders them unknowable.

I

Is Nancy alive or dead in the morning? This is the ''overwhelming question'' raised by Faulkner's ''That Evening Sun.'' Readers have sought an answer both outside the story and in. Malcolm Cowley thought he had found proof of Nancy's murder in a passage from *The Sound and the Fury* (published 1929, two years before the story) in Caddy's reference to some bones left from the time ''when Nancy fell in the ditch and Roskus shot her and the buzzards came and undressed her,'' but Stephen Whicher shattered that claim by demonstrating convincingly that these bones belonged to a horse or pony, not a human being. Other readers have claimed proof for Nancy's survival by pointing to *Requiem for a Nun* (1951), Faulkner's novel written twenty years after ''That Evening Sun'' as a sequel to *Sanctuary* (1931), in which Nancy is alive and well in the employment of Gowen and Temple Drake Stevens at a date subsequent to her employment by the Compsons in ''That Evening Sun.'' But if Faulkner is capable of resurrecting a three-years-dead Quentin Compson from *The Sound and the Fury* to serve as narrator in ''That Evening Sun,'' he is equally capable of resurrecting a several-years-dead Nancy from ''That Evening Sun'' to serve as a central character in *Requiem for a Nun*. In any case, the story must be read and interpreted on its own terms. It is unreasonable to think that Faulkner intended readers of the short story in 1931 to interpret it on the basis of evidence which he would not provide them until twenty years later.

Though probably none would deny that the ending of the story is technically indeterminate, many commentators believe that an answer is implied. Critics who believe Nancy slain have expressed themselves with enormous conviction. John V. Hagopian, explicitly inquiring whether Nancy's awareness of Jesus waiting in the ditch may not be an hallucination, rejects the possibility. ''It would be foolish to wonder if Nancy will actually be killed; of course she will—all the lines of force in the story move powerfully in that direction.'' Edward J. O'Brien declares that, though ''the climax is implicit, . . . we can have no doubt what is going to happen.'' Wilbur L. Schramm echoes him, saying that at the end we walk out of Nancy's life, ''perfectly sure of what is going to happen.'' Those who take this side seem to do so mostly because of the force and intensity of Nancy's own conviction—a conviction so compelling that they call it ''knowledge.'' Norman Holmes Pearson writes that Nancy ''hates to see the coming of the dark, not because her sweet man left the town, but because he has returned to it to take a revenge which Nancy knows she cannot escape, nor the Compsons prevent.'' The use of the verb ''knows'' rather than ''thinks'' is frequently how these critics express their assurance. Commentators on the survival side view Nancy's mental state quite differently. Robert Heilman refers to it as one of ''terrified hallucination.'' Jim Lee calls it ''insanity caused by . . . guilt.'' If my informal tally is reliable, critics who believe that Nancy will be murdered outnumber their opponents by almost three to one.

In this paper I propose to show that the question of Nancy's survival is only the climactic example of a long series of questions which the story raises and leaves unanswered, that ambiguities about fact and motivation are central to its technique, and that the case for Nancy's death is much, much weaker than its proponents realize. I shall argue that Faulkner *meant* the story to end with a question mark to which no train of inferences would supply a truly reliable answer.

II

Just as Caddy throughout the story keeps asking questions which are seldom answered by the adults, so the story itself keeps raising questions for which no sure answers are provided by its author. We may always, of course, conjecture, and sometimes infer, but rarely can we rest in certainty, though we sniff like bloodhounds back and forth through the story searching for clues.

That many of these questions are deliberately raised and left unanswered can be demonstrated. Faulkner's resurrection of dead Quentin to narrate the story, rather than using an omniscient narrator, is part of his method. It is not that Quentin is an unreliable narrator. Indeed he has remarkably precise recall of what he has seen or heard or smelled. Uncertainties arise not because of defects in his memory but because of gaps in his knowledge. He can report accurately what was reported to him, he can repeat precisely what people have said, but these abilities do not guarantee the truth of their

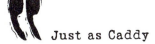

Just as Caddy throughout the story keeps asking questions which are seldom answered by the adults, so the story itself keeps raising questions for which no sure answers are provided by its author."

saying. In addition there is much that Quentin has not heard and does not know. And some matters, like motivation, may be unknowable *except* to an omniscient narrator.

Here is a partial list of questions raised by the story which cannot be certainly answered: (1) Why is Nancy so often late for cooking breakfast? (2) Why is she arrested? (3) Why does she attempt suicide? (4) Has Nancy slept with more than one white man? (5) Who fathered Nancy's unborn child? (6) Does she know? (7) Does Jesus know? (8) Why does Mr. Compson tell Jesus to stay off their place? (9) Why does Jesus leave Nancy? (10) Where does he go? (11) How long does he stay? (12) Does he come back? (13) What causes Nancy's disturbance in the kitchen? (14) Is Aunt Rachel Jesus' mother? (15) Why might Jesus be ''mad'' at Nancy? (16) Why does Nancy think he is angry with her? (17) For what does Nancy feel guilty? (18) Why did Mrs. Lovelady commit suicide? (19) What happened to her child? (20) What happened to Nancy's pregnancy? (21) Is Nancy alive next morning?—I shall address some, but not all of these questions.

Three questions of minor importance should convince us that Faulkner's creation of uncertainties is deliberate:

Why did Mrs. Lovelady commit suicide? What happened to her child? Nancy tells Mr. Compson, ''Anyway, I got my coffin money saved up with Mr. Lovelady.'' Quentin explains:

> Mr. Lovelady was a short, dirty man who collected the Negro insurance, coming around to the cabins or the kitchens every Saturday morning to collect fifteen cents. He and his wife lived at the hotel. One morning his wife committed suicide. They had a child, a little

girl. He and the child went away. After a week or two he came back alone. We would see him going along the lanes and back streets on Saturday mornings.

Quentin's remarks about Mrs. Lovelady and the child are a complete digression from the plot of the story. No reader would have missed anything had Quentin stopped at the end of his first explanatory sentence, or even short of it. But Faulkner has him go on to add two mysteries, neither of which is resolved. We must suppose, however, that Faulkner included this material for a reason. Mr. Lovelady makes his living from the economic exploitation of blacks. His wife's suicide *may* spring from a conflict with her husband over his profession. The husband is described as "a short, dirty man." Nancy's husband is "a short black man" with a "dirty"-looking razor scar on his face, and Nancy too attempts suicide. If a parallel is intended, its significance is that the white attitude toward blacks causes conflict not only *between* but *within* the races. In each of the story's three married couples— Jesus and Nancy, Mr. and Mrs. Compson, Mr. and Mrs. Lovelady—conflict is generated or exacerbated by the relationship of one of the pair with a person or persons of the opposite color.

Is Aunt Rachel Jesus' mother? Again Faulkner deliberately introduces uncertainty. When Mr. Compson asks Nancy, "Cant Aunt Rachel do anything with [Jesus]?" most readers would have been quite satisfied with the simple explanation "Aunt Rachel was Jesus' mother." Instead, Quentin goes on to describe Aunt Rachel, and ends with "They said she was Jesus' mother. Sometimes she said she was and sometimes she said she wasn't any kin to Jesus." A reasonable inference is that she is his mother, or she wouldn't say so, but that, when he does something outrageous, she prefers to deny kinship. Still, Jesus never speaks of her; Nancy expects no help from her; no scene in the story shows Jesus at her house. We are left with a possibility, not a certainty.

The creation of uncertainty is patently part of Faulkner's strategy in writing this story. Let us now turn to more crucial questions.

Why is Nancy so often late for cooking breakfast? "About half the time," Quentin tells us, the children had to summon her by throwing stones at her house until she appeared, leaning her head around the door with no clothes on, to say, "I ain't studying no breakfast." Jason shouts, "Father says you're drunk. Are you drunk, Nancy?" Quentin continues: "So we thought it was whisky until that day they arrested her again. . . ." Here Quentin's narration swings in a wide arc through a revelation of Nancy's prostitution to an account of her suicide attempt and ends with the jailer's asserting that "it was cocaine and not whisky, because a nigger full of cocaine wasn't a nigger any longer." Four reasons are therefore suggested for Nancy's behavior: that she's drunk; that she's been engaging in prostitution; that she's high on cocaine; plus Nancy's own explanation, "I got to get my sleep out." An astonishing number of critics accept the explanation that Nancy is a dope-addict, though the jailer is a brutal bigot whose reasoning, cast in syllogistic form, is (a) No Negro has sufficient courage to attempt suicide unless he's high on cocaine; (b) Nancy is a Negro and has attempted suicide; (c) therefore Nancy is high on cocaine. Others, perhaps reasoning that Nancy would not have the courage to challenge Mr. Stovall in public unless she were drunk, accept Mr. Compson's explanation to his children about her behavior, disregarding the probability that Mr. Compson would prefer to give them such an account than expose them at their age to the harsh facts of prostitution (the one thing we *know* Nancy to be guilty of) and disregarding also the implications of Quentin's statement, "So we thought it was whisky *until*. . . ." But the facts are that nowhere in the story is Nancy shown taking cocaine or drinking anything stronger than coffee, and that, despite her overwhelming terror later in the story, she is not naturally a timid woman, as shown by her taunting her violent husband with the assertion that the child she is carrying is not off his "vine" as well as by her challenging Mr. Stovall. Nancy's explanation, together with her unclad appearance, supports the prostitution theory. But Nancy's nakedness and her need of sleep can be equally well explained by supposing that she stayed awake late making love with her husband. We tend to forget that Nancy's house is Jesus' house too; but the children chunk stones at it from a distance, not just out of thoughtless disrespect, but because their father told them "not to have anything to do with Jesus."

Why is Nancy arrested? Prostitution? Use of illegal drugs? Being drunk and disorderly? Disturbing the peace? All we can be sure of is our admiration for Faulkner's conjuring up a past history of arrest with a single word ("again"). We are not told how often or why.

Why does Nancy attempt suicide? The reasons are probably multiple, may be unknown to Nancy herself, and are best left to the imagination of the reader. The function of her attempt in the story is clearer. The depth of her despair here, put beside the violence of her jealous reaction to Mr. Compson's suggestion that Jesus has probably "got another wife" in St. Louis, reveals Nancy's emotional extremes and prepares for her paroxysm of fear when she hears that Jesus has returned.

Who fathered Nancy's unborn child? Several commentators confidently name Mr. Stovall as the father, since he is the only candidate named; others more cautiously attribute paternity only to an unknown white man, their caution validated by Mr. Compson's rebuke to Nancy, "If you'd just let white men alone." We cannot be sure, however, whether Mr. Compson speaks from certain knowledge, or whether his rebuke simply combines the universal tendency to generalize from one instance with the Southern white's tendency to give black behavior the least favorable interpretation. Moreover, Jesus' claim that he can "cut down the vine" that Nancy's "watermelon" came off of is a valid threat only if Mr. Stovall is the only white man she has slept with. How else would he know whose "vine" to cut? A third possibility, that Jesus himself is the father, is seldom considered. Yet how can Nancy know who made her pregnant if she was living with Jesus while having sexual relations with another? That Nancy and Jesus have been living together is indicated by the general acceptance of them as husband and wife, by the children's approaching no nearer than the ditch to Nancy's house, by Jesus' taking breakfast in the Compson kitchen when Nancy begins cooking there, by Jesus' eloquent statement that "when white men want to come in my house, I ain't got no house," and by Nancy's announcement of Jesus' departure: "one morning she woke up and Jesus was gone." On the basis of the published story alone, we must acknowledge a possibility that Nancy, in declaring that her "watermelon" didn't come off Jesus' "vine," is baiting Jesus with a possibility, not a certainty.

Evidence from outside the story, however, does certify Faulkner's intention as being that Jesus should *know* the child not to be his. In submitting the story for publication in the *American Mercury*, Faulkner modified the passage about Nancy's pregnancy (in response to its editor H. L. Mencken's protest that it was "somewhat loud for a general magazine") as follows:

> When Dilsey was sick in her cabin and Nancy was cooking for us, we could see her apron swelling out; . . .[Jesus] said it was a watermelon that Nancy had under her dress. And it was Winter, too.

"Where did you get a watermelon in the Winter?" Caddy said.

"I didn't," [Jesus] said. "It wasn't me that give it to her. But I can cut it down, same as if it was."

Faulkner restored the original wording—both more effective and more ambiguous—for the story's first book publication in *These Thirteen* later that year.

Why does Jesus leave Nancy? Nancy wakes up one morning "and Jesus was gone." The almost casual way she tells it does not suggest that they had quarreled. Nancy says, "He quit me. Done gone to Memphis, I reckon. Dodging them city *po*-lice for a while." Had Jesus simply tired of dodging the Jefferson "*po*-lice" and sought temporary respite in the larger city? Later, Nancy says, "He said I done woke up the devil in him and ain't but one thing going to lay it down again." But Nancy makes this remark after the presumed return of Jesus; if he said it to her, he must have said it sometime *before* he left, for there has been no communication between them since. The threat (presuming Jesus actually made it and Nancy has correctly interpreted it) would explain Nancy's outbreak of fear on hearing of his return. But if Jesus intends to murder her, why must he go away first and then come back to do it? And why does Nancy's fear not date from his making the threat? Might she not have "invented" the remark to rationalize the fear that has arisen in her *after* his departure?

Where does Jesus go? Nancy says, "Done gone to Memphis, I reckon." Father says, "He's probably in St. Louis now."

Why might Jesus be "mad" at Nancy? Why does she think he is? When Mr. Compson suggests to Nancy that Jesus has "probably got another wife by now," Nancy's reaction is immediate: "If he has, I better not find out about it. I'd stand right there over them, and every time he wropped her, I'd cut that arm off. I'd cut his head off and I'd slit her bell and I'd shove—." Reacting this way, Nancy might very well think that Jesus would react the same way when the cases are reversed and she sleeps with another man. But, as critics have pointed out, when Jesus is told that the watermelon is not off his vine, he threatens the father, not Nancy. Moreover, he must have known about her prostitution earlier, for his speech about "When white man want to come in my house, I ain't got no house" voices a sense of injustice that must have been smouldering for a long time. Not until the moment when he tells Nancy, *if* he does, that she "done woke up the devil in him" does Jesus manifest any anger toward Nancy. The problem is to explain the delay. But the parallel between Jesus' sleeping with a hypothetical "St. Louis woman" and Nancy's sleeping with Mr. Stovall is inexact. In the one case Jesus is loving a new woman and has forgotten Nancy. In the other, Nancy is sleeping with Mr. Stovall for money and has not at all forgotten Jesus. Still, Jesus feels the indignity keenly and makes a violent threat, just as Nancy does, though against the father, not against Nancy. We hear nothing of his attempting to carry out that threat, however. The only violence in the story is committed by whites against blacks. And even supposing that Jesus knows who the father is, there is little possibility of his being able to carry out the threat, so supreme is white power in Jefferson. Though Mr. Stovall has slept with Nancy several times, has refused to pay her, has knocked her down and kicked her teeth out, and possibly fathered her child, Jesus has pretty clearly never attacked Mr. Stovall. Nancy continually protects herself against Jesus by sleeping in the Compsons' house or surrounding herself with Compson children, knowing that Jesus is unlikely to attack her in their presence. Meanwhile, we may conjecture, Jesus' anger and frustration seethe inside him, and his indignity is daily pressed upon him as Nancy's belly swells. Such being the case, is it illogical to believe that the anger originally directed toward the unknown father might be redirected toward Nancy? Nancy herself undergoes an emotional transition, from blaming others to blaming, at least partially, herself. At the beginning of her terror, she says, I ain't nothing but a nigger. "It ain't none of my fault." But near the end she says, "I reckon it belong to me, I reckon what I going to get ain't no more than mine." Nancy is capable of changing from an initial defiant taunting of Jesus ("It ain't off your vine") to a feeling of guilt over her physical infidelity to the man who "always been good" to her. Whether we accept a change in Jesus' feelings or not will depend on how much credence we give to Nancy's report that he said she "done woke up the devil in him and ain't but one thing going to lay it down again." Nancy's feelings change; there are good reasons why Jesus' feelings *might* change; and there are reasons why Nancy should believe they have changed, whether they have or not. The mere act of his leaving her would explain *that*.

What happens to Nancy's pregnancy? It is puzzling that Nancy's pregnancy, forced so vividly on our attention early in the story, should never be mentioned again. There are three possibilities: Nancy has had an abortion; she has had a miscarriage or stillbirth; she is still pregnant at the end of the story.

A recent critic contends that "the following enigmatic paragraph can hardly be read in any other way than as a symbolic confirmation of an abortion":

> "Father said for you to go home and lock the door, and you'll be all right," Caddy said. "All right from what, Nancy? Is Jesus mad at you?" Nancy was holding the coffee cup in her hands again, her elbows on her knees and her hands holding the cup between her knees. She was looking into the cup. "What have you done that made Jesus mad?" Caddy said. Nancy let the cup go. It didn't break on the floor, but the coffee spilled out, and Nancy sat there with her hands still making the shape of the cup.

There is nothing enigmatic about this paragraph. It is simply a graphic description of Nancy's terror. Nancy's sitting with her hands still making the shape of the cup she has dropped, like other symptoms of her terror, exhibits a violent disjunction between the signals received and sent out by her brain. In her suicide attempt, after putting the noose around her neck, she can't make her hands let go of the window ledge. In her cabin she keeps her hand on the hot lamp without realizing that the hand is burning. But if one insists on reading the paragraph symbolically, it is a much apter symbol for miscarriage than for abortion, for Nancy's dropping the cup and spilling its contents is involuntary. But, indeed, the abortion-theory must be dismissed. In Mississippi, before the turn of the century, a black woman of Nancy's class and education would not have had access to abortion at her stage of pregnancy. Still, if Nancy has had either abortion or miscarriage, it is strange that Quentin, keenly observant of physical detail, should not mention that Nancy's belly was "flat" again. A colleague of mine suggests that the sentence "Jason's legs stuck straight out of his pants where he sat on Nancy's lap" may be intended to convey this information. Possibly so. We can not be certain.

Does Jesus come back? So strong is Nancy's conviction of Jesus' return that few commentators question it, yet all the reasons supporting it are undermined by uncertainty.

Our first news of Jesus' return is received on the night that Nancy sits by the cold stove in the Compsons' kitchen, scared to go home:

> "I am going to walk down the lane with Nancy," [father] said. "She says that Jesus is back." "Has she seen him?" mother said. "No. Some Negro sent her word that he was back in town."...

What we are given here is *at the very least* a fourth-hand report. Quentin tells us that father said that Nancy said that "some Negro" said. Though there is not need to question the reliability of Quentin or of father, the last two members in the series are increasingly unreliable. The phrase "sent her word" (rather than "told her") suggests moreover the probability of one or more additional intermediaries. What evidence the first Negro had, how the word was sent, what the word was, whether it was transmitted accurately, and whether Nancy interpreted it correctly—all these factors are left undetermined.

The next suggestion of Jesus' return is the disturbance in the kitchen when the Compson household is awakened by Nancy's terrified ululation. When Caddy asks, "Was it Jesus? Did he try to come into the kitchen?" Nancy can only answer, "I ain't nothing but a nigger. God knows." Whether Nancy was frightened by an intruder, whether that intruder was Jesus, or whether the whole affair was a bad dream—these matters are left unresolved. Nancy herself seems not to know the answers.

The chief support for Jesus' return seems simply the intensity of Nancy's own subjective conviction. Dilsey asks, "How do you know he's back? You ain't seen him." "I can feel him," Nancy says. "I can feel him laying yonder in the ditch." "Tonight?" Dilsey asks. "How come you know it's tonight?" "I know," Nancy replies. "He's there waiting. I know. I done lived with him too long. I know what he is fixing to do fore he know it himself." Nancy may well have lived with Jesus long enough to have a feeling for how his mind works; but this hardly gives her absolute power to predict his actions, let alone the precise *time* of his actions. There is no evidence that she had foreseen Jesus' leaving her, and there is some suggestion that she was surprised when it happened. She woke up one morning "and Jesus was gone." If she failed to predict this event when she went to bed with him the previous evening, why should one think she could predict the date on which Jesus would attempt to kill her when she has been out of communication with him for weeks? Dilsey's question is crucial: "How come you know it's tonight?" There is no rational answer to Dilsey's question. There *is*, however, a strong psychological reason why Nancy's terror should peak this night. Dilsey's return to work has deprived Nancy of the security offered by the Compson house. For the first time in weeks she is faced with the prospect of spending the night alone in her cabin.

Nancy's intuitions are, for her, convictions; and she expresses them with such force that many readers accept them as truth. Yet it is difficult to believe that, in the lapse of time between the first report of Jesus' return and Nancy's night of terror, there would be no confirmation of his return. If Jesus is back, why has nobody seen him? It is also hard to imagine why Jesus would lie for hours in an uncomfortable ditch in order to take his revenge. There are easier ways. And Nancy's words strain credulity when she tells Mr. Compson, "He looking through that window this minute, waiting for yawl to go," just as they strain it when Mr. Compson escorts her home on the first night after she has heard of Jesus' return: "I can feel him now, in this lane. He hearing us talk, every word, hid somewhere, waiting." In Nancy's mind, after his "return," Jesus is omnipresent.

A final piece of evidence for Jesus' return would seem, at first sight, objective enough. "I got the sign," Nancy says. "It was on the table when I come in. It was a hogbone, with blood meat still on it, laying by the lamp." But *when* did she get the sign? If she means when she returned to the cabin with the children, the children would have seen it too, as would Mr. Compson when he arrived. (If she had removed it, the children would have seen her remove it, and she could not have removed it so far that she could not have *showed* it to Mr. Compson). If she refers to sometime earlier in the day, why had she not mentioned it to Dilsey when Dilsey asked, "How do you know he's back? You ain't seen him?" We are left with strong reasons to believe that the "sign" is a desperate last-ditch invention of Nancy's feverish mind designed to keep Mr. Compson in the cabin. (It should be pointed out that Mr. Compson's "He's not here. I would have seen him" is equally an invention—a display of false confidence designed to calm Nancy down. When Nancy replies, "He waiting in the ditch yonder," Mr. Compson first says, "Nonsense," but then, "Do you know he's there?" Even *he* is impressed by the force of Nancy's conviction.)

Is Nancy alive next morning? It is now time to construct the most plausible account of the story we can imagine for each of the two suppositions about its ending:

(A) Nancy, washerwoman, cook, and prostitute, is made pregnant by a white man. Her violent husband, Jesus, angered by the pregnancy, makes what is either a castration or a murder threat against the father, and voices his indignation in a fine speech about "I cant hang around white man's kitchen. But white man can hang around mine. . . ." Frustrated, however, by his powerlessness to carry out his threat, he gradually turns his anger against Nancy and tells her she "done woke up the devil" in him and only her death will "lay it down again." Perhaps to prevent himself from carrying out this threat, he leaves town. His anger, still frustrated, drives him back. Nancy, hearing of his return, knowing his violent nature, and aware of his threat, knows he has come back to kill her, and is so overcome by fear that Mr. Compson feels obliged to escort her home at night. When Mrs. Compson objects to being left alone, a pallet is fixed for Nancy in the kitchen. After Jesus makes an unsuccessful attempt one night to break into the house, Nancy's fear turns to terror. Denied the protection of the Compson house after Dilsey's return, she entices the children to come home with her and pretends that their father is with them. She knows Jesus will strike this night because she is unprotected and because he has left a "sign," which, in her disturbed state, she had not mentioned to Dilsey. When Mr. Compson, who has come after the children, refuses to stay with her, her will breaks, and she resigns herself to the death that surely awaits her.

(B) Nancy's suicide attempt, to which her pregnancy is a contributing cause, displays the conflicting impulses and emotional extremes to which she is subject. In the kitchen sometime later, she taunts Jesus with the assertion that the "watermelon" under her skirt "never came off[his] vine." Jesus' anger is directed, not against her, however, but against the unknown father and against white men in general. When Jesus leaves her, her response is at first casual, but during his absence she questions the reasons for his departure and her own role in it. She is torn between the desire to relieve herself of responsibility ("I ain't nothing but a nigger. It ain't none of my fault") and a need to acknowledge her guilt ("Jesus always been good to me. Whenever he had two dollars, one of them was mine"). She shows that her feelings toward Jesus run deep when she tells Mr. Compson what she'd do if she caught Jesus with another wife. The false rumor that Jesus has returned intensifies her inner conflicts and feelings of guilt, and she convinces herself that Jesus has come back to kill her ("I ain't going to see him but once more, with that razor in his mouth"). She imagines that Jesus had threatened her life before he left ("He done say I woke up the devil in him"), and she irrationally feels him lurking everywhere, waiting, hearing all she says. She so vividly hallucinates

an attempted attack by Jesus in the Compsons' kitchen one night that afterwards she is unsure what actually happened. Her terror psychologically peaks on the day when Dilsey returns to the kitchen, depriving her of her sanctuary. Her guilt and her fear mount together ("I hellborn," she tells Jason. "I going back where I come from soon"), and she turns to the desperate expedient of enticing the Compson children to her cabin. When Mr. Compson dismisses her fears as "Nonsense," her imagination creates the "proof" of the hog-bone with blood meat still on it. When this too fails, her will breaks, and she resigns herself to what she falsely believes her fate, now fully accepting her guilt ("I reckon it belong to me. I reckon what I going to get ain't no more than mine").

The first account is the more emotionally compelling, as demonstrated by the reactions of commentators. The second bears up better, I think, under rational scrutiny of the facts. But neither account can be proved. Each rests on undemonstrable assumptions, each embraces long sequences of conjecture (the first, especially, about the progress of Jesus' feelings; the second about Nancy's).

If we ask ourselves Faulkner's *intention* in the story, we must conclude that Faulkner wished to end it with an unresolvable question mark. First, Faulkner takes great pains to emphasize that question mark. On the final three pages of the story, the question is put before the reader six separate times. Nancy four times asserts that Jesus is waiting in the ditch, and Mr. Compson four times dismisses the assertion as "Nonsense." After that, Mr. Compson twice answers Caddy's questions with assurances that nothing is going to happen and that Jesus has gone away. Even so, Quentin is unpersuaded. "Who will do our washing now, Father?" he asks. The Compson family are divided on the answer. Second, the uncertainty about the ending is *not* caused by any gap in Quentin's knowledge. Quentin certainly knows whether Nancy was alive or not the next morning. This uncertainty exists because Faulkner deliberately stops the story before Quentin reaches the next morning. Finally, the question of Nancy's survival is the crowning uncertainty in a story whose consistent method is uncertainty. The other uncertainties lead up to and feed into the final uncertainty.

IV

"*That Evening Sun*" is about fear and the gulf separating the white and black communities which is both cause and result of that fear. The uncertainties of the story serve both subjects. Many of the gaps in Quentin's knowledge arise from the separation of the two communities; most of the uncertainties feed into our final uncertainty about the outcome of the conflict between Nancy and Jesus. This unresolved personal conflict reflects the larger unresolved social conflict of which it is a symptom. Fifty years after the Emancipation there has been no improvement in white-black relationships. Finally, the uncertainties of the story, especially the final uncertainty, intensify the fear and horror felt by the reader: Nancy's fear is multiplied as if by many mirrors. If Mr. Compson had seen clearly where Jesus was hiding in the ditch, or if Nancy had seen clearly that Jesus was not there, the force of Faulkner's masterpiece would be sadly diminished. Unresolved, the story haunts the consciousness and conscience of the reader far beyond its formal limits.

Source: Laurence Perrine, "'That Evening Sun': A Skein of Uncertainties," in *Studies in Short Fiction*, Vol. 22, No. 3, 1985, pp. 295–307.

Sources

Brooks, Cleanth, *William Faulkner: The Yoknapatawpha Country*, Yale University Press, 1963.

Cantwell, Robert, Review in *New Republic*, October 21, 1931, p. 271.

Carothers, James B., "Faulkner's Short Story Writing and the Oldest Profession," in *Faulkner and the Short Story*, edited by Evans Harrington and Ann J. Abadie, University Press of Mississippi, 1992.

Ferguson, James, *Faulkner's Short Fiction*, University of Tennessee Press, 1991.

McDonald, Edward, Review of *These 13*, in the Philadelphia *Record*, October 4, 1931, p. 14-B.

Peden, William, Review of *Collected Stories*, in *Saturday Review of Literature*, August 26, 1950, p. 12.

Review of *These 13*, in *Time*, August 28, 1950, p. 79.

Skei, Hans H., *William Faulkner: The Novelist as Short Story Writer*, Universitetsforlaget, 1985.

Trilling, Lionel, Review in *The Nation*, November 4, 1931, p. 491–92.

Further Reading

Cash, W. J., and Bertram Wyatt-Brown, eds., *The Mind of the South*, Vintage Books, 1991,

This widely popular nonfiction work was first published in 1941 and has ever since been recognized as a path-breaking work. The book presents examinations of the Southern class system and its legacies of racism, religiosity, culture.

Inge, M. Thomas, ed., *Conversations with William Faulkner*, University of Mississippi Press, 1999.

This collection of interviews ranges from Faulkner's early years as a writer in 1916 to the early 1960s when he was composing his last novel. These interviews build a profile of Faulkner in his daily world and home. They also capture the many myths that were perpetuated about Faulkner and that he helped foster.

Kartiganer, Donald, and Ann J. Abadie eds., *Faulkner at 100: Retrospect and Prospect*, University of Mississippi Press, 2000.

This work is a collection of presentations by literary scholars given at the 1997 Faulkner and Yoknapatawpha Conference in Oakland, Mississippi. Though each entry is slight (covering about twenty mintues per speech), they cover a wide range of aspects within Faulkner's works.

Minter, David L., *William Faulkner: His Life and Work*, John Hopkins University Press, 1997.

Minter's book draws on published and unpublished interviews with Faulkner, his letters, and his writings to present the many fascinating angles of Faulkner's personality.

Williamson, Joel, *William Faulkner and Southern History*, Oxford University Press, 1995.

Williamson's text is both a biography of William Faulkner and an examination of Faulkner's fictional worlds. The book becomes an analysis of Faulkner's history, and through presentations of him and his ancestors, it unfolds an intriguing insight into Southern culture.

What We Talk About When We Talk About Love

Raymond Carver

1981

The short story "What We Talk About When We Talk About Love," by Raymond Carver, is the title story in his first volume of short fiction by a major publisher. Upon publication, *What We Talk About When We Talk About Love* received immediate and glowing critical acclaim, earning front page coverage in the *New York Times Book Review* as well as a favorable review in the *New York Review of Books*. Adam Meyer explains that "this was to be the volume that would firmly establish Carver as an important writer." The stories in *What We Talk About When We Talk About Love* are considered the epitome of Carver's sparse, minimalist writing style. Marshall Bruce Gentry and William L. Stull refer to the volume as Carver's "minimalist masterpiece." Meyer explains that "the collection has been nicknamed the 'minimalist bible,' and when readers and critics consider Carver a minimalist they generally have this volume in mind." Meyer concludes that "because it is the volume that established Carver as a major literary figure, it has remained the collection most associated with him." Gentry and Stull note that "the bare-boned collection proved immensely influential on a younger generation of short-story writers coming of age in the 1980s."

The entire action of the story takes place over the course of an evening, during which two married couples, Nick, who is also the narrator, and Laura, and Mel and Terri, sit around the kitchen table drinking gin and discussing the topic of "real love." The dynamics between the two couples are

contrasted through their gestures and interactions with one another. Nick and Laura are still in the glow of early love, and their behavior toward one another is affectionate and respectful. Mel and Terri, on the other hand, have been together five years, and their surface-level civility to one another barely masks a deep-seated anger and resentment. Mel's alcoholism, and increasing drunkenness over the course of the evening, sets a tone of increasingly intensified menace to the whole conversation.

This story addresses typical Carver themes of marriage and divorce, alcoholism, despair, and the difficulty of communication.

Author Biography

Raymond Carver was born on May 25, 1938, in Clatskanie, Oregon. His father was a manual laborer, and Carver worked as a laborer at various jobs from the early 1950s through the late 1960s. In 1957, at the age of eighteen, he married sixteen-year-old Maryann Burk, who eventually became a teacher, and with whom he had two children within the first two years of their marriage. They moved to California, where Carver attended Humboldt State College (now California State University at Humboldt) and received his bachelor's degree in English in 1963, while at the same time working in a sawmill to support his family. In 1966, Carver earned a master of fine arts degree in creative writing from the University of Iowa. His short story, ''Will You Please Be Quiet Please?'' was selected for *The Best American Short Stories of 1967*, an annual publication. His stories were selected for the O. Henry Award in 1973, 1974, 1975, and 1983. 1976 saw his first major book publication, a collection of stories written between 1962 and 1975 entitled, *Will You Please Be Quiet Please?*.

From 1971 to 1979, Carver taught at several colleges and universities, including: as a lecturer in creative writing at the University of California at Santa Cruz (1971–1972); as a lecturer in fiction writing at the University of California at Berkeley (1972–1973); as visiting professor of English at the Writers Workshop, University of Iowa (1973–1974); as a lecturer at the University of California at Santa Barbara (1974–1975); as a member of the faculty writing program at Goddard College (1977–1978);

and as visiting distinguished writer at the University of Texas at El Paso (1978–1979).

Carver and Maryann separated in 1976 and he was hospitalized for his alcoholism four times between 1976 and 1977. In the summer of 1977, he quit drinking for good—one of his proudest achievements in life. His second major collection of short stories, *What We Talk About When We Talk About Love*, was published in 1981. 1983 saw the publication of his third major collection, *Cathedral*. He and Maryann divorced in 1983; in 1988, he married poet Tess Gallagher. Carver died later that year of lung cancer at the age of 50. His fourth major story collection, *Where I'm Calling From: New and Selected Stories* was published, shortly before his death. Several collections of his short stories and poems were published posthumously. Director Robert Altman adapted a number of Carver's stories to the screen, combining them into a single narrative feature film as director of the movie entitled *Short Cuts*.

Plot Summary

The action of the story, ''What We Talk About When We Talk About Love,'' takes place over the course of an evening, in which two couples, Nick and Laura, and Mel and Terri McGinnis, sit around the kitchen table at the McGinnis' apartment, drinking gin and talking, before they all go out to dinner together. No one so much as gets up from the table over the course of their conversation, except to get out a second bottle of gin. The story takes place in Albuquerque, New Mexico, although, as the narrator explains, ''we were all from somewhere else.'' Mel, a forty-five year old cardiologist, is divorced, and Terri is his second wife. Terri is also divorced and Mel is her second husband. Mel and Terri have been married for four years, together for five. Nick and Laura are married, and have been together only eighteen months.

As the story opens, the narrator explains that ''The gin and tonic water kept going around, and we somehow got on the subject of love.'' Mel, who had once gone to seminary school, claims that ''real love was nothing less than spiritual love.'' They then begin to discuss Terri's former husband, Ed, who was physically abusive to her, had threatened Mel on several occasions, and eventually shot himself in the head, dying three days later. Mel argues that that is not real love, while Terri insists that Ed did love her. While Nick and Laura's relationship

Raymond Carver

seems to be completely harmonious, and their inter-actions with each other kind and affectionate, Mel and Terri's interactions take on a tone of controlled menace, barely covering a deep-seated resentment between the two of them.

The conversation continues on the subject of love while Mel becomes increasingly drunk. He gives an example of what he considered to be "real love." He tells them about an elderly couple who had gotten into a terrible car accident when they were hit by a teenage boy. Both of them nearly died, but they continued to survive, although both were covered from head to toe in bandages. Mel explains that, one day, the old man explained to him in tears that he was upset that, although he and his wife's beds were next to each other in the hospital room, he could not turn his head to see her face, because of his bandages. Mel is taken with the idea that this man loved his wife so much it was nearly killing him not to be able to look at her: "I mean, it was killing the old fart just because he couldn't *look* at the . . . woman."

Mel, now clearly drunk, decides that he'd like to call and talk to his kids, who live with his ex-wife, Marjorie. He explains that Marjorie is allergic to bee stings, and part of him would like to appear at her front door and release a swarm of bees into her

house. But he is baffled that he feels such hatred for her now, when he knows that he did once truly love her. Mel then decides against calling his children, and all four finish off the last of the gin. Mel erratically turns his glass of gin upside, allowing it to spill all over the table. "Gin's gone," he says. "Now what?" Terri responds. At this point the narrator ends the story with a description of the four friends, sitting in silence around the table: "I could hear my heart beating. I could hear everyone's heart. I could hear the human noise we sat there making, no one of us moving, not even when the room went dark."

Characters

Laura

Laura is Nick's wife. They have been together for a year and a half. She is thirty five years old and a legal secretary. The narrator describes her as "easy to be with." Nick's depiction of Laura is based on the continuing "honeymoon" tone of their relation-ship. Laura's comments and her expressions of affection for Nick are presented in marked contrast to the biting tenor of the exchanges between Terri and Mel.

Mel McGinnis

Mel is a friend of the narrator, and husband of Terri. He is a cardiologist and is described as: "forty-five years old. He was tall and rangy with curly soft hair. His face and arms were brown from the tennis he played." Mel, clearly an alcoholic, is the dominant voice in the conversation between the two couples, and the tone of the conversation changes as he becomes increasingly drunk. Mel is the one who continues to focus on the question of "what we talk about when we talk about love." He brings up Terri's abusive ex-husband as a negative example of love. He then talks about an old couple who were almost killed in a car accident as an example of the "love" he's talking about. Mel's behavior also changes with his drunkenness, as "when he was sober, his gestures, all his movements, were precise, very careful." As he becomes drunker, his com-ments to his wife take on an increasingly menacing tone, and he begins to seem capable of the abusive behavior Terri's ex-husband had exhibited toward her. He eventually decides that he wishes to call his kids, who live with his ex-wife, then decides not to. He effectively turns the conversation between the two couples to the silence with which the story ends when he dumps his shot-glass upside down, spilling its contents on the table.

Nick

Nick is the narrator. He is thirty eight years old but beyond that does not describe himself or what he does for a living. He primarily plays the part of observer, as his contributions to the conversation are minimal. Nick's perspective on his relationship with Laura, whom he's been with for a year and a half, is in marked contrast to his observations of the menacing tone of the relationship between Mel and Terri. He is clearly in love with Laura and believes their relationship to be in the category of true love. Because Nick is the first-person narrator, the reader is given only his perspective of the other characters and is left to wonder if perhaps his relationship with Laura is bound to take the bitter turn toward the veiled hostility of Terri and Mel's relationship.

Teresa

Teresa is the second wife of Mel, who is also her second husband. She is described as: "a bone-thin woman with a pretty face, dark eyes, and brown hair that hung down her back. She liked necklaces made of turquoise, and long pendant earrings." The topic of "love" first revolves around a discussion of her abusive former husband Ed, who tried to kill her, made threats to Mel, and eventually shot himself in the head, taking three days to die from it, during which Terri stayed at his bedside. Terri's behavior toward Mel walks a line between caution and menace; like Mel's comments to her, her comments to him, while infused with terms of endearment, such as "honey," smack of a deep-seated bitterness that is never directly expressed. It seems that, in her marriage to Mel, she is in some ways repeating her relationship with her abusive ex-husband.

Terri

See Teresa

Media Adaptations

- A collection of Carver's short stories was adapted to the screen and made into a composite narrative film entitled *Short Cuts* (1993), directed by Robert Altman.

Themes

Love

The central theme of this story is love. The two couples spend the evening drinking gin and discussing the nature of "real love." The narrator explains that "we somehow got on the subject of love." It is Mel who insists on returning to the topic of love. He believes that "love was nothing less than spiritual love." They then turn to the topic of Terri's abusive former husband Ed, who eventually shot himself in the head and died. Terri and Mel, both of them married for the second time, debate whether or not Ed really loved Terri. She claims that Ed "loved her so much he tried to kill her." Mel insists that "that's not love."

Mel eventually describes to them an example of what he considers to be "real love," the old couple who had nearly died in a car accident. This conversation about, as Mel puts it, "what we talk about when we talk about love" is many-layered, however. While they discuss the topic, getting drunker all the while, Terri and Mel exhibit an increasingly menacing tone to their interactions with one another. Although they are soft-spoken and civil on the surface, they express a deep-seated anger and resentment toward one another. The narrator, Nick, meanwhile, clearly perceives his relationship with his wife Laura as one of real love, and their warm, affectionate, harmonious interactions with one another seem to demonstrate this. However, as Mel becomes drunker, the atmosphere of subtle but distinct menace seems to pervade the entire room, leaving the two couples sitting in the dark in silence.

Topics for Further Study

- While he consistently disclaimed the label, Carver's writing style, particularly in the stories of the collection *What We Talk About When We Talk About Love*, is consistently referred to by critics in terms of "minimalism." The term minimalism has also been used to describe stylistic trends in both art and music. Find out more about minimalism in either art or music and pick a minimalist artist in either of these mediums to learn more about. How does the minimalist style of Carver's story translate into the medium of the artist or composer you have chosen?

- Carver has often cited the nineteenth-century short story writer and playwright Anton Chekhov as one of the greatest influences on his own writing. Read a short story by Chekhov. In what ways does Carver's writing style seem to draw from that of Chekhov? In what ways is Carver's style markedly different from Chekhov's?

- A central focus of the discussion between the four characters in Carver's story is on the abusive behavior of Terri's former husband, Ed. Find out more about the prevalence and conditions of domestic violence today. What resources are available to battered women in your town,

county, or state? What laws exist at the local, state, or national level to protect battered women? What are some of the difficulties faced by battered women in trying to leave an abusive relationship?

- Film director Robert Altman has adapted several of Carver's short stories into a composite feature-length narrative film entitled *Short Cuts*. Read at least one of the stories in the published collection *Short Cuts*, and then watch the film. In what ways does the film translate the atmosphere, characterization, and dialogue of Carver's written stories into the film medium? What elements of these stories are lost in the translation? In what ways does the film medium add to the meaning of the short stories?

- Robert Altman is a much-praised filmmaker in his own right. Carver himself was an admirer of Altman's film *Nashville*. Learn more about Altman's directing career, his other films, and the most notable elements of his film style. In what ways are Altman's sensibilities as a filmmaker similar to Carver's sensibilities as a writer? In what ways is Altman's style completely different from that of Carver's?

There is a sense that the dark underbelly of "real love" has been exposed, and the characters are left in utter despair, unable to move or speak.

Communication

A central theme of Carver's stories is communication between people, especially people in relationships. His characters almost universally lack the ability to articulate their true feelings or to effectively make use of language in conducting their relationships. Carver's minimalist style of writing is especially suited to the exploration of the theme of communication. In minimalist writing, nine-tenths of the story's meaning is submerged below the surface level dialogue and interactions between the

characters. Likewise, for the characters themselves, conversation seems to be a means of masking or evading, rather than expressing, their true feelings. The "action" of this story consists primarily of conversation between the four characters, who never even get up from their chairs over the course of the story. Yet while much of the story is taken up with dialogue, the communication between the members of each couple is indicated by their physical gestures, their silences, and, most of all, what the words that remain unspoken.

Marriage and Divorce

Carver's characters have often been divorced at least once and are often remarried. Carver himself first married at age eighteen, later divorced, and remarried shortly before his death from cancer. The characters in this story have experienced divorce and remarriage. Mel's first wife is Marjorie, with whom he has had children, and whom he now supports financially. Terri's first husband was Ed, an abusive man who eventually shot himself. Mel and Terri are now remarried to each other. Nick, who has also been divorced, is now married to Laura. The subject of divorce and remarriage is an important element of the story's focus on the theme of love. Mel first brings up the topic of Terri's abusive former husband, and the two of them debate whether or not Ed truly loved her.

Mel later mentions his ex-wife, whom he once truly loved, but whom he now hates. Mel uses the example of remarriage as evidence of the impermanence of love. He contrasts such short-lived marriages with that of the old couple, who maintained "real love" for one another even through their hardship. Yet despite this touching anecdote, the story as a whole is pervaded by a tone of pessimism as to the permanence of "what we talk about when we talk about love."

Alcoholism

Alcoholism is a pervasive theme in Carver's stories. Carver himself was an alcoholic for over ten years. During his final year of drinking, he was hospitalized on four separate occasions for his alcoholism. He took his last drink in 1977, upon which he became dedicated to recovering from his alcoholism. He has stated in numerous interviews that he was more proud of having quit drinking than of anything else he'd ever done. This story is pervaded by alcohol and alcoholism. All four of the characters spend the evening sitting around drinking gin and tonic. The narrator explains that "the gin and the tonic water kept going around." While they all become drunk, Mel is clearly an alcoholic, and the conversation is most affected by his increasing drunkenness. His interactions with Terri become more bitter, and he becomes even less attuned to those around him. As the story ends, Mel purposefully dumps his glass of gin upside down, allowing it to spill all over the table. He states that the gin is all gone, and it seems as though the conversation runs out with the gin, leaving the two couples in silence and despair.

Style

Narration

The story is told from the first-person restricted point-of-view. The narrator, Nick, describes the interactions between the two couples only from his own perspective. Nick portrays his relationship with his wife, Linda, in glowing terms, full of warmth, affection, and mutual respect. Given the atmosphere of the story, and the tone of the conversation, however, the reader is invited to speculate if perhaps Nick's idealized perception of his marriage may eventually develop the tone of "benign menace" characterized by the relationship between Mel and Terri. Because the story is related in the past tense, the narrator suggests a feeling of nostalgia on Nick's part, for this early period of his marriage.

Setting: "Carver Country"

The story is set around the kitchen table of the McGinnis', in Albuquerque, New Mexico, although the narrator explains that "we were all from somewhere else." This is significant in that many critics agree Carver's settings are not regionally specific, but that his characters and the lives they lead describe a specific segment of white, working-class American life many have dubbed "Carver Country." Carver's widow, the writer Tess Gallagher, has edited a book entitled *Carver Country*, which includes photographs that capture the flavor of "Carver Country," accompanied by excerpts from Carver's letters, stories, and poems. In her introduction, Gallagher explains that "Carver Country was, in fact, an amalgam of feelings and psychic realities which had existed in America, of course, even before Ray began to write about them." She goes on to describe the atmosphere of the world of Carver's fiction as pervaded by "a current of benign menace." Others have described "Carver Country" as "Hopelessville, USA" because his characters occupy a class standing that leaves them without hope for financial or personal improvement. While the characters in this story seem to be more of the professional class (Mel is a cardiologist), the atmosphere in which they exist does carry "a current of benign menace" in terms of the relationship between Mel and Terri, which is characterized by a surface-level civility thinly covering a deep-seated anger and resentment. Over the course of their conversation, an atmosphere of "hopelessness" about the possibility of real love descends upon the two couples.

Closing Imagery

Critics have debated about the way in which Carver characteristically ends his stories. His endings have been described as "tableaus," providing a visual image, frozen in time, and infused with ambiguity. This story has such an ending: "I could hear my heart beating. I could hear everyone's heart. I could hear the human noise we sat there making, not one of us moving, not even when the room went dark." There is no direct information indicating the future of each of the couples, leaving the reader to speculate on indirect elements of the story. Some critics have criticized Carver's ambiguous endings as cliché and unsatisfying to the reader. Others, however, have praised the "photo-realist" detail of Carver's tableau endings and asserted that the ambiguity invites the reader to actively engage in the story and characters, in order to draw his or her conclusions as to their fate.

Historical Context

John Gardner

John Gardner (1933–1982), an American novelist and poet, was one of Carver's first writing teachers. Gardner is perhaps best known for his novel *Grendel* (1971), which is a retelling of the traditional Beowulf story from the perspective of the monster. His novel *October Light* (1976) won the National Book Critics Circle Award. Gardner was also a critic, and wrote two books aimed at aspiring writers: *On Becoming a Novelist* (1983) and *The Art of Fiction* (1984), both published after his death.

John Cheever

John Cheever (1912–1982) was a close friend of Carver, as well as his colleague and fellow fiction writer. In contrast to Carver, whose stories centered on the working poor, Cheever, a novelist and short story writer, was known for his middle-class suburban settings and characters. Among his best known works are *The Enormous Radio and Other Stories* (1953), *The Wapshot Chronicle* (1957), his first novel, which won a National Book Award, and *The Stories of John Cheever* (1978), which won the Pulitzer Prize for Fiction. Because of his clear prose style and ability to capture the social milieu of suburban America, critics have dubbed him "the Chekhov of the suburbs."

Robert Altman and Shortcuts

Screenwriter and film director Robert Altman (born 1925) adapted a collection of Carver's short stories to the screen in the 1993 feature film *Short Cuts*. Altman first won national attention for his film *M*A*S*H* (1970), which takes place at a Mobile Army Surgical Hospital during the Korean War, but is a commentary on the Vietnam War. Altman became known for his innovative style, which utilized an ensemble cast, stressed atmosphere and character over plot, and made use of multiple microphones to create an affect of overlapping dialogue. Altman's other films of note include *Nashville*, about a political election set in the milieu of the country music scene; *McCabe and Mrs. Miller* (1971), a revisionist Western starring Warren Beatty and Julie Christie; *The Long Goodbye* (1973), based on the style of the Raymond Chandler detective novel; and *Come Back to the Five and Dime, Jimmy Dean, Jimmy Dean* (1982), based on a stage play and starring Cher. *The Player* (1992) includes an all-star ensemble cast in a spoof of the milieu of the Hollywood film industry.

Minimalism

Carver's writing style has been referred to as "minimalist," because of his rigorously sparse prose. Minimalism began as a movement in the visual arts, primarily in the United States, in the 1960s. The minimalists were responding to the abstract expressionism of the 1950s. Minimalism in the visual arts was based on the principal that a work of art should not refer to anything real, but only to its own visual properties. Minimalism in music was largely inspired by minimalism in the visual arts. Minimalist music is characterized by simple, repetitive compositions. Philip Glass (born 1937), whose style is characterized by monotonous repetition and sparse composition, was a leading composer in minimalist music in the 1960s. Some of his most famous compositions are the operas *Einstein on the Beach* (1976), and *The Voyage* (1992), which was commissioned by the New York Metropolitan Opera.

Alcoholics Anonymous

Carver's stories often include characters who are alcoholics, and depict the ways in which alco-

Compare & Contrast

- **1960s–1970s:** The dominant trend in fiction is in the style of experimental, "postmodern" writing. The American short story is considered to be at a low point.

  1990s: Carver's turn to "neo-realist" subject-matter, written in a "minimalist" style, which goes against the grain of postmodern fiction, is credited with both revitalizing the genre of the American short story, and inspiring a generation of writer's attempting to imitate his minimalist style. Because of the large number of Carver imitators, however, a backlash against minimalist writing soon follows. Carver's entire oeuvre is now seen in a broader perspective, and Carver is indisputably recognized as the foremost American short fiction writer of his generation.

- **1960s–1970s:** While Carver's story, published in 1982, focuses on the theme of domestic violence, the term itself is not mentioned. The battered women's movement, which begins in the early-to-mid-1970s, grows out of feminist efforts at anti-rape legislation. Early efforts to help battered women include providing safe refuge for women and children escaping abusive situations, and lobbying efforts to protect women from abuse.

  1990s: The awareness of the problem of battered women grows throughout the 1980s and 1990s: there is increased funding for and availability of battered women's shelters, increased sensitivity to the problems of battered women in law enforcement training, the passing of numerous laws designed to protect battered women, including anti-stalking laws adopted in many states and laws against marital rape, and the effective use of "battered women's syndrome" in court.

- **1930s:** Alcoholics Anonymous is founded by two friends, with the seminal text of the organization, *Alcoholic's Anonymous*, appearing in 1939.

  1990s: By the late twentieth century, there are approximately two million members of Alcoholics Anonymous throughout the world.

holism can affect relationships between people. Carver himself was an alcoholic for over ten years, until he took his last drink in 1977. The organization Alcoholics Anonymous (AA), devoted to helping alcoholics quit drinking and stay sober, was an important influence on Carver's life, and he considered his recovery from alcoholism to be his greatest achievement in life. Alcoholics Anonymous originated in 1935 when two friends, William Griffith Wilson (1895–1971), a stockbroker, and Robert Holbrook Smith (1879–1950), a surgeon, got together to help each other quit drinking. They published the book *Alcoholics Anonymous* in 1939, which put forth the program they had devised. There are now approximately two million members of AA throughout the world. According to Encyclopaedia Britannica, there are an estimated 5,400,000 alcoholics in the United States at any given time.

Critical Overview

Raymond Carver is best known for his four major collections of short stories. His first collection published by a major press, *Will You Please Be Quiet, Please?* (1976), comprised stories written over a period of fourteen years. The second, *What We Talk About When We Talk About Love* (1981), established his national reputation as a leading short story writer. The third, *Cathedral* (1984), is considered Carver's masterpiece. The fourth, *Where I'm Calling From: New and Selected Stories* (1988), includes major revisions of previously published stories.

Carver is perhaps best known for his characterization of the sector of struggling white, working poor Americans and the atmosphere of despair and defeat in which they take place. Adam Meyer claims that "of the writers who attempted to depict the history of this 'blue collar despair,' none did so as fully and accurately as Raymond Carver.'' Carver himself was born into a working poor family, his father a laborer at a sawmill, and Carver occupied a variety of blue-collar jobs before landing his first white-collar job. Critics have dubbed this milieu ''Carver Country,'' indicating that it represents a significant sector of American life, regardless of regional specificity.

Adam Meyer explains that ''one thing Carver Country is not is a particular geographic location,'' noting that ''the great majority of Carver's stories . . . take place in regionally anonymous indoor settings.'' Meyer describes typical Carver characters as: ''primarily employed, when they are employed at all, as blue-collar workers—waitresses, mill or factory workers, mechanics, mail-carriers, sales clerks, motel managers, hairdressers. For relaxation they play bingo, watch television, or go fishing or hunting.'' Describing the atmosphere of Carver's stories, Meyer points out that the characters' ''marginal lives are filled with failure, deterioration, disenchantment, and despair, leading many critics to designate Carver Country 'Hopeless-ville.'''

Tess Gallagher, however, has defended the positive spirit of ''Carver Country,'' despite the struggles of his characters: ''In his stories Ray had been able, in a likeness to the voices and perceptions of the people themselves, to reveal the spiritual tenacity by which these people survived in spite of their limited means, and his readers at all economic levels of the population had been moved toward new awareness.''

Carver is widely credited with inspiring a renaissance in the short story form in American literature. Meyer states that ''although Carver was reluctant to claim too much personal credit for this resurgence'' in the short story form, ''there is no doubt that he played a significant part in that development.'' Meyer also notes that ''Carver played a significant part in another revival, that of realist writing.'' While the 1970s were dominated by experimental, ''postmodern'' literary form, Carver wrote stories about real people in real settings. Gentry and Stull point out that, during the 1980s, ''Carver was regularly cast as a 'godfather' to younger American neorealists, a role he neither claimed nor wanted.''

Upon publication, *What We Talk About When We Talk About Love* received immediate and glowing critical acclaim, earning front page coverage in the *New York Times Book Review* as well as a favorable review in the *New York Review of Books*. Meyer explains that ''this was to be the volume that would firmly establish Carver as an important writer.'' The stories in *What We Talk About When We Talk About Love* are considered the epitome of Carver's sparse, minimalist writing style. Marshall Bruce Gentry and William L. Stull refer to the volume as Carver's ''minimalist masterpiece.''

While Carver himself disliked the use of the term, and considered it partly an insult, many aspiring writers attempted to copy this style for years to come. Runyon asserts that ''Carver has been the most influential minimalist . . . while at the same time the least representative.'' Runyon has stated that this volume ''is the most minimalist of Carver's collections.'' Asserting that ''the stories have been pared to the bone,'' Runyon explains, ''In this volume Carver went the farthest he ever had towards a terse-ness that is almost silence.'' Adam Meyer claims that the writing style in this volume is ''an exaggerated form of minimalism,'' later referring to it as ''the finest book minimalism has to offer.'' He goes on to state that these stories ''continue to embody minimalism at its most distinctive,'' explaining: ''The collection has been nicknamed the 'minimalist bible,' and when readers and critics consider Carver a minimalist they generally have this volume in mind.'' Meyer concludes that ''because it is the volume that established Carver as a major literary figure, it has remained the collection most associated with him.'' Gentry and Stull note that ''the bare-boned collection proved immensely influential on a younger generation of short-story writers coming of age in the 1980s.''

Gentry and Stull assert that ''by the late 1980s there could be little doubt that [Carver] was the foremost short-story writer of his generation.'' Meyer claims that ''Carver's influence'' on American literature ''is undeniable.'' He explains that ''at the time of his death in 1988 . . . Carver was seemingly at the height of his powers and popularity. Since his death, though, his popularity has continued to grow, along with critical estimation of his work.''

Criticism

Liz Brent

Brent has a Ph.D. in American culture, specializing in cinema studies, from the University of Michigan. She is a freelance writer and teaches

What Do I Read Next?

- *Will You Please Be Quiet, Please?* (1976) is Carver's first major collection of short stories. It includes works developed over a period of fourteen years.

- *What We Talk About When We Talk About Love* (1981) is Carver's second major short story collection. It is considered to be the epitome of Carver's "minimalist" style.

- *Cathedral* (1984) is collection of short stories considered Carver's masterpiece. The title story, "Cathedral" is recognized as Carver's best.

- *Where I'm Calling From: New and Selected Stories* (1988) is Carver's fourth major collection of short stories. It includes revised versions of previously published stories.

- *Carver Country: The World of Raymond Carver* (1990), with photographs by Bob Adelman, is a posthumously published collection of photographs that capture the flavor of the struggling working class world depicted in most of Carver's stories. It includes an introduction by his widowed wife, the poet Tess Gallagher, and excerpts from letters, poems, and stories by Carver.

- *Remembering Ray: A Composite Biography of Raymond Carver* (1993), edited by William L. Stull and Maureen P. Carroll, is a collection of essays by friends and fellow writers close to Carver, describing their experiences with him. The book is organized chronologically, according to the various locations around the country in which Carver lived.

- *Conversations with Raymond Carver* (1990), edited by Marshall Bruce Gentry and William L. Stull, is a collection of previously published interviews with Raymond Carver, organized chronologically.

---

courses in American cinema. In the following essay, Brent discusses Carver's use of figurative language.

Carver is best known for his minimalist writing style, as embodied in a sparse use of language and paired down prose. He is also known as a neorealist, capturing the working class milieu of blue-collar America with his mundane, naturalistic, everyday dialogue. Nevertheless, he does make use of figurative language throughout "What We Talk About When We Talk About Love" by exploring its central themes of love, relationships, communication, and alcoholism. Through the imagery of the knight's armor, the beekeeper's protective clothing, the "pill" and the word "heart," Carver demonstrates that the surface level conversation of his four characters is only the tip of an emotional iceberg.

Since the character of Mel dominates the conversation, much of the figurative language is expressive of his own feelings about the subject of love. The image of the human "heart" takes on figurative connotations in the story, as it is referred to both in the mechanical sense, of the functioning of the human heart, and the symbolic sense, as the organ of love. Mel is a cardiologist, a doctor who operates on people's hearts. The opening sentences of the story, in retrospect, play on the irony of Mel, a heart doctor, claiming to be an expert on matters of the heart: "My friend Mel McGinnis was talking. Mel McGinnis is a cardiologist, so sometimes that gives him the right." Mel even describes his own work as that of "just a mechanic," marking the difference between expertise in heart surgery and knowledge of "true love." When he tells the story of the old couple injured in the near-fatal car accident, the word "heart" again takes on a double meaning. Mel concludes his story, in which the old man and woman are so bandaged up that they cannot see each other even though their beds are next to each other in the same hospital room, by stating that "the man's heart was breaking because he couldn't turn his goddamn head and see his god-

> The image of the human 'heart' takes on figurative connotations in the story, as it is referred to both in the mechanical sense, of the functioning of the human heart, and the symbolic sense, as the organ of love."

damn wife.'' Mel is using the word ''heart'' in the figurative sense here, but it also refers back to the fact that Mel himself had been the attending cardiologist for the old couple in the aftermath of the car accident.

Another central element of figurative speech in this story revolves around Mel's mention that, if he could come back in a different life, he would want to be a ''knight.'' Mel's fascination with the armor worn by a knight is perhaps a heavyhanded image of Mel's need to protect himself emotionally against the ravages of love. Mel explains that ''you were pretty safe wearing all that armor.'' The image is extended to suggest that Mel's protective emotional armor has failed to protect him against the dangers of new love: ''It was all right being a knight until gunpowder and muskets and pistols came along.'' Mel goes on to expand upon his fascination with the protective armor of knights: ''what I liked about knights, besides their ladies, was that they had that suit of armor, you know, and they couldn't get hurt very easy.'' Mel is expressing a desire to be protected from getting ''hurt'' at an emotional level in his relationships with others.

At this point, the discussion of the knight turns on a pun that comes out of Mel's misuse of the term ''vessel'' when he means ''vassal.'' A vassal is a servant to another, and Mel, using vessel by accident, attempts to point out that even knights were subservient to others. The idea of servitude is extended symbolically when Mel points out, ''But then everyone is always a vessel to someone.'' At this point Terri corrects him, supplying the proper term, vassal for vessel.

Mel's incorrect use of vessel has further figurative implications. Mel is an alcoholic, and a vessel is an object designed to contain something, usually in reference to a liquid, as a cup or chalice. Through this play on words, the connection is made to Mel's use of alcohol, which he drinks out of a vessel, or glass, as his means of protective armor against emotional injury. Furthermore, a vessel, such as an ''empty vessel'' may be read figuratively to indicate that everyone is a vessel to be filled with the love, false or true, of another.

Nick, the narrator, points out to Mel that the armor worn by knights had its drawbacks. Nick's comment extends the metaphor of the armor as emotional armor in explaining that one's emotional defenses, or armor, can end up suffocating the knight in the name of protecting him from harm:

> But sometimes they suffocated in all that armor, Mel. They'd even have heart attacks if it got too hot and they were too tired and worn out.

The image of the heart comes up here, implying that the armor Mel uses to protect himself from emotional suffering in the name of love (a ''heart attack'') can be the very cause of his suffering. In reference to Mel's alcoholism, his use of alcohol to protect himself from heartache may actually lead to a heart attack in terms of the demise of his marriage and other personal relationships, as well as some form of heart attack in the sense that alcoholism can be fatal. (This may seem like a leap of logic, but, given that this story was written not long after Carver nearly died from alcoholism and eventually quit drinking, it is not an unreasonable interpretation.) Mel's interest in armor as a means of protecting himself from love is made clear when he adds that, were a knight to be made vulnerable by the weight of his armor, ''Some vassal would come along and spear the bastard in the name of love.''

The imagery of ''taking a pill'' combines several figurative themes in the story. As Mel becomes more clearly drunk, his conversation acquires an antagonistic edge.

> 'He's depressed,' Terri said. 'Mel, why don't you take a pill?' Mel shook his head. 'I've taken everything there is.' 'We all need a pill now and then,' I said. 'Some people are born needing them,' Terri said.

Here, the characters themselves are consciously using the phrase ''to take a pill'' in a figurative sense. But the pill imagery also echoes with the fact that Mel is a doctor, whose job is, in general terms, to give people pills to make them feel better. Mel's own pill is clearly alcohol, and his comment that ''I've taken everything there is'' expresses a deep despair at ever finding a cure for his personal heartaches.

The figurative language combining the use of alcohol, as contained in a vessel, or the swallowing of a pill, as administered by a doctor, as a means of curing the emotional pain caused by love, is also expressed in Terri's explanation that her abusive ex-husband, Ed, drank rat poison when she left him. Like Mel's consumption of alcohol, or his figurative need "to take a pill," Ed's consumption of rat poison is his own self-destructive attempt to medicate his own emotional pain in the face of his "love" for Terri. Terri explains the effect of the poison; Ed's life was saved at the hospital, "but his gums went crazy from it. I mean they pulled away from his teeth. After that, his teeth stood out like fangs." The image of Ed's teeth turning into fangs symbolizes the fact that Ed, an extremely violent and abusive man, is akin to a beast who threatens Terri with his fangs. More indirectly, there is a suggestion that, just as Ed's drinking of rat poison in an attempt to cure his emotional pain turns him into a fanged beast, so Mel's drinking of alcohol in an attempt to cure his own emotional pain may be turning him into a beast, posing a threat of danger to Terri.

Mel later uses the imagery of a beekeeper's protective clothing to express a similar desire for some form of protection from love. In discussing his ex-wife Marjorie, he explains that she is allergic to bees, saying that "if I'm not praying she'll get married again, I'm praying she'll get herself stung to death by a swarm of f—ing bees." He then makes what is perhaps his most outwardly menacing gesture toward his wife: "'Bzzzzzzz,' Mel said, turning his fingers into bees and buzzing them at Terri's throat."

Mel's expression of hatred for his ex-wife and his wish that she would die is used as a thinly veiled expression of a similar hatred for Terri. The gesture of buzzing his fingers around her neck combines the figurative image of murder by bee sting into a more literal physical gesture threateningly aimed at Terri's throat. The armor imagery is echoed here in his description of the beekeeper's protective clothing:

> Sometimes I think I'll go there dressed like a bee-keeper. You know, that hat that's like a helmet with the plate that comes down over your face, the big gloves, and the padded coat? I'll knock on the door and let loose a hive of bees in the house.

The double implications of the word heart come back into play in the closing image of the story. As the two couples sit in the dark in silence,

the narrator explains, "I could hear my heart beating. I could hear everyone's heart." The narrator uses the literal image of a silence so profound that he can actually hear the beating of his own and the others' hearts to express a symbolic feeling that he can "hear everyone's heart." It is as if the excess of human emotion aroused by the discussion of true love hums about the room without any hope of articulate expression between the two couples. The term vessel, mentioned earlier, is also echoed with Mel's enigmatic gesture in the closing moments of the story, when he turns his glass of gin upside down on the table. Mel has emptied his vessel of alcohol, the "gin's gone," and they are left with nothing but an ominous feeling of emotional emptiness.

Although Carver is considered a minimalist writer, whose stories take on meaning more in what is not said than what is said, his use of figurative language gives depth to his stories by expanding upon their central themes.

Source: Liz Brent, Critical Essay on "What We Talk About When We Talk About Love," in *Short Stories for Students*, The Gale Group, 2001.

Adam Meyer

In the following essay, Meyer describes the minimal nature of "What We Talk About When We Talk About Love," and examines the story's themes of "the difficulty of sustaining relationships" and "the effect of alcoholism as a contributing factor to that difficulty."

Carver had stopped drinking by the time *Furious Seasons* was published, but he had not yet returned to writing. When he did, his stories were markedly different from what they had been. The obsessions were the same, but the stories were much darker, reflecting the hell of marital discord and alcoholism that Carver himself had experienced. Their style, moreover, was an exaggerated form of minimalism. Whereas he had once worried that a story like "Neighbors" might be "too thin, too elliptical and subtle," Carver was now writing stories that would make "Neighbors" appear positively lush. As one critic has pointed out, in these new texts "language is used so sparingly and the plots are so minimal that the stories at first seem to be mere patterns with no flesh and life in them. . . . Characters frequently have no names or only first names and are so briefly described that they appear to have no physical presence at all; certainly they have no distinct identity." Carver, looking back on the volume several years after its initial publication, told an interviewer that the texts in *What We Talk About When We Talk About Love* were "so pared down. Everything I thought I could live without I just got rid of, I cut out." Urged on by his editor Gordon Lish, he began implementing Hemingway's "theory of omission. If you can take anything out, take it out, as doing so will make the work stronger. Pare, pare, and pare some more." That phrase could in fact serve as a motto for *What We Talk About When We Talk About Love*, although critics have more often pointed to the following lines from "On Writing" : "Get in, get out. Don't linger." The stories here are indeed shorter, on average, than those in *Will You Please Be Quiet, Please?* and *Furious Seasons*. They also have a more desolate outlook, which is amplified by their astringency of tone. Nowhere is Carver's minimalist aesthetic more clearly visible than in the five stories from *Furious Seasons* that reappear here in reduced versions, having been "subjected to rigorous cutting." Although Carver eventually reacted against this extremely pared-down style, the stories in *What We Talk About When We Talk About Love* continue to embody minimalism at its most distinctive. The collection has been nicknamed the "minimalist bible," and when readers and critics consider Carver a minimalist they generally have this volume in mind. Because it is the volume that established Carver as a major literary figure, it has remained the collection most often associated with him, even if it is, as we shall later see, his least representative. . . .

The title story is the collection's longest and undoubtedly its greatest achievement, as well as being a fitting climax to the volume. Although its plot is rather thin, several of the obsessions that have run through the collection—the difficulty of sustaining relationships, the effect of alcoholism as a contributing factor to that difficulty, the problem of communication—are given their most extensive treatment. As the four characters (the narrator, Nick; his wife, Laura; their friend Mel McGinnis, a cardiologist; and his wife, Terri) sit around the table drinking gin, Carver is able to turn the question of love in several different directions. For this reason, more than one critic has likened the story's situation to Plato's *Symposium*, which does indeed seem to be the model for the dialogue. Nevertheless, "the relative articulateness of these characters by no means enables them to reach a satisfactory conclusion." The only resolution reached in this version of the symposium is that we really have no idea What We Talk About When We Talk About Love.

As the story opens, Terri, Mel's second wife, states that Ed, "the man she lived with before she lived with Mel[,] loved her so much he tried to kill her." Mel argues, however, that she cannot really call Ed's emotions love. Having been a divinity student before he became a doctor, Mel feels that true love must contain a spiritual dimension. He argues that "'the kind of love I'm talking about is [an absolute]. The kind of love I'm talking about, you don't try to kill people.'" Terri's continuing insistence that what Ed felt was love only serves to anger Mel, and we begin to see signs of strain in their own relationship. To show what real love is, Mel tells the story of an old couple he had treated in the hospital. While recovering from a terrible car accident, the husband became depressed because, due to his bandages, "'he couldn't turn his g–dd–n head and *see* his g–dd–ed wife.'" This old couple symbolizes for Mel what the old couple in the gazebo meant for Holly, a sign of stable and long-lasting love. During his narration, however, he and Terri begin to argue more openly. When Terri kids Mel about sounding drunk, he quietly responds, "'Just shut up for once in your life. . . . Will you do me a favor and do that for a minute?.'" Mel begins to explain about the old couple's injuries, how they had only lived because they were wearing their seat belts, and Terri interrupts to say that Mel's story is a public service message. Mel doesn't find her jest the least bit funny. He is concerned with the true meaning of love, and he presses the point about the length of this older couple's commitment because, as he points out, all four of this symposium's participants have been married more than once. As the story points out, "the greatest obstacle to any ideal love turns out to be the transitoriness of love." Mel notes that "'sometimes I have a hard time accounting for the fact that I must have loved my first wife too'" and he reminds the other couple that they "'both loved other people before [they] met each other.'" He even goes on to say that, should any of them die, he feels it wouldn't be long before the widowed person would remarry. This doesn't sit well with Terri, naturally, and the tension mounts.

Counterpoised to the disintegrating relationship of Mel and Terri are Nick and Laura, still-glowing newlyweds who, "in addition to being in love . . . like each other and enjoy one another's company." When Laura is asked whether she would call Ed's feelings toward Terri love, for example, she says, "'who can judge anyone else's situation?,'" and Nick tells us that "I touched the back of Laura's hand. She gave me a quick smile. I picked up Laura's hand. It was warm, the nails polished, perfectly manicured. I encircled the broad wrist with my fingers, and I held her.'' Such physical intimacy continues throughout the story, although Terri tells them that they're '''still on the honeymoon''' and must '''wait awhile''' to see what married life is really like. She seems to be making fun of them, yet her "remarks contain a hint of regret; she would like very much, it seems, to receive gestures of affection like those between Nick and Laura." They are still in the first throes of love, whereas her marriage to Mel seems to have become stale.

At the end of the story, the gin is all gone and the four people, who had been planning to go eat at a new restaurant, seem exhausted and reluctant to move. Terri says that she will '''put out some cheese and crackers,''' but she makes no move to do so. Suddenly the story's tension level increases dramatically. Nick states that "I could hear my heart beating. I could hear everyone's heart. I could hear the human noise we sat there making, not one of us moving, not even when the room went dark." As with other Carver stories of menace, such as "The Bath," the final note here is one of suspension, of tension threatening to explode but not yet ignited. The conversation began in the light of afternoon, but the participants fall silent in the dark of night and the story ends "in anxious isolation, enervation, and stasis." Although one critic has asserted that "these moments together, deeply imbued with shared sensibilities, make up for the antagonisms, the regrets, the flirtations, [and] the spilled gin," such comments seem to miss the mark. Carver's use of the word "noise" in the passage indicates that, rather than having achieved some kind of peace beyond words, the four talkers have reached a point where no communication is effective, where nothing can be heard. The seemingly imminent explosion may be the one between Mel and Terri, but Nick and Laura are necessarily dragged into it and implicated as well, since the newly married couple cannot avoid seeing themselves as Mel and Terri in a few years. As with all of Carver's first-person narratives, furthermore, we must ask ourselves who Nick is telling the story to, and when. The implication here is that he is fondly remembering that evening as a time when he and Laura shared a closeness that perhaps no longer exists.

Ultimately, the answer to Mel's question '''What do any of us really know about love?''' appears to be "not very much." A humorous digression in the middle of the story underscores this point. Mel,

> **As the four characters (the narrator, Nick; his wife, Laura; their friend Mel McGinnis, a cardiologist; and his wife, Terri) sit around the table drinking gin, Carver is able to turn the question of love in several different directions."**

whose definition of love is based on "the chivalric code," asserts that he would like to have been a knight, because armor made it harder to get hurt. The narrator tells him, however, that sometimes the knights would die because they got too hot in their suits or because they fell off their horses and didn't have the energy to stand up, whereupon they could be trampled by their own horses or killed by rivals. What follows is a subtle but telling bit of dialogue:

> "That's right," Mel said. "Some vassal would come along and spear the bastard in the name of love. Or whatever the f–k it was they fought over in those days." "Same things we fight over today," Terri said. Laura said, "Nothing's changed."

When it comes to talking about love—and understanding what we mean when we do so—Carver indicates treat we are still in the dark ages.

Perhaps the most quoted quip concerning *What We Talk About When We Talk About Love*, and for good reason, comes from Donald Newlove's review of the collection; he writes that the book includes "seventeen tales of Hopelessville, its marriages and alcoholic wreckage, told in a prose as sparingly clear as a fifth of iced Smirnoff." Newlove here highlights the main features, both of matter and manner, that unify the collection and give it a great deal of cumulative impact. By the end of the volume, having seen so much despair and so few spots of promise, we are as fatigued and numbed as the characters themselves. In these stories, then, Carver brilliantly weds his minimalistic style to his dispiriting themes. About the end of "One More Thing," for example, Hamilton E. Cochrane notes that "this conclusion reflects the unfinished business that is

L. D.'s life. L. D. can make no sense of it—can make no connections, draw no conclusions—and the fragmentary and inconclusive form of the story itself seems to reinforce this.'' This marriage of form and content marks the style that Carver would become best known for, and that would so influence younger writers.

Many critics, particularly ones who don't like him, continue to take their measure of Carver from *What We Talk About When We Talk About Love*, which is, indeed, the finest book that minimalism has to offer. Yet, as Jay McInerney has noted, ''Carver's career as a story writer and prose stylist had several distinct phases; only his [third] collection, *What We Talk About When We Talk About Love*, can really be called minimalism—a conscious attempt to leave almost everything out.'' Carver himself noted that it ''had been in many ways a watershed book for me, but it was a book I didn't want to duplicate or write again,'' and, following *What We Talk About When We Talk About Love*, Carver's stories did indeed change again, becoming broader, fuller, and more generous. We have passed through the narrowest point of the hourglass of Carver's minimalism—as exemplified by the truncations of the *Furious Seasons* stories—and we are now ready to broaden the form again as we turn to *Fires* and, especially, *Cathedral*.

Source: Adam Meyer, ''The Middle Years: 'What We Talk About When We Talk About Love,''' in *Raymond Carver*, Twayne, 1995, pp. 86–87, 108–11, 113.

Ewing Campbell

In the following essay, Campbell discusses the "several varieties of emotion existing under the single rubric of love" in "What We Talk About When We Talk About Love."

Readers often complain that nothing happens in stories like ''What We Talk About When We Talk About Love.'' Two couples in this story—Mel and Terri McGinnis and Nick and Laura—sit around a table, drinking gin and talking about love. Several varieties of emotion, existing under the single rubric of love, enter into the conversation either in passing or at length—spiritual love, carnal love, chivalric love, idealized devotion, and even the sort of complex torment that exhibits itself in abuse, often murder, and sometimes suicide. Mel the cardiologist does most of the talking, and much of that about Terri's former lover, Ed, who abused her, threatened murder, and finally succeeded on his second attempt at suicide.

Mel's other anecdote focuses on an elderly couple injured in a car wreck. The injured husband drifts into depression because the bandages prevent his seeing his wife while they are in the hospital.

That is it—ostensibly. But of course that is not all there is to the story. The little ironies and revelations of the story help to develop a complete narrative that no summary can ever sufficiently provide. Although not explicit, they are capable of revealing the inability of these characters to see themselves or each other honestly.

The most graphic scene is Terri's anecdote: Ed beat her one night, dragging her around the room by her ankles, repeating, ''I love you, I love you, you b—.'' She says Ed loved her so much he tried to kill her. Terri's interpretation of such evident ambivalence agrees with Ed's—it is love. That an individual deems his life not worth living without her must seem to her the highest testimony of her value. That Ed might have killed himself as one last attempt to punish her or that he might have taken his life as an act of self-loathing is unacceptable to Terri. That interpretation would devalue her.

Up to a point it is advantageous for Mel to see more clearly than Terri. If he sees that Ed's passion hardly qualifies as love, he need not feel quite as emotionally threatened by the dead lover, but only up to a point. It would not, for example, enhance Mel's self-image for him to see the parallel between Ed's violence toward Terri and his violent feelings toward his former wife. ''She's allergic to bees. . . . I'm praying she'll get herself stung to death by a swarm of f–ing bees.'' Then again a moment later, ''Sometimes I think I'll go up there dressed like a beekeeper. You know, that hat that's like a helmet with the plate that comes down over your face, the big gloves, and the padded coat? I'll knock on the door and let loose a hive of bees in the house.'' Nor does Nick, the narrator of the story, his girlfriend, or Terri seem to notice the parallel pattern. It remains invisible to all but the reader.

At the same time, Mel may sense his own susceptibility to sentimentality (in his desire to be a knight), immediate gratification (in eating, drinking, and getting high), and compulsiveness, features of arrested emotional development shared with Ed, for he says about himself, ''I like food. . . . If I had to do it all over again, I'd be a chef, you know?'' Mel's alcoholism and attraction to pills also testify to this self-gratifying impulse. Spiritual love, the idealized state of chivalric love, and the devotion of the elderly couple, having made a strong impression on him, may represent antidotes to or, at least, havens from his emotional immaturity. Or, as is more likely, extensions of that immaturity, for such imaginary escapes are further proof of underdevelopment.

He characterizes the years he spent in the seminary as the most important years of his life, yet he left that life. He maintains that had he the opportunity to come back in a different life, he would come back as a knight, an impossible, sentimental wish. Moreover, he idealizes the elderly couple's love when he asserts that their example ''ought to make us feel ashamed when we talk like we know what we're talking about when we talk above love.'' This idealized state amazes Mel, who says, ''I mean, it was killing the old fart just because he couldn't *look* at the f–ing woman.''

Nothing happens. Four people sit around a table talking about love. Or so it seems, but the term needs defining. Distinct, sometimes opposite states are experienced under the name of love: spiritual devotion, sexual attraction, fellowship, emotional dependence, and more. From Mel's incredulity, the reader can rightly infer that nothing he has ever felt as love could be favorably compared with what he found in the elderly man who was depressed because he couldn't see his wife. Whatever these characters sitting around the table drinking gin speak of when they talk about love, it is different from what he has seen in the hospital.

Different enough for him to realize that their talk around the table and elsewhere never approaches the real thing, and yet Mel remains partly blind to the truths of love and self. Not so the careful reader, for a while at least, because Carver dramatically juxtaposes varieties of experience that, when seen together, sharpen their lines of difference and no longer pass unquestioned for love. In life though, just as in literature, moments of the most vivid clarity soon fade, leaving us to fall back on signs and symbols to guide us in love or in life.

Source: Ewing Campbell, ''Breakthrough: 'What We Talk About When We Talk About Love,''' in *Raymond Carver: A Study of the Short Fiction*, Twayne, 1992, pp. 45–47.

Sources

Gallagher, Tess, *Carver Country: The World of Raymond Carver*, Scribner, 1990, pp. 8, 11–12.

> Nothing happens. Four people sit around a table talking about love. Or so it seems, but the term needs defining. Distinct, sometimes opposite states are experienced under the name of love: spiritual devotion, sexual attraction, fellowship, emotional dependence, and more."

Gentry, Marshall Bruce, and William L. Stull, eds., *Conversations with Raymond Carver*, University of Mississippi Press, 1990, pp. xii, xiii, xvi.

Meyer, Adam, *Raymond Carver*, Twayne, 1995, pp. ix, 1, 20, 21, 27, 86, 87, 113.

Runyon, Randolph Paul, *Reading Raymond Carver*, Syracuse University Press, 1992, pp. 4, 85.

Further Reading

Carver, Raymond, *Short Cuts: Selected Stories*, Vintage, 1991.
This collection contains previously published short stories by Carver, on which Robert Altman's film *Short Cuts* was based. It has an introduction by Altman that discusses the processes of adapting a number of short stories to a single composite narrative film.

Carver, Raymond, and Tom Jenks, eds., *American Short Story Masterpieces*, Delacorte, 1987.
This work is a collection of what the editors determined to be the best American short stories written between the 1950s and the 1980s.

Cheever, John, *The Stories of John Cheever*, Knopf, 1978.
This book is a collection of short stories, originally published between 1946 and 1975, written by Carver's close friend, colleague, and fellow author.

Foote, Shelby, ed., *Anton Chekhov: Early Short Stories, 1883–1888*, Modern Library, 1999.
Foote has collected the early stories of the playwright and fiction writer that Carver has most cited as having

influenced his own writing—the Russian writer, Anton Chekhov.

———, *Anton Chekhov: Later Short Stories, 1888–1903*, Modern Library, 1999.
This book presents the later stories by Anton Chekhov.

Gallagher, Tess, *At the Owl Woman Saloon*, Scribner, 1997.
This work is a collection of short stories by Carver's second wife and widow, the poet and fiction writer Tess Gallagher.

Gardner, John, *On Becoming a Novelist*, Harper, 1983.
Gardner's book provides advice to young writers aspiring to write novels. This book includes a forward by Raymond Carver.

Hemingway, Ernest, *The Complete Short Stories of Ernest Hemingway*, Scribner's, 1987.
This book of short stories is by the American writer to whose sparse prose and terse dialogue Carver's writing style is often compared.

Keyssar, Helene, *Robert Altman's America*, Oxford University Press, 1991.
This work is a critical analysis of the films of Robert Altman, who adapted Carver's short stories to the screen in the film *Short Cuts*.

Glossary of Literary Terms

A

Aestheticism: A literary and artistic movement of the nineteenth century. Followers of the movement believed that art should not be mixed with social, political, or moral teaching. The statement "art for art's sake" is a good summary of aestheticism. The movement had its roots in France, but it gained widespread importance in England in the last half of the nineteenth century, where it helped change the Victorian practice of including moral lessons in literature. Edgar Allan Poe is one of the best-known American "aesthetes."

Allegory: A narrative technique in which characters representing things or abstract ideas are used to convey a message or teach a lesson. Allegory is typically used to teach moral, ethical, or religious lessons but is sometimes used for satiric or political purposes. Many fairy tales are allegories.

Allusion: A reference to a familiar literary or historical person or event, used to make an idea more easily understood. Joyce Carol Oates's story "Where Are You Going, Where Have You Been?" exhibits several allusions to popular music.

Analogy: A comparison of two things made to explain something unfamiliar through its similarities to something familiar, or to prove one point based on the acceptance of another. Similes and metaphors are types of analogies.

Antagonist: The major character in a narrative or drama who works against the hero or protagonist. The Misfit in Flannery O'Connor's story "A Good Man Is Hard to Find" serves as the antagonist for the Grandmother.

Anthology: A collection of similar works of literature, art, or music. Zora Neale Hurston's "The Eatonville Anthology" is a collection of stories that take place in the same town.

Anthropomorphism: The presentation of animals or objects in human shape or with human characteristics. The term is derived from the Greek word for "human form." The fur necklet in Katherine Mansfield's story "Miss Brill" has anthropomorphic characteristics.

Anti-hero: A central character in a work of literature who lacks traditional heroic qualities such as courage, physical prowess, and fortitude. Anti-heroes typically distrust conventional values and are unable to commit themselves to any ideals. They generally feel helpless in a world over which they have no control. Anti-heroes usually accept, and often celebrate, their positions as social outcasts. A well-known anti-hero is Walter Mitty in James Thurber's story "The Secret Life of Walter Mitty."

Archetype: The word archetype is commonly used to describe an original pattern or model from which all other things of the same kind are made. Archetypes are the literary images that grow out of the "collective unconscious,'' a theory proposed by psychologist Carl Jung. They appear in literature as incidents and plots that repeat basic patterns of life. They may also appear as stereotyped characters. The ''schlemiel'' of Yiddish literature is an archetype.

Autobiography: A narrative in which an individual tells his or her life story. Examples include Benjamin Franklin's *Autobiography* and Amy Hempel's story ''In the Cemetery Where Al Jolson Is Buried,'' which has autobiographical characteristics even though it is a work of fiction.

Avant-garde: A literary term that describes new writing that rejects traditional approaches to literature in favor of innovations in style or content. Twentieth-century examples of the literary *avant-garde* include the modernists and the minimalists.

B

Belles-lettres: A French term meaning ''fine letters'' or ''beautiful writing.'' It is often used as a synonym for literature, typically referring to imaginative and artistic rather than scientific or expository writing. Current usage sometimes restricts the meaning to light or humorous writing and appreciative essays about literature. Lewis Carroll's *Alice in Wonderland* epitomizes the realm of belles-lettres.

Bildungsroman: A German word meaning ''novel of development.'' The *bildungsroman* is a study of the maturation of a youthful character, typically brought about through a series of social or sexual encounters that lead to self-awareness. J. D. Salinger's *Catcher in the Rye* is a *bildungsroman*, and Doris Lessing's story ''Through the Tunnel'' exhibits characteristics of a *bildungsroman* as well.

Black Aesthetic Movement: A period of artistic and literary development among African Americans in the 1960s and early 1970s. This was the first major African-American artistic movement since the Harlem Renaissance and was closely paralleled by the civil rights and black power movements. The black aesthetic writers attempted to produce works of art that would be meaningful to the black masses. Key figures in black aesthetics included one of its founders, poet and playwright Amiri Baraka, formerly known as LeRoi Jones; poet and essayist Haki R. Madhubuti, formerly Don L. Lee; poet and playwright Sonia Sanchez; and dramatist Ed Bullins. Works representative of the Black Aesthetic Movement include Amiri Baraka's play *Dutchman,* a 1964 Obie award-winner.

Black Humor: Writing that places grotesque elements side by side with humorous ones in an attempt to shock the reader, forcing him or her to laugh at the horrifying reality of a disordered world. ''Lamb to the Slaughter,'' by Roald Dahl, in which a placid housewife murders her husband and serves the murder weapon to the investigating policemen, is an example of black humor.

C

Catharsis: The release or purging of unwanted emotions—specifically fear and pity—brought about by exposure to art. The term was first used by the Greek philosopher Aristotle in his *Poetics* to refer to the desired effect of tragedy on spectators.

Character: Broadly speaking, a person in a literary work. The actions of characters are what constitute the plot of a story, novel, or poem. There are numerous types of characters, ranging from simple, stereotypical figures to intricate, multifaceted ones. ''Characterization'' is the process by which an author creates vivid, believable characters in a work of art. This may be done in a variety of ways, including (1) direct description of the character by the narrator; (2) the direct presentation of the speech, thoughts, or actions of the character; and (3) the responses of other characters to the character. The term ''character'' also refers to a form originated by the ancient Greek writer Theophrastus that later became popular in the seventeenth and eighteenth centuries. It is a short essay or sketch of a person who prominently displays a specific attribute or quality, such as miserliness or ambition. ''Miss Brill,'' a story by Katherine Mansfield, is an example of a character sketch.

Classical: In its strictest definition in literary criticism, classicism refers to works of ancient Greek or Roman literature. The term may also be used to describe a literary work of recognized importance (a ''classic'') from any time period or literature that exhibits the traits of classicism. Examples of later works and authors now described as classical include French literature of the seventeenth century, Western novels of the nineteenth century, and American fiction of the mid-nineteenth century such as that written by James Fenimore Cooper and Mark Twain.

Climax: The turning point in a narrative, the moment when the conflict is at its most intense. Typically, the structure of stories, novels, and plays is one of rising action, in which tension builds to the climax, followed by falling action, in which tension lessens as the story moves to its conclusion.

Comedy: One of two major types of drama, the other being tragedy. Its aim is to amuse, and it typically ends happily. Comedy assumes many forms, such as farce and burlesque, and uses a variety of techniques, from parody to satire. In a restricted sense the term comedy refers only to dramatic presentations, but in general usage it is commonly applied to nondramatic works as well.

Comic Relief: The use of humor to lighten the mood of a serious or tragic story, especially in plays. The technique is very common in Elizabethan works, and can be an integral part of the plot or simply a brief event designed to break the tension of the scene.

Conflict: The conflict in a work of fiction is the issue to be resolved in the story. It usually occurs between two characters, the protagonist and the antagonist, or between the protagonist and society or the protagonist and himself or herself. The conflict in Washington Irving's story "The Devil and Tom Walker" is that the Devil wants Tom Walker's soul but Tom does not want to go to hell.

Criticism: The systematic study and evaluation of literary works, usually based on a specific method or set of principles. An important part of literary studies since ancient times, the practice of criticism has given rise to numerous theories, methods, and "schools," sometimes producing conflicting, even contradictory, interpretations of literature in general as well as of individual works. Even such basic issues as what constitutes a poem or a novel have been the subject of much criticism over the centuries. Seminal texts of literary criticism include Plato's *Republic*, Aristotle's *Poetics*, Sir Philip Sidney's *The Defence of Poesie*, and John Dryden's *Of Dramatic Poesie*. Contemporary schools of criticism include deconstruction, feminist, psychoanalytic, poststructuralist, new historicist, postcolonialist, and reader-response.

D

Deconstruction: A method of literary criticism characterized by multiple conflicting interpretations of a given work. Deconstructionists consider the impact of the language of a work and suggest that the true meaning of the work is not necessarily the meaning that the author intended.

Deduction: The process of reaching a conclusion through reasoning from general premises to a specific premise. Arthur Conan Doyle's character Sherlock Holmes often used deductive reasoning to solve mysteries.

Denotation: The definition of a word, apart from the impressions or feelings it creates in the reader. The word "apartheid" denotes a political and economic policy of segregation by race, but its connotations—oppression, slavery, inequality—are numerous.

Denouement: A French word meaning "the unknotting." In literature, it denotes the resolution of conflict in fiction or drama. The *denouement* follows the climax and provides an outcome to the primary plot situation as well as an explanation of secondary plot complications. A well-known example of *denouement* is the last scene of the play *As You Like It* by William Shakespeare, in which couples are married, an evildoer repents, the identities of two disguised characters are revealed, and a ruler is restored to power. Also known as "falling action."

Detective Story: A narrative about the solution of a mystery or the identification of a criminal. The conventions of the detective story include the detective's scrupulous use of logic in solving the mystery; incompetent or ineffectual police; a suspect who appears guilty at first but is later proved innocent; and the detective's friend or confidant—often the narrator—whose slowness in interpreting clues emphasizes by contrast the detective's brilliance. Edgar Allan Poe's "Murders in the Rue Morgue" is commonly regarded as the earliest example of this type of story. Other practitioners are Arthur Conan Doyle, Dashiell Hammett, and Agatha Christie.

Dialogue: Dialogue is conversation between people in a literary work. In its most restricted sense, it refers specifically to the speech of characters in a drama. As a specific literary genre, a "dialogue" is a composition in which characters debate an issue or idea.

Didactic: A term used to describe works of literature that aim to teach a moral, religious, political, or practical lesson. Although didactic elements are often found in artistically pleasing works, the term "didactic" usually refers to literature in which the message is more important than the form. The term may also be used to criticize a work that the critic finds "overly didactic," that is, heavy-handed in its delivery of a lesson. An example of didactic literature is John Bunyan's *Pilgrim's Progress.*

Dramatic Irony: Occurs when the reader of a work of literature knows something that a character in the work itself does not know. The irony is in the contrast between the intended meaning of the statements or actions of a character and the additional information understood by the audience.

Dystopia: An imaginary place in a work of fiction where the characters lead dehumanized, fearful lives. **George Orwell's** *Nineteen Eighty-four,* and Margaret Atwood's *Handmaid's Tale* portray versions of dystopia.

E

Edwardian: Describes cultural conventions identified with the period of the reign of Edward VII of England (1901-1910). Writers of the Edwardian Age typically displayed a strong reaction against the propriety and conservatism of the Victorian Age. Their work often exhibits distrust of authority in religion, politics, and art and expresses strong doubts about the soundness of conventional values. Writers of this era include E. M. Forster, H. G. Wells, and Joseph Conrad.

Empathy: A sense of shared experience, including emotional and physical feelings, with someone or something other than oneself. Empathy is often used to describe the response of a reader to a literary character.

Epilogue: A concluding statement or section of a literary work. In dramas, particularly those of the seventeenth and eighteenth centuries, the epilogue is a closing speech, often in verse, delivered by an actor at the end of a play and spoken directly to the audience.

Epiphany: A sudden revelation of truth inspired by a seemingly trivial incident. The term was widely used by James Joyce in his critical writings, and the stories in Joyce's *Dubliners* are commonly called "epiphanies."

Epistolary Novel: A novel in the form of letters. The form was particularly popular in the eighteenth century. The form can also be applied to short stories, as in Edwidge Danticat's "Children of the Sea."

Epithet: A word or phrase, often disparaging or abusive, that expresses a character trait of someone or something. "The Napoleon of crime" is an epithet applied to Professor Moriarty, arch-rival of Sherlock Holmes in Arthur Conan Doyle's series of detective stories.

Existentialism: A predominantly twentieth-century philosophy concerned with the nature and perception of human existence. There are two major strains of existentialist thought: atheistic and Christian. Followers of atheistic existentialism believe that the individual is alone in a godless universe and that the basic human condition is one of suffering and loneliness. Nevertheless, because there are no fixed values, individuals can create their own characters—indeed, they can shape themselves—through the exercise of free will. The atheistic strain culminates in and is popularly associated with the works of Jean-Paul Sartre. The Christian existentialists, on the other hand, believe that only in God may people find freedom from life's anguish. The two strains hold certain beliefs in common: that existence cannot be fully understood or described through empirical effort; that anguish is a universal element of life; that individuals must bear responsibility for their actions; and that there is no common standard of behavior or perception for religious and ethical matters. Existentialist thought figures prominently in the works of such authors as Franz Kafka, Fyodor Dostoyevsky, and Albert Camus.

Expatriatism: The practice of leaving one's country to live for an extended period in another country. Literary expatriates include Irish author James Joyce who moved to Italy and France, American writers James Baldwin, Ernest Hemingway, Gertrude Stein, and F. Scott Fitzgerald who lived and wrote in Paris, and Polish novelist Joseph Conrad in England.

Exposition: Writing intended to explain the nature of an idea, thing, or theme. Expository writing is often combined with description, narration, or argument.

Expressionism: An indistinct literary term, originally used to describe an early twentieth-century school of German painting. The term applies to almost any mode of unconventional, highly subjective writing that distorts reality in some way. Advocates of Expressionism include Federico Garcia Lorca, Eugene O'Neill, Franz Kafka, and James Joyce.

F

Fable: A prose or verse narrative intended to convey a moral. Animals or inanimate objects with human characteristics often serve as characters in fables. A famous fable is Aesop's "The Tortoise and the Hare."

Fantasy: A literary form related to mythology and folklore. Fantasy literature is typically set in non-existent realms and features supernatural beings. Notable examples of literature with elements of fantasy are Gabriel Garcia Marquez's story "The Handsomest Drowned Man in the World" and Ursula K. LeGuin's "The Ones Who Walk Away from Omelas."

Farce: A type of comedy characterized by broad humor, outlandish incidents, and often vulgar subject matter. Much of the comedy in film and television could more accurately be described as farce.

Fiction: Any story that is the product of imagination rather than a documentation of fact. Characters and events in such narratives may be based in real life but their ultimate form and configuration is a creation of the author.

Figurative Language: A technique in which an author uses figures of speech such as hyperbole, irony, metaphor, or simile for a particular effect. Figurative language is the opposite of literal language, in which every word is truthful, accurate, and free of exaggeration or embellishment.

Flashback: A device used in literature to present action that occurred before the beginning of the story. Flashbacks are often introduced as the dreams or recollections of one or more characters.

Foil: A character in a work of literature whose physical or psychological qualities contrast strongly with, and therefore highlight, the corresponding qualities of another character. In his Sherlock Holmes stories, Arthur Conan Doyle portrayed Dr. Watson as a man of normal habits and intelligence, making him a foil for the eccentric and unusually perceptive Sherlock Holmes.

Folklore: Traditions and myths preserved in a culture or group of people. Typically, these are passed on by word of mouth in various forms—such as legends, songs, and proverbs—or preserved in customs and ceremonies. Washington Irving, in "The Devil and Tom Walker" and many of his other stories, incorporates many elements of the folklore of New England and Germany.

Folktale: A story originating in oral tradition. Folktales fall into a variety of categories, including legends, ghost stories, fairy tales, fables, and anecdotes based on historical figures and events.

Foreshadowing: A device used in literature to create expectation or to set up an explanation of later developments. Edgar Allan Poe uses foreshadowing to create suspense in "The Fall of the House of Usher" when the narrator comments on the crumbling state of disrepair in which he finds the house.

G

Genre: A category of literary work. Genre may refer to both the content of a given work—tragedy, comedy, horror, science fiction—and to its form, such as poetry, novel, or drama.

Gilded Age: A period in American history during the 1870s and after characterized by political corruption and materialism. A number of important novels of social and political criticism were written during this time. Henry James and Kate Chopin are two writers who were prominent during the Gilded Age.

Gothicism: In literature, works characterized by a taste for medieval or morbid characters and situations. A gothic novel prominently features elements of horror, the supernatural, gloom, and violence: clanking chains, terror, ghosts, medieval castles, and unexplained phenomena. The term "gothic novel" is also applied to novels that lack elements of the traditional Gothic setting but that create a similar atmosphere of terror or dread. The term can also be applied to stories, plays, and poems. Mary Shelley's *Frankenstein* and Joyce Carol Oates's *Bellefleur* are both gothic novels.

Grotesque: In literature, a work that is characterized by exaggeration, deformity, freakishness, and disorder. The grotesque often includes an element of comic absurdity. Examples of the grotesque can be found in the works of Edgar Allan Poe, Flannery O'Connor, Joseph Heller, and Shirley Jackson.

H

Harlem Renaissance: The Harlem Renaissance of the 1920s is generally considered the first significant movement of black writers and artists in the United States. During this period, new and established black writers, many of whom lived in the region of New York City known as Harlem, published more fiction and poetry than ever before, the first influential black literary journals were established, and black authors and artists received their first widespread recognition and serious critical appraisal. Among the major writers associated with this period are Countee Cullen, Langston Hughes, Arna Bontemps, and Zora Neale Hurston.

Hero/Heroine: The principal sympathetic character in a literary work. Heroes and heroines typically exhibit admirable traits: idealism, courage, and integrity, for example. Famous heroes and heroines of literature include Charles Dickens's Oliver Twist, Margaret Mitchell's Scarlett O'Hara, and the anonymous narrator in Ralph Ellison's *Invisible Man.*

Hyperbole: Deliberate exaggeration used to achieve an effect. In William Shakespeare's *Macbeth,* Lady Macbeth hyperbolizes when she says, ''All the perfumes of Arabia could not sweeten this little hand.''

I

Image: A concrete representation of an object or sensory experience. Typically, such a representation helps evoke the feelings associated with the object or experience itself. Images are either ''literal'' or ''figurative.'' Literal images are especially concrete and involve little or no extension of the obvious meaning of the words used to express them. Figurative images do not follow the literal meaning of the words exactly. Images in literature are usually visual, but the term ''image'' can also refer to the representation of any sensory experience.

Imagery: The array of images in a literary work. Also used to convey the author's overall use of figurative language in a work.

In medias res: A Latin term meaning ''in the middle of things.'' It refers to the technique of beginning a story at its midpoint and then using various flashback devices to reveal previous action. This technique originated in such epics as Virgil's *Aeneid.*

Interior Monologue: A narrative technique in which characters' thoughts are revealed in a way that appears to be uncontrolled by the author. The interior monologue typically aims to reveal the inner self of a character. It portrays emotional experiences as they occur at both a conscious and unconscious level. One of the best-known interior monologues in English is the Molly Bloom section at the close of James Joyce's *Ulysses.* Katherine Anne Porter's ''The Jilting of Granny Weatherall'' is also told in the form of an interior monologue.

Irony: In literary criticism, the effect of language in which the intended meaning is the opposite of what is stated. The title of Jonathan Swift's ''A Modest Proposal'' is ironic because what Swift proposes in this essay is cannibalism—hardly ''modest.''

J

Jargon: Language that is used or understood only by a select group of people. Jargon may refer to terminology used in a certain profession, such as computer jargon, or it may refer to any nonsensical language that is not understood by most people. Anthony Burgess's *A Clockwork Orange* and James Thurber's ''The Secret Life of Walter Mitty'' both use jargon.

K

Knickerbocker Group: An indistinct group of New York writers of the first half of the nineteenth century. Members of the group were linked only by location and a common theme: New York life. Two famous members of the Knickerbocker Group were Washington Irving and William Cullen Bryant. The group's name derives from Irving's *Knickerbocker's History of New York.*

L

Literal Language: An author uses literal language when he or she writes without exaggerating or embellishing the subject matter and without any tools of figurative language. To say ''He ran very quickly down the street'' is to use literal language, whereas to say ''He ran like a hare down the street'' would be using figurative language.

Literature: Literature is broadly defined as any written or spoken material, but the term most often refers to creative works. Literature includes poetry, drama, fiction, and many kinds of nonfiction writing, as well as oral, dramatic, and broadcast compositions not necessarily preserved in a written format, such as films and television programs.

Lost Generation: A term first used by Gertrude Stein to describe the post-World War I generation of American writers: men and women haunted by a sense of betrayal and emptiness brought about by the destructiveness of the war. The term is commonly applied to Hart Crane, Ernest Hemingway, F. Scott Fitzgerald, and others.

M

Magic Realism: A form of literature that incorporates fantasy elements or supernatural occurrences into the narrative and accepts them as truth. Gabriel Garcia Marquez and Laura Esquivel are two writers known for their works of magic realism.

Metaphor: A figure of speech that expresses an idea through the image of another object. Metaphors suggest the essence of the first object by identifying it with certain qualities of the second object. An example is ''But soft, what light through yonder window breaks?/ It is the east, and Juliet is the sun'' in William Shakespeare's *Romeo and Juliet.* Here, Juliet, the first object, is identified with qualities of the second object, the sun.

Minimalism: A literary style characterized by spare, simple prose with few elaborations. In minimalism, the main theme of the work is often never discussed directly. Amy Hempel and Ernest Hemingway are two writers known for their works of minimalism.

Modernism: Modern literary practices. Also, the principles of a literary school that lasted from roughly the beginning of the twentieth century until the end of World War II. Modernism is defined by its rejection of the literary conventions of the nineteenth century and by its opposition to conventional morality, taste, traditions, and economic values. Many writers are associated with the concepts of modernism, including Albert Camus, D. H. Lawrence, Ernest Hemingway, William Faulkner, Eugene O'Neill, and James Joyce.

Monologue: A composition, written or oral, by a single individual. More specifically, a speech given by a single individual in a drama or other public entertainment. It has no set length, although it is usually several or more lines long. ''I Stand Here Ironing'' by Tillie Olsen is an example of a story written in the form of a monologue.

Mood: The prevailing emotions of a work or of the author in his or her creation of the work. The mood of a work is not always what might be expected based on its subject matter.

Motif: A theme, character type, image, metaphor, or other verbal element that recurs throughout a single work of literature or occurs in a number of different works over a period of time. For example, the color white in Herman Melville's *Moby Dick* is a ''specific'' *motif,* while the trials of star-crossed lovers is a ''conventional'' *motif* from the literature of all periods.

N

Narration: The telling of a series of events, real or invented. A narration may be either a simple narrative, in which the events are recounted chronologically, or a narrative with a plot, in which the account is given in a style reflecting the author's artistic concept of the story. Narration is sometimes used as a synonym for ''storyline.''

Narrative: A verse or prose accounting of an event or sequence of events, real or invented. The term is also used as an adjective in the sense ''method of narration.'' For example, in literary criticism, the expression ''narrative technique'' usually refers to the way the author structures and presents his or her story. Different narrative forms include diaries, travelogues, novels, ballads, epics, short stories, and other fictional forms.

Narrator: The teller of a story. The narrator may be the author or a character in the story through whom the author speaks. Huckleberry Finn is the narrator of Mark Twain's *The Adventures of Huckleberry Finn.*

Novella: An Italian term meaning ''story.'' This term has been especially used to describe fourteenth-century Italian tales, but it also refers to modern short novels. Modern novellas include Leo Tolstoy's *The Death of Ivan Ilich,* Fyodor Dostoyevsky's *Notes from the Underground,* and Joseph Conrad's *Heart of Darkness.*

O

Oedipus Complex: A son's romantic obsession with his mother. The phrase is derived from the story of the ancient Theban hero Oedipus, who unknowingly killed his father and married his mother, and was popularized by Sigmund Freud's theory of psychoanalysis. Literary occurrences of the Oedipus complex include Sophocles' *Oedipus Rex* and D. H. Lawrence's ''The Rocking-Horse Winner.''

Onomatopoeia: The use of words whose sounds express or suggest their meaning. In its simplest sense, onomatopoeia may be represented by words that mimic the sounds they denote such as ''hiss'' or ''meow.'' At a more subtle level, the pattern and rhythm of sounds and rhymes of a line or poem may be onomatopoeic.

Oral Tradition: A process by which songs, ballads, folklore, and other material are transmitted by word of mouth. The tradition of oral transmission predates the written record systems of literate society.

Oral transmission preserves material sometimes over generations, although often with variations. Memory plays a large part in the recitation and preservation of orally transmitted material. Native American myths and legends, and African folktales told by plantation slaves are examples of orally transmitted literature.

P

Parable: A story intended to teach a moral lesson or answer an ethical question. Examples of parables are the stories told by Jesus Christ in the New Testament, notably ''The Prodigal Son,'' but parables also are used in Sufism, rabbinic literature, Hasidism, and Zen Buddhism. Isaac Bashevis Singer's story ''Gimpel the Fool'' exhibits characteristics of a parable.

Paradox: A statement that appears illogical or contradictory at first, but may actually point to an underlying truth. A literary example of a paradox is George Orwell's statement ''All animals are equal, but some animals are more equal than others'' in *Animal Farm.*

Parody: In literature, this term refers to an imitation of a serious literary work or the signature style of a particular author in a ridiculous manner. A typical parody adopts the style of the original and applies it to an inappropriate subject for humorous effect. Parody is a form of satire and could be considered the literary equivalent of a caricature or cartoon. Henry Fielding's *Shamela* is a parody of Samuel Richardson's *Pamela.*

Persona: A Latin term meaning ''mask.'' Personae are the characters in a fictional work of literature. The persona generally functions as a mask through which the author tells a story in a voice other than his or her own. A persona is usually either a character in a story who acts as a narrator or an ''implied author,'' a voice created by the author to act as the narrator for himself or herself. The persona in Charlotte Perkins Gilman's story ''The Yellow Wallpaper'' is the unnamed young mother experiencing a mental breakdown.

Personification: A figure of speech that gives human qualities to abstract ideas, animals, and inanimate objects. To say that ''the sun is smiling'' is to personify the sun.

Plot: The pattern of events in a narrative or drama. In its simplest sense, the plot guides the author in composing the work and helps the reader follow the work. Typically, plots exhibit causality and unity and have a beginning, a middle, and an end. Sometimes, however, a plot may consist of a series of disconnected events, in which case it is known as an ''episodic plot.''

Poetic Justice: An outcome in a literary work, not necessarily a poem, in which the good are rewarded and the evil are punished, especially in ways that particularly fit their virtues or crimes. For example, a murderer may himself be murdered, or a thief will find himself penniless.

Poetic License: Distortions of fact and literary convention made by a writer—not always a poet—for the sake of the effect gained. Poetic license is closely related to the concept of ''artistic freedom.'' An author exercises poetic license by saying that a pile of money ''reaches as high as a mountain'' when the pile is actually only a foot or two high.

Point of View: The narrative perspective from which a literary work is presented to the reader. There are four traditional points of view. The ''third person omniscient'' gives the reader a ''godlike'' perspective, unrestricted by time or place, from which to see actions and look into the minds of characters. This allows the author to comment openly on characters and events in the work. The ''third person'' point of view presents the events of the story from outside of any single character's perception, much like the omniscient point of view, but the reader must understand the action as it takes place and without any special insight into characters' minds or motivations. The ''first person'' or ''personal'' point of view relates events as they are perceived by a single character. The main character ''tells'' the story and may offer opinions about the action and characters which differ from those of the author. Much less common than omniscient, third person, and first person is the ''second person'' point of view, wherein the author tells the story as if it is happening to the reader. James Thurber employs the omniscient point of view in his short story ''The Secret Life of Walter Mitty.'' Ernest Hemingway's ''A Clean, Well-Lighted Place'' is a short story told from the third person point of view. Mark Twain's novel *Huckleberry Finn* is presented from the first person viewpoint. Jay McInerney's *Bright Lights, Big City* is an example of a novel which uses the second person point of view.

Pornography: Writing intended to provoke feelings of lust in the reader. Such works are often condemned by critics and teachers, but those which can be shown to have literary value are viewed less harshly. Literary works that have been described as pornographic include D. H. Lawrence's *Lady Chatterley's Lover* and James Joyce's *Ulysses.*

Post-Aesthetic Movement: An artistic response made by African Americans to the black aesthetic movement of the 1960s and early 1970s. Writers since that time have adopted a somewhat different tone in their work, with less emphasis placed on the disparity between black and white in the United States. In the words of post-aesthetic authors such as Toni Morrison, John Edgar Wideman, and Kristin Hunter, African Americans are portrayed as looking inward for answers to their own questions, rather than always looking to the outside world. Two well-known examples of works produced as part of the post-aesthetic movement are the Pulitzer Prize-winning novels *The Color Purple* by Alice Walker and *Beloved* by Toni Morrison.

Postmodernism: Writing from the 1960s forward characterized by experimentation and application of modernist elements, which include existentialism and alienation. Postmodernists have gone a step further in the rejection of tradition begun with the modernists by also rejecting traditional forms, preferring the anti-novel over the novel and the anti-hero over the hero. Postmodern writers include Thomas Pynchon, Margaret Drabble, and Gabriel Garcia Marquez.

Prologue: An introductory section of a literary work. It often contains information establishing the situation of the characters or presents information about the setting, time period, or action. In drama, the prologue is spoken by a chorus or by one of the principal characters.

Prose: A literary medium that attempts to mirror the language of everyday speech. It is distinguished from poetry by its use of unmetered, unrhymed language consisting of logically related sentences. Prose is usually grouped into paragraphs that form a cohesive whole such as an essay or a novel. The term is sometimes used to mean an author's general writing.

Protagonist: The central character of a story who serves as a focus for its themes and incidents and as the principal rationale for its development. The protagonist is sometimes referred to in discussions of modern literature as the hero or anti-hero. Well-known protagonists are Hamlet in William Shakespeare's *Hamlet* and Jay Gatsby in F. Scott Fitzgerald's *The Great Gatsby.*

R

Realism: A nineteenth-century European literary movement that sought to portray familiar characters, situations, and settings in a realistic manner. This was done primarily by using an objective narrative point of view and through the buildup of accurate detail. The standard for success of any realistic work depends on how faithfully it transfers common experience into fictional forms. The realistic method may be altered or extended, as in stream of consciousness writing, to record highly subjective experience. Contemporary authors who often write in a realistic way include Nadine Gordimer and Grace Paley.

Resolution: The portion of a story following the climax, in which the conflict is resolved. The resolution of Jane Austen's *Northanger Abbey* is neatly summed up in the following sentence: ''Henry and Catherine were married, the bells rang and everybody smiled.''

Rising Action: The part of a drama where the plot becomes increasingly complicated. Rising action leads up to the climax, or turning point, of a drama. The final ''chase scene'' of an action film is generally the rising action which culminates in the film's climax.

Roman a clef: A French phrase meaning ''novel with a key.'' It refers to a narrative in which real persons are portrayed under fictitious names. Jack Kerouac, for example, portrayed various his friends under fictitious names in the novel *On the Road.* D. H. Lawrence based ''The Rocking-Horse Winner'' on a family he knew.

Romanticism: This term has two widely accepted meanings. In historical criticism, it refers to a European intellectual and artistic movement of the late eighteenth and early nineteenth centuries that sought greater freedom of personal expression than that allowed by the strict rules of literary form and logic of the eighteenth-century neoclassicists. The Romantics preferred emotional and imaginative expression to rational analysis. They considered the individual to be at the center of all experience and so placed him or her at the center of their art. The Romantics believed that the creative imagination reveals nobler truths—unique feelings and attitudes—than those that could be discovered by logic or by scientific examination. ''Romanticism'' is also used as a general term to refer to a type of sensibility found in all periods of literary history and usually considered to be in opposition to the principles of classicism. In this sense, Romanticism signifies any work or philosophy in which the exotic or dreamlike figure strongly, or that is devoted to individualistic expression, self-analysis, or a pursuit of a higher realm of knowledge than can be discovered by human reason. Prominent Romantics include Jean-Jacques Rousseau, William Wordsworth, John Keats, Lord Byron, and Johann Wolfgang von Goethe.

S

Satire: A work that uses ridicule, humor, and wit to criticize and provoke change in human nature and institutions. Voltaire's novella *Candide* and Jonathan Swift's essay ''A Modest Proposal'' are both satires. Flannery O'Connor's portrayal of the family in ''A Good Man Is Hard to Find'' is a satire of a modern, Southern, American family.

Science Fiction: A type of narrative based upon real or imagined scientific theories and technology. Science fiction is often peopled with alien creatures and set on other planets or in different dimensions. Popular writers of science fiction are Isaac Asimov, Karel Capek, Ray Bradbury, and Ursula K. Le Guin.

Setting: The time, place, and culture in which the action of a narrative takes place. The elements of setting may include geographic location, characters's physical and mental environments, prevailing cultural attitudes, or the historical time in which the action takes place.

Short Story: A fictional prose narrative shorter and more focused than a novella. The short story usually deals with a single episode and often a single character. The ''tone,'' the author's attitude toward his or her subject and audience, is uniform throughout. The short story frequently also lacks *denouement*, ending instead at its climax.

Signifying Monkey: A popular trickster figure in black folklore, with hundreds of tales about this character documented since the 19th century. Henry Louis Gates Jr. examines the history of the signifying monkey in *The Signifying Monkey: Towards a Theory of Afro-American Literary Criticism,* published in 1988.

Simile: A comparison, usually using ''like'' or ''as,''of two essentially dissimilar things, as in ''coffee as cold as ice'' or ''He sounded like a broken record.'' The title of Ernest Hemingway's ''Hills Like White Elephants'' contains a simile.

Social Realism: The Socialist Realism school of literary theory was proposed by Maxim Gorky and established as a dogma by the first Soviet Congress of Writers. It demanded adherence to a communist worldview in works of literature. Its doctrines required an objective viewpoint comprehensible to the working classes and themes of social struggle featuring strong proletarian heroes. Gabriel Garcia Marquez's stories exhibit some characteristics of Socialist Realism.

Stereotype: A stereotype was originally the name for a duplication made during the printing process; this led to its modern definition as a person or thing that is (or is assumed to be) the same as all others of its type. Common stereotypical characters include the absent-minded professor, the nagging wife, the troublemaking teenager, and the kindhearted grandmother.

Stream of Consciousness: A narrative technique for rendering the inward experience of a character. This technique is designed to give the impression of an ever-changing series of thoughts, emotions, images, and memories in the spontaneous and seemingly illogical order that they occur in life. The textbook example of stream of consciousness is the last section of James Joyce's *Ulysses.*

Structure: The form taken by a piece of literature. The structure may be made obvious for ease of understanding, as in nonfiction works, or may obscured for artistic purposes, as in some poetry or seemingly ''unstructured'' prose.

Style: A writer's distinctive manner of arranging words to suit his or her ideas and purpose in writing. The unique imprint of the author's personality upon his or her writing, style is the product of an author's way of arranging ideas and his or her use of diction, different sentence structures, rhythm, figures of speech, rhetorical principles, and other elements of composition.

Suspense: A literary device in which the author maintains the audience's attention through the build-up of events, the outcome of which will soon be revealed. Suspense in William Shakespeare's *Hamlet* is sustained throughout by the question of whether or not the Prince will achieve what he has been instructed to do and of what he intends to do.

Symbol: Something that suggests or stands for something else without losing its original identity. In literature, symbols combine their literal meaning with the suggestion of an abstract concept. Literary symbols are of two types: those that carry complex associations of meaning no matter what their contexts, and those that derive their suggestive meaning from their functions in specific literary works. Examples of symbols are sunshine suggesting happiness, rain suggesting sorrow, and storm clouds suggesting despair.

T

Tale: A story told by a narrator with a simple plot and little character development. Tales are usually relatively short and often carry a simple message. Examples of tales can be found in the works of Saki, Anton Chekhov, Guy de Maupassant, and O. Henry.

Tall Tale: A humorous tale told in a straightforward, credible tone but relating absolutely impossible events or feats of the characters. Such tales were commonly told of frontier adventures during the settlement of the west in the United States. Literary use of tall tales can be found in Washington Irving's *History of New York,* Mark Twain's *Life on the Mississippi,* and in the German R. F. Raspe's *Baron Munchausen's Narratives of His Marvellous Travels and Campaigns in Russia.*

Theme: The main point of a work of literature. The term is used interchangeably with thesis. Many works have multiple themes. One of the themes of Nathaniel Hawthorne's ''Young Goodman Brown'' is loss of faith.

Tone: The author's attitude toward his or her audience may be deduced from the tone of the work. A formal tone may create distance or convey politeness, while an informal tone may encourage a friendly, intimate, or intrusive feeling in the reader. The author's attitude toward his or her subject matter may also be deduced from the tone of the words he or she uses in discussing it. The tone of John F. Kennedy's speech which included the appeal to ''ask not what your country can do for you'' was intended to instill feelings of camaraderie and national pride in listeners.

Tragedy: A drama in prose or poetry about a noble, courageous hero of excellent character who, because of some tragic character flaw, brings ruin upon him- or herself. Tragedy treats its subjects in a dignified and serious manner, using poetic language to help evoke pity and fear and bring about catharsis, a purging of these emotions. The tragic form was practiced extensively by the ancient Greeks. The classical form of tragedy was revived in the sixteenth century; it flourished especially on the Elizabethan stage. In modern times, dramatists have attempted to adapt the form to the needs of modern society by drawing their heroes from the ranks of ordinary men and women and defining the nobility of these heroes in terms of spirit rather than exalted social standing. Some contemporary works that are thought of as tragedies include *The Great Gatsby* by F. Scott Fitzgerald, and *The Sound and the Fury* by William Faulkner.

Tragic Flaw: In a tragedy, the quality within the hero or heroine which leads to his or her downfall. Examples of the tragic flaw include Othello's jealousy and Hamlet's indecisiveness, although most great tragedies defy such simple interpretation.

U

Utopia: A fictional perfect place, such as ''paradise'' or ''heaven.'' An early literary utopia was described in Plato's *Republic,* and in modern literature, Ursula K. Le Guin depicts a utopia in ''The Ones Who Walk Away from Omelas.''

V

Victorian: Refers broadly to the reign of Queen Victoria of England (1837-1901) and to anything with qualities typical of that era. For example, the qualities of smug narrow-mindedness, bourgeois materialism, faith in social progress, and priggish morality are often considered Victorian. In literature, the Victorian Period was the great age of the English novel, and the latter part of the era saw the rise of movements such as decadence and symbolism.

Cumulative Author/Title Index

Nationality/Ethnicity Index

Antiguan

Subject/Theme Index